INTRODUCTION TO
HUMAN RESOURCE
MANAGEMENT

INTRODUCTION TO
HUMAN RESOURCE
MANAGEMENT

third edition

Paul Banfield | Rebecca Kay | Dean Royles

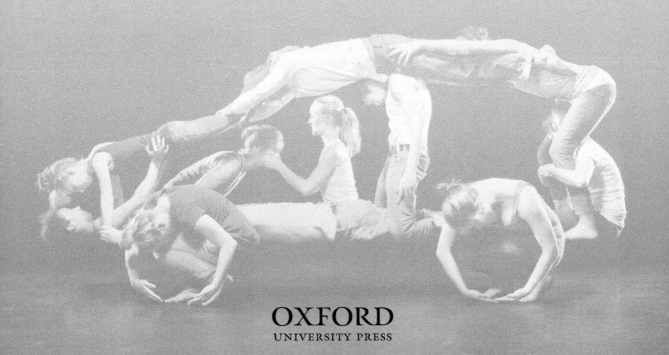

OXFORD
UNIVERSITY PRESS

Great Clarendon Street, Oxford, OX2 6DP,
United Kingdom

Oxford University Press is a department of the University of Oxford.
It furthers the University's objective of excellence in research, scholarship,
and education by publishing worldwide. Oxford is a registered trade mark of
Oxford University Press in the UK and in certain other countries

© Oxford University Press 2018

The moral rights of the authors have been asserted

First edition 2008
Second edition 2012

Impression: 2

Published in the United States of America by Oxford University Press
198 Madison Avenue, New York, NY 10016, United States of America

British Library Cataloguing in Publication Data

Data available

Library of Congress Control Number: 2017952322

ISBN 978-0-19-870282-5

Printed by CPI Group (UK) Ltd, Croydon CR0 4YY

Contents in Brief

Contents in Full

xi

List of Case Studies

About the Book

Most authors claim that their book is different, and by implication, better than many others currently in use. Often, however, the differences, where they exist, are more superficial than substantial and tend to relate to the choice and range of HRM subject areas rather than the way these areas are treated. We feel that many contemporary introductory HRM books are very similar in terms of style, approach, and coverage and that they tend to be written by academics in a style that fails to reflect the realities, uncertainties of organizational life, and the nature of the challenges facing those with responsibilities for HRM. This led us to believe that there was a need for a book on HRM that approached the subject in significantly different ways.

What seemed to us to be missing from much of the literature available to tutors and students was a perspective on HRM that combined a strong academic underpinning with a realistic and informed understanding of how the HR function has evolved within organizations, as it seeks to contribute in the most appropriate way to how organizations function. In this third edition, more than in the previous two, we have tried to locate and make sense of the HR function within complex and dynamic organizational environments, as part of the wider management function and as a specialist department tasked with specific responsibilities and contributions. In other words, we have tried to represent HR 'as it is' and how it is perceived as well as how it is meant to be, an approach that combines criticality with change and opportunities for improvement in the way the HR function is managed. This approach involves being more open and honest about the relationship between HR activities and their associated outcomes (often taken for granted). In doing so, we question the unproblematic way in which HR is often presented, for example, in relation to its contributions to employee behaviour and business performance.

It is one thing to have a concept of a book that you would like to write—one that aspires to overcome the gap between 'theory' and 'practice'—but quite another to produce one that actually achieves this and provides students with a set of analytical tools and frameworks that are academically rigorous, while offering important insights into the realities, uncertainties, and compromises that HR practitioners and line managers constantly face. Only our readers will be able to say whether we have achieved our objective, but we believe that we have made significant progress in that direction, for the following reasons:

1. The book is informed by contributions from two senior HR practitioners, although Rebecca Kay has now moved on to a new career in education, and an experienced academic and consultant. Dean Royles, the new member of the writing team, brings an even greater range of experience and insight into HR and senior management as a result of his career in the NHS, with Paul Banfield providing the academic content and analytical and conceptual frameworks. Our intention has always been to draw upon contributions to the understanding of HR from the most influential writers on the subject from the UK, Europe, and the USA and interpret these through our experience. The result is a fusion of both academic and professional insights which explore how HR as an academic subject is represented and how it is practised and experienced in the workplace.

2. We take a holistic and integrated approach to HRM which avoids presenting it as a series of separate activities and as an isolated management function detached from wider organizational and business interests and priorities. The emphasis in Chapter 1 on the importance of adopting a systems perspective on organizations and the HR function means that both are represented as dynamic concepts and as representing complex and multifaceted phenomena.

3. The text offers an abundance of real-life examples of organizations, situations, and HR departments that illustrate the diversity of thought and practice. All chapters offer a range of challenging student activities, mini-cases (insights), and end-of-chapter case studies which cover a range of organizational

and business contexts, both in the UK and overseas, many provided or informed by practising managers and HR professionals.

4. The text actively encourages students to shape and extend their own learning and understanding of HRM by presenting them with real-life situations that can be discussed either in a seminar/group context or on a private study basis. Moreover, the book is written in a style that seeks to engage with the student through the way the text constantly raises questions, providing critical comment, and opening new lines of enquiry/thought.

5. The extensive online resources provide all the teaching and learning materials needed to support each chapter, removing the need for lecturers to look for additional class and test materials, and giving students the resources they need to build their understanding and to check what actually happened in many of the real-life case studies.

How to Use This Book

KEY TERMS

Each chapter opens by defining the key terms which are to
be explored within that chapter. Read through these before
you begin the chapter to make the ideas and arguments that
follow easier to understand.

LEARNING OBJECTIVES

Clear, concise learning objectives outline the main concepts
and themes to be covered within the chapter. These lists will
help you review your learning and effectively plan revision,
ensuring you have covered all key areas.

STUDENT ACTIVITIES

Put your knowledge to the test by completing the student
activities found in every chapter. Often research-based or
involving problem solving, these activities are designed to
help you engage with the subject and encourage you to learn
through practice. They will support you in developing transferable skills such as group work and giving presentations.

HRM INSIGHTS

These mini case studies present the kinds of scenarios and
challenges experienced in the real world of business, such as
sourcing talented staff and managing strikes in essential services. Accompanied by questions, they prompt you to consider how the theories and models apply in practice.

PRACTITIONER INSIGHTS

Learn from the real-life experiences of HRM professionals in
worldwide businesses and public services through the practitioner insights in each chapter. Practitioners from a range of
organizations reflect on a challenge they have faced to help
you see how such issues are overcome.

RESEARCH INSIGHTS

RESEARCH INSIGHT 1.1

Gouldner, A. W. (1954), *The Wildcat Strike* **(Antioch Press).**

Although Gouldner's (1954) classic account of a labour rela contains many references to organizational features and b introductory chapter, focusing particularly on what he calls within and between the two organizational domains.

Broaden your understanding by reading the summaries of key publications outlined in the research insights. These will help you direct your learning of the topics covered in each chapter and encourage you to delve deeper.

KEY CONCEPTS

KEY CONCEPT Unintended consequence

Unintended consequences, sometimes called quences, are outcomes that are not the ones can be positive but when the term 'unintended consequenc describes something that is negative.

Strengthen your theoretical and analytical grounding by consulting the key concept boxes, which outline new terms that have a specific meaning and are part of the language of HRM.

SIGNPOSTS

I will venture the prediction that we will succeed in inc organizational settings only as we succeed in creating (Heil et al., 2000)

 For an example of one company's attempt to k the Online Resources Extension Material 1.1.

McGregor's emphasis on the importance of understandi izational success is the theme of more recent contributi beings (Amabile and Kramer, 2007, 2011; Lewis, 2011).

Look out for signposts which point to related coverage in another chapter or to where relevant extension material can be found in the online resources to take your learning further.

CASE STUDIES

CASE STUDY ABB

This case study provides interesting insights into most successful executives, and demonstrates th people within the wider context of managing th
    This is a story about the merger, in 1987, of tv and the Swedish firm ASEA—and the role of on tives, Percy Barnevik. It is taken from the book

End-of-chapter case studies and accompanying questions integrate many of the key issues and activities covered in the chapter to demonstrate the challenges faced in HRM and to present an illustration of the theory in practice. They will enable you to contextualize the issues discussed in the chapter and consider how HRM affects organizations as a whole.

REVIEW QUESTIONS

? REVIEW QUESTIONS

1. To what extent is organizational success a function c support your conclusion?

2. What are the current and future challenges that orga manage people?

3. What might happen that will increase the level of co increase, is this likely to be because of what employe

Reinforce your learning and aid your revision with end-of-chapter review questions covering the main themes and issues raised in the chapter.

FURTHER READING

» FURTHER READING

Effron, M. et al. (2003) *Human Resources in the 21st Cer*

Osterhaus, E. (2013) 'The HR department of 2020: 6 bo softwareadvice.com/the-hr-department-of-2020-4

Roehling, M. V. (2005) 'The future of HR management: *Management*, 44(2).

Sage-Gavin, E. and Foster-Cheek, K. (2015) 'The transfc *Strategy*, 38(3), 8–10.

Want to know more? Gain a deeper subject understanding, and explore alternative ideas and contributions to the mainstream treatment of HRM with these selected further reading suggestions.

How to Use the Online Resources

This book is accompanied by a package of online resources that are carefully integrated with the text to assist the learning and teaching of the subject. Students can benefit from extension material, multiple-choice questions, web links, and an interactive glossary; whereas lecturers can make use of a question test bank, suggested answers to questions in the book, seminar activities, and PowerPoint slides.

 Go to www.oup.com/uk/banfield3e/ to find out more.

Acknowledgements

Many people have contributed to this and earlier editions of the book—ex-students who are no doubt now successful professionals, colleagues who have provided important insights into the way people are managed at work, and other managers who have shared their personal experiences and reflections with us to help make the book much better than it would otherwise have been. To all these we offer our thanks and gratitude.

I dedicate this book to my three wonderful children, Sally, Judy, and David who have filled my life with so much love, happiness, and contentment, not to mention five adorable grandchildren. There are no words that express my love for you.

Paul Banfield

I would like to acknowledge the valuable contributions of Francesca Fowler, Beverley Hodson, and Katy Edmonds to this book. I would also once again like to thank my father Neil Kay, for his pride and encouragement and my brother, Steven Kay, for his guidance.

I would also like to thank the many people who have inspired and encouraged my development, thinking, and values in delivering a professional HR service and business partnership throughout my career, including Leigh Thomasson, Tony McLoughlin, Sally Cabrini, and Francesca Fowler.

Rebecca Kay

I'd like to thank my wife Karen and children Holly, Josh, Jake, and Beth who have encouraged me throughout my career in the traditional Yorkshire manner—with a heavy dose of sarcasm. And I love them for it.

Dean Royles

Foundations
of HRM

PART
1

Managing People at Work: Challenges and Opportunities

1

Introduction

This book is written primarily for university and college students who are either specializing in human resource management (HRM), possibly in the context of a CIPD-approved programme, or are taking an HR module as part of a degree that includes the study of the human aspects of work and management. But students rarely stay students forever; they complete their courses and move on into the world of work, becoming HR professionals, managers, entrepreneurs, and executives in many different kinds of organizations. An increasing number will run their own businesses, initially in the small and medium-sized enterprises (SME) sector, and will, among many competing demands, have to deal with the kind of 'people issues' described by Tony Watson. The following quotation is taken from his influential book on management and the organization of work, and reflects the experiences, sense of frustration, and uncertainty articulated by one manager. It is an extract from part of a conversation between the author and manager.

> So the problem is?
> It's the people management thing. It's handling the people who work for me. They are a constant headache. I've tried to read the books and I've been on people management courses. I didn't miss one of the OB classes on my MBA course. But I still despair at the difficulty I have with managing the people in my function; sorting out who is going to do what, getting them to do things I want, getting them to finish things on time, even getting them to be where I want them. And that's before I get into all the recruiting, training, appraising and all that stuff.
> (Watson, 2002)

This book serves two different but related purposes. The first and most obvious is to help readers, as students, grasp the essentials of HRM as an academic field of study and help them meet their course and professional body requirements—and we hope that it will take you well beyond these. But we believe that describing *what* HRM involves and referring to what others have written about it is only a necessary but not sufficient requirement for preparing students for academic and professional examinations. Prescriptions of so-called 'good or best practice' and lists of advantages for certain HR interventions may seem useful, and some may be, but the experiences of the vast majority of managers, and we quote a sample later in the chapter, suggest that the reality of managing people is far more complex, problematic, and challenging than it is often represented. It is also important to question what is 'known' and practised, rather than unquestioningly accepting its efficacy and without understanding its relevance to the different contexts and the particular circumstances and conditions surrounding any claimed-for success. Moreover, indicating what should be done or is being done in other organizations without a third party knowing how to do it or understanding the reasons why a particular HR intervention was made raises important questions about what other factors might need to be taken into account when advocating the transferability of HR practice from one organization to another. What appears to work in one organization may not work in another, and assumptions made about what is to be copied might not be applicable from one to another. Pfeffer and Sutton, writers we will refer to throughout the book, are particularly concerned about managers following unthinkingly the latest fad and 'new management practice'. They caution against the attractive but misleading belief that becoming a better manager is based on knowing what successful managers do and then somehow trying to learn from and then copying their behaviours, a practice sometimes known as benchmarking. Citing Toyota as an example, they argue that:

> Toyota's success is not a set of techniques but its philosophy—the mind set of total quality management and continuous improvement it has embraced.
> (Pfeffer and Sutton, 2006)

They quote a manager who attended one of their classes and realized the danger of an unthinking or casual approach to benchmarking. He said:

> **We have been benchmarking the wrong things. Instead of copying what others do, we ought to copy how they think.**
> (Pfeffer and Sutton, 2006)

As students, then, there is a need to go beyond prescriptions about good practice and develop the habit of questioning why things are being recommended, what the evidence is that supports such prescriptions, and perhaps the most important attribute—develop an independence of thought and a critical mindset, not necessarily to reject what is being presented, but to actively engage with it and apply tests of relevance and appropriateness. We hold the view that many of the explanations and therefore remedies for the kind of people problems common to many organizations may be found in textbooks and that managers can learn from others through benchmarking and the application of 'good practice'. But the challenges of changing behaviour and improving and creating better workplaces also involves leaders, managers, and employees looking *within* their own organizations and at themselves to find answers to the questions that are most important to them. Organizations are not, of course, islands but part of an increasingly interconnected world, yet it is within rather than without that understanding and the sources of improvement lie.

The second purpose of the book is to emphasize the importance of understanding that everything 'done by HR' doesn't necessarily work and that many HR interventions and practices do not produce the outcomes either intended or expected of them and can in fact produce serious and damaging unintended consequences. It is too simplistic to talk about 'good' or 'bad' HRM because these are such subjective terms (although reference is frequently made to good and bad managers), but we can more usefully talk about effective and ineffective HRM practices and reach conclusions about what is achieved based on the use of appropriate evaluation criteria. The importance of establishing the effectiveness of what is done within an HRM context cannot be overstated, nor can seeking to understand the nature of cause–effect relationships even where these may be complicated and mediated by other factors. Many HRM practices are controversial in terms of their value and what they contribute to outcomes at the individual and/or organizational level, an issue that is taken up in more detail in Chapter 2, where the link between HRM and performance is critically evaluated. But the continuing controversy over the claimed contributions of HRM, which we believe, for the majority of organizations, is evidentially based means that a questioning rather than an accepting approach to its role and assumed importance is justified and necessary.

Parts, but not all of the HRM and wider management literature do address the question of effectiveness and why initiatives fail as well as succeed but despite the often-heard claim that 'we are learning from our mistakes', there is a worrying lack of evidence that managers actually do engage in the kind of double-loop learning described by Argyris (1999) as the basis of deeper insights and understanding of why things don't work. For example, given that much of what is involved in HRM is concerned with change—introducing new incentive schemes, new organizational structures, and cultural initiatives as well as more specific initiatives such as value-based selection—should HR practitioners be concerned about the claim made by Nohria and Beer (2000) that:

> **the brutal fact is that about 70% of all change initiatives fail**

Most organizations still invest time and energy in complex and time-consuming performance appraisal (PA) systems and selection procedures, but how many of them would be considered to be successful, and if not are the reasons for the lack of success fully understood? Frequent reorganizations that consume time, resources, and energy are justified on the basis of cost savings and/or efficiency improvements, but how much do they really achieve, and equally important, how much do they cost? Presenting outcomes in terms of success or failure is probably not that helpful—there are of course different degrees of success and failure and often the answer depends on who is asked and when—but there is an expectation that what is done within and by HRM is more likely to have on balance net positive rather than negative outcomes.

The **benefits** and gains following from the implementing of the HR initiative or intervention	Divided by the total **costs** associated with developing	Equals the net gain/loss arising from that intervention

Figure 1.1 An investment model of HRM

Calculating or estimating the value of outcomes means that the costs as well as gains/benefits have to be taken into account and where transactional and opportunity costs are included in the calculations together with the costs of any unintended consequences, the gains from any HR initiative—reducing for example absenteeism rates or introducing a new incentive system—need to be substantial to make the initiative net value adding. In very general terms, Figure 1.1 represents an investment model of HRM based on the costs and benefits of the HRM initiative.

Of course, there are real challenges in being able to accurately calculate the value of costs and benefits, but, without some ability to establish whether HR is making a positive difference and adding rather than reducing value, its overall status and importance will inevitably be challenged.

The position taken here is that the outcomes that follow from HR interventions are problematic and uncertain; we simply can't be sure that the objectives associated with any HR activity or procedure will be met simply because the activity is carried out. In extreme cases, not only may HRM interventions not work, that is, they produce no discernible benefits, but they actually produce negative outcomes. What is even more of an issue is that these are often not immediately known but emerge some time later and may not actually be recognized as negative. The reasons for this are often complex but are frequently to do with stakeholders not wishing to admit and accept their ideas and actions have 'failed' and a tendency to over-state benefits and understate negative outcomes. Failure through rationalization becomes success, which may serve political purposes but hardly contributes to a genuine understanding of what is actually achieved. The following story of a 'good idea' that didn't work illustrates the concept of unintended consequences and a failed initiative.

> **During the time of British rule in colonial India, in order to free Delhi from a plague of snakes, the City's governor put an incentive scheme in place for their capture by introducing a bounty on cobra skins. The bounty was quite high as cobras are tricky to catch. And so, instead of the snakes being caught in the city, it became a sound business idea to start farming them. All of a sudden, the number of bounty claims increased disproportionately. The local authority realised what was going on and responded by abandoning the incentive scheme. And as they were no longer profitable, the cobras were released from the farms into the city, exacerbating the original problem.**
> (Obloj, 2013)

The point of the story is obvious and needs little elaboration other than to note that when managers introduce 'solutions' to problems, the solution might itself become a new problem!

Another more recent example provides further evidence on the problematic nature of many managerial interventions. In the same article, Obloj claimed that firms are often tempted to accept the unintended costs of financial incentive schemes in the hope that any productivity increases generated by the scheme will outweigh them. He went on to say that while this may be true in some cases, there are reasons to be cautious of using powerful compensation mechanisms to drive performance, citing the case of Lloyds Bank and the heavy financial penalties incurred over the mis-selling of PPI as a result of 'serious failings' in its sales incentives system. He argued that the effectiveness of such systems changes over time and that while there may be productivity gains early on, the adverse consequences manifest themselves more and more as employees learn the loopholes in the system and figure out how to work it.

One of the most influential of contemporary HRM writers, Dave Ulrich, whose work is considered in detail in Chapter 2, is particularly concerned to distinguish between what he calls HR activities and HR outcomes, arguing that much more needs to be done to connect the two together. The story of the Indian incentive scheme also reminds us of the concept of unintended consequences which relates to outcomes that are either not thought of or intended but which often follow new initiatives and practices. Not all are negative but the use of the concept is usually associated with things that 'go wrong', as they did in the snake example.

> **KEY CONCEPT Unintended consequences**
>
> Unintended consequences, sometimes called unanticipated consequences or unforeseen consequences, are outcomes that are not the ones foreseen and intended by a purposeful action. They can be positive but when the term 'unintended consequences' is used to describe a particular outcome it usually describes something that is negative.

Workforce planning is another area of HR where the problem of unintended consequences can be illustrated. As an example, HR specialists in the NHS are frequently in the news because of staffing crises or the lack of suitably trained doctors and nurses and seem to be engaged in a constant battle to overcome what are both long-term and periodic shortages. At the time of writing this chapter, a prominent headline in a national newspaper read:

NHS looks to India to fix A & E staffing shortages
(*Daily Telegraph*, 15 January 2014)

There are many explanations for what seems to be chronic staffing shortage in emergency medicine, and in the past the most attractive and appropriate answer might have been that there were too few doctors training and that the obvious solution was to train more. Up to a point almost certainly, but there is a need to look beyond the obvious and more attractive explanations and become intellectually curious about that part of 'the picture' that is hidden. This means looking for explanations which are less obvious, which may be unpalatable or ideologically difficult to countenance and often require more sophisticated strategies to remedy the problem. And this goes to the heart of our approach to learning about and practising HR. It is a question about 'knowing' the kind of problem that has to be addressed, understanding its causes (rather than addressing symptoms), and then being able to, with a degree of confidence, predict the likely outcomes that will follow any new policy and action. This means that people need to be sure that they:

- Are engaging in a rigorous diagnostic process.
- Are framing the problem in the right way.
- Understand what the problem is and how important it is.
- Distinguish problem symptoms from underlying causes.
- Are able, within resource constraints, to fix or control the problem.
- Find unconventional and innovative ways that are 'resource light'.
- Don't produce a 'solution' that is worse than the original problem.
- Can deal with any unintended consequences.

As we make clear throughout the book, most situations that HR professionals and managers face can be seen through different lenses or by the application of different mental models and they need to be aware of which they are using and then recognize both their strengths and limitations. We are all limited to a degree by our own 'blindness' and those working within the context of HRM are no different! We often interpret situations in ways that make them easier to understand but in so doing we can distort and oversimplify; the things we would rather not see but which can be particularly important are often conveniently ignored or rationalized away.

STUDENT ACTIVITY 1.1

Read the article by Pfeffer (2005), 'Changing mental models: HR's most important task human resource', *Human Resource Management*, 44(2), 123–8. Summarize the article's key points and begin to think about your own ways of 'seeing' HR and the mental models used in your organization and the implications that follow.

So, with the NHS example in mind, what can we say about these shortages of A&E doctors? Well, the problem may not only be about the number of doctors who are trained but also one of retention and utilization. In what is increasingly a global market for medics there is a greater likelihood that doctors will increasingly look for opportunities outside of the NHS for promotion and career development opportunities. Note: moving to other hospitals within the NHS is much less of a problem than staff leaving the country to work abroad, and globalization also works in the interests of the NHS through foreign doctors moving to the UK.

There is evidence that while medical students are keen to train in emergency medicine, many drop out or emigrate to work in countries such as Australia where staffing levels are higher, with one study suggesting that the number of young doctors trained in the UK or Ireland but who are now working in Australian A&E departments has risen by 60 per cent in the past five years. In 2015, it was reported by the Australian Bureau of Statistics that 13 per cent of all GPs in Australia and 22 per cent of all specialists came from the UK (*Daily Telegraph*, 5 November 2015). Simply increasing the numbers trained here without changing anything else perpetuates the loss, at least in the short to medium term (see also *The Guardian*, 27 December 2013).

Let's consider two further examples where a solution to a problem produced unexpected consequences. The first involves the increasing number of females entering the medical profession. Few would argue that this is anything other than a positive step forward in the attempt to increase female participation in the professions generally, but, and it is a but that has to be acknowledged, this trend is not without its implications. The growing proportion of females in medical schools was the theme of an article written by Professor J. Meirion Thomas who reported that by 2017, for the first time, there will be more female than male doctors in the UK. He goes on:

> Although I am a feminist—in the NHS hospital in which I work as a surgeon, some of the best doctors are women—this shift of the gender balance in medicine is a worrying trend. I believe it is creating serious workforce problems, and has profound implications for the way the NHS works. For many years—until the Sixties—fewer than 10 per cent of British doctors were female. Then things changed. For the past four decades 60 per cent of students selected for training in UK medical schools have been female . . . I fear this gender imbalance is already having a negative effect on the NHS. The reason is that most female doctors end up working part-time—usually in general practice—and then retire early. As a result, it is necessary to train two female doctors so they can cover the same amount of work as one full-time colleague. Given that the cost of training a doctor is at least £500,000, are taxpayers getting the best return on their investment?
> (*Mail Online*, 2 January 2014)

However politically sensitive this argument might be, and it is likely to prove controversial, from an intellectual perspective can the possibility that changes in the gender composition of the labour force may be a factor in the shortage of A&E doctors be disregarded? In the wider debate about women in the workforce and the need to correct historical inequalities and biases, the long-term workforce planning implications may have been taken into account by decision makers and the impact on the supply of labour accepted, but it is difficult to know whether this is the case. There is also the question of medical school capacity to train more doctors to compensate for the effect Professor Meirion Thomas identified (although recent government policy changes are addressing this issue) and the ethical issues in attracting doctors from overseas and depriving less developed countries of a vital human resource. There are two agendas at work here and the question of which one takes priority is a political not an HR one. But the point being made is not about whether this commitment to encourage more females to study and practise medicine is 'right' but rather whether its consequences for the supply of labour were fully understood and planned for.

The second example relates to the effect of external regulation on working conditions and labour supply. The European Working Time Directive was implemented in 2009 and tightly regulated the time that junior doctors are allowed by law to work. The thinking behind the Directive was that doctors should be protected from having to work excessive hours which can be detrimental to their own well-being and the safety of hospital patients. But there is a general perception that the reduction of working hours to a maximum of forty-eight per week was having an adverse effect on the utilization and development of junior doctors. Evidence for this, however, is less than clear. Morrow et al. (2012a) found that there have been a number of interesting and important adaptations to working practices in response to the Working Time Directive that had not necessarily been intended or foreseen. These are:

- the redesign of working hours, shifts, and rotas, including specific initiatives for night-time services;
- the redistribution of trainee workload to other professionals, usually nurses or other groups, although sometimes to other doctors;
- the use of technology to improve monitoring and time management, or to facilitate more flexible learning.

In this particular example, a change in one part of the 'system', which reflected the health and safety agenda, impacted negatively on another—the utilization and development of staff—but what was not foreseen was how the 'system' would adapt and produce 'solutions' that while unforeseen were nevertheless effective. As this example illustrates, not all unintended and unknown consequences are negative, but many can be and need to be identified and addressed as soon as possible.

Making a Difference

As we said earlier, the students of today will soon become the professional managers and business people of tomorrow, and the challenges they face in these roles will be very different to those they faced in lectures, seminars, and the examination hall. The reason for this is obvious; as a student, passing or failing at whatever level has consequences primarily for the individual. It matters of course whether the learning experiences have been interesting and developmental and whether course work assignments and examinations have been passed, but in a future role the consequences of success and failure are of a very different order. Decisions taken or conversely not taken by managers and HR professionals not only have implications for their own positions and standing but far more importantly affect other people: their subordinates, colleagues, and possibly trade union representatives—and will of course affect the business or organization as a whole; indeed, from a systems perspective the wider community could also be affected. The more senior the position, the more good or harm the manager can do! Getting things right and doing the right things in the right way most of the time may be thought of as aspirational rather than as a realistic objective, given the challenges and difficulties managers face on an ongoing basis, but it can be a very useful template for action and decision-making. Of course, the answer to the question 'right for whom' is not always straightforward and doing 'the right things in the right way' raises issues of conflicting goals, interests, and ethical standards. Nevertheless, when it comes down to the fundamentals of managing people making a positive difference, meeting as many different interests as possible, making employees feel good about themselves and their jobs, and helping to ensure organizational success have to be the outcomes managers strive to deliver. Interestingly, the existential question asked of Alban, quoted in the preface to Weisbord's book on productive workplaces (2012):

> do we make any difference?
>
> (p. xxiii)

is both a compelling and provocative one and a test that can be used throughout our lives. There are numerous ways people at work can make a difference but because this book is written from a managerial perspective, the following story was chosen because it relates to the behaviour of a manager and its effect on an employee.

 HRM INSIGHT 1.1 The marriage invitation

As with all the stories in this book, this is essentially true and based on what actually happened, although names have been changed to preserve confidentiality.

Martin Wilson was a qualified accountant with considerable experience of financial and management accounting in industry. He built a reputation for honesty and incisiveness and was recognized as someone who could find out what the problems of a business were and had the ability to come up with solutions that worked. Not long after he retired from his job as finance director of a medium-sized engineering company located in Yorkshire, he received a call from a friend who owned the same kind of company not far from his home. His friend outlined a series of production and financial problems that were proving difficult to resolve and asked Martin if he would consider running the company as its CEO for a year to try to sort things out.

After considering the offer, Martin agreed and took over in early 2009. The company employed about 450 people and had a divisional structure, each one headed by a director. There was a small personnel department which dealt with recruitment and employment issues but it didn't extend its activities much beyond that. His approach to management was to find out as much as he could about the business before deciding what action to take. So, in his first two weeks, as well as looking at the books and finding out how each of the divisions was doing, he began a series of visits to all the manufacturing units to get a first-hand view of the manufacturing processes and working conditions. He wanted to get a feel for how things were done. He did this by walking around, observing, and talking to managers and operatives.

After a few weeks, he thought he had built up a picture of where the business was and what needed to be done, but he still visited each part of the business on a regular basis, taking time to talk to people, know their names, and find out what they thought about their jobs, management, and the business as a whole. He believed in listening as much as talking.

During the Easter of that year he was surprised to receive a wedding invitation; it was from one of the shop-floor operatives who he had got to know as a result of his frequent visits around the factory. Of course, it was a surprise to him to receive something like that from someone who was neither a friend nor relative, so he went to have a word with him to try to find out what was behind the invitation. When he met with him shortly after receiving the invitation he told him—his name was David James—that he was surprised by the invitation but that he would certainly be at the wedding, but he was still curious about the reason for it. So, he said, 'David, given that we don't really know each other that well, why invite me to your wedding?' The reply came as something of surprise! David said, 'Well, in all the time I've worked here none of the directors ever bothered to talk to me like you did and you were the first to ask me my name and talked to me as an equal—I mean like informally and friendly. So, I wanted to show my appreciation for something that is important to me and I thought the wedding invitation would do just that.'

Questions

1. Why did Martin's behaviour have such a powerful influence on David James?
2. What stopped other directors from engaging in the same behaviour?
3. How could something that Martin wasn't even aware of doing have had such an effect?
4. What was being affected by Martin's behaviour?

A consistent theme of this book is the importance of understanding how, and the extent to which, the behaviour of managers influences employees emotionally and psychologically and how this in turn affects their behaviour, not only in terms of job performance but also in relation to propensity to stay, attendance, and engagement levels. We believe that it is important to distinguish the impact of the behaviour of managers from the effects of formal HRM practices and activities and suggest that where these practices and activities are appropriate to the situation *and* are supported by positive managerial behaviour the outcomes are likely to be beneficial for all stakeholders. Uncaring and unthinking managers can make a very significant difference to the performance and well-being of their subordinates and the organization as a whole, as can those managers who are engaged with their staff, understand human motivation, can communicate effectively, and build trust within relationships. It is a different difference! Both kinds of managers make a difference but one is negative and the other positive, and the implications for the well-being of the individual and organization of having one or the other type of manager in control are far-reaching and often profound. We hope that those students who use and read this book will become better managers than they might otherwise have been, but also become different people in small but important ways; people who combine a high level of emotional intelligence with a strong philosophy of management, high but realistic ethical standards, and good practical and professional skills. And, above all, avoid becoming the kind of manager described by writers such as Sutton (2010), Frost (2003), and Buckingham and Coffman (2005), whose contributions to our understanding of what could be described as dysfunctional managers are reviewed later in the chapter.

All managers in whatever discipline or function have a major responsibility for managing people: those that work for them directly and those that they are able to influence indirectly. The importance of influence as an integral element in any relationship is critical to developing a deeper understanding of employee behaviour. Influence doesn't only come from managers but that which does often has a powerful effect. Paradoxically, managing is more often seen as a technical function with managers involved in planning, acquiring, using, and controlling resources, managing information, decision-making, and so on, and much of the so-called classic approach to management certainly emphasizes such functional responsibilities (Clegg et al., 2015). But there is a danger that, if these are seen as the only things that managers do, the crucial human side of management will be ignored or downplayed. Watson, in the first edition of his book, alluded to this problem of manager detachment when he said that:

> **Managers are pressurised to be technical experts, devising rational and emotionally neutral systems and corporate structures to 'solve problems' and 'make decisions' about how to run the business. These scientific and rational–analytical practices give reassurance but can leave managers so distanced from 'the managed' their capacity to control events is undermined.**
> **(1994)**

The effect on people of having an unthoughtful and uncaring manager can in extreme cases be psychologically and emotionally damaging and long lasting.

A popular belief is that the primary reason people leave their jobs is because of pay, but according to a recent survey carried out by the Gallop organization involving over one million workers in the United States, a bad boss or supervisor is the number one reason people leave, reflecting the way they have been treated and the hostile environment created by their managers (Oien, 2016).

This idea that 'managers can damage the health of their workers' is one that several of the writers referred to in this chapter subscribe to. This suggests that while many managers are highly competent and effective in the way they manage their staff, others are less so and there is a further category whose contributions actually undermine well-being and performance. One of the most influential contemporary writers on management is Robert Sutton, a member of faculty at Stanford University in the USA. In his blog, Sutton lists the twelve things he believes in about management, the first one being:

> **Sometimes the best management is no management at all—first do no harm!**

The idea that managers can do harm should not surprise anyone who has read about the Enron Corporation and the damage done to its employees and other organizations by its CEO Jeffrey Skilling and many other senior managers. And the disastrous rule of Fred Goodwin at RBS, although partly explained by a reckless business strategy, is also linked to his approach to leadership and management. A 2012 report into the crash of RBS:

> condemned the former chief executive's 'aggressive, macho management style' that created a culture where staff were locked in constant fear of losing their jobs, and his lieutenants were said to have stopped employees speaking out about problems.
> (*The Scotsman*, 2012)

STUDENT ACTIVITY 1.2

Watch the film about Enron and its demise at https://www.youtube.com/watch?v=AiWKPQAWuug, thinking carefully about the corporate culture that was created and the different management practices that characterized the organization.

Sutton (2007) is also well known because of his belief that organizations need to reduce the malign influence of 'bad' managers by applying what he calls 'the no-asshole rule' which reflects the importance of preventing people who represent a negative and destructive influence on other people from joining the organization or removing them from it. Sutton's belief that people and organizations suffer from managers and ordinary employees who fit his description of what an asshole is and does, is undoubtedly controversial and the purpose of mentioning it is not to support or challenge his thinking and beliefs but rather to present it as a potentially relevant contribution to the debate about the kind of influences managers can exercise. He states that the most important reason he wrote the book is because demeaning people does terrible damage to others and to their companies, arguing that even though there are occasions when being an asshole helps people and companies 'win', his view still is that if you are a winner and an asshole, you are still an asshole. The question that springs to mind here is whether to be a winner you have to be an asshole or whether success over the longer term is compromised if managers strive to win at all costs and feel that this requires them to act like one.

Perhaps the most influential management writer of his generation, Peter Drucker (2007), used less colourful but equally unequivocal language when he wrote:

> So much of what we call management consists of making it difficult for people to do work.
> (quoted in Amabile and Kramer, 2011)

But the idea that getting the 'best out of people' necessarily involves managers being tough and putting pressure on staff is one that resonates with many people, particularly those who hold the set of assumptions about peoples' attitudes towards work which McGregor labelled Theory X. We consider McGregor's work later in the chapter. The point being made here is that pressurized working environments staffed by so-called 'macho managers' may indeed be successful, although whether this success extends into the long term is much more problematic. The difference between acceptable levels of pressure and high but realistic standards and damaging and stressful behaviour is one of degree not kind and the evidence about the most effective people management strategies is almost certainly going to be contentious and inconsistent. One reason for this is that the context in which managers manage differs and changes, often quite rapidly. The evidence we use, and we accept that it is selective, suggests that long-term success is unlikely to be maintained if managers undermine, use fear and coercion, bully and belittle their staff, but many organizations do seem to survive despite managers behaving as 'assholes' to use Sutton's terminology. There is evidence supporting the use of certain strategies, approaches, and practices but it is often qualified, challenged, and sometimes rejected and the difficulty of course is to know what to believe. The famous economist Hayek (1974) argued that we should look for what he called 'pattern predictions' to understand the nature of relationships, and in the context of HRM these would be represented by behaviours, activities, configurations, and situations which seemed to be consistently linked to favourable outcomes for both the organization and its employees. The need is for evidence which is consistent, persuasive, and verifiable. In the penultimate section we address directly the question of evidence and the work of those associated with evidence-based management.

Making a difference is the basis of the annual *Sunday Times* survey of companies that are nominated by employees as outstanding places to work in. The following activity generates genuine insights into companies that have succeeded in making a difference and provides insights into management and organizational practices that are associated with high-performing businesses and satisfied employees.

STUDENT ACTIVITY 1.3

The *Sunday Times* carries out an annual survey of different sized and sector companies which have been voted as the best companies to work for by their employees. These are companies that are making a difference! See http://appointments.thesundaytimes.co.uk/article/best100companies

Look at the latest survey reports. Then:

1. Split into two or three groups depending on size and available time. In all seminar activities provided in this book, it is highly advisable that the number in each group should not exceed five/six. This is to avoid the tendency of some members becoming disengaged and peripheral.

2. The task of group 1 is to research the top ten best big companies to work for.

3. Group 2 has the same task but focusing on the top ten best small companies.

4. If appropriate, group 3 can look at the top 10 not-for-profit companies.

5. Each group should then present a PowerPoint presentation of no more than six slides and lasting no more than ten minutes each, using a mixture of words, symbols, images, and other forms of visual representations (this technique is called 'rich pictures'). The emphasis is on creativity and clarity of message. In open discussion, explore the findings produced by all three groups and draw appropriate inferences and conclusions. The emphasis is on showing the relationship between HRM practices and outcomes for different stakeholders.

In the same way that employees represent different asset values and make different contributions to the organization they work for, managers also vary significantly in terms of their asset value, or to use another expression, their human capital value. But an important distinction needs to be made between what individual managers are valued at and the value of the contributions they actually make. Because managers are by definition in positions of authority and exercise a degree of control over their staff, we would argue that their potential to generate added value is in general terms higher than that of an employee. But the reverse equally applies; managers have greater potential to generate 'negative' added value, by which we mean that on balance they do more harm than good and the reason for this is obvious. The kind of manager Sutton wishes to keep out of organizations has the potential to undermine the productive behaviours of all those they have influence over, through direct contact, and as a result of the working environment they help to create.

As a yardstick, it could be argued that a ratio of 1:1 represents a situation where a manager's net added value is zero: where the negative contributions are broadly equivalent to the value of their positive contributions. Managers who are effective at managing people would be associated with a higher net added value figure because their benign impact stimulates and encourages all their staff to perform at higher levels. A ratio of plus 1:8 might represent that end of the positive part of the continuum. At the other extreme a ratio of minus 1:8 indicates not simply an incompetent manager but one who is causing serious damage and incurring unnecessary lost performance and production. Put simply, a bad employee will cost the organization far less than a bad manager because of the much more extensive impact that managers have. It follows therefore that the higher in the organization, the greater damage/added value individual managers are associated with.

Consider the following practical example of the costs associated with bad managers. In 2004, the CIPD estimated that the costs associated with replacing someone who left was £4k for an employee and £7k for a manager. In 2014, a report published by Oxford Economics revealed that replacing members of staff incurs much higher costs for employers, estimated to be £30,614 per employee. (The survey focused on professional workers.) This is made up of the cost of lost output as the new employee becomes fully competent and the logistical cost of recruiting and absorbing a new worker.

While it is impossible to be sure about why people leave or the number that do so primarily because of their manager, the Gallup findings suggest this is the main reason people leave. And while the figure of £30k is representative, rather than definitive, the point is that bad and ineffective managers cost money!

However, the issue is not only about the costs incurred when managers demotivate their employees and negatively impact their performance and contributions; it is also about those managers who have a consistently positive impact on these factors and what that means for both employee and organization. Interestingly, such a difference is by no means unique to work organization; the same phenomenon is found in schools, universities, and other institutions. Research into the differential impact teachers make found that:

> the magnitude of variation in the quality of teachers, even within schools, is startling. Teachers who work in a given school, and therefore teach students with similar demographic characteristics, can be responsible for increases in math and reading levels that range from a low of one half year to a high of one and a half years of learning in each academic year.
> (Hanushek, 2011)

Note: in the light of these findings and arguments it is difficult to argue that selection is not perhaps the most important of all HRM activities and decisions.

So far, we have linked the effective management of people to two key variables:

- the appropriateness and effectiveness of the strategies, policies, and practices associated with HRM; and
- the quality and effectiveness of managers and the way they manage their staff.

But these are only two of the four variables that need to be considered in our analysis of people management. The other two are highlighted by Watson (2006) when he said:

> the study of the organization and management of work, and by implication the management of people, has to combine two inter-related factors. One is the study of worker behaviour—the drives, motivations, aspirations and emotions that people display in their work roles and which help to explain their value, performance and contribution as economic resources, and the other is what he describes as the 'already existing and emerging organizational structures and patterns.
> (p. 2)

For him, this interplay between human and structural factors represents perhaps the central dynamic of organizational life and understanding how it plays out in each organization offers incredibly important insights and explanations into the behaviour of people and the success or failure of HR practices.

The same point is made by Weisbord (2012) in the context of training effectiveness. He argues that existing job descriptions, work demarcations, patterns of influence, and restricted information were factors that if left unchallenged and unchanged would almost certainly limit the effectiveness of any skills development programme. His statement that managers need to:

> fix structures first then watch how people straighten up and fly right

suggests that focusing on attempting to change worker behaviour and performance in isolation from the context in which they are delivered, and particularly the constraints that limit what they are required or allowed to do, will be unlikely to succeed. In this sense, we might consider that one of the key functions of HRM is or should be one of liberation: freeing people from unnecessary and constraining restrictions. In Chapter 2 we review the use of different metaphors to describe 'HR' but the interesting idea that HR practitioners are 'liberators' isn't one of them!

It might be considered that the structural characteristics we have identified as having an important limiting effect on employee behaviour are unintended and can easily be removed. This would for many large-scale organizations, particularly in the public sector, be an inappropriate conclusion. Many of the consequences of these structural factors on employee behaviour are actually intended. Organizations are many things but one thing they do represent is *structures of control*. They are designed to ensure conformity, obedience, and to eliminate behaviour that challenges the existing locus of power and patterns of authority which are invariably invested in the management hierarchy. Over the decades, the coercive nature of organizational control has been partly replaced by control based on consent as the costs in lost labour utilization and both collective and individual resistance became unacceptable. As Morgan argues, organizations that still retain historical structural forms with their formalized procedures, routines, hierarchies, and roles will:

> **limit rather than mobilise the development of human characteristics, moulding human beings to fit the requirements of mechanical organizations rather than building the organization around their strengths and potential.**
>
> **(1986)**

All organizations exercise different forms of control over the people they employ; what distinguishes them is in the form and degree of control and its effectiveness. The position taken here is that fitting people into jobs, structures, and hierarchies can only work up to a point and that point is reached when the strategy creates resistance, unintended consequences, low performance, and an unhealthy psychological environment. It fails precisely because it forces people to behave in ways that are in conflict with their innate humanness and requires them to be less than they are. As Herzberg (1991) once said in a lecture:

> **treat me as I am, not how you want me to be.**

But from a managerial perspective the alternative statement might be something like:

> **be as I need you to be and do what I need you to do**

Making a difference can be applied to almost any situation: a new sports coach, a different teacher, a special book, and so on. Applied to the practice and study of HRM and management in general we know from our own experiences that not all lecturers have the same value or make the same impressions, some of which stay for a long time and have a lasting effect! The same principle applies to management writers and the contributions they make. In this book, the selection of writers and books referred to have been chosen because they have been influential and made a difference to our understanding of what the management of people involves and how it can be made more effective. Some of these contributions will be familiar but others less so. Very few students, for example, are likely to have heard of Robert Townsend, although McGregor, because of his frequently referred to Theory X and Y, is better known today. But Warren Bennis described Townsend as the management guru of the 1960s and claimed that:

> **Despite appearances, Bob Townsend is not just a Sixties happening. His words still ring true, truer than they seemed almost forty years ago. Like McGregor, he may have been stricken with a case of unwarranted optimism. Doug thought we'd have an anti-Theory X vaccine by 1980. It is undeniable that Theory Y has gained more adherents and robustness over the years with a new vocabulary of 'HR talk' like empowerment, transparency, agency, and so forth. And there are certainly more enlightened and emboldened leaders and scholars making some headway toward creating cultures of growth and learning. But it will always be a struggle.**
>
> **(Townsend, 2007)**

And O'Toole argued that:

> Townsend was the first true, modern corporate leader (defined as one who manifests vision, integrity, and courage in a consistent pattern of behaviour that inspires trust, motivation, and responsibility on the part of followers, who in turn become leaders themselves).
> (Townsend, 2007: xiii)

He added:

> Townsend hated bureaucracy and bloated central headquarters. His advice: 'Fire the P.R. Department'. Ditto the law, purchasing, and other staffs headed by 'V.P.'s. Fire the Personnel Department', he said most famously, not only because those supernumeraries produce little at great expense but, more important, because no significant contribution to corporate excellence had ever been led by an H.R. department. So why not get rid of it?
> (Townsend, 2007: xiii)

So, Townsend was a practising manager, an owner, and a leader who wrote about his experiences and was both highly critical of many managers and organizations while at the same optimistic about what could be achieved. He took over control of the Avis Rent a Car company in the 1960s when it was loss-making. Several years later he sold it to Hertz and was asked by the CEO of Hertz what he had done to turn the business around. The CEO intimated that he must have made extensive changes. Townsend replied by saying that he hadn't. What he had done was to talk to lots of people and asked the same questions, which were

- Who are the people who are stopping things that need to change from happening?
- Who were obstructing progress and generally, using the words of Sutton, were being 'assholes' but Townsend called them lemons?
- Who were what he called 'the unsung heroes'—the people who were striving to do better, who had the right ideas to turn the company around but were being thwarted and marginalized?

After listening to what the employees had to say, Townsend acted. He essentially got rid of the 'lemons' and promoted the unsung heroes; he identified and liberated talent while at the same time removing the dead weight of those who couldn't or didn't want to change and were holding the company back. As a contemporary of the 1960s the relevance of his ideas could easily be questioned by today's managers and HR professionals. But on closer inspection his analysis of what was wrong with organizations then is arguably still valid in important respects today and continues to inform much of today's management thinking although less so practice. As an example, for many years Nortel Networks, a Canadian telecoms business, developed an HR strategy based on what it called structured differentiation. This meant that it devised different practices and policies to reflect the different value and contributions of its best people: this didn't mean the majority of employees were ignored; rather, that they rewarded, developed, and utilized differently and in ways that reflected differences in ability, value, commitment, and potential. So, while organizations share many common features, as do people, difference is an equally important concept and making a difference is an outcome that can be linked to how:

- leaders lead;
- managers manage;
- organizational cultures and working environments develop;
- HRM policies and practices are designed and implemented; and
- individual characteristics, attributes, and motivations translate into behaviours.

Interestingly, difference and differentiation is at the heart of Michael Porter's work on strategy, and in Chapter 3 we apply these concepts to HRM, looking at how added value can be achieved through doing the same things better, by doing things differently, or by doing different things compared to their competitors.

Developing a Systems and Holistic Perspective

The frequently competing and conflicting interests and forces that exist within and outside organizations constitute what is often described as the context within which employment and work takes place, and any meaningful understanding of what influences the way people behave and are managed at work has to have regard to the nature of organizations, their environments, how they function, and how we conceptualize them. This section addresses these questions.

The focus of much that goes on 'within' HRM quite rightly is on individual behaviour, but individual behaviour is much more than a function of individual motivation. We use the term 'the organizational environment' to mean the totality of the influences that have a potential bearing on what employees and managers do. The external environment, whether this is competitive or state regulated, has a major influence on the kinds of challenges and opportunities each organization faces and many of the decisions taken by managers reflect their understanding and interpretation of these external forces. There are circumstances when these pose an existential threat and require appropriate and often urgent action. Economic recession, loss of competitive advantage, technological change, and unforeseen events all require managerial responses that usually impact on their employees either directly or indirectly. So, we can see for example that the focus of workforce planning during an economic downturn will reflect the need to reduce headcount or wage costs and in an upturn ensure sufficient supplies of labour are available to meet an increasing demand for staff. The key to understanding the challenges facing HRM is to recognize the dynamic and rapidly changing nature of the external environment and the implications this has for the strategies and policies needed to react to it.

Consider the case of the North Sea oil and gas sector and the changes it has had to adapt to over the last few years. Both of the situations described below occurred and probably overlapped since 2008.

According to recent research by Oliver Wyman (formerly Mercer Management Consulting):

> **over the next decade, attracting and retaining skilled workers will be one of the biggest risks to industry success.**
> (Orr and McVerry, 2007)

They argue that upstream and midstream businesses are expected to be the most affected, as large numbers of experienced workers retire and competition for new talent heats up. They point out that this is not just an HR issue in terms of the numbers that need to be recruited but one that recognizes that knowledge, not assets, will be the source of future value growth in the sector, and a shortage of well-qualified professionals will constrain the abilities both to grow in scale and to compete in an ever more crowded field.

But the following was written in 2015:

> Oil explorers predict 10,000 more job losses in North Sea sector. Two of the biggest independent oil explorers in the North Sea have predicted a further 10,000 jobs will be lost from the sector, indicating a growing acceptance that oil prices are stuck in a prolonged slump.
> (*Financial Times*, 18 October 2015)

Examples like this suggest that while much of what HR does reflects relatively stable and predictable circumstances it also has to deal with the unpredictable and often contradictory events over which it has little or no control. Does this mean that if the external environment is dynamic and to a degree unpredictable the nature of HRM has to be equally dynamic, responsive, and to a degree unpredictable too? We would argue that this is the case but only in relation to operational activities and priorities; what should be an enduring feature of HRM, and is for what might be described as enlightened organizations, is the way people are treated and managed at work. There is of course a tension between these two dimensions of HRM; on the one hand reacting quickly to environmental change and existential threats and on the other developing a long-term commitment to employees, rewarding them fairly and treating them with respect. The potential and often real conflict between these dimensions cannot be resolved in any finite way but it can be managed in ways that minimize the damage to employee interests caused by organizations reacting to environmental change.

Losing one's job for whatever reason can often cause financial and psychological damage, and few organizations today can guarantee a job or employment for life; but while it might be thought that economic circumstances give managers little choice in relation to cutbacks and downsizing—and realistically this is often the case—the ability to maintain a commitment to the well-being of their employees can still to a significant extent be maintained because:

- Where job losses are needed to cut costs, reducing employment costs can be achieved by alternative means such as cutting back on overtime, implementing a generalized pay reduction, including managers, and allowing people to leave who are close to their preferred retirement age. In other words, the pain can be shared or different cost-reduction strategies can be deployed. Some years ago, while attending an HR conference in Beirut one of the authors had a conversation with an internationally known French management consultant who specialized in performance management. He said that one of his conditions for taking on a new job was that no one would lose their job unless it was managers who lost theirs! Not always possible to achieve but it was his strong belief that workers should not be punished for the mistakes of their managers.

- Where job losses are inevitable, two points can be made. First, job losses may be reversed if and when economic conditions improve. The following account by William Beckett shows that this strategy can mitigate what might otherwise have been a permanent loss. Second, the **way** in which people are treated during the process of redundancies is critical to maintaining the organization's commitment to its employees' well-being. Leaving packages, support in finding alternative employment, continued links with the organization, counselling, and creating a sense of fairness in the way things are done are all things that HR can do to demonstrate this concern for employees.

The following Practitioner Insight captures these two aspects of HRM perfectly: a rapidly changing external environment and the actions of a CEO who was required to take appropriate action in response.

PRACTITIONER INSIGHT William Beckett CEO of Beckett's Plastics
The following is a description of what the company experienced during the recent economic recession and the action it took to stave off closure. It shows what the company did in order to survive a rapid and steep fall in its orders and highlights the choices management made that ensured its survival.

One of the important things I realized was that previous experience helped in the way I reacted to the 2009 recession. It was also apparent that speed of action was essential to our survival; I know of many other companies whose management delayed taking the necessary action which often came too late to save the businesses. As soon as we realized how badly affected our sales were going to be we immediately started looking at the management accounts to look at cash flow and where we could start reducing costs. Initially that didn't affect our employees. For example, we cancelled all our cleaning contracts and took responsibility for cleaning the premises ourselves—the directors shared responsibilities for this—even to cleaning the toilets. We needed to set an example that said we all share the pain of saving the company!

The problem was that this saved only half a job and that wasn't nearly enough: we quickly realized that we had to make cuts in the labour force, but we did this in as fair a way as possible but always having regard for the need to protect and secure key skills. We had to make a 20 per cent cut in shop-floor workers and then over 40 per cent in our sales and administration team, but even that wasn't enough. We then instituted cuts in hours and a cut in wages with the directors taking the biggest cut in remuneration. Overtime and pension contributions were also halted.

This meant that the remaining staff had to do more to cover the work of those who had left, so we had to rely on their willingness and goodwill to keep things going. The decline in sales reached 55 per cent in August 2009 and by that time we had made further redundancies and instituted short-time working. We also made important changes to shift patterns which meant that we were working more efficiently and this also benefited the operatives who found they had more leisure time to enjoy. Our productivity went up because in the worst of the recession the factory was only open for three days each week and this meant we saved on many of our variable costs.

Although these actions seem extreme they simply reflected a need to reduce costs to reflect a drastic fall in income and cash flow—another month of falling sales would almost certainly have meant that the company went under! And they worked because after August sales increased and we began to bring back those employees who had been temporarily laid off even though we were still losing money. In total, we lost £120k in that year. And despite the effect of the cuts on our staff they were incredibly supportive of what we were doing and there was a strong sense of 'being in this together'. No one left for other jobs and we were able to offer those we made redundant their jobs back towards the end of 2009 and into 2010.

The situation now is that the order book is double what it was in 2009. We have increased working hours, re-employed many old staff, and are looking to recruit skilled workers again. So, many of the cuts have been reversed as business has improved and the company is on an upward trajectory again.

On reflection, the final point I would make relates to leadership and the importance of understanding the nature and scale of the problem you are faced with. Employees in these circumstances need to feel that the right decisions are being made for the company and that management is doing everything it can to protect all employees in the best way that it can. In these circumstances, when all stakeholders share the cutbacks and additional responsibilities and where management sets a clear example, people will rally together and work towards a common goal.

The forces that impact on people are not exclusively located in the external environment. While the management of people has at some point to reflect economic and financial imperatives (hard forces), it also expresses what we can call softer and more subtle influences that exist in the form of ideologies, values and beliefs, cultural features, interpersonal influence, and psychological forces which together with work processes and structural patterns collectively shape and constitute the internal environment within which people experience their world of work.

Viewing organizations as complex, multidimensional entities, made up of interdependent subsystems that are in a dynamic relationship with each other and connected to a constantly changing external environment is a conceptualization that either explicitly or implicitly informs all of the subsequent chapters in this book. Consider for a moment what this might mean from a practical perspective. Taking training as an example, apart from the difficulties of showing the link between training interventions and its intended outcomes, one of the enduring criticisms levelled at training is that it frequently fails to work as well as expected! Why is this the case? For those who subscribe to a systems perspective, the answer is obvious:

> **Attempting to solve job performance issues with training will not work when other factors such as reward systems, job design and motivation are the real issues.**

In other words, viewing 'people problems' in isolation, disconnecting the human dimension from its context and ignoring less obvious influences on behaviour will always compromise the effectiveness of different HR interventions and initiatives.

The following examples illustrate some of the critical distinctions and relationships that need to be understood and incorporated into the 'organizational picture' and perceptions of managers and HR professionals.

- **The coexistence of the informal and formal organization** where the informal organization can be understood as the network of relationships, norms, feelings, and perceptions that are hidden from management and may not even be fully understood or articulated by those who inhabit 'that world', while the formal organization is represented by the system of roles, rules, and procedures, lines of authority, and the organization of work subject to managerial control.

The comment made by Frederic Bastiat (1995), the French economist, that we tend to focus on:

> **that which is seen, while we ignore that which is not seen**

seems to have particular relevance here. For many managers, particularly the more senior ones, the informal organization is often invisible to them; they rarely inhabit that world, although in one sense they are part of it, and fail to appreciate its significance for the behaviour of employees. But managers do need to understand and appreciate the functions the informal organization serves for employees, which are:

1. providing a sense of belonging;
2. providing support and help in times of stress and uncertainty;
3. providing alternative channels of communication; and
4. providing mechanisms of social control to limit the power of managers.

So, the existence of overlapping and parallel 'worlds of work' poses a particular challenge to managers, more so to those at lower levels in the hierarchy. One reason is that they are closer to the informal organization and are more susceptible to its influences than managers more remote from 'the shop floor'. Second, while it might be attractive to manage the informal organization by ignoring it or by making concessions there is real danger that this might be seen to confer a kind of legitimacy, however provisional and limited this might be, which can have long-term implications for stability and management control.

RESEARCH INSIGHT 1.1

Gouldner, A. W. (1954), *The Wildcat Strike: A Study of Worker-Management Relationships* (Antioch Press).

Although Gouldner's (1954) classic account of a labour relations situation was written over fifty years ago, it still contains many references to organizational features and behavioural patterns that are relevant today. Read the introductory chapter, focusing particularly on what he calls the indulgency pattern, a phenomenon that emerges within and between the two organizational domains.

- **The inner working life and the external working environment** Unlike the informal organization which is essentially social in character, the inner working life can be defined in more psychological terms, represented by Amabile and Kramer as:

the confluence of perceptions, emotions and motivations that individuals experience as they react to and make sense of the events of their workday.

(2011: 20)

These are the day-to-day events that exist outside of people at work that affect them either directly or indirectly through the way they are perceived and interpreted. In other words, we cannot fully understand people's behaviour and their reactions to HR interventions and managerial actions without connecting their inner selves to the range of influences and stimuli that affect them at work. Behaviour is not simply a function of motivation, but the interaction between the inner and outer worlds of work.

- **The relationship between the production or technical system and the social system** This relationship was originally described by Emery and Rice as the sociotechnical system. To read a comprehensive account of the concept, see Appelbaum (1997). Earlier research focused on the way in which changing technologies in mining affected the social interactions between miners and how these in turn affected production and output. In more contemporary organizations the sociotechnical concept can be applied to the creation of high-performing work teams and the way the organization of work—roles, responsibilities, functions, etc.—need to be changed in order to facilitate a different social organization which offers more in relation to output and satisfaction levels.

Systems thinking then emphasizes the importance of:

- interconnecting subsystems;
- system interdependence;
- holistic thinking;
- permeable boundaries; and
- potential conflict of interest between those who are part of and identify with different system elements.

The point we are making here is a fundamental one. For those working in HRM there has to be some form of conceptual framework which they can use to help them make sense of what has to be managed; managing people is about much more than people! Failure to understand and manage relationships, behavioural patterns, hidden features of the organization, and potential causes of tension and conflict will inevitably undermine the effectiveness of what we usually think of as the main activities and functions of HRM. New ways of looking at and thinking about the organizations within which people live and work will always challenge existing conceptualizations and beliefs but are necessary if human potential is to be realized. As Lewis states

positivity, ethical actions, affirmative bias and whole-system approaches hold out the exciting and tantalizing possibility of building sustainable, flourishing and inspirational organizations.

She goes on:

Organizations are living entities within a living world. This means that we need to give up our ideas of organizations as dead machines and instead understand them as complex, adaptive systems.

(2011)

There are different ways of representing a systems perspective. Weisbord identifies the human system, work system, and reward system as the key components, while Trist and Rice talk primarily about the sociotechnical systems interacting. For our purposes, we propose the model in Figure 1.2 that combines four major subsystems that can be broken down into their component parts which interact with each other and connect to the external environment.

21

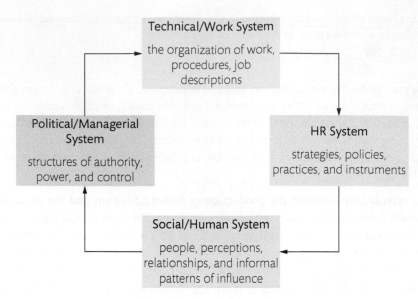

Figure 1.2 A systems representation of an organization's internal environment

RESEARCH INSIGHT 1.2

To take your learning further, read the following article:

Boudreau, John W. (2015), 'HR at the tipping point: The paradoxical future of our profession', *People + Strategy,* 38(4).

The article provides a comprehensive assessment of the major social, economic, and technological forces affecting the way people are managed and their impact on HR. After reading the article consider the major challenges facing HR and how it needs to change to deal with these challenges.

Evidence-Based Management

We have already made numerous references to the ideas and beliefs of both academics and practising managers in our analysis of what HRM is about, its objectives, and to a limited extent we have looked at the evidence in support of these ideas and beliefs. But now is the time to address the much wider question of what constitutes evidence and what does evidence-based management mean? EBM is not only relevant to HRM although for obvious reasons this is where our primary interest lies, but relates to medicine, education, as well as management in general. It is an approach to any activity that involves 'practice' and is based on the idea that any form of practice needs to be based on a substantial and reliable body of evidence.

Pfeffer and Sutton (2006) made the case for EBM when, in the context of analysing why some organizations performed consistently better than their competitors, they said that success stemmed from the systematic examination of evidence about what went right and what went wrong. We have already made the point that not all HRM interventions are successful but we did not explain why this is so. The lack of success may be because:

- the situation is so complicated that managers struggle to understand the nature of the problem or challenge they are dealing with;
- the environment changes so rapidly that 'solutions' quickly lose their impact and relevance;

- managers and HR professionals lack the necessary knowledge and skills to make a positive difference;
- many of the variables that managers/HR professionals need to influence are outside of their control.

All of the above may to a lesser or greater degree be credible explanations for initiatives and practices that don't work particularly well, but Pfeffer and Sutton offer another explanation. At the core of their criticisms of current management practice is the conviction that too many managers fail to recognize and engage with the available evidence relevant to what they are doing and as a result take decisions and design interventions that subsequently turn out to be wrong, inappropriate, or ineffective.

The Centre for EBM, based in Geneva, argue:

> **The starting point for evidence-based management is that management decisions should be based on a combination of critical thinking and the best available evidence. And by 'evidence', we in general just mean information. This information may come from scientific research, but internal business information and even personal experience can count as 'evidence'. In principle, then, all managers base their decisions on 'evidence'.**
> (Barends et al., 2014)

Pfeffer and Sutton go on to say that many managers pay little or no attention to the quality of the evidence they rely on to make decisions and as a result their decisions are often based on so-called 'best practice' and success stories of famous CEOs and on organizations recognized for their outstanding performance. For them, evidence-based practice seeks to address this state of affairs by helping managers critically evaluate the validity, generalizability, and applicability of the evidence they have in hand and how to find the best available evidence to support professional practice.

The idea that managers may not rely on the best available evidence on which to base their decisions and actions might seem counter-intuitive, but while Pfeffer and Sutton agree that there is an expectation that management decisions would be based on the best evidence, that managers systematically learn from experience, and that organizational practices would reflect sound principles of thought and analysis, they argue that the reality is often different, where:

> **decisions are frequently based on hope or fear, what others seem to be doing, what senior leaders have done and believe has worked in the past, and their clearly held ideologies—in short lots of things other than the facts.**
> (2006: 5)

This raises of course crucial questions about what represents good or best available evidence, what form do 'facts' take, and what does EBM mean for the exercise of leadership and managerial judgement.

Barends et al. (2014) explain that the basic idea of evidence-based practice is that good-quality decisions should be based on a combination of critical thinking and the best available evidence and that while all management practitioners use evidence in their decisions, many pay little attention to the quality of that evidence. The result is bad decisions based on unfounded beliefs, fads, and ideas popularized by management gurus. But exactly where is this evidence to be found and what does it consist of? According to Barends et al. (2014), relevant evidence can take the following forms:

- Findings from academic research—but given the proliferation of management and HRM journals it is becoming increasingly difficult to identify 'good' research from that which is methodologically flawed and unreliable.
- Organizational evidence in the form of data, facts, and figures—but the usefulness of this is dependent on the ability to measure the right things in a reliable way. We would argue that a fundamental weakness of HRM practice in the UK is that very few organizations possess the capability to measure what is important in terms of outcomes and link these back to HRM interventions.
- Experiential evidence which involves learning from and using the professional experience and judgement of HRM practitioners and line managers. Different from intuition, opinion, or belief,

professional experience is accumulated over time through reflection on the outcomes of similar actions taken in similar situations. This raises the question though of how that experience is made sense of, collated, and interpreted.

- Stakeholder evidence—feedback from those who have an interest in HRM and what it does and achieves but here the question is about the way in which this feedback is communicated and how it is received.

Being able to identify sources and categories of evidence does not, as has been indicated, tell us much about its quality and reliability so the issue is by no means straightforward. Perhaps the most important issue, though, is how the evidence is used and by whom. Creating meaning from experiences is at the heart of this process of individual and collective learning and experiences—ours and those of others—represent one of the most important and accessible sources of evidence that managers can use to inform their beliefs and approaches to managing people. Probably all managers rely on their personal experiences to guide them in the way they manage people but this may operate at the unconscious rather than conscious level and may not involve sharing experiences and collective learning. The test, therefore, of whether an organization is engaged in EVB can take the form of the following question:

Is knowledge about what we do and what we achieve in the way we manage people being consciously collated and evaluated and HRM practices either validated or changed as a result of this active engagement with experience?

The important assumption underpinning this question is that managers *want* to learn from experience and use the information they have to improve what they do and how they do things. Unfortunately, this assumption may not be valid in all situations and for all managers. The reality is, that leaders and senior managers as well as professionals can have their own agendas and priorities, as the examples of Enron and RBS showed, where evidence of poor performance, wrongdoing, and unethical behaviour was either ignored or suppressed. The Francis Report (2013) into failings in one of the UK's NHS hospital trusts provided a powerful insight into the way professionals, managers, and leaders can become complicit in cover-ups and deliberately ignoring professional practice that damaged people's health. In the section of the report dealing with the analysis of evidence, Francis said:

While it is clear that, in spite of the warning signs, the wider system did not react to the constant flow of information signalling cause for concern, those with the most clear and close responsibility for ensuring that a safe and good standard care was provided to patients in Stafford, namely the Board and other leaders within the Trust, failed to appreciate the enormity of what was happening, reacted too slowly, if at all, to some matters of concern of which they were aware, and downplayed the significance of others. In the first report, this was attributed in a large part to an engrained culture of tolerance of poor standards, a focus on finance and targets, denial of concerns, and an isolation from practice elsewhere. Nothing I have heard in this Inquiry suggests that this analysis was wrong. Indeed the evidence has only reinforced it . . . The Trust's culture was one of self-promotion rather than critical analysis and openness.

(2013: 43)

The lesson from this extract from the Francis Report for HRM and EVB is clear—the collective experiences of people can only constitute 'evidence' in support of or against current thinking and practice if the organizational culture encourages people 'to know' and its leaders are prepared to act on that knowledge.

Sutton, who we quoted earlier as saying that managers 'should do no harm', might also have been implicitly recommending that where the evidence for specific HRM practices suggests they are not effective or in extreme cases are producing outcomes far removed from what was intended, then these practices should be stopped and replaced by more effective interventions or redesigned. The question that needs to be answered by those involved in managing people in whatever capacity is whether this requirement is being met. It is of course important not to take an overly critical position on this issue and to recognize the challenges it involves, but in the context of selection methods, the design of reward systems, and the use of training interventions there is both anecdotal and research-based evidence that ineffective practices are still being adopted and implemented. The work of Coens and Jenkins (2000) is particularly interesting in this regard. They looked at the use of performance appraisals and investigated why they frequently fail to deliver what they were intended to. They concluded that on the whole they do not work because appraisal:

- impedes the reception of feedback;
- fails to motivate people;
- doesn't result in improvement and development;
- produces distorted data about the contribution a person makes;
- undermines human spirit and changes a committed employee into a demoralized person whose performance falls and who probably will look for alternative employment.

Presenting their views is not meant to suggest that there aren't any positive experiences from being appraised or that we necessarily agree with them; rather it is to raise a fundamental question about the continuation of and support for a core HRM practice for which they argue there is very little evidence to support its continued use. They claim that the studies and surveys carried out over many years, often by supporters and defenders of appraisal, offer scant evidence of its success. In support of their position, they quote a US survey that found more than 90 per cent of appraisal systems were not successful and another from a leading HR consultancy that found most employers expressed overwhelming dissatisfaction with their performance management systems, and although somewhat dated now, they also quote a 1997 survey of HR professionals that found only 5 per cent were very satisfied with their systems for managing performance. So, if the evidence suggests these systems are not effective why are they retained? The paradox that this example throws up is that HR practices for which the evidence is overwhelmingly negative still continue to be used!

 Signpost to Chapter 3: A Strategic Perspective on HRM, for exploration of the idea that HR's strategic contribution comes from doing things either better than competitors or doing things differently.

In the context of performance appraisals, the argument we have presented is that the procedurally driven approach that Coen and Jenkins (2000) were so critical of could and arguably should be replaced by a different approach to helping people improve the performance at work; a different approach that actually works!

Coen and Jenkins try to explain what they call 'this complex enigma' and provide an alternative that offers the prospect of the intended outcomes of performance appraisal being achieved when they offer their answer to the question 'why do people want to keep a process that has never worked?' They believe that the continued unjustified attachment to it is because its purposes are worthy and that abandoning appraisals would mean abandoning these purposes. They claim that people will

> think that no appraisal means no feedback, no help on career and performance issues. They believe no appraisal means arbitrary decisions about pay adjustments and career advancement. They also cling to the illusion that people need appraisal to tell them where they stand.

They conclude:

> Each organization has two choices in dealing with the futile process of appraisal. Choice one is to appease everyone by continuing the practice, promoting the illusion that appraisal works and pretending not to notice the harmful side effects. Choice two is to begin an organization-wide initiative of education in which you help people understand why appraisal fails and then, together, work on strategies to replace appraisal, looking for genuinely new ways to actually deliver on the high hopes that were placed on appraisal.

One of the enduring challenges of basing practice on evidence of what works or is likely to is that cause–effect relationships are very difficult to establish because there are so many mediating factors that affect outcomes. Often the best that can be achieved are associations or patterns that link an intervention with an outcome but of course the behaviour of people is subject to a wide range of influences and the idea that it is possible to isolate the effects of one is clearly untenable. But the need to establish what Pfeffer and Sutton call 'the internal logic' (Hayek used the term 'pattern predictions') that explains relationships, despite this uncertainty, is a challenge that needs to be accepted. The alternative is that managers continue to copy what others do, continue to use things that have 'worked' in the past, rely on questionable evidence of success and base practice on fads and myths. What might explain the reasons for this?

- It's easier to believe that the problem of a defective selection procedure, appraisal system, or incentive scheme is linked to lack of skill and understanding, a diagnosis that usually results in more training, or is due to a design defect which can be resolved by minor modifications in the way the system/scheme operates.

- People base decisions and take action on the basis of what they know. This knowledge base may be dated and limited. Evidence in the form of knowledge therefore needs to be constantly updated and tested for its relevance and currency.

- Learning from experience is often an undeveloped management skill and infrequently practised. Collective as well as individual learning is a particularly productive way of creating new knowledge and awareness.

- Knowledge has to be tested in relation to its origins and reliability, and how it is interpreted can give rise to doubts as to its meaning and significance.

- Not all evidence is of the same quality. Pfeffer and Sutton quote an eminent physician, described as the founder of modern evidence-based medicine, who screens out 98 per cent of published articles on the basis that they are only interested in the best and soundest research.

The challenge to those who work in HR and those with wider people management responsibilities is clear, although by no means an easy one to deal with. But Pfeffer and Sutton are convinced that this challenge has to be confronted. They argue that the movement towards a more evidential basis for managerial practice requires a mindset with two critical components:

- A willingness to put aside belief and conventional wisdom—what they describe as the dangerous half-truths that many embrace—and instead act on the facts.

- An unrelenting commitment to gather the facts and information necessary to make informed and intelligent decisions and to keep pace with new evidence and the use of new facts to update practice.

The final contribution to our understanding of EBM and its significance to HRM comes from more recent work from Pfeffer (2014), in which he locates EBM in the wider context of management theory and the way its development is influenced by the requirements of management publications. This is relevant because one of the stated sources of good evidence that supports practice is academic research and papers published in journals. Notwithstanding the fact that there is little interaction between academic research and HRM practitioners—according to Briner (2007), there are with one exception no publications about evidence-based practice for this management function as there are for many other professions—it is important to understand what is being researched and published and to make an assessment of its value.

Pfeffer's argument is that far too many journal articles are concerned with 'new theory' and the discovery of new facts rather than with the testing and replication of already existing theoretical ideas. Does new mean better or more useful just because it is 'new'? He claims that this interest in new theory produces writing that 'is filled with theoretical pretense rather than insight' and that the absence of testing or possibly even a concern with testability results in developing theories that may not be very useful in either a practical or a scientific sense. Contrasting EBM in medicine with that in management, Pfeffer claims that:

Medicine is concerned with rigorous findings about disease processes and treatment outcomes. Replication is encouraged. Management publications discourage replication and mostly want new, clever ideas, regardless of their applicability, substantive importance, or even their ability to cumulatively advance understanding.

(2014: 462)

In conclusion, the case for EBM in HRM is compelling but basing HRM practice on a more convincing evidential basis is dependent on two critical factors:

● HR professionals and other managers recognizing the limitations of their existing approaches to managing people and being prepared to be much more questioning and critical about the practices and interventions they currently employ.

● The ability to find the evidence that will point them in the right direction and which indicates the changes that need to be made in what and how they do things in order to achieve better outcomes.

But, according to Briner (2007), a common misunderstanding of evidence-based practice is that it means acting only on the basis of 'good' evidence. He argues that this is problematic, and that there will always be concerns about what good evidence actually means. Rather, he states, it is about combining the best available evidence with practitioner expertise in order to make decisions about what to do.

Evidence-based practice is not easy—nor is it the only way to improve the quality of decision-making and hence the effectiveness of practice. However, it seems that adopting an evidence-based approach is the most promising means of both challenging and developing HR practitioners and improving HR practice. This means fundamentally being able to establish links between what is done and what outcomes are achieved.

27

RESEARCH INSIGHT 1.3

To take your learning further, read the following:

Briner, Rob (2007), 'Is HRM evidence-based and does it matter?', Institute of Employment Studies.

The article provides an explanation of what EBM involves and explores the implications of applying this approach to strategy and decision-making to the HR function.

Employees as human beings

What people want from work and employment has been briefly touched upon earlier but we now need to look more closely at what 'being human' means so that we can try to explain how and why, in their role as employees, people behave in the ways that they do. A useful starting point is to examine the assumptions made about people that are used, often unconsciously, to help managers make sense of what managing them involves. Perhaps the most well-known contribution to our understanding of the attitudes and behaviours of employees comes from the work of Douglas McGregor who we referred to earlier in the chapter. McGregor combined extensive industrial experience with a distinguished academic career in management. He is particularly well known for the way that he developed his two sets of assumptions about worker motivation and behaviour which he labelled 'Theory X' and 'Theory Y' (McGregor, 1960).

Theory X assumptions are based on a belief that:

● the average human being has an inherent dislike of work and will avoid it if he or she can;

● because of their dislike of work, most people cannot be trusted to do a good job, and therefore need to be controlled and closely supervised;

● people generally prefer to be directed, dislike taking on responsibility, will not change much beyond what they already are, and desire a high level of security.

He argued that holding this view of workers would logically lead managers to create working environments and organizational controls that reflect the unreliable and problematic nature of their employees' work ethic and commitment.

Theory Y assumptions, on the other hand, are based on a different view of people and the way in which they are likely to behave at work. They reflect a view that:

● people enjoy work as a natural and necessary part of the human experience;

● tight control and the use of punishments are not the only or most effective ways to make people work;

● employees are capable of self-motivation and self-direction, and can, under certain circumstances, show a high level of commitment to management and the organization for which they work;

● the average person is capable of learning and changing, and will be prepared, under certain circumstances, to take and exercise responsibility for his or her and others' actions.

The conclusion reached by McGregor is that, because of the existence of Theory X-based management practices, which he argues are based on a simplistic and partial understanding of people, there is a significant gap between what people are doing and giving at work, and what they are capable of. This is a point taken up by O'Reilly and Pfeffer (2000), who argue that, because of Theory X assumptions or the inability and reluctance to create environments that reflect a Theory Y view of their workers, many organizations are failing to unlock the hidden value and potential that their employees offer. They claim that:

> this 'hidden value' is not scarce or unique, but rather can be found in all companies. It resides in the intellectual and emotional capital of the firm and is in the minds and hearts of its people. Although organizations we describe have used this potential, to achieve great success, most companies squander this resource even as they bemoan its scarcity.
> (O'Reilly and Pfeffer, 2000)

HRM INSIGHT 1.2 Murray's story

Murray is a university lecturer, working in one of the UK's 'new' universities. He is married and has three children. He has three degrees and is recognized by his peers and colleagues for his teaching excellence and dedication to his students. Nothing particularly unusual about that, but there is more. He is the only academic known to the authors who has for many years provided anyone who asked or had an interest in his work with copies of all his teaching materials. This means he gives his electronic files to his colleagues so that they can use and benefit from them. He is an expert in research methodology and teaches quantitative and qualitative methods. Students and staff who ask for his help in understanding how to use the statistical package SPSS get his help; he supports his doctoral students well beyond the level he might be contractually expected to, but that's how he is. He doesn't ask for anything in return for what he does. He recognizes positive traits in people where they exist but is equally aware that life generally and his work life in particular has its difficulties and challenges; he really isn't recognized for what he is and what he has done by those who manage him, perhaps because they feel threatened by his reputation, qualifications, and expertise; he also has a tendency to speak his mind, maybe too often. But he retains his positivity and enjoys life. The thing about Murray is that when he was in his twenties and working as a mining engineer, he broke his back in an accident and was left paralysed from the waist down. He spent two years in hospital recovering. As a consequence of his accident, he became diabetic and needs to inject himself with insulin several times a day. I was with him once at a conference in Ireland. At the disco afterwards, looking at him flying across the dance floor in his wheelchair with a woman across his knee, I just thought, 'what a very special person'.

So, the point of the story is? People can interpret it how they want, but for me it means that even in adversity people can be positive and display virtuous behaviour. He learned to come to terms with his condition and didn't let it change him from the kind of person he always was but who could have become very different. That he is not given the recognition he deserves says more about his managers than anything else. And, in a very practical context, why isn't one of the core selection criteria used in HRM to do with positivity and positive human characteristics? Murray represents the antithesis of the jerks and assholes that Sutton argues should be kept out of organizations. Perhaps we need to think of a way of describing people like Murray who are exactly the kind of people who are needed to enrich and strengthen organizations. Townsend called them 'unsung heroes'; in talent management terminology they would be 'stars'. Whatever the term is, it has to combine two elements. First, their competence, expertise, and economic value to the organization; second, it has to express their positive human qualities and what they give to others they work with. I call them 'the good guys'.

The significance of this argument can hardly be overstated: it is quite simply that there is, in most organizations, a productive potential that managers are failing to access and utilize because they base their approach to management on mistaken assumptions about the nature of employee motivation or fail to recognize the talent that people possess and wish to use at work. Moreover, because many managers either implicitly or explicitly identify with a Theory X view of employees, organizations and managerial practice reflect this minimalist perspective which has the effect of becoming a self-fulfilling hypothesis because employees treated as if they are 'Theory X people' will conform to that stereotype even if they display 'Theory Y' characteristics. And where people are thwarted from making the contributions they want to the result is that they either leave or become disillusioned.

KEY CONCEPT Reciprocity

Reciprocity refers to a response to a positive action with another positive action. When someone is perceived to have extended a kindness, been considerate, or done something that perhaps wasn't necessary but which was appreciated and valued, it creates a feeling of wanting to do something in return; to repay that which was done to you but not necessarily in the same form. People who are treated well by their manager or the organization may well reciprocate with higher levels of loyalty and commitment and deliver higher levels of discretionary effort. Reciprocity, however, tends to be generated when that which is done to someone and valued is not expected but is unexpected and discretionary and is probably symbolic rather than material in form.

The full richness and insights of McGregor's thinking and writing is often lost to the majority of students who would probably find difficulty in going beyond a set of Theory X and Y statements. In fact, these are not theories at all but sets of assumptions that managers hold about their employees! In fact, in a book devoted to re-examining his contribution to our understanding of human behaviour at work (Heil et al., 2000), the authors argued that McGregor was frustrated by the way management approached organizational improvements. For him, they asked the wrong questions in the wrong places. As an example, he believed that asking the question many managers today ask and continue to seek an answer to—how do you motivate employees?—is misconceived. McGregor's answer is that you don't! He believed that people are naturally motivated and driven by their own set of values and motivations, and that this means they have to be treated as individuals first and foremost. This view may clash with the established orthodoxy, and be rejected by some. But the point about his position is not fundamentally whether people are self-motivated or need to be motivated by external influences—and realistically both sources of motivation need to be recognized. It is a question of how managers choose to frame the problem.

 Signpost to Chapter 12: Managing Performance, for a more detailed exploration of motivation and the role of managers in influencing employee behaviour.

What he offers those interested in change and improvement are not simple prescriptions based on wishful thinking but a challenge based on understanding human nature and what building successful organizations and working environments involves. He said:

> I will venture the prediction that we will succeed in increasing our utilization of the human potential in organizational settings only as we succeed in creating conditions that generate a meaningful way of life. (Heil et al., 2000)

 For an example of one company's attempt to build a business based on McGregor's beliefs, see the Online Resources Extension Material 1.1.

McGregor's emphasis on the importance of understanding the human side of work and what drives organizational success is the theme of more recent contributions to our understanding of employees as human beings (Amabile and Kramer, 2007, 2011; Lewis, 2011). In her book on positive psychology at work, Lewis emphasizes the importance of positivity or 'feeling good' in peoples' lives, where positivity refers to the balance of positive emotions and experiences over negative ones. She claims that:

> It is becoming clear that this ratio profoundly affects both individual and organizational wellbeing.

The arguments developed by Lewis and others such as Csikszentmihalyi (2004) (watch the podcast at https://www.ted.com/talks/mihaly_csikszentmihalyi_on_flow?language=en) are based on a psychological perspective that links human well-being to positive experiences and positive emotions that are associated with increased performance. Lewis claims that modern organizations can be run and managed in such a way that they are good for the people who work in them—they generate well-being and positive emotions—and are good for business. It is essentially the same argument as that put forward by McGregor and Herzberg.

It is highly likely that those companies identified by the annual *Sunday Times* survey display the same features to a lesser or greater degree that Lewis identifies as being key components of a positive organizational environment. These are:

- **Positive deviance**—describes an organization that is flourishing, benevolent, generous, and recognizes people and their contributions and where positive actions on the part of people are encouraged and valued. She contrasts this kind of organization with those that have a deficit orientation which involves focusing on preventing things from happening, seeking consistency and conformity, eliminating errors and inefficiencies, and seeking to achieve minimum standards of behaviour and performance. We would describe such organizations in similar negative terms but in addition suggest that they suppress or fail to recognize that which is good about the human condition and create at best a neutral and at worst an unhealthy psychological environment.

- **Virtuous actions**—these are behaviours that have a positive impact on others—co-workers, customers, etc.—and are undertaken without the intention of creating a reciprocal response although this may well occur. Within the workplace these can include:
  - being helpful;
  - sharing information and ideas;
  - being generous;
  - forgiving people for genuine mistakes;
  - helping them to learn;
  - engaging in feedback to people that emphasize their strengths and contributions.

Quoting the work of Cameron (2003), Lewis showed that high levels of virtuousness associated with trust, optimism, compassion, integrity, and forgiveness are positively correlated to the organization's perceived as well as its objective performance, expressed in financial terms.

- **Affirmative bias**—this means focusing on the best rather than the worst; it means an emphasis on strengths, capabilities, potential, and possibilities rather than threats, weaknesses, and problems. Realistically organizations and people experience negativities as well—when things go wrong, mistakes are made, plans don't work out and unintended consequences occur, but within affirmative organizations such negative events do not elicit a simplistic or rigid response which can itself be perceived negatively. The frequent use of suspensions by many public sector organizations as part of a disciplinary process and the early formalization of disciplinary procedures are indicative of an organization where negative perceptions and a procedure-following mindset characterize decision takers. Of course, organizations need procedures to assist in the way disciplinary, and other situations are managed, but they have to be perceived to be fair in the way they are designed and implemented and used to support management's judgement rather than a replacement for it.

 Signpost to Chapter 5: Ethics and Leadership in HRM, for a consideration of the importance and application of the concept of fairness in organizations.

The idea that the happy worker was a productive worker characterized many of the contributions to the human relations literature of the 1960s and 1970s but was challenged later by supporters of a much harder approach to people management in the 1980s and 1990s (macho management), but interestingly has received more recent support. Research based on the work of academics at the University of Warwick and the London Business School (LBS) has provided interesting new insights into this relationship. Based on experimental and real-life studies the paper written by a team from Warwick led by Andrew Oswald (Oswald et al., 2014) posed the question does 'happiness' make human beings more productive? They claim that the evidence they accumulated shows that it does. And work from the LBS also suggests that there is a link between not just happier workers, but between happier companies and shareholder returns over a long period of time. It was found that between 1994 and 2009, the 100 best companies to work for in the United States, as measured by *Fortune* magazine, outperformed their peer group by 2.3 per cent per year. Without the hard evidence, it is difficult to make definitive claims, but we would argue that for many of the *Sunday Times* best companies to work for a similar causal relationship exists between the state of employee well-being/happiness and organizational performance.

Research findings are considered more reliable than anecdotal stories about individual companies but why should these be discounted? The following two statements from well-known international companies suggest that the link between employee well-being and organizational success is becoming embedded at least in certain private sector businesses (Black, 2009).

> At Google, we know that health, family and wellbeing are an important aspect of Googlers' lives. We have also noticed that employees who are happy . . . demonstrate increased motivation . . . [We] work to ensure that Google is . . . an emotionally healthy place to work.
> (Lara Harding, People Programs Manager, Google)

> Supporting our people must begin at the most fundamental level—their physical and mental health and wellbeing. It is only from strong foundations that they can handle . . . complex issues.
> (Matthew Thomas, Manager–Employee Relations, Ernst & Young)

What general conclusions can be reached from both research findings and organizational practice?

- First, managers and professionals involved in managing people/HRM need to pay more attention to the emotional well-being of their employees.

- Second, if workplace happiness is positively associated with productivity, then HR specialists need to look at ways of strengthening that relationship by developing policies that focus on increasing and sustaining a positive emotional state.

- And, third, they have to challenge those managers who persistently and intentionally undermine employees and in so doing restrict their performance and contributions.

In making these recommendations, it is important to also point out that we are not advocating managers 'getting soft with employees'. There will be a small number who definitely fit McGregor's Theory X description and are unlikely to significantly change their behaviour under any managerial regime; there may be organizations where they fit in, but in most they probably shouldn't be employed unless there are extenuating circumstances. But for the majority of staff the evidence is clear: create the right emotional, psychological environment and combine this with managers who are not control freaks but support and develop their people and build in opportunities for people to use all their skills and abilities.

 For sections on 'The employee as a resource' and 'Management', see the Online Resources Extension Materials 1.2 and 1.3.

Summary

This introductory chapter is subheaded 'Challenges and Opportunities', and we have tried to outline an approach that goes well beyond describing what HRM 'does' and the many different prescriptions associated with so-called 'best practice'. Rather, we have begun to develop an analytical framework that locates HRM within a distinctively organizational and managerial context but one in which people as well as policies, procedures, and activities are seen as the central focus for HRM. The evidence we have reviewed all points to the same conclusion: that it is through and with people that organizations can enjoy higher performance and long-term success. We have emphasized the importance of linking 'the doing' with outcomes and learning from the experiences of success and failure. The points made below represent some of the strategically important challenges and opportunities faced by managers and HR professionals but each organization will need to construct its own specific list to reflect its unique situation and requirements.

- The need for agility and flexibility. The so-called agile organization is one that can, in respect of its internal operations and mental models, readily adapt to competition, uncertainty, and change. This means that organizations need flexible structures, less hierarchy, resilience, an entrepreneurial mindset, and openness.

- Increasing worker productivity will be a requirement for all organizations; more has to be achieved with less as they search for competitive advantage, respond to budgetary cuts, and seek to operate in 'smarter ways'. Making workers more productive will require a whole systems perspective to be applied and the ability of managers to go beyond the obvious in their search for ways of achieving this. Liberating workers from constraints that limit what they give, addressing the problem of non-productive work, increasing levels of discretionary effort, and encouraging innovation and creativity will become increasingly important to those working in organizations where these requirements are necessary to ensure their continuing success.

- Recognizing that long-term reductions in employee numbers will be an inevitable outcome of the growth in artificial intelligence, robots, and expert systems. Much routine work will become automated; certain skills will become redundant while others will increase in value. As has already been seen, there will be an increase in the number of independent workers networked to different organizations, who may have a changing portfolio of jobs and become less of an employee and more of a service provider. There will be far fewer people to manage! Social media will play an increasingly important role in communication with people and of course will transform the way the informal organization functions; it will also offer different opportunities to influence people and reduce management's traditional control over communications and the social production of meaning.

- For HR, the days of developing and implementing policies applied to 'everyone' will be increasingly replaced by more individualized and tailored employment and service packages. HR will become focused on the individual rather than the collective but at the same time it will need to generate sustainable cooperation between people in the production of goods and services; more people will need to know how to learn and work together.

Much of what is covered in the next chapter addresses these issues and the challenges facing HRM and the extent to which the HR function is meeting them, but we conclude this chapter with a case study of a company that combines a strong and consistent approach to the way it manages its people with a determination to succeed in the highly competitive world of engineering.

 Visit the online resources that accompany this book for self-test questions, web links, and more information on the topics covered in this chapter, at: www.oup.com/uk/banfield3e/

 ## REVIEW QUESTIONS

1. To what extent is organizational success a function of the 'human dimension'? What is the evidence to support your conclusion?

2. What are the current and future challenges that organizations face with regard to the way in which they manage people?

3. What might happen that will increase the level of conflict between employers and workers? If conflict does increase, is this likely to be because of what employers and managers do, or not do, or is it likely to be generated by factors beyond their control?

4. Why is a philosophy of management important and where can this be found?

33

 ## CASE STUDY   ABB

This case study provides interesting insights into the managerial and personal philosophy of one of Europe's most successful executives, and demonstrates the fundamental importance of locating the management of people within the wider context of managing the business.

This is a story about the merger, in 1987, of two engineering companies—Brown Boveri from Switzerland and the Swedish firm ASEA—and the role of one of Europe's most well-known and successful chief executives, Percy Barnevik. It is taken from the book *ABB—The Dancing Giant*, by Bareham and Heimer (1998). ABB was chosen because it represents an example of a company that enjoyed phenomenal growth, financial success, and an international reputation for its ability to operate a highly decentralized international business. It is described by Bareham and Heimer as a 'globally connected corporation operating a loose-tight network of processes, projects and partners that is held together by highly committed people and strongly held principles'. Its approach to business, the way in which it is organized, and the approach taken to the management of its employees, certainly in the 1990s, set it apart from many of its contemporaries and brought it to the attention of management writers such as Warren Bennis, who were interested in Barnevik's leadership style and global/local business model (Bennis, 1993).

Always recognizing that further improvements might be made, the company emphasized the crucial role played by its employees, particularly its cadre of managers, and the importance of creating a culture of:

continuous learning and change, wherever higher targets and constant transition are seen as normal and positive, not threatening and negative. We will make it happen only by instilling a creative
and entrepreneurial attitude in all our employees who welcome change as a challenge.

(Bareham and Heimer, 1998)

In addition to his personal qualities and business acumen, Barnevik also had a strong commitment to the
company's people, and was able to articulate a distinctive philosophy of management and organization. In
Developing ABB's People and Corporate Glue, Barnevik is quoted as saying:

It is fantastic how much business is really about people issues. You never cease to be surprised
whether you are a lawyer or an engineer, or if you have a business education, that the question
really is: can you communicate, ignite people, be believable, build trust? We talk about having
bright strategies. But at the end of the day it comes back to execution. Can you create a culture,
leadership, make people buy in, and feel part of it?

(p. 317)

Barnevik's successor as CEO, Goran Lindahl, has a similar belief in the importance of the company's human
resources, with a particular emphasis on attracting and developing new talent, a role that is seen as being
the prime responsibility of line management.

What comes through clearly is the way in which ABB makes strong demands on its people: it is not a
company that offers its employees an 'easy ride'. According to Bareham and Heimer, employees—and particularly management—are expected to work extremely hard, perform well, and be technically very good.
The existence of internal competition and profit-and-loss centres means that business unit performance
is regularly reported, and this has the effect of encouraging people to feel ownership and of meaningful
autonomy deep down within the business.

The company also sets high standards in its recruitment of new staff, with all newly appointed professional staff expected to have:

- a good education;
- strong analytical skills;
- good communication skills;
- an interest in, and openness to, other cultures; and
- energy to drive the business.

As far as developing people is concerned, ABB has a very simple approach: after recruiting talented people,
give them early responsibility and subject them to a range of informal and formal development strategies.
The line drives both sets of activities, with the personnel function supporting the line with leading-edge
development strategies rather than with complicated models and elaborate processes. As the head of the
corporate management resourcing function, Arne Olssen, is reported to have said:

Exposing talented people to demanding assignments and providing feedback and support—this is
the key to management development.

Olssen articulates ABB's management development philosophy very clearly, when he states that managers
develop:

- 70 per cent on the job;
- 20 per cent by the influence of others; and
- 10 per cent as a result of courses and seminars.

Without it being explicitly stated, it is reasonable to assume that the same principles and philosophy also
applied to the development of the company's non-management employees.

The company also believes very strongly in the integrity of those it employs at all levels which is supported by creating an environment where all of its employees can be open about identifying risks, asking

questions, and raising concerns, and a system of zero tolerance for violations of its integrity policy. The importance of trust is claimed to be central to its culture. The company website states that:

> Trust is built through transparency and honesty. To be successful, we must build each stakeholder's trust through the integrity of our words and our actions.

And according to the company's general counsel/chief integrity officer:

> ABB is committed to fostering a culture where integrity is woven into the fabric of everything we do ... We want integrity to be embedded in our businesses and processes, and reflected in our employees' behavior. This means acting responsibly as individuals and as a company.

And ABB's new CEO in reaffirming the company's commitment to ethical behaviour states that its performance is measured not only by the results achieved, but also how these results were achieved.

While the period during which Percy Barnevik was the CEO of ABB is associated with success and growth, problems emerged around the time of his retirement when it was discovered that highly questionable decisions had been taken by top management over pension rights for Barnevik. The company was in financial difficulties in 2002 and had a large debt pile that needed servicing. Companies such as ABB often experience crises after a long period of success, but despite its difficulties in the early part of the millennium its commitment to its people and its expectations of them remained constant; what changed was the introduction of much stronger formal mechanisms such as codes of conduct, ethical standards, and a more open and transparent culture to ensure that its people and the company not only performed well but did so in ethically acceptable ways.

Sources: Barham, K. and Heimer, C. (1998) *ABB, The Dancing Giant: Creating the Globally Connected Corporation* (Pitman), http://www.abb.com

Questions

1. What role does HR play in expressing the company's commitment to ethical behaviour, trust, and personal responsibility? How does HR support the company's commitment to ethical standards and a transparent culture?

2. What are the distinctive features of the company's culture? What effect do these have on employee behaviour?

3. What specific examples of management development practices would fit with the company's approach to this activity?

4. How would both employees and managers be judged in terms of their individual performance?

 Insights and Outcomes: visit the **online resources** at **www.oup.com/uk/banfield3e/** for an up-to-date summary of issues related to talent management.

 **FURTHER READING**

Effron, M. et al. (2003) *Human Resources in the 21st Century*, Wiley.

Osterhaus, E. (2013) 'The HR department of 2020: 6 bold predictions', at: http://new-talent-times. softwareadvice.com/the-hr-department-of-2020-413

Roehling, M. V. (2005) 'The future of HR management: Research needs and direction', *Human Resource Management*, 44(2).

Sage-Gavin, E. and Foster-Cheek, K. (2015) 'The transformation of work: Will HR lead or follow?', *People + Strategy*, 38(3), 8–10.

35

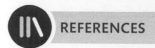

Amabile, T. M. and Kramer, S. J. (2007) 'Inner work life: understanding the subtext of business performance', *Harvard Business Review* (May).

Amabile, T. M. and Kramer, S. J. (2011) *The Progress Principle*, Harvard Business School Press.

Appelbaum, S. H. (1997) 'Socio-technical systems theory: An intervention strategy for organizational development', *Management Decision*, 35(6).

Argyris, C. (1999) *On Organizational Learning*, Blackwell.

Bareham, K. and Heimer, C. (1998) *ABB—The Dancing Giant*, FT/Pitman.

Barends, E. et al. (2014) 'Evidence-based management: the basic principles', Center for Evidence-Based Management, at: https://www.cebma.org/wp-content/uploads/Evidence-Based-Practice-The-Basic-Principles.pdf

Bastiat, F. (1995) *Selected Essays on Political Economy*, Foundation for Economic Education.

Black, C. (2009) 'Healthy people–healthy profits', Business in the Community Report, at: http://webarchive.nationalarchives.gov.uk/+/http:/www.dwp.gov.uk/docs/hwwb-healthy-people-healthy-profits.pdf

Boudreau, J. W. (2015) 'HR at the tipping point: the paradoxical future of our profession', *People + Strategy*, 38(4).

Briner, R. (2007) 'Is HRM evidence-based and does it matter?', Institute of Employment, at: https://www.cebma.org/wp-content/uploads/Briner-Is-HRM-evidence-based-and-does-it-matter.pdf

Buckingham, M. and Coffman, C. (2005) *First, Break All the Rules*, Pocket Books.

Cameron, K. (2003) 'Organizational virtuousness and performance', in K. S. Cameron, J. E. Dutton, and R. E. Quinn (eds.), *Positive Organizational Scholarship*, Berrett-Koehler, pp. 48–65.

CIPD (2004) 'Measuring the cost of staff turnover and putting a value on retention'.

Clegg, S., Kornberger, M., and Pitsis, T. (2015) *Managing and Organization*, Sage.

Coens, T. and Jenkins, M. (2000) *Abolishing Performance Appraisal*, Berrett-Koehler.

Csikszentmihalyi, M. (2004) *Good Business: Leadership, Flow, and the Making of Meaning*, Viking.

Drucker, P. (2007) *The Practice of Management*, Routledge.

Francis, R. (2013) *Report of the Mid-Staffordshire NHS Foundation Trust*, Public Inquiry Executive, summary.

Frost, P. J. (2003) *Toxic Emotions at Work*, Harvard Business School Press.

Gouldner, A. (1954) *The Wildcat Strike*, Antioch Press. [complete book can be accessed at https://libcom.org/files/gouldner-alvin--wildcat-strike-a-study-in-worker-management-relationships.pdf]

Guardian, The (2013) 27 December, at: http://www.theguardian.com/society/2013/dec/27/exodus-nhs-doctors-australia

Hayek, F. A. von (1974) 'The pretence of knowledge', prize lecture, Nobelprize.org, Nobel Media AB, 11 December, at: http://www.nobelprize.org/nobel_prizes/economic-sciences/laureates/1974/hayek-lecture.html

Heil, G. et al. (2000) *Douglas McGregor Revisited*, Wiley.

Herzberg, F. (1991) *Herzberg on Motivation*, Penton Education.

Lewis, S. (2011) *Positive Psychology at Work*, Wiley-Blackwell.

McGregor, D. (1960) *The Human Side of Enterprise*, McGraw-Hill.

Mayo, A. (2001) *The Human Value of the Enterprise*, Nicholas Brealey.

Mayo, A. (2012) *Human Resources or Human Capital*, Gower.

Morgan, G. (1986) *Images of Organization*, Sage.

Morrow, G. et al. (2012a) *The Impact of the Working Time Regulations on Medical Education and Training: Literature Review*, Report for the General Medical Council, August, at: http://www.gmc-uk.org/The_Impact_of_the_Working_Time_Regulations_on_Medical_Education_and_Training___Literature_Review.pdf_51155615.pdf

Morrow, G. et al. (2012b) 'Preparedness for practice: The perceptions of medical graduates and clinical teams', *Medical Teacher*, 34(2).

Nohria, N. and Beer, M. (2000) 'Cracking the code of change', *Harvard Business Review* (May–June).

Obloj, T. (2013) *Guardian*, 11 December, at: https://www.theguardian.com/sustainable-business/financial-incentives-bonus-schemes-lloyds-fine

Oien, L. (2016) see http://businesspaths.net/Articles/12/people-quit-their-boss-not-their-job

and http://www.gallup.com/services/178517/state-global-workplace.aspx

O'Reilly, C. A. and Pfeffer, J. (2000) *Hidden Value*, Harvard Business School Press.

Orr, B. and McVerry, B. (2007) *Talent Management Challenge in the Oil and Gas Industry*, Wiley, at: http://www.oliverwyman.com/content/dam/oliver-wyman/global/en/files/archive/2007/GAS24_05proof_orr.pdf

Oswald, A. J. et al. (2014) 'Happiness and productivity', University of Warwick, UK/IZA Bonn, Germany, at: https://www2.warwick.ac.uk/fac/soc/economics/staff/eproto/workingpapers/happinessproductivity.pdf

Oxford Economics (2014) 'The cost of brain drain: Understanding the financial impact of staff turnover', February.

Pfeffer, J. (2005) 'Changing mental models: HR's most important task', *Human Resource*, 44(2).

Pfeffer, J. (2014) 'The management theory morass: Some modest proposals', in J. A. Miles (ed.), *New Directions in Management and Organization Theory*, Cambridge Scholars Publishing, ch. 19.

Pfeffer, J. and Sutton, R. I. (2006) *Hard Facts, Dangerous Half-Truths and Total Nonsense*, Harvard Business School Press.

Sutton, R. I. (2007) *The No Asshole Rule: Building a Civilized Workplace and Surviving One That Isn't*, Warner Business Books.

Sutton, R. I. (2010) '12 things good bosses believe', *Harvard Business Review*, May.

Sutton, R. blog, at http://bobsutton.typepad.com

Townsend, R. C. (2007) *Up the Organization: How to Stop the Corporation from Stifling People and Strangling Profits*, Jossey-Bass.

Watson, T. J. (1994) *In Search of Management: Culture, Chaos, and Control in Managerial Work*, Routledge.

Watson, T. J. (2002) *Organising and Managing Work*, FT/Prentice Hall.

Watson, T. J. (2006) *Organising and Managing Work*, Pearson Education.

Weisbord, M. R. (2012) *Productive Workplaces*, Jossey-Bass.

The Evolution of the HR Function: A Critical Perspective

2

Learning Outcomes

As a result of reading this chapter and using the online resources, you should be able to:

- recognize that definitions and meanings in HRM are socially constructed and are constantly being reconstructed;

- understand the origins and evolution of HRM;

- explain the reasons for the change in approach and emphasis from personnel management to HRM;

- engage in an initial exploration of HR and its contribution to individual and organizational performance; and

- explain why the role of the line manager is critical to the management of human resources.

Introduction

One of the interesting features of modern life is that there are often different ways of saying the same thing. By that we mean that the phenomenon we are trying to explain is clearly understood but is described using words or terms that carry broadly the same meaning. But there are also situations where the use of a different language to describe a phenomenon reflects important differences about the very nature of that phenomenon: in other words, it means genuinely different things to different people. To illustrate this point, consider for a moment something as ordinary as motor cars. It might, at one level, seem relatively straightforward to describe what they are and what they represent, but it isn't quite that simple. Many people would see cars as representing a popular form of personal transportation, while others might view them as a status symbol and reflection of personal wealth and prestige. From a different perspective, cars are seen as a source of pollution and a hazard to personal health and safety and in the context of global warming a major contributor to climate change. The point is that conversations about cars have different starting points and agendas shaped by the particular interests and perspectives of those involved. In other words, cars mean different things to different people and exactly the same point applies to HRM (more recently abbreviated to HR). Most commentators would probably agree that there has been a worrying lack of consensus about what it means and represents, and the continuing existence of the many definitions, models, and theories about HRM and the constant search by those leading the HR profession for an identity and role confirms the belief of some that HR still has an 'identity crisis' (Bolza, 2016; Flynn, 2014). These and many other contributions to the debate about what HRM means suggest that little has changed since its emergence in the 1990s stimulated the academic community into searching for answers to the question—'Is HRM something new and different or something new but essentially the same as personnel management?' Although this question has been thoroughly investigated—and we consider the question in detail later in the chapter—new questions about HR's role and identity continue to emerge which suggests that doubt, uncertainty, and controversy continue to exist. At one level, this involves trying to establish whether HR is primarily an administrative, operational, or strategic function and at another highlighting the kinds of roles and contributions it should be making but which it is currently failing to play and deliver. The question then, 'what is HRM' (HR) is an important and a natural one to ask by those students who may be seeking to enter the profession and by managers who have to work with HR professionals in the management of people at work. It is the aim of this chapter to try to provide insights into the debate and an understanding of the reasons behind the continuing controversy about what HRM means and is or should be about. We choose to avoid embarking on a search for an 'answer' because such an approach implies that a single answer exists and the task is one of discovering it after which the controversy becomes resolved. In our opinion, this is not a particularly helpful or fruitful way to generate genuine understanding. Why? Well, it implies that there is only *one* question that needs to be answered, or that interested parties are in *agreement* over what are the most important questions about HR. We would argue that neither proposition is valid, and that where there are 'answers' to be found they are unlikely to be unproblematic, bringing the search to a conclusion. Rather, they are much more likely to generate other questions that have the potential of disclosing deeper insights into what HRM means. Trying to establish meaning in HR is not a straightforward or finite process!

Ask different organizational stakeholders the same question(s) and it will almost certainly elicit a varied set of answers that reflect the different expectations and experiences of HR associated with these different groups. Perhaps the question we should be asking is not what HR is but what people think it is *and* what it should be. This question takes us into the realm of seeing meanings and descriptions of what is seen as being socially generated rather than scientifically proven. This approach recognizes the existence of multiple rather than a single meaning or definition. While it is beyond the remit of this chapter to consider the philosophical frameworks relevant to the social sciences, it is important to see these two different ways of trying to understand HR as a phenomenon, defined as something that is observed to exist or happen, especially one whose cause or explanation is in question, in relation to two 'competing' approaches to the world we inhabit. These may not be familiar to first-year students but will be important in the context of research methods and when dissertations are being undertaken. They are positivism and social constructionism.

> **KEY CONCEPT** Positivism
>
> The term used to describe an approach to the study of society, or phenomena, that relies specifically on scientific evidence, such as experiments and statistics, and the discovery of facts, to reveal the 'true' nature of how society operates or the phenomenon being studied.

The approach taken here is one based on the social construction of reality, where meaning is socially produced and continues to be reproduced to reflect the nature of relationships, power, and ideology and the need for actions and behaviour to be seen to be socially legitimate. This allows us to ask the question not what does HR mean, but *which* meaning has greater heuristic value: in other words which or which combination of definitions offers the most useful insights into our understanding of HR? This is not an unimportant point because as we have stated above and will explore later, as an academic subject and managerial function it continues to be associated with uncertainty about its nature, importance, and contribution to organizational success. For some, it is *the* key management function because it deals with an organization's most valuable resource—people—but for others it has a much more limited significance, being little more than a necessary administrative activity. However challenging it might be (most people prefer certainty and simplicity to uncertainty and complexity), students need to be critical and questioning in their search for meaning and understanding, and to recognize that conceptual confusion rather than conceptual clarity characterizes the study and practice of HRM—that ambiguity and paradox are part of the process of making sense of what it means.

There are two important literature contributions that help with the challenge of generating and evaluating meaning and in understanding the nature of social phenomena. The first involves the work of Karl Weick (2001) and his interest in what he calls the process of 'organisational sense-making'. He wasn't interested specifically in HRM, but his theorizing and ideas are particularly helpful to those who are interested in making sense of what HRM 'is' and what it represents. Weick argues that the task of sense-making:

> resembles more closely the activity of a cartographer. There is some terrain that mapmakers want to represent and they use various modes of projection to make this representation. What they map, however, depends on where they look, how they look, what they want to represent, and their tools for representation.

He goes on:

> It is the job of the sense-maker to convert a world of experience into an intelligible world. That person's job is not to look for the one true picture that corresponds to a pre-existing, pre-formed reality . . . Instead the picture that is suggested is that there is nobody here but us scratching around trying to make our experience and our world as comprehensible to ourselves in the best way we can . . . There isn't any one true map of the earth, of human existence or of ultimate reality . . . there are only maps we construct to make sense of the welter of our experience.
> (2001: 9)

Applying this reasoning to the study of HRM, the search for a simple consensus of what it means and involves is almost certainly a distraction. There are as many definitions as there are textbooks on the subject and each of these represents one person's attempt to establish clarity and involves little more than one contribution to the multidimensional and ever-changing map of HRM. HRM is fundamentally a social construct: it is a term used to denote an area and activity of management; it represents a very flexible boundary within which 'things' associated with this activity take place but where these boundaries and activities are constantly changing within and between organizations, differences that reflect unique situations and different evolutionary paths. There are of course a number of core HR activities that are common to most organizations, but their significance, the way they are carried out, and the contributions they make to organizational success are not the same because although organizations share similar characteristics and operations they are still unique. This means that the HR function can also be thought of as being similar but different to those in other organizations.

HRM does not exist in any objective sense: it's not possible to see or touch it; it is perceived differently by different people, but while it doesn't have a physical existence it does have a social existence, or, more accurately, it has social existences—it is made sense of by people in their own ways and from their own experiences, interests, and perspectives. Although this is to reify HRM, little wonder then that 'it' is unsure of what it is or what its role should be.

KEY CONCEPT Reification

This term is used widely in the social sciences. It refers to the process of giving things that are inanimate, for example social constructs, human characteristics such that they become an independent, living entity. For example, when we talk about organizations as having objectives, of thinking, of having a conscience we reify them. The same thing happens to HRM/HR—it is almost always, but wrongly, represented as having an independent existence because we often have to simplify and make complex phenomena accessible.

The second contribution comes from the work of the French philosopher Michel Foucault. His interest lies in the field of language and the way meaning and legitimacy are socially constructed: he is known for his development of the concept of *discourse* and the way that meaning and understanding is generated through the development and use of language (Barratt, 2008). For him, language is developed around particular points of interest or activity and the nature of that activity is described by language which gives the activity meaning. The language used both expresses and influences people's perceptions; it sets the agenda and helps to create the conceptual map and framework within which that activity takes place. He sees language not as a neutral or technical instrument but as something that expresses political power and serves important functions, particularly those concerning the need for legitimacy. The importance of this argument for HRM lies in the fact that HRM is not only studied—and the dominant discourse around it will influence what is studied and for what purpose—but that HRM is also practised—it involves decisions, actions, and attempts to control people's behaviour. The distinction between 'hard' and 'soft' HRM is an example of language that shapes perceptions, structures the debate, and directs action. Words are also used to describe relationships and responsibilities and in the world of work these need to be seen to be legitimate so that organizations can continue to function in the way that they do. The dominant discourse (there can of course be more than one but only one that is dominant) on HRM is one that expresses a particular view about people in organizations and how they are managed. It is characterized by a normative, consensus-oriented perspective on the management of people which largely rejects the idea that conflict between management and employees is inherent in the capitalist system of work and organization and promotes the idea that differences between these two interest groups are at worst material—salaries and the way people are treated—not structural and inherent. This discourse also promotes the idea that managerial control and hierarchy are legitimate and necessary for the organization to continue to function, and while accepting that the questioning and even challenging of existing political structures may itself possess a degree of legitimacy, further maintains that any challenge to these has to be kept within tight boundaries. As a consequence, the 'norm' is one where relationships are based on cooperation and implied consent and where challenges to the continuation of management control are deemed in principle to lack legitimacy although in certain situations may be understandable. This discourse thus provides and denies legitimacy!

When owners/managers talk about providing opportunity for work, others talk about employees being exploited; when managers act in ways that are perceived to be in the interests of the business others talk about the undermining of workers' rights; the interests of the organization (remember reification) are essentially defined and articulated by its leaders. It goes on! When people in organizations disagree over things, it's almost as though they were talking a different language! And, of course, they are in the sense that there is more than one discourse in play at any one time. The legitimation and justification of managerial action is a critical function of the dominant discourse and this can be illustrated by the concept of rationality. Managerial behaviour is almost always defined in terms of its being rational and therefore necessary and logical: rationality is also a source of legitimacy. On the other hand, employee behaviour which challenges managerial control is usually defined as being irrational and therefore lacking in legitimacy which in turn justifies management attempts to suppress or ignore it. We explore the concept of rationality in HRM later in the chapter. So, to conclude this introduction, the main point that we are making is that the study of HRM as an academic discipline is in certain ways as challenging as the management of people is in a practical sense and it is to the latter that we now turn.

STUDENT ACTIVITY 2.1

Read the following article by Truss et al. on the differences between 'hard' and 'soft' HRM.

Truss et al. (1997) 'Soft and hard models of human resource management: A reappraisal', *Journal of Management Studies,* **34, 53–73.**

Look for examples of reification and the way language is used to justify the distinction between these two different forms of HRM. Particularly look for the justifications behind this distinction and consider whether such a binary distinction is valid.

The Emergence of Personnel Management

As we noted in Chapter 1, there is a wealth of anecdotal evidence to support the view that, while technology, product, or service development, and organizational change are frequent priorities, the challenge with which managers at all levels seem to have the most difficulty is managing people. These are the challenges that can consume a disproportionate amount of management time and energy, and, paradoxically, despite the sustained investment in management education and training, there is little evidence that today's managers feel confident that they have found the answers to all the questions and challenges that face them.

But what specifically are these questions and challenges? Without being exhaustive, the following list represents arguably the most common and persistent questions to which managers struggle to find convincing answers:

● What makes employees 'tick' and how can they be motivated?

● What do people want from work and what is the best way to reward them?

● Where am I going to get well-qualified staff from and what do I have to do to keep them?

● How am I going to get my workers to be more flexible and deliver higher levels of discretionary effort?

● How can I find the right balance between treating my workers fairly and with consideration, but at the same time ensuring that wider organizational interests are not compromised?

● How can I reduce or eliminate the causes of conflict and build a loyal and committed workforce?

If, as is argued here, these are questions that are relevant and important to *all* 'managers'—from chargehands and supervisors to the most senior executives in both public and private sector organizations—how do they relate to personnel management and HRM, as specialized approaches to the management of human resources?

One way of making the connection is to see the emergence of a specialized people management function as an expression of the difficulties and problems general or line managers faced in the second half of

Figure 2.1 Diagrammatical representation of the shift in responsibility from the line manager to personnel specialists in the 1970s–1980s

the twentieth century as the work environment became more volatile and the pace of change began to accelerate. As management, in general, became more differentiated and specialized, the people management aspect began to acquire a distinctive identity, developed more specialist roles, and became increasingly professionalized. This new domain was occupied by a new kind of manager who brought expert knowledge and experience in employing and managing people and claimed to offer 'solutions' to the kinds of problems outlined above. (Interestingly many of these personnel managers came from the armed forces.) The need for a special kind of people manager who could negotiate with the unions, develop training strategies, extend welfare policies to the workforce, and introduce new reward systems coincided with an increasing sense that line managers had neither the time nor experience to actively engage in these new areas of people management and initially at least seemed comfortable with the idea that they should cede responsibility for them to the personnel specialists. Figure 2.1 illustrates the shift in key aspects of people management from the line manager towards the personnel specialist during the latter part of the twentieth century. Interestingly, one of the significant changes in the early part of the twenty-first century affecting HRM/HR has been a reversal of this trend and a redefinition of the relationship and responsibilities between the line manager and personnel specialist.

 For a summary of the origins of personnel management see the Online Resources Extension Material 2.1.

The debate about the respective roles and contributions of line managers and people management specialists has been an enduring feature of the literature on HRM. On this, the work of Hutchinson and Purcell (2003) has been particularly influential in exposing the tensions and contradictions in the relationship between the two. In its extreme form, this twentieth-century practice of moving responsibility for key aspects of people management away from line management and into centralized personnel departments effectively disenfranchised line managers, and became one of the most important sources of criticism levelled at people management specialists. Whether line managers were reluctant to lose their people management responsibilities or saw the benefits of centralized expertise is difficult to say. But more recent research (CIPD, 2005, 2010) has found evidence that line management's loss of HR responsibility may have had serious consequences because:

> front line managers played a pivotal role in terms of implementing and enacting HR policies and practices . . . where employees feel positive about their relationship with their front line managers they are more likely to have higher levels of performance or discretionary behaviour and clearly this particular line manager responsibility can never be delegated to a remote, centralized department.

The importance of the line to the way in which people are managed and the outcomes that are generated was recognized decades ago by Tyson and Fell (1986), who argued that:

> All managers of people are 'personnel managers' in the literal sense, that is they have a personnel function to perform.

This means that (using the more contemporary expression) all managers can be seen to be HR managers because part of their responsibility involves managing people. Managers who do not, therefore, recognize and fulfil their HRM role can be said to be failing to meet the full range of their managerial responsibilities.

Confusion surrounding the question of responsibility and the controversy accompanying the role of centralized HR departments are fundamental problems that HR still faces. It is not a problem that can ever entirely be resolved, and remains a potential source of tension between line managers and HR professionals. Will the centralized HR department, staffed by HR specialists, prove ultimately to be the preferred model or will its alternative, based on the key role of line managers, come to dominate thinking and practice? Christensen (1997) argues that the future of HR lies in the importance of being able to:

> differentiate between human resource management and the human resource department.

He also describes the situation in which, after asking for the HR strategy or plan, senior managers are often presented with a description of current and future activities of the personnel or HR department, which, he argues, more often than not has little obvious connection to the business. Later in the chapter we quote Dave Ulrich making exactly the same point but some twelve years later! Christensen goes further in this differentiation between the personnel or HR department and what can only be interpreted as the 'real HR' when he claims that 'the Human Resource Plan doesn't necessarily have anything at all to do with the HR Department', arguing that the HR plan belongs to the business. Accepting that there is a lack of clarity in terms of who is responsible for HRM, he offers the opinion that:

> Managers and HR professionals of the future will understand that line managers are the 'people managers' of their organizations and as such, they are ultimately accountable for human resource management.
> (Christensen, 1997)

The conclusion that can be reached at this point is that the growth of a specialist people management function—the question of what it is called is considered later—has the potential of making major contributions to the way in which people are recruited, selected, trained, and rewarded. While these specialists may have a key role in the design of policies and procedures, it is the line managers who have the responsibility *for delivery* and this can never be fully taken or given away. As a consequence of this realization, the trend over the past ten years or so has been for the line to re-engage more explicitly and directly in the management of its employees, with HR specialists playing a less executive, but more supportive and advisory role.

A consequence of the line re-engaging directly with employees—and one that has major implications for the size of specialist HR departments and for those working in them—is that fewer HR professionals will be needed in this new HR 'architecture'. Reilly and Williams (2006) refer to British Airways halving its HR department in 1989, devolving much of its HR responsibility to line management, and to the BBC, who more recently cut over half of its specialist HR jobs. Clearly, there is an ongoing tension and dynamic between the line and HR specialists, with some organizations abandoning centralized departments altogether in favour of a decentralized and devolved approach to the management of people; others, particularly in the public sector, continue to retain well-resourced HR departments and a key role for the HR specialist.

Arguably the most important question that emerges from the growth of specialist 'people managers' and different approaches to the way in which people are managed is, however, not about differences of definition and conceptual models, but rather about *what* works and *why*. Tyson and Fell (1986) articulated this concern when they posed the question:

> Given that the appointment of these specialists is one answer to the question of how to manage people, how effective is it?

STUDENT ACTIVITY 2.2

Pritchard, K. (2010) 'Becoming an HR strategic partner: Tales of transition', *Human Resource Management Journal,* **20(2), 175–88.**

Read this article by Pritchard which looks at the way in which HR specialists work with and support line managers. The article provides interesting insights into the different and complementary contributions HR specialists and line managers can make to the management of people.

After reading the article, work in two groups to produce presentations, one which analyses the key contributions HR specialists can make to managing people and the second which does the same for line managers. After viewing both presentations, the group should collectively discuss the strengths and limitations of both the HR specialist and line managers in this activity.

So, the growth of HR as a specialized management function can be related to either the unwillingness or lack of capability of line managers to address emerging people management challenges but in a wider context can also be seen to be driven by:

1. The growth in the size and complexity of organizations during the second half of the twentieth century and the increasing specialization of management, where the existing management functions of production, finance, and administration were joined by the new functions of quality, strategy, marketing, and HR, within which the emergence of talent management, workforce planning, and the internationalization of the labour force represented and reflected a new HR agenda.

2. The growth in 'new ideas' about managing people and the emergence of a coherent body of knowledge based on new theoretical models, concepts, and research outputs that supported the use of particular strategies, policies, and practices based on their perceived link to organizational success. The evolution of a specialist management function was not simply about the balance of responsibilities between HR and line managers and organizational complexity and change, but was also affected by the emergence of a more sophisticated understanding about the link with people and organizational success and what needed to be done to strengthen this relationship: the evolution of HR was driven by developments in knowledge and ideas.

The rise of PM as a distinctive specialist management function was characterized, and to a significant extent still is, by changes in what it claimed to be and do. This partly reflected the changing environment in which organizations operated and how this translated in PM/HRM priorities and roles shaped by senior managers, but also it expressed a desire by PM/HRM professionals to 'carve out' a piece of the management territory. Advancing the interests of the HR department in particular was achieved in several ways but taking on more roles and responsibilities was certainly one that led to it growing in size, number, and justified its claims for greater resources. But as a consequence of this growth in the boundaries of HR and its internal differentiation, the question that began increasingly to be asked was, 'what is its primary function and what is the nature of its contribution?'

One way to answer this question is to use metaphors and analogies which, through relatively unsophisticated language, provide a route into the world of meaning (Morgan, 2006). According to Longo (2012), metaphors also serve to put order and clarity in those situations dominated by vagueness and dubiety. She states:

> the more ambiguous a situation is, the more important metaphors become for ordering the situation and making sense of our organisational experience.

Metaphors in HRM help to define what, in its departmental form, it represents and does. Some of the earliest used are presented by Storey (1989) and are briefly summarized below.

- **Acolyte of benevolence**—this metaphor was used to capture the welfare function that developed in the late nineteenth and twentieth centuries, driven by the paternalism of mainly Quaker employers such as Cadbury, Rowntree, and the Lever Brothers. HR was welfare and the welfare officer was responsible for its distribution and management.

- **The humane bureaucrat**—this manifestation of HR reflected the 1950s and 1960s when organizations became larger and more internally differentiated. Personnel officers emerged to cope with the administrative and procedural demands around employment, selection, training, and placement. Tyson and Fell (1986) used the metaphor 'Clerk of Works' to describe the same kind of work and role.

- **The negotiator**—this role reflected the post-war era of trade unionism, collective bargaining, and what became known as industrial relations, where a key part of the personnel department became focused on managing industrial conflict and negotiating with the unions.

- **The organization man**—Tyson and Fell used the term 'Architect' to describe the evolution of what in the later part of the twentieth century became known as organization development. This aspect of personnel work involved taking a more holistic approach to the way organizations were structured and how individual parts fitted together.

- **The manpower analyst**—here personnel developed capability in manpower planning with an emphasis on 'getting the numbers right' and forecasting future labour requirements.

- **The trainer**—this expression of personnel was given a particularly important boost as a result of the creation of industry training boards and more recently has evolved into a learning/development role.

More recent metaphors include strategist, internal consultant, change manager, business partner, policeman, and social engineer. Of course, as HR continues to evolve and change, new metaphors and models of the HR function will emerge and either replace or overlap with the earlier ones, some of which no longer accurately describe what HR does but are still retained within the organization's memory and still influence perceptions.

KEY CONCEPT Organizational memory

Sometimes called institutional or corporate memory, organizational memory is the accumulated body of data, information, and knowledge created in the course of an individual organization's existence.

The existence of so many different metaphors in HR is one source of confusion about what HR means and what it wants to be known for: the proliferation of metaphors provides HR with multiple identities and roles, but while this may be the inevitable outcome of the growing complexity of managing people it also contributes to the doubts of those who still need to be persuaded that the HR department is making the important contributions it claims. For, as Longo points out, different individuals can represent the same phenomenon by using different metaphors that fit their perceptions, views, and interests. Indeed, the same individual might potentially use a different metaphor at different times to represent the same occurrence depending on his/her changing feeling, state of mind, or interests.

STUDENT ACTIVITY 2.3

Split into two groups. Group one takes the social engineer and policeman metaphors and creates a presentation on what they mean in terms of HR, why the role is important, but also how they could be damaging to HR's reputation within the organization. The second group has to create two new metaphors that will be relevant to HR into the future and explain what these mean and why they will be considered important. The groups present to each other and discuss.

The Rise of HRM

The term HRM has its origins not in the UK, but in the USA during the 1980s, and is associated with the work of such writers as Tichy et al. (1982) and Beer et al. (1985). For some, but not all, it came to represent a fundamentally different approach to the management of people, based on new assumptions about employees, about the changing nature of work, and about how best to maximize the potential of an organization's human resources. Many UK organizations were quick to embrace this new development and many personnel departments became, almost overnight, HRM departments; personnel officers/managers were transformed into HR officers/managers who assumed or aspired to a more strategic role although as we shall see later, in reality for many the changes in what they did were far less significant than they wanted them to be. Not all organizations embraced HRM, in that they preferred to retain the 'personnel management' title, on the grounds that this avoided the impersonal association with their employees as 'human resources', but, over time, more and more specialized 'people' departments became known as HR departments (Hendry and Pettigrew, 1990).

There is, however, still argument and disagreement over what this new development actually represented, although most of it is confined to academics and is of less importance than it used to be. Those actively involved in the management of people appear to have been less concerned about titles and concerned more with practice and with the effects on employee behaviour and performance linked to new ideas about commitment, involvement, resource utilization, and the role of the line manager.

But the academic debate is not without interest or relevance for those who practise HR and a number of important contributions to this debate need to be analysed. The key issue—that of whether HRM is, or is not, different to personnel management—is considered by Hoque and Noon (2001), who quote David Guest, arguing that the HRM label *does* represent something new and distinctive, and John Storey (1992), who suggests that there are twenty-seven points of distinction between the two. Yet, Karen Legge (1995) begins her book on HRM by quoting a caller on BBC4, who described HRM as:

> **a posh way of describing a personnel manager . . . but it goes a bit further than that.**

In trying to make sense out of what appear to be quite different views, Hoque and Noon (2001) argue that:

> **the key issue is whether departments that have adopted the HR title operate differently from those that have retained the personnel title.**
> (2001: 6)

They suggest that, based on extensive anecdotal evidence, the introduction of the HR title has meant little more than a 'change of name on the door'. A further contribution to this controversy came from Gennard and Kelly (1994), who researched the views of personnel directors and concluded that the debate over differences between personnel management and HRM was largely sterile: many of the organizations from which they had gained information displayed evidence of fundamental changes in employment and management practices, but many did not adopt the HR label to indicate or justify these changes. In other words, practitioners were embracing many of the ideas of HRM, but were not necessarily adopting the label or changing the departmental title. Simply looking for evidence of difference by focusing on nominal changes in department titles is not, therefore, likely to be particularly helpful. In a later telephone-based survey of a wider sample of practitioners, Grant and Oswick (1998) found that 50 per cent of their sample was convinced that HRM was something different to personnel management; 37 per cent believed that there was no difference.

A further source of confusion lies in the way in which HRM is split into two forms, with a distinction made between 'hard' and 'soft' types. The *hard* approach emphasizes the quantitative, strategic aspects of managing people as organizational assets. A *soft* approach instead highlights the importance of communication, motivation, leadership, and the mutual commitment of employees and employers. Unfortunately, using such simplistic terms to represent complex phenomena not only has the effect of trivializing the debate, but also of presenting the practitioner with what appears to be a choice between one or the other interpretations. More usefully, it is better to present the challenge as one of incorporating both approaches into the practice of HR and being sensitive to the conditions and circumstances which require an emphasis to be given to one or the other to reflect changing circumstances and requirements.

For students coming to this debate for the first time, trying to understand the issues and to make sense of the ambiguous language and sometimes inaccessible academic arguments can be a frustrating experience. Tony Watson recorded the story of one student, who was left confused and uncertain about the way the academic debate was presented to her. HRM Insight 2.1 is an abbreviated version of what she recounted to Watson.

HRM INSIGHT 2.1 The story of Sue Ridgebridge

This story is told in detail by Tony Watson (2002). The essence of the story is the confusion and frustration experienced by a student being 'taught' HRM at a UK university.

The student, Sue Ridgebridge, starts her story by explaining that, when the organization she worked for changed the title of the specialized people management function from 'personnel' to 'human resources', it represented little more than a continuation and development of what had previously been done under the personnel banner. She speculated that the reasons behind the change were more to do with being fashionable and the need to be seen to be moving away from the welfare tradition of personnel management towards something more business-oriented.

As far as the experience of being taught HRM was concerned, Sue had a particular problem: she was confused about whether HRM was to do with the general business of managing people or represented a particular approach. She had real difficulty in understanding what one of her tutors meant when he said that 'Human Resource Management is a particular approach to human resource management'! As someone who had spent most of her working life in a personnel department, she also felt aggrieved when her tutors emphasized that the distinctions between personnel management and HRM were to do with the former's:

- short-termism;
- tendency towards a reactive, firefighting approach to problems;
- association with collectivism;
- inability to move away from transactional, towards transformational, management;
- lack of a strategic dimension.

When presented with John Storey's list of twenty-seven differences between personnel management and HRM her response was to cross out HRM and retitle the table '27 differences between good personnel management and bad personnel management' (see also Watson, 2006).

Insights and Outcomes: visit the **online resources** at **www.oup.com/uk/banfield3e/** for some additional points on this HRM Insight.

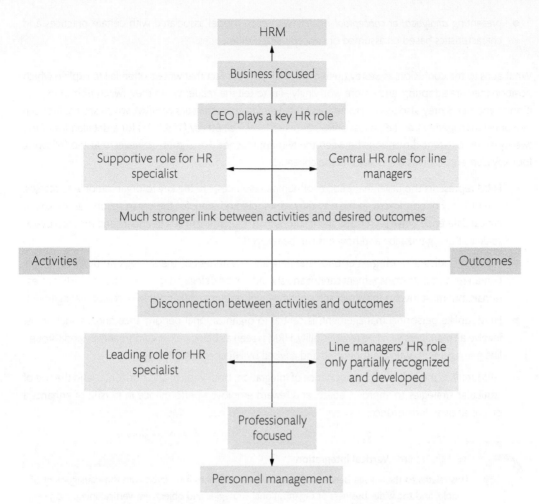

Figure 2.2 A comparison between personnel management and HRM

The point about HRM Insight 2.1 is that it highlights the problem that students can experience when being introduced to the subject for the first time, and illustrates the difficulties they have in understanding the terms and labels used by academics, many of which tend to confuse rather than enlighten. It also provides justification for Watson's comment that:

> these criticisms are well founded and . . . there is a serious ambiguity in the HRM literature about its analytical and prescriptive elements.
> (2002)

Figure 2.2 represents some of the main differences between PM and HRM as articulated by various academic writers. The obvious problem, as pinpointed by Ridgebridge in HRM Insight 2.1, is that these are analytical differences rather than necessarily being actual ones. And one of the many paradoxes found in the debate about HRM and PM is that the CIPD, which has been in the forefront of promoting the HRM model of HRM (managing people), chose to retain the term 'personnel' in its corporate title.

What complicates the search for a greater degree of clarity in the characteristics of, and relationship between, these two approaches to the management of people is that academic writers rarely make it known to the reader whether they are offering:

- definitions and descriptions based on *practice*—in other words, whether they are studying these two approaches empirically and making comparisons between the two based on observed and discovered differences; or

- presenting *analytical or conceptual models*, with each model associated with certain practices and characteristics based on assumed or conceptualized differences.

What adds to the confusion, as Storey quite rightly claims, is the fact that writers often fail to explain which position they are adopting, and—more worryingly—fail to tell the reader when they switch from one position to another. Storey also sets out to establish the defining characteristics of HRM, which set it apart from personnel management at the philosophical, or belief, level. See Storey (1992: 34) for a detailed list of the twenty-seven different dimensions between the two approaches. He argues, however, that the following four key elements express the essence of the concept.

- HRM represents the belief that people, or human resources, are the key to organizational successes. The majority of employees, in the way they contribute and work for the organization, can make the critical difference between success and failure, and management needs to understand the employees' value to the organization and how this can be realized.

- HRM embodies a much greater understanding and awareness of the strategic importance of the human resource. Its management cannot and should not be delegated to and reserved for HR professionals, but must involve the direct and ongoing involvement and leadership of senior management.

- HRM, unlike personnel management, is central to organizational performance and, as such, must involve all managers with line responsibility. HRM is seen as being delivered primarily by and through line management, who are supported and advised by HR specialists.

- HRM reflects the belief in the importance of integration, both vertical and horizontal, and the use of particular strategies to improve, utilize, and reward employee performance in pursuit of enhanced organizational performance.

KEY CONCEPT Vertical integration

This relates to the linkage between the policies and practices associated with the management of people, and the wider business or organizational strategies and objectives. Vertical integration can be based on the cascading down of corporate priorities and objectives, which then inform and give direction to HR priorities, policies, and practices. Alternatively, it can be based on representatives of HR informing senior management of the current and future state of human resource capacity and capabilities, which helps to ensure that corporate strategy is grounded in a realistic understanding of what is, or will be, available to deliver the strategy.

KEY CONCEPT Horizontal integration

This relates to the linkage between different HR activities and practices, and emphasizes the importance of looking at what HR does holistically, rather than as separate and disconnected elements. The concept also expresses the need for consistency in the sense that the way in which the activities are carried out reflects understood and agreed strategic objectives. For example, adopting an individualist, rather than a collectivist, approach to the management of people implies the use of individual reward and development practices if consistency in practice is to be achieved.

Whether these defining features of HRM are actually delivered and experienced in practice—that is, whether they become operationalized—is another matter and realistically it is much more about the *degree* to which organizations choose to or are able to implement them. But these differences at least suggest that HRM is an approach that involves, or should involve, a more systematic and sophisticated engagement with employees and managers as part of the process of adding value to the organization through the efforts and contributions of all its employees.

Table 2.1 Summary of the main differences between personnel management and HRM

Personnel management	HRM
Emphasis on collectivity	More emphasis given to individuals
Generalized HR solutions	More tailored and bespoke solutions
Centralization of HR responsibility	Greater devolution of authority and responsibility for managing people
Increasing role for HR specialists	Senior managers and those in line positions seen as key to delivering effective HR 'solutions'
Associated with maintaining status quo and stability	Associated with maintaining stability and driving through changes in structures, practices, and capabilities
Associated with trade unionism and managing conflict	Associated with capabilities, performance, and outcomes
'Can't do' mindset	'Can do' mindset
Thought to be reactive	Associated with a more proactive orientation
Associates employees primarily as an economic resource and a cost	Much more emphasis on employees as a source of resourcefulness
More operationally oriented	Operates at the strategic and operational levels
Lacking in sufficient integration of activities	Strong emphasis on vertical and horizontal integration

Although, in one sense, it matters little what label is used to give an identity to these underlying beliefs, because it is the beliefs themselves that are important, for many practitioners the label *is* important because it symbolizes the departure from one approach to the management of people and the adoption of another. This other approach is considered more in tune with changes in the nature of work, the organizational pressures to 'deliver', and the need for a more flexible, committed, and productive labour force. The HRM label and approach to managing people can be seen therefore as being a symbol of a transition and change in the prevailing mindset as well as representing material changes in professional practice. These changes in practice are presented in Table 2.1.

Strategic Human Resource Management (SHRM)

One of the questions inevitably asked by students of HR is: 'If human resource management represents, among other things, a more strategic approach to the management of people, what is strategic human resource management (SHRM) about and how is it different?' This is a question that has merit and deserves a considered answer. The first thing to say is that SHRM is not a third distinctive and different approach to the management of people, with its own twenty-seven differences that help to establish its separate identity. For many who use this term, it means little more than recognizing the strategic dimension of HRM. In this sense, as Boxall and Purcell (2000) state, when the adjective 'strategic' is applied to HRM, in many cases, it means nothing at all.

But SHRM, for some academics and practitioners, does represent something more than the strategic dimension of HRM and this 'more' can be explained in three ways. First, SHRM is concerned with the way in which the management of people is critical to, and contributes towards, organizational effectiveness, and while this link was a claimed feature of HRM, SHRM identifies specific activities that connect the domain of HRM more explicitly to the strategic needs and interests of the organization. Put in a slightly different way, this means that while HRM is associated with the integration of its activities at the horizontal level, SHRM is more concerned with integrating HRM activities vertically, ensuring that these 'fit' with the strategic direction in which the organization is moving.

 Signpost to Chapter 3: A Strategic Perspective on HRM, for further development of the concept of integration.

Second, strategic choice is about making critical decisions in the key areas of managing people, such as rewards, relations, training and development, recruitment and selection, and performance management, and involves management deciding on whether to:

- commit to an individualist approach to employee relations or to recognize and negotiate with trade unions;
- reward employees on merit, performance, and potential, or on the basis of the jobs they do and length of service;
- employ only talented people or those that are available;
- base the development of employees on learning or training;
- adopt a 'one size fits all' approach to the development of HR practices or to develop more tailored and individualized policies and practices.

SHRM might, in the context of strategic choice, be seen to represent the processes and decisions that shape the organization's philosophy towards its employees and how they are managed in relation to the above strategically important areas. A good example of this is the development of talent management, the meaning of which is explored in Chapter 4. In the evolution of SHRM the concepts of differentiation and segmentation assume strategic significance and coexist with the two forms of integration to provide organizations with a strategic identity in the context of managing people.

 Signpost to Chapter 4: Talent Management, for a more detailed explanation of the concepts of differentiation and segmentation as applied to employees.

The third way of making sense of SHRM is to see it in terms of the development of what Becker et al. (2001) call the 'strategic HR architecture'. This concept expresses the full range of HR activities, interventions, policies, and practices, and links these to the effect they have on the value-creating potential of all employees, and how this added-value potential is actually measured and utilized. The idea of HR having an 'architecture' might seem somewhat fanciful and abstract, but the value of using this term lies in the idea that there is a coherent design behind HR; that someone has thought about design principles, has thought about the function of HR and produced a vision of how HR should 'look' in terms of its structures, internal relationships, emphases, and how to make it 'fit for purpose'. The alternative would be a management function that just evolved over time with little thought to its purpose and how it functioned.

 STUDENT ACTIVITY 2.4
One of the more interesting developments in the architecture of HR has been the implementation of the business partner model. This is much more than the sharing of responsibilities between HR and 'the line' and involves HR working to support the line in its pursuit of business objectives and the way it manages people.

Read '"You can't put in what God left out": not everyone can be a strategic business partner', by Nick Holley. What is Holley's central argument about the reasons for business partnering failing to deliver, and what if anything can be done to overcome these problems?

The Link between SHRM and Performance

One of the central tenets of SHRM is that the HR function makes, or should make, contributions which either individually or collectively contribute to organizational goals and to its long-term success. There are, however, difficulties in showing this link and establishing its strength because:

- Current measures of organizational success are predominantly concerned with financial and quantitative measures. With so many HR practices focusing on what could be described as 'soft' or intangible aspects of behaviour and individual performance the difficulty of measuring changes in key areas such as engagement, flexibility, creativity, motivation, and well-being represents a significant challenge for HR practitioners.

- Even where progress is made in producing more relevant and credible measures of HR outputs there is still the problem of linking these directly to organizational measures of success which are influenced by other factors in addition to the impact of HR. And, as we pointed out in Chapter 1, much that HR departments still do lacks any strategic impact at all.

For many, however, despite these two problems, the fundamental question that needs to be answered by those who claim HR is or is becoming strategic in its orientation is:

Does HRM make a difference to organizational performance?

David Guest's early work (1997) linked theories of HRM to theories of organizational performance and offers important insights into this critical relationship. It resulted in numerous new research projects designed to generate hard evidence that would support the claims of those who believed that, not only did HRM have the potential to deliver strategically valuable outcomes, it was actually achieving this, or at least in organizations that embraced this new approach to managing people (Purcell, 2003).

One of the enduring difficulties with HR, particularly in its departmental form, is showing conclusively that what HR does is directly connected to value-adding behaviours and improved organizational outcomes. (As we show in Chapter 12, employee performance is much more susceptible to the influence of line managers than HR professionals.) As Legge (2005) argued, it is extremely difficult if not impossible to establish clear-cut cause–effect relationships where what HRM 'does' can be unambiguously connected to particular outcomes even at the level of employee behaviour: it becomes even more problematic when attempts are made to link HR activities to organizational changes.

The work of Jaap Paauwe and colleagues in the Netherlands reflects the continuing academic interest in the HRM–performance relationship (Paauwe and Boselie, 2008). After reviewing numerous articles and research papers into the HRM–performance link, they reached an interesting conclusion. They claim that academics and practitioners need to look beyond the more obvious HR activities such as staffing and human resource planning—and we would suggest others such as appraisal systems and reward schemes. They say:

> A real contribution to performance . . . will only happen once we approach HRM from a more holistic and balanced perspective, including part of the organizational climate and culture, aimed at bringing about the alignment between individual values, corporate values and societal values.
> (Paauwe and Boselie, 2008)

They adopt a conceptual approach that allows them to argue that many of the activities undertaken by HR represent 'hygiene factors' which if not done well will cause problems for the organization, but which in themselves, and even collectively, will not produce the step-change improvements that produce sustained competitive advantage. (Herzberg used the same term to describe a number of factors that stop individuals from reducing their effort and performance but do not constitute factors that explain high performance which according to him is determined by a different set of factors.) The obvious point here is that not all of HR's activities are of the same value and that different activities make different kinds of contributions. This raises the question—which activities are producing strategically valuable outcomes and which are value-sapping?

One way of interpreting Paauwe and Boselie's argument is that HR needs to think more holistically in the search for better ways to impact organizational performance, one of which might be expressed in terms of organizational capability building. This refers to an organization's ability to create, mobilize, and utilize its key resources—in this case its human resources—to maximum effect. The concept emphasizes the key strategic role that HR can and must play if the organization is to optimize the contribution from all its employees. The concept is also important because it helps to redefine what HR represents: it is seen less as a series of activities and responsibilities and more as a resource and capability builder and a business function that exercises maximum leverage in the way this resource and its capabilities are used. This kind of theorizing has much in common with the work of Boudreau and Ramstad and their emphasis on HR concentrating on key pivot points which offer substantial opportunities to gain maximum leverage from human resources by developing and using strategically important capabilities. More about this is said in Chapter 3.

From the early research carried out by Patterson et al. (1997) to more recent insights into the value of what HR is capable of delivering (Boxhall and Purcell, 2016), academics have been trying to establish which HR practices are directly linked to business results, and which 'bundles' of practices have a greater impact on 'bottom line' outcomes. Holbeche (2009), after considering the importance of the human contribution to organizational success and competitive advantage, refers to the findings of Patterson et al. (1997), which suggested that:

> **Good personnel policies and practices can improve productivity and performance by enhancing skills and giving people responsibility for making the best use of their skills, but the combination of policies and practices which produces these effects varies by context.**
> **(1997: 91)**

The problem with this kind of statement, however, is that while 'good' policies and practices are identified, the extent to which they are successfully applied and implemented is not considered as a critical factor nor is the effect on the ability to implement changes of the wider organizational environment. One of the difficulties those who have identified 'bundles' of HR practices that are associated (we can't say they have a causal effect) with improved measures of organizational performance have, is showing the effect of such organizational variables as structure, culture, and stability on this relationship. By this we mean whether the same effects have been observed, and in the same degree, in different kinds of organizations and in different organizational states. This may mean that two organizations appearing to employ the same set of HR practices may well experience significantly different effects on the same measures of organizational performance.

What does seem to be an essential requirement in the transformation of HR into a strategic management function is the existence of a set of connected indicators or measures that focus on the critical outputs of HR activities and link these to strategically important organizational outcomes which are known or are believed to be influenced by what HR does and achieves. But in a later book on the subject Paauwe et al. (2013) attempt to highlight the continuing controversy of the HR–performance link. They begin chapter 1 by quoting from three different sources:

● 'Based on four national surveys and observations on more than 2000 firms, our judgement is that the effect of a one standard deviation change in the HR system is 10–20% of a firm's market value.'

● 'The existing evidence for a relationship between HRM and performance should be treated with caution.'

● 'After hundreds of research studies we are still in no position to assert with any confidence that good HRM has an impact on organisation performance.'

There are at least three explanations for this lack of agreement:

1. Methodological differences are at the heart of the problem and until there is a more reliable and consistent approach to testing the relationship, inconsistent results are to be expected.
2. There is a positive relationship but its strength varies between organizations and over time.
3. What HR does, in its departmental form, has very little if any impact on organization performance, despite claims to the contrary, although the wider HR function, where people management is influenced by organization leaders and line managers, may have a more positive impact.

Part of the problem of showing a relationship between HR and performance may also lie in the choice of HR and organization output measures. Examples of HR outputs are:

- changes in labour productivity;
- changes in labour supply and labour costs;
- changes in the quality/capabilities of the workforce;
- changes in retention, engagement, and satisfaction levels;
- changes in discretionary effort and individual performance;
- changes in employee flexibility.

Some of the above lend themselves to being systematically measured but others less so; how, for example, can labour flexibility and effort/performance be reliably measured? We also have to ask how many of the activities of the HR department actually contribute to any and all of these outputs?

Examples of organizational outcomes are:

- ratio of labour costs to total costs;
- results of employee and other surveys on attitudes to the organization;
- levels of industrial unrest;
- levels of employee contributions to innovation and creativity;
- brand reputation;
- customer satisfaction levels.

But then financial outcomes also need to be considered and built into the picture as indicated in Figure 2.3. As with all similar models, what is represented or suggested fails to convey the complexity and problematic nature of this hypothesized relationship and needs to be viewed with a healthy degree of scepticism. As we

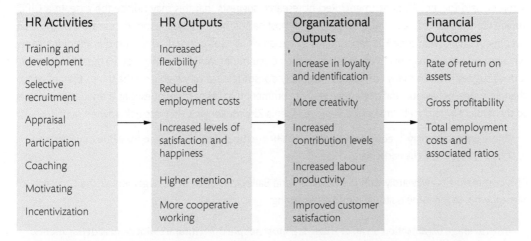

Figure 2.3 Diagrammatical representation of the HR–performance relationship

have already pointed out, very few writers go as far as to claim that what HR does causes the kinds of outputs and outcomes identified in the model. Yet there is clearly a significant body of research that does support a relationship between the two and intuitively it is logical to think that the way people are managed and used at work will have some effects on the variables we have included in the model (the list is not exclusive). The problem though is how much of an effect—it can be negative as well as positive—and precisely how does the transmission of effect/influence work at each stage? Perhaps at some future point and after further and more focused research a more convincing answer(s) than we have now will be found, but until then, our position is best summed up by the words of Herzberg who once said:

It works whether you believe it or not.

We would add, 'it works whether you can prove it or not', but how well and for how long is uncertain.

STUDENT ACTIVITY 2.5

Although not developed specifically as an HR tool, Kaplan and Norton's balanced scorecard model can be applied to HR and provides opportunities for developing different kinds of measurements and metrics.

Listen to this podcast and think about the relevance and applicability of the model to HR: https://www.youtube.com/watch?v=l_Z78iKDRcs

Then in a group agree on your own list of HR activities (carried out by the department and line managers) that you think could have an effect on HR and organizational outputs, and on how you measure both.

RESEARCH INSIGHT 2.1

You will benefit from reading

Gates, S. and Langevin, P. (2010) 'Human capital measures, strategy, and performance: HR managers' perceptions', *Accounting, Auditing & Accountability Journal,* **23(1).**

The article offers insights into the perceptions of HR managers of ways of measuring human resource capital and the use of these measures to support strategy development.

Despite the quotation from Herzberg and the belief that the quality of people an organization employs and how they are used must have some effect on 'things that matter', the question remains: in what way and to what extent is the HR department and its staff responsible? In Chapter 1 and later in Chapter 12 convincing evidence is provided to support the idea that a person's line manager, and to an extent his/her co-workers, have a significant impact on emotional and psychological well-being and performance levels, but can the same be said for the HR department? Recent research suggests that this may not be the case. In a CIPD survey reported by *People Management* (2016), almost half of the employee respondents said they had had no direct contact with their HR departments in the previous twelve months and one-quarter didn't know who carried out the majority of the HR work in their organization. While this may not tell the whole picture, it does suggest that for many employees HR simply doesn't feature very highly on the things that influence their attitudes, behaviour, and performance. In a comment that raises more questions than it does answers to the issue of whether HR 'makes a difference', Ksenia Zheltoukhova, CIPD research adviser, said:

There is a role to play in educating people that HR are the people to come to for values, culture and career progression in particular.

This comment sits awkwardly with the views of Katie Bailey, professor of management at the University of Sussex, who, in the same editorial is quoted as saying:

In an average organisation on an average day, most people don't interact with central departments. And when they do, it's inevitable it will be more routine.

Because all managers, whether specialists in HR or not, are in an important sense 'managers of people', that is, human resource or personnel managers, the contributions that each party makes to desirable and undesirable outcomes is difficult to separate out and measure. This means that it is possible for one party to blame the other when things go wrong and to claim the credit when things go well. Much depends, of course, on the nature of working relationships between specialists and line managers and the way in which the HR operates, but the problem of separating out and measuring the influence on employees and on other key HR outputs of the HR department and leaders/line managers is a difficult and enduring one.

Although nominally offering an advisory service, the HR specialist can be seen by line managers to be taking on executive responsibilities and introducing practices and policies that, although purportedly in the interests of the organization as a whole, can be perceived as intrusive, unhelpful, and having little relevance to the line manager's priorities and agendas. In seeking to develop their functional expertise and professional identity, those who work in HR can become detached from 'the needs of the business', and, as a consequence, run the risk of being seen as 'marginal' and adding little of value. The article by Nick Holley is particularly interesting in this regard because of the potential mismatch between the competences and experience HR professionals bring to the 'table' and what line managers and CEOs require them to be able to be and do to support the business. Perhaps the most important realization that HR has to face up to is that HR needs to be more about the business than about people. According to Rita McGrath, professor at the Columbia Business School:

> **Companies should insist that nobody gets to have an important job in HR unless they have managed a profit and loss process, developed a strategy or delivered major organisational change.**
> (*People Management*, 2016)

An example that might illustrate the feeling that HR has its own agenda would be in relation to diversity training. Diversity and equality are issues which have become increasingly important in contemporary society, particularly in the public sector. Many organizations have taken strong ethical positions in relation to the way all people are treated and respected, but excessive emphasis on diversity training may be perceived by line managers as having little direct relevance to matters of production or to 'bottom-line performance', although such a commitment may have important reputational and brand significance. There is the additional question about the effectiveness of training that focuses on attitudes and social behaviour rather than skills and competences. In the absence of the 'business case' being made for diversity training, beyond legal requirements, is it legitimate to raise questions about its value to organizational subunits? Until there are agreed criteria for measuring HR's contributions and valid metrics designed to monitor changes in these criteria, questions about relevance and contribution are likely to continue to be raised (CIPD, 2016).

So, the question regarding the link between what HR does and performance, which is in many respects similar to Ulrich's concern about HR activities and outcomes, continues to produce very different answers.

STUDENT ACTIVITY 2.6

This activity involves an element of role playing. Split into two groups and allocate to each group the role of HR specialists or line managers. The organizational setting can be public or private sector but the exercise will work better if the private sector is used. The line manager group should discuss the contributions it values most from HR and what it feels offers little value. The HR group should identify the services and contributions it offers to the line and rank this list in order of what the HR group thinks is of greatest value to the line. The two groups then come together and share their ideas and seek explanations for any difference in the two lists. Then they should discuss the implications of their work for what the HR department does.

For an opportunity to see the problematic nature of the link between what HR does and HR outcomes, see the case study in the Online Resources Extension Material 2.2.

The Future of HR

As we noted earlier in this and in Chapter 1, questions about HR's value and contribution in its departmental form have been asked by organizational leaders and line managers as well as a number of influential commentators and academics; these are not new questions, and as we have tried to explain, they reflect ambiguities and paradoxes that are deeply rooted within most medium and large-scale organizations. This means that at least part of predicting what HR will be like over the next two decades will depend on finding answers to the following questions:

● Will HR departments shrink in size as HR administration is outsourced and/or made more efficient as a result of IT developments?

● Where will professional HR expertise be located and how will it be used?

● Will HR be able to make the kinds of strategic contributions expected of it?

● What kinds of agenda items and priorities will HR be associated with?

● What kinds of experience and expertise will HR need to confront the challenges it faces?

● What new HR models will be developed by academics?

The starting point for offering insights into these questions must be with the internal but particularly the external environment, both of which create pressures and exert influence on how people are managed and used at work. Care should be taken to avoid an overly deterministic position on these forces but clearly environmental change has and will continue to provide explanations for what HR does and what it is expected or required to do. Organizational leaders will continue to be responsible for shaping corporate strategy and philosophies about how people should be managed, but these too are subject to external influence, particularly from legal regulation, changing social values, competition, and the growth of the digital economy. Perhaps the most important internally driven change will come from the increasing deployment of technology, particularly in information management, robotics, and artificial intelligence. Whether these influences will change the 'ends' HR pursues or the 'means' it employs is debatable, but the position taken here is that both will be affected to some degree. What we can be fairly sure about, however, is that trying to find new and more effective ways of making people more productive, engaged, committed, and loyal, which will be achieved by a small number of what we call 'advanced organizations', will prove problematic for the majority. The reason for this is the existence of an underlying and inherent tension between the interests of people as employees and their economic status as economic resources. Watson (2003) described this tension when he talked about the 'paradox of consequences' which he defined as:

> **The tendency for the means adopted by organisational managers to achieve particular goals to fail to achieve these goals since these 'means' involve human beings who have goals of their own which may not be congruent with those of managers.**

And however much managers try to convince their employees that both sets of goals are in fact congruent, the reality that most employees periodically experience is that this is not the case and a win–win situation is replaced by one of win–lose in relative but sometimes absolute terms. People value and have a need for security over uncertainty, fairness over randomness, recognition over invisibility, status over anonymity, and contribution over exploitation: most organization requires subordination, conformity, obedience, and control so that it can function in predetermined ways. What reduces the tension between organizational interests and those of employees is what we call, 'expressions of humanity'. By this we mean the way people are treated at work and whether employees see this treatment as fair, reasonable, and justified. What we don't know is how well a future HR will be able to meet the legitimate expectations of the organization as an employer *and* the interests of its employees and how far it can and will go to create a secure psychological and emotional working environment where fairness, equity (this does not always mean equal), and reasonable treatment prevails. The evidence we have is that the HR department may struggle to deliver against these requirements. The worst-case scenario is one in which the HR department fails to 'support the business' (the CIPD research we quoted above identified a serious credibility problem in this respect), and fails to prevent managerial excesses that damage the self-respect, confidence, and well-being of employees. Paradoxically, recent attempts to make work a 'safer', fairer, and better regulated place, although well intentioned may be undermined by the unintended consequences that we can see following on from a number of major HR initiatives. To use another metaphor, HR risks being identified as the organization's 'social conscience', concerned more with social engineering than becoming a key strategic player, where the social behaviour of employees takes precedence over their work behaviour. Of course, the two are not unrelated but there is an important difference between them, where efficiency, performance, and key business objectives become subordinate to how people communicate and relate to other people. HR procedures and practices in employment, development, appraisal, and discipline may come to reflect an emphasis on that which is 'organizationally correct' rather than that which supports and drives the business and is fair and reasonable. This concern with the social at the perceived expense of the economic and fair reflects an HR agenda and social mindset, where they exist, that risks undermining the ability of the organization to function effectively. By this we mean where excessive regulation, greater intolerance, tighter procedural control, excessive centralization, and uniformity results in a dysfunctional, unhealthy, risk-averse, and conformist culture. In a recent *Wall Street Journal* article, it was stated that:

Companies seeking flat management structures and more accountability for employees are frequently taking aim at human resources. Executives say the traditional HR department—which claims dominion over everything from hiring and firing to maintaining workplace diversity—stifles innovation and bogs down businesses with inefficient policies and processes. At the same time, a booming HR software industry has made it easier than ever to automate or outsource personnel-related functions such as payroll and benefits administration.
(Webber and Feintzeig, 2014)

In a new book on feminism in the workplace, Elsesser (2015) has identified what she calls a 'sex partition', which is found in organizations that have embraced socially correct standards of behaviour, which she believes impedes women from building vital networks of contacts within the workplace because men in senior positions are fearful of being accused of socially improper behaviour and as a result become disengaged from women employees. Elsesser found that many companies in the USA are contributing to this situation out of fear of legal action, and to avoid this they are sending staff on sexual harassment training courses, following up on any allegation of sexual harassment however minor. She cites examples of men who have been called in by their HR departments for simply opening a door for a female colleague or complimenting a woman on a new suit. She concludes:

Stories like these spread around workplaces, instilling a fear that innocent remarks will be misinterpreted.

We are not suggesting that this kind of situation is typical in the UK but rather that there are indications that HR in some organizations is moving in this direction. But an HR agenda and mindset that overemphasizes the importance of socially correct behaviours is likely to raise the question again—what is HR for? This leads people to question whether the balance of roles and activities is appropriate to meet the legitimate expectations of different stakeholders and interests.

Another insight into the future of HR is provided by Michie et al. (2015), who talk about it moving from centres of expertise to centres of excellence; the diffusion of HR into non-functional structures and constellations of activities—developments or recommendations that may involve meaningful changes in the HR architecture, but worryingly raise questions as to what they actually mean by these descriptions and whether we are being presented with a new language to describe existing situations or genuinely new models of HR. All management functions evolve and change over time and we should not be surprised that the same imperatives that influence marketing and finance also affect HR, but is this constant search for something 'new' obscuring our ability to identify the core of what HR represents and what works, which is the point made by Pfeffer in his criticism of management theory.

Another contribution to the debate about HR in the future comes from the work of Ulrich et al. (2009, 2012). Dave Ulrich in particular is well known for his analysis of HR and of the criticisms he has levelled at it as well as his influential prescriptive models. In this latest work, he again raises the question of the HR mindset and its agenda. At the beginning of the book, Ulrich talks about their approach to trying to understand what HR does as part of the process of interviewing HR professionals: he says they always ask them to 'tell us about the business', as a way of finding out the current state of HR in the companies they visited. The answers they received highlight the pervasive problem that the authors highlighted in their earlier writings—how do senior HR professionals explain their role?

> **Most replies start with discussing the latest challenges or innovations in HR practices (hiring people, training leaders, building incentive compensation, doing HR analytics and so forth), relating to business leaders (having a voice at the table, getting buy in), or managing the increased personal demands of the HR job ... That is, HR professionals almost invariably talk about their current initiatives in leadership training, recruiting, engagement, rewards—the areas where they focus their attention on the job.**

His response to this pattern of responses is not difficult to predict! He states:

> **These efforts are important, but they are not the business. They are in support of the business.**

He goes on to argue that the real business is about the external environment, the key stakeholders, and the strategies that should be providing competitive advantage; the mindset of HR should reflect this external reality rather than express the activities of the department. But, as we noted earlier, the external environment is not just about business and competitive forces and to deny the relevance of social values, new ideologies, and the external regulation of employment would be wholly inappropriate. It may be, however, that Ulrich and his colleagues are raising the question of primacy and what HR's core contribution to the organization should be.

Implicit in their analysis of what HR departments were doing is the belief that many had not made the transition from what they call wave 1 which is characterized by a focus on administration to waves 2 and 3—HR practices and HR strategy respectively—to wave 4—HR from the outside in. There is nothing particularly original or illuminating in this representation of HR's evolution but it certainly suggests that those who are responsible for setting the HR agenda should not be limited to HR professionals. This conclusion is supported by a recent CIPD study (2016) into what leading members of the profession felt about the current state of HR. In the foreword to the report, Karen Minicozzi acknowledged that while business and HR are mostly aligned on what the key business priorities are, there is a real disconnect between what HR believes it can do, what the wider business believes HR should focus on, and what it is actually capable of delivering. The report found that close to three-quarters of HR leaders surveyed believe they have the right people strategy to help the organization achieve its future goals. However, this confidence is not shared by non-HR business leaders, with just one-quarter agreeing with this statement. Put in a slightly different way, there is genuine and broad-based doubt outside of the HR department that it is focusing on the things that would make a difference 'to the business', and, arguably more worrying, even if HR did commit to these activities there is a lack of confidence that they could deliver in these areas.

A key theme of Ulrich and Brockbank's (2005) book is that of added value, which has to be of concern for future HR. The concept of adding value is in one sense unproblematic, but in another is more complex and operationally challenging. Part of the difficulties with HR engaged in activities that add value is over what this actually means. Value can be expressed in terms of objective and 'hard' criteria—we can measure added value by volume and value, but it also has a subjective dimension where adding value is linked to individual perception and different stakeholder perspectives, rather than unequivocal measurements. Take for example employee well-being policies. While such policies are in principle difficult to argue against, what do such policies actually achieve, assuming they are successful, and what is the 'value' of any claims for 'value-adding outcomes'? Although there have been developments in HR metrics, quantifying the value of such policies is still difficult and any claims made by HR are unlikely to go without challenge. There are, of course, the often-ignored costs associated with such policies, and any meaningful attempt to measure added value needs to reflect the balance between costs and outcomes, in other words net added value. If the outcomes of such policies do affect important issues, such as engagement and commitment levels and attendance patterns, the ability to prove causal links will, despite improvements in HR metrics, still be a challenge. Perhaps believing they work in the way claimed may be sufficient if all stakeholders share the same belief (CIPD, 2007).

STUDENT ACTIVITY 2.7

Read the *Personnel Today* article 'How can HR prove it really adds value?', 3 September 2012, http://www.personneltoday.com/hr/how-can-hr-prove-it-really-adds-value

Summarize the main points made in the article and then consider the difficulties HR might experience in moving in the directions suggested.

The interest in creating greater clarity about what HR actually achieves and costs, as a basis for making better decisions on what HR should be concentrating on, is at the heart of what is called human capital analytics (HCA), associated with the work of people like Jac Fitz-enz (2010). He argues that HR should not only focus on creating value but that it needs to be able to measure this value in financial and objective ways. The origins of this form of HR lie in the recognition by some leading HR practitioners (e.g. Fitz-enz) that the dominant paradigm in the 1980s and 1990s, which was about running the HR department, needed to be changed to that of managing human capital. (This is a good example of what is called a paradigm shift.) So, a future HR may become much more closely aligned to the management of human capital and less involved in administration (but this point has been made for some considerable time!) HCA involves HR in developing metrics that support and validate all that HR does in important areas such as strategy, workforce planning, providing intelligence to business leaders about performance, and productivity changes. In the UK, the term, 'HR dashboard' is used to represent the visual display of HR metrics that measure performance of key processes, ratios, and outcomes, but the use of metrics in HR is not without its challenges or difficulties particularly in relation to what we have described as HR's social dimension.

Another development affecting the future HR architecture is the trend towards outsourcing of HR's administrative responsibilities (CIPD, 2016). This essentially means that more specialized and efficient resources are contracted to do the administrative tasks associated with the 'hiring and firing' of people and data management which in turn reduces the costs of the contracting organization through a reduced HR head count and lower fixed costs. A second effect is that, free from time-consuming and resource-intensive work, the HR department can refocus its professional staff towards more value-adding activities. The effect of HR outsourcing is potentially significant in relation to the structure of the HR function. This 'transformation' is highlighted by Lawler et al. (2004):

> We argue that the field of HR is being split in half. Much of the traditional, administrative, and transactional work of HR—payroll, benefits administration, staffing policies, training logistics, and so forth—must be carried out more efficiently. Most large firms have either built service centres and invested in HR technology or outsourced these transactions. What is left after transactional HR has been automated, centralized eliminated or outsourced forms the heart of this book. The HR Value Proposition.

What emerges from the visions of these academics is a picture of a future HR which is characterized by:

- A reduction or elimination of its *transactional* work which will continue to be done but not within the HR department.

- An increase in its *transformational* role. By that we mean it will engage with strategically important and value-adding areas of the business where changes in people—capabilities, motivation, and flexibility—can make a big difference to how the organization works and what it achieves.

- A change in the kind of *people* who occupy key HR positions. Increasing emphasis will be given to experience and expertise found outside of HR. For too long HR has been an insular and exclusive profession, where CIPD qualifications and experience in HR departments are seen as essential prerequisites for senior HR roles. This is changing and the trend towards appointing 'non-HR' people as HR leaders will continue.

- A *relocation* of responsibilities for important people management decisions to line managers *and* employees as new organizational forms develop, centralized functions shrink in size and become strategic rather than operational, and 'one size fits all' solutions are replaced by flexible and bespoke ways of managing people.

What is the evidence that supports this view of a future HR? We have already referred to several well-known and influential US commentators; now in this final part of the chapter we summarize the views of a group of experts who participated in a CIPD (2015a) survey on changing HR operating models. John Bersin, from a consultancy perspective, identifies a similar transition to that presented by Ulrich et al., but calls the fourth and final stage high-impact HR, characterized by a strong service delivery capability and sophisticated talent management programmes. In key areas such as recruitment, the emphasis has moved from traditional practices towards 'network recruiting', where the drivers of success are employment brand, candidate relationship management, the use of analytics to determine who are the best candidates, and strong and local relationships with hiring managers. Learning has replaced traditional training practices and has moved towards a 'self-learning' digital-learning environment, where individuals can learn on-demand and decide between formal and informal learning and where training is *integrated* into career management and professional development goals. Another notable feature of this advanced form of HR is the existence of more specialists being located closer to the business, where they can work with line managers to create the most value.

Boudreau and Lawler consider the future structure of HR and how it can develop a stronger strategic role. They refer to Charan's (2014) article in which he calls for corporate HR functions to be split into two parts, one dealing with employment and compensation administration with a reporting line to the organization's chief financial officer and the other concerned with leadership and organization development, but staffed by talented people from operations and finance who would rotate through the role on their way to the top of the organization. Although Boudreau and Lawler consider this proposal too simplistic, they also recognize its resonance with many business leaders and offer some support for Charan's new HR model:

> **Having HR leaders gain firsthand experience as business leaders throughout their careers seems likely to prepare them more fully for true business partnership than does having only HR jobs.**

They go on to say:

> **Perhaps even more important is having leaders outside of HR rotate into the function, which is also associated with a stronger HR strategic role. Such rotations enhance the business awareness of the HR function because the inward rotations bring valuable expertise from outside.**

Writing in the same publication Nick Holley reflects on the very different skill sets required of those who work as HR business partners compared to those occupying more traditional HR roles within the department. Quoting the work of Elliott Jaques on work levels of complexity, Holley argues that not all HR practitioners have the necessary skill set to become successful business partners, and that asking level 3 HR people to do level 4 work is unfair, inappropriate, and will almost certainly result in disappointment. It's very interesting to note that as many of those who contributed to the CIPD's publication on HR operating models focused on HR experience, expertise, and capability as those who were interested in the operating models themselves.

In the CIPD (2016a) report on leaders' views of the HR profession, what emerged as shared priorities for both HR and non-HR leaders in the future was a continuation rather than a change of priorities. Managing costs remains at the top of the list and has become a permanent rather than a temporary feature of HR work. (The practitioner insight below supports this belief in the importance of controlling employment costs.) Both parties also agreed on the importance of increasing the agility/flexibility of the organization and the need to develop strategies to drive productivity growth. Interestingly, none of the five future priorities identified in the report mentioned diversity, equality, or the ethical dimension of work, but rather highlighted the business dimension of HR. Does this suggest that current HR practice and future priorities are misaligned or that the survey failed to reflect the diversity of both HR practice and future organizational priorities? It could of course hide the fact that this aspect of HR is too important to be left to the HR department and is increasingly within the remit of CEOs.

 For additional material on the future of HR, see the Online Resources Extension Material 2.3.

PRACTITIONER INSIGHT Roger Collins, director of HR & OD in an NHS trust hospital—HR in the NHS: leading on the pay bill challenge

From 2000 to 2008, the role of the HR practitioner in the NHS was to increase the size of the workforce; the NHS planning framework during that period set out very clear targets for expanding workforce numbers, but now we face a very different situation. Pay makes up approximately 70 per cent of total spend in the NHS and now the focus is very much on pay bill reduction as part of an integrated approach to cost improvement programmes, ensuring that where potential pay bill savings are identified, the impact on the quality of clinical care provided for our patients is not diminished. This is a real challenge. In our organization, HR is firmly established as a key member of the board team, although this is not uniform across all NHS organizations. However, the workforce agenda is common to all trusts and other NHS bodies.

There is a real need for the HR function to not only look at where pay bill savings can be made, but also how we engage our wider workforce in meeting these financial challenges. Our trust has just started an open conversation with our workforce regarding potential pay bill savings areas and local staff representatives are aware of the challenge facing the organization. But there is an inherent tension in the need to make savings locally and a fierce desire to maintain national terms and conditions of service on the part of trade union representatives. For our workforce, I don't feel that saying that we need to save £48 million over the next four years really resonates, so we have developed new approaches to getting this message across, breaking down the total figure to the challenge of saving £1 for every £20 we currently spend. As a trust, we have two key campaigns running, Employment Over Earnings and War on Waste. We want to maintain employment for as many of our existing staff as we can, but we also need them to mobilize and join management to identify and drive out waste in all areas of our organization.

We are very mindful of our corporate and social responsibility. Sixty per cent of our business is in Cumbria and we know that near on 50 per cent of the employed population in Cumbria works in the public sector, so taking posts out of the public sector potentially damages the whole of the Cumbrian economy.

Future supply lines into our organization have to be maintained too, so we are actively engaging with local schools and colleges to ensure that when we are in a position to recruit. The talent pool out there remains engaged and aware of the rewarding employment opportunities the NHS and the wider public sector has.

In order to manage our organizations successfully now and ensure future sustainability, we need to workforce plan effectively, but this needs to be integrated with our financial and clinical plans and also needs to be mindful of the technological changes which impact upon our clinical delivery. The challenge is huge, but we have to prove that we are an asset to our organization and not an overhead.

To conclude this section, Table 2.2 offers a way of understanding the different paradigms and conceptualizations associated with the HR function, and provides opportunities for establishing differences in the value-adding outcomes of each model of HR.

Table 2.2 Ways of conceptualizing the role and purpose of HR

Requirement	Label	Problems	Consequences	Justifications
To care for the physical, psychological, and emotional well-being of employees	The welfare role and function	Can focus too narrowly on employee interests—no explicit recognition of 'business interests'	HR seen as 'soft' and 'woolly'; seen by line managers as of little relevance	Continues to be of fundamental importance in how people are managed and how they behave or perform at work
To solve problems and fix things	The firefighting role	Largely a reactive role—involves HR dealing with symptoms, rather than addressing underlying causes and problems	HR is often 'busy', but its agenda and focus is limited and misses out on other important areas of contribution	Fixing problems and 'putting out fires' is important: small 'fires' can develop into larger, and more threatening, situations
To maintain systems and procedures, with an emphasis on administrative conformity	The conservative and process role	Can focus too narrowly, with little regard for outcomes; HR seen as coercive and reactionary	HR has negative reputation—seen as adding little value and becomes marginalized	Efficient administration is always important and a certain level of procedural regulation is legally prescribed
To build capability	HR's strategic contribution and strategic alignment	Can lose sight of the importance of efficient administrative and effective operational interventions	Associated with outsourcing of non-strategic functions and devolvement of many key operational responsibilities to line managers	Easily spoken about and more often than not aspirational; requires different mindsets and skill sets on the part of HR professionals working in this way
To support the business and line managers	The 'business partner' role	Requires specialist skills and wider business experience to be effective	Raises questions about the 'professional' dimension of HR	Often ignores tensions between business and professional interests; is 'being good for the business' the only reference point for HR professionals to use to justify their actions?

Summary

There is little doubt that HR, as a specialist management function, faces a challenging future: a future that, for some, involves something of a metamorphosis. There also seems to be a consensus that it has to change before it can meet the requirements and expectations of other organizational stakeholders, and be accorded the status and credibility that the function is seeking. Whether the change, as Rucci (1997) believes, will involve its demise (in its departmental form) is more problematic and contentious. So, what are the changes to which HR needs to commit to preserve its future? They can perhaps be expressed in relation to the following:

- Acquiring and applying a much stronger business orientation in designing and delivering HR activities and services. This has major implications for the skills and mindset of HR professionals and in relation to their recruitment and selection. The employment of people from outside of the HR profession to senior HR positions is a trend that is likely to continue.

- Being clearer about the priorities they pursue and why certain activities have been prioritized. This will inevitably mean that the HR agenda and the deployment of HR resources is influenced, if not determined, by the 'users' of HR—i.e. by employees, line managers, and senior executives, as well as HR professionals.

- Developing their functional expertise. This involves developing skills and competences that allow HR to deliver 'solutions' and to offer advice and support to managers that is founded on a body of professional theory that has been tested and refined in countless situations. If line managers retain a degree of dependence on HR experts, then the expertise offered has to deliver the contributions and outcomes that those line managers need.

- Building personal credibility and a reputation for reliability and professionalism. As long ago as 1993, Buckingham and Elliot, in their article on what distinguishes successful from less successful HR managers, found that those rated as 'above average' in performance were associated with:

  - the ability to motivate others;

  - the ability to build relationships;

  - the ability to seek and build commitment;

  - the possession of a conceptual mindset, and a clear perspective on their role and its purpose.

They concluded:

> This mindset may be defined as a philosophy of Personnel Management and a conceptual ability to define the significant contribution that the personnel professional can make to the organisation. This philosophy is strongly rooted in clear perceptions about, and a real commitment to, the value of good employees and of their contribution to the company.

Despite this important contribution to what characterizes a successful HR function the sense that HR, in many organizations, still suffers from the 'wrong' mindset and employs staff with an outdated or inappropriate skill set is still evident and supports the notion that not all the 'right' people are working in HR.

The future of HR will undoubtedly be influenced by developments in technology, in changing organizational forms, and in relation to the capability of line managers in taking on much more responsibility for the management of their staff. It might also be argued that its future is in the hands of those who work in HR and whether they can rise to the challenges confronting the profession.

 Visit the **online resources** that accompany this book for self-test questions, web links, and more information on the topics covered in this chapter, at: **www.oup.com/uk/banfield3e/**

65

? REVIEW QUESTIONS

1. What are the contributions of HR professionals and line managers to the behaviour and performance of employees?

2. What is the difference between human resource management and Human Resource Management?

3. In the context of the knowledge economy, what particular employment and HR practices will be necessary if organizations are going to maximize the performance and contributions of knowledge workers?

4. What will be the issues and pressures affecting HR in five years' time?

The material for this case study is taken from a presentation given at a CIPD national conference.

The Royal Mail, prior to recent changes, employed over 200,000 people and had been a national institution for over 300 years. In the early part of this century, however, it began to suffer serious performance and financial problems. It was known for poor industrial relations and accounted for nearly 50 per cent of working days lost because of strikes. It was a business that was near to insolvency, and was renowned for low pay and long hours, and an over-reliance on agency workers. It was, in other words, a business that had failed to adapt its internal structures and culture to a rapidly changing external environment in which increasing competition was the most important development.

The HR function, defined in terms of those who worked in and for the specialized HR department, was costing the business £200 million each year. Approximately 3,700 people were employed in HR, which meant that the ratio of HR staff to total employees was near to 1:55 (i.e. for every 55 employees, there was one member of HR). The primary role of HR was in relation to the trade unions, which defined the state of the company's employee relations. But, increasingly, HR had become associated with numerous policies and procedures covering almost every aspect of the employment and management of people. Unfortunately, the increasing influence of the centralized HR function had led to a defranchising of line managers, who felt unable to engage directly with their staff.

The need to transform HR as part of changing the culture of the organization was based on a clear understanding of how the 'people' side of the business needed to change. It involved:

- an overall reduction in costs;

- a modernization of employment processes and procedures;

- the professionalization of the HR function;

- a change in the relationship with trade unions;

- adding more strategic value;

- empowering line managers;

- driving change.

The transformation was achieved by creating a new HR architecture, based on a very clear distinction between the different contributions that HR was required to make. The 'new' HR was based on three distinctive domains:

- establishing functional expertise that supported the line;

- creating business partners that worked with the line;

- a shared service capability that delivered administrative efficiency.

The transformation was not achieved without considerable investment in the development of HR staff, supplemented by the injection of new talent to lead the changes. The newly appointed 'business partners' were assessed against a demanding competence framework and there was an emphasis away from 'doables' to 'deliverables', with a new focus on how HR could add value to the business.

The results of the transformation were both impressive and challenging. The ratio of HR staff to employees rose to 1:130. A new attitude and relationship with the trade unions resulted in a reduction in industrial disputes and restrictive work practices, and a reduction in head count of 34,000.

The clear message, however, was that this was the beginning rather than the end of a process. Further competition pressures meant that Royal Mail needed to become more competitive, leading to increasing pressure on jobs and the need to raise productivity levels even higher. For HR, there was 'no hiding place', but its key contributions could only be made as a result of a very different HR architecture and a new relationship with line managers.

Questions

1. What particular competences do the organization's HR 'business partners' need to be able to work effectively with line managers?

2. What are shared service centres and how do they operate?

3. What needs to be done to allow line managers to take direct responsibility for managing their staff?

4. What happened to those HR staff that were lost to the company?

 FURTHER READING

Boudreau, J. W. (2010) *Retooling HR: Using proven business tools to make better decisions about talent*, Harvard Business School Press.

Boudreau, J. (2014) 'It's time to retool HR, not split it', *Harvard Business Review*, August, at: https://hbr. org/2014/08/its-time-to-retool-hr-not-split-it, 7

Boudreau, J. W. and Lawler, E. E. (2009) *Achieving Excellence in Human Resource Management: An Assessment of Human Resource Functions*, Stanford University Press.

Buyens, D. and Verbrigghe, J. (2015) 'Adding value and HRM practice: Evidence-based HR', in M. Andresen, C. Nowak (eds.), *Human Resource Management Practices, Management for Professionals*, Springer.

CIPD (2010) 'Next generation HR time for change—Towards a next generation for HR'.

 REFERENCES

Barratt, B. (2008) 'The later Foucault in management and organization studies', *Human Relations*, 61(4): 515–37.

Becker, B., Huselid, M. A., and Ulrich, D. (2001) *The HR Scorecard*, Harvard Business School Press.

Beer, M. et al. (1985) *Human Resource Management: A General Manager's Perspective*, Free Press.

Bolza, M. (2016) 'Dealing with the HR identity crisis', HC Online, 15 February, at: http://www.hcamag. com/hr-news/dealing-with-the-hr-identity-crisis-211747.aspx

Boxall, P. and Purcell, J. (2000) 'Strategic human resource management: Where have we come from and where should we be going?', *International Journal of Management Reviews*, 2(2), 183–203.

Boxall, P. and Purcell, J. (2016) *Strategy and Human Resource Management*, 4th edn, Palgrave.

Buckingham, G. and Elliot, G. (1993) 'Profile of a successful personnel manager', *Personnel Management*, 25(8), 26–9.

Charan, R. (2014) 'It's time to split HR', *Harvard Business Review* (July).

CIPD (2005) 'Outsourcing human resources: A framework for decisions'.

CIPD (2007) 'What's happening with well-being at work?', at: http://www.cipd.co.uk

CIPD (2010) 'The role of line managers in HR', at: http://www.cipd.co.uk/hr-resources/factsheets/role-line-managers-hr.aspx

CIPD (2015a) 'Changing HR operating models', 17 February, at: https://www.cipd.co.uk/knowledge/strategy/hr/operating-models

CIPD (2015b) 'HR business partnering', revised, September.

CIPD (2016a) 'HR outlook. HR leaders' views of our profession, winter 2015–16', at: https://www.cipd. co.uk/Images/hr-outlook_2016-winter-2015-16-leaders-views-of-our-profession_tcm18-11009.pdf

CIPD (2016b) 'HR outsourcing', September.

Christensen, R. N. (1997) 'Where is human resources?', quoted in D. Ulrich, M. R. Losey, and G. Lake, *Tomorrow's HR Management*, Wiley.

Elsesser, K. (2015) *Sex and the Office: Women, Men, and the Sex Partition That's Dividing the Workplace*, Taylor Trade Publishing.

Fitz-enz, J. (2010) *The New HR Analytics: Predicting the Economic Value of Your Company's Human Capital Investments*, AMACOM.

Flynn, S. (2014) 'Overcoming the identity crisis in human resources', *Human Resource Management International Digest*, 22(2), 1–3.

Gennard, J. and Kelly, J. (1994) 'Human resource management: The views of personnel directors', *Human Resource Management*, 5(1), 15–32.

Grant, D. and Oswick, C. (1998) 'Of believers, atheists and agnostics: Practitioner views on HRM', *Industrial Relations Journal*, 29(3), 178–93.

Guest, D. E. (1997) 'Human resource management and performance: A review and research agenda', *International Journal of Human Resource Management*, 8, 263–76.

Hendry, C. and Pettigrew, A. (1990) 'Human resource management: An agenda for the 1990s', *International Journal of Human Resource Management*, 1(1), 17–43.

Holbeche, L. (2009) *Aligning Human Resources and Business Strategies*, Routledge.

Holley, N. (2015) '"You can't put in what God left out": Not everyone can be a strategic HR business partner', CIPD, http://www.cipd.co.uk/research/changing-hr-operating-models/hr-business-partner.aspx

Hoque, K. and Noon, M. (2001) 'Counting the angels: A comparison of personnel and HR specialists', *Human Resource Management*, 11(3), 5.

Hutchinson, S. and Purcell, J. (2003) 'Bringing policies to life: The vital role of front line managers in people management', CIPD.

Lawler, E. E. III et al. (2004) *Human Resources Business Process Outsourcing: Transforming How HR Gets Its Work Done*, Jossey Bass.

Legge, K. (1995/2005) *Human Resource Management: Rhetorics and Reality*, Palgrave Macmillan.

Longo, R. (2012) 'Using metaphors to explain and shape organisational culture', *HR Professionals*, at: http://rosariolongo.blogspot.co.uk/2012/08/using-metaphors-to-explain-and-shape.html

Michie, J. et al. (2015) *Do We Need HR?: Repositioning People Management for Success*, Palgrave.

Morgan, G. (2006) *Images of Organisation*, Sage.

Paauwe, J. and Boselie, P. (2008) 'HRM and performance: What's next?', CAHARS Working Papers Series, Paper 474, at: http://digitalcommons.ir/cornell.edu/caharsswp/474

Paauwe, J., Guest, D., and Wright, P. (2013) *HRM and Performance: Achievements and Challenges*, Wiley.

Patterson, M. et al. (1997) *The Impact of People Management Practices on Business Performance*, IPD.

People Management (2016) 'UK employee survey: 48% of staff haven't talked to HR in the last year', at: http://www2.cipd.co.uk/pm/peoplemanagement/b/weblog/archive/2015/12/23/48-of-staff-haven-t-talked-to-hr-in-the-last-year.aspx#

Pritchard, K. (2010) 'Becoming an HR strategic partner: Tales of transition', *Human Resource Management Journal*, 20(2), 175–88, at: http://eprints.bbk.ac.uk/6477/1/HRMJ%20Becoming%20a%20HR%20strategic%20partner%20BIRON%20version.pdf

Purcell, J. (2003) *Understanding the People and Performance Link: Unlocking the Black Box*, CIPD.

Reilly, P. and Williams, T. (2006) *Strategic HR: Building the Capability to Deliver*, Gower.

Rucci, A.J. (1997) 'Should Human Resources survive? A profession at the crossroads', in D. Ulrich, M. R. Losey, and G. Lake, *Tomorrow's HR Management*, Wiley.

Storey, J. (ed.) (1989) *New Perspectives on Human Resource Management*, Thompson Business Press.

Storey, J. (1992) *Developments in the Management of Human Resources*, Blackwell.

Tichy, N., Fombrun, C., and Devanna, M. A. (1982) 'Strategic human resource management', *Sloan Management Review*, 23(2), 47–64.

Truss, C. et al. (1997) 'Soft and hard models of human resource management: A reappraisal', *Journal of Management Studies*, 34(1), 53–73.

Tyson, S. (2007) 'The management of the personnel function', *Journal of Management Studies*, 24(5), 523–32.

Tyson, S. and Fell, A. (1986) *Evaluating the Personnel Function*, Hutchinson Education.

Ulrich, D. and Brockbank, W. (2005) *The HR Value Proposition*, Harvard Business School Press.

Ulrich, D. et al. (2009) *HR Transformation: Building Human Resources from the Outside in*, McGraw-Hill.

Ulrich, D. et al. (2012) *HR from the Outside In: Six Competencies for the Future of Human Resources*, McGraw-Hill.

Watson, T. J. (2002) *Organising and Managing Work*, FT/Prentice Hall.

Watson, T. J. (2003) *Sociology, Work and Industry*, Routledge.

Watson, T. J. (2006) *Organising and Managing Work*, 2nd edn, FT/Prentice Hall.

Webber, L. and Feintzeig, R. (2014) 'Companies say no to having an HR department', *Wall Street Journal*, 9 April.

Weick, K. (2001) *Making Sense of the Organisation*, Blackwell.

A Strategic Perspective on HRM

3

Introduction

In Chapter 2, reference was made to the way in which thinking and practice around the management of people has evolved and become more sophisticated and differentiated over time, although whether this also means it has become more effective is a quite different question, and one for which there is no straightforward answer. Many of the more forward-looking and successful organizations seem to have developed HR strategies and practices that have delivered engaged, motivated, and productive workforces while others in the private and public sector struggle to create the kind of internal culture that helps to generate and liberate the potential of their people. As the external environment becomes less predictable and more volatile, organizations need to react to unforeseen changes as well as those associated with the more predictable economic cycle—the recent decision to exit the EU by the UK (termed Brexit) is a good example of the kinds of uncertainties businesses have to face, although not all are on this scale. The implications of external change for HR will differ depending on a number of key variables such as size, economic sector, competitive forces, and whether the organization is national or international in structure and focus, but it is likely that sooner or later organizations will either reduce or increase their head count depending on the kind of change they are reacting to: for some it may mean doing both in relation to different employee groups. It also means that existing employment and management strategies will become less relevant and effective as the conditions which they were originally designed for no longer exist. As an example, nearly one million public sector jobs have been lost since 2010 which means that HR departments in local authorities would have moved from a position where they recruited to maintain and possibly increased employment levels to one where substantial job losses and termination programmes needed to be implemented (ONS, 2015). At the time of writing, the world's oil, gas, and commodities businesses are rapidly downsizing, cost-cutting, and retrenching and the financial sector is still unclear about the implications of Brexit but is braced for job losses as financial institutions relocate part of their business to Europe. In these circumstances, the role of HR must change to reflect different priorities and new challenges: it must embrace a stronger and more focused strategic role to protect its credibility and reputation as a key management function. Stakeholder expectations are almost certainly going to increase during periods of uncertainty and the need for organizational adaptation.

This chapter is about making sense of what being strategic means and what HR, in its departmental and generalized forms, is meant to be and do to be seen to be a 'strategic player'. In the context of an external environment that can be volatile and/or stable, and often both, the nature of HR's strategic contributions and what senior managers expect of it will reflect the need to adapt and adjust but also maintain and strengthen that which defines the organization's core values and philosophy: yet another example of paradox and complexity in HRM.

Several writers on strategic HR have produced research that identifies this in terms of a range of core and unchanging activities which suggests that irrespective of the external environment HR should continue to focus on developing human capital, building commitment and engagement, and working to create a high-performance working culture (Jackson and Schuler, 2000; MacDuffie, 1995). The problem that a rapidly changing competitive and business environment creates, however, is that what is considered to be of strategic value and importance under 'normal' conditions may not enjoy that status as the environment changes and things become more challenging in relation to supply/demand for labour, external regulation, and changing labour markets. In other words, some HR activities and contributions may always be considered to be of permanent strategic value while others may be strategic in a contingent sense: HR has a long-term strategic role to play but also needs to make critical strategic contributions in the short term where crises and the need for rapid adjustments are experienced. The problem with strategic is not what it is but what it means to different stakeholders as they are responding to environmental pressures and a world where states of certainty and uncertainty are constantly changing.

If being strategic means (as we shall see later in the chapter strategic has several meanings) being adaptable and changing in response to internal and external forces, HR can be legitimately criticized for not being strategic or not being strategic enough. As we noted in Chapter 2, in many organizations much of what is done by the HR department is essentially administrative in nature, involving contractual issues, routine communications with staff, data processing, and the management of existing HR processes and systems. Can these in any way be considered strategic? Or can they under certain conditions assume strategic significance? The problem with labels is that they only identify one characteristic or trait and are reductionist, where complex phenomena are reduced to being more easily understandable by the use of language. But it is legitimate to question whether HR as a management function possesses sufficient flexibility and capability to reorient and refocus itself to address different organizational challenges and priorities. Again, we are confronted with the same question—just what does being strategic mean for the HR function?

As an example of the difficulty of establishing what is strategic, it was reported in the *Daily Telegraph* (10 May 2016) that the Aberdeen-based Wood Group is planning to cut 300 more jobs and reduce the wages of many of its contractors. The argument presented by the head of its Oil Services arm is that the decision to cut jobs and pay packets is necessary to cut back inflated wages and salaries that grew faster than industry standards in the past few years. One could argue that the cost-cutting exercise is in fact of strategic significance, as it helps to improve the company's competitive position. But if this is achieved at the expense of industrial action and a weakening of employee engagement we could argue that this could be on balance strategically weakening rather than strengthening the company's position even after the reduction in employment costs have been achieved. The question then becomes not simply one of strategic intent but of strategic impact, intended or otherwise. Referring again to the concept of unintended consequences, if being strategic means doing things that contribute to competitive advantage, which often means being better than competitors, surviving and growing, then certain strategies or strategic action will not just affect that aspect of the organization it is directed towards but will almost certainly affect other aspects which it was not intended to influence. This is, as we stated in Chapter 1, because organizations are complex entities with parts or elements which connect to each other in ways that are known but are difficult to predict, manage, and control. This is why it is important to distinguish between strategic aspiration, strategic action, and strategic impact which can be both positive and negative. For an explanation of what strategy means in the public sector, see Driver (2014).

RESEARCH INSIGHT 3.1

Blomme, R. J. (2012) 'Leadership, complex adaptive systems, and equivocality: The role of managers in emergent change', *Organization Management Journal*, **9(1).**

The ability to respond to external change and environmental volatility through organizational change will inevitably involve and affect human resources (HR) and the HR function. According to Blomme (2012), managers have to act in a way that is different from the traditional role of the administrative leader to become successful change leaders. (Note Ulrich's latest model of HR which emphasizes the importance of HR being a strategic change leader.)

Blomme's article uses complexity theory and the work of Karl Weick and Ralph Stacey as a basis for explaining how successful change is achieved and the role of managers in this process. Read the article with the objective of understanding complexity theory and how this is used to inform the process of strategic organizational change.

The question of whether HR is or could become a strategically important management function is one that, despite the existence, at least in academic circles, of a version of HR called strategic HRM (SHRM), continues to be asked, with many line managers and senior executives expressing concern over the function's lack of strategic orientation and impact. Before we consider how and why HR should become a strategic function, it is worthwhile reflecting on the challenge that it faces and needs to overcome if it is to acquire this status. As we noted in the previous chapter, many criticisms of HR reflect the frustrations experienced by line managers and senior executives over the function's inability to realize its strategic potential and promise despite the claims made on its behalf. The frequently stated belief that

people are an organisation's most important asset
(Bassi and McMurrer, 2007)

frequently clashes with the reality of a function mired in bureaucratic and non- or low-value-adding activities which define it in administrative and operational rather than strategic terms. The challenge for HR is to explain how it is going to acquire, develop, and use this vital asset in ways that confer competitive advantage, add sustainable value to the organization, and assist it in transformational change—outcomes that most would see as being strategically important. We would argue that this challenge has not always been effectively addressed by HR professionals and the absence of an adequate explanation from them as to why they struggle to become strategically focused continues to fuel the doubts of those who view HR as an underachieving management function. We saw in the previous chapter that one of the responses of HR professionals to the criticisms around HR's perceived strategic impact was to claim that the problem was one of a lack of understanding on the part of non-HR people, rather than a lack of contribution from HR! On the other hand, it would be far too easy to lay the blame for the continuing concerns expressed about HR in terms of individual and professional limitations and deficiencies, although these have been raised in relation, for example, to the lack of success in certain organizations of the HR business partner model. In our view, explanations for HR's failing to deliver strategic outcomes are as likely to be found in the ambiguities and structural/relationship difficulties outlined by writers such as Legge (2005) as in the personal and professional limitations of HR staff. However, as we have noted, bringing people into HR from other management functions and with different backgrounds is seen as one way of creating a sharper business (strategic) edge to its activities. These ambiguities and relationships represent important mediating factors that influence and limit how HR can operate and what it can realistically do to change the performance-related behaviour of people and be seen to contribute to organizational success through making strategically important contributions. Many of these limitations, by their very nature, are inherent and cannot be fully resolved or eliminated; they exist within almost all organizations but not necessarily in the same degree as organizational structures and managerial philosophies vary in form and content. This means that moving to a more strategic level of contribution isn't only about doing things differently and better and looking more critically at the effectiveness of some of the things it currently does, but also involves HR's understanding what else might have to change, outside of its own 'boundaries' to facilitate and enable HR's search for strategic impact. To illustrate this point, is the resolution of the paradox contained in the existence on the one hand of prescriptive models of strategic HRM, or, on the other hand, the other continued criticism that HR is not strategic enough, found in changes *within* HR or changes in key aspects of the internal *environment* in which it operates, or a combination of both?

 For a description of HR's 'strategic pathway', see the Online Resources Extension Material 3.1.

 KEY CONCEPT Ambiguity
Ambiguity can be understood to relate to lack of clarity or meaning in something: the difficulty in seeing and understanding, for example, the relationship between HR activities and individual and organizational outcomes.

 KEY CONCEPT Paradox
Paradox is different in that it is a concept that describes a situation which contains conflicting and possibly contradictory ideas, behaviours, and/or elements.

In the *Abilene Paradox*, Harvey (1996) refers to the work of the eminent sociologist Robert Rapaport who was interested in this question and offered an explanation as to why certain situations appeared to be paradoxical. For us, the fundamental paradox is why, if people are supposedly the key to competitive advantage and organizational success, does the function closely associated with the management of people suffer from persistent criticisms over its value and contribution?

Taking his line from Rapaport, Harvey believes that all paradoxes deal with absurdity, or at least involve behaviour that doesn't make sense to others, although it does to those directly involved! From an HR perspective, this might be expressed by asking why some HR departments spend most of their time and resources engaged in activities that fail to deliver outcomes that are strategically important to other stakeholders, and, in extreme cases, why HR is as much a part of the problem as it is a part of the solution to an organization's underperforming human resources. According to Harvey:

> paradoxes are generally paradoxes only because they are based on a logic or rationale different from what we understand or expect. Discovering that different logic not only destroys the paradoxical quality but also offers alternative ways for coping with similar situations. Therefore, part of the dilemma facing an Abilene-bound organization may be the lack of a map—a theory or model—that provides rationality to the paradox.
>
> (1996)

This explanation suggests that the reason paradoxes continue to exist is because the people involved have yet to find a coherent explanation for the existence and continuation of that which appears, using Harvey's language, absurd—or hard to understand. The route to resolving a paradox, then, is to understand the reasons it exists. In the case of HR this means finding explanations for why HR, in many cases, is failing to become the strategic management function it claims to be and others want and expect it to be.

In other words, until we understand *why* HR is not, in the eyes of many, delivering important strategic contributions, the necessary changes in either mindset or the way HR operates are unlikely to be realized. As Harvey says, it will be only when a new and liberating logic emerges that the paradoxes affecting HR will be fully understood and challenged. As an example of what this 'new' logic might look like, we might point to a greater emphasis on self-management, liberating people from bureaucratic control, taking responsibility for strategic contributions away from the HR department and relocating it at board level and treating the HR department primarily as a business and not a 'people' function. Only by *changing* the way HR works and its agenda, and questioning long-held practices about how people should be managed will people make the kinds of contributions that confer competitive advantage and long-term success.

Further examples of what we mean by paradox in HR can be found in the writings of Paul Mooney (2001). At the beginning of chapter 6 of his book, Mooney quotes an experienced HR practitioner who says:

> Our people are too important, too valuable and too capable of doing important work to waste on routine and repetition.

The paradox in this case is that valuable and talented people are not being fully utilized at work because not all their talents are being used or required, or obstacles are being put in the way of their wanting to do more. And the obvious question is why organizations continue to under-utilize costly and valuable human resources, often forcing staff to restrict their efforts and suppress their desire to do more. Mooney also argues that the relationship between the cost of delivering administrative, operational, and strategic value-added activities is in inverse proportion to the value they generate. In other words, while the administrative work of a 'typical' HR department costs 50 per cent of its total budget/resource base it adds something in the region of 15 per cent in added value. Conversely, HR's strategic contribution, he argues, costs around 15 per cent of the budget but generates 50 per cent of total added value. While there are of course issues over how costs and added value are conceptualized and measured, the basic point seems to be fairly obvious and allows us to ask the question:

> Why are so many of HR's departmental resources spent on activities that produce relatively little added value?

The resolution of these kinds of paradoxical situations would appear to lie in HR embracing a much more strategic role and putting much less of its available resources on lower-value-adding activities such as administration, but as we have pointed out this does not seem to have happened for the majority of HR departments. Simply stating an intention to be 'more strategic' is not in itself a sufficient condition to make the transition from its administrative and operational roots to a more elevated and strategic role within the organization. As we note later in the chapter, HR seems to be strong on rhetoric yet weak on strategic contribution. The need for an efficient administrative set-up is not being questioned; what is, is the idea that administration contributes the same value as strategically relevant activities. We quoted the article by Driver (2014) above, which looks at strategy in the public sector. Although he wasn't talking about HR per se he was critical of what he called strategies that are just aspirational rather than those that produce meaningful outcomes. For him, a strategy should

> guide organisations to create assets effectively and efficiently, and guide organisations to help people to use those assets to their benefit.

 Signpost to Chapter 13: Managing Rewards, for further examples of paradox in HR and human behaviour, specifically in relation to the use of financial incentives.

What Does Strategic Mean for HR?

Bassi and McMurrer (2004) provide an answer to this question in the context of continuing globalization and increasing competition when they claim that:

> The relentless force of globalization has left only one sustainable path to profitability for firms operating in high-wage, developed nations—to compete based on superior human capital capabilities and strategies. Any benefits that were historically associated with superior technology and access to capital (both physical and financial) are now far too short-lived to provide a sustainable advantage.

Two points emerge from this. First, it goes beyond the simple statement that people are an organization's most important asset by emphasizing the need to gain competitive advantage through the contributions that they make. Second, it links the acquisition and development of key human resource capabilities to strategies that harness and apply these to strategically important organizational objectives. Being strategic in HR doesn't just mean creating capabilities; it also requires that they are used. This means that:

> people not only need to be connected to their job but to each other and their organization.
> (Bassi and McMurrer, 2004)

The link between people and their attitudes, competences, and behaviour, and how these impact on the organization is a theme that characterized the report of the UK Government's Accounting for People Taskforce (2003).[1] In the report, one of the task force members commented that:

> An organisation's success is the product of its people competence. That link between people and performance should be made visible and available to all stakeholders.
> (John Sunderland, Executive Chairman, Cadbury Schweppes)

Interestingly, the argument made by some HR professionals that the lack of recognition for the function's strategic contribution might be as much to do with awareness and communication as much as substance, seems to be at least partially supported by this comment. But realistically the absence of recognition cannot

[1] A successor to the original Taskforce for People, Accounting for People 2.0, was established in October 2010. See *Human Capital Handbook* (2010) HubCap.

be explained away wholly by reference to a lack of awareness; a genuine problem over utilizing its human resources to their full potential still remains a key part of the answer as to why organizations fail to achieve long-term success. To address this challenge and 'become more strategic', those working in HR need to answer the question:

under what conditions and as a result of what HR strategies does individual and organizational performance move to a sustainably higher level?

It has to be recognized that there is never likely to be a single strategic 'lever' that can transform HR's status within the organization, but from the different literature contributions we can suggest at least five broad approaches:

1. Focus on talent and develop HR strategies based on differentiation and segmentation.

2. Focus on building an organizational culture that supports high-performance working, increased levels of employee engagement and functional flexibility.

3. Focus on creating synergies by increasing the level of integration between different HR activities and between these and the business.

4. Changing the HR architecture and the nature of the HR discourse and develop new models of HR that transform the function into one that is seen as strategic by key stakeholders.

5. Develop a range of metrics/HR analytics that show changes in key financial and performance indicators in strategically important relationships.

We have already indicated that the search for strategic status and contribution is affected by a lack of consensus over what strategic means. According to Sullivan (2005) the term 'strategic' is one of the most commonly used words in business and management, and is sometimes overused. He argues that this overuse is part of the problem—it confuses the 'real' meaning of the term. In support of this position, he provides an interesting insight into why so many people associate themselves and their contributions with being strategic when he states that:

The word is just as likely to be uttered by senior executives as it is by people that feel that they need to be 'more strategic' in order to be recognized or successful.
(Sullivan, 2005)

Sullivan's comment suggests that there is a certain status or cachet associated with being seen to be acting in a strategic way or engaging in a strategic discourse but which may not necessarily translate into strategic effect or impact. For him:

being strategic means having an impact on the things that are most important to an organization—the corporate goals and objectives.

Talking strategically does not necessarily mean that HR is engaged strategically or has acquired a strategic mindset, and the illusion that the language of strategy implies strategic action, although attractive, is dangerous and is one that not only Sullivan warned against. In his seminal article for the *Harvard Business Review* many years ago, Whickam Skinner said:

Since Hawthorne, successive waves of people-problem solutions and programs have washed and tumbled through industry. In some desperation, managers have steadily invested in supervisory training, organizational behaviour, interpersonal behaviour, T-groups, sensitivity training, employee attitude surveys, job enrichment, flexible benefits, and expanded fringe benefits—bigger pensions, subsidized insurance, more holidays, shorter work days, four-day weeks, and canned communications packages—and now companies are attempting to revive the 'work ethic' with human resources departments. Big programs, but where are the payoffs?
(Skinner, 1981)

One of the reasons he gives for HR talking big but failing to deliver is to do with what he calls critical problems in the corporate management of personnel, such as the place of HRM in corporate decision-making, the role and priorities of those who work in HR departments, and a lack of HRM expertise in senior executives, points that were made in the previous chapter. In other words, Skinner was identifying a lack of strategic focus and an inability to implement high-impact policies and practices that could have made a difference to organizational performance.

Similar questions about the extent to which, despite much talk and new ideas, little in HR seems to have moved on, have been posed by other writers. Kearns, for example, some twenty-five years after Skinner's article was published expressed the same concerns when he asked 'How much has HR changed?' (2004). His rather depressing answer is that despite the increasing specialization and evolution of HRM (he refers to the emergence of strategic HRM and human capital management as examples):

> **Any independent observer could be forgiven for asking whether all the name changes have just been cosmetic or if they signify any real, substantive differences.**
> **(Kearns, 2004)**

And the sense that HR's claims to 'be a strategic' function are more rhetorical than real resonates with Haffendon's view that being strategic became somewhat 'fashionable', with a:

> **large category of HR Directors who are faddists bent on chasing best practice and the latest quick fix, regardless of the needs of the business.**
> **(2002)**

Despite the growing evidence that many organizations have built strategically oriented HR functions (Birdi et al., 2008; Huselid, 1994) a sense that many changes are still at the superficial level and often limited to participation in a strategic discourse, persists. In his critical but widely read article, Hammonds (2005) tells the story of the HR director, Julie Muckler, who gave a talk to fellow professionals entitled 'How to transform your staff into strategic business partners'. As a member of the audience, he recalls after the talk that he had:

> **no idea what she's talking about. There is mention of 'internal action learning' and 'being more planful in my approach'. PowerPoint slides outline Wells Fargo's Home Mortgage's initiatives in per-formance management, organization design, and horizontal-solutions teams. Muckler describes leveraging internal resources and involving external resources—and she leaves her audience dazed. That evening, even the human-resources pros confide they didn't understand much of it, either.**

Hammonds asks the question about what is driving the strategy disconnect between what HR professionals seem to be saying and doing and the reality of a much more muted strategic impact. Referring to the work of Linda Gratton (1999) he makes two important points:

1. The majority of HR professionals, although they often possess strong technical expertise and are professionally qualified, struggle to offer a vision of the future and how the organization, as a whole, works and needs to change.

2. There is real difficulty in trying to successfully align HR strategy to business strategy for the simple rea-son that business strategy can change quickly and arguably is in a constant state of flux. It is also very difficult, if not unrealistic, to constantly adapt aspects of HR such as its recruitment, compensation, and employment policies to maintain this notional alignment.

An alternative way of making sense of HR's strategic role and contribution was presented during an unscript-ed talk at the 2009 CIPD Centres Conference during which the speaker, representing the CIPD, argued that there is real frustration among HR professionals because they feel they are not being taken seriously enough and that their contributions are not being recognized by line managers and senior executives. His proposed solution—and way of resolving the paradox—was to argue that HR should adopt a language that these stakeholders could understand and engage in a narrative with them to get the message across. The point he was making was that HR *is* engaged in making strategic contributions; the problem is that this is not recognized by people 'outside' the HR department because they don't really understand what HR is doing. To paraphrase, HR is acting strategically but other people don't recognize this and to overcome this disconnect HR needs to communicate better.

There may well be some merit in this view and undoubtedly a clash of discourses can make it difficult for people to relate to how different management functions and contributions operate. But, on the other hand, it also has to be accepted that the problem may not be that managers do not understand HR's contribution and as a result fail to recognize its strategic contribution, but rather that they are very much aware of what HR does and are justifiably critical of its policies and practices as lacking strategic significance and impact. Are we dealing with a problem of communication, perception, or substance? Probably a mixture of all three! But what this situation reinforces once again, is that there is not one but rather multiple realities existing at the same time, complicating the process of reaching a common position and understanding.

In the UK, Linda Holbeche (2009) offers both support and criticism of HR's strategic contribution and evolution into a value-adding rather than a largely administrative and support function. On the positive side, she sees evidence of HR departments becoming, as she describes it, as

players within the organisational hierarchy and have made the transition into value-adding and valued functions.

Adapting the Wyatt-Haines (2007) functional ladder to HR, the four levels being:

1. generally ineffective;
2. following;
3. enabling;
4. leading;

she argues that there are increasing numbers of HR departments that are moving up the value ladder which requires the ability to display strategic anticipation and the ability to create value. More negatively, she argues that one of the key challenges facing HR is to free up capacity to become more strategic, assuming of course there is a consensus on what this means within organizations—and reaching agreement on what constitutes added-value activities. She believes that reaching agreement with line managers on what HR can and should do to add value will continue to be difficult for many in HR and that there is still too much reliance on HR metrics as defensive instruments that 'prove' value is being added rather than showing that genuine and strategically important contributions are being generated. She believes that the evidence on what HR departments do and achieve suggests that they have become

caught like a rabbit in the headlights, away from the safe place of the old role at the curb-side yet unable to move forward to a new, more dynamic place.
(Holbeche, 2009: 19)

She goes on:

In many cases practitioners reverted to what they knew best, what they felt was expected of them by line managers, and where they gained the most personal satisfaction. Inevitably perhaps, HR value and the merits of HR transformation continued to be called into question.

Being strategic is not a 'tick-box' exercise nor is it easily established partly because there can be an objective and subjective dimension to this; being strategic can be perceived (subjective) as well as being measured (objective). Nor is there an end state at which point HR can claim to have finally become strategic; in a dynamic and changing environment the nature of the strategic challenge is constantly changing and priorities are frequently redefined. It is also important to recognize that the nature of HR's strategic contribution is not always the result of rational planning activities but can result from reacting quickly to crises and unforeseen events. And, finally, the nature of strategic contributions is likely to change in relation to the stage in the development of the organization and its location on the organizational life cycle. HR's strategic contribution will inevitably change as the organization moves from its early, formative stage to a period of growth, maturity, decline, and either rebirth or extinction (Mitsakis, 2014).

RESEARCH INSIGHT 3.2

You may wish to read the following article:

Phelps, R., Adams, R., and Bessant, J. (2007), 'Life cycles of growing organizations: A review with implications for knowledge and learning', *International Journal of Management Reviews*, 9, 1–30.

The article reviews the literature on life-cycle growth models, traces the development of a growing sophistication of conceptualizing growth, and highlights some of the limitations of the literature. Consider the kinds of interventions they recommend and the role of HR in leading or contributing to these.

So, after highlighting the challenges and difficulties of 'knowing' what strategic means for HR is there any way of bringing together the different ideas and contributions on what it does or should mean? Figure 3.1 offers a picture of what the strategic dimension of HR might look like.

According to Michael Porter (1996), there is a real danger of failing to distinguish between operational effectiveness and strategy. He argues that if all organizations adopt similar operational practices, in other

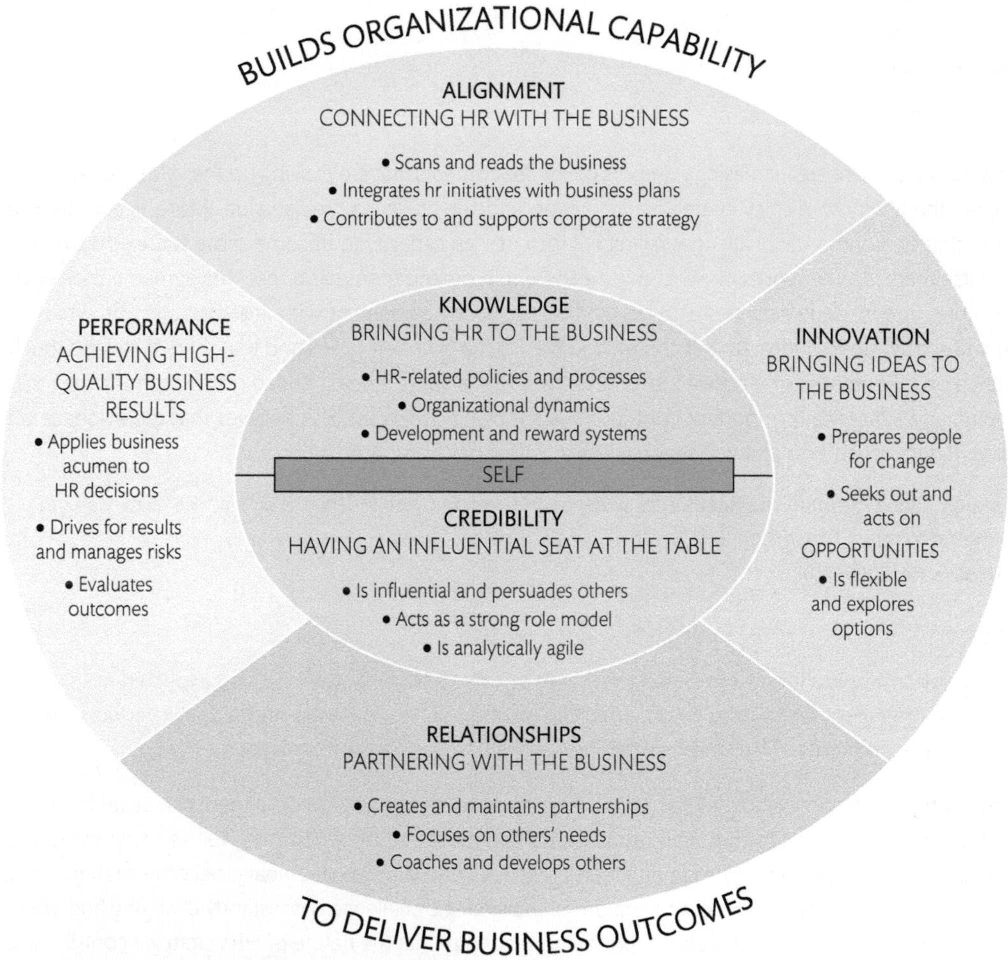

Figure 3.1 A diagrammatic representation of what a strategic HR function involves
Source: Australian Public Services Commission (2003), © Commonwealth of Australia, reproduced with permission.

words how they use resources, no strategic competitive advantage will be gained by any unless such practices result in higher levels of profitability or other improvements *in strategic performance*. He states that:

> **Operational effectiveness means performing similar activities better than rivals perform them. Operational effectiveness includes but is not limited to efficiency. It refers to any number of practices that allow a company to better utilise its inputs by, for example, reducing defects in products or developing better products faster. In contrast, strategic positioning means performing different activities from rivals or performing similar activities in different ways.**
> (Porter, 1996)

Porter's contribution to the debate on what makes something strategic is important for HR because his emphasis on difference is at odds with the 'best practice' approach to SHRM which suggests, in a somewhat simplistic way, that there exists a set of universally effective HR practices that are associated with enhanced organizational performance. However, according to Purcell:

> **What is most notable about the best practice model is there is no discussion on company strategy at all. The underlying premise of this view is that organizations adopting a set of best practices attract super human resources, talent and competencies. 'These superior human resources will, in turn, influence the strategy the organization adopts and is the source of its competitive advantage.'**
> (Milkovich and Newman, 2002: 30)

Therefore, for this approach, policy *precedes* strategy.

Supporters of this 'best practice' approach to HR strategy believe that there is sufficient evidence from research into the link between HR practices and organizational performance to suggest the existence of mutually compatible 'bundles' of HR policies that promote high levels of employee motivation and commitment (MacDuffie, 1995; Pfeffer, 1994). These are thought to include selective hiring, extensive training, employment security, a structure that encourages employee participation, and certain kinds of pay policies and practices. This list might also include other well-known HR activities such as developing competency frameworks, 360-degree feedback, performance appraisal systems, and development centres. Questions that emerge from this way of providing HR with its route map to strategic contribution, but don't seem to be adequately answered, include:

- Where does the list stop and how many HR activities/elements constitute the bundle?
- Are all the individual elements of the bundle equally important?
- Does context play any part in influencing their strategic impact?
- Does it matter how the different elements are bundled together and precisely what does 'bundling' mean?

The point Porter makes about the difference between operational effectiveness and strategy is significant. HR departments that are successful in improving the way they do things do so because they deliver measurable improvements in cost reductions, productivity, cycle times, customer satisfaction levels, and so on, but to be strategically effective, HR needs to demonstrate the impact of what it does that goes beyond the operational level in ways that result in competitive advantage. (This term is less applicable to public sector organizations but as old public sector monopolies are broken, greater competition between institutions does emerge.) But if all organizations are copying each other in their HR activities, then none will achieve a competitive advantage: they will only improve their operational effectiveness relative to how they were before but not in relation to organizations they are in competition with; if everyone makes the same operational changes, then competitive advantage relationships remain largely unaltered. His view is that improvements in operational effectiveness only translate into strategic changes if similar activities are done in different ways or if there are differences between what one HR function does compared to another and that these differences are significant in generating and preserving a competitive advantage. Although Porter does not make this point, we would argue that his analysis also extends to HR departments actually stopping doing certain things that have little or no operational value, but simply consume valuable resources. Strategic value and competitive advantage come from either significantly reducing the costs of delivering HR services and/or reallocating professional resources to other and more value-adding activities such as developing the function's ability to mobilize its resources, build capability, and to support corporate objectives.

 Signpost to Chapter 4: Talent Management, for an indication of how certain organizations are implementing different HR strategies for different groups of employees.

STUDENT ACTIVITY 3.1

This is a collective exercise. Split into two groups: one representing a local authority or hospital, the other a UK-based private sector manufacturing company operating within the EU. Working independently, each group highlights the strategically valuable contributions HR can make in supporting each organization's objectives. (These have to be established first.) Each group then presents a two-sided flip chart sheet summary of its decisions. After each presentation, the presenting group has to explain how its ideas about HR's contributions can be seen to be strategically important.

The engrained belief that many of the activities HR engages in add value at the operational level and therefore must have strategic significance may well express little more than 'taken for granted assumptions' that are rarely questioned or tested empirically.

References made in the previous chapter to the increasing interest in evidence-based management suggest that the retention of existing HR practices and an unquestioning belief in their efficacy needs to be subject to a more rigorous process of questioning and evidence-based evaluation to justify their continuation. This point, that HR can act strategically by questioning rather than accepting the case for certain practices and policies is critical to the 'new HR' and is being increasingly reflected by those committed to looking carefully at the available evidence. For example, Beverly Alimo-Metcalfe during her presentation on engaged leadership at the 2008 CIPD National Conference, made it clear that she was not convinced by the argument that competences and being competent were strongly linked to organizational performance, yet she stated that many organizations are still developing competency frameworks and investing significant resources in their implementation and improvement. Is this justified, or is their growth more to do with 'fashion' and HR professionals simply copying what others are doing, based on the belief that if other organizations employ these then it must be right?

Not all HR activities and contributions are at or should be at the strategic level; adding value and making contributions to the way an organization's human resources are managed can take place at different levels, and it is unrealistic to link each and every HR initiative and practice to a strategic intention and outcome. On the other hand, the consequences of not engaging at all at the strategic level are real and damaging to HR's standing in the organization, and the hype about HR's strategic role may well have raised expectations which are difficult to meet without radical changes in how the HR function operates. This is particularly the case when line managers' perceptions still reflect a non-strategic HR function, a view confirmed by Lawler's (2007) research that found that the amount of time reported by HR professionals devoted to being a strategic business partner, in 2004, was no more than in 1995—23 per cent.

He also found that line managers believed that HR was far less involved in strategy than it thinks it is. And despite the influence of their writings, the comment by Ulrich and Brocklebank (2005) that 'HR's role is to root out discrimination whenever it appears' hardly suggests that such a prioritization of activities will shift this perception.

If HR's strategic role and contribution is defined in terms of rooting out discrimination, the question is not whether this role is important or not but how it will be perceived by other stakeholders whose agendas and priorities may well be defined in terms of surviving economic recessions, coping with funding reductions, and remaining competitive in an increasingly difficult and uncertain world. Nor does it provide a convincing rebuttal to Hammonds's rather biting critique and challenge to HR expressed in his statement that:

> After close to 20 years of hopeful rhetoric about becoming 'strategic partners' with a 'seat at the table' where the business decisions that matter are made, most human-resources professionals aren't nearly there. They have no seat, and the table is locked inside a conference room to which they have no key. HR people are, for most practical purposes, neither strategic nor leaders. (2005)

Such critical views are not necessarily representative of all line managers and senior executives, and many HR professionals are likely to take issue with them. But the point being made is that being aspirational is not enough and that in a stakeholder model of the organization it is those who depend on HR and are the recipients of its 'services' that will define what adding value means, what is strategic, and whether HR is acting effectively as a strategic business partner. The following practitioner insight represents one senior HR professional's views about what helps in understanding HR's strategic contribution to the organization.

PRACTITIONER INSIGHT Trevor Lincoln, former people director at Eaga

Eaga was a FTSE 250 company with headquarters in Newcastle, UK. Its main business was in home insulation but it also operated as an outsourcing arm offering a range of business services through call centre operations. The business was founded in 1990 in Newcastle upon Tyne as the Energy Action Grants Agency (EAGA) Partnership to administer the Home Energy Efficiency Scheme in the local area. In 2000, it was then restructured to become an employee-owned business, and was ultimately taken over by Carillion in April 2011.

For as long as I can remember during my career in HR there has been a debate about the contribution of HR to business strategy. My experience tells me that businesses will not be successful without HR, not just supporting the delivery of business strategy but, more importantly, helping shape it. HR has the opportunity to either drive the business or become a passenger—a back seat driver constantly nagging at managers telling them what they should and should not do. The degree to which HR becomes the driver or takes a free ride is in my view determined by the qualities and competence of HR professionals:

1. Commercial acumen, so that they understand the commercial world, and can influence the strategic plans the business has to conquer it.

2. Flexibility to interpret and apply the raft of employment legislation in a way which protects and supports the commercial intent of the business.

3. Most importantly of all, their ability to define a rock-solid set of behavioural values which permeate the business, influencing the development of the organization's culture and commercial orientation.

This does not mean plastering values posters on the office wall, or reproducing them in glossy brochures and doing nothing else. Quite the contrary, it means HR's role is to define these values in such a way that everyone in the organization understands them and how they fit within their role. When the organization reaches the point at which its values are strongly embedded, the strategic influence of HR flourishes.

In Eaga we will not compromise our values for anyone or anything. We recruit, we promote, we performance manage, and we recognize talent through measuring performance against both performance objectives (what the individual achieves) and Eaga values (the way in which they achieve this). Our values are underpinned by a set of job competencies so that employees know exactly what they need to do to demonstrate that they are living the Eaga values. This applies to leaders at all levels of the organization. What has this to do with business strategy you might ask? The answer is that it has everything to do with business strategy and it has not come about by accident.

Three years ago, Eaga took the unusual step of taking all of its commercial managing directors plus their senior HR and corporate services colleagues out of the business for one week to visit some of the world's top companies. Over the course of the week the group studied these organizations and compared them to Eaga. The majority of the discussions during that week were not at all about commercial imperatives—instead they were about the values which underpin our business. The discussions were led by HR and resulted in a strategy defined jointly by HR, corporate services, and the commercial MDs which has influenced our business ever since. These values are embodied in the following statement:

Eaga cares for its partners, customers and communities with integrity, respect and enthusiasm.

It was agreed that the business could only be successful if we put our employees (partners in Eaga's case) first. In doing so they would treat our customers and the communities we live and work in well, which would then lead to the long-term commercial success of the business. To reinforce this, HR now has peer representation on Eaga's executive, operating, and divisional boards ensuring strategic influence at each.

What Can HR Learn from the Strategy Gurus?

Recognizing the strategic issues facing HR and working to develop HR strategies that have a high impact—it does not necessarily follow that all strategies have the same strategic impact—is helped by drawing upon the thinking and contributions of influential writers on strategy and strategic management. To fully understand the complexities and challenges facing HR in its search for a more strategic role, we have to go outside the strategic HRM literature and learn from the wider world of corporate strategy and strategic management. In doing so the intention is to identify key concepts and theories that can be applied to HR and from which HR practitioners can learn about strategy in the corporate world.

Perhaps the most influential book on strategy written in the UK in the last fifteen years is by Johnson et al. (2014) *Exploring Strategy*. In this edition, they define strategy as:

the direction and scope of an organisation over the long term: which achieves advantage for the organisation through its configuration of resources within a challenging environment, to meet the needs of markets and to fulfil stakeholder expectations.

But this definition addresses the question of what strategy involves rather than offering a conceptualization of what strategy *is*, which is arguably more useful for the HR practitioner, although the idea that strategy involves the reconfiguration of resources is potentially very helpful. This is what Minzberg offers in his influential 1987 article. He begins by stating that:

The field of strategic management cannot afford to rely on a single definition of strategy, indeed the word has long been used implicitly in different ways even if it has been defined formally in only one.

He argues that explicit recognition of multiple definitions can help practitioners and researchers alike manoeuvre through this difficult field. Interestingly, although Minzberg accepts the existence of multiple definitions of the word strategy he doesn't see this as a problem but an advantage, recognizing that there is not one way of making sense of this complex concept but several with each having their own uses and merits. Think about what we said about sense-making in Chapter 1, where multiple rather than a single meaning emerge to reflect the subtle differences in the way people define and make sense of the same phenomenon.

His five different interpretations of strategy are:

1. Strategy as a plan

Seen as some form of consciously intended action, strategy represents a way forward, a set of actions and a use of resources that directs the organization (or the HR function) to do certain things in intended ways which are rational and consistent over time. Strategy as a plan represents a statement of the direction of travel, how we are going to get there, and what resources we need to ensure we successfully achieve our intended objectives.

In an HR context, strategy as a plan has been strongly associated with human resource planning, which involves the careful analysis of human resource requirements in the context of labour market conditions and the external product or service environment. The objective of such plans is to achieve the optimum balance between the demand and supply of labour over a given period. But workforce planning as it is now more commonly called does not generate the HR plan, and from comments made earlier the HR department's plan may not represent the HR plan: the latter being the product of a corporate planning process. So, while we can see the logic in defining strategy as a plan, from an HR perspective we need to ask whose plan it is and what is its coverage and scope.

Unfortunately, plans do not always work out in the way intended; plans are often only as good as the information and analysis that informs them, and crucially plans can quickly become outdated and dysfunctional, as external conditions change. Plans can also be 'good' and 'bad' in the sense that the assumptions, expectations, and intelligence they are based on can be accurate and realistic or outdated and erroneous. Simply having a strategy—in the form of a plan—guarantees nothing other than you have a plan of action.

Strategies as plans can be intended and deliberate, following a rational line of thinking and pointing in a particular direction, or they can be emergent and flexible and much more closely related to the environment the organization operates in. Paradoxically, not having a formal plan but simply responding as quickly and as effectively as possible to environmental change can be equally strategic in the sense that this way of thinking and acting can have a more positive effect on the organization's performance than an HR plan that doesn't work! As an example, the speed of the onset of the 2008 economic recession invalidated many recruitment, development, and reward strategies (as plans) with these being rapidly abandoned and replaced by responses more in tune with harsh economic and financial realities. Equally, many organizations' recruitment plans were subject to careful scrutiny immediately after the EU referendum in 2016. And not all HR plans are necessarily strategic in the sense that they may fail to generate operational change and enhance operational effectiveness and have little or no impact on the organization's competitive position. Paradoxically, some HR plans may be devoid of strategic impact even though the plans are effectively implemented!

2. Strategy as pattern

According to Minzberg, strategy can also be understood as a pattern of behaviour, whether intended or not. In other words, there is consistency as opposed to randomness in what organizations do. A helpful way of relating strategy as a pattern to the HR context involves contrasting what is described as HR's reactionary and firefighting role with one based on foresight and proactivity. Being forward-looking and 'ahead of the curve'—and shaping rather than responding to events—is often represented as a more preferable strategic pattern, but, given that we have emphasized that the strategic value of any action is to be found in its impact, either pattern could be more or less strategic than the other.

Another example of strategy as pattern can be found in an organization's approach to recruitment. One of the common threads linking companies rated highly by their employees as places to work is the emphasis they give to developing and promoting staff from within. This pattern of action arguably produces a more reliable labour supply chain and greater employee engagement, both highly desirable and strategically valuable.

3. Strategy about what

Whether plan or pattern, strategies need to be about something. The question that concerns the specific content, focus, and purpose of HR strategies is one that will be heavily influenced by the organization's unique history, position in its environment, and internal competences. Specific HR policies and practices are always about 'something' and the relative emphasis given to each reflects a belief in their relevance and value to the organization, although put to the test many HR departments might be less than convincing in the way they defend every practice and policy they are involved in! But strategy as content and focus is also about implementation—it's not simply what HR does but how well it can implement its chosen policies. According to Porter (1996) being strategic can mean performing similar activities in different ways and this can mean developing more effective ways of implementing chosen policies.

STUDENT ACTIVITY 3.2

Successful implementation is often key to any strategy and even though the strategy itself can be potentially effective, failure to implement it means its potential is never realized. The following article involves looking at strategic management implementation from an operations management perspective and aims to highlight key practices associated with effective strategic implementation.

Saunders et al. (2008) 'Implementing strategic initiatives: A framework of leading practices', *International Journal of Operations & Production Management*, 28(11), 1095–1123.

After reading the article, identify:

1. The factors that seem to be associated with implementation failure.

2. The main implementation frameworks the authors refer to and consider their relative merits and weaknesses.

3. The main findings of the study, in particular what practices are associated with implementation success, and relate these to the role and contribution of HR.

Of the many strategies that HR is engaged with, in terms of content and focus, the following are some of the most frequently found in practice:

- **Strategies for managing talent**—should this focus be on buying in talent and emphasize the criticality of the recruitment and selection process or should the emphasis be given to growing and nurturing existing employees? What are the plans or chosen pattern for this?

- **Strategies for managing performance**—this involves deciding on the use of different instruments and practices that are thought to stimulate employee performance. Do we rely on formal mechanisms such as appraisal processes, reward systems, and targets, or rather emphasize the creation of a high-performance work environment characterized by cooperation, engagement, enjoyment, and personal growth and achievement?

- **Strategies for managing costs**—does this involve reducing head count, time worked, or wages/salaries, and are reductions across the board or targeted?

- **Strategies for managing rewards**—are these based on a collective or individual approach to employees? Are rewards linked to or independent of performance? What is the balance between financial and non-financial rewards?

- **Strategies for managing ethical standards and behaviour**—does this involve creating a particular kind of working culture where the required values and standards are embedded, or HR acting as a kind of 'police force', where enforcement rather than compliance characterizes the chosen strategy?

- **Strategies for managing trade unions (TUs)**—are TUs recognized and given negotiating rights? Is collective bargaining legitimized as the main form of decision-making in relation to the determination of and changes in terms and conditions of employment? Are employee communications directed through TU representatives or based on direct contact with individuals?

Finally, strategies about 'what' fundamentally involves choice. First, in the sense of which aspects of employment and HR are going to be emphasized, and, second, choosing the specific way(s) in which the preferred action plans are going to be implemented to deliver the required outcomes and impact.

4. Strategy as position

This can be understood in terms of strategy differentiation—how an organization differentiates itself in relation to competitors. Perhaps the best example of this in HR is the way certain organizations position themselves within the labour market and relative to competitor organizations—the aim often is to be the employer of preferred choice. This positioning is more commonly known as employer branding and can be understood as:

> How an organization markets what it has to offer to potential and existing employees. Marketers have developed techniques to help attract customers, communicate with them effectively and maintain their loyalty to a consumer brand. Employer branding involves applying a similar approach to people management.

The deliberate positioning of an organization through distinguishing itself from its competitors involves making commitments and promises to provide a particular kind of working and employment experience to prospective employees and in so doing engage with people who are attracted to the particular kind of cultural environment being offered (CIPD, 2010).

5. Strategy as perspective

The fifth conceptualization of strategy is arguably the most difficult to grasp but is potentially the most powerful because it is the most enduring. Strategy in this respect is, according to Minzberg, similar to what personality is to the individual. It might be better understood through such concepts as philosophy, ideology, and culture, or the character of the organization. The power of this way of understanding strategy is that it is associated with a collective and shared set of understandings and ways of being that transcend changes in the external environment and generate a sense of deeply rooted commitment to patterns of behaviour.

In relation to strategy as plan, position, purpose, or pattern, strategy as perspective stands out as the one where HR could make the most important strategically valuable contribution but realistically the one that it is least likely to understand and deliver on its own. The ability to shape the collective mindset and change organizational culture is one that HR in its departmental form could potentially contribute to but is unlikely to lead. This is the role of the organization's leader(s) whose vision and values help to shape the defining features of how the organization functions.

The work of Gary Hamel and C. K. Prahalad (1994) has long been recognized within the world of business and business strategy as having a seminal influence on corporate and business leaders.

In their 1993 article, they present a summary of conventional thinking on strategy that emphasizes:

- Fit or the relationship between the organization and its environment; in the case of HR this idea translates into the fit between HR strategy and corporate strategy and the fit or integration between different HR strategies.
- The allocation of resources in ways that generate the best returns from investments made.
- A long-term rather than a short-term perspective.

Without rejecting the importance of these three elements, they offer an alternative view of strategy in which 'the concept of *stretch* supplements the idea of fit' and that '*leveraging* resources is as important as allocating them'.

The concept of leveraging resources is particularly relevant to HR. Strategic contribution comes as much, if not more, from how human resources are used as having the right quantity and quality of resources in place at the right time. This position reflects O'Reilly and Pfeffer's (2000) belief that the problem with an HR strategy based on hiring the most talented people, while important for many organizations, detracts attention from the far more strategically significant requirement of increasing the talent and productive value of *all* of an organization's employees. And the notion of leveraging the human resource to increase its productivity is consistent with the point made in Chapter 1 that one of management's fundamental objectives in the way human resources are managed is to constantly increase the level of resource utilization—getting more from the same or, even better, more from less. The search for continuous improvements in employee productivity is not only important for operational effectiveness but also has strategic potential. One important consequence is that companies can afford to increase real wages/rewards as productivity increases, wage improvements which are non-inflationary! The question, however, is whether what HR does actually embraces the objective of improving labour productivity. According to Sullivan (2011), while increasing productivity is one of the most critical goals in business it is not something that HR professionals see as a legitimate part of what they do.

> While most HR professionals acknowledge that their job entails establishing policy, procedures, and programs governing people management, few attempt to connect such elements to increasing employee output (volume, speed, and quality) per each dollar spent on labor costs (or as an easier to measure alternative, revenue per employee).

According to Hamel and Prahalad, there are two basic approaches to achieving greater resource productivity. These are:

1. Downsizing and head-count reductions, or, as they say, 'becoming lean and mean'.

2. Resource leveraging that seeks to get the most out of the available resources, in other words to get more from what you have.

They argue that a resource-leveraging strategy is more energizing than the downsizing route which is likely to have a demoralizing effect on employees and has the potential of actually reducing productivity which can result in further cutbacks; in other words what starts off as a planned reduction in resource costs can lead to a downward spiral of productivity as reduced costs trigger reduced human resource outputs which can often be proportionately greater than the savings from reduced input costs. However, we also know that realistically both of these strategies have an important role to play in most industry sectors because they meet different strategic requirements. The first is to ensure that the supply and cost of an organization's human resources is broadly in line with demand and financial resources, while the second reflects the longer-term importance of building capability and leveraging resources to maximum effect. The strategic choice presented to HR is not which strategy to adopt but how to incorporate both in ways that meet short-term needs for economic adjustment and flexibility and longer-term growth.

They claim that management can leverage its resources (including human resources) in five basic ways, four of which can be related to HR.

1. Concentrating resources: convergence and focus

They describe this in terms of organizations having a strategic focal point or strategic intent—it's what defines what the organization is about and known for. In marketing, this is known as the 'strap line'—a statement which summarizes its focus and represents a reference point for employees to use to help them stay aligned and in tune. In HR, the equivalent is what Purcell called 'The Big Idea'—that unifying concept that defines the organization's purpose or *raison d'être* (Purcell, 2003).

They claim that convergence prevents the diversion of resources and that focus prevents their dilution at any given time, arguing that:

> Without focused attention on a few key operating goals at any one time, improvement efforts are likely to be so diluted that the company ends up as a perpetual laggard in every critical performance area.

 See the Online Resources Extension Material 3.2, which links strategy to change management and the performance gap.

2. Accumulating resources: extracting and borrowing

In an HR context, this involves an organization maximizing its resource base through the way it learns from experience. Strategic advantage comes from harnessing the power of learning in ways that support operational effectiveness. This way of leveraging an organization's human resources touches on subjects such as the learning organization, organizational learning, and knowledge management, which requires, according to

Hamel and Prahalad, a corporate climate which allows people to challenge long-standing practices—not something many employees would feel comfortable about, or explicitly encouraged by many management teams. Learning from experience is a key source of leverage but it is paradoxically also a threat because learning from and using experience invariably involves at least the potential for challenging the status quo. They make this point very clearly when they say that:

> **Unless top management declares open season on precedent and orthodoxy, learning and the unlearning that must precede it cannot begin to take place.**
> (Hamel and Prahalad, 1993)

Note: a strategic perspective that emphasizes learning, honesty, and openness is to be found in the government's response to bad practice and cover-ups in the NHS (Department of Health, 2015).

The implications of gaining strategic leverage through the use of experience for the HR function are obvious and not necessarily surprising. But this is not really the issue: what is, is the *ability to deliver* high-impact outcomes based on learning strategies that go beyond the mere delivery of training but based on a clear understanding of how learning can be used to increase operational effectiveness and generate competitive advantage. We might, with some justification, argue that most organizations fail to generate the strategic benefits that come from the 'power of learning', and in the context of the HR function we might also wish to pose the question: how does HR learn?

STUDENT ACTIVITY 3.3

Read the blog and listen to the podcast by Shelley White (21 June 2013): 'Start with Why: The Power of Student-Driven Learning', at: http://plpnetwork.com/2013/06/21/start-why-power-student-driven-learning

Then as a group use the workplace and the employee scenario and write down two sets of statements, one that describes the workplace equivalent of what White believes characterizes schools and second a set of statements that describes what *should* characterize the workplace if the power of learning is to be realized.

3. Complementing resources: blending and balancing

This source of leverage is concerned with how organizations are structured and how this affects the way they function. It is about how organizations, based on hierarchy, levels, divisions, and departments, create internal barriers that inhibit people working together. This is often expressed by reference to 'silos' which represent inflexible working arrangements and internal restrictions on what people can do and who they can work with. Blending, for Hamel and Prahalad, is essentially about the integration of organizational units and resources; it is about working together in ways that reflect a systems view of organizations. From an HR perspective, this has implications for the level of flexibility that exists in working arrangements and relationships and the degree to which managing is separated from rather than integrated within the sociotechnical system.

4. Conserving resources: recycling, co-opting, and shielding

This is about the productivity of resources—the extent to which any given skill, knowledge, or competence is actually used and how frequently it is used to drive the business forward. It is also about the ability of an organization to move its resources to wherever they can make a more valuable contribution. According to the authors, there are extensive opportunities for knowledge and resources to be recycled, but whether this happens depends on the state of the organization's internal culture and processes. Perhaps the best example of recycling and co-opting can be found in the idea of communities of practice (Lave and Wenger, 2007). These involve people who have a shared or similar interest in a particular profession or area of work and involve the creation, processing, and sharing of knowledge. Membership can be flexible and involve co-optation. Essentially, such communities represent a key resource that can be used to turn tacit knowledge into explicit knowledge and offer tried-and-tested solutions to different parts of an organization. The implications of this strategy for HR also lie in the question of how to retain knowledge that can be lost as people leave and how knowledge can be accessed and leveraged through various formal and informal mechanisms.

The interesting point about Hamel and Prahalad's concept of leveraging value and generating strategic contribution from stretching organizational resources is that it can so easily be related to developments in HR, whether in terms of new approaches to generating learning-rich experiences, to unblocking existing sources of knowledge, to creating flexible and organic communities of people who have similar interests, and finally to working across boundaries in flexible and integrated ways. The crucial question is, however, whether HR professionals are aware of the potential such developments represent and whether they are able to realize this potential.

Are HR Strategies Uniquely Different?

Whatever form HR strategies might take—and at this point it is important to emphasize the distinction between specific strategies that emerge from within HR departments in response to key human resource challenges and those that have their origins at the corporate level and relate to top management's strategic decisions—an important question to ask is whether these are specific and unique to each organization. How different are HR strategies and are they, in themselves, the source of competitive advantage? Boudreau and Ramstad (2007) argue that most HR strategies are similar in focus and content and it would be difficult to identify which strategy belonged to which organization. They claim that:

> Talent and organisation decisions are often based on very broad and generic strategic goals such as 'increase innovation' or 'provide world class customer service'. Or they reflect workforce goals that are important but common to most organisations such as 'retain more baby boomer technical talent', 'increase diversity', 'or build next-generation leadership'.

At one level, most HR departments would claim to have strategies, probably in the form of plans or patterns, but strategies that are intended to confer competitive advantage and generate high-impact outcomes not only need to be effectively implemented but need to focus on aspects of behaviour, structure, and culture. Boudreau and Ramstad describe these strategically important areas as 'pivot points'. (We explore this in more detail in Chapter 4.) Their argument is that HR strategy needs to reflect and focus on those key pivot points in the employment and management of people because they have the potential to permanently change behaviour in ways that confer significant and sustainable improvements in performance. Different organizations may have different pivot points but identifying them involves applying the same analytical process of questioning to establish precisely where they exist for individual organizations. Boudreau and Ramstad suggest that HR and corporate leaders need to work together in finding answers to these questions:

- Where does our strategy require that our talent and organization be better than our competitors?
- Where do our talent and organization systems need to be different from our competitors and why?
- Where should we pay more and who should we increase the rewards to?
- Where should we spend more on our pivotal talent programmes and practices and what could we expect to get from this?
- If we shifted our strategic goals, does the organization have sufficient flexibility to change when required? If not, how can we increase organizational flexibility and capability?

These and other strategic questions, according to these writers, offer organizations a way of identifying their critical pivot points and the opportunity to move away from generic prescriptions and external benchmarking and towards the development of tailored strategies that will move the organization forward rather than simply support the status quo.

What does this mean in practical terms? One way to make strategy 'real' is to look at what this meant for organizations in the 2008 recession. Many organizations linked strategy to survival, and for many this was the only strategically important objective they were dealing with, but others defined their strategy in terms of emerging from the recession stronger and better placed to take advantage of new opportunities. The key point here is that strategy, both corporate and within HR, reflects how people *frame* the problem(s) they are faced with and their ability to visualize a future desired state that they want the organization to be in. It seems to us that having a strategy and thinking strategically above all else means that someone has a vision of a future state that is realistic and achievable. But this raises another important paradox; that of continuity and change.

Stacey (2012) argues that in the context of environmental uncertainty and complexity organizations need to be 'agile' in order to survive and beyond that to gain and retain competitive advantage, and that the ability to outperform another firm is based on its ability to rapidly and repeatedly disrupt the current situation in order to create a new and more effective basis for competing. The problem with this position is that constant disruption and change affects an organization's ability to effectively function in the present. This dilemma was recognized by Brown and Eisenhardt (1998) who advocated a strategy that combined the necessary degree of structure and stability that would allow the organization to continue to function with sufficient fluidity and adaptability to allow it to respond to known and 'unknown' environmental change. The implications of this view of strategy for HR is obvious; the function has to develop its own strategic contributions that reflect and support the organization in its search for the appropriate 'balance' between supporting the status quo and changing it. The conclusion we would reach on the basis of reviewing the literature on HR's strategic role and contribution, or lack of it, is that it places too much emphasis on preserving the status quo and insufficient emphasis on facilitating change and adaptation.

Gary Hamel provides an insight into the kinds of changes HR needs to be engaged in in a podcast for the CIPD. In trying to make sense of what organizations needed to do he said:

> we're going to have to find ways to get our employees to bring their creativity and their passion to work every day. I think the companies that do well over the next few months, the next few years are going to have a very important set of skills but those may not be the same skills that will see them through beyond this crisis. For that we need organisations that are fundamentally more adaptable, more innovative, and more engaging places to work than they are right now. Some companies I think are already moving in that direction, most have a long ways to go.
> (Hamel, 2009)

From his comments, we can see that the examples of strategically important pivot points are:

- The degree to which organizations are flexible and adaptable to environmental changes.
- The degree to which their employees are creative and innovative.
- The extent to which organizations engage with their employees and provide psychologically and emotionally rewarding places to work.
- Having the right leaders and leadership capabilities to confront new challenges and take advantage of opportunities to grow the business.

And why are these important? Because there is extensive evidence that positive measures of flexibility, creativity, and engagement are consistently associated with high performance at the individual and organizational levels (Buckingham and Coffman, 1999; Khilji and Wang, 2006). The task for HR then becomes one of establishing the strategic links between specific aspects of employee and management behaviour and organizational performance and developing effective strategies that bring about the desired changes in those aspects of work and organization that will impact the greatest on organizational performance.

What makes HR strategies different between organizations is less to do with the strategic intentions expressed through mission statements and departmental strategy documents than their ability to identify and focus on the key things that need to be *changed*, rather than simply improved. This inevitably involves leading and leadership, and confronting the resistance and possibly conflict that certain kinds of change involve. A key question is:

> **does behaviour change as a result of changes in the structure and culture of an organization or does a change in behaviour precede and facilitate structural and cultural change?**
> (Pfeffer, 2005)

Going back to what was said in Chapter 1, the most fundamental aspect of organizations and HR is people and the way they behave. Strategies that focus on structures and processes without incorporating ways of influencing behaviour in desired ways are unlikely to enjoy anything other than limited and short-term success.

STUDENT ACTIVITY 3.4

CIPD Podcast 109—'Looking ahead to 2016', available at: https://www.cipd.co.uk/podcasts/looking-ahead-to-2016#

Listen to the podcast featuring Cary Cooper and consider his assessment of what are organizations' strategic challenges for the future. Relate these to the HR function within your own organization or one you are familiar with. Then consider some of the difficulties HR may experience in meeting these challenges.

The Concept of Fit and Integration

In considering whether HR strategies are more generic than unique and how they can be made more specific to the organization, we need to return to the concepts of 'fit' and 'integration' which we briefly considered in Chapter 2. To avoid confusing the issue we treat the two terms as having the same meaning, although depending on how they are defined there can be subtle differences in meaning. Fit is used in the context of 'best fit', as opposed to the concept of 'best practice' to describe a critical relationship which is that between what HR does and what the organization either needs or is capable of accommodating. Farnham argues that:

> **Organizations need to identify the HR strategies which 'fit' their enterprises in terms of product markets, labour markets, size, structures, strategies, and other factors.**
> (Farnham, in Pilbeam and Corbridge, 2002)

He offers three kinds of 'best-fit' models:

1. One that links HR to an organization's life or business cycle. The importance of this point lies in the realization that, while many HR practices and activities appear to be present at all stages of the life cycle, their relative importance changes to reflect the different demands on the development journey.

2. One that links HR's contribution to the different strategies and structural configurations of organizations. Here, the emphasis is on HR's understanding how cultural and structural forms and preferences generate the context within which HR needs to operate and make its contributions. For example, many public sector organizations are organized on rigid hierarchical lines and operate in predominantly formal ways. The concept of best fit in this situation suggests that the design and operation of appraisal systems, for example, will also reflect both hierarchy and formality. A second example of this particular model can be found in the design of performance and reward systems. In a cultural environment where individuals rather than teams are seen as the primary social and work unit, the design of jobs, the degree of functional flexibility, and the use of individual rather than collective rewards will

need to 'fit' this culture. On the other hand, in organizations that claim to be value-driven, HR will be expected to reflect the importance of these values in every aspect of employee behaviour and in the way HR selects, develops, and promotes employees; hierarchy becomes less important than behaviour and HR needs to orient its activities and contributions to reflect these different priorities. One of the most difficult challenges facing HR in organizations that are increasingly emphasizing the importance of value-driven behaviour is to make the transition from enforcing rules to promoting and encouraging values.

3. The third best-fit model matches HR strategies to business strategies. This involves HR actively engaging with current and planned business strategies and working to support them. Strategies which stress creativity and innovation will require HR to tailor their selection criteria to ensure that creative and innovative people are employed and that these virtues are rewarded in the pay and reward systems more than conformity or length of service. The tight control of costs, reflecting a competitive strategy based on price, will require HR to be particularly sensitive to increases in wage/salary and employment costs, and seek to minimize labour costs without undermining productivity levels. In the 2008 recession, the survival of many private sector businesses depended on HR looking at ways of reducing costs, but in that recession, unlike previous ones, retaining skilled employees was considered to be strategically important in the context of expected future growth. This meant that reducing head count, while often a temporary 'survival' strategy, ran in parallel with wage reductions, temporary lay-offs, and reduced working time rather than permanent and forced redundancies (Risling, 2010).

The concept of strategic integration–fit can take three different forms:

1. **Horizontal integration.** In this form, the different activities and contributions associated with HR work need to be mutually supportive and designed in a holistic way rather than exist as unconnected and isolated interventions. The concept of connectivity is also useful in explaining what horizontal integration involves. Strategic impact comes from the synergistic effects of the different but closely interwoven and mutually supportive activities.

2. **Vertical integration.** Here, HR is outward-looking and connected to the wider organization, sensitive to its values and beliefs, its corporate strategy, and contextual challenges.

3. A third type, described as **functional integration**, is less frequently referred to in the HR literature, but refers particularly to the way the HR and production functions work in conjunction rather than in isolation. Examples of this in action include work and job design, performance-related pay systems, high-performance team working, and production system design which can be seen as closely related to the concept of sociotechnical systems. The concept of sociotechnical systems is an example of this type of integration, where the human and technical systems are designed together to ensure the requirements of both are met rather than existing in competition with each other.

The significance of fit–integration for our understanding of what strategic HR means and what in practice is involved is clear. To be strategically relevant, activities and HR outputs have to:

- be connected and supportive of each other;
- facilitate business goals and objectives;
- create synergies where they impact on other management functions;
- help to create a working environment within which critically important behaviours are encouraged and rewarded;
- if the organization has 'a big idea', be seen to contribute in one way or another to *this*.

Figure 3.2 illustrates the meaning of both vertical and horizontal integration.

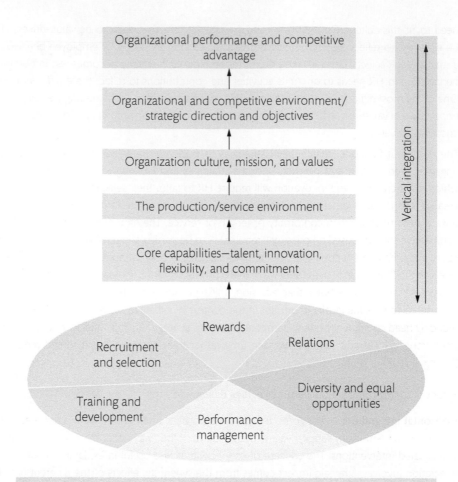

Figure 3.2 A representation of vertical and horizontal integration as applied to HR
Source: Reprinted by permission of Harvard Business Review Press. From *Human Resource Champions*, by D. Ulrich, Boston MA, 1997, p. 24. Copyright © 1997 by the Harvard Business Publishing Corporation; all rights reserved.

HRM INSIGHT 3.1 **Introducing a leadership training programme at Midshire University**

Midshire, one of the UK's 'new' universities, had been structured around ten departments, each with its own management team and administrative support. Central functions, based on finance, marketing, the registry, facilities, and HR, coordinated a series of common services and procedures for all academic departments, with the 'centre' operating very much as a bureaucracy, exercising hierarchical control over its constituent parts.

Over time, the HR department had grown from rather modest proportions to what had now become a large and influential part of the university, employing approximately sixty staff, split evenly between professional and administrative employees. Its main operational role was in maintaining good relations with TUs, providing advice to the senior management teams within the departments, managing grievance and disciplinary cases, and providing a centralized, course-based training service. Its reputation within the university ranged from being seen as an expensive overhead, to being seen as a well-managed but largely administrative service, to, for the majority of university staff, a somewhat remote and detached set of people who didn't have much interest in, or experience of, what most staff actually did and the environment in which they worked.

As a result of a major reorganization in 2012, which resulted in the merger of the ten academic departments into three new super colleges, it became apparent that many of the newly appointed senior managers lacked the strategic management skills that they needed to take on these important leadership roles. In addition, the results of the annual staff survey indicated that many employees, in both academic and non-academic roles, had considerable concerns about the quality of leadership in general and felt that this was an important matter that had to be addressed if the aspirations of the university's vice chancellor were to be met.

Responding to a request from the vice chancellor, the head of HR contacted an external provider of leadership training and held discussions about what would represent the most appropriate way of dealing with this problem. What emerged was a sophisticated course in leadership, delivered off-site and consisting of three separate two-day sessions using a mixture of both experiential and classroom-based learning.

The reaction of those who participated in the training was that, while the experience of being on the course had been interesting and developmental, the big problem was that little, if anything, had changed in the university and that the course on its own was not able to address the problem of a lack of leadership among management. The results of the staff survey the following year confirmed that staff continued to feel that the university had a serious leadership deficit.

Questions

1. What action should have been taken and by whom prior to, during, and after the course to ensure that there was a high level of integration within the whole learning experience?

2. What other HR and management changes might the HR department have made to ensure that the new leadership course was horizontally integrated?

3. What should have been the respective contributions of the HR specialists and line managers in making sure that the investment in both time and money delivered the necessary outcomes?

 Insights and Outcomes: visit the **online resources** at **www.oup.com/uk/banfield3e/** for answers to the HRM Insight questions.

The Resource-Based View of the Firm

The resource-based view of the firm (RBV) is a perspective or way of understanding what confers and sustains competitive advantage (Figure 3.3). The approach emerged in the 1980s and 1990s, based particularly on the work of Barney (1991) and Prahalad and Hamel (1990). The supporters of RBV argue that organizations should look inside the company to find the sources of competitive advantage instead of looking into the external environment to achieve the same objective because that is where most organizations can contribute most. According to Rothaermel (2012), between 30 and 45 per cent of a firm's competitive advantage is based on its internal resource base, with the effects of the industry it is in explaining a further 20 per cent and the remainder accounted for by other influences.

But within the RBV approach to competitive advantage, not all resources have the same strategic status. The VRIO classification distinguishes one type of human resource or capability from another on the basis of:

- its *value*;

- its *rarity* or scarceness;

- the ease or cost associated with *imitating* the resource or capability;

- the degree to which it is *organized* and utilized to capture and realize its inherent value.

Central to this way of thinking is the belief that an organization's stock of human resource is not fixed but subject to renewal and expansion through carefully considered recruitment and selection policies, and increases in competence and capability through effective learning interventions, both of which can contribute to improvements in performance and productivity. In thinking about people as a flexible rather than fixed resource, the often unstated assumption is that the resource can only increase its contribution. This is not the case; people, depending on a number of influences, can become less efficient and productive, and it becomes critical for HR to understand the reasons why this might occur, to take appropriate action to prevent it happening. People can be and do more or less depending on a wide range of factors and influences,

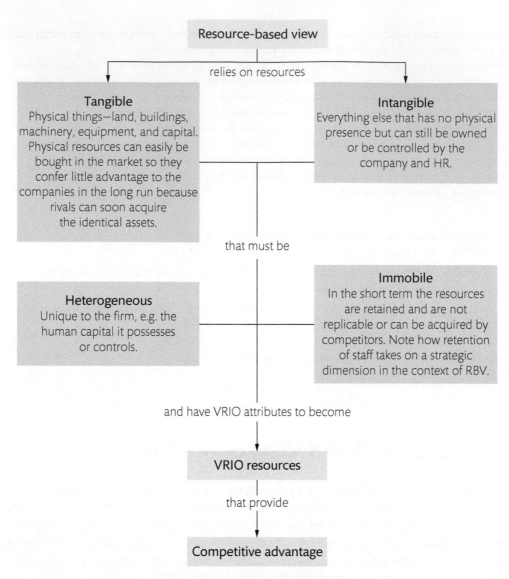

Figure 3.3 The RBV model of competitive advantage
Source: O. Jurevicius, 'Resource Based View', *Strategic Management Insight*, 14 October 2013.
Reproduced with kind permission of Ovidijus Jurevicius.

most of which are located in the working environment not in the HR department. In the Podcast featuring the views of Cary Cooper, one of his major concerns is over the growth in what is known as 'presenteeism' and the damaging effect low performance levels have on productivity (Johns, 2010).

This way of understanding the opportunities and challenges of managing people at the strategic level is consistent with Hamel and Prahalad's concept of resource stretching and owes much to the influential work of Barney (1991). In this article, Barney argues that the key relationship is that between the way human resources are used and the organization's chosen strategy to deliver competitive advantage and resultant changes in its performance.

The emphasis from the resource-based view of organizations tends to be on the development of human capital capabilities so that 'the same becomes more' and through this improvements in operational effectiveness translate into increases in strategically important measures of organizational performance. According to Kamoche (1996), this means that people need to be seen as the 'source of resourcefulness', and that a central focus of HR is to grow as well as use the resource in ways that result in or contribute to competitive advantage. But if all organizations understand this and make similar commitments to and investments in training and development how does any single organization improve the value of its human capital at a greater rate or to a higher level than its competitors? According to Analoui (2007), to make a distinctive contribution to competency development an organization's resources must be unique and distinctive, and Porter, whom we referred to earlier in the chapter, argues that strategic advantage comes from organizations doing things differently from their competitors or doing different things better. So, the dilemma for HR professionals, while sharing a common HR agenda with most comparable organizations, is that they have to find ways to improve efficiency and productivity that drive competitive advantage and which are unique to their own organization. But knowing what to do and talking about it in strategy meetings is not the same as being able to initiate and successfully deliver organizational change, starting with HR itself (Blomme, 2012). Without the willingness and capability to change itself and then parts of the wider organization, HR will continue to suffer from what Whickam Skinner (1981) criticized the function for many years ago—talking about what it does but lacking substance.

What does this mean in practical terms? Well, one way of making sense of this challenge is to take a concrete example: performance management. Doing something different might involve abandoning traditional forms of performance appraisals altogether, a strategy justified by a significant body of evidence that indicates many PA systems do not work, contribute little if anything of value to performance, and paradoxically can result in performance and productivity falls (Coens and Jenkins, 2000). Simply disengaging from what most other organizations do in this respect has the potential of saving significant resources and may prevent a reduction in what people actually produce and contribute to. We should ask the question: what does performance appraisal contribute to improved worker productivity? Of course, it serves a number of other purposes, but without evidence that it positively impacts on this key source of competitive advantage, its utility will be subject to legitimate questioning.

An example of doing things differently, again using performance appraisal as an example, would be to replace formal and highly structured systems driven by HR with informal systems owned and controlled by line managers and their teams of employees. What is lost is consistency and conformity, but in its place are diverse and relevant practices that reflect important differences and opportunities in the organization. As we argue consistently throughout the book, a one-size-fits-all model of HR, whether it relates to recruitment, PA, rewards, talent, or training is increasingly inconsistent with a view of people as individuals and of organizations as flexible. But the risks involved as perceived by HR rather than the opportunities lost are likely to continue to affect its ability or willingness to accept diversity of practice.

Taking recruitment and selection as a second example, what different things could be done or the same things done differently? Instead of employing people directly organizations could outsource work and build flexible supply chain networks to deliver all but the core work of the organization. In other words, you stop most of the normal recruitment and selection activities and let other organizations take on this responsibility at a price which is considerably below the costs of undertaking this in-house. Would this run the risk of affecting the quality of selection decisions? This is clearly an important question and in practice it would be difficult to establish, but, again, we have to ask whether existing methods result in the employment of the 'right' kinds of people? This might involve:

- Establishing whether all the relevant information about applicants and shortlisted candidates was being presented to decision makers.

- Questioning whether the essential and required attributes were appropriate to the job and organization.

- Looking at who is involved in making decisions and whether they have the necessary experience and insight.

- Avoiding groupthink and overstating the importance of candidates being 'safe'.

- Taking a holistic view of applicants' and candidates' achievements, attributes, and potential.

Doing the same things differently would involve retaining recruitment and selection responsibilities in-house but relying much more heavily on online recruitment and assessment—in other words leveraging technological resources while retaining human expertise and competency for the final stages of the selection process. Managed well, this approach could not only significantly reduce costs and cycle times but also result in better selection decisions. Related to the field of recruitment and selection, most organizations use job descriptions to help them draw up person specifications that in turn support the assessment and selection of applicants. Why? Some, but fewer, organizations don't use them for reasons which they fully understand. As an example, the highly successful engineering company Gripple, based in Sheffield, have rejected job descriptions completely. An article in the *Daily Telegraph* (Hurley, 2010) claims that the founder of Gripple has deliberately avoided the growth of formal structures and procedures, as his company has grown into a £30-million business, and one of the things he has decided not to adopt are job descriptions. Hugh Stacey is reported as saying:

> **Job descriptions stop people doing things. If someone sees a ball dropping do they catch it or do they say it's not my ball?**

This might be a trivial example, although the management of Gripple certainly believe that job descriptions actually inhibit positive behaviour and flexibility, but the principle is what is important. Doing something differently from his competitors—and not having job descriptions is only one example of his approach to managing people—distinguishes him because, in his mind, the approach Gripple has adopted works and helps to contribute to competitive advantage. Why? Because his employees are so much more productive and value-adding because, in part, they are free from traditional structures of formal control.

Attempting to preserve its traditional interest in uniformity and consistency, influenced by contemporary concerns over equality and equal treatment, however understandable, may also involve HR becoming complicit in the under-utilization of the organization's key resource and in failing to support the organization in its need for productivity, adaptability, and flexibility. This dilemma is real, involving important choices about priorities and what takes precedence, but whichever direction HR leans towards consequences will follow.

Summary

Of all the different elements within HR, as it is taught in colleges and universities, the one that frequently causes students most difficulty is HR strategy. It's not immediately obvious why this is the case. Is it the way it is taught, the abstract and academic nature of much of the material presented to students? Or possibly because the 'theory' of strategy doesn't lend itself to easy application within HR? Whatever the explanation, this chapter set out to overcome some of these difficulties and to present an analysis of strategy and strategic contribution firmly within an HR context by using valuable and important concepts and contributions from the field of corporate strategy. After reading the chapter, we hope it will be clear that SHRM does not mean the same as the strategic analysis of HR. The following are some of the key points that we believe students, many of whom are likely to work in HR, need to reflect on:

- Despite having the potential to make strategically important contributions that support corporate objectives, HR is still subject to the criticism that it doesn't understand what this means and often fails to deliver.

- The reasons for this unfulfilled potential lie primarily in the behaviours, competences, agendas, and mindsets of HR professionals and in the unique ambiguities associated with the HR function.

- Being 'strategic' and making strategically important contributions is not something that happens because HR practitioners engage in a strategic discourse or associate themselves with the strategic dimension of HR. Being strategic comes from having a strategic as opposed to an administrative and operational mindset and from delivering contributions that other stakeholders define as being of strategic value.

- The concept of fit–integration suggests that HR needs to understand organizations as consisting of complex and dynamic subsystems, and only by fully understanding these dynamic relationships can HR move towards achieving what at best can only be a temporary fit–integration. Fitting and being integrated are at best temporary and provisional rather than absolute and permanent states. The challenge never ends!

- The idea of leveraging human resources to generate competitive advantage is central to what being strategic represents. This means that HR strategies which maximize the utilization of people and continue to grow their potential without undermining their commitment and level of engagement are those that are likely to make the greatest strategic contribution. One of the ironies of contemporary organizational life is that many people actually feel undervalued and underused while others feel that work is too stressful and pressurized; both conditions suggest that management is failing to make the most of its people. What are the strategies that resulted in these two undesirable states and what strategies can change them?

- Finally, being strategic fundamentally means understanding the implications for behaviour and performance of the decisions managers make and the choices they are confronted with. We have argued that the available evidence suggests that the most successful organizations are those that relate decisions and choices to values, beliefs, and shared mindsets which endure and remain consistent through transformation and change.

Visit the **online resources** that accompany this book for self-test questions, web links, and more information on the topics covered in this chapter, at: **www.oup.com/uk/banfield3e/**

? REVIEW QUESTIONS

1. What does strategic mean for the organization?

2. As head of an organization's HR department what would you say to your CEO to support your claim that the department was strategically significant?

3. What often prevents HR from realizing its strategic potential?

4. What are the future strategic challenges facing HR?

Q CASE STUDY   The role of HR in strategic change

In this case study, the experiences of one HR manager are recounted as part of a 'story' of strategic change and HR's role and contribution to this.

Background to organization: Irish-based company ABC Ltd is the market leader in their sector and has been operating on the island for over seventy years. It is heavily unionized with 90 per cent of employees active members of four different unions, and it negotiates separately with production, distribution, sales, and clerical and management unions.

Prior to a takeover in the 1990s by an international company, the company was managed locally by a board of directors based in the Dublin head office. Traditionally the culture of the company has been very paternalistic—'We are one family and we all look after each other.' There was a very strong emphasis on the mentality that no one ever got kicked out of the family no matter how troublesome they were. Change never happened without complete consensus with the unions and without exchange of a monetary benefit to the affected group of employees. Traditionally the style of leadership within the company was very transactional and task-oriented; employees' views and opinions were never sought for any strategic change projects.

The majority of the employees in the Irish Republic have been doing the same job for the past thirty to forty years with little differentiation in their day-to-day tasks and therefore anything new or different that is asked of them is treated with suspicion and mistrust. This group of 'Theory X' employees tends to be closed and secretive in their manner, risk-averse with low team spirit, and status. They adopt a predominantly 'what's in it for me?' attitude and are not open to change.

Change in ownership: The international company that took over the Irish organization was very innovative and was successful in exploiting niche markets.

The company developed into an international organization by creatively adapting to the changing business environment. They established themselves as a leading participant in their markets. The organization believes that change creates opportunities—management analyse change and capitalize on it as effectively as they can. They look for the unusual and see how it can help their business—this helps differentiate them in the marketplace. The organization fosters a culture of learning from each other and ensures knowledge is shared internally. This is a culture they like to see mirrored throughout their individual companies and it represented a huge change for the Irish organization.

ABC not only wanted to change to 'better' practices as a company, it also wanted to introduce formal policies and procedures that would govern every aspect of the management of its people. Such formality had never existed in the business previously and the new management were convinced that this was critical to its future success. But they were also aware that there would be resistance to this change.

It was identified that to achieve the desired outcome they would involve and engage with everybody in a meaningful way. The desired outcome of ensuring that all our people are aligned and intrinsically motivated would be taken into account both in 'what we do' and in 'how we do it'.

The management initially communicated the need for this change in practice through an employee briefing session chaired by the CEO where all affected employees were invited to attend. This session was then followed up by a written business briefing which was not only issued to all staff but also copied to the union officials (an act that was never done before).

The management team made a commitment to all employees and union officials at the onset of the engagement process stating the following:

People will not be surprised by what we do.

All the people within the area have the opportunity of contributing to suggestions and ideas before any decisions are made.

We engage with staff and give them the opportunity of contributing to planning the best way of implementing and achieving our plans.

We will work on the principle that the support of the people is critical to the success of any decision.

We will respect the union agreements that are in place in the business and will not change custom or practice without proper consultation and communication with all.

Taking into account all suggestions and ideas, ultimately it is the responsibility of the leader to make the decision. We must always make the best decisions in a timely fashion for the company in the long term.

Role of HR in this change programme

Once the initial briefings took place with all affected employees and their union representatives the HR manager arranged a series of training days[2] for the senior and middle management teams where they could view the initial draft of the proposed policies and make their suggestions and recommendations on the content, the language, and the tone of the policy—and to ensure that they understood the rationale of each one. The drawback of this method of engagement is that the pace of learning can be slow. It was identified though that due to the complexity of this change, that is, fundamentally changing the culture of the company, that the pace of change needed to be slow to allow all managers to fully understand and gain a sense of ownership of the processes, so that they could in turn become agents of change.

Table 3.1 illustrates the time allocated to these off-site training sessions.

[2] Training days were held off-site and overnight so managers could focus on really examining what the rationale was behind each policy. Learning exercises used on training days were group exercises, role play, case study analysis, group discussion, and debate.

Table 3.1 Overview of facilitated policy training days for management

Policy to be discussed	No. of delegates	No. of days allocated to training
Disciplinary	10	2
Grievance	10	2
Dignity and respect	10	2
Absenteeism management	10	2
Leave policy	10	2
Recruitment and selection	10	2
Performance management	10	3

The middle management team of ABC was now in effect the change agent in this process and the CEO and HR manager were the facilitators or sponsors of this project. Over the following eighteen-month period (change of this magnitude for a heavily unionized company is very slow) the middle management team started to move away from their traditional roles of instructing, directing, and controlling staff. They started to move away from focusing solely at the macro and micro levels within the organization (transactional/autocratic leadership trait) and started to encourage commitment and engagement from their followers. We could start to see these managers moving towards the resonant leadership style in that they were in tune with those that surrounded them and they were intuitively aware and understood the needs and wants of others. Middle managers discussed and debated with their followers about the rationale of the policies. They then reported back to senior management and HR with their thoughts and suggestions so that a robust set of agreed and negotiated policies and procedures could be designed, agreed, and implemented in the business.

Figure 3.4 illustrates the methodology that the organization adopted during this change programme.

Effectiveness of employee engagement and involvement in the change process: Throughout the process of engagement and again once the policies had been agreed and implemented the HR manager conducted an exercise with a sample group of individuals that were involved with the change programme. The purpose of this exercise was to ascertain on a continuum of employee involvement (Blyton and Turnbull, 1998) where they rated the level of employee involvement throughout the change programme. The group of employees sampled came from the following functions:

Senior Managers (A)
Union Shop Stewards (B)
Union Officials (external stakeholder) (C)
Middle Manager (D)
HR Manager (E)
Employee (F)

For comparative purposes, these groups were asked to identify where they felt they fit best on the continuum at the initial stages of the programme and at the final stage. As illustrated in Figures 3.5 and 3.6, all groups moved along the continuum by the end of the process which illustrated to all that the methodology used in the management of this change process had indeed been effective.

The exercise clearly illustrated when an individual felt that they were involved in the change programme rather than the feeling that change was happening to them they became more aligned with the goals of the organization, thus allowing the change to be more effective.

In the strategic change programme, the HR manager was intrinsically involved in the offset of this strategic programme. She worked side by side with the CEO and senior management team advising on the communication rollout of the change and language to be used to relate to those affected the most by the change, that is, employees. She became a coach for the middle manager and an adviser for the employees.

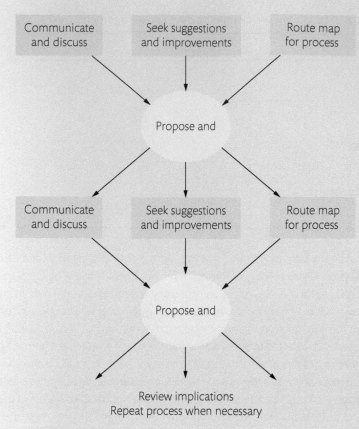

Figure 3.4 The methodology of introduction of change (we will constantly repeat the following sequence until we are satisfied that all issues are addressed)

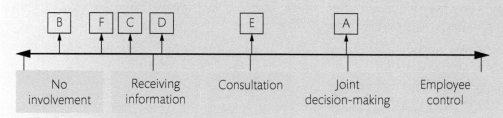

Figure 3.5 Continuum of employee involvement (initial stage of change programme)

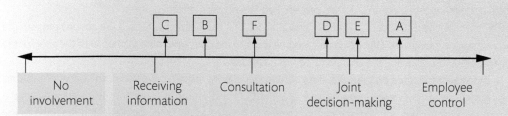

Figure 3.6 Continuum of employee involvement (post implementation of change programme)

In this role, the HR function moved away from a task-oriented administrative role to a more strategic business partner position. It was important that during this time the HR manager was able to converse with senior management in their language—business language—and relate everything back to how this change programme would ultimately add value to their business.

Questions

1. Which of the five definitions of strategy were in operation within the company?

2. What were considered to be the key pivot points?

3. What were the drivers for strategic change?

4. Given that relying on training as a way of implementing strategic change so often fails, what was it about the way training was used in the company that achieved the desired changes?

5. How could the company have dealt with managers and employees who resisted the changes being made?

FURTHER READING

Boxall, P. and Purcell, J. (2016) *Strategy and Human Resource Management*, Palgrave.

CIPD (2010) 'Building productive public sector workplaces. Part four. Boosting HR performance in the public sector'.

Kets de Vris, M. (2011) 'Creating authentizotic organisations: Well-functioning individuals in vibrant companies', *Human Capital Handbook*, 1(3), at: http://www.ketsdevries.com/news/pdf/Human_Capital%20Handbook_V1N3Sep2011.pdf

Paaue, J. et al. (2013) *HRM & Performance*, Wiley.

Stacey, R. D. (1995) 'The science of complexity: An alternative perspective for strategic change processes', *Strategic Management Journal*, 16(6).

Also read the slides and watch the presentation on strategy and HR on https://www.youtube.com/watch?v=ZMnJc_XKlwE

REFERENCES

Analoui, F. (2007) *Strategic Human Resource Management*, Thomson Learning.

Barney, J. B. (1991) 'Firm resources and sustained competitive advantage', *Journal of Management*, 17(1), 99–120.

Bassi, L. and McMurrer, D. (2004) 'What to do when people are your most important asset', at: http://mcbassi.com/wp/resources/documents/WhenPeopleAreYourMostImportantAsset.pdf

Bassi, L. and McMurrer, D. (2007) 'Maximizing your return on people', *Harvard Business Review* (March).

Birdi, K. et al. (2008) 'The impact of human resource and operational management practices on company productivity: A longitudinal study', *Personnel Psychology*, 61(3).

Blomme, R. J. (2012) 'Leadership, complex adaptive systems, and equivocality: The role of managers in emergent change', *Organization Management Journal*, 9(1).

Blyton, P. and Turnball, P. (1998) *The Dynamics of Employee Relations*, Palgrave Macmillan.

Boudreau, J. and Ramstad, P. (2007) *Beyond HR: The New Science of Human Capital*, Harvard Business School Press.

Brown, S. L. and Eisenhardt, K. (1998) *Competing on the Edge: Strategy as Structured Chaos*, Harvard Business School Press.

Buckingham, M. and Coffee, C. (1999) *First Break All the Rules*, Pocket Books.

CIPD (2010) 'Employee branding and total reward', at: http://www.cipd.co.uk/binaries/employer-branding-and-total-reward_2010.pdf

Coens, T. and Jenkins, M. (2000) *Abolishing Performance Appraisal*, Berrett-Koehler.

Department of Health (2015) 'Learning not blaming', at: https://www.gov.uk/government/uploads/system/uploads/attachment_data/file/445640/Learning_not_blaming_acc.pdf

Driver, P. (2014) 'Why most public sector strategies aren't actually strategies at all', *Guardian*, 8 April.

Gratton, L. (1999) *Strategic Human Resource Management*, Oxford University Press.

Haffenden, M. (2002) 'Strategic visions', *Personnel Today* (October).

Hamel, G. (2009) CIPD Podcast 32, at: http://www.cipd.co.uk/hr-resources/podcasts/32-gary-hamel.aspx

Hamel, G. and Prahalad C. K. (1993) 'Strategy as stretch and leverage', *Harvard Business Review* (March–April).

Hamel, G. and Prahalad C. K. (1994) 'Competing for the future', *Harvard Business Review* (July–August).

Hammonds, K. H. (2005) 'Why we hate HR', *Fast Company*, 98.

Harvey, J. (1996) *The Abilene Paradox*, Jossey-Bass.

Holbeche, L. (2009) *Aligning Human Resources and Business Strategy*, Routledge.

Hurley, J. (2010) 'Offshoring a false economy, says employee-owned Gripple', *Daily Telegraph*, 15 October.

Huselid, M. A. (1994) 'Documenting HR's effect on company performance', *HR Magazine* (January).

Jackson, S. E. and Schuler, R. S. (2000) *Managing Human Resource: A Partnership Perspective*, Southern-Western College Publishing.

Johns, G. (2010) 'Presenteeism in the workplace: A review and research agenda', *Journal of Organizational Behaviour*, 31(4), 519–42.

Johnson, J. et al. (2014) *Exploring Strategy*, Pearson.

Kamoche, K. (1996) 'Strategic human resource management within a resource capability', *Journal of Management Studies*, 33(2), 213–33.

Kearns, P. (2004) 'How strategic are you? The six killer questions', *Strategic HR Review*, 3 (March–April).

Khilji, S. E. and Wang, X. (2006) '"Intended" and "implemented" HRM: The missing linchpin in strategic human resource management research', *International Journal of Human Resource Management*, 17, 1171–89.

Lave, J. and Wenger, E. (2007) 'Communities of practice', at: http://infed.org/mobi/jean-lave-etienne-wenger-and-communities-of-practice

Lawler, E. (2007) 'Why HR practices are not evidence-based', *Academy of Management Journal*, 50(5), 1033–6.

Legge, K. (2005) *Human Resource Management*, Palgrave Macmillan.

MacDuffie, J. P. (1995) 'Human resource bundles and manufacturing performance: Organizational logic and flexible production systems in the world auto industry', *Industrial and Labor Relations Review*, 48, 197–221.

Milkovich, G. T. and Newman, J. M. (2002) *Compensation*, 8th edn, McGraw-Hill/Irwin.

Minzberg, H. (1987) 'The strategy concept. 5 P's for strategy', *Californian Management Review* (Fall).

Mitsakis, F. V. (2014) 'Human resource management (HRM), economic crisis (EC) and business life cycle (BLC): A literature review and discussion', *International Journal of Human Resource Studies*, 4(1).

Mooney, P. (2001) *Turbo-charging the HR Function*, CIPD.

Office for National Statistics (2015) 'Public sector employment', at: http://www.ons.gov.uk/ons/rel/pse/public-sector-employment/q1-2015/stb-pse-2015q1.html

O'Reilly, C. A. and Pfeffer, J. (2000) *Hidden Value*, Harvard Business School Press.

Pfeffer, J. (1994) *Competitive Advantage Through People*, Harvard Business School Press.

Pfeffer, J. (2005) 'Changing mental models: HR's most important task', *Human Resource Management*, 44(2), 123–8.

Pilbeam, S. and Corbridge, M. (2002) *People Resourcing*, Financial Times/Prentice Hall.

Porter, M. E. (1996) 'What is strategy?', *Harvard Business Review* (November).

Prahalad, C. K. and Hamel, G. (1990) 'The core competence of the corporation', *Harvard Business Review* (May/June), at: http://globex.coe.pku.edu.cn/file/upload/201606/27/1756365219.pdf

Purcell, J. (2003) *Understanding the People and Performance Link: Unlocking the Black Box*, CIPD.

Risling, C. (2010) '7 human resource strategies to use in a recession', at: http://ezinearticles.com/?7-Human-Resource-Strategies-to-Use-in-a-Recession&id=2216451

Rothaermel, F. T. (2012) *Strategic Management: Concepts and Cases*, McGraw-Hill/Irwin.

Saunders, M., Mann, R., and Smith, R. (2008) 'Implementing strategic initiatives: A framework of leading practices', *International Journal of Operations & Production Management*, 28(11), 1095–1123.

Skinner, W. (1981) 'Big hat no cattle', *Harvard Business Review* (October/September).

Stacey, R. (2012) 'Responding to complexity and uncertainty: The agile organisation', posted 29 August, at: http://complexityandmanagement. wordpress.com/2012/08/29/responding-to-complexity-and-uncertainty-the-agile-organisation

Sullivan, J. (2005) *Rethinking Strategic HR*, CCH.

Sullivan, J. (2011) 'Increasing employee productivity: The strategic role that HR essentially ignores', 16 May, at: https://www.eremedia.com/ere/ increasing-employee-productivity-the-strategic-role-that-hr-essentially-ignores

Ulrich, D. and Brocklebank, W. (2005) 'Role call', *People Management*, 16 June.

Whyatt-Haines, R. (2007) *Align IT*, Wiley.

Operational Challenges

PART

2

Talent Management: Strategies and Models

4

Introduction

It is unusual to find contemporary HR textbooks that don't have a chapter or a significant section of one devoted to TM. Ever since McKinsey published the *War for Talent* report in 1998, the subject of talent and how it should be managed has become an important part of the HR discourse, with the CIPD in particular contributing to its popularity growing status with the profession (CIPD, 2015).

The existence of talent departments and talent budgets within organizations and the growth in the number and range of TM strategies is also testament to the spread and perceived importance of TM as a coherent body of thought and practice. On the other hand, the argument that, as part of the evolutionary process of HRM, it represents not much more than another and the latest iteration of what HRM 'is' in the never-ending search for an identity and purpose, is one that also has credibility. We noted in Chapter 3 that HR has been criticized before for appearing at times to follow the newest 'fad', and consistent with our approach throughout the book, we need to try to establish what TM actually means or could mean before we attach too much significance to it. It is also interesting to speculate whether TM should be considered part of strategic HRM, given that many of the writers we referred to in Chapter 2 saw an organization's 'talent' as the key to competitive advantage. So, it is legitimate to ask whether TM is old wine in new bottles, where the only difference is one of semantics, with talent replacing but meaning essentially the same as people. Is there anything fundamentally or even mildly different from what is meant by TM compared to people or personnel management? Are we faced with the same introspection and attempted legitimation that was seen when HRM emerged in the 1990s? The purpose of this chapter, therefore, is to critically engage with the literature on this topic to establish whether TM represents a new and distinctive approach to the management of people or whether it is little more than a new interpretation with a different emphasis.

This picture of a relatively new perspective on HRM which has attracted considerable interest in both professional and academic circles but which also suffers from a lack of clarity, is one that resonates with the views of Lewis and Heckman (2006), who in an earlier and critical review of the field said:

> **Given the number of consulting firms engaging in talent management and the growing number of articles and books on the topic, one might also believe 'talent management' to be a well-defined area of practice supported by extensive research and a core set of principles. We find that such is not the case.**

But despite the findings of Lewis and Heckman, it is undeniably the case that the interest in talent and its management is genuine and continues to grow, although whether there is a 'bandwagon effect' at play is difficult to know: in the same way that most HR professionals suddenly became strategic practitioners as HRM replaced personnel management, the same need to be moving with the times and embracing the latest 'version' of HRM may be a factor in this popularity. Part of the problem in trying to assess the significance of TM is that, while it has become embedded in the HR discourse, there is a worrying lack of agreement about what it actually means. This lack of consensus may in itself be much less of a problem than might originally have been thought; why for example is a consensus over meaning necessary and important? We saw in the previous chapter that the different meanings of strategy as outlined by Minzberg created a greater depth of understanding, where multiple meanings enriched rather than confused the study and practice of HR strategy and it *may be* that the same applies to TM. So, it may not matter if academics define it and view TM from different perspectives as long as there is some degree of substance and consistency in their definitions. Is it not acceptable to view the lack of consensus not as a weakness but as the inevitable outcome of a complex and evolving process of discovery, driven by research, model building, and greater conceptual insight. Remember what Weick said when we quoted him in Chapter 2, that making sense of something from the social world does involve people deciding on what is important, what needs to be emphasized, and what are the key relationships that need to be highlighted, and realistically some of those involved in the sense-making process are not neutral when it comes to making these decisions and choices. For example, TM consultancies have a vested interest in promoting the idea that it is a new and potentially powerful concept that can 'transform' organizations and academics are equally affected by pushing the conceptual and theoretical boundaries through greater academic recognition and reputation. So, from a student perspective, while specific definitions of a phenomenon are useful, they should be considered only as starting rather than end points in the sense-making process.

So, before we progress to an exploration of specific TM models and their application, there are important questions to be asked about the form talent takes, over the relationship between TM and other HR 'labels', and whether conceptually and practically TM represents a separate coherent body of thought and practice. Specifically, we need to address the more strategically important question:

> Is TM something which is both new and different and if so how is it different such that it offers HR professionals and senior line managers opportunities to leverage their human resources in ways that contribute to organizational success in whatever way that is defined?

TM: Conflicting Scenarios

Before we explore and evaluate the different meanings and conceptualization of TM and in order to provide a helpful indication of arguably the dominant narrative around talent, it is worth considering the example of a specific industry and reflect on the kinds of talent issues, projections, and recommendations people in that industry are focusing on. Oil and gas was chosen because it is a global industry and well known to most people and because it illustrates the different and often conflicting challenges managing talent involves. While the economic and employment conditions in the sector are different to other industries and certainly to the public sector, they only differ in degree and not in kind (Devine and Powell, 2008). This sector, therefore, provides a realistic and familiar context within which concerns over talent and the 'talent agenda' can be easily understood. Although, as we will see later in the chapter, TM is about much more than ensuring qualified people are either in place or ready to be promoted as vacancies occur, the oil and gas sector does show the particularly strong links that exist between it, demographic change, workforce planning, and employee resourcing.

At a recent conference on the role of HR in the global oil and gas business, Derek Massie, former senior vice president for HR at a major oil and gas drilling company, made the following prediction, that:

> half of the oil and gas workforce globally could retire by 2015 and that the growing demand for oil 'far outstrips' the talent resources the industry has available. In the context of the domestic oil and gas industry, he added that the UK is facing a talent drain of its own as workers are moving away from the North Sea and exploring other more 'glamorous' options.
> (Newcombe, 2013)

And in an article that pre-dated Massie's warning, consultants from the US oil and gas practice, Oliver Wyman (formerly Mercer Management Consulting) claimed that:

> over the next decade, attracting and retaining skilled workers will be one of the biggest risks to industry success.
> (Orr and McVerry, 2007)

They argue that upstream and midstream businesses are expected to be the most affected, as large numbers of experienced workers retire and competition for new talent heats up. They point out that this is not just an HR issue in terms of the numbers that need to be recruited but one that recognizes that knowledge, not just physical assets, will be the source of future value growth in the sector, and a shortage of well-qualified professionals will constrain the abilities both to grow in scale and to compete in an ever more crowded field.

Orr and McVerry revealed a number of key issues that the industry needed to address as a matter of priority in order to improve the future talent outlook. The most important of these are:

● an ageing workforce, particularly in the western hemisphere;

● the ability to attract and retain qualified talent across the global oil and gas industry;

● an experience gap which has the ability to significantly affect their power to compete in the global market; and

● the ability to find experienced candidates with the skills needed to meet anticipated demand.

The authors claim that approximately 70 per cent of companies contacted by Oliver Wyman indicated this last challenge as their highest-priority issue with one-third of all respondents citing it as 'critical'. And because the business model of many service firms is based on their ability to offer oil and gas companies a high-quality workforce with specialized industry knowledge, a shortage of experienced workers in the labour market will inevitably affect their ability to deliver value to customers. Natural attrition and retirement are expected to intensify the demand for experienced people. By implication, shortages of skilled and experienced workers will impact on the wages/salaries and benefits paid to them, pushing the overall employment costs of these firms ever upward. And the growth of the knowledge economy means that knowledge workers expect increasing access to personal and professional development opportunities as part of a more sophisticated contractual relationship with their employers, so not only does this scenario project a global shortage of talented oil and gas workers but in addition highlights their increasing reward expectations.

This view is confirmed by the finding that over 85 per cent of respondents cited providing 'opportunities for career progression and personal development' as a high/critical priority issue. Knowing the human resource challenges facing the industry is one thing: addressing them effectively is quite another and the survey again pointed to the need for company executives to think very carefully about the efficacy of their existing resourcing and TM policies and practices. It pointed out the limitations of relying too heavily on the internal solutions—seeking more flexibility from existing employees, providing more career development experiences or paying more—because of the lack of sustainability and cost of these options in the long term. Instead the authors of the article argue that strategies focused on developing local pools of talent are expected to have the greatest impact. They conclude:

> **Rather than current piecemeal approaches, what will be needed to address this challenge effectively is an integrated, top-down talent management strategy that ensures that a company can maintain and grow its workforce in line with its long-term business goals.**

 Signpost to Chapter 10: Workforce Planning and Measurement, for an explanation of the role of the internal labour market as a source of labour supply.

Interestingly, several of those who commented on Massie's speech questioned the extent and depth of this talent shortage, based on their different experiences of the sector—a point that we will return to shortly—but this combination of demographic change affecting the supply of labour and increasing demands for goods and services increasing the demand for labour is not something that is unique to the oil and gas industry. In the UK at least, what are being presented as secular and long-term changes are leading both HR professionals and academics to reach similar, if not the same conclusions; that talent is becoming and will remain scarce into the foreseeable future and in order to compete for this diminishing resource organizations need to develop appropriate and effective TM strategies, which presumably means doing different things from those that are currently part of their employee resourcing strategies. In the same way that companies in the technology sector need to constantly innovate and develop new products and business models to remain competitive, it could be argued that the same imperative applies to the management of people, where innovation in how organizations acquire and manage is equally necessary to compete successfully in the 'talent war'. Despite short-term fluctuations in the health of individual sectors and the cyclical impact on labour demand, most observers would argue that the picture presented by both Massie and Mercer is broadly in line with long-term economic trends and forecasts (World Economic Forum, 2016).

They are not alone or the only party projecting this long-term economic vision of talent shortages. In 2007, the CIPD commissioned research into this topic and in a previous report made the following statement:

> **Persistent skills shortages, the changing demographics of the UK workforce, its increasing diversity and the work–life balance agenda have led to increased competition for individuals who are capable of making the greatest difference to organisational performance. In the current tight labour market this has given rise to what has been labelled 'the war for talent'. The ability to attract and retain higher-quality individuals than competitor organisations is increasingly a strategic priority for business. How this is to be achieved is a growing preoccupation for chief executives and senior managers, and those responsible for the design and delivery of HR strategies that proactively support the needs of the business.**
>
> **(CIPD, 2007)**

This representation of what is the 'talent shortage' narrative can be traced back to the McKinsey report referred to earlier. In this the authors claim that:

> **Many American companies are already suffering a shortage of executive talent. Three-quarters of corporate officers surveyed said their companies had 'insufficient talent sometimes' or were 'chronically talent-short across the board'. Not surprisingly, search firm revenues have grown twice as fast as GDP over the past five years.**

STUDENT ACTIVITY 4.1

Read the McKinsey presentation of 2001, at http://www.slideshare.net/dkdmadhubhashini/the-warfortalentmckinsey and the article in *Fast Company*, at http://www.fastcompany.com/34512/war-talent, then answer the following questions:

1. What assumptions are being made by the authors of both contributions to the TM debate? Consider their validity and whether alternative assumptions exist.

2. Why does there have to be a 'war for talent'? Is there an alternative, or complementary strategy to one that involves competing in the labour market for talented people? Are there any costs associated with this 'war'?

3. How reliable are the demographic profiles being presented? What else needs to be taken into account in addition to an ageing population in forecasting future talent requirements?

The dominant narrative that emerges from these and many other contributions to the debate about talent and how it is managed is one that places qualitative and quantitative shortages of labour at its heart: that demographic change combined with increasing demand pressures will make the search for talent, particularly executive talent in the case of the McKinsey report, more important and probably more challenging than it has been in the past. While such a narrative is persuasive and supported by industry survey data, there is a need to exercise considerable caution in both the analysis of talent shortages and in the conclusions and recommendations that follow. Much more rigour needs to be applied in establishing the meaning of talent, where it is located, and how it can be accessed. Moreover, the contexts in which organizations operate vary widely and are constantly changing, and it cannot be intellectually acceptable to treat all organizations as though they experienced the same and unchanging TM requirements and challenges.

There is a need therefore to discriminate between different contexts and the way these can change in an often unpredictable direction which can very quickly render existing TM strategies outdated, inappropriate, and potentially dysfunctional. The concepts of differentiation and alignment that were considered in the previous chapter and will be raised again below are very relevant to developing a more multidimensional and critical model of TM. By this we mean that while an individual organization might have experienced shortages or surpluses of labour similar to others in the same sector it is in a unique position regarding present and future requirements and can, to a certain extent, shape its own future as long as any TM strategies are clearly aligned to the company and not the industry.

We started this section by presenting evidence and views that reflected the close association between TM and workforce planning and demographics. Consistent with the need just outlined to be more questioning and open to different contributions to the debate on talent, it is worth revisiting the example of the oil and gas industry. In one of the comments posted in response to Massie's speech, one HR director made the following interesting points:

- A significant proportion, 23 per cent, of workers aged 55 and over in the sector intend to continue working beyond retirement age. The significance of this intention should not be underestimated! It resonates with the point made in Chapter 1 on the impact a longer and more active working life was having on the labour participation rates and the supply of experienced and skilled labour.

- The loss of skilled workers did not necessarily mean the loss of their knowledge. As will be made clear, techniques to 'expropriate' knowledge limit the extent to which knowledge is both owned and retained by the individual. Although we could argue that talent is more than knowledge and that the ability to appropriate talent might therefore be more limited, increases in the existence and use of artificial intelligence (AI) does suggest that that talent and the person are not synonymous.

- Many companies under-utilize human resources. Using existing talent more productively impacts on the need for 'new talent' in the form of people.

Another commentator wrote:

> This claim that half of the entire oil and gas workforce could retire by 2015 is ludicrous, particularly given that the UK Government increased the retirement age a short while ago. It really shows up the mentality of those who are still attempting to support the myth of a skills 'shortage' at a time of massive skills glut.

A BBC online bulletin (2014) on the industry in the North Sea reported that:

- Oil companies and service providers are cutting staff and investment to save money.

- This has happened before, and the industry adapts, but the adaptation is one of slashing people, slashing projects, and reducing costs wherever possible, and that's painful for our staff, painful for companies and painful for the country.

- 'It's close to collapse. In terms of new investments—there will be none, everyone is retreating, people are being laid off at most companies this week and in the coming weeks. Budgets for 2015 are being cut by everyone.'

- Sir Ian Wood, veteran oil man and government adviser, predicted a wave of job losses in the North Sea over the next eighteen months.

Two very different scenarios indeed! But how can they be explained? In this case, the reason seems to be almost entirely related to the dramatic reduction in the price of crude oil linked to mainly changes in supply as output from the USA as a result of a huge investment in fracking bears fruit. But the very volatility in both supply and demand may well mean that by the time this book is published the situation could well be very different and indeed, difficult to predict. While many industries are far less volatile than oil and gas, most do experience significant levels of uncertainty in the demand for their products and services which impacts on their demand for labour. But not only is the need for talent affected by changes in the product/services markets: other important changes are perhaps less obviously impacting on the supply side as indicated above. Of these the following are of real significance:

- increases in the flexibility of labour which includes both functional and geographical forms;
- increases in the productivity of labour;
- technological change;
- labour market reforms;
- economic migration;
- education and training.

While these developments might be considered to have more impact on the quantity of labour/talent, they will also impact on the qualitative side; in some cases, increasing the need for certain types of labour and in other categories decreasing demand. But the central point is that not all organizations will be affected in the same way and to the same degree. And from this, it is logical to argue that the kind of TM strategies that organizations need will also need to differ to reflect different situations and perhaps even more importantly be sufficiently flexible to remain relevant as circumstances and requirements change. Making the general point: HR strategies that are no longer relevant are not only inappropriate but they are also counterproductive and costly.

HRM INSIGHT 4.1 Sourcing talented staff

Angie Reynolds is the CEO of a hi-tech business based in London. Angie established the company ten years ago with funding from venture capitalists that still retain a 40 per cent stake in the business although they are not involved in its management or development. Of the forty-five staff currently employed, thirty are graduates with either first or second degree qualifications in computing or software engineering; the remainder work in administration, finance, and sales. The HR function is largely outsourced although an HR administrator is employed to manage basic employment procedures. Because of the company's success—it has enjoyed double-digit growth rates over the past five years—problems are beginning to emerge, principally with regard to management capacity and over shortages of programmers and software engineers who together create the software solutions clients have commissioned. Although turnover levels have historically been low, more staff have left to develop their careers elsewhere, and Angie is spending more time trying to replace them. Future growth is now being compromised by the difficulties of attracting and retaining core staff. Angie has been advised to develop a TM strategy and has had preliminary discussions with an HR consultancy specializing in talent solutions. Either in groups or individually and representing the HR consultancy:

- What further information would you want Angie to provide?
- How can the level of managerial expertise and capacity be increased to support the management of the business?
- How would you establish whether Angie was paying above or below market rates for the roles in her business?
- Provide Angie with four possible sources of new core staff and recommend two to her, explaining to her your thinking and reasons behind your recommendations.
- Suggest to Angie what she could do to reduce the turnover rates without having an excessive impact on employment costs.

TM: Definitions and Approaches

If TM strategies need to be flexible to reflect changing economic situations, is the concept of talent itself equally problematic and contingent? It is to this question that we now turn. We referred earlier in the chapter to the important contributions Weick (2001) has made to the process of sense-making and giving meaning to social phenomena. He wasn't talking specifically about talent when he presented his ideas but much of what he said has relevance here. Our position is clear; as we stated above, there is far less utility in seeking to establish the 'right' definition or ascribing the 'right' meaning to TM than in recognizing and being comfortable with different but equally valid definitions and meanings based on the different experiences and situations confronting HR practitioners and senior managers. We start therefore, from the premise that definitions and meanings emerge *from* rather than being imposed *on* a social setting/context and that such contexts change or remain the same, as do the definitions and meanings that emerge as part of an ongoing process of interpretation by those directly involved and external theorists. So, instead of what TM means, we should instead ask what can it mean, what does it to mean for different parties, and how does the relevance of different meanings change as contexts change? This perspective has two important consequences:

1. It avoids students asking and academics trying to answer the question—what is the right definition?
2. HR practitioners need to look within the organization to access the different and shared experiences of its key stakeholders to provide a mediated and multidimensional definition of the term.

There will, however, be an inevitable attempt to search for and create common or at least mutually compatible interpretations and meanings if for no other reason than too many meanings can be a source of confusion particularly where language obscures and a lack of a common language makes it difficult to generate the kind of shared mental models needed to formulate TM strategies (Pfeffer, 2005).

As we stated earlier, there seems to be a lack of a consensus over what TM means and involves. Lewis and Heckman went as far as to claim that:

> **A review of the literature focused on talent management reveals a disturbing lack of clarity regarding the definition, scope and overall goals of talent management.**
> **(2006: 39)**

While Ashton and Morton's comment that:

> **good TM is of strategic importance**
> **(2005: 28)**

raises the obvious question of what is the difference between good and bad TM and how to recognize both forms?

Lewis and Heckman argue that different definitions or explanations confuse TM decisions from processes and outcomes, but the definition by Collings and Mallahi (2009) seems to overcome this criticism because they do in fact link processes and outcomes when they say that strategic TM is concerned with:

> **activities and processes that involve the systematic identification of key positions which differentially contribute to the organisation's sustainable competitive advantage, the development of a talent pool of high potential and high performing incumbents to fill these roles, and the development of a differentiated human resource architecture to facilitate filling these positions with competent incumbents and to ensure their continued commitment to the organisation.**

Interestingly, as the research and subsequent literature on TM has progressed, there has been a recognition that definitions and meanings can and should be more inclusive and flexible rather than exclusive and fixed, reflecting exactly the kinds of situational and contextual factors we have referred to (CIPD, 2015). In their most recent survey the CIPD found wide variations in the way talent is defined across sectors and organizations, with many organizations preferring to formulate and adopt their own interpretations rather than accept universal or prescribed definitions. The report also produced two definitions that offer deeper insights into the topic.

- **Talent** consists of those individuals who can make a difference to organizational performance either through their immediate contribution or, in the longer term, by demonstrating the highest levels of potential.

- **TM** is the systematic attraction, identification, development, engagement, retention, and deployment of those individuals who are of particular value to an organization, either in view of their 'high potential' for the future or because they are fulfilling business/operation-critical roles.

Analysing other literature sources produces four other distinct strains of thought that indicate how TM might be understood and practised. These are:

1. Equating it to a collection of typical human resource department practices, functions, activities, or specialist areas such as recruiting, selection, development but doing these things faster, via the internet, or by outsourcing or across the enterprise rather than within a department or function.

2. Equating TM to workforce and succession planning and focusing on creating and maintaining talent pools and flows throughout the organization but particularly servicing higher levels and critical jobs.

3. Seeing TM as a separate activity that while sharing common processes and objectives with employee resourcing, operates in a differentiated way by concentrating on a smaller and more important—by virtue of their special talents—group of people.

4. Talent, as a resource within and part of all people, needs to be nurtured, developed, and deployed to generate the maximum possible sustained impact on what the organization does and achieves.

Of these four interpretations and approaches the first two add little to suggest TM is in any meaningful way different from employee resourcing except in relation to emphasis, although the third and fourth do offer potentially interesting and useful insights into how TM could be different. The idea that it does or should focus on recognizing and investing in those people with special or rare talents suggests this approach to TM is about differentiation and a focus on scarce and valuable capabilities.

KEY CONCEPT Differentiation

In the context of TM, differentiation can have two meanings. First, from an employee perspective it means that one (or more) organization stands out from other potential employers as being different and more attractive as a place to work. Differentiation in this sense is based on the organization, through the way it rewards, develops, and values its employees, positioning itself differently from its competitors. The second meaning applies to the organization's employees and reflects that they possess different existing human capital values and potential and the way an organization rewards, develops, and uses its employees will differ in relation to these different values and potential.

PRACTITIONER INSIGHT Jean Goodwin, HR adviser

From working as an HR adviser in various contexts and from discussions with fellow CIPD professionals it is clear that there is no one best recruitment or TM strategy to fit all circumstances. There are, however, common elements of good practice, and careful planning consistently reduces the potential for failure, for example, in skills shortages. In managing their talent pool, some small engineering companies make the most of their older engineers through providing private healthcare to maintain their health and retain their scarce skills for longer which has the additional benefit of making the employees feel valued. In the public sector, where dealing with large numbers of applications can be problematic, other roles are difficult to fill; replacing some of those graduate roles experiencing high turnover rates with apprentices who are trained and qualified on the job can improve retention rates and increase employee commitment levels.

In a globalized environment where efficiency and productivity are paramount, organizations are increasingly adopting flexible job profiles based on broader competencies rather than the more prescriptive job descriptions of the past. To be consistent with this, new approaches to interviewing are needed with questions based on those broader competencies rather than questions around specific skills for a particular job, which may not exist in the not too distant future. Online pre-screening processes, as frequently used in the retail sector and for civil service roles, address the match between organizational and individual employee values ensuring that suitable candidates reach the interview stage. The aim is to ensure that the successful candidate will work well within the organizational culture and have the flexibility to adapt to changes in the business or service environment which impact on their role. In other contexts, because of the transient nature of the employment, for example, for students working in hospitality roles, understanding the life cycle of job tenure is more relevant in correctly positioning large-scale recruitment drives, perhaps in college job fairs, to coincide with the point in the college year when students are likely to be considering temporary employment.

In my experience, what is essential to the successful development and implementation of TM strategies is for HR professionals to really understand their own organizational and external context and to be ready to deal with what is out (or in) there. Embracing the value of diversity in every sense of the word can be a great preparation for the unknown, whether it is to reflect the changes in customer or service user bases or to provide the novel perspectives which could potentially lead to competitive advantage for an organization. Diversity here is not just about embracing difference as prescribed by the Equality Act 2010, but also in safeguarding that, within a workforce who reflect your organizational values, you take steps to avoid employee 'clone syndrome', for example, to avoid the 'group speak' of board members coming from one particular background who may miss issues arising from outside their experience. Employees expect an organization to practise TM fairly and to be seen adopting diversity as a core value can support this view. After all, the next employee having the skills to move your organization forward is quite capable of accessing employer rating websites (such as Glassdoor) for negative comments and can take their valuable talent elsewhere.

Perhaps the most influential and original treatment of talent comes from the work of Boudreau and Ramstad (2007). In their book, *Beyond HR: The New Science of Human Capital*, they present 'Talentship' as the successor to HR rather than something that exists within it, a position that represents a change in kind rather than of degree and involves a new language, focus, and mindset. Talentship doesn't involve replacing existing HR architecture, based on the need for compliance and control and the provision of expert services; rather, it represents an extension of the HR paradigm where the emphasis is on decision-making processes and the decisions that are taken over and about the organization's human resources. They describe their book as providing:

> a decision science for talent and organisation resources and how organisation leaders must learn the principles of that decision science to improve their talent decisions.

Interestingly, their definition of talent is not distinctively different from that of other writers and commentators: they define it as:

> the resource that includes the potential and realised capacities of individuals and groups and how they are organised.
> (2007: 2)

But the way they see strategically important decisions about people as *pivotal*, is. They think of pivotal as a lever where a small change at the fulcrum—the pivotal point—causes very large changes in outcomes/effects. Once identified, pivot points allow managers to make selective investments and changes in ways that produce disproportionate and high-value effects. They also make the very important distinction between pivot points that relate to processes and activities (indirectly involving people) and pivotal people. However, they question whether organizations know where their pivotal talent is, and by inference who possesses such talent, which undermines their ability to make the right investment decisions. We can from this 'lack of knowledge' make two points:

1. TM at least involves accepting and recognizing the fact that certain people possess different and more or less valuable talents and potential than other employees.

2. TM can only be successfully practised if the organization actually knows who possesses this higher-value talent and what form this talent takes.

Boudreau and Ramstad equate this 'new' approach with a different and more scientific attitude towards decision-making, claiming that the decision science for talent and organization that drives this evolution will change the game for the way people are managed. They argue that:

> **Talentship builds organisation effectiveness by improving decisions that affect or depend on human capital, where they make the biggest difference and wherever they are made.**
> **(2007: 4)**

The point made in Chapter 1 about people's asset value and the differential value of their contributions is consistent with Boudreau and Ramstad's emphasis on the need to engage in what they call 'talent segmentation'. Knowing where the marginal value of contributions and changes in the organization of work are the greatest and why is at the heart of their advocacy, as is their rejection of treating everyone the same.

It might seem to some that the claim made by Boudreau and Ramstad that they have developed or are articulating an approach to the way an organization manages its people that is significantly different from a more traditional HR approach, has definite merit. Whether it represents a new science of decision-making is more debatable. But what is of particular significance is the emphasis they give to people and their behaviour rather than the organization of activities and the delivery of HR services. In addition, the importance they attach to the measurement of behaviour that is performance critical and the use of the data generated to make informed decisions that change things that matter is very distinctive and different. In the context of TM, this means that knowing who are the most valuable people and why, and then knowing how to maximize the leverage they possess has to be based on a much more systematic understanding of cause and effect relationships.

STUDENT ACTIVITY 4.2

This activity offers the opportunity to appreciate what Boudreau and Ramstad's ideas might mean in a practical context. Read the blog by Greta Roberts (October 2015): 'The beginner's guide to predictive workforce analytics', at http://www.talentanalytics.com/blog/the-beginners-guide-to-predictive-workforce-analytics/#.Vh6Fuk2ROaI.twitter

After reading the blog, consider the implications for 'traditional' HR departments of this new emphasis and approach to decision-making.

While all of the above approaches and definitions offer something of value, many are saying essentially the same thing, and other contributions are less than helpful. Egerova (2014) believes that because most of the currently used processes of TM (she doesn't say what these are) were created almost half a century ago, it is time to create a new model. She identifies 'one of the new approaches' as integrated TM, which she defines as:

> **an innovative and holistic approach to talent management, which enables an organization to adequately and flexibly respond to changes in the business environment. The concept of integrated talent management integrates the business strategy, the human resources strategy, talent management processes and organizational culture.**
> **(2014: 5)**

So, now we have something called integrated TM which is presented as different from and above not only TM, but an organization's human resource and business strategy, its TM processes, and its culture! In our opinion this is a wholly unrealistic and highly questionable conceptualization that unnecessarily makes claims that cannot be substantiated. To be fair to Egerova, Collings and Mellahi (2009) talk about strategic TM which reminds us of the debate about HRM and SHRM. It seems pointless and unproductive to try to distinguish between two forms of TM (more may be on the horizon), whatever distinctions might be made by academics.

Why does TM need integrating? Isn't the very conception presented by Boudreau and Ramstad based on talent decisions that reflect a high level of awareness of vertical and horizontal connectivities and relationships? Rather than provide helpful insights that deepen our knowledge of TM, such 'theorizing' and the interest in 'new' models and approaches undermines the search for empirical-based evidence on the effectiveness or otherwise of TM strategies and practices and unnecessarily complicates the TM terrain and narrative. As Pfeffer (2014) observes in his insightful work on the problems facing management theory, the emphasis on theory over measurement and particularly the emphasis on new theory has resulted in the articulation of numerous theoretical ideas, many seeking recognition for simply being new. He goes on:

> Within the social sciences, only the discovery of a new fact is credited, a statement that certainly applies to management and organization studies. No big surprise, then, that since the field asks for, and in fact demands, new theory, we have new theory and new concepts in abundance. Whether this is good for either theory or practice is, of course, quite another matter. This emphasis on the new and unique as important for publication, rather than on rewarding the testing and replication of already existing theoretical ideas, and the emphasis on theory over the presentation of interesting data, has had some negative effects, many of which are predictable and some of which may at first glance seem surprising. One predictable consequence has been the proliferation of 'theories' and also writing that is filled with theoretical pretence rather than insight.

In exactly the same way that people differ in terms of their productive value, so too do journal articles and academic papers that claim to present new theoretical insights. The view we adopt is one similar to that presented by Pfeffer—that little is gained from adding more theoretical insights and new approaches to the already overcrowded field of, in his case, TM; what really needs to be the focus of research is the testing of existing TM theories/models, with an emphasis on deepening our understanding and the production of reliable evidence about what practices are effective and under what circumstances. Finally, the focus should be on developing a range of metrics to allow managers to measure return on investment in TM activities and programmes.

RESEARCH INSIGHT 4.1

To take your learning further, you may wish to read:

Vaiman, V. and Collings, D. J. (2013) 'Talent management: Advancing the field', *International Journal of Human Resource Management*, **24(9).**

The article provides an overview of the literature on TM and summarizes the main contributions on the subject.

Talent as Human Capital

One way of making sense of the growing use of the term talent is to relate it to the notion of human capital (introduced in Chapter 1). Human capital has two dimensions: the social and economic. From a social perspective, human capital represents the collection of knowledge, talents, skills, capabilities, intelligences, and wisdom that people possess, although not in equal or indeed fixed amounts. Economically, these attributes of people have a value which is determined by their contribution to the production of goods and service and to wealth-creating process. So, talent might be understood as just another way of describing human capital; the more human capital a person has, the more talented he/she may be considered—and the more value that person represents to the organization. It might be expected that the rewards a person receives will reflect broadly the value he/she represents to the organization but this assumed relationship is not always reflected in actual rewards received. This is because:

- talent/value can be hidden or denied;
- talent may not be used or allowed to be used in ways that reflect its potential;
- rewards are not sufficiently flexible to reflect changes in talent/value;
- rewards reflect other influences in addition to people's value.

Human capital has long been associated with the resource-based view of the firm (RBV) which sees an organization's unique resources and human capabilities as explaining differences in competitive advantage. Clearly, what we mean by talent is very close to or identical with those human capital attributes such as education, experience, skills, and capabilities, and the characteristics of top managers explored in the RBV literature (Barney, 1991). This kind of analysis allows us to reach two tentative conclusions:

1. Reference to top managers suggests that the meaning of talent can be linked to the characteristics and capabilities of a particular type of managerial or professional employee rather than or as well as of employees in general. So, again, competitive advantage might be more closely linked to the special talents of a small proportion of an organization's employees rather than or as well as reflecting aggregate talent levels.

2. Talent is associated with intangible assets or capabilities rather than tangible assets such as machinery, plant, technology. This means that we cannot assume the same ways of managing plant and machinery will be appropriate to managing talent. It also means talent can be difficult to measure and control.

Alvesson, in the context of his study of knowledge-intensive industries, makes an important distinction between what he calls human capital advantage and human process advantage:

> **The former relates to the employment of talent, the latter to difficult to imitate, highly evolved processes within a firm, such as cross-departmental co-operation and executive development.**
> **(2004: 139)**

From this, it follows that the critical issue in managing talent is to recruit and retain people with the best qualifications and capabilities, given existing and projected work requirements. This seems to be a fairly obvious statement but identifying high-value/talented people within the assessment and selection process requires skill levels that are not always in evidence or allowed to be applied when the selection process becomes overly procedurally driven. But the real value of Alvesson's contribution lies in his recognition that human capital, that is the individual and collective knowledge, skills, and capabilities, is only part of the TM challenge; the other is represented by the organizational processes and relationships both formal and informal that connect people together, creating human capital synergies. Alvesson's recognition of the importance of effective human processes that result in these synergistic outcomes is closely associated with the concept of social capital defined by the OECD as:

> **networks together with shared norms, values and understandings that facilitate co-operation within or among groups.**

Talent, seen from this perspective, is not only something that is owned or possessed by individuals but rather is the product and outcome of common experiences, shared understandings, mutually acceptable norms of behaviour, and a shared language, all of which become embedded in and contribute to the way culture is formed and shaped by the way people connect to each other. We might say, therefore, that a certain kind of talent is socially produced and is constantly being reproduced by the organization not although necessarily formally managed by it.

There's much debate over the various forms that social capital takes, but one fairly straightforward approach divides it into three main categories:

- Bonds: links to people based on a sense of common identity ('people like us')—such as family, close friends, and people who share our culture or ethnicity.

- Bridges: links that stretch beyond a shared sense of identity, for example to distant friends, colleagues, and associates.

- Linkages: links to people or groups further up or lower down the social ladder. The potential benefits of social capital can be seen by looking at social bonds. Friends and families can help us in lots of ways—emotionally, socially, and economically. In the United Kingdom, for example, a government survey found that more people secure jobs through personal contacts than through advertisements. Such support can be even more important in countries where the rule of law is unreliable. Interestingly, talent does not just represent value to the organization but to the person and to the communities that he/she is part of. And when an organization employs someone they are in fact potentially gaining access to the person's social as well as economic capital (OECD, 2007). The converse is also the case: losing a person means a loss of economic capital *and* social capital.

 See the Online Resources Extension Material 4.1 for further insights into the importance of social capital and social networks for attracting and retaining talent.

Again, in evaluating the contribution of both human capital and human processes to the organization, Alvesson accepts that managers may have to prioritize the two elements differently, or to put it in strategic terms, develop different human capital strategies. On the one hand, they could attempt to recruit the brightest and best available in the labour market but on the other they could accept the limitations with this, particularly the question of costs and uncertainties of recruiting and retaining 'the best' and decide to focus on their existing employees, work to make them more skilful and flexible, and emphasize the importance of developing optimal systems and procedures that facilitate social learning, cooperation, and high performance.

Of all the component elements of human capital perhaps the most frequently referred to is knowledge; talent then becomes defined in terms of what people know and what they and the organization do with this knowledge. Spender (1996) argues that knowledge and the organization's ability to generate knowledge is at the heart of the theory of the firm, and Alvesson claims that

> **Few people seem to doubt that knowledge is of the utmost significance for contemporary business and working life and that many researchers take it for granted that the foundation of industrial economies has shifted from natural resources to intellectual assets.**
> (2004: 4–5)

Interestingly, Alvesson makes the distinction between knowledge as an attribute of an individual—what a person knows—and knowledge that is embedded in an organization's culture. If knowledge can usefully be seen to be an indication of or synonymous with talent it must also be recognized that knowledge, and, by inference, talent, can exist outside as well as within the individual. This distinction equates to that made by Nonaka and Takeuchi (1995) between tacit knowledge which is internalized and controlled by the individual and explicit knowledge which is knowledge that has been 'captured' or appropriated by the organization and incorporated into operating systems, procedures, and processes. Pivotal points can be people or pools of people but they can also be found in organizational processes. Figure 4.1 shows the two forms of knowledge and their dynamic interaction.

This distinction is important for our understanding of what constitutes knowledge at the conceptual level because it points very clearly to the need to challenge one of the core elements of the dominant narrative on talent—that it is only something that people possess. Whether this point is accepted may come down

From/To	Tacit	Explicit
Tacit	*Socialization* Creates *sympathized* knowledge through the sharing of experiences, and the development of mental models and technical skills. Language unnecessary.	*Externalization* Creates *conceptual* knowledge through knowledge articulation using language. Dialogue and collective reflection needed.
Explicit	*Internalization* Creates *operational* knowledge through learning by doing. Explicit knowledge like manuals or verbal stories helpful.	*Combination* Creates systemic knowledge through the systemizing of ideas. May involve many media, and can lead to new knowledge through adding, combining, and categorizing.

Figure 4.1 The Nonaka and Takeuchi model of knowledge

Source: Ikujiro Nonaka and Toshihiro Nishiguchi (eds.), *Knowledge Emergence: Social, Technical, and Evolutionary Dimensions of Knowledge Creation* (Oxford University Press, 2001), figure 2.1 'The SECI Process', p. 18. By kind permission of Oxford University Press.

to how knowledge and talent are defined and the nature of the relationship between them. Few would argue, though, against the proposition that successful organizations invest heavily in knowledge capture and retention which is at the heart of AI and 'smart machines'. The idea of machines being talented in the way people are is however always likely to be contentious, perhaps because talent is often equated with creativity and almost unique abilities. This raises the possibility that if talent as knowledge can be appropriated by the organization then the scarcity of talented people problem could be partially alleviated by the development of strategies that facilitate appropriation, which in the long term reduces the need for organizations to be constantly competing with each other for talented and scarce human resources.

Of course, talent is not simply about knowledge, important though this component is; talent is about much more. But what? Consider the following points:

- We need to think about how knowledge is used and applied and how productive it is. The concept of knowledge or talent productivity is one that organizations need to consider very carefully as part of the way they manage talent. Do talented people who possess special and valuable attributes and competences actually use them, or are they encouraged to use them to their full potential? This raises the question of how important management strategies, motivation, and the working environment are in the liberation and application of talent (Keursten et al., 2003).

- Talented people are not only defined by what they know and achieve but also by what they are like as people and their ability to work effectively with others. The work of Daniel Goleman (2004) in developing the concept of emotional intelligence and linking this to leadership, highlights the importance of such factors as:

  - self-awareness;
  - self-regulation;
  - motivation;
  - empathy;
  - social skill;

to our understanding and appreciation of the importance of talented people relating to their inner selves and their external environment. Increasingly, the proposition that talent alone, expressed as what people know and can do, is a necessary but not sufficient condition for long-term organizational success is one that seems to be difficult to argue against. In a similar vein, Gardner (2007) articulates a belief that people—and he doesn't differentiate although there is an implicit sense that he is thinking about leaders and those that are going to make a difference to society—need to think in different ways. He argues that to deal with what is expected as well as what cannot be anticipated, a person needs to possess or cultivate different ways of thinking which he describes as:

- a disciplined mind;
- a synthesizing mind;
- a creative mind;
- a respectful mind;
- an ethical mind.

'Talent', seen from this perspective, then becomes a way of thinking as well as knowledge and the capability to achieve things. The point that emerges from these two references is that being talented is not enough; talent has to be applied, and this application has to be tempered by several key cognitive and emotional influences that also connect to an ethical framework. In this sense, we are talking about talent being channelled in the right direction and applied to the achievement of outcomes that are both self-serving and socially responsible.

Talent as Hidden Potential

Much of the earlier literature on talent reflected a view that talent was something that was scarce, special, and undermanaged, particularly in the context of business organizations where the shortage of talented managers as well as other professionals was seen as an urgent and challenging issue. This notion that talent is associated with a limited number of 'special' people is critical to understanding the range of TM strategies advocated by consultancies like McKinsey who advise companies on how to, among other things, retain their talented people. In the context of encouraging them to stay, they comment:

> **Making sure top performers' compensation is significantly higher than that of their average colleagues is a relatively straightforward way to keep the exit price high and raise barriers to poaching. When a senior manager at GE was told a division was going to give its highest performers a 10 percent salary increase and its average performers 5 percent, he said, 'Ten percent? Not nearly aggressive enough! Go for 15 percent, 20 percent, or 30 percent!'**
> (Chambers et al., 2007)

But what if the problem is framed differently? We have consistently argued that how managers and HR professionals make sense of the challenge and then frame the problem that has to be addressed is critical to the choice of strategies the organization deploys to meet the challenges it faces. While this still remains a key point, what also has to be recognized is that unless the challenges are accurately identified and understood, the choice of strategies becomes compromised. As an example, what if the basic premise that talent is both scarce and restricted to a relatively limited number of people is only partially correct? Not only would the way the problem or challenge being framed be different, so too would the actions and strategies taken by management as a consequence of this different understanding.

This is precisely the position adopted by O'Reilly and Pfeffer (2000) in their book *Hidden Talent*. While accepting that organizations need great people, and that effective recruitment and retention are important, they argue that companies need something else which is actually more difficult to achieve. They believe that talent is much more about organizational cultures and systems and management practices that produce extraordinary results from almost anyone. Their argument is simple but persuasive. If talent is seen as something only the top 10 per cent of people possess then the only effective strategy companies have is to compete with each other for this scarce resource, which can only result in a zero-sum game and the cost of paying talented people keeps rising. Winning the 'war' can therefore be costly and not without undesirable consequences. They see the alternative or complementary strategy of building an organization which encourages and facilitates all employees to perform to the limits of their abilities while more difficult to achieve is one that will produce long-term success and satisfaction and is much harder to copy. Instead of buying talent, they propose that the talent that exists within each employee is recognized, nurtured, and utilized. Talent from this perspective is seen as hidden, not scarce, and flexible in the sense that it can emerge as abilities are recognized and liberated and can grow in absolute terms as people's potential is also recognized and developed. Their central argument is encapsulated in the following statement:

> Hiring and retaining talent is great. Building a company that creates and uses talent is even better. (2000: 2)

This line of thinking is closely related to another important insight into the way organizations function—the unintended but damaging consequences associated with suppressing identification with and commitment to organizational interests, putting obstacles in place to higher levels of effort and performance and demotivating people. According to O'Reilly and Pfeffer (2000) TM involves, among other things:

- the removal of obstacles and blockages that prevent talent being recognized and used; and
- creating a stronger relationship between individual and the organizational interests, which isn't just about encouraging people to identify with the organization but also about leaders connecting with the workforce.

In this respect, they quote George Zimmer, founder and then CEO of the US retail company, Men's Wearhouse:

> Most business practices repress our natural tendency to have fun and socialise. The idea seems to be that in order to succeed you have to suffer . . . I believe an organisation that is authentically built on servant leadership, where people are not just trying to acquire for themselves and where they see cooperative effort that is all around them, ends up affecting things in very metaphysical ways. When people feel connected to something with a purpose greater than themselves, it inspires people to reach for levels they might otherwise not attain . . . Our business is based on human potential.

O'Reilly and Pfeffer are redefining the narrative on talent and placing it within a much wider analysis of the kind of organizational environment that helps to bring the best out in people and of course the reverse being an analysis of the kind of environment that suppresses human endeavour and the human spirit. They argue that:

> Those companies that have developed positive and constructive, as opposed to toxic, workplaces won't ever notice a talent drought because they currently enjoy, and will continue to enjoy, a surfeit of applications and loyal employees.

In this, they are saying something quite profound but which many UK and foreign-owned companies identify with: efforts to develop a positive employer brand, becoming an employer of first choice, and creating an emotionally secure and purposeful working environment characterize many of the most successful companies not only in the UK but worldwide. There is both a transactional and transformational element in the way they recognize the importance of aligning an organization's purpose with the spirit of their employees, offering them a sense of community, security, and mutual trust that facilitates the capture of employees' emotional as well as intellectual energies.

Consider the extract below taken from a newspaper article which relates to a recent visit to Apple's London offices by Tim Cook CEO:

> Staff rarely choose to leave Apple of their own volition: in many cases, they work there for years. The company enjoys extremely high levels of employee retention and loyalty—and from the scene in the Covent Garden store in London on Friday morning, the last stop on a whirlwind tour of Europe and Israel by the Apple boss, it's not difficult to see why.
>
> Cook and *The Telegraph* entered a rear entrance; nobody at the store bar the manager knew of the visit. I have witnessed many shop, office and factory visits before, with bosses being received in a variety of ways. In some cases, they were welcome but often they were met with indifference or, of course, outright hostility. But the reaction at the Covent Garden store was off the charts: the staff gasped, and then burst into spontaneous, loud applause as soon as they spotted Cook, who walked in behind them.
>
> (Heath, 2015)

Much of what this 'alternative' narrative is about is leadership which is not confined to the business context. There are numerous examples from sport where a group of players with the same level of talent that they had under one manager/coach will perform significantly better under another. As an example, consider the case of the English Rugby Union team that were knocked out of the 2015 World Cup at the first stage. With largely the same players, England became a different side under the new head coach Eddie Jones. They were undefeated in 2016, winning thirteen consecutive matches, including the Six Nations Grand Slam and all three matches against Australia, in Australia. What explains this transformation in sustained performance? Partly it was about creating a new vision—of being the best and winning the next world cup. Second, there was a change in mindset of the players who not only wanted to be the best but believed they could be. Third, a new approach to training was introduced to make the squad fitter, faster, and more aggressive. Finally, it involved setting high and demanding standards in everything the squad and the coaching staff did, with no exceptions or excuses. Time and time again the same group of employees/players perform differently and better for different managers/leaders and coaches—and the secret is? It's in the mind.

 Signpost Chapter 5: Ethics and Leadership in HRM, for different conceptualizations of leading and leadership.

 STUDENT ACTIVITY 4.3

Think of the organization you work for or have experience of in relation to its structure, culture, and management practices.

1. Consider whether the *full range* of talents that people have are recognized and understood by managers, and if not why not. Use a scale of 1–10 where the lower figure represents a serious under-utilization. Which talents are not being recognized?

2. Assess whether these talents are being *fully utilized*; if not, why not?

3. Identify any blockages to the use of talent and establish the cause.

4. Think about what managers could do differently to remove these blockages or at least reduce their impact.

5. What kind of reaction do your CEO/senior managers get when they appear informally on the premises? If they don't engage at the informal level, what might this say about the way they manage talent?

Bringing together the different conceptualizations of talent considered above, we can construct a basic talent model, shown in Figure 4.2. As a seminar activity, you could take Figure 4.2 and develop a more sophisticated version and present it for critical discussion.

Figure 4.2 A basic talent model

HRM INSIGHT 4.2 **The John Carney story**

John Carney worked as a management strategy lecturer in Midtown University located in one of the UK's older industrial cities. He had enjoyed a successful managerial career in a major utility company, reaching senior management level with extensive experience of managing major projects. He had an extensive professional network and was highly respected for his ability to 'make things happen'. The department he worked for at the university was headed by an accountant who had spent most of his working life in either professional practice or lecturing, and had developed a rather conservative and risk-averse approach to managing the department. John arranged to see his departmental head and presented him with a proposal that John thought would be of real interest and contribute to the department's full cost income. John outlined the proposal which involved:

- Working with the UK Department of Enterprise on an EU-funded business growth development project in the Czech Republic.

- The university being designated the 'academic partner' with responsibility for supplying management experts who would visit small and medium-sized companies in the Republic to help develop managerial capapabilities.

- The university would be paid 1.5 times the salaries of those staff involved with all travel, administration, replacement, and management costs covered in full.

The head told John that he needed to think about the proposal and discuss it with the university's director of enterprise. A week later John received an email to the effect that the university would not be participating in the project and despite further meetings this decision remained unchanged.

Questions

1. What effect do you think this decision had on John Carney and other members of staff?

2. What opportunities were lost by the decision?

3. What might have explained the decision of the head not to participate in the project?

TM from an Applied Perspective

As with all management theories, concepts, and models, however interesting they might appear, the only meaningful test of their value, at least to managers, is whether they help in making sense of a particular phenomenon or activity and offer insights into how it could be better managed. If we equate TM, as many have done, with existing aspects of HR, then we retain the existing paradigm with changes only experienced in terms of improvements in the way such activities as recruitment and retention strategies, career and succession planning and development are carried out. But if we see TM from the perspective of Boudreau and Ramstad—as involving the application of a different mindset with an emphasis on optimizing marginal value gains through the manipulation of key human and organizational pivot points—then there are genuine and significant opportunities for developing new ways of managing based on the idea of greater segmentation and differentiation of human resources. Their emphasis on a new 'decision science paradigm' where all TM decisions are closely aligned with leveraging higher-value outputs provides a much-needed alternative perspective, emphasizing less what TM involves and more about what it should be contributing to. The purpose of this final section is, therefore, to explore and review developments in TM practice to critically evaluate the claims of those who believe that effective TM is key to achieving organizational success. The question we are interested in is: what do organizations do or should they do to translate the potential TM offers into concrete organizational actions that produce the outcomes that contribute to this?

In their introductory chapter to the *Talent Management Handbook*, Berger and Berger (2011) articulate a TM model that they claim is used by high-performing organizations. Their model is based on three inter-related components:

- a talent creed;
- a talent strategy; and
- a talent system.

Creed

Berger and Berger (2011) define creed as consisting of a widely publicized set of core principles, values, and mutual expectations that guide individual and collective behaviour. A creed described in this way is akin to a philosophy which we refer frequently to throughout the book as the foundation and defining feature of many successful businesses. This creed, they argue, to be effective, needs to be incorporated into all the important TM activities such as in selection criteria and standards, competency definitions, performance criteria, and development processes. Such a creed represents a set of guiding principles and framework within which people/talent as well as the business are managed.

A creed isn't about differentiation and segmentation but it could well represent an important pivot point. A creed equates to a statement about what the organization is like, how it operates, how it treats its staff, and how it connects to its external community. As such it represents a blueprint for its culture and we know that organizations with strong and supportive cultures are associated with high performance and long-term success.

One of the more interesting elements in what organizations are increasingly committed to as part of their creed relates to employee well-being. Initially defined in terms of physical health and wellness it now embraces psychological and social components: for example are employees enthusiastic and positive about their jobs or frustrated, stressed, and unhappy? Do they feel part of a community from which they give and receive support and rewards? A TM mindset would see well-being as a potentially important pivot point that would justify investments in creating an environment in which well-being was highly valued and desired (Mehta, 2016). Payoffs would be in the form of reduced sickness absence and associated costs, higher retention levels, and a more productive workforce. A similar argument could be made for employee engagement as an area to invest in. The CIPD (2012) reported a significant relationship between high levels of workforce engagement and top-performing organizations. Towers Perrin (2003), after comparing companies with low and high engagement levels, found that on three measures of financial performance those with high engagement scores performed significantly better than those with low scores. Notwithstanding methodological issues, such statistical correlations and strong associations do point to the value of incorporating employee well-being and engagement into any TM strategy explicitly through its creed.

Strategy

According to Berger and Berger (2011) the purpose of a TM strategy is to make explicit the types of investments in people an organization needs to make to ensure future success. Components of this strategy involve:

- Cultivating and investing in the what they call super-keepers, which is just another way of describing the small percentage of highly talented and valuable employees, the loss of whom would severely damage the long-term future of the organization. Of course, the idea that organizations should differentiate employees based on talent value sits uneasily for some who believe that employees should as far as possible be treated the same; that pay and other rewards should be determined by people's job/grade rather than performance/value. This is a position more strongly associated with public sector institutions and collective bargaining, but it is one that is increasingly under pressure as its limitations and failure to reflect real differences in talent, abilities, and value become more apparent and difficult to justify.

- Retain key position backups—this is essentially about having an effective succession planning programme in place that produces high-quality replacements for designated key positions. Not all need to be key and much depends on what criteria are used to differentiate position importance but this is another example of differentiation in use. Berger and Berger suggest the following criteria to help identify which positions need backup:

  - Immediacy—short-term loss of incumbent would seriously affect profit, revenue growth, and other important objectives.
  - Uniqueness—the position requires competences that are unlikely to be found outside the organization or industry.
  - Demand—labour market pressures create high levels of competition for the people who can do the job.
  - Strategic impact—losing the incumbent without a qualified replacement would affect future success.

A critical part of any TM strategy is the approach taken to the way the organization invests in its people, and by investments we mean the allocation of resources and opportunities. There are different areas/activities that provide investment opportunities but the ones below probably constitute the more familiar and used ones:

- **Rewards.** Chapter 13 deals with the management of rewards in detail; the point to be made here is that managers have choices in the kinds of rewards they offer employees and particularly in the way these are allocated. Wage and salary grades offer annual incremental gains irrespective of value or performance and through collective bargaining annual wage increases are paid to everyone, again irrespective of any criteria other than being employed. The question is, are these reward practices consistent with an approach linking rewards to talent, value, and achievement? This may be seen as controversial, but HRM Insight 4.3 illustrates how thinking and practice even in the public sector is changing as far as TM is concerned.

Signpost to Chapter 13: Managing Rewards, for insights into different organizational reward strategies.

HRM INSIGHT 4.3 Changing reward practices with UK teaching

Historically, the payment of teachers in the state system has been determined and regulated by the process of collective bargaining. This has led to a grade structure which provides annual incremental increases within each grade and the opportunity to receive higher pay through promotion into another pay grade. In addition, annual pay increases are applied to all grade pay points. The problem that became increasingly obvious was that 'bad' teachers were being paid the same as 'good' teachers in the same grade and older but perhaps less effective teachers could be, and in certain cases were, being paid considerably more than younger but more talented teachers.

While not the only explanation of poor achievement standards in some state schools, the lack of pay and reward flexibility was recognized by many, although not by teaching unions, as a contributory factor. In a Department of Education publication (2013), new regulations were announced that allowed head teachers in all state schools to develop pay policies tailored to their schools' needs, helping them attract and retain talented teachers in the subject areas they know they need. In was claimed that:

Evidence shows that improving the quality of teaching is essential to raising standards in schools. According to the Sutton Trust, the difference between a very good teacher and a bad teacher may be equivalent to a whole year's education for a disadvantaged pupil.

We made a similar point in Chapter 1, on the different outcomes that can be achieved from people with different talents and motivations. HRM Insight 4.3 illustrates this in a specific context. It also illustrates how significant productivity improvements can be achieved through changes in TM practices.

- **Training.** Historically, training was often associated with what was euphemistically called 'the sheep dip' approach, where, irrespective of need or interest all people within the same group or category were required to attend training courses on the same topics. Today, although there is more choice and flexibility with regard to training courses much training that is made available is still based on collective participation, with everyone exposed to the same experience. Although there has been an increase in the emphasis given to learning rather than training, the critical question is still about the criteria used to decide on the allocation of training/learning resources and opportunities. A TM mindset would probably result in resources being concentrated rather than widely distributed with much higher expectations of outcomes being applied to the participants. Participation is no longer enough; relevance, value, and behavioural outcomes are increasingly being questioned and expected. In addition, questions such as the following can help in the allocation decisions:

  - Has the person had these kinds of opportunities before and have they taken advantage of them?
  - Has the person's value to the organization increased as a result of these opportunities?
  - Should the emphasis now be on the use of newly acquired competencies and experiences rather than on further development opportunities?
  - Has the person involved been identified in any succession planning plan?

Given that segmentation and discrimination, for the right reasons, seem to be central features of a TM strategy, the basic premise must be that the allocation of resources has to be socially fair but economically justifiable. Here we have to confront the possible existence of competing ideologies, where on the one hand equal opportunities and the requirement to avoid wherever possible discrimination in the way people are treated may conflict with more objectively based criteria to do with value, potential, performance, and estimates of returns on investment in human capital. According to Berger and Berger (2011) many US organizations are classifying their employees according to their value and long-term potential and distribution (nominal) within the workforce, as follows:

- Super-keepers (3 per cent)—employees who greatly exceed expectations and are seen as critical to the future success of the organization.

- Keepers (20 per cent)—employees who exceed expectations and are predicted to continue to do so in the future.

- Solid citizens (75 per cent)—employees who are doing an acceptable to good job and who generally meet expectations.

- Misfits (2 per cent)—employees who have performed at below expectation and are unlikely to change in the future.

The process by which people are located into these categories can vary and reflect contextual circumstances and practices, but the appraisal of performance, annual reviews, and career progression profiles can all provide data that allows segmentation decisions to be made. These decisions help to create an overview of the employee population profile in terms of the actual proportion in each category and form the basis of investment and resource allocation decisions.

The interest in segmenting the workforce and the development of different segmentation models is not new and reflects developments in other management disciplines; it could be argued that:

Just as a marketer segments or stratifies their clients, products, and services according to their value, the same principles should apply to segmenting the workforce. Segmentation is the key to treating workforce assets as a portfolio that can be analysed and managed.

Many writers on TM believe that segmentation and the choice of segmentation models is fundamental to analysing and understanding the workforce and developing a rational and consistent approach to addressing the people management dilemmas and challenges in the twenty-first-century workplace. But although segmentation models have been in existence for many years, most are based on the hierarchical organization where position in the hierarchy, wage/salary, and job responsibility are used to indicate limits of authority and influence and possibly 'importance'. But in the context of contemporary approaches to TM the limitations of these models and the lack of any explicit reference to value and future rather than historical importance they are increasingly seen as dated and inappropriate. Wage/salary and organizational levels don't necessarily indicate the importance of a role or person to the achievement of the business strategy and impact on business outcomes (i.e. value creation, competitive advantage). The decision of companies to strip out layers of management, often at senior levels, not only indicates a trend to flatter organizational hierarchies but also suggests that many senior managers are considered as expensive costs rather than as value-adding assets. Rolls-Royce, for example, is reported to have doubled the number of senior management job cuts in Derby for 2016 to 400 and is stepping up the cull of senior managers, cutting almost one-fifth of the 2,000 bosses worldwide while at the same time the company has been hiring on the factory floor (Kollewe, 2016).

More specifically, hierarchical segmentation models don't provide definitive answers to the following key workforce questions:

- How do various roles and contributions relate to the business strategy and desired outcomes?

- How do you determine what really are the critical roles in your organization and which people should you be investing disproportionally in, that is developing people in-house to take on key roles?

- Which key roles should be filled from outside and why?

- Which jobs/job categories can be outsourced? A TM strategy may involve sufficient flexibility to allow certain work to be done by external organizations with greater expertise than is possessed in-house.

- How should the attraction, engagement, and retention strategies differ for these various roles?

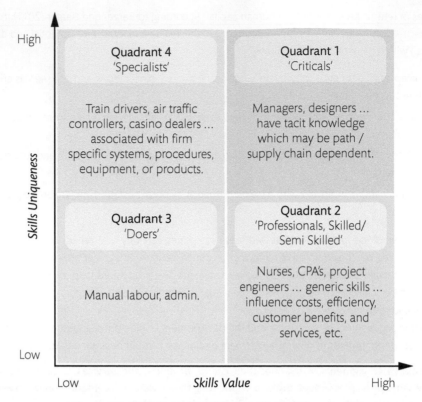

Figure 4.3 Skills-based workforce segmentation model

Source: Beames, C. 'Workforce Segmentation: A Skills' Based Approach', http://www.businessperform.com/talent-management/skills-based-workforce-segmentation.html. Reproduced with the kind permission of Colin Beames.

Contemporary segmentation models, often based on skills or competences, but implicitly incorporating measures of value, offer insights into these questions, and help managers make better investment and other human capital decisions. Based on the generic skills segmentation model in Figure 4.3, the link between relationships, skills, value, and investment decisions can clearly be seen.

RESEARCH INSIGHT 4.2

To take your learning further you may wish to read:

Melton, J. et al. (2011). 'Using employee segmentation to bring out the best in your workforce', *Bain & Company Insights* (12 August).

This article will help you develop more insight into the business and ethical case for treating people differently based on economic and financial considerations.

TM system (TMS)

TM creeds and strategies, to be effective, need to be implemented and that is the function of the TMS, which can be understood as:

A set of procedures and processes that translate an organization's talent creed and strategy into a diagnostic and implementation programme designed to achieve desired outcomes and objectives.

Most TMSs rely heavily on assessment techniques and the rating of one person by another or a group of others, based on different kinds of information, diagnostic processes, and monitoring activities. Assessment is arguably at the centre of any systematic process that results in informed investment and career development decisions precisely because the outcome of assessment techniques is information and knowledge about each individual. Without such understanding of what a person has done, is doing, and probably will be able to do any decision becomes problematic and based more on subjectivity than on verifiable facts.

There are different kinds of *assessment practices* but the most common seem to involve:

- **Competency assessment.** There are numerous bespoke and generic competences, many designed for managerial work and professional occupations such as teachers and medics and for specific occupations and crafts (see Goleman, 2004). The challenge is, however, not only in establishing the relevance of the model for particular organizations and the strength of the relationship between competency scores/levels and performance outcomes, but in the way that they are assessed and the reliability of the assessment process. Fundamentally, competences can be assessed through the gathering of objective evidence, from different rating techniques, or through more subjective judgements and feedback from different stakeholders. But competency assessment only allows inferences to be made about a person's ability to do the job, not how well they do it or how much value the person represents to the organization. As such, competences frameworks and the assessment of competences are less important to organizations developing a TM approach to managing people than they might be to those characterized by bureaucracy and hierarchy.

- **Performance appraisal (PA).** This is perhaps the most commonly used rating technique despite continued criticism about its effectiveness (Coens and Jenkins, 2000). In its formal expression, PA involves usually one person rating or assessing the previous year's performance of a subordinate, but this process essentially is about what has been, or is thought to have been achieved, and in certain schemes how outcomes have been achieved, based on evidence from different sources. As with many rating techniques, the quality of the evidence used is critical to their value as is the ability of the rater to avoid bias in the way judgements are made. Past performance does not guarantee future performance but it can be indicative and predictive when other sources of information are taken into account.

- **Potential forecasting.** By definition, this is more problematic than reviewing past performance, but, as we have argued earlier, potential is a key factor in assessing a person's human asset value. A person's potential contributions and capabilities will be enhanced as a result of appropriate developmental investments and this means that potential is a variable and is contingent on other factors. In sports, a person's potential to be better and possibly the best tends to be identified earlier than later in his/her sporting career based on performance, achievements, and comparisons with others.

Many of the above practices involve the use of measurement scales. Although the choice of how performance and potential are measured and expressed might not seem to be of particular importance this is not the case. Numerical scales from 1 to 5 for example and numerical scales with accompanying definitions and explanations can be influential in affecting choices and decisions made. First, there is the question of what they mean and second how they should be interpreted. Many decisions affecting selection for jobs, promotion, and training/development are subject to the effects of the design and application of measurement scales which often involve simple categories of ranking, achievement, potential, and performance. People involved in the use of measurement instruments and techniques will know that the process of scoring individuals can never be wholly objective and can reflect personal bias and political considerations and pressures, where the desirability of a particular outcome influences the interpretation and rating of particular criteria.

 See the Online Resources Extension Material 4.2 for further insights into the use of HR data in the development of TM strategies.

The two main *diagnostic processes* used in TM are succession planning and career planning. With the former, decisions are taken as to which are the critical positions that might require to be filled under different scenarios, three of the most frequently experienced being retirement, promotion, and career advancement outside the host organization. Predicting which jobs/job holders need suitably qualified people to be ready to take over with the minimum of disruption is a key objective of TM.

Career planning involves assessing the career paths of those identified as having special talents and potential and is closely linked to succession planning. Critical to this process is the ability to identify people who exhibit the indicators of future leadership potential and/or have the potential to take on key responsibilities relatively quickly. Career plans which may also be described as development plans involve a range of different activities and involvements, including:

- participation on management development programmes;
- leadership training;
- work shadowing;
- secondments;
- individual/group projects;

and are designed to prepare people for both planned and unexpected promotions, replacements, and key deputy roles.

Many organizations engage in one or more of these assessment and diagnostic practices, but those with a coherent and integrated approach to TM are characterized by what Dave Ulrich said distinguished effective HR functions from those that were frequently criticized for their lack of strategic impact—the ability to engage in important and relevant activities that also produce strategically valuable outcomes. Bringing together the results of diagnostic assessment processes to formulate a dynamic picture which integrates changing organizational requirements with current and future human capital capabilities is what helps to give TM its distinctiveness and relevance to the more competitive and fast changing environments of the twenty-first century where the quality of human capital (talent) is often the key to competitive advantage and success.

RESEARCH INSIGHT 4.3

To take your learning further, you may wish to read:

Gandhi, D. and Kumar, P. (2014) 'Succession planning: Developing leaders for tomorrow to ensure organizational success', *International Journal of Business & Management*, 2(3).

What are the key arguments presented by the authors that support the use of succession planning? What developmental experiences are linked to the creation of leadership capabilities?

The final element in the TM system involves a *monitoring and controlling function* that provides feedback and intelligence on the effectiveness of the TM strategy and on the kinds of decisions that need to be made to avoid the following situations:

- Too many people in the talent pipeline in relation to expected future opportunities.
- Current position holders not classified as high performers or with potential to become one who are blocking the advancement of others.
- Problem employees defined as those with performance problems being left in post without appropriate action being taken. This can include training where lack of competency is considered the major cause of underperformance, the opportunity to improve, or in other cases transfer/termination.

- The allocations of rewards and development opportunities spread too thinly with consequential reduced impact.
- Where those not included in mainstream leadership or management development programmes are not provided with any opportunities to learn, improve, or increase their contributions.

As with any form of HR intervention, the importance of trying to establish whether it has been effective is critical to taking appropriate action—to continue with the strategy, modify it, or implement an alternative. Precise measures of effectiveness are unlikely to be available and realistically it makes sense to think in terms of looking for indicators of success. Berger and Berger offer three criteria to support the monitoring process:

1. **Quality**—are people ready in sufficient numbers to take over key roles and is there evidence that the process of succession and replacement is working. They also suggest that while it is not possible to establish causal relationships, evidence needs to be collected on changes in possible key indicators such as retention rates, surpluses and shortages, number of blocking employees/managers, and engagement levels, recognizing that most of these are likely to reflect other HR interventions and practices in addition to those directly related to the TM strategy.

2. **Timeliness**—are the decision-making processes associated with the management of talent operating within an appropriate time frame, and are the inputs from senior managers and other stakeholders being made at the right time to have maximum effect.

3. **Credibility**—do managers and employees understand and believe in the strategy and the implementation system and does it meet the tests of ethical acceptability and fairness.

Summary

- There is little doubt that the interest in talent is growing and that many organizations are beginning to explore new ideas and approaches to the way they acquire, utilize, and retain talented people. From a review of selected literature, it is clear that for some the terms talent and TM mean something very similar to people and people management (HR). But other writers locate TM or talentship as Boudreau and Ramstad prefer to describe it, as the core of what HR represents.

- A different mindset and approach is needed to the way people are managed and used in organizations to maximize their contributions and grow as human beings and productive resources. Moving towards a talent mindset within an HR framework will require an assessment of long-standing practices, particularly those relating to reward and development.

- It is almost inevitable that a focus on the individual will gradually gain greater importance, challenging the default position where treating everyone by reference to common standards tends to dominate thinking and shapes what HR does. By this we mean that the individualization of HR, driven by the TM movement, will replace many HR practices where people are grouped together, treated as having the same value and potential and requiring the same opportunities and rewards appropriate to their position and occupation.

- Implementing effective TM strategies that do have a strategic impact will almost certainly require HR to be strategically engaged and to develop flexible practices that are also consistent with organizational values.

Visit the **online resources** that accompany this book for self-test questions, web links, and more information on the topics covered in this chapter, at: **www.oup.com/uk/banfield3e/**

REVIEW QUESTIONS

1. What are the different ways talent can be conceptualized?

2. What does 'investing in talent' involve and why is it justified?

3. What are pivot points and what are the key pivot points in TM?

4. Is career development only about succession planning? If not, why not?

CASE STUDY   TM in Continental Travel

Continental Travel was founded by Alex Wilson twenty-five years ago. Alex was a French teacher who travelled every year during the holidays to the south of France; it was during one of his trips that he began to think about organizing holidays for people there. His original idea was that he would focus on the 'mature' market and provide guided tours from the UK to France. Over the years the business grew rapidly as the baby-boomer generation retired and had the time and money to enjoy travel and holidays. The company organized tours in over twenty countries worldwide but Europe was still the destination for the majority of customers.

Alex based his business in Derby where, over the years, turnover reached £35m and his staff grew to sixty, a number that excluded the self-employed tour guides the company used. The management structure was uncomplicated, with Alex as CEO responsible for building the business and adding new destinations, and a company secretary responsible for legal, financial, and administrative matters. The bulk of the staff were employed in general administration, finance, customer liaison, and operations, with each section supervised by a single, experienced person.

Jenny Harper had worked for Continental Travel for eleven years and had worked her way up to operations manager. This was a key role and involved the detailed organizing and planning of each tour; she had a team of twelve who reported to her, but no deputy. As the business grew, additional staff were recruited but apart from employment procedures and legal compliance there was little in the way of an HR function. There were no formal appraisals, developmental activities, or forward planning of HR requirements.

Alex had recently attended a CIPD-organized conference on TM and had realized just how little the business actually managed its people and their talents, but as work pressures grew and competition increased, he knew that he needed to do something!

Questions

1. What are Alex's priorities in developing a more proactive TM strategy?

2. What kind of career development policy would make sense in the context of the company's size and opportunities?

3. If anything happened to Alex, what might the company need to have in place?

4. What can be done to alleviate the pressure Jenny is working under?

5. How can those staff with real potential be identified and nurtured?

Insights and Outcomes: visit the **online resources** at **www.oup.com/uk/banfield3e/** for suggested answers to these case study questions.

FURTHER READING

Aguinis, H. and O'Boyle E. (2014) 'Star performers in twenty-first-century organizations', *Personnel Psychology*, 67(2), 313–50.

CIPD (2016) 'The future of talent in Singapore 2030'.

Dries, N. (2013) 'The psychology of talent management: a review and research agenda', *Human Resource Management Review*, 23(4), 272–85.

REFERENCES

Alvesson, M. (2004) *Knowledge Work and Knowledge-Intensive Firms*, Oxford University Press.

Ashton, C. and Morton, L. (2005) 'Managing talent for competitive advantage: Taking a systemic approach to talent management', *Strategic HR Review*, 4(5).

Barney, J. (1991) 'Firm resources and sustained competitive advantage', *Journal of Management*, 17(1), 99–120.

BBC (2014) 'North Sea oil industry "close to collapse"', 18 December, at: http://www.bbc.co.uk/news/business-30525539

Berger, L. A. and Berger, D. R. (eds.) (2011) *The Talent Management Handbook*, McGraw-Hill.

Boudreau, J. W. and Ramstad, P. M. (2007) *Beyond HR: The New Science of Human Capital*, Harvard Business School Press.

Chambers, E. G. et al. (2007) *The War for Talent*, McKinsey Quarterly, at: http://www.executivesondemand.net/managementsourcing/images/stories/artigos_pdf/gestao/The_war_for_talent.pdf

CIPD (2007) 'Research insight on talent management'.

CIPD (2012) 'Managing for sustainable employee engagement', at: https://www.cipd.co.uk/binaries/managing-for-sustainable-employee-engagement-developing-a-behavioural-framework_2012.pdf

CIPD (2015) *Resourcing and Talent Planning 2015* [survey report].

Coens, T. and Jenkins, M. (2000) *Abolishing Performance Appraisals*, Jossey-Bass.

Collings, D. G. and Mellahi, K. (2009) 'Strategic talent management: A review and research agenda', *Human Resource Management Review*, 19(4), 304–13.

Devine, M. and Powell, M. (2008) 'Talent management in the public sector', *Ashridge Journal*, (autumn), at: https://www.ashridge.org.uk/Media-Library/Ashridge/PDFs/Publications/TalentManagementInThePublicSector.pdf

Egerova, D. (2014) 'Talent management—Towards the new perspectives', *Problems of Management in the 21st Century*, 9(2), at: http://oaji.net/articles/2014/450-1410981423.pdf

Gardner, H. (2007) *Five Minds for the Future*, Harvard Business School Press.

Goleman, D. (2004) 'What makes a leader?', *Harvard Business Review* (January).

Heath, A. (2015) 'Apple watch will replace your car keys, says Tim Cook', *The Telegraph*, 27 February.

Keursten, P. et al. (2003) 'Knowledge productivity in organizations: Towards a framework for research and practice', paper presented at AHRD Academy of Human Resource Development (Conference Proceedings, vol. 2, pp. 892–9). Minneapolis, 27 February–2 March.

Kollewe, J. (2016) 'Rolls-Royce to cut 400 senior management jobs', *Guardian*, 28 July.

Lewis, R. E. and Heckman, R. J. (2006) 'Talent management: A critical review', *Human Resource Management Review*, 16, at: http://www.cnproje.com/pdf/l23.pdf

McKinsey Quarterly (1998) *The War for Talent*.

Mehta, N. (2016) 'Keeping employee wellbeing at the heart of your talent management strategy', *HR Review*, 8 April.

Melton, J. et al. (2011). 'Using employee segmentation to bring out the best in your workforce', *Bain & Company Insights*, 12 August.

Newcombe, T. (2013) 'Half the entire oil and gas workforce could retire by 2015, warns former SVP HR, Seadrill', at: http://www.hrmagazine.co.uk/hro/

news/1076591/half-entire-oil-gas-workforce-retire-2015-warns-svp-hr-eadrill#sthash.sZhYo5E4.dpuf

Nonaka, I. and Takeuchi, H. (1995) *The Knowledge-Creating Company*, Oxford University Press.

OECD (2007) *Human Capital: How What You Know Shapes Your Life*.

Orr, B. and McVerry, B. (2007) 'Talent management challenge in the oil and gas industry', *Natural Gas and Electricity* (December), 18–23.

Pfeffer, J. (2005) 'Changing mental models: HR's most important task', *Human Resource Management*, 44(2).

Pfeffer, J. (2014) 'The management theory morass: Some modest proposals', in J. Miles (ed.), *New Directions in Management and Organization Theory*, Cambridge Scholars.

Pfeffer, J. and O'Reilly, C. A. (2000) *Hidden Value*, Harvard Business School Press.

Spender, J. C (1996) 'Making knowledge the basis of a dynamic theory of the firm', *Strategic Management Journal*, 17(2).

Towers Perin (2003) 'Engaged employees drive the bottom line', at: http://www.twrcc.co.za/Engaged%20employees%20drive%20the%20bottom%20line.pdf

Vaiman, V. and Collings, D. J. (2013) 'Talent management: Advancing the field', *International Journal of Human Resource Management*, 24(9).

Weick, K. (2001) *Making Sense of the Organisation*, Blackwell.

World Economic Forum (2016) 'Employment trends', at: http://reports.weforum.org/future-of-jobs-2016/employment-trends

Ethics and Leadership in HRM

5

Introduction

Without being precise, recent concerns over the ethical dimension of business and more specifically the role and contribution of HR in ensuring ethical standards and ethical behaviour at work, might be linked to events that have happened since the new millennium and to the impact on public consciousness of a number of more recent high-profile scandals and public reports into organizational failings. Whether public concern with organizational ethics is greater now than it used to be is difficult to know, if indeed it is knowable, but a recent survey by the Institute of Business Ethics found that 38 per cent of the British public believe that business behaviour is in general not ethical (Wheldon and Webley, 2013).

In Chapter 1 we highlighted the case of the Enron Corporation in the US as an example of corporate greed, management dishonesty, and questionable accounting practices. But Enron is only one of many examples we could highlight that raise serious issues and questions about the acceptable limits of corporate behaviour. The economic recession of 2007/8 was the result of economic forces that few were able to predict, and its causes are still being debated. However, at least one major explanation for the wrongdoings of international banks and the behaviour of some of their staff in the way they mis-sold financial products, lies in the absence of a sufficiently strong ethical framework within those organizations. We could also point to the effect of personal greed, the dysfunctional effects of financial reward systems, and the absence of effective management controls as factors that contributed to the systemic failings in corporate behaviour. Of course, it would be wrong to suggest that business in general was guilty of unethical practices but there was and probably still is a perception that the financial sector at least behaved as though it had little or no responsibility to act ethically; it was almost as though ethics was something business didn't have to worry about.

The public sector has also not been immune from criticisms about low standards of corporate behaviour. We mentioned the Francis Report into the North Staffordshire Hospital Trust in Chapter 1, in which Francis found evidence of poor leadership, dysfunctional departments, below acceptable standards of care, and systemic failings that were not addressed by senior management. The BBC has also come in for serious criticisms for its ethical standards and lack of open and transparent management, with the former human resources director being criticized by the Parliamentary Public Accounts Committee for potentially misleading them over the oral evidence she gave in December 2013 on BBC severance packages for senior executives (House of Commons Public Accounts Committee, 2013).

We explore in more detail both of these examples of corporate wrongdoing later in the chapter. The point is that while levels of unethical behaviour may not be significantly different now than they were in the last millennium, there is a greater public awareness of and suspicion about ethical practices and standards and the effect of this concern is one of the forces driving organizations to develop new policies of corporate responsibility (CR) and ethical codes of conduct for their employees. We may, as a consequence of historical cases of unethical behaviour, have moved into an era where corporate and individual failings are tolerated far less than they may have been in the past.

All organizations are required to act in ways that ensure compliance with legal rules that regulate the way they do business and manage their employees, but what is the requirement for ethical behaviour not regulated by the law?

One point of view is expressed by the economist Milton Friedman (1970):

The social responsibility of business is to its shareholders ... The business of business is business.

But is behaving ethically a legal requirement? In one sense, the answer is 'no' if we define ethics as something which is additional to legal standards of what is right and wrong, but ethical behaviour, as we saw in the ABB case study in Chapter 1, is often at the heart of what a company wishes to be known for and defines the way it wishes to be seen and judged. The concern to be seen as an organization with high standards of ethical behaviour is driven by three forces:

1. **Legal changes** that prohibit such behaviours as taking or offering bribes in the process of doing business. The 2010 Bribery Act offers guidance on how organizations can develop policies that reduce

and control the risks of bribery, regulate the acceptance of gifts, hospitality, or donations, and avoid conflicts of interest. It is worth pointing out, however, that practices considered unethical and now illegal in the UK would be considered as not only acceptable but expected in other countries.

2. **Public opinion** that is increasingly sensitive to and aware of corporate behaviour and influenced by such activities as tax avoidance schemes and excessive corporate remuneration packages.

3. **The positive and reputational effects** of being ethical and in an HR context treating staff with respect and consideration. In a recent report on fairness, the CIPD found evidence that suggested that having a strong and positive ethical culture not only reflects public expectations and meets legal regulation but is also 'good for business'.

> **organisations that treat their employees with fairness, integrity and sensitivity are more likely to find that those employees respond with increased commitment and productivity.**
> (CIPD, 2014)

But what do we mean by ethics?

KEY CONCEPT Ethics

Ethics can be understood as the moral principles that govern a person's behaviour or the conducting of an activity. In this sense, ethics relate to individual and collective behaviour and the way an activity or function is carried out. Ethics involves standards about what is right and wrong and how things are done.

While this is a starting point, for the purposes of our interest in corporate behaviour and the role of HR we need to go beyond this initial explanation. For example, are ethical standards universal or relative? From a business perspective, we know that certain business practices in one country which would be judged as perfectly acceptable would be seen as ethically wrong in another. This means that reaching judgements about what is right and wrong depends on the standards and cultural values used to reach that judgement. Ethics in this sense are relative. We also need to avoid the mistake of assuming that two different people observing the same situation will always reach the same conclusion about its ethicality. Perception based on experience, ideology, and different social values may result in different conclusions being reached. It is also necessary to recognize that there may well be an element of pragmatism applied to the way judgements about ethical behaviour are reached. That is, the context and exigencies affecting the situation need to be taken into account. Ethical judgements in the workplace are rarely free from contextual impact.

The existence of ethical dilemmas also needs to be recognized, which means that different ethical standards or frameworks may compete for primacy and complicate the process of reaching ethical judgements. Take the well-known example of child exploitation. It is estimated that there are over 211 million children worldwide aged 15 or under in paid work. Child labour is widespread throughout Africa, Asia, Latin America, and the Caribbean, though there are also some 2.5 million working children in developed economies. Asia has the largest number of working children, accounting for 60 per cent of the world's total (Ethical Trading Initiative).

It would be easy to conclude that this is child exploitation on a grand scale but the report makes the point that the reason why so many children are working is because of poverty, debt, ignorance, and cultural norms; simply saying that it is wrong and that multinational companies should stop trading with local firms that employ child labour would have significant and negative consequences for the children and their families. Righting one 'wrong' by potentially worsening the situation of children and their families is not necessarily improving things. The existence of such dilemmas means that ethical questions can rarely be managed or resolved without consideration of the consequences that might follow, intended and unintended. The recently introduced National Living Wage is a case in point; the increase in hourly wage rates is considered to be ethically justified because it increases the income of the lowest paid workers but may, according to the Office for Budgetary Responsibility, result in 60,000 jobs being lost. In a report on standards in public office, the author, after advocating the creation of an ethical framework to help structure activities and behaviour, also said that:

> We acknowledge there is a need for any such framework to be risk-based, flexible and proportionate: In the standards field proportionality is concerned with the balance between propriety, accountability and efficiency in the context in which decisions are made and the outcomes intended.
>
> (HMSO, 2014)

The report identified what it called the 'Seven Principles of Public Life', which highlight the characteristics expected of those working in the public sector. They are:

- selflessness;
- integrity;
- objectivity;
- accountability;
- openness;
- honesty; and
- leadership.

Ethics in the public sector, both corporate and individual, are then judged against these seven principles or reference points. This example shows that judgements about right and wrong or good and bad can only be reached by reference to criteria or standards, and questions need to be asked about how such standards were decided and by whom.

Business ethics is also concerned with corporate and individual standards of behaviour but in a different context. It involves the study of proper business policies and practices regarding potentially controversial issues, such as corporate governance, insider trading, bribery, discrimination, corporate social responsibility (CSR), and fiduciary responsibilities. While sharing similarities with business ethics, management ethics has its focus on the way people are treated at work while at the same time acknowledging Friedman's argument that corporate management should also fulfil its economic goals and legal responsibilities in ways that meet social norms and expectations about the conduct of business.

But from our perspective, ethics is not simply about the rights and wrongs of *what is* done but also about *how things are done*; we are interested in the environment in which people work, physical and psychological, how they are paid and disciplined and how they are treated by their managers and colleagues, and above all the kind of leadership they are subjected to. To illustrate this focus on people and the importance of how they are treated at work, consider a situation where an organization has to make people redundant; for the survival of the business this may at times be necessary and cannot be considered to involve the unethical abuse of managerial power, but the process of selecting people for redundancy, the information they are provided with, the help or lack of it in finding alternative employment can all be considered from an ethical perspective. For some, therefore, a concern for ethics is not something that is bolted on as an afterthought but rather something that is an integral part of working and of organizational life.

It is obvious from this brief introduction that ethics is in many ways a controversial subject and goes far beyond simply establishing the rights and wrongs of a situation. Interpretation, perception, different ethical standards and moral principles, social and cultural norms, and organizational creeds all need to be considered before reaching ethical judgements about corporate and individual behaviour. It follows, therefore, that the role of HR in establishing and monitoring ethical standards of behaviour and ethical practices will also be controversial and problematic and this question is explored in more depth later in the chapter.

One final point which should help to clarify any uncertainty over terms and meanings; the concepts of morals and morality are often used synonymously with ethics and ethicality and given that ethics and morals mean the same (ethics is Greek and morals Latin) this is not an issue. The dictionary definition of morals is:

principles concerning the distinction between right and wrong or good and bad behaviour

which is essentially how we have defined ethics. Social values are the reference points that help us make decisions about right and wrong and ethical decisions are guided by the underlying values of the individual and the corporate values of the organizations. Values might be understood as principles of conduct or standards of behaviour such as caring, being honest, keeping promises, pursuing excellence, showing loyalty, being fair, acting with integrity, respecting others, and being a responsible citizen. The seven principles of public life, referred to in the HMSO report, are examples of important and desirable behavioural standards that reflect underlying social values.

STUDENT ACTIVITY 5.1

Read the blog by James O'Toole (2015) on ethical challenges in human resources, available at: https://www.scu.edu/ethics/focus-areas/business-ethics/resources/ethical-challenges-in-human-resources
Then discuss the contents in your seminar group. Prepare a presentation addressing the following questions, using one PowerPoint slide for each.

- What does 'ethics' mean and what is it about?
- Why is ethics an important issue in organizations?
- What are six questions that will help to establish whether an organization is ethical?
- How is legal compliance different from ethical behaviour?
- Does HR focus too much on legal compliance and not enough on ethics and ethical behaviour?
- In an induction session on ethics, what kind of points would you want to make if you were describing an ethical organization?

Perspectives on Workplace Ethical Dilemmas

We have already made the point that ethics (standards about what is right and wrong) and ethical behaviour (how we actually live our lives) is not some 'bolt-on' attribute but something which is integral to being human. We all make decisions in our work and non-work environments that reflect either conscious or unconscious ethical standards that we acquire from different sources, some of which become incorporated into the individual mind while others remain external reference points. At work, we are faced with a different behavioural context in which many of the rules about what we should and should not do are imposed by management or external agencies. The legitimacy of these rules and the extent to which they clash with our own values and beliefs as to what is right and wrong will affect our response to them. How things are done is often as important as what is done and the test that is frequently applied to the way we are treated at work is that of fairness. The concept of procedural justice captures the importance people attach to the way they are treated and the need to act in ways that are both legitimate and procedurally fair. We will consider both concepts later in the chapter.

From an HR perspective, HR professionals and other managers involved in the function are constantly faced with challenges and circumstances that raise ethical questions. But given the nature of organizations, where the existence of multiple stakeholders means that decisions have to reflect different interests, the ethical question is not only one concerned with what is right or wrong (where organizational rules and procedures make it relatively easy to establish this, although not always) but also with the effect on these different interests of the decisions managers are constantly taking. Ethics is not then simply about right and wrong in relation to ethical and procedural standards but about the *effects* and *consequences* of decisions on the interests of others. This does not mean that all stakeholder interests have equal standing—the primacy of those associated directly with management and indirectly with shareholders or 'the public interest' is generally accepted and legally confirmed—but it does mean that these effects and consequences for others cannot be ignored by managers.

PRACTITIONER INSIGHT Dean Royles HR director: ethics and management in the NHS

NHS management seems to be portrayed in much of the press as a pantomime villain. Managers are presented as grey suits more interested in money and financial balance than in patient care: surprisingly so, because the majority of line managers in the NHS are in fact clinicians. And, in my experience, the majority of those that aren't clinicians are just as patient-centred as their clinical colleagues. I don't want to sound complacent and it is clear that there has been some poor practice, as evidenced in the Francis Report into the events at Mid-Staffordshire hospital—where financial sustainability seemed to trump patient care and in the treatment of some NHS whistle-blowers.

However, many managers are trying to navigate complex ethical dilemmas in their decision-making. Seeking to balance the Nolan principles of openness and honesty with maintaining public confidence and access to essential services, and trying to be fair, equitable, and compassionate to staff while wanting to ensure the highest possible standards of care for patients often involves difficult judgement calls. For example, managers and HR practitioners in particular get approached by staff asking if they can speak to them in confidence. It seems innocuous enough and the staff member clearly wants to tell you something of importance. The employee then explains concerns they have. You believe this information impacts on care and/or the well-being of other staff. Do you maintain or breach the confidentiality? What is your professional responsibility? Is the staff member a whistle-blower and wants to feel supported? If you don't do anything will they feel let down? It's a tough dilemma. You learn over time, and the hard way, to preface these conversations explaining to the staff member or colleague who wants to share something in confidence that you may need to breach that confidence if it is about patient care or impacts on your professional duties and responsibilities. You also explain appropriate and safe ways for them to be able to raise concerns.

Or, you're chairing a disciplinary panel hearing on gross misconduct. It's a case that relates to poor patient care and experience. It is a very long-serving member of staff. The facts are pretty clear, but you know that depriving someone of their employment, and possibly livelihood, is one of the most significant decisions you will take. Do you demonstrate compassion and give the staff member another chance? If you do, will other staff members believe standards have been lowered? If they reoffend, how do you explain to patients and the patients' relatives that the staff member had done this before? What's the right choice to make? What are the ethical considerations? In essence, it's not the big strategic and financial decisions that cause you the sleepless nights, it's taking these decisions that impact on people's lives that present the toughest choices and give the ethical dilemmas.

Another example of ethical dilemmas involves situations where the press approach your communications department. A member of staff has 'leaked' information about the criminal past of another member of staff. The newspaper tells you that the whistle-blower is concerned about patient care. They plan to run the story that evening. The organization is aware of the background of the employee with the criminal past and has undertaken a risk assessment to ensure safe and high-quality care. The crime had taken place twenty years ago and there have been no problems since. How much do you disclose? Could it breach personal data confidentiality? If the story appears in the press, will it put patients off accessing potentially life-saving care out of misplaced fear? How do you reassure the whistle-blower who may have raised the concerns out of a genuine belief without breaching the confidence of other staff?

The ethical considerations for staff managers and clinicians when providing a public service are enormous. There seem to be competing stakeholders and choices. There are no absolute right answers, just judgements. These judgements may have been very different thirty years ago when we lived in a more paternalistic time. Social media, increased public scrutiny, and access to information through freedom-of-information legislation all make these ethical judgement calls ever more complex. How people make them with sound patient-centred values increases the odds of making the right call. It will however never be the right decision for everyone.

HR practitioners/managers constantly have to navigate their way through challenging ethical situations and have to make choices and take decisions on the basis of their experience, professionalism, and what is known or believed, but they cannot know what the outcomes and consequences of their actions will be in any precise sense. Employees may believe that management action will be against their individual or collective interests, whereas the reality might be the opposite and of course the reverse situation can occur where people believe management are acting in their interests but the consequences may be quite different to the original belief. But ethical dilemmas are not restricted to managers in their professional roles; individual employees are faced with situations which require decisions to be made that have an ethical dimension—whether to tell the truth or lie about the reason for being absent from work, for example. Consider the further example of a situation in which people have to choose whether to lie or tell the truth outlined in Student Activity 5.2.

STUDENT ACTIVITY 5.2

The situation involves a UK police force. A recently qualified constable working in a local police station is on patrol with an experienced and older colleague when they observe a black man acting suspiciously. They approach him and tell him that they have grounds to believe he was dealing in drugs and they have a legal right to search him. He initially refuses and is abusive to the police, but he is pushed to the ground by the older constable who slaps the man and uses abusive and racially charged language. The man is not in possession of any drugs and claims he is the victim of racist behaviour. After his release and on their return to the station, the older officer tells his colleague that they both have to agree on 'their story' and that in their report they need to avoid any reference to rough treatment and abusive/racist language. The younger officer has to decide whether to tell the truth or in some way lie.

For the activity:

- Split into two groups.

- Group one is to list the consequences for the police force, the older officer, and his younger colleague of lying or not telling the whole truth about what happened.

- Group two does the same for the three stakeholders of telling the truth.

- The two groups come together to discuss the two lists, and consider the options the younger officer has and what she should do.

Then read Baekgaard, O. (1984) 'The cost of whistleblowing', *Multinational Monitor* 5(6), on the case of Stanley Adams versus Hoffman La-Roche (available at: http://multinationalmonitor.org/hyper/issues/1984/06/baekgaard.html) and discuss in relation to the activity.

The brief ethical dilemma in Student Activity 5.2 highlights the importance of understanding the possible different consequences that follow from the choices people make. While it might be thought that being truthful is always better than lying, the consequences of being truthful and acting ethically also need to be considered in understanding individual decisions. The advantages of not being completely truthful are explained by Pfeffer (2015), in his book on leadership that we refer to in the last section of the chapter. But the point we would make here is that being honest and truthful is not without consequences, some of which may be damaging to the interests and well-being of the individual.

Costs are a kind of consequence, and understanding the costs of different courses of action may be a helpful way of overcoming ethical dilemmas. Of course, many decisions are taken quickly without their costs being fully thought through, and however attractive it might seem, trying to base decisions on the balance of costs and benefits is not always possible because we are trying to predict outcomes that have not yet happened. We also know that some individuals despite knowing the costs of doing that which is right and sticking to their principles will not change their minds. We might think of medics working in a war zone who stay with their patients despite personal danger, or people with strong religious convictions who risk persecution and even death for failing to recant and confess their religious beliefs.

HRM INSIGHT 5.1 **Patagonia**

Patagonia is an outdoor gear and clothing business founded in 1974 by Yvon Chouinard for whom climbing and extreme sports dominated his life until he became an entrepreneur and CEO of the company. Decades before other businesses embraced the green movement and sought reputations for social responsibility, Patagonia spearheaded campaigns to use eco-friendly materials and fabrics in its clothing and pioneered sustainable manufacturing practices, turning the outerwear industry on its head. Chouinard wanted to shape the way Patagonia was run, and not just the products it sold.

Early on, Chouinard laid out values for how he wanted to work: employees, including the founder himself, should be able to take off time for enjoying activities such as going on climbing expeditions that had drawn the people to Patagonia in the first place. They also should 'work with friends' and with family members close at hand. The company promotes such values by hiring people with a shared love of the outdoors and by spreading employee benefits to all such as a shared eating place instead of building an executive-only dining room.

Also at the heart of Patagonia's values is a love of the natural environment. Whether they are surfing, skiing, climbing a mountain, or paddling a kayak, Patagonia's employees and customers are enjoying the beauty of the world's wild places. Chouinard readily admits that this poses a dilemma. He values protection of the beautiful planet he enjoys, but at the same time, manufacturing clothing uses up resources and causes pollution. For example, toxic chemicals are needed to tan leather, and polyester is made from crude oil. This was his fundamental dilemma—how to reconcile his personal values without compromising the company's business success. For Chouinard, the resolution of this dilemma involves meeting two objectives: reducing as far as possible any harm his business does to the environment and then contributing a proportion of the company's earnings to preserving and protecting the environment. That understanding of the company's purpose is summed up by Patagonia's mission statement:

Build the best product, cause no unnecessary harm, use business to inspire and implement solutions to the environmental crisis.

Some of the ways in which Patagonia fulfils that mission involve the choices of materials used, the benefits offered to its employees, and the standards it sets for suppliers. Clothing designs emphasize reliance on materials that do minimal damage—for example, organic cotton and fleece made from recycled soda bottles. The company has established standards for measuring the environmental performance of the manufacturers it buys from, and it uses those criteria in selecting contractors. Furthermore, since 1985 the company has donated 1 per cent of its revenues (not just profits) to organizations working to protect the environment (http://www. patagonia.com/company-history.html).

Interestingly, the point of HRM Insight 5.1 isn't about how ethical dilemmas can be resolved—in the case of Patagonia they weren't actually resolved at all but persisted and paradoxically this is what allowed the company to continue to do all it reasonably could to minimize any harm it caused to the environment and support other companies in their commitment to environmental protection. In this sense, the dilemma represented a permanent catalyst or force for achieving its values and realizing its social responsibilities. But HRM Insight 5.1 also illustrates how competing value systems can be accommodated and reconciled through compromise and accommodation.

In a recent research report, the CIPD (2015) offered an interesting contribution to our understanding of workplace ethics and the kinds of choices and dilemmas people face. The report claims to be an aid to ethical decision-making by describing the possible ways of thinking about work using different philosophical perspectives. It identifies eight lenses, none of which the report argues represent the 'right' or 'wrong' ways of making decisions in the workplace; rather, they represent different ways of making sense of workplace ethical dilemmas. This kind of framework is particularly useful for the organization as a whole as well as the HR function in its attempts to create a meaningful and practical way of both making ethically justified decisions and also helping to resolve ethical issues. Of course, the choice of which lens to apply can itself be controversial and is unlikely to be value-free. But choice in this context does allow managers and employees to claim legitimacy for their decisions and behaviour, which in turn recognizes that legitimacy can come from different ideological and ethical sources.

The eight lenses through which people can look and make 'ethical sense' of situations and requirements are:

1. **Fairness**—defined in terms of everyone in an organization being able to agree to something, whatever their place in it may be. We look in more detail at fairness in ethical decision-making later, but the problem with this approach is that it is idealistic rather than pragmatic and fails to take account of the way fairness is defined and used by different interest groups. There is no doubt however that the fairness lens is widely used in organizations to help decide on the rights and wrongs of very different situations from the way disciplinary procedures operate, to pay relationships, and selection criteria.

2. **Well-being**—work should be good for us! The idea behind this lens is that work is one of our main central life interests and is the place where many of our social and psychological needs are met—or at least should be. To meet this requirement workplaces should be designed to promote well-being for its own sake, not just to create goods and services as efficiently as possible. Notwithstanding the conceptual and practical challenges of defining what well-being is or should be—and the assumption here seems to be that all employees would see it in the same way—the problem with this lens is that organizations are rarely designed with this in mind, although management generally understands the importance of maintaining the physical and psychological health of their workers.

3. **Merit**—jobs and their rewards should track talent and hard work. Again, a laudable objective but issues arise over what merit is and how it can be measured. It also clashes with ideas about equal pay and payment based on the job a person does. Decisions on and about merit are often contested and contestable: so, although it may be, in theory, 'right' to use merit as a way of justifying different treatment, it is not without difficulties.

4. **Rights and duties**—everyone has rights to do some things and to be free of some things, and everyone has duties not to violate others' rights. This lens concentrates less on what rights are conferred on people by the law, which can change, and more on the universality of certain rights such as the right to join a trade union, to be treated equally regardless of gender and race, and to equal pay which should be enjoyed regardless of any consequences that might follow. In Chapter 13 we identify a set of rights developed by the International Labour Office which support the way people are paid and which represent a set of ethical standards against which company pay policies and practices can be judged, but the idea promoted by the CIPD research paper that such rights should be available to people regardless of any consequences is again controversial and fails to adequately reflect competitive forces and financial realities. We might also question the ability of this lens to help resolve ethical dilemmas without any reference to personal responsibilities which might be attached to these rights.

5. **Markets**—jobs and their rewards should follow from voluntary market exchanges. This lens suggests that primacy is given to the interactions of market forces of supply and demand which can be considered ethically neutral. The CIPD (2015) report states that:

   > **Any distribution of positions and their rewards which results from exchanges and agreements between individuals, within the rules, is an ethically acceptable distribution, whether or not it tracks merit or any other pre-existing pattern. Need and in fact merit are subordinated to the determination of the market which is the arbiter of pay and position and an ethical reference point. The problem here is to do with the way labour markets actually work and whether references to existing market rates to justify high managerial salaries are in fact justified or simply an excuse for excessive pay levels.**

6. **Democracy**—no one should be subject to a regime in which they have no say. This lens suggests that people affected by a decision should be involved in making it. So, for example, employees should be involved in decisions over how their workplace is organized and run. The idea of employees having a 'voice' at work enjoys contemporary support from many sources. It owes much to earlier develop-

ments in worker participation and industrial democracy, practices that are supported by EU directives (Hall, 2008). The question that arises here is about the extensiveness of these rights to participate in decision-making processes when private sector organizations are not based on democratic principles but on property and ownership rights, and the public sector reflects bureaucratic rather than democratic principles of control.

7. **Character**—each of us should work to develop the best ethical character for our roles. According to the report, a person's character is a set of deep, consistent, closely connected psychological tendencies to feel and act in the right way. It might be also thought of in terms of virtuous behaviour and is consistent with the kind of human features we highlighted in 'Murray's story' in HRM Insight 1.2. According to this lens, people are judged by their ability and determination to do what is right rather than following procedures or orders. However, most people understand from experience of working that 'doing things right' often takes precedence over doing the 'right thing'.

8. **Handing down**—this is an environmental lens which focuses on the extent to which people understand and accept their responsibility for protecting and preserving the environment for future generations. This lens is closely linked to the notion of CR and the importance of organizations in particular recognizing that they have responsibilities that extend beyond shareholders and customers. HRM Insight 5.1 on Patagonia is a good example of how this lens can be used and applied to determine the ethical behaviour of the company concerned.

As we have noted, the identification of these eight ethical lenses offers important insights into organizational ethics and illustrates the choices people have in making ethical judgements. Choice exists in how we reach ethical conclusions but so does conflict. As Bateman and Snell (2015) state:

Ethics becomes a more complicated issue when a situation dictates that one value overrules others.

The final element in this section which deals with ethical dilemmas and the challenges involved in making ethical choices and decisions concerns differences between men and women. Evidence on this is by no means conclusive but there is evidence to suggest that women tend to act more ethically than men or at least choose different ethical reference points.

According to Bateman and Snell (2015):

Studies have implied they are, at least by some measures. Surveys of business students found an increase in their interest in studying ethics, with a greater increase among women. Compared with their female counterparts, undergraduate male students in business and psychology showed stronger unethical attitudes and a tendency to behave unethically. When business students took an ethics curriculum, women made greater strides than men in improving their moral awareness and decision-making processes.

Dobrin (2014) suggests that other studies point in this direction. He quotes a study by Roberta Bampton and Patrick Maclagan (2009), which states that women tend to justify actions based on an ethics of compassion while men adhered more to proper procedures or law and rules. The research included asking men and women how they behave in the same circumstances. In one example women found it unacceptable for a company to manufacture equipment used by police and military to extract information from prisoners, while many more men didn't object to the practice. In the second, given the choice of an organic farm or buying cheaper products overseas that would harm the environment because of carbon emissions and use of fuel, nearly all men in the survey would make the switch to increase profits while about half the women did. Dobrin posed the question—'does this mean that women have the ethical edge?' He argued that this wasn't necessarily the case, suggesting that both reason and adherence to rules *and* compassion/care can be equally valid ethical standpoints. And of course the simplistic assumption that all women and men act in the same way is becoming less acceptable as evidence grows that women can display 'male' traits and men women's. One explanation for the mixed results is that most situations don't rely upon one moral value alone—as we noted above, different ethical lenses can be applied to the same situation to help make decisions. Ethics is about values and what is right and wrong, but it is also about reason; it is about emotions and it is about judgement.

The point about the reference to emotions affecting people's judgements is a particularly important one and is something that we have emphasized throughout the book. The underlying assumption about the ethical decisions people make is that they are acting consciously and rationally when they make these decisions. This may well be the case but the influence of that which occupies our subconscious and emotional self and its effect on our decisions also needs to be recognized. In fact, according to Banaji et al. (2003), people are far less ethical than they believe they are:

> Most of us believe that we are ethical and unbiased. We imagine we're good decision makers, able to objectively size up a job candidate or a venture deal and reach a fair and rational conclusion that's in our, and our organization's, best interests. But more than two decades of research confirms that, in reality, most of us fall woefully short of our inflated self-perception. We're deluded by what Yale psychologist David Armor calls the illusion of objectivity, the notion that we're free of the very biases we're so quick to recognize in others.

Even more interesting, is the idea that these unconscious or implicit biases and opinions can be contrary to people's consciously held and explicit beliefs which raises again the notion of ethical conflict within the individual which that person may not even be aware of. Banaji et al. argue that the existence and prevalence of these biases suggests that even the most ethically conscious person can unwittingly be influenced by deeply rooted thoughts and feelings on what are believed to be objective and ethically grounded decisions.

STUDENT ACTIVITY 5.3

First, read the following article:

Bampton, R. and Maclagan, P. (2009) 'Does a "care orientation" explain gender differences in ethical decision making? A critical analysis and fresh findings', *Business Ethics*, 18(2).

Then collectively produce three or four short vignettes or short stories that involve an ethical dilemma. Just use your own experience and imagination to do this. Then split the group on gender lines and get each group to decide on what they would do to address/solve the ethical question. Consider the decisions of both groups: does gender seem to be a relevant factor in the decisions that were taken?

Fairness at Work

> Evidence suggests that organisations that treat their employees with fairness, integrity and sensitivity are more likely to find that those employees respond with increased commitment and productivity.
> CIPD (2013a)

This statement points to an important conclusion about organizational ethics: that being ethical is not only a desirable and the 'right' thing to do and be but it also has tangible and significant benefits for the organization. In this sense, it represents a very similar position to the one we identified in Chapter 1 where treating people well and trying to create a psychologically supportive workplace was associated with high performance and increased productivity. Are we now suggesting that being an ethical employer and treating people fairly has the same effect? In all probability, treating people fairly is part of a wider spectrum of employer strategies that collectively and positively impact on employee behaviour, but it is difficult to avoid the conclusion that fairness permeates many of the expectations people bring to the workplace. For example:

● Paying a fair wage in relation to what I do and achieve.

● Operate fair recruitment and selection procedures.

- If I am disciplined apply rules fairly and without bias.
- Be fair in the way you treat me.
- Operate appraisal systems fairly.

But being treated fairly doesn't mean special treatment. As we explore the concept, it becomes clear that fairness can be interpreted in different ways. But as a starting point it might be interpreted as:

Being treated by someone as they would like to be treated.

This means almost the same thing that Herzberg said was important for employees when he is quoted as saying:

Treat me as I am not how you want me to be.

This is of course only one way to understand what fairness can mean and is only a starting point, but it is a thought-provoking position nevertheless.

Fairness is closely related to ethics and is integral to the kind of language and discourse found in most contemporary workplaces. It could be argued that fairness or justice (they can be seen to be almost identical in their meanings) are, in the context of how people are treated and managed at work, at the heart of the ethical debate.

Justice means giving each person what he or she deserves or, in more traditional terms, giving each person his or her due. Fairness over pay and rewards more generally carries the same meaning but fairness can also mean being judged, appraised, or evaluated without bias or prejudice. But as Banaji et al. (2003) argue, the ability to be fair in the way we judge and appraise others is compromised by the existence of unconscious bias. They claim that:

Most fair-minded people strive to judge others according to their merits but our research shows how often people instead judge according to unconscious stereotypes and attitudes, or 'implicit prejudice'.

They believe that because implicit prejudice arises from the normal and unconscious tendency to make associations, and for people to reach conclusions on the basis of these associations, it is distinct from conscious and explicit forms of prejudice, such as racism and sexism. They also claim that this distinction explains why people who believe they are free from conscious prejudice may still hold and display biases in the decisions they take and how they behave. Their research found that while people tend to report little or no conscious bias against so-called 'minority groups' they do display significant biases on implicit measures. If their research is credible and supported by other research results, which they claim it is, then we are left with the inevitable conclusion that there are two sources of fairness/unfairness, the conscious and explicit and the unconscious and implicit. What is difficult to establish is the degree to which they are consistent or inconsistent with each other but the possibility is that when people say and believe they are acting fairly they may not be quite as much as they thought, and the perception and interpretation of their behaviour by others may be different to what was expected and intended.

Another way of defining fairness or justice is to relate it to the Aristotelian principle that equals should be treated equally and unequals unequally. Applying this principle to the workplace means that people should receive the same treatment or be given the same opportunities unless they differ in ways that are relevant to the situation. For example, if two people are doing the same job and to the same level of performance, then treating them fairly means paying them the same. But if one is paid more than the other simply because he is a man, or because he is white, then we have an injustice—an unfairness—because race and sex are not relevant to normal work situations. Although the principle is clear and helps establish the fairness or otherwise of a situation (and therefore whether it is right or wrong; acceptable or unacceptable) difficulties can arise over what constitutes a material difference. Paying people the same rate who are doing the same job would be considered fair, but not paying someone more as a consequence of working longer hours would probably not.

This raises the difficult question of whether people doing the same job but at different levels of performance should be paid the same. First, there are two competing criteria to determine fairness of pay—the job and job performance. Which one takes precedence? In reality, some organizations offer the same basic pay but then provide a performance-related bonus to the higher achiever, a situation that allows both criteria to be fairly applied. But in many public sector organizations the only determinant of pay is often the job they do and the grade they are on. This situation creates the potential for perceived unfairness where people receive the same wage but for widely differing levels of job performance.

In Chapter 4, we highlighted the differentiation and segmentation strategies of many organizations without raising the question of the ethical basis of this strategy, but based on the idea that it is unfair to treat different people the same (based on performance, potential, and innate talent) the ethical basis of such discriminating practices seems to have a strong foundation. Aguinis and Bradley (2015) advocate the establishment of management practices to manage and produce star performers, ranging from recruitment practices, development activities, to rewards based on performance. They argue that pay dispersion, where pay differentials are increased should not be avoided in an attempt to appear 'equal' as star performers need to be compensated according to their performance level. They believe that organizations should promote transparency and fairness in policies, to reduce the resentfulness and animosity felt by some non-star performers. By this they mean that managers need to communicate clearly and explain why people are being treated differently and that rather than being seen as unfair because it promotes inequality such practices are inherently fair and therefore ethical.

RESEARCH INSIGHT 5.1

To take your learning further, read the following article:

Swailes, S. (2013) 'The ethics of talent management', *Business Ethics: A European Review,* **22(1).**

This article focuses on a particular aspect of HR—the management of talent—and looks at the ethics behind discriminating and segmenting the labour force. After reading it, consider whether the ethical case for treating a few, special employees has been convincingly made. A discussion around this question can also be the basis of a group/seminar activity and presentation.

Looking at the question of pay between men and women, the principle of equal pay, that is men and women doing similar work or work of similar value should get paid the same amount (assuming they work the same hours and in the same conditions), has been part of UK law for the best part of four decades. Even so, there's still confusion about the circumstances in which people can be paid more for doing the same work.

Employers must pay men and women equally if they are doing 'like work', which is work that is the same or broadly similar; or work that is of equal value (for example, in terms of effort, skill, or other demands); or work that is rated as equivalent under a job evaluation study. But the situation is more complicated because if an employer can show that there's a genuine reason for any difference in pay that's not based on the sex of the individual, then the equal pay legislation may not apply and by inference the pay difference is seen as fair and reasonable (ACAS, 2013). Experience or length of service may be the basis for someone being paid more than another, but is this acceptable? In law, it may be because longer service and greater experience is often associated with improved job performance which can then justify a pay differential. According to ACAS (2013), there are exceptions to using experience as a justifiable reason for a pay differential. Experience can't be put forward as an excuse for pay inequality in every situation. Their guidance on this states that:

If there's 'serious doubt' that it's appropriate to justify a pay gap on length of service, then an employer has to show that it goes 'hand in hand' with experience and that experience enables the worker to perform duties better. It's particularly difficult for employers to justify a pay gap if the difference in experience or service between parties is based on a period spanning more than five years, and there could be an increased risk of indirect age discrimination against younger claimants as well.

As far as pay is concerned, certainly in the UK, the law only regulates pay relationships (but not absolute pay levels) between men and women but it does regulate the pay of young people and low-paid workers through national minimum rates (earnings is something quite different). Legal rules can be taken as an indicator of the ethicality of certain kinds of pay relationships, based on the principle of equality between men and women (although it does not always follow that that which is legal is also ethical). But where difference between employees is not based on sex or other unacceptable criteria such as age, race, or religion, but is related to a person's productive value to the organization, then treating people differently, although there are serious ethical questions about the extent of pay differences, is considered by many to be fair and right (*Guardian*, 2016). Conversely, there is often a sense of perceived unfairness associated with treating people equally when there exist significant material differences in performance and talent within a group of people, but whether this perception is shared by both parties is problematic.

STUDENT ACTIVITY 5.4

Read the following story and consider whether the pay differential is legal and ethical. How would you explain and justify the decision to increase the woman's pay and manage the situation that has emerged?

A colleague of mine who very recently started working here is being paid a higher hourly rate than me and my other colleagues, I have discovered. This woman is very experienced and qualified, but so am I. (Not as much as her, but more so than some others working here.) I don't see any evidence that her job performance is any different from mine.

The aforementioned colleague has made a song and dance about how poor the pay is compared with what she was used to, particularly after being told in her job interview that pay rates were comparable with 'the market rate'. And after a meeting with the manager she was promised an increase would be given to her, which it has, last month. She seems to think she can swan into our workplace, claim to be better than the rest of us and feel justified in asking for a pay increase. Management just seem to have caved in and given her one. I know we don't have any wage grades to allow for pay to reflect experience, qualifications, etc., but I really feel the rest of us have been unfairly treated here and we are not happy about it.

We have already made the point that fairness and justice are frequently used as alternative terms that carry the same or very similar meanings; for example, the concept of justice is associated with fairness, entitlement, and equality; judicial processes and procedures are expected and required to meet the tests of fairness and reasonableness. But it is important to distinguish between the different kinds of justice that exist in the workplace. According to Velasquez et al. (2014), the most important forms are:

- Distributive justice

    This refers to the extent to which society's institutions ensure that benefits and burdens are distributed among society's members in ways that are fair and just. When the institutions of a society distribute benefits or burdens in unjust ways—favouring one group at the expense of others—conflict of one sort or another is likely to emerge to reflect feelings of unfairness. Within the workplace, the obvious example of an interest in distributive justice is in the field of rewards. In the private sector, sharing in the 'fruits of success' involves decisions on the distribution of profits between different stakeholders: shareholders receive dividends and managers/employees pay increases and bonuses. In the public sector, the situation is less obvious; although there are numerous performance-related bonus schemes in existence, most apply to senior managers. But the question is: how are profits to be distributed and what criteria will be used to decide on the distribution of resources?' Looking at annual wage increases, the question becomes one of which interest group/individual receives what in relation to others. In Chapter 13 we talk about the importance of relative pay changes in detail: here we are highlighting the fact that if one group/individual receives a higher pay award than another there is every possibility, in the absence of such differences being legitimized, of discontent and potentially conflict being generated. Distributive justice is the same as substantive justice—people get what they deserve. But do they?

 Signpost to Chapter 13: Managing Rewards, for insights into the way perceptions legitimize reward differences.

- **Retributive or corrective justice**

Refers to the extent to which punishments are fair and just. In general, penalties are held to be just to the extent that they take into account relevant criteria such as the seriousness of the breach of rules, motivation, and an employee's record. In the context of discipline at work, people expect the penalties applied to be reasonable, fair, and proportionate and for an appeal system to be in place to ensure that the 'correct' decision and outcome is reached. Most organizations have works rules that link disciplinary breaches to different levels of sanctions, but outcomes are influenced by procedures, so procedural regularity is often directly related to the acceptability of disciplinary decisions.

- **Compensatory justice**

Refers to the extent to which people are fairly compensated for their injuries, hurt feelings, or losses as a result of procedurally incorrect or unlawful managerial decisions. Breaches of the common law duty of care have resulted in national compensation schemes for workers in the coal, steel, and asbestos industries where specific and verifiable occupational illnesses and diseases have been seen to have been caused by certain kinds of working conditions and industrial environments. Compensation for workers unfairly dismissed or where anti-discrimination laws have been broken involve reference to compensatory justice, but in the UK at least, financial and other remedies for wrongful treatment are more often than not laid down in acts of parliament or through official guidance and precedent. But in relation to job losses either through redundancy or compromise agreements organizations can set their own standards of compensation above the minimum laid down. What is a fair price for losing one's job is determined by exiting company policy or through negotiations.

- **Interactional justice**

Refers to the quality of interpersonal treatment employees receive when procedures are implemented (Colquitt et al., 2001). Interactional justice can take two forms:

- **interpersonal treatment**—where employees expect to be treated with politeness, dignity, and respect;

- **informational justice**—where employees expect to be given the information they need to understand the situation. For example, a planned closure or redundancy; employees will have expectations relative to this, and the information will be communicated to them by managers and organizational leaders.

According to Colquitt et al. (2001), the fairness or otherwise of interactional justice is determined by the extent to which managerial action and behaviour:

- is justified;

- involves truthfulness;

- is associated with respect; and

- conforms to conventionally accepted standards of behaviour.

- **Procedural justice**

  This elevates and emphasizes the importance of how things are done rather than the outcomes or consequences of actions and decisions directly. But there is an implicit if questionable assumption that if the way decisions are taken and procedures designed meets certain standards and requirements, particularly that of fairness and non-discrimination, then the outcomes will also be fair and legitimized. This may not always be the case because:

  > **When it comes to fairness what is important is not the reality itself, but the subject's perception of reality.**

  Procedural justice is also closely associated with legitimacy, reputation, and management based on consent. It is a critical element in many of the key areas of HR such as recruitment and selection, appraisal, redundancy, discipline, and dismissal. In a case of dismissal that went to appeal, it was concluded that the case demonstrated the importance of adopting fair procedures and principles of natural justice before an employer takes any action against an employee. Employers should be mindful of the following:

  - Management must give the person a *fair hearing* in advance of the decision being made.

  - Particular managers (decision-takers) involved in the case should not be compromised and biased by, for example, being involved in earlier stages of the case. It is particularly important to ensure that the decision maker has not had any prior involvement in the matter before being assigned to investigate or make a decision.

  - Managers involved should not have been the subject of any previous allegations made by the person under investigation, nor have prior knowledge of the issue before being given responsibility to investigate or decide on the case.

  - An employer should ensure that an employee receives a fair hearing which normally means it involves oral evidence being presented, that the person under investigation should be given prior warning of the meeting, and that the allegations should be sent in writing to that person prior to the hearing so that he/she has time to consider them.

  - Any relevant documentary evidence should be sent to the person in advance of the hearing, for example copies of policies or works rules.

  - The person under investigation should be given the opportunity to call witnesses in their own defence and to cross-examine those witnesses who give evidence against them if they wish to do so.

  - The person under investigation is entitled to be represented (rather than simply accompanied) by a person of their choice at any hearing/meeting. That person might be a colleague, a friend, a relation, a trade union official, or even, in some cases, their solicitor.

  - Finally, the decision maker should usually give reasons for their decision.

  It was concluded that it might seem that these 'fairness requirements' are on the onerous side but where dismissal is potentially involved, tribunals are clearly applying high standards of compliance.

Fairness in organizations is not only important because it represents a way of establishing the rights and wrongs of a situation (because fairness can be established subjectively as well as objectively the same situation can be deemed to be both fair and unfair by different stakeholders) and is associated with positive work behaviours, but also because there are consequences that might follow from workplace unfairness, a point illustrated in Research Insight 5.2.

RESEARCH INSIGHT 5.2

Read the following article to further your learning:

Dineen, B. R. et al. (2004) 'Perceived fairness of web-based applicant screening procedures: Weighing the rules of justice and the role of individual differences', *Human Resource Management,* **43(2–3).**

Dineen et al. write about fairness in web-based recruitment and consider the ethical challenges and requirements facing online recruiters. They consider the main determinants of fairness as experienced by applicants and the importance of procedural justice in the screening of online applications.

CIPD (2013a) is a report that provides interesting insights into fairness or its absence in the workplace. In addition to providing what the authors call the different contours of fairness or the different ways we can understand it, they comment on the consequences to organizations of being perceived as acting fairly or unfairly. They argue that being fair and ethical (again it's important to point out that this is not about achieving some notional end state but of acting fairly in things that matter to people) produces positive attitudinal and behavioural reactions. Where the organization acts in an unethical and unfair manner in the way it treats its employees it is likely to experience higher turnover, lower productivity, reduced discretionary effort, and increased discontent/conflict. The report quotes US research that suggests unfair practices cost US employers $64billion annually linked to cases involving harassment, discrimination, and bullying (Level Playing Field Institute, 2007). There may well be issues over the methodology of this research and the attribution of financial costs but there can be little doubt that employers can pay a high financial price through reputational damage, legal costs, compensation payments, and lost productivity for consistently acting unfairly towards their employees.

One of the noted tendencies of people who feel that they are treated unfairly is not to raise this officially or at least not to persevere with official complaints if nothing is done about the claim or complaint. They may feel unsure about how management will react, and feel apprehensive about bringing a complaint into the formal domain. But there may well be consequences even though a formal complaint has not been made. People may leave, suffer cognitive dissonance—the existence of conflicting standards or norms—or simply get on as best they can. This means that the 'true' level of unfairness, if measured by the number and frequency of formal complaints, is unlikely to be known. Of course, we are not talking about unfair free organizations—that would be unrealistic as well as naive. And we are not talking about unfairness only in terms of managerial behaviour towards employees. Consistent with the emphasis we have given throughout the book to the informal organization, it has to be noted that unfair behaviour and unethical behaviour is perceived to exist within the employee community, directed at both colleagues and upwards towards managers, although these cases are likely to be less frequent and damaging on the whole than where managers abuse their power or fail to use it to address unacceptable behaviour.

Much of what we consider to be unfair is structural; that is, it resides in procedures or systems in the form of rules, criteria, and levels of discretion. But other forms of unfairness and unethical behaviour results from either individual behaviour or cultural practices. Senior managers may know about these things and choose to ignore or actively condone them. Willie Brown, Professor of Industrial Relations at Cambridge, coined the terms 'errors of omission' and 'errors of commission' to describe the kinds of mistakes managers can and do make. Doing something that is knowingly in breach of ethical standards will rightly be questioned and challenged, although in cases like Enron (see Chapter 1) this didn't happen because the wrongdoing was perpetrated by senior managers. To use Sutton's term again, 'assholes' usually inhabit senior positions within hierarchies! But knowing something is wrong and failing to address it, an act of omission, is equally questionable but can be understood. Think about Harvey's explanation of the Abilene paradox and the dangers associated with whistle-blowing. Making sense of unfairness means that we need to go beyond its obvious and formal manifestations and explore its cultural origins and the extent to which it has become informally tolerated or legitimized within certain areas of the organization. Unfair practices that can be established and

153

evaluated can be more easily addressed than practices that are less obvious and culturally embedded, but both types present challenges to HR in terms of its ability to create a fairer working environment characterized by higher ethical standards. It is to the role of HR in ethics that we now turn.

HR and Ethics

The chapter so far has focused on creating awareness and understanding of the way ethics impinge on organizational life and how fairness is frequently used as a way of establishing the rights and wrongs of a situation. Concerns over unethical behaviour and the commitment of many organizations, but by no means all, to address the challenges of CR appear to be increasing, driven by publicity about corporate fraud, excessive pay, bullying at work, and increased societal expectations about the exercise of corporate power. But where does the HR function stand in this world of heightened expectations, where more and more people are demanding that action be taken to address the ethical wrongs associated with corporate life? In this section, we address the question directly and review the arguments in favour of a more proactive role for HR, considering the views of different stakeholders on what HR should be doing to make a significant contribution to the objective of creating a more ethical workplace within the context of a 'business-driven' environment.

CIPD (2013b) noted that:

> the great majority (81%) of HR managers see their contribution to the corporate responsibility agenda as vital and a similar proportion (78%) believe that they make a valuable contribution to driving and promoting it in practice.

This should not perhaps be surprising, as HR has, in the minds of some, acquired a reputation for championing new initiatives and claiming at least part ownership of that which it believes will increase the function's status. But the report also highlights a gap between how the function views itself and its role and the views of other managers of that role. While not all HR professionals are convinced that their function has a major role to play in advancing CR, a far greater proportion outside HR is less convinced. The report concluded that HR's aspirations and efforts were not matched by its actual influence, impact, and visibility although the report found evidence that general managers want and expect HR to make more of a contribution than it currently seems to be making. But the argument that HR has more to offer, but will only be able to make this increased contribution if it is at the heart of the ethical debate, has close parallels to the debate on HR's strategic contribution or lack of. If the HR function doesn't enjoy high corporate status, what does this mean for its ability to take a leading role in raising ethical standards? We are confronted by the same paradox we explored earlier in the book—that HR's influence, in this case on the ethical behaviour of managers and employees, is linked to its corporate status and prestige. Yet this is often withheld precisely because senior managers do not feel confident that HR can actually deliver what it claims it can!

Given that HR in the public sector is predominately an employment and administrative function, the question arises as to what specifically HR can or should be doing to fulfil its ethical role. It seems that this is almost certainly going to be limited to its role as the designer and enforcer of procedures that are aimed at shaping language, attitudes, and behaviours; HR has once again been associated with the 'policeman' role, but in this particular manifestation it is the role of the 'ethics police'. In the private sector, there is more evidence of HR departments taking on a wider and more strategically relevant role. As private sector organizations place increasing emphasis on their reputation for ethical standards and for the way they treat their employees, it might be expected that HR in this sector is taking a leading role in the task of applying and culturally embedding these standards and practices within the organization. But in the private sector HR is also associated with the design and application of ethical rules and procedures. While this role is understandable and is a reflection of the increased importance given to ethical behaviour, the question that needs to be asked is why do many senior managers lack confidence in HR's ability to deliver better standards of behaviour? Has involvement in this role also been at the expense of some of its other core activities?

In addition to trying to ensure people conform to ethical policies and procedures what specifically could HR focus on to help create a feeling that organizations are functioning in an ethically acceptable way? The following are examples of what this might involve:

- Helping to make the recruitment process more inclusive and open to a wider population. For example, the increasing use of personal recommendations and referrals from existing employees may well be discriminatory and can result in many suitably qualified candidates being excluded from the process.

- Looking carefully at assessment criteria and the way they are applied to ensure only those that are appropriate and relevant to the job and expectations of wider contributions are used in the selection process.

- Demonstrating a concern with those who were not successful in the selection process, ensuring that procedural justice and a concern for their feelings and expectations characterized their experiences.

- Ensuring that success and failure in selection can be justified by reference to acceptable and necessary differences between applicants rather than the bias of selectors.

- Ensuring that the selection of people for redundancy conforms to best practice as outlined by ACAS codes of practice, and that those chosen are provided with appropriate levels of compensation and support in finding alternative employment.

- Ensuring that the abuse of power by managers is recognized and appropriate action taken at the earliest possible moment.

But areas of ethical interest and concern extend well beyond recruitment and the termination of employment. Table 5.1 identifies other areas of ethical concern from the perspective of both HR professionals and employees.

Interestingly, many of the examples from both parties either directly or indirectly involve the behaviour of managers rather than that of HR professionals and the work of the HR department. This points again to one of the important ambiguities we discussed in Chapter 3, that much of 'HR' is actually the responsibility of senior managers, line managers, and supervisors rather than the HR department. In the context of ethical

Table 5.1 Most common areas of workplace conduct causing ethical concern, from perspective of HR professionals and employees

HR perspective	Employee perspective
Favouritism in hiring, training, and promotion decisions	Failure to discipline or punish bad or abusive behaviour
Failure to maintain confidentiality of customers or employees	Pressure to compromise standards
Potential discrimination in appraisals and in allocating pay/non-pay reward	Low trust in senior managers
Maintaining a safe and healthy work environment	Retaliation against those reporting misconduct
Subcontractor conduct within outsourcing and off-shoring	Bad behaviour by managers setting a poor example for everyone else
Harassment and bullying	Corruption
Generation stereotyping	

Source: Carter, A. (2015), 'Ethical dilemmas in HR practice', in Tamkin, P. (ed.), *HR in a Disordered World: IES Perspectives on HR 2015*, Institute for Employment Studies.

or unethical behaviour, HR has to work with and through other managers to achieve the organization's ethical objectives. Whether this challenge is effectively met depends very much on the standing of the HR department and its influence at the 'top table'. Inevitably, senior managers and particularly the CEO will play an important leadership role in both establishing ethical standards and expectations—think about ABB (Chapter 1) in this context—and ensuring they are met, which will almost certainly involve HR through its monitoring, advisory, and reporting role. This is a point reinforced by CIPD (2013b) which identified Toyota as an example of a corporate body in which the senior management team includes CR in its core business planning processes. Their head of HR, corporate planning, and CSR believes it is critical for senior management to take a leading role in embedding ethics within the company through incorporating it into strategic decisions and planning activities:

> If you don't find it there, it's very difficult to ingrain its importance in individual objectives or any other process.
> (CIPD, 2013b)

But there are some who argue that HR is uniquely placed to make a major contribution to changing ethical standards. They claim that HR's 'expertise' in leadership, people management practices, and employee communications means that it can contribute to the raising of ethical awareness and help to establish ethical standards throughout the organization (CIPD, 2010). HR's leadership role either directly or indirectly comes through strongly in both reports (2010, 2013) which contain specific references to HR's promoting learning and development in values-based leadership, helping to nurture leaders throughout the organization to become more self-aware, and taking responsibility for setting ethical standards. But in her keynote address at a recent ethics conference at Leeds Business School, the group secretary of M&S suggested that meeting the ethical challenge wasn't going to be straightforward and achieved simply through leadership training:

> Developing standards and values frameworks are the easy part: it is how you engage employees in living up to organisation values in practice that is the leadership challenge
> (Mellor, 2014)

While the rhetoric of the HR fraternity displays optimism about its role in creating a more ethical organization, whether this is justified remains open to question. The reality at the moment at least suggests the function has major challenges to overcome before its claims are backed up by actual progress in achieving higher ethical standards in the workplace. Mellor's statement highlights the fact that creating an ethical framework consisting of values, creeds, and codes of conduct is a necessary first step. The more difficult challenge is to ensure that these ethical references are embedded within individuals to become part of the organizational culture—the creation of a shared ethical mindset to use Pfeffer's terminology.

A striking feature of CIPD's findings (2013b) is that those working in HR consistently rated HR's role in developing organizational values and an ethical culture higher than other managers and felt the function could and should take on a broader role and make a greater contribution to CR.

> HR is uniquely placed to understand and engender the right employee attitudes, bringing them more in line with the organisation's purpose and reviewing policies on desired behaviours and ensuring people are held accountable for their behaviour.

That only 56 per cent of the managers surveyed (and we have to question how representative this sample is of managers in general) supported this view can be seen either as a positive or negative statement. But of more interest are the reasons why many managers doubted either HR's role or its capability in meeting the ethical challenge. Does this reflect a more general questioning of HR's ability to transcend its historical traditions and limitations, or does it reflect other factors that constrain its ability to challenge unethical practices and behaviour?

Perhaps the picture is more complicated than appears to be the case. The assumption underpinning the discussion so far is that HR is or should be the main influence in shaping and monitoring an organization's ethical framework (subject of course to CEO-level overall direction). But this may not be the 'model' in all organizations. Larger organizations may have dedicated ethics departments in addition to those dealing with HR, and while research suggests that the ethics and HR functions recognize the importance of working effectively together, in a survey of ethics and compliance staff and HR professionals from 214 global companies, 77 per cent of respondents said they would like to see a more collaborative approach between the two functions than is currently the case (Foley, 2014a). The survey found that despite the potential and necessity for collaboration between the two functions, it was not uncommon for tensions and perceived lack of cooperation to exist between the two. In a 2008 survey of global companies by Ethics Resource Centre and Society for Human Resource Management, 30 per cent of respondents cited differences in the way ethical problems were expressed and interpreted as the key obstacle towards successful collaboration between the two functions, with 18 per cent citing potentially disruptive areas such as lack of mutual professional respect and HR staff feeling that they were not taken seriously enough in their 'ethical partner' role (Foley, 2014b).

While it can be credibly argued that HR is generally responsible for key systems and processes which underpin the effective delivery of messages that the organization wishes to convey about ethics, it is much more questionable to claim that HR is or should be directly responsible for ensuring ethical standards of behaviour throughout the organization. The reason for this is due to lack of contact between HR professionals and most employees. Most non-managerial employees most of the time have no direct contact with HR, and with the introduction of shared service centres and IT-led information systems the need and opportunity to talk directly with one is becoming even more limited. Because of this lack of direct contact, HR professionals would find difficulty in justifying any claim that they can influence the behaviour of employees except through the design and content of works rules, codes of behaviour, and HR processes/ systems.

A second factor that helps to explain HR's difficulties in claiming to or being expected to lead the organization's position on ethics is the simple fact that HR departments are not established for that purpose but rather to more generally 'manage' the organization's people as efficiently and effectively as possible. This will always throw up challenging ethical dilemmas, as was illustrated by the recent case of the BBC. The corporation was heavily criticized in 2013 for agreeing 'excessive' payoffs to senior managers leaving the organization. During her defence of its decisions to a committee of MPs, the then head of HR, Lucy Adams claimed that:

> **HR is not required to act as an organisation's 'conscience' in times of crisis.**
> (Jeffery, 2014)

When being questioned later by an audience of her peers at the 2014 HR Directors Business Summit in Birmingham, she admitted she should have 'challenged harder' as senior managers received payoffs totalling a reported £61 million. Her defence of the corporation's decision to sanction severance payments was based on the need to cut employment costs.

> **We were trying to save money. We have 2 per cent staff turnover in some areas of the BBC, with people who have been there 20 or 25 years. We took £20 million a year off the cost base and 30 per cent of senior managers left.**
> (Jeffery, 2014)

What stands out from this particular case is the change in public expectations on ethical standards. Corporate misbehaviour is increasingly coming under greater scrutiny as is HR's passive or active involvement in this. So, what might be expected of HR in relation to its contributions to higher ethical standards and better corporate governance? In addition to the points we made above which were largely about employment issues, in a wider, corporate role, HR could become involved in:

- Commenting on questionable financial risks or risk taking that might damage an organization's long-term interests.
- Being aware of any compliance or reporting risks where these may involve breaching legal or regulatory requirements.

- Identifying fraud risks which would damage the organization and its reputation.
- Limiting the risk of personal and confidential information being stolen or used inappropriately (Leigh, 2013).

Additionally, HR might be expected to contribute towards:

- **Creating a psychological environment** where people do not feel threatened or fearful of the behaviour of others and which allows employees to fulfil their potential and increase their productive contributions. Ethics isn't just about stopping certain kinds of specific behaviours but also about promoting that which enhances the human spirit.
- **Designing instruments, processes, and systems** that deliver against business requirements but in ways that do not involve unfair and unnecessary discrimination and which are designed in ways that do not encourage or reward dysfunctional behaviour.
- **Encouraging transparency, honesty, cooperation, and trust** in the way people relate to each other and in the way the organization functions.
- **Creating effective monitoring systems** that people understand and trust, and act appropriately on the results generated by such systems.
- **Setting standards that others can follow.**

> **STUDENT ACTIVITY 5.5**
> The aim of this activity is to explore in more depth the claim that the BBC and its HR department acted wrongly in agreeing to 'excessive' redundancy payments. Read the report produced by the National Audit Office on severance payments and wider benefits for senior BBC managers, available at https://www.nao.org.uk/wp-content/uploads/2013/07/10193-001_BBC_BOOK.pdf
> Think carefully about the following questions and reach your own conclusions:
>
> - Was the BBC excessively generous in the level of redundancy payments to senior managers?
> - Was the BBC in breach of its statutory responsibilities in its decisions over redundancy payments?
> - Was it acting in breach of an ethical code or standard in the way it structured these payments? If so, which?
> - Did the BBC's defence of its actions over these payments represent an ethically defensible position? If so, what was it?
> - Could the head of HR be legitimately criticized for these decisions? If so, on what grounds?
> - What general conclusions can be reached about the whole episode?

The Leadership Illusion

It seems reasonable to believe that uncertainty in our lives increases the importance of trust and of having leaders in whom we can trust. This is the conclusion of a joint CIPD/University of Bath report (Hope-Hailey and Gustafsson, 2014). The need for greater certainty is similar in its importance to people to the need for belonging that Harvey (1988) identified as an explanation for the Abilene paradox syndrome. According to the report, this need for greater certainty has implications for what people expect from those in authority:

> In essence people need more reassurance that their leaders or institutions are reliable. They expect more ability, benevolence, integrity and predictability from their leaders because they feel a fear about the future.

Distrust in organizations undermines personal relationships and inhibits cooperation leading to an unhealthy psychological environment and reduced organizational effectiveness: trust on the other hand helps to bind people together in mutually beneficial relationships, supports innovation/change, and contributes to a sense of psychological security that makes us more productive. Trust in leaders is generally believed to be based on four elements (CIPD, 2014):

1. **Ability**—describes perceptions of leadership competence in doing their job or fulfilling their role.

2. **Benevolence**—describes a concern for others beyond the leader's own needs, showing levels of care and compassion to others.

3. **Integrity**—defines how trustworthiness is linked to being seen as someone who adheres to principles of fairness and honesty while avoiding hypocrisy and deceit.

4. **Predictability**—emphasizes how leadership behaviour has to be consistent or regular over time. It allows people to be comfortable relying on the leader.

An important distinction needs to be made between organizational trust and trust based on relationships, or personal trust. Organizational trust is based on practices, policies, and codes of conduct that create a framework which shapes and influences behaviour; relationally embedded trust exists in both the formal and informal domains and rather than creating compliance generates more powerful behavioural outcomes such as loyalty, consent, and legitimization. It is precisely because relational trust produces these powerful effects that leadership is seen to be the key to influencing employee behaviour in terms of higher ethical standards.

 For a detailed explanation of the meaning of trust, see the Online Resources Extension Material 5.1.

A school of leadership that has been particularly influential in the last decade is that associated with authenticity (Leroy et al., 2012). Authentic leadership can be understood as an approach to leadership that emphasizes building the leader's legitimacy through honest relationships with followers. Generally, authentic leaders are seen as positive people with truthful self-concepts and high self-awareness who promote openness and generate trust (Avolio and Gardner, 2005). The idea is that leaders should 'be themselves', be trustworthy, share their personal side with employees, occasionally stepping out of their formal role to engage informally with people. Those who promote authentic leadership believe that it is perfectly natural for them to acknowledge their fallibility and to admit their flaws, which helps to promote honesty and openness among their followers who are likely to trust them more because of this. Such leaders are also more likely to recognize that mistakes are an inevitable and necessary part of learning and 'becoming more', and that works discipline needs to be applied appropriately and with consideration.

As well as being associated with positive ethical outcomes, leader behaviour (the wrong kind) has also been identified as a contributory factor in many cases of public and private sector organizational failings in many Western countries. In ABB, Percy Barnevik was heavily criticized for showing a lack of ethical behaviour over the excessive pension contributions he authorized for himself, while the unethical behaviour of the collective leadership of Enron has been thoroughly documented. Interestingly, in Barnevik's case the same person was lauded for his leadership and achievements (and ethical stance) but later criticized for financial greed. In the NHS, both the Kirkup Report (2015) and the Francis Report into failings in the Mid-Staffordshire hospital in 2013 identified leadership failings as critical factors that help explain why dysfunctional cultures developed and were allowed to continue. Certainly, within the NHS, improving the quality of leadership was seen as a key recommendation in both reports and it is often the case that in failing private sector companies changing the leader (CEO) is the preferred and first strategy for turning the business around.

Referring to the NHS, Michael West (2014) talked about the importance not of the leader, but of collective leadership which is leadership of all, by all, and together with all. This rather different conceptualization means moving away from the dominant command-and-control and hierarchical-based leadership models that dominate most large-scale organizations and creating a quite different leadership culture. It means attracting, developing, and sustaining leaders who are committed to working together to create a leadership culture underpinned by core values. Collective leadership means leaders and teams working together across and within boundaries in organizations in the interests of patient care and community health.

> This requires us to change the way we think about leadership by seeing leadership as the responsibility of all—anyone with expertise taking leadership responsibility when appropriate.

Improving the quality of leaders and creating leadership capabilities throughout the organization is seen then as the 'way forward' in terms of driving organizational performance (Dinwoodie et al., 2014) and addressing ethical and cultural issues. This impetus to improve leadership has predictably led to a huge growth in what we would call 'the leadership industry'. This consists of those individuals, consultancies, universities, and leadership centres that offer 'leadership solutions' to organizations that believe leadership, good and bad, is both the problem and solution as far as their efforts to become 'better' is concerned.

This final section takes a much more critical perspective on the claims of many in the leadership industry who, we suggest, present an overly simplistic and one-dimensional picture of what leaders need to be like to fulfil the expectations others have of them. It seeks to understand why leaders, even the most revered, sometimes act unethically and why unethical behaviour is not simply associated with both 'good' and 'bad' leaders but is a characteristic of the human condition generally. It does so by using the analysis and insights developed by Jeffrey Pfeffer (2015), in which he presents a well-argued critique of the leadership industry and of the leadership myths that have been perpetuated by those whose business is leadership and particularly leadership training.

Pfeffer begins his analysis by presenting an interesting paradox: that the ever-growing leadership industry and particularly its training and development component, that continues to recommend that leaders inspire others, generate trust, act authentically, be truthful, and so on, coexists with what he says is overwhelming evidence that workplaces are filled with disengaged and disillusioned employees who do not trust their leaders. Consider two questions in response to his statement.

1. On a personal basis, how many leaders, and by that we mean those in authority and with responsibility for the performance of a significant part of an organization and significant numbers of staff, do you or have you trusted implicitly?

2. Has there been any noticeable and permanent change in the behaviour of people who have attended leadership training programmes? This does not necessarily mean that the leadership course was uninteresting or that the participant didn't feel satisfied with it but that it led to positive behavioural change that lasted.

The position taken here is that most people will and are likely to continue to answer no to both questions! It is a stance supported by others who have expertise and experience in the field. Pfeffer quotes such a person who argued that the leadership industry:

> [has failed] in any major, meaningful, measurable way to improve the human condition [and that] the rise of leadership as an object of our collective fascination has coincided precisely with the decline in leadership in our collective estimation.
> (2015: 5)

Pfeffer is not only critical of the claimed-for contributions made by the leadership industry, but also of a number of its central recommendations, one of which is for leaders to be authentic. As we stated above, authentic leadership has become arguably the most popular of the contemporary leadership models and one of the model's implied assumptions is that leaders who are true to themselves make better leaders, but is it the case that more effective leaders also display the characteristics associated with authenticity? Pfeffer presents a counter-intuitive yet convincing case that being authentic is pretty much the opposite of what leaders must be. He claims that:

> Leaders do not need to be true to themselves. Rather, leaders need to be true to what the situation and what those around them want and need from them.

Does this mean that leaders can abandon their core values and beliefs whenever it is considered expedient? Almost certainly not, but it does suggest that where leaders are genuinely concerned about the impact of technological change or the financial health of the business they need to display not concerns and fears but optimism, confidence, and positivity to their staff. Without being too cynical, the comment that

sincerity—if you can fake that you've got it made

suggests that the belief in a leader's sincerity may be more important than his/her *being* sincere. Pfeffer is particularly critical of the authentic leadership movement, based on his belief that:

- Although well intentioned, it is values laden and offers little to either science or practice.
- It is heavily reliant on prescriptions rather than systematic analysis and scientific research and is associated with lots of 'shoulds' and 'oughts'.
- It does not reflect accurately what effective leaders do and paints a one-dimensional image of leader behaviour.
- It offers recommendations that are almost certainly not implementable and may be fundamentally misguided.

One of the most interesting of Pfeffer's comments is that as people move onwards and upwards in the organization their freedom to act on personal beliefs and feelings—in other words to act more authentically—is constrained by the requirements of being effective and successful. He refers to internationally known leaders such as Kennedy and Mandela who were known for their integrity and authenticity but who had less well-known private lives that didn't fit this image and who over the years made and remade themselves to reflect the different challenges that they faced. They may have been true to themselves but they were also flexible and pragmatic when they needed to be. The inference is that being 'too' authentic would have made them less not more effective leaders!

Ethical behaviour is also considered to involve being truthful, but what does this actually mean? Is it realistic to expect leaders to be truthful all the time and in all circumstances? We may think that this is what we would like to find or hope to discover, but are organizations the kind of places where this is encouraged and supported? Of course, integrity is strongly associated with some of the best-known leaders of industry and commerce (see Collins, 2001: ch. 2), but, according to Pfeffer, openness and honesty are not default behaviours in most organizations. This does not necessarily mean lying is endemic, but not telling the truth, misrepresenting, hiding information, failing to disclose important information, and so on probably are in varying degrees. Harvey's identification of the power of groupthink and the distorting effect of the need to belong and to be psychologically safe help us to understand why this might be the case. The fact that most messengers *are* 'shot' if the message is bad news helps us to understand why leaders are often told what they want to hear!

Pfeffer isn't advocating lying, by any means, he is only acknowledging that building a culture of truth-telling is a difficult task. It requires considerable effort and conviction, and that telling the truth can be unpleasant and have serious consequences for individuals and organizations. Hiding the truth, as evidenced by the Francis and Kirkup reports into NHS failings, can become culturally acceptable and clearly serves particular purposes and interests. Lying or not telling the truth may also be prevalent in many organizations because there are no negative consequences for doing so and no perceived positive outcomes for truth-telling.

So, what does Pfeffer have to say about trust and leadership? Well, he quotes research that suggests that worldwide fewer than one in five respondents in a survey believed government or business leaders would actually tell the truth when confronted with a difficult issue (2015: 135). In the UK, a recent Ipsos Mori poll (2016) found that politicians are still trusted less than estate agents, journalists, and bankers. Civil servants were trusted to tell the truth by 59 per cent of respondents, NHS managers by 49 per cent, and business leaders by only 35 per cent. So, despite millions and over the years billions of pounds spent on leadership training and development and ethics training only 35 per cent of business leaders are trusted. There is clearly an issue to be analysed, understood, and addressed here.

He also thinks that while most people are predisposed to trust leaders there is good reason to temper that trust and be more cautious in who is trusted and about the reasons for trusting others. Again, Pfeffer makes the point that breaking the trust others place in leaders may not be as important as first thought because in many cases the consequences of breaking someone's trust are not that significant. Loss of trust in an institution or organization may have serious consequences, but only if the ability to apply sanctions exists; where it doesn't, what can the aggrieved party do? He believes that there are advantages in not trusting too much and that being sceptical about what leaders say and promise is a form of protection from their potential misbehaviour and dishonesty. This idea does of course contradict those who believe leaders should work to increase the degree of trust that exists within the organization and is certainly not consistent with the thinking underpinning authentic leadership, but it is a thought-provoking thesis which should be taken seriously.

One reason for this is because leaders may and probably are, at times, unable to keep the promises they make to employees and other stakeholders because of the changing circumstances they have to deal with and the different priorities that have to be juggled. We spoke earlier about the ethical dilemmas and it is unquestionably the case that leaders need to be adept at managing these. Another is that, as colleagues get promoted and friends move on, new social groupings and power centres emerge—older and more trusting relationships based on shared experiences and long-term cooperation are replaced by ones that have yet to, and indeed may not, replicate the ones lost. Trust is not easily transferable!

This brief but important critical perspective on leadership is not meant to undermine the belief in the importance of 'good' leadership nor the attempts to address the challenges of unethical behaviour through a leadership improvement strategy. It represents rather a note of caution to those who might adopt an overly optimistic position on the ability of leaders to set new and higher ethical standards and to eliminate or at least reduce the unethical behaviour of others. Human nature, organizational politics and dynamics, and powerful sociopsychological forces come into play when we look for explanations of why trust, integrity, and honesty seem to be in such short supply in contemporary organizations. But that statement in itself may be based on misconceptions and engrained stereotypes rather than hard facts. It is very difficult to know. But even those leaders who are used as role models possess a 'darker side' where the need to be politically successful or because of personal interests often means they are not as honest and truthful as they appear to be. It is worth pointing out that those who judge others in terms of their ethical standards and behaviour are more than likely to exhibit in their own behaviour that which they are critical of in others.

 For a personal account of the ideas and the justification supporting Pfeffer's book, see the Online Resources Extension Material 5.2.

Summary

- The fairness or otherwise of something can be determined by objective and subjective references; the more that reliance is given to the latter, the more there will be disagreement over whether something is fair, because different stakeholders will use their own references to support their particular interpretation.

- Organizations are environments in which power and authority is legitimately concentrated in the hands of leaders and managers. Power can corrupt and where there are limited opportunities to hold those in power to account, or people are apprehensive about raising questions about behaviour, unethical and unprofessional practices can develop.

- Acknowledging the existence of ethical dilemmas means that actions and behaviours can be 'right' and 'wrong'.

- Seeing the solution to questionable ethical practices in the form of more ethical leadership behaviour (authentic leadership) is, despite its popularity, not the only, and may be not the most effective way towards changing organizational ethics.

- The position of HR in relation to ethical behaviour is complicated. First, HR itself needs to put its own house in order and look at the fairness and procedural justice of the mechanisms used in the way people are recruited, rewarded, appraised, and disciplined.

- HR might wish to claim to be the organization's conscience but the evidence suggests not all managers are convinced this is a role it should or could take on. Furthermore, being perceived as primarily a policing and compliance function might undermine its influence and capacity to contribute to other aspects of HRM.

 Visit the **online resources** that accompany this book for self-test questions, web links, and more information on the topics covered in this chapter, at: **www.oup.com/uk/banfield3e/**

 ## REVIEW QUESTIONS

1. What is meant by ethical dilemmas and how do they arise?

2. Why is it so difficult to establish the fairness or otherwise of behaviour and decisions that some may perceive as being unfair?

3. What different kinds of justice are there and which are likely to be most relevant to the management of people?

4. Realistically, what are the kinds of things HR can do to reduce unethical behaviour in organizations?

5. Why does the HR department lack credibility in the eyes of some senior managers when it comes to its claims for a key role in improving organizational ethics?

163

CASE STUDY The bullying head of department

Alex Wilson had enjoyed a long and rewarding career as a university lecturer. Despite organizational changes in his department, which meant that he lost certain managerial responsibilities and influence, he was reasonably contented with his lot. He planned to spend the last few years before he retired working with students and writing. That was until he received a call from an ex-colleague who had moved to work in a private management college some years earlier and who was looking to recruit experienced staff to support the expansion of the college's faculty. Alex thought long and hard about the opportunity that had been presented to him; he was interested in what was being offered—the chance to get involved with some interesting management development programmes and the experience of working outside the public sector—but he wondered if, at his age, it was the right thing to do.

After being invited to visit the college and talk to the departmental faculty, some of whom he knew from conferences and other professional events, Alex was invited to apply for a specific post, which he did and was subsequently appointed. His ex-colleague who headed up a different school within the department helped with his informal induction and explained the department's five-year development strategy, although Alex was located in a different school, working under its head, Catherine Palmer. Catherine was someone he had met professionally over the years but in a very different capacity. Now she was his line manager.

It didn't take long for Alex to realize that the management style practised by his head was very different from what he had been used to in his previous institution. Staff meetings were highly structured and chaired by Catherine Palmer who worked closely with three of her senior colleagues to ensure staff conformed to her expectations and requirements. Her style was exclusive rather than inclusive, and she restricted discussion on important issues to the bare minimum. Alex was amazed to find that in meetings hardly anyone was prepared to ask questions and no one challenged the head or said anything that could be interpreted by her as being critical of her decisions. In addition, his own work was frequently criticized by her on the basis that 'that's not how we do things here' and he had a feeling that she was being excessively critical over unimportant things. Things deteriorated after his six-month appraisal with her during which she expressed her disappointment over his work, making it clear that she expected him to conform to the culture that prevailed in the school and department which was led by someone she worked closely with and had been a colleague of for several years. It was obvious that the departmental head and Catherine shared the same commitment to a style of management based on the principles of command and control and used their positional power to enforce compliance from more junior and middle-ranking staff.

What became more apparent, though, was that Catherine picked on people she didn't like—those few who were prepared to question the way she was managing the school. From conversations with colleagues, it was clear to Alex that people were being bullied and treated unfairly in several ways. One was the overly critical feedback they received from Catherine informally without any recognition of the positive contributions they were making. Second, her practice of bringing individuals in for formal 'performance chats' left them demoralized and demotivated. Third, there was a serious lack of trust and a fear of doing or saying anything wrong. Most people tried to just get on with their jobs and accept things, but it was clear to Alex that things were far from right.

He knew the college had a policy on harassment and bullying, but was unsure how seriously his complaint would be taken if he raised his concerns formally. He was in a quandary; should he just accept the way things were, or do something? And, if he decided to act, what should he do?

Questions

1. Is the situation experienced by Alex acceptable within the range of legitimate management behaviour in an environment where the school and department's business objectives were being met?

2. It was surprising to Alex that HR hadn't become involved already—what explanations are there for this?

3. Is there any action Alex could take informally to raise his concerns?

4. What was missing in the way the college was being led that could have identified the problems Alex had experienced?

5. Are there any ethical dilemmas at play here?

 Insights and Outcomes: visit the **online resources** at **www.oup.com/uk/banfield3e/** for suggested answers to these case study questions.

 FURTHER READING

Business Ethics Briefing (2014) 'Collaboration between the ethics function and HR', issue 40 (April), at: http://www.ibe.org.uk/userassets/briefings/b40_hr.pdf

CIPD (2012) 'Responsible and sustainable business: HR leading the way' [online], at: http://www.cipd.co.uk/hr-resources/research/responsiblesustainable-business-hr-leading.aspx

Danley J. et al. (1991) 'HR ethical situations', *Human Resources Management*, 26, 1–12.

Dow, J. (2014) 'Leadership Ethics', Business Ethics Conference, Leeds Business Schools Leeds University, 2–3 April, at: http://www.leeds.ac.uk/arts/info/125163/consultancy_and_training/2412/business_ethics_conference_2014/2 [video presentation]

Institute for Fiscal Studies (2014) *Public Sector Pay in the UK*, Report R97.

Klotz, A. C. and Bolino, M. C. (2013) 'Citizenship and counterproductive work behaviour: A moral licensing view', *Academy of Management Review*, 38(2).

ACAS (2013) 'Myths of the workplace: Everyone should get equal pay for doing the same work', at: http://www.acas.org.uk/index.aspx?articleid=4198

Aguinis, H. and Bradley, K. (2015) 'The secret sauce for organizational success: Managing and producing star performers', *Organizational Dynamics*, 44(3).

Avolio, B. J. and Gardner, W. L. (2005) 'Authentic leadership development: Getting to the root of positive forms of leadership', *Leadership Quarterly*, 16.

Baekgaard, O. (1984) 'The cost of whistleblowing', *Multinational Monitor*, 5(6).

Bampton, R. and Maclagan, P. (2009) 'Does a "care orientation" explain gender differences in ethical decision making? A critical analysis and fresh findings', *Business Ethics*, 18(2).

Banaji, M. R. et al. (2003) 'How (un) ethical are you?', *Harvard Business Review* (December).

Bateman, T. S. and Snell, S. A. (2015) *Management: Leading and Collaborating in a Competitive World*, McGraw-Hill Education, ch. 5.

CIPD (2010) 'Next generation HR: time for change: towards a next generation for HR', at: http://www.cipd.co.uk/hr-resources/research/next-generation-hr-time-for-change.aspx

CIPD (2013a) *The Changing Contours of Fairness* [research report].

CIPD (2013b) *The Role of HR in Corporate Responsibility* [research report].

CIPD (2014) *Cultivating Trustworthy Leaders* [research report].

CIPD (2015) 'Ethical decision-making: Eight perspectives on workplace dilemmas'.

Collins, J. (2001) *From Good to Great*, Random House.

Colquitt, J. et al. (2001) 'Justice at the millennium: A meta-analytic review of 25 years of organizational justice research', *Journal of Applied Psychology*, 86(3).

Dineen, B. R. et al. (2004) 'Perceived fairness of web-based applicant screening procedures: Weighing the rules of justice and the role of individual differences', *Human Resource Management*, 43(2–3).

Dinwoodie, D. L. et al. (2014) *How Leadership Strategy Drives Business Results*, Center for Creative Leadership.

Dobrin, A. (2014) 'Are women more ethical than men?', *Psychology Today*, 11 June.

Ethical Trading Initiative [n.d.] 'Child labour', at: http://www.ethicaltrade.org/issues/child-labour

Foley, P. (2014a) 'Ethics and HR departments need to work together', Ethical Foundation, 30 May, at: http://www.ethicalcorp.com/people-careers/ethics-and-hr-departments-need-work-together

Foley, P. (2014b) 'Ethics and the HR department—A happy marriage?', at: http://www.hrbullets.co.uk/unplugged/ethics-and-the-hr-department-a-happy-marriage.html

Francis, R. (2013) *Report of the Mid Staffordshire NHS Foundation Trust Public Inquiry*, at: https://www.gov.uk/government/uploads/system/uploads/attachment_data/file/279124/0947.pdf

Friedman, M. (1970) 'The social responsibility of business is to increase its profits', *New York Times Magazine*, 13 September.

Guardian, The (2016) 'Boardroom pay under spotlight as City AGM season begins', at: https://www.theguardian.com/business/2016/mar/27/boardroom-pay-under-spotlight-as-city-agm-season-begins

Hall, M. (2008) 'EU regulation and the UK employee consultation framework', at: https://www2.warwick.ac.uk/fac/soc/wbs/research/irru/publications/recentconf/mh_-_lse_workshop_paper.pdf

Harvey, J. B. (1988) *The Abilene Paradox*, Jossey-Bass.

HMSO (2014) *Report on Ethical Standards for Providers of Public Services*.

Hope-Hailey, V. and Gustafsson, S. (2014) *Cultivating Trustworthy Leaders*, CIPD/University of Bath research report.

House of Commons (2013) 'BBC severance packages', at: https://www.publications.parliament.uk/pa/cm201314/cmselect/cmpubacc/476/476.pdf

Institute of Employment Studies (2015) *HR in a Disordered World: IES Perspectives on HR 2015*, ed. P. Tamkin, at: http://www.employment-studies.co.uk/system/files/resources/files/506_1.pdf

Ipsos Mori (2016) https://www.ipsos-mori.com/researchpublications/researcharchive/3685/Politicians-are-still-trusted-less-than-estate-agents-journalists-and-bankers.aspx#gallery[m]/1

Jeffery, R. (2014) 'Lucy Adams: "HR isn't an organisation's conscience"', *People Management*, 6 February.

Kirkup, B. (2015) *The Report of the Morecambe Bay Investigation*, at: https://www.gov.uk/government/uploads/system/uploads/attachment_data/file/408480/47487_MBI_Accessible_v0.1.pdf

Leigh, A. (2013) 'The harsh reality of human resources', 27 October, at: http://www.ethical-leadership.co.uk/human-resources-and-ethics-66

Leroy, H. et al. (2012) 'Authentic leadership and behavioural integrity as drivers of follower commitment and performance', *Journal of Business Ethics*, 107(3).

Level Playing Field Institute (2007) 'Corporate leavers survey 2007: The cost of employee turnover due solely to unfairness in the workplace', at: https://www.lpfi.org/sites/default/files/corporate-leavers-survey.pdf

Mellor, A. (2014) Keynote presentation, Business Ethics Conference, Leeds Business School, Leeds University, 2–3 April, at: http://www.leeds.ac.uk/arts/info/125163/consultancy_and_training/2412/business_ethics_conference_2014/2

O'Toole, J. (2015) 'Ethical challenges in human resources', at: https://www.scu.edu/ethics/focus-areas/business-ethics/resources/ethical-challenges-in-human-resources

Pfeffer, J. (2015) *Leadership BS*, Harper Business.

Swailes, S. (2013) 'The ethics of talent management', *Business Ethics: A European Review*, 22(1).

Velasquez, M. et al. (2014) 'Justice and fairness', Markkula Center for Applied Ethics, at: https://www.scu.edu/ethics/ethics-resources/ethical-decision-making/justice-and-fairness

West, M. (2014) 'Collective leadership: Fundamental to creating the cultures we need in the NHS', at: http://www.kingsfund.org.uk/blog/2014/05/collective-leadership-fundamental-creating-cultures-we-need-nhs

Wheldon, P. and Webley, S. (2013) 'Corporate ethics policies and programmes', Institute of Business Ethics, at: http://www.ibe.org.uk/userfiles/codes_survey_2013_interactive.pdf

International HRM

6

Key Terms

Global organization An organization that employs a workforce in different countries throughout the world, with a view to maximizing performance by sourcing or providing goods and/or services in a globally based market, and in which decisions are driven by markets rather than by geography.

National culture A complex system of norms, social values, behaviours, expectations, and legal frameworks that gives an identity to a particular country.

Multinational companies (MNCs) Multinational companies that have a national base, but which operate and trade multinationally.

Expatriate worker An employee deployed overseas, usually sourced from his or her country of origin.

Culture shock The psychological and emotional reaction associated with exposure to different cultural environments.

Learning Outcomes

As a result of reading this chapter and using the online resources, you should be able to:

- explain the implications for the human resources (HR) function of globalization;

- recognize the social and cultural differences between countries, and their effect on employment and management practices;

- understand the concept of a global organization, and the implications for global employment and for global HR policy and practice;

- support staff on overseas assignments and secondments; and

- understand the role of the international HRM (IHRM) practitioner and the responsibilities that he or she has.

Introduction

IHRM is a field of growing importance in the HR arena, a development that reflects the increasing importance of international business and the dominant position of global institutions in business, government, and NGOs in the politico-economic system. The emphasis on maximizing performance by treating business and resources in a global rather than country-specific context, applies increasingly to HR, and this perspective informs and shapes how many are employed and managed. Senior and middle managers experience frequent overseas placements and secondments, often in a number of countries, and are frequently required to travel to and work in different overseas locations. CEOs spend a considerable amount of their working time travelling and communicating with international customers, governments, and their overseas subsidiaries. Management for many has indeed become truly international.

With the onset of more cost-effective transport systems, supply chains, and swifter, more effective methods of communications, organizations that previously operated in a number of countries, but sourced and supplied from within, are now seeing the benefits of global sourcing and supply, with more complex and interdependent supply chains operating with increasingly tight timescales. Equally, economic expansion, particularly in China and India, and the forecast for higher growth rates overseas has led many organizations to the conclusion that they need to have the organizational capability to operate in these countries and across national borders, to benefit from this predicted growth. This can mean many different things, but common to most is the importance of flexibility in the way organizations are structured, resourced, and function.

To be a truly global organization, it is not sufficient simply to operate in a number of countries. The global organization has to possess the capability of operating and managing at a level at which service to its customers is not restricted by local and regional geographies. Products and services can be sourced from the optimum location, and price and quality, rather than national identity, become critical business criteria. The search for raw materials to fuel world economic growth, and the search for markets for goods and services as this growth creates new wealth and greater demand is having a profound effect on the way in which senior executives think about business. Success in this global arena is a function of a number of key factors, but the ability to generate and sustain the organizational capability to operate in these markets is absolutely critical and the human resource is an integral component of the competitive organizational capability that global companies need to maintain and increase their international presence (Hira and Hira, 2005).

Few, if any, HR practitioners in the private sector are now immune from the effects of globalization and the internationalization of business, and it is difficult to think of any oil, gas, or energy company, to continue with the sector example from Chapter 4, that is not in some sense international or global. In the UK, however, globalization and international business have less direct effects on the 'business' of the public sector. The aim of this chapter is to explore and explain the implications of this inexorable trend for those with specific responsibilities for the human resource in this different and arguably more challenging environment. Before we outline those areas of HR that have been influenced either directly or indirectly by the opening up of borders and the increasingly free movement of goods, services, and people, it is worth remembering that this is not a new, or indeed recent, phenomenon. The pace of change has undeniably increased over the past twenty years—but transnational movements of goods and people/labour have been a feature of society for hundreds if not thousands of years. As an example, when the Egyptians built the Pyramids, while most workers were probably local, it is almost certain that many of the skilled workers employed came from outside Egypt—from different countries in the Middle East and beyond. This is a view that accords with the research of David (1997), who, basing his evidence on ancient artefacts found near to the Pyramids, argued that:

> The workforce at the town may therefore have included elements from a number of countries, as well as native-born Egyptians.

The construction of Britain's canal and rail networks in the eighteenth and nineteenth centuries certainly depended heavily on 'foreign' labour, in the form of Irish 'navvies'. Before this, the forced migration of the French Huguenots into England in the sixteenth and seventeenth centuries represented a major source of skilled labour, expertise, and know-how that transformed the country's textile industry. In the nineteenth century, the expansion of the British Empire was dependent on engineers, traders, and others living and working overseas. In the twentieth century, immigrants from the West Indies and the Asian subcontinent provided a much-needed source of labour for the UK's textile and steel industries. From a US perspective, inward migration into the USA from Europe created an endless supply of labour and capital which drove the growing US economy and facilitated extensive trading relationships. The point is that flows of labour into the UK and elsewhere, doing business abroad, and the employment of technical experts and managers on overseas contracts and secondments are not new phenomena; what *is* new is the scale and complexity of these developments, and their implications for social and economic change and the role of the HR practitioner and the HR function.

In the context of an introductory text, it is not practical to try to cover all aspects of IHRM and, for the purposes of this chapter, the following are of concern:

● the use of UK expatriate staff to work on overseas projects;

● the cultural issues related to establishing overseas businesses and outsourcing the production of goods and services;

● employing and managing a diverse workforce;

● new developments in HR in Asia;

● competences of the IHRM manager and those needed for working successfully abroad.

Globalization

The internationalization of management has, for some, become an expression of what has become known as 'globalization' (Edwards and Rees, 2006). Accepting that there is an ongoing debate about what this actually means, Edwards and Rees believe that, as far as IHRM is concerned, the most important aspects of globalization are:

● global production, meaning that transnational corporations produce, distribute, and sell goods and services around the world;

● global organizations, for which the ability to resource and manage global production systems impacts directly on HR and management, both of which have to come to terms with social and cultural differences.

Each of these is facilitated by the growth in global financial systems and the expansion of global communications networks.

Globalization is also associated with the rapid, and relatively recent, development of a 'global economy'. What this means is that national economic and social identities and differences are becoming less distinctive, and arguably more irrelevant, as market forces and free trade move national economies and economic organizations towards a more convergent and universalistic state (Edwards and Rees, 2006). While the effects of globalization are clearly accelerating, including the idea of systems of finance, production, and trade that are 'without boundary', care must be taken not to overstate the effects that this has on national employment systems, and on the social and cultural differences that not only exist between national economies, but within them.

Globalization can also be thought of as the integration of economies, industries, markets, cultures, and policy-making around the world. It describes a process by which national and regional economies, societies, and cultures have become integrated through the global network of trade, communication, immigration, and transportation. In the past, globalization was often primarily focused on the economic side of the world, such as trade, foreign direct investment, and international capital flows, but more recently the term has been expanded to include a broader range of areas and activities such as culture, media, technology, political, and even climate change. Globalization is not however without its critics (see Global Policy Forum) and the recent political developments in the UK and USA suggest that resistance to the economic and political implications of free trade, uncontrolled migration, and the free movement of capital is increasing.

But thinking about the debate on globalization and the impact that this is having on HR, what does it actually mean for the HR practitioner in terms of his/her work? Without representing an exhaustive list, the following represent situations that are related to the growth of transnational corporations and a converging global economic system.

- More people are working for transnationals in an HR capacity. Increasing numbers of newly qualified and experienced HR practitioners are employed by 'global' enterprises, such as Gazprom (the Russian gas supplier), or work for overseas companies that set up UK or Irish subsidiaries. These new employment contexts raise interesting questions about the way in which social and cultural differences are managed within the workplace and the status that HR enjoys within these organizations. A particularly important issue here relates to gender and the extent to which females working for overseas companies face problems of acceptance and discrimination (Wirth, 2002).

- UK-based organizations are, because of inward migration and a more diverse indigenous workforce, employing more people from different social, cultural, and religious backgrounds. Managing diversity has become less of an aspiration for those organizations seeking to adjust to demographic change and more of a reality. CIPD (2013) reports that one in three UK employers is actively recruiting migrant workers to work in such diverse industries as the NHS, agriculture, food processing, and hospitality. The implications of this for recruitment and selection, and induction practices, as well as for communications, welfare, and training, are obvious.

- Increasingly, HR practitioners, particularly more senior ones, have to undertake overseas assignments or secondments, or are responsible for organizing the expatriation and repatriation of other managers.

- HR professionals are developing new approaches to individual and organizational learning, and generating knowledge-sharing networks that connect to the different parts of the transnational/global organization.

- HR professionals in global organizations are also developing ways of communicating with people in different parts of the world, and building the capability to track and monitor employment numbers, costs, and the outcome of management development programmes across national boundaries.

- The growth of global labour markets and the development of global talent management strategies which involve multinational and global organizations sourcing key executive and leadership roles from wherever top talent can be found (Al Ariss, 2014).

Figure 6.1 presents the different challenges and responsibilities facing the international HR manager at the strategic level.

One of the growing trends in IHRM is the trend towards increasing the outsourcing of non-critical parts of the function (Cisek and Ozer, 2011). The question which arises from this development is whether the way in which HR outsourcing works in regions such as South East Asia reflects Western models and practices or has its own distinctive characteristics. Research Insight 6.1 offers an opportunity to answer this question.

International transactions and administration	Building capability and resource development
• Pay and conditions • Legal issues • Recruitment and selection • Induction • Database maintenance • Managing expatriation and repatriation	• Fast-tracking and developing managers • Career and succession planning • Developing knowledge management systems • IT-driven learning
Business-driven activities	Developing and implementing strategy
• Reorganization • Efficiency drives • Supporting overseas startups, e.g. new factories • Outsourcing, e.g. overseas call centres	• Strategic HR planning • Performance and reward management • Managing closures, acquisitions, and mergers • Culture building

Figure 6.1 The four dimensions of the international HR manager's role and contribution

RESEARCH INSIGHT 6.1

To take your learning further you may wish to read the following article:

Chiang et al. (2010) 'Examining human resource management outsourcing in Hong Kong', *International Journal of Human Resource Management*, **21 December, 15.**

This article focuses on the strategic significance of outsourcing in the Asian context. It draws on several important HRM perspectives in explaining outsourcing practices and concludes that the practice is still in its development phase and subject to a number of key constraints and considerations.

Despite the current state of the world economy, the global supply of talent is short of its long-term demand trend, and the gap is a challenge for employers everywhere as this shortage in the supply of talent is likely to continue to increase, notably for highly skilled workers and for the next generation of middle and senior leaders (Kapoor, 2008). He argues that most emerging nations with large populations, including Brazil, Russia, India, and China, may not be able to sustain a net surplus workforce with the right skills for much longer and that now, more than ever, organizations need to place greater emphasis on attracting human capital rather than financial capital. As noted in Chapter 1, economic success will be increasingly based on the ability to attract and retain human capital where as well as financial capital, creativity, innovation, and leadership are still very much the product of human enterprise. From our perspective, the most important feature of a globalized economy is the creation, for many knowledge-based jobs, of a global labour market and an internationally mobile labour force. Organizations working in this global environment are still subject to the laws of supply and demand and need to react to different market conditions, but it is increasingly likely to be the case that effective HRM will be a key differentiator between those companies who succeed and those that don't. Global staffing and global leadership development are the two components of global HR with the greatest potential for achieving leverage and strategic advantage, and only the multinationals that are willing to adapt their HR practices to changing global labour market conditions will be able to attract, develop, and retain the right talent. As a consequence, they will build the kind of global capabilities successful organizations need.

STUDENT ACTIVITY 6.1

Read the blog by Jonathan Portes on the economic case for migration, February 2016, published by the Institute for Economic Affairs, at https://iea.org.uk/blog/the-economic-case-for-migration Critically consider the argument that the free movement of labour is necessary for economic growth and identify the challenges this might bring for organizations that depend on global flows of labour for success.

Perhaps the most important effect of globalization on the HR function has been to emphasize HR's strategically vital role in managing talent globally; in other words, all or most of what HR does in and for international and global businesses supports the search for, use of, and retention of talented people. In the context of what we said in Chapter 4 this involves both sourcing distinctively talented individuals and creating a workforce that is trained, motivated, and engaged. In their recent global human capital trends survey (Deloitte University Press, 2015) the Deloitte Consultancy firm generated data from over 3,000 managers and HR professionals in over 100 countries to try to establish the business and HR agendas that were shaping global talent management activities and objectives. Four major themes were identified and their associated specific activities and trends are indicated below:

1. **Leading** This involves addressing the challenge of strengthening organizational *leadership* by investing in new and innovative leadership development models and actively exploring new approaches to *learning and development* as they confront increasing skills gaps.

2. **Engagement** Organizations are recognizing the need to focus on *culture and employee engagement* as they struggle to build and maintain feelings of loyalty and increase retention levels that support the business. There is also a greater recognition that organizations need to build a *flexible and responsive workforce* which involves taking a more sophisticated approach to managing all aspects of the workforce, including hourly, contingent, and contract staff. The recent issues in the UK over the employment status of Uber drivers and other supposedly self-employed staff working in the gig economy, is evidence of the importance of this activity.

3. **Reinventing** This involves *reinventing HR* so that it can deliver greater business impact and drive HR and business innovation. Effective *HR and people analytics* will increasingly characterize HR's new approach to developing new capabilities and approaches appropriate to the task of meeting the expectations of senior executives in relation to its organizational contributions. The importance of knowing more about staff is also reflected in the emphasis given to HR *expanding its data strategies* by harnessing and integrating third-party data about their people from social media platforms.

4. **Reimagining** This involves the *simplification of work* and working environments in response to information overload and increasing organization and system complexity. It also involves looking for opportunities in robotics and AI as 'intelligent talent' to either replace people or work in collaboration with them while at the same time rethinking the design of work and the skills their employees need to succeed.

Signpost to Chapter 4: Talent Management: Strategies and Models, for insight into organizational practices to acquire and develop talented staff.

The point is that globalization and the increased competition that follows is driving businesses and HR functions that are exposed to these forces to embrace these themes and activities at an ever-faster pace. In terms of international businesses, therefore, globalization is probably the main driver for change in the way organizations function and HR is structured and operates to support the business.

International HRM

IHRM, as an area of academic study, followed the emergence of HRM/strategic HRM (SHRM), and shares the same strategic focus and emphasis on vertical and horizontal integration, human resource capability, and human capital development. Its antecedents lay in the comparative study of industrial relations, which focused on national differences in employment and managerial practices, the collective organization of labour, and conflict resolution mechanisms (Ferner and Hyman, 1998). It has, however, evolved into a distinctive, and increasingly recognized, subject in its own right, as the implications of globalization and international business have impacted on the use of human resources and the role of the HR professional (Brewster et al., 2011; Harzing and Pinnington, 2015).

As far as IHRM is concerned, academics have tended to adopt one of two approaches. In the first approach, it is seen as essentially HRM 'writ large', and associated with domestic and national agendas transferred and relocated into an international arena.

A definition that fits this approach is given by Scullion (1995), who claimed that IHRM could be understood as:

> **the HRM strategies, policies and practices which firms pursue in response to the internationalization of business.**

This approach gives particular emphasis to the international context and transnational requirements associated with such activities as:

- recruitment and selection;
- performance and reward strategies;
- the management and control of diverse workforces;

and a definition that reflects the same approach but goes further would be:

> **International HRM is concerned with identifying and understanding how global and international organisations manage their geographically dispersed worked force in order to leverage their HR resources for obtaining local as well as global competitive advantage**
> **(Brewster et al., 2011)**

In this second definition, IHRM is viewed in a more strategic sense in ways that mirror the HRM/SHRM debate, and highlights the importance of leveraging maximum contributions from an organization's global human resources in the pursuit of competitive advantage. Seen in this way, IHRM encompasses the above three sets of activities, but additionally involves:

- facilitating organizational learning and knowledge management across borders and between internationally dispersed operating units (Glaister et al., 2003);
- the internationalization of management throughout the organization, reflecting its global presence and operations;
- the internationalization of organizational culture to reflect multiple dimensions of diversity.

But as with HRM, there is a lack of consensus as to what IHRM means and involves with different authors giving emphasis to particular features and activities and ignoring others, which may be perfectly reasonable in terms of our reference to 'the cartographer' and sense-making in Chapter 2. Scullion and Linehan (2005), after reviewing some of the earlier definitional attempts, concluded that despite the absence of a consensus as to what IHRM represented most definitions expressed a focus on the HRM issues, challenges, strategies, and practices that affect organizations as they become international in both business and human resource terms. Another way of understanding what IHRM involves, and which captures its strategic and flexible aspect is provided by Dickmann et al. (2008) who see IHRM in terms of:

> how MNCs manage the competing demands of ensuring that the organisation has an international coherence in and cost-effective approach to the way it manages its people in all the countries it covers, while also ensuring that it can be responsive to the differences in assumptions about what works from one location to another.

From the perspective of the HR practitioner, the internationalization of business has had the effect of adding new responsibilities to those previously restricted to a regional and national perspective, such as the employment and management of expatriate workers and 'foreign' nationals which, as a result of the EU and increased globalization, has created in many countries a diverse, and at the higher end, a highly mobile labour force. It has also created new levels of complexity and challenge resulting from organizations extending their operations internationally and, as a consequence, having to come to terms with the implications of different cultures, business environments, and legal systems.

Harris et al. (2001), in their study of the implications of globalization on HR, capture the essence of these challenges when they argue that:

> Whilst managers in organisations working in a single-country environment are still subject to the twists and turns of external events, the manager working in an international environment must try to assess the impact of multi-country, regional and global trends. Hardly surprising, choices in this context become complex and ambiguous.

Specific differences relate to:

- language;
- employment laws;
- different political climates;
- different stages of social and economic development;
- different values and attitudes;
- religious differences; and
- differences in social institutions and authority structures.

Harris et al. suggest that a domestically based company developing an international dimension will need to think carefully about:

- the kind of HR strategy that will facilitate the transition and operation as an international organization;
- the implications of such a transition for the kind of managers the organization requires and the competences they will need to be effective in different contexts;
- whether it will be appropriate to develop a standardized set of employment policies and practices, or to allow flexibility and variability to reflect local and regional differences;
- strategies for resourcing, rewarding, and managing the performance of employees;
- employee recognition and representational issues; and
- corporate communications and data management.

Having to manage people as well as a business in a different cultural environment can be a particularly difficult challenge in part because employees may not exhibit the same attitudes and behaviours that an expatriate manager is used to. In the Practitioner Insight, a colleague of one of the authors talks about some of the historical characteristics still being experienced in an ex-communist eastern European state.

PRACTITIONER INSIGHT Edin Veljovic, HR consultant, Serbia

How is HR different in Serbia, for example, how do laws, customs, and attitudes to work differ?

Being an HR consultant in various sectors in Serbia (both in profit and non-for-profit organizations) provided me with insights about typical challenges that stand in front of HR managers in these sectors. One has to be careful and to distinguish three main contexts in which HR has to operate. The first consists of MNCs that operate in Serbia. Employees who work in these companies pose more (pro)Western attitudes to work, that is, they are task-oriented, well educated, familiar with the lifelong learning (training) concept of work, and they spend long hours on their jobs. The main challenges of the HR managers in this sector are related to managing expectations, hiring, and when necessary managing lay-offs and dealing with job uncertainty.

The second consists of small and medium enterprises (SMEs). The SMEs' owners are predominately entrepreneurs and they do not have clearly developed structures and functions within their organizations. Given that, in local SMEs, the role of HR is attached to one of the existing functions (marketing, quality, or administration) or the owner/CEO is the main HR figure, these functions are very fragile. It could be said that HR, in terms of the life-cycle concept, is in its emergent and developmental stage. Such unstructured and vulnerable partnerships between business and the HR function creates enormous potential for development of HR capacity within the company, working closely with the CEO. Only recently, CEOs of SMEs realized that they have to bring both more structure and (international) experience into SMEs' HR functions. There is a huge need for training of HR people especially in the domains of recruitment, selection, creating of job descriptions, employee development, and reward systems. Employees in this sector, usually, have attended a state university that has obsolete learning methodologies, and which favours knowledge rather than the skills to engage that knowledge. Commonly, employees from SMEs lack critical skills and their attitude to work is more reactive than proactive in spite of owners' entrepreneurial influence that cascades right through the businesses. Their view of business is that it belongs to the owner(s) and it is not their role to nurture it. Nevertheless, once exposed to interactive training and the influence of external consultants their reaction/response is highly positive.

The third context consists of employees from public sector or state-(pre)owned companies. There is usually an HR function which is connected with the legal department. It is predominantly administrative and bureaucratic, solving employees' different legal issues such as salaries, sick, and maternity leaves, and fits closely to the 'clerk of works' model of personnel management. The employees in these organizations have less flexible attitudes to work. They are time-driven, that is, they rarely work long hours and are more interested in their rights than duties, tasks, and deadlines. The lay-offs usually happen if a company is privatized and new shareholders want to make it more efficient and effective. However, these companies have strong union history as heritage from socialistic times that protect employees' rights.

175

The Practitioner Insight focuses on the challenges managers face in leading organizations and their employees from an existing to a more challenging state of being where old certainties and securities are replaced by a much more challenging world where change rather than stability rules.

From a UK perspective, the road to internationalization can take different forms, from recruiting internationally, outsourcing production, buying overseas companies, and setting up overseas subsidiaries. Many long-established companies such as Shell and BP, because they have always been international, have extensive experience of doing business internationally and of managing internationally. The same cannot be said of relatively new companies who are beginning to look beyond their existing national boundaries with a view to becoming 'international'. This kind of expansionist strategy will sooner or later have implications for their HR function which, depending on the scale and speed of the process, will be faced with a range of different kinds of challenges as it develops new capabilities and responsibilities. HRM Insight 6.1 illustrates a particular kind of problem that overseas expansion can involve.

TNN International is a UK-based global manufacturer and supplier of air-conditioning systems. Due to predicted expansion in overseas markets, TNN would like to appoint a sales manager to manage its South American operations and to coordinate the activities of a potentially growing team of sales representatives based in Mexico. This position has been advertised internally. Applicants include an expatriate British sales representative, who is employed on a considerably more generous package than are the other candidates, due to his expatriate status and who was involved in the start-up of the South American operation because of personal contacts with local agents. There are two Mexican applicants, both of whom joined the operation from a competitor, and both have had a significant influence in growing sales. Finally, there is a female sales representative, currently based in South Africa, who has been extremely successful in developing this market and, for family reasons, is looking to move to Mexico. The successful candidate will be responsible for managing the remaining team members who have, to date, reported to the international business manager in the UK. You have heard unofficially from other international sales agents that the expatriate British worker is adamant that he will not work for a Mexican because this will affect his credibility with his customers. You have also independently heard that the two Mexican male candidates have expressed a determination to not work for a woman for 'cultural' reasons, stating that the Mexican customers will not accept working with a female manager. The UK business has a clear fair employment policy that it extends to all of its international businesses, but this is the first time the policy has been tested in this way.

Questions

1. How should the informal complaints of the expatriate British worker and the two Mexican workers be addressed prior to the selection process?

2. What selection methods might be used to establish a fair basis for making the recruitment decision?

3. What action might need to be taken after the conclusion of the selection process?

4. Should the company's commitment to treat employees in a non-discriminatory way be maintained in the context of its overseas expansion where cultural differences do exist? If so, what changes might be considered appropriate?

Many oil, gas, and pharmaceutical companies have been operating internationally for years and have developed extensive experience of managing internationally. But smaller exploration businesses who are developing new energy sources and emergent but expanding pharma businesses may lack this experience and supportive infrastructure. They need to develop their HR function, linking its operation explicitly to the business strategy in ways that develop its human resource capability in line with the business' growth and expansion. Interestingly, many of the HR challenges and problems that these companies face when they become 'international' and seek to build for future expansion are similar to those faced by organizations operating only in a domestic context. There are, however, important differences to do with managing change, creating consistency and uniformity of practice, and challenging entrenched perceptions about gender, culture, and contribution.

According to Harzing and Pinnington (2015) cultural differences will be reflected in differences in the way employees are managed and in the way HR policies and practices evolve. Moreover, making reference to neo-institutional theory Farndale et al. (2008) argue that HR practices need to gain a degree of legitimation from key stakeholders, where changes are being introduced to existing 'ways of doing things'. This requirement to show a degree of sensitivity to entrenched beliefs and what might appear to be unacceptable prejudices and restrictions, particularly at the informal level, suggests that companies expanding abroad need to make some concessions, at least during a transitionary period, to the situation that currently exists. At the formal level, Harzing and Pinnington go further, arguing that:

> As those institutional bodies and their views of what is legitimate vary from country to country MNCs have to adapt their HRM policies in each location.

But the wider issue of the degree to which HR practices should diverge to reflect cultural differences, or converge in ways that express a centralized and uniform set of HR policies and practices remains contentious. Most MNCs will probably approach the question in a pragmatic rather than ideological way, finding different solutions to similar problems as they are confronted by different institutional and cultural forces.

HRM Insight 6.2 illustrates the challenges, and some of the key issues, facing the HR manager in a French-owned electronics company operating in Ireland. It concentrates on establishing a new HR function staffed by HR professionals, and on the difficulties of implementing agreed HR policy in the face of managerial inertia and resistance.

HRM INSIGHT 6.2 Developing the HR function in an international company

International Electronics was established in France in 2003. Despite some initial problems, the company grew from a €20 million company in 2005 to a company with a turnover of €350 million in 2017.

As the company increased its production and turnover, the strategic decision was taken to establish a manufacturing plant in Ireland and its Cork factory was established in 2015. Because of its success and the favourable economic environment in Ireland, Cork became the predominant manufacturing site for the company's complete product range. In terms of its general HR approach, the company has slightly different policies to reflect differences in local legislation but, overall, has a set of corporate policies and practices which it expects all of its subunits to adhere to, but it lacked a centralized HR function.

In 2015 the decision was taken to appoint an HR director who was based in France, with a brief to introduce formalized systems and procedures into the company and to ensure that overseas subsidiaries understood and followed company standards and expectations. As a result of her appointment as HR director, Catherine Dupre oversaw the recruitment of several key managerial personnel, one being the head of HR in Cork. The appointee, Ciara O'Sullivan, who qualified as an accountant before moving into HR, began work in January 2016 when the head count stood at 180.

As the only female in the eight-strong management team, Ciara was faced with a number of important questions: where to start; what to do first; how to begin to contribute to the company's operational and strategic objectives, and so on. It soon became apparent that her first priorities were to find out what policies were in place, who was responsible for what, and whether any procedures had been established to support these practices.

One of her first tasks was to conduct an audit of the organization from an HR perspective. This involved one-to-one meetings with colleagues on the senior management team to establish their levels of need in areas such as recruitment and selection, induction, the socialization of new employees, contracts of employment, and general administration, training and development methods and records, and, finally, performance management and appraisal.

As it transpired, this was only the tip of the iceberg. As well as dealing with all of the above, Ciara experienced a significant degree of negativity towards the HR function that was, in certain respects, more difficult to deal with than some of the more straightforward matters. As she remarked:

> While most would see this function as necessary and indeed useful, some managers find it the complete opposite: literally a thorn in the side of progress.

In trying to introduce change, she was constantly confronted with the phrase 'but this is the way it's always been done', and began to wonder what it was about change and the introduction of new processes that upset a small minority of individuals. One explanation was that they felt threatened by the introduction of more formal control mechanisms or that they would have to conform to the same standards as the rest of the employees. Whatever the case, their initial reaction was to justify and defend the status quo.

One event that captured the difficulties facing Ciara was the need to shed a small number of temporary workers, due to a short-term downturn in business predicted to last four weeks. The management team had agreed the need for this and the situation was not unusual for those workers who were employed on a contingent basis. The key decision, however, was which employees should be let go? Although not in itself a difficult question to answer, it led to a great deal of discussion and disagreement.

One suggestion was that the LIFO ('last in, first out') method should be used because it was a practice that had been used in the past, although not very successfully. The problem was complicated because Ciara had, in the preceding period, implemented an intensive recruitment drive to find suitable, flexible, and adaptable employees for one particular area of the factory. Having heavily invested in this process, and having spent valuable resources on medical examinations and training, she felt that the application of the LIFO criteria was not in the best interest of the company. She preferred to use the criterion of functionality, which meant that employees would be chosen on the basis of their role and value to the company.

One part of the plant was chronically overstaffed and had a surplus of staff working on contingent contracts. It seemed obvious to Ciara that the small number who needed to be let go could be selected from this group, but this suggestion was immediately rejected by the relevant manager, who told Ciara (politely) to mind her own business and 'stop interfering in things [she knew] nothing about'.

The manager in question, in defence of the LIFO approach, argued:

This is the way it's always been done. Why fix it, if it isn't broken?

Tensions arose between Ciara and several of the management team over the way the situation should be handled and the longer the impasse continued, the more the company was haemorrhaging valuable resources in the form of higher wage costs and unproductive workers. She decided to pick up the phone and talk to the managing director about the problem and, if necessary, involve the HR director. Politically, however, this was not without its problems because, while the group HR director had overall responsibility for employment matters, she left the Cork site very much in the hands of Ciara.

Questions

1. Why did the company feel it was necessary to establish a centralized HR function in 2008, and what challenges did the HR director face in establishing the function?

2. What support might Ciara have expected from the HR director and managing director in her efforts to get HR embedded in the Cork plant?

3. What action might Ciara have taken to overcome the resistance to change generally and the employment problem specifically?

4. Should she have involved senior managers from headquarters? If yes, in what capacity and what might the consequences have been?

The International HR Manager and Culture

KEY CONCEPT Culture

Culture, as a force and a phenomenon, exists within professions, religions, organizations, and geographical regions. Historically, the focus of interest was on national cultures, but more recently organizational cultures have become included in the study of cultures. 'Culture' can be understood as the shared beliefs, values, and understandings that define and distinguish one group from another. It is what Hofstede et al. (2010) call 'the collective programming of the mind'.

A more helpful and realistic definition of culture is provided by Spencer-Oatey (2008):

Culture is a fuzzy set of basic assumptions and values, orientations to life, beliefs, policies, procedures and behavioural conventions that are shared by a group of people, and that influence (but do not determine) each member's behaviour and his/her interpretations of the 'meaning' of other people's behaviour.

From a managerial perspective with a focus on people working internationally and on how they are managed, it is important to avoid an oversimplified approach to the understanding of culture but equally to concentrate on those aspects that are relevant to this particular perspective. Spencer-Oatey (2012), as part of a detailed exploration of the concept, suggests that culture is manifested at different levels in the form of:

- observable artefacts and behaviour—surface level;
- learned values and beliefs—expressed through language and patterned behaviour—deeper level; and
- basic underlying assumptions about relationships, one's role, and what is right—internalized beliefs about the world and people—at the core of people.

Culture affects behaviour and interpretations of behaviour. Although certain aspects of culture are physically visible, the meanings that people give to them are not, and are only known and interpreted by those who are familiar with them. For example, a gesture such as the 'ring gesture' (thumb and forefinger touching) may be interpreted as conveying agreement, approval, or acceptance in the USA, the UK, and Canada, but as an insult or obscene gesture in several Mediterranean countries, and the shaking of the head in India means yes rather than no, which is the opposite in the UK and other Western countries.

Culture can be differentiated from both universal human nature, which is entirely inherited, and unique individual personality, which is inherited and learned. Culture, which is specific to a group or category, is entirely learned. Culture is also associated with groups and communities that share common belief and behavioural systems. As almost everyone belongs to a number of different groups and occupies different social roles, people unavoidably carry several layers of mental programming within themselves (equivalent to cultural identities) corresponding to different levels of culture. This might be better understood in terms of membership of different subcultures which we identify with and are members of. These cultural identities that people associate with and which are most relevant to behaviour at work involve:

- a national identity;
- a regional and/or ethnic and/or religious and/or linguistic affiliation, as most nations are composed of culturally different regions and/or ethnic and/or religious and/or language groups;
- a gender level, according to whether a person is male, female, or transgender;
- a generation level, which separates grandparents from parents from children;
- role category, e.g. parent, son/daughter, teacher, student;
- a social class level, associated with educational opportunities and with a person's occupation or profession;
- an organizational or corporate level according to the way employees have been socialized by their work organization.

We could also argue that while national culture can be learned it can't easily be changed; what can be attempted, however, is to impose elements of a 'culture of work' that reflects the requirements of organizations who operate within a broadly capitalist mindset and exhibit the same or similar practices wherever they operate. This raises the important question of cultural compatibility and cultural conflict, where elements of a national culture clash with organizational attempts to impose a different working culture (Mayer and Louw, 2012).

The culture which people identify with influences and shapes their behaviour in relation to their environment. Cultural clashes exist if people are exposed to different belief and value systems, but fail to learn to adapt to such differences. From an IHRM perspective, the inability to understand and manage culture and cultural differences is often the reason why expatriate assignments fail, and why some immigrants and migrant workers in the UK find difficulty in assimilating into the UK way of life.

Despite the feeling that globalization and the convergence of economic systems is reducing national differences, it would be wrong to ignore the continued existence of cultural differences between nations—differences that impact both directly and indirectly on the employment and management of people. At one level, such differences manifest themselves in restrictions: for example, on the employment of women and the types of work they are allowed to do. While the emancipation of women in Western societies has resulted in very high labour market participation rates and increasing female representation across occupational boundaries, in other societies, there remain significant cultural and legal restrictions on what women are allowed to do and be. While child labour has been outlawed in most Western societies, it is seen as culturally acceptable and economically necessary in a number of African and Asian countries, giving rise to difficult ethical questions and dilemmas.

 Signpost to Chapter 5: Ethics and Leadership in HRM, for an explanation of ethical dilemmas and the use of different ethical lenses.

Less obvious cultural differences restrict or make it socially unacceptable to engage in certain behaviours that might be taken for granted in other cultures. For example, in particular countries or organizations, the status and position of people in the organizational hierarchy carries far more formal importance than it would in other national contexts, creating a strong sense of deference from those of lower status and in subordinate positions. In itself, the reluctance on the part of those lower down the hierarchy to question those in more senior positions may not be a problem, but it will affect the ability of the organization to introduce more egalitarian and democratic practices, such as 360-degree appraisal systems, open discussion forums, and the ability to address the challenges of groupthink. Cultural sensitivity and the ability to manage in situations of cultural difference, and indeed of cultural conflict, consequently become an important requirement for expatriate managers and those who work across borders; understanding these cultural differences and the challenges they represent is a key responsibility of the HR manager with responsibility for managing such people. Cultural differences can be found in many aspects of HR particularly in the way certain HR activities are carried out, as HRM Insight 6.3 illustrates.

HRM INSIGHT 6.3 A different approach to selection

Ahmed Hassan is head of the International Computer Group operating throughout the Middle East. The business involves designing and contracting for the installation of computer networks and the supply and maintenance of component parts. His and the company's reputation is based on a strong underpinning philosophy about doing business, wherever that might be, with reliability, international quality standards, and a strong ethical approach to business at its heart. The company has grown in size and profitability, and continues to develop new markets in the region and beyond. Ahmed's approach to recruitment and selection is heavily influenced by the concept of the family, and family relationships transferred into the world of business. He relies heavily on members of his extended family to run the business and several occupy key management positions. Trust as well as technical competence defines his approach to the employment of people.

Ahmed's approach to management is based on strong values and beliefs and trust in his staff. He offers attractive remuneration packages and expects his employees to reflect his personal and business values. The quality of his staff is the key to the success of his business and new recruits need to buy into the ethos of the company. Because of the expansion of the business a new senior technical post was created, but because of limited availability in the local labour market Ahmed advertised in India and received several responses with accompanying CVs. One in particular caught his attention and he arranged to fly to Delhi to interview him. He invited the applicant for dinner and began to ask him about his background and experience. The conversation continued until towards the end of the meal Ahmed put his hand in his pocket and pulled out an employment contract and said 'I would like to offer you the job'. This surprised the applicant who, after recovering his composure, said that he needed time to think. Later the following day the applicant called and said he would accept the job and they met to agree the details around salary, conditions, and start date.

This event took place quite recently and the following questions need to be thought through very carefully if you are to understand that the UK approach to recruitment and selection reflects our legal system and social values, but is not intrinsically better than anyone else's.

Questions

1. What was Ahmed basing his decision to offer the job on?

2. How does this way of deciding whether someone is suitable or not differ from the general approach taken in the UK?

3. Is the UK approach likely to produce a decision that means the integrity of procedure will always identify the applicant who will add value to the organization and perform the job to the required standards?

4. What do you think happened in the following years?

 Insights and Outcomes: visit the **online resources** at **www.oup.com/uk/banfield3e/** for comments on this HRM Insight and answers to the questions.

National cultures are important because they help people to understand:

- what they are and how they fit into society;
- how they relate to each other;
- what social conventions are important and why;
- how they perceive work and what it means in the broader context of their lives;
- the importance of time and the significance of space in relation to personal and professional relationships.

Successfully working across cultural boundaries is often associated with the person moving into, and feeling comfortable within, a different cultural environment. This inevitably involves being prepared to learn new social and business conventions, and to adjust psychologically to different values and cultural norms. The corollary of this is equally valid: the inability to cope with cultural difference is associated with ineffective performance and failed overseas assignments, secondments, and postings. As Hofstede et al. (2010) point out:

> Culture is more often a source of conflict than of synergy. Cultural differences are a nuisance at best and often a disaster.

 STUDENT ACTIVITY 6.2

Read the article by Stroppa, C. and Spieß, E. (2010) 'Expatriates social networks: The role of company size', *International Journal of Human Resource Management*, 21(13), which concerns the support provided to expatriate workers. Then produce answers to the following:

1. Explain the different kinds of support that should be made available to expatriate workers on overseas assignments.

2. What would a support network look like and who/what would be part of it?

3. How would the support provided to expatriate workers prior to leaving and after returning differ?

Hofstede's work has been particularly influential in identifying national cultural identities and the differences in the ways in which people behave and organizations function. As a result of his research, he found that nationality affected many cultural assumptions and business practices, with the key cultural differences being explained by the following five variables.

- Power distance

  This refers to the degree to which members of a society or organization accept and expect that power is distributed unequally. This dimension also represents the degree of inequality that exists within social institutions and, while all societies reflect differences in the distribution of power and the resulting pattern of inequality, some are more unequal than others.

● Individualism

This represents the degree to which people identify themselves as individuals or as members of a social group (or 'collectivity'). In certain Western societies, social ties are loose and the interests of the individual are given primacy; in other societies, such as that of Japan, there is a strong collectivist ethic and group identity. This might mean, as a generalization, that effective team and group working is more difficult to achieve in the USA than it is in Japan, or at least in Japanese companies that reflect Japanese cultural work practices. Equally, Japanese culture might inhibit individuality and creativity.

● Masculinity/femininity

This concept refers to the distribution of roles and relationships between genders. In different cultures, men are characterized, to varying degrees, by a tendency to be assertive and competitive, while women are regarded as caring and seeking to avoid conflict, although such descriptions are increasingly less appropriate in competitive working environments. Women working in cultures that are closer to the masculinity pole have a tendency to 'behave like men', that is, they become competitive and assertive, believing that becoming 'more like men' is necessary to achieve personal and professional recognition and success.

● Uncertainty avoidance

Uncertainty avoidance represents the extent to which a society exhibits a tolerance for uncertainty and ambiguity. On an individual level, it helps to predict how well a person from a culture that has a low tolerance of uncertainty and ambiguity would cope if, for example, he or she were to work in an organization within which uncertainty and ambiguity were frequently experienced. Uncertainty-avoiding cultures try to minimize the possibility of the 'unknown' by developing strict laws and rules, and by adhering to philosophical and religious teachings that produce a greater number of social 'absolutes'. People who live and work in uncertainty-accepting cultures are likely to be more tolerant of different opinions, rely on fewer rules, and adopt a more questioning and relativist approach.

● Long-term versus short-term orientation

This describes the 'time horizon' of a society or organization, or the importance that it attaches to the future as compared to the past and present. From the point of view of working and doing business in different cultures knowing where they score in this dimension can be very important because it can help managers to appreciate the time needed to build relationships, to become accepted, and to be trusted. Eastern nations tend to score especially high on this dimension, while Western nations score low and developing nations very low (high, in this sense, meaning a long time horizon).

RESEARCH INSIGHT 6.2

To further your learning, read the following article:

Dartey-Baah, K. (2013) 'The cultural approach to the management of the international human resource: An analysis of Hofstede's cultural dimensions', *International Journal of Business Administration,* **4(2).**

This article explores a culture approach to IHRM, as well as providing insights into the way human resource practices need to be culturally sensitive as organizations extend their international and global operations.

The following terms are useful in understanding the different cultural stances people can take in the context of cultural interpretations:

● **Ethnocentric**—this can refer to the practice, often unconscious, of judging other cultures from the perspective of one's own. The starting point therefore in anyone taking an ethnocentric position is with that person's own national culture. An ethnocentric position can also be the basis of an unfavourable comparison between the home culture and one that is different: people will always make cultural comparisons but the important question is how these comparisons are interpreted and made sense of.

- **Polycentric**, on the other hand, describes a position and perspective that recognizes the existence of many different national cultures which are in principle equally valid and justifiable to national identities and difference. No one culture is seen as inherently better than another.

- **Culture shock** is a term used to describe the anxiety and feelings of surprise, disorientation, and confusion felt when people have to operate within a different culture or social environment. It is often the outcome of the negative experience of moving from a familiar culture to one that is unfamiliar. But it is not simply the effect of the new that is potentially destabilizing: it is also linked to the shock and discomfort of being separated from family, friends, and the other things that matter in a person's life, such as church, social club, pub, and local shops.

For many people, the experience of moving to a different cultural environment, without the benefit of any acculturation experiences, can be expressed in terms of four stages. Not everyone passes through all of the phases, of course; much depends on the individual, their duration in the new location, and whether the move involves an individual or group.

1. The 'honeymoon' phase

   This is not always experienced and depends on the nature of the new location, but when everything new seems to be 'different and better', those affected may experience a temporary sense of pleasure.

2. The 'distress' phase

   At this point, which may occur after a few days, weeks, or even months, new things are seen in a different light and begin to be compared unfavourably with those 'at home'. Small irritations become exaggerated, and feelings of loss and loneliness can develop.

3. The 'autonomy and independence' phase

   After a period of time, people become more confident in and familiar with their 'new' environment. They have, either consciously or subconsciously, engaged in a social learning process, which changes their perceptions of their new environment from being different to being normal. Entering this phase also implies a degree of social integration, as opposed to social and psychological isolation.

4. The 'reverse culture shock' phase

   Perhaps the most well-known example of this phase is that of soldiers coming home after time spent in a war zone: coming to terms with the very different conditions and relationships in a peacetime environment can produce very serious and lasting psychological effects. Although not as intense as those of soldiers, the experiences of expatriates and their families returning to the UK after a two- or three-year secondment or assignment abroad can involve similar psychological stresses and difficulties of adjustment (Gunn, 2003).

STUDENT ACTIVITY 6.3

Read the following article on the management of repatriation:

Tyler, K. (2006) 'Pre-assignment planning, ongoing communication and mentoring help retain valuable repatriates', Expatriate Foundation.

What are the recommended actions companies should take in the way they manage this process and what might undermine their effectiveness?

HRM INSIGHT 6.4 Virginia Power Tools

Virginia Power Tools is a large multinational company quoted on the New York Stock Exchange. It manufactures and sells high-precision power tools to the automotive industry worldwide. The resignation of the managing director of the UK arm of the business, who has been headhunted by a competitor company, has prompted Virginia to place the executive immediately on garden leave for the duration of his notice, pending negotiations over his departure, because Virginia is concerned about conflicting interests. Virginia estimates that it may take up to twelve months to select and recruit a replacement and the company has therefore decided to second an existing US employee, Bob Homer, vice president of a similar-sized operation in the USA, to the UK. He will both run operations and lead the recruitment of a replacement.

While it is anticipated that this secondment will initially last for twelve months, there is a possibility that the company's commitment to acquire businesses overseas as part of its global expansion programme may result in further UK-based assignments for Bob. Bob is married with two children, aged three and six years.

Questions

1. What alternatives, in terms of benefits and support, might form part of the package to encourage Bob to move to the UK?

2. What arrangements might need to be considered to support Bob's family?

3. What arrangements will the UK HR team need to put in place to enable Bob to be employed in the UK?

4. Is there a case to use external specialist companies to provide support for Bob and his family? If so, what might this involve?

5. To reinforce your learning from this HRM Insight, read the article by Reiche and Harzing (2009).

See the Online Resources Extension Material 6.1 for insights into the management of overseas assignments.

Alternative International HR Models and Practices

From a UK ethnocentric perspective, the study of IHRM often involves looking at the HR practices found in other developed countries, but more usually today at the emerging economies of South East Asia. The approach tends to focus on how HR practices are different from those in the UK and to judge them against UK established criteria and practice. In other words, the point of departure is HR in the UK and the UK context becomes the reference point against which comparisons are made. Rarely is the UK judged in relation to different practices and alternative models of HR. So, HRM Insight 6.3 will almost certainly be read by UK students in terms of their practices and experiences and many will interpret the actions of the company head as not only different from what would have happened in the UK but wrong too! However, the important point to make is that it was only 'wrong' in the context of UK practices and legislative requirements. From a different social and cultural perspective Ahmed Hassan's approach was perfectly understandable and from a business perspective eminently sensible. He knew the company and what the job involved in detail; he also knew the technical and personal competencies he needed to find in applicants. It may not have been written and formalized and he may not have followed 'procedure' but if his decision was validated by how well the successful applicant subsequently performed then we can say that, to use a Weberian concept, his behaviour was materially rational; that is, he achieved a successful outcome. It could also be considered to have been formally rational in the sense that it reflected not the rules and requirements of a bureaucracy but the values and beliefs of a family business in a country where trust as well as expertise is highly valued. Limitations and deficiencies in the UK approach to recruitment and selection that result in 'the wrong' people being employed through procedural rigidity and decision-making errors are more familiar to managers and business leaders rather than academics and HR professionals. James Hurley (2011) indicates what some of these might be:

> **Companies that complain about skills shortages preventing them from hiring are just as likely to be undermined by their own recruitment processes as weak applicants.**

He continued by quoting a senior UK manager who said:

> **Too often, internal 'specialists' take insufficient time to understand requirements, define the job description and then turn those into an operating brief.**

Although this is an example of how similar things are done in different ways in other countries, it provides another indication of where internationally oriented HR specialists can learn from others, rather than assuming that the UK or USA model of HR is the given starting point in any consideration of international practice. It is also worth remembering the point made by Michael Porter in Chapter 3 that being strategic often involves acting differently from competitors in the way the same activities are carried out. And in research undertaken by the CIPD and Bridge Consulting, Connor (2010) provides more extensive evidence that companies in South East Asia in particular are not merely following UK and Western practice, but are developing their own distinctive approach to HR. In his report Jerry Connor asks how relevant HR can be if the so-called best practice approach to HR has not led to an improvement in the status and reputation of the HR function. He goes on by stating that:

> **In Europe this has been extrapolated by the tendency, especially where the Ulrich model had been implemented without a truly compelling overriding purpose, for the function to become ever more specialised and fragmented.**

He continues by asking the rhetorical question:

> **Is it enough to build a function built on a collection of expertise around core people priorities? Or do we need to be bolder and build the capability to generate rule-breaking insight and to act as guardians of the long-term commercial success of our organisations?**

His research, based on interviews with leaders of Asian businesses, suggests that the new form of HR being developed there appears to bypass and avoid some of the issues that are being raised in Europe. The different HR agenda reflects very different situations and requirements where growth and expansion and technological change define the context in which business is done and the role and contribution HR is expected to play and make. Clearly the legislative framework in that part of the world is different but the report also suggests that there is a different HR mindset, particularly among companies operating in an international context and global marketplace. According to Connor:

> **Asia represents one of the most fast-moving and creative business environments in the world today. And it has some of the world's most dynamic and creative HR leaders.**

Connor believes that because of the very different situation in the emerging and rapidly growing Asian economies a new 'form' of HR is developing in response to and in support of more dynamic and outward-looking businesses. He goes on to say that the:

> **great news is that, in the course of our research, we've found something more exciting, the so-called 'Next Generation' (beyond Western best practice) HR in small pockets. While the Western models of HR founded on Ulrich-inspired logic have merit, it is crucial to appreciate that there are two underlying issues that, if addressed early in the life of HR in Asia, will enable the development of the 'turbo-charged' HR that is so needed in the region.**

These two issues are:

- the purpose and positioning of the function; and
- building critical capabilities within the HR function that extend beyond a 'people remit'.

Connor's research is based in Asia but focused on companies that are very much international in their trading and business activities. It may be that international businesses, precisely because they operate in such fast changing and demanding environments have created the conditions where this 'next generation' model of HR has emerged from that associated with best practice and a focus on people rather than the business. It could also be argued that it is the Asian rather than the international context that is the most important influence on this development, with its distinctive context and development trajectories. Whatever the case might be, there is a subtle but significant difference in the way that these next-generation HR functions see themselves and in what they think they are there for. This is manifest specifically in the way they see themselves as business functions first with a people and culture brief that is there to support the business agenda. For them, HR is an applied business discipline. It means they are actively involved in acts of leadership in the business that sit outside of the classic people arena. Crucially, the underlying purpose is about driving short- and long-term business success. He believes this has clear echoes with developments in certain UK-based international businesses where those HR departments focusing on driving sustainable business performance are avoiding the trap of becoming too internally facing and disconnected from the business context they operate in. This is in contrast with those HR functions that have a much more limited sense of purpose, are focused on following 'best practice' without questioning why, and have a mindset where following procedure and being conformist are seen as more important than making a difference. These functions are applied people functions and are concerned with 'pure' HR and people issues. While they may claim to add value that may be more to do with attempting to legitimize its role than reflecting any meaningful contributions at the strategic level. It is very easy for this kind of HR to become disconnected from the business, and despite the rhetoric of those who work in HR, be seen as little more than a transactional and administrative function rather than a key driver of long-term success.

We would argue that this relationship between rapid economic growth and the innovative approach to HR found by Connor is not a coincidence, but an inevitable outcome of the interplay between economic forces and the international war for talent. As Yeung et al. (2008) claim:

> **the growth and globalisation of firms in Asia and the evolution of HRM in the region are two faces of the same phenomenon.**

The four elements of Asia's 'new' model of HR indicate the degree to which practice in emerging and growth-oriented countries not only reflects economic conditions and imperatives but also national and regional cultures. These elements are:

- Insightful thinking

    The report by Connor indicates an important paradox: on the one hand, Asian culture and business practice is based on the idea of telling people what to do and expecting them to do it unquestioningly. But the economic challenge requires much more insightful thinking that has to go beyond top business leaders, affecting the organization as a whole. Again, we see parallels with Porter's idea that to be strategic HR needs to explore opportunities to be different and being different requires the ability to question, challenge, and have insight. One of the examples given of what being insightful involves relates to a rejection of the distinction between corporate strategy and HR strategy. According to Connor:

    > **There is no need to talk about the HR strategy supporting the business strategy. They are one and the same thing.**

- Community

    Building a particular type of social organization or organizational culture is seen as one of the key priorities for the new Asian model of HR, and one of the key influences on this is the importance of the family and family-type relationships within business organizations. Many of those interviewed as part of the research project questioned the perceived Western emphasis and value of individualism and internal competition, which can be seen to conflict with core values such as community and networked relationships that generate high levels of mutual trust and loyalty. This feature came out strongly in the selection case study we discussed earlier in the chapter. However, such distinctions are now ones of degree rather than kind and, as is seen later, the value of competition and competitiveness is recognized much more in Asia today than in earlier phases of its economic development. The notion that globalization is creating forces that are gradually resulting in the convergence of national systems of management and HR is an interesting one!

● Purpose

The report highlights the importance and power of what it describes as 'purpose'—the sense of identification and pride that many aspiring professionals seem to have and to want. National pride and a self-belief in the 'rightness' of what organizations do and the contributions they make are key drivers that help to explain the zeal and commitment of employees to their organizations and what they stand for. Self-interest coexists with a belief in a higher interest, whether this be organizational, national, or cultural, and HR is seen to have an important role in facilitating this fusion of different levels of engagement and involvement. The report notes that HR leaders:

> are looking to build deep and enduring engagement, tapping into the passion, dreams and aspirations of their people to power long-term growth

and one way this can be achieved is through the power of a higher and often ethically attractive interest or cause that is articulated and projected by organizational leaders including those in HR.

● Performance

Again, the emphasis given to individual performance is potentially in conflict with cultural values and a feeling of loyalty to other employees. However, the report offers insights into the way HR leaders are increasingly trying to create a stronger commitment to achieving high performance and trying to manage this effectively without undermining the strength and importance of traditional values. For some organizations, this involves encouraging a degree of competition that is not inconsistent with Asian educational systems, where the pursuit of excellence is a defining feature. In others, the coaching by expatriates of indigenous staff creates a pool of people who are able to replace those on short-term contracts and represent this 'bounded competitiveness'. A third example of creating high-performing organizations links back to the recruitment of talented new people whose personal drives and capabilities are seen as equally important as their ability to undertake specific jobs.

IHRM, while sharing similarities with its national variant, has developed in different directions to address challenges that are different either in degree or kind. Perhaps the most significant of these is the new model of HR identified by Connor as emerging in Asia. The paradox associated with this model is the HR function isn't primarily about people at all; rather, it is another business function whose primary 'material' is people, with the shift in mindsets opening up radically different approaches to the way people are managed and used at work. Competition for talent and the challenges associated with an international labour force and the employment of expatriate workers are additional factors in propelling IHRM to find original solutions to new or more complex problems, such as the need to develop managerial competences necessary for the international manager to succeed. It is to this final topic we now turn.

STUDENT ACTIVITY 6.4

Read **Connor, J. (2010)** *The Growth Option: Turbo-Charging HR's Impact in Asia*, CIPD.

After reading the report, identify practices highlighted in it that could be used in the UK to improve the status and effectiveness of the HR function.

International Management Competences

Understanding the cultural and business environments in which international managers have to operate, and the potential difficulties associated with the repatriation and expatriation process helps HR staff in the decisions they have to make in the recruitment, selection, and development of these managers. Integral to the successful management of these processes is the ability to identify the key skills and competences that those working overseas need to possess. The case study at the end of the chapter provides insights into what these might be, but this is only one person's account of what major overseas assignments involve and it is important to look carefully at what research tells us about these competences. Moreover, how are these skills and competences actually acquired? Do the critical challenges for IHRM lie in the assessment and selection of managers who are expected to work overseas or in designing effective learning experiences that develop the required psychological and behavioural characteristics and strengths?

One of the most interesting findings from research into the recruitment and selection of international managers, and one that confirms a view expressed elsewhere in this book, is provided by Paul Sparrow (2006). As a result of his work, commissioned by the CIPD, he found that:

> The majority of expatriate skills are learnt through experience—they learn how to manage across cultures in most instances without education in cross-cultural skills.

This suggests that the key HR decision is taken at the assessment and selection stage, at which point evidence of the ability to learn from experience and to be able to cope with potentially stressful environments becomes an important differentiator.

Sparrow's report identified the following characteristics as being associated with the successful expatriate manager.

- **Professional and technical competence, and experience on the job**

    This area also included general maturity, knowledge of the company, and experience of performing the job in the 'home' organization.

- **Personality traits and relational abilities**

    Included under this heading are also important communication skills, but not only those involving language ability. The category also relates to personal maturity, tolerance, respect for the host country, and adaptability.

- **Perceptual dimensions and life strategies**

    This area relates to, among other things, the ability to learn from experiences, and the avoidance of being judgemental and evaluative in relation to different social values and social conventions. In other words, it relates to avoiding an ethnocentric stance.

- **Self-maintenance factors**

    These characteristics relate to the ability to function independently, to cope with stress and pressure, and to exhibit confidence in carrying out specific tasks.

- **Leadership and motivational factors**

    This final area of competency relates to the development of relationships, the use of initiative and the ability to take appropriate action, and a general interest in working overseas.

The outcome of Sparrow's research into relevant managerial competences is certainly consistent with the personal account of Chris Atkin (see the case study at the end of the chapter), and with other individuals' 'stories' of what working overseas involves and the demands such work makes of managers who have to carry out important duties in an often unusual and demanding environment. Based on his work, Sparrow offers an interesting and useful competency framework, which rests on the three fundamental attributes that those working overseas need to have: emotional stability; confidence and relationship building; openness to different experiences. This framework is presented in Figure 6.2.

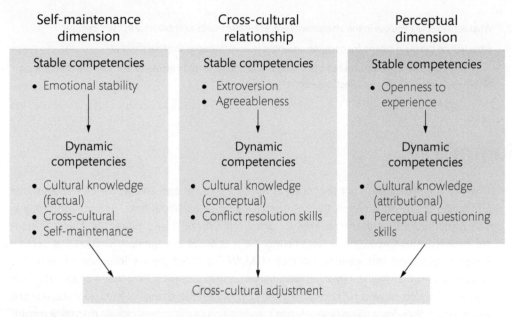

Figure 6.2 A competency model for overseas working
Source: This material is taken from *International Recruitment, Selection and Assessment* (Sparrow, 2006), with the permission of the publisher, the Chartered Institute of Personnel and Development, London.

RESEARCH INSIGHT 6.3

To take your learning further, read the following article:

Cascio, W. F. and Boudreau, J. W. (2016) 'The search for global competence: From international HR to talent management', *Journal of World Business*, **51(1).**

This article explores the new and additional competences global managers need to be successful and links these to their selection and development.

STUDENT ACTIVITY 6.5

This is a demanding activity that requires careful planning and preparation. It is also one that needs to be done collaboratively. Groups can set their own parameters on the scale and level of sophistication of the exercise, and can add detail to the context. To give the exercise extra realism, your tutor might play the role of the managing director and give you feedback on your proposals.

You are a team of HR practitioners working for a global engineering company, with manufacturing and distribution centres in India, China, and Japan. Currently, these centres are managed by local staff, who report directly to the UK-based head of overseas production. Because of continuing expansion of the centres and the building of an additional unit in Malaysia, the managing director has decided that the current reporting lines are no longer appropriate. He has decided to create the new position of managing director for Asia, with executive responsibilities for all of the company's business in that region. The appointee would report directly to the UK-based MD. Your job is to provide the MD with a shortlist of three candidates from which he will make the final choice.

He wants to be kept informed of developments on this new appointment and wants you to report back to him with answers to the following questions:

1. What is your recruitment strategy?

2. What is your person specification?

3. What activities will you use in the assessment centre? He also wants to know how this will operate.

4. What will be the main criteria for deciding on who is to be included in the final shortlist?

5. Six months after the appointment has been made, what criteria would you use to evaluate the effectiveness of the whole recruitment and selection process?

Summary

- Diversity in employment is not only being driven by the ethnic, age, and gender differences within UK society, but by globalization, the internationalization of the labour force, and economic migration. All of these are trends that are likely to continue. In Chapter 2 we explored the different historical influences that shaped the development of the specialized management function that became known as personnel management and then HRM. We identified the key influences of social and religious values, management theory, trade unionism, and industrial conflict. Now we can add further seminal influences on what HR is becoming and how its agenda is changing: internationalization and globalization. Workforce diversity is only one manifestation of this; others include managing expatriate workers and supporting their families, developing new management strategies for recruiting and developing in a global labour market, coping with cultural differences, and complying with different employment regulations and traditions. At the same time, HR continues to be tasked with delivering administrative efficiency and providing operational support to managers, while not forgetting the importance of maintaining effective communications with staff, gaining employee commitment, and providing a positive and stimulating working environment.

- The implications for HR of these challenges are profound, and are unlikely to be met unless organizations develop the 'right' level of HR capacity and capability to equip them to operate in this new and more demanding context. This may not involve employing more HR staff: interestingly, some of the organizations that have been in the forefront of developing new models of HR have employed outsourcing, IT-enabled HR services, and service flexibility to generate their status as truly international and global (examples being the Royal Bank of Scotland and Diageo).

- It is not only the shape of the HR 'architecture' that changes: perhaps as significant are the implications for the HR professional. New, business-related skills are becoming increasingly critical, both for personal and professional credibility, and for the function's standing with other stakeholders. New competences linked to operating and managing in an international context will be crucial in the development of new HR tools and interventions, such as those needed to facilitate learning and knowledge sharing within the international organization. And, as always, the ability to develop and relate HR strategies to operational performance will continue to be valued and expected from those in HR. Not only is HR being shaped by the forces of internationalization and globalization, so too is the profile of those who work in the function.

 Visit the **online resources** that accompany this book for self-test questions, web links, and more information on the topics covered in this chapter, at: **www.oup.com/uk/banfield3e/**

REVIEW QUESTIONS

1. How do cultural differences affect HR and the management of people?

2. Why do individuals and organizations have to become less ethnocentric and more polycentric when operating in an international context?

3. What key attributes and competences does the HR professional working for an international company need?

4. What is the link between diversity and internationalization?

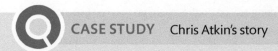

CASE STUDY Chris Atkin's story

The following is based on an interview with the subject.

Chris Atkin can be reliably described as an 'international manager', with over thirty-nine years' experience of travelling and 'doing business', in Europe initially, then in the Middle and Far East, in South Africa, and in Australasia. He might best be described as an 'international commuter', because his job as sales director for Dormer Tools meant that he was frequently away for up to four weeks at a time. Dormer Tools was a world-class producer of engineering cutting tools, used in almost all metal manufacturing processes. It sold a range of high-quality products through a network of international distributors and agents. Starting out as a management trainee, he spent the first five years with Dormer in manufacturing, and then moved into sales and marketing, after the managing director suggested that his outgoing personality might make him well suited to that function.

Early experiences of working in the Middle and Far East created an element of culture shock, when he was exposed to very different traditions, values, and ways of working. It became clear to him that becoming culturally aware and sensitive was a precondition of building trust and mutual understanding with potential business partners and clients. Using Saudi Arabia as an example, it was clear that it was very much a 'man's world', certainly during the time he worked there, and there would be no contact or socialization with female family members. Of course, times change and, at the recent wedding of the daughter of one of his business associates in Dubai, around one hundred people attended, and although males and females dined separately, they all came together afterwards.

Reflecting on 'doing business abroad', Chris thought that the following were important points to remember.

- Don't make promises that can't be kept—people have long memories and, if you let them down, they will remember and refuse to do business with you again.

- Be aware of how business is conducted in different parts of the world—Saudis, for example, like to barter before agreeing a deal and the need for them to feel that they have achieved a good deal means that negotiating skills, and the ability to keep something in reserve as a concession, are important.

- Preserving a strong ethical stance in business dealings is important—realistically, in certain countries, potential customers will seek additional commissions or will link a sale directly to an 'illegal payment'. It is important, when negotiating contracts, to remember the long-term benefits to one's personal reputation and the safety of avoiding questionable business dealings.

One of the points that came over clearly in the interview was the need for UK managers working abroad to have certain competences, the most important for Chris being as follows.

- **The ability to work alone, along with personal endurance and resilience**

  In the early period of his international role, there was little backup from the home company and telecommunications were far less developed than they are now. The ability to make business decisions in relative isolation was an important requirement.

- **Understanding the implications of 'getting business'**

  This means thinking about whether the manufacturing plant's capacity to produce and deliver products in the quantities agreed and on time was an important requirement.

● **Problem solving and problem preventing**

This involves seeing beyond 'the deal' and taking a longer-term, more holistic, perspective, as well as being able to resolve difficulties that might be preventing a deal from being concluded.

● **The ability to help customers to solve technical problems**

This means not only selling the cutting tools, but offering advice on the machines that will use them, helping with maintenance issues, and advising on operative training.

● **Language and cultural understanding**

Learning the basics of Arabic, for example, was very helpful for the business side of his work, but also facilitated social interaction and personal acceptance.

Talking about the support he received from what was called 'personnel' in those days, Chris accepted that, in the 1970s and 1980s, the function in his company was not as developed and influential as it is now. Even so, he admitted that he never really understood what it was about! The people who worked in it always seemed busy, but were not business-oriented and lacked a real identity, although this changed under the influence of developments in HRM, with the HR manager now sitting in on commercial discussions with other senior managers. Chris's main recollection of his 'own HR people', however, was that they were 'a race apart', physically isolated from other management functions in the same building and only visible during a strike or the threat of industrial action.

The main 'HR' interventions with Chris were conducted by the managing director, rather than by HR staff, and involved annual appraisals, the setting of performance targets, and the development of strategies for developing new markets. His advice to HR is to spend more time with the people who are working abroad, discover what they need to know and the support they require, and find out where they are going, so that intelligence can be gathered about these countries to help the managers to prepare for their assignments, particularly if families are also involved.

Finally, one particular experience that Chris had is worth recounting. Invited by a Saudi sheik to a traditional Bedouin feast, he was presented with a dish of rice that contained sheep's eyes—a delicacy in certain parts of Saudi Arabia. Knowing that, when offered one, he could not refuse to accept it because to do so would be construed as an insult to his hosts, he accepted it and a second when this, too, was offered. The experience wasn't particularly pleasant, but on the basis of understanding the importance of social etiquette, he built up a lifelong friendship with his host, who later presented him with a complete set of traditional Arabian clothing as a token of his respect, something that Chris experienced as a very humbling occasion.

Questions

1. With international secondments and overseas business travel now much more frequent than they used to be, what is the role of HR in supporting this?

2. What competences do members of HR staff need to have to be effective in preparing and supporting expatriates?

3. What can be done to avoid or limit the effect of culture shock?

4. Consider HR's role in developing an ethical code of practice for managers working and doing business abroad.

 **FURTHER READING**

Briscoe, D. R., Schuler, R. S., and Claus, L. (2009) *International Human Resource Management: Policy and Practice for Multinational Enterprises (Global HRM)*, 3rd edn, Routledge.

Farndale, E. et al. (2010) 'The role of the corporate HR function in global talent management', *Journal of World Business*, 45, 161–8.

Ngo, H.-y. et al. (2011) 'Human resource flexibility in foreign subsidiaries: An empirical investigation in Hong Kong', *International Journal of Business Studies*, 19(2).

Scullion, H. and Collings, D. (2010) *Global Talent Management*, Routledge.

Seers, L. (2010) *'Next Generation HR', Time for Change—Towards a Next Generation for HR*, CIPD.

Thoo, L. and Kaliannan, M. (2013) 'International HR assignment in recruiting and selecting: Challenges, failures and best practices', at: http://www.macrothink.org/journal/index.php/ijhrs/article/viewFile/4610/3783

REFERENCES

Al Ariss, A. (2014) *Global Talent Management: Challenges, Strategies, and Opportunities*, Springer.

Brewster, C. et al. (2011) *International Human Resource Management*, CIPD.

Chiang et al. (2010) 'Examining human resource management outsourcing in Hong Kong', *International Journal of Human Resource Management*, 21(15).

Cascio, W. F. and Boudreau, J. W. (2016) 'The search for global competence: From international HR to talent management', *Journal of World Business*, 51(1).

CIPD (2013) 'The state of migration: Employing migrant workers', at: https://www.cipd.co.uk/binaries/the-state-of-migration-employing-migrant-workers_2012.pdf

Cisek, I. and Ozer, B. (2011) 'The effects of outsourcing human resource on organisational performance: The role of organisational culture', *International Journal of Business and Management Studies*, 3(2), ISSN: 1309-8047, at: http://www.sobiad.org/ejournals/journal_IJBM/arhieves/2011_Vol_3_n_2/13isik_cicek.pdf

Connor, J. (2010) *The Growth Option: Turbo-Charging HR's Impact in Asia*, CIPD, at: http://www.cipd.co.uk/NR/rdonlyres/EF81FAED-89A2-4A14-BB42-10B26C8C22DE/0/5348NextGenHRFINALPROOF.PDF

David, R. (1997) *The Pyramid Builders of Ancient Egypt: A Modern Investigation of Pharaoh's Workforce*, Routledge.

Deloitte (2015) *Global Human Capital Trends 2015*, Deloitte University Press, at: https://www2.deloitte.com/content/dam/Deloitte/at/Documents/human-capital/hc-trends-2015.pdf

Dickmann, M., Sparrow, P. R., and Brewster, C. (2008) *International Human Resource Management: A European Perspective*, Routledge.

Edwards, T. and Rees, C. (2006) *International Human Resource Management*, FT/Prentice Hall.

Farndale, E. et al. (2008) 'Co-ordinated vs liberal market HRM: The impact of institutionalisation on multination firms', *International Journal of Human Resource Management*, 19(11).

Ferner, A. and Hyman, R. (1998) *Changing Industrial Relations in Europe*, Blackwell.

Glaister, K. W., Husan, R., and Buckley, P. J. (2003) 'Learning to manage international joint ventures', *International Business Review*, 12(1), 83–108.

Global Policy Forum [n.d.] 'The threat of globalization', at: https://www.globalpolicy.org/globalization/defining-globalization/47948-the-threat-of-globalization.html

Gunn, N. (2003) 'Repatriation the right way', *Expatica HR*, www.expatica.com

Harris, H., Brewster, C., and Sparrow, P. (2001) *Globalisation and HR*, CIPD.

Harzing, A.-W. and Pinnington, A. (eds.) (2015) *International Human Resource Management*, Sage.

Hira, R. and Hira, J. (2005) *Outsourcing America: What's Behind Our National Crisis and How We Can Reclaim American Jobs*, AMACOM.

Hofstede G., Hofstede G. J., and Minkov, M. (2010). *Cultures and Organizations: Software of the Mind: Intercultural Cooperation and Its Importance for Survival*, McGraw-Hill.

Hurley, J. (2011) 'Employers a risk to recruitment', *Daily Telegraph*, business section, 8 February, p. B7.

Kapoor, Bhushan (2008) http://www.jimsjournal.org/6%20Bhushan%20Kapoor.pdf

Mayer, C.-H. and Louw, L. (2012) 'Managing cross-cultural conflict in organizations', *International Journal of Cross Cultural Management*, 12(1), 3–8.

Reiche, S. and Harzing, A. W. (eds.) (2009) 'International assignments', in *International Human Resource Management*, Sage, ch. 5.

Scullion, H. (1995) 'International human resource management', in J. Storey (ed.) *Human Resource Management: A Critical Text*, Routledge.

Scullion, H. and Linehan, M. (2005) *International Human Resource Management: A Critical Text*, Palgrave Macmillan.

Sparrow, P. (2006) *International Recruitment, Selection and Assessment*, www.cipd.co.uk

Spencer-Oatey, H. (2008) *Culturally Speaking: Culture, Communication and Politeness Theory*, 2nd edn, Continuum.

Spencer-Oatey, H. (2012) 'What is culture? A compilation of quotations', GlobalPAD Core Concepts, at: http://go.warwick.ac.uk/globalpadintercultural

Stroppa, C. and Spieß, E. (2010) 'Expatriates social networks: The role of company size', *International Journal of Human Resource Management*, 21(13), 2306–22.

Tyler, K. (2006) 'Pre-assignment planning, ongoing communication and mentoring help retain valuable repatriates', Expatriate Foundation, at: http://expatriatefoundation.org/course/international-hr-management-repatriation

Wirth, R. (2002) 'Breaking through the glass ceiling: women in management', presentation at the First ILO International Conference on Pay Equity Between Women and Men: Myth or Reality.

Yeung, A., Warner, M., and Rowley, C. (2008) 'Growth and globalization: Evolution of human resource management practices in Asia', *Human Resource Management*, 47(1), 1–13.

Recruitment and Selection

7

Key Terms

Hiring or employing The overall process of taking on new staff from outside the organization.

External recruitment The process of identifying and attracting potential employees to an organization to fill current or future vacancies.

Internal recruitment The process of identifying current employees who may be suitable for newly created vacancies or for replacing staff who leave.

Assessment The tools and techniques used by an organization to identify and measure, either qualitatively or quantitatively, the skills, knowledge, and potential of applicants.

Selection The process, culminating in the decision to fill a vacancy from internal or external applicants, used by the organization to choose the most suitable candidate from a pool of applicants.

Learning Objectives

As a result of reading this chapter and using the online resources, you should be able to:

- understand the importance of attracting high-performing employees to an organization;

- define and manage the processes involved in recruitment and selection;

- identify and develop different recruitment strategies for an organization;

- understand the professional and ethical standards that are appropriate in recruitment and selection; and

- understand the relationship between recruitment and selection and other HR activities.

Introduction

No matter how sophisticated the systems, processes, and technology of an organization, it is the capabilities and commitment of its employees that ensure its success. Without the optimum combination of people at different levels, with appropriate capabilities, knowledge, and motivation, individual and organizational performance will suffer. It is therefore essential to the success of the organization to ensure that recruitment and selection is effective, and delivers the highest calibre of employees at optimum cost. At the beginning of the twenty-first century writers such as Gratton (2000) and Michaels et al. (2001) were emphasizing that the only unique and sustainable source of competitive advantage came from the inspiration, knowledge, and effort of employees; that is, of the organization's 'human capital'. Human capital is a valuable asset for organizations, which resides within the people that comprise the workforce and can easily be reduced if employees lose interest and motivation in their work and permanently lost through people leaving the organization. Maintaining and strengthening the human capital base is one of the main strategic challenges facing the human resource professional, and recruitment and selection is key to achieving this goal. But not only is effective recruitment and selection relevant to how well people can do their jobs it is also important for other HR activities and processes. In other words, the ability to motivate, to train and develop, and to promote is heavily dependent on the kind of people who are selected and employed. In particular industrial sectors such as catering, retail, and hospitality, the ability to deliver a consistently high-quality experience to customers is critical to organizational success. In his article on service quality, Ueno (2010) identified seven factors that are critical for the management of service quality of which recruitment and selection is one with three others—training, team working, and empowerment—heavily dependent on the employee attributes and potential which can only be initially established and assessed during the recruitment and selection process. Of course, the ability to deliver high performance and service delivery is not completely dependent on the quality of new recruits—culture, communications, trust, and relationships are also influential. How an organization *uses* and *retains* its people will clearly affect the contribution of human capital to the organization's overall performance. Nevertheless, there is a strong case to be made for recognizing that recruiting and selecting the 'right' employees is absolutely critical to an organization's ability to grow and prosper. This view is reflected in the work of such writers as Jack Welch, a previous head of General Electric (GE), who argues that:

> **Nothing matters more in winning than getting the right people on the field.**
> (Welch and Welch, 2005)

But attracting and selecting the 'best' candidates is neither an easy task, nor is it risk free. Burrows (2004) justifiably argues that the challenges of introducing and integrating new recruits from outside a company cannot be underestimated or treated lightly. He also believes, however, that as long as the proper tools are used in the assessment process, applicants' ambitions and personal motivations are understood, and coaching is used to ensure the rapid integration of new recruits, the chances of meeting these challenges will be much greater than if these requirements were ignored or misunderstood. Notwithstanding this, mistakes can be made and the 'wrong' people hired, with unfortunate implications for the organization and for the employee.

Collins (2001) offers an opinion on the importance of being as sure as one can about a person's suitability before making the job offer:

> **When in doubt, don't hire, keep looking . . . A company should limit its growth based on its ability to attract enough of the right people.**
> (Collins, 2001)

In the context of trying to avoid employing 'the wrong' people it is worth remembering Robert Sutton's advice about keeping the 'assholes' out of the organization (see Chapter 1), and noting that the aim of the selection process is not only to hire the person that fits all or as many requirements as possible (and this does not necessarily mean the one who scores highest on the assessment form), but to identify and reject those that are or could become 'assholes'. But according to Mariah DeLeon (2015), writing for the *Entrepreneur* magazine, people who do not stand out as being problematic and are employed can still represent decision-making errors because they:

- Will still need to be paid even though they may not be performing to expectations, and if additional or remedial training is required this represents an additional and unexpected cost. Furthermore, if the decision is made to terminate the contract this may involve significant direct costs and indirect costs in the form of replacing the unsatisfactory employee.

- Through retraining, poor work performance, and interpersonal conflict contribute to productivity falls in the department they work in as valuable managerial time has to be given to addressing the problems they create.

- Damage morale and undermine established relationships.

But pressure to fill positions quickly can often result in the wrong decisions being made—decisions that are not always easily rectified.

If an organization's current recruitment and selection is not risk free can the assessment and selection of applicants be carried out in such a way that the 'best', or the 'right', person will always be identified, and the 'wrong' people kept out of the organization? The answer to this is, unfortunately, that 'no', it cannot be guaranteed. Recruitment and selection is not an exact science and, no matter how thorough and 'objective' the processes undertaken is, there is always a possibility that the chosen candidate will not perform to the expected standards, unexpectedly leave the business, or fail to grow and develop as was initially hoped. Extraneous pressures can interfere with the decision-making process, and subjectivity and bias can undermine procedural rigour. Indeed, the procedure itself can be flawed and be compromised by design faults, skill deficiencies, and groupthink. It is important to recognize, however, that much better decisions and fewer mistakes can be made if a thorough process is followed, involving the gathering of as much relevant and objective information as possible, and using the expertise and judgement of different stakeholders at each stage of the process, an example of which is summarized in Figure 7.1.

Why Is It Important to Make the Right Recruitment and Selection Decisions?

Apart from the obvious importance of attracting talented people into the organization, why is the recruitment and selection process so important? It is important because:

- each employment decision can add to, or subtract from, the overall quality of the workforce;

- the ability of managers to continuously generate greater levels of added value from each employee is heavily influenced by what each new recruit brings into the organization and what each is capable of becoming;

- as a result of the increase in employment protection rights, it has become more difficult to correct mistakes in employment decisions once a person has been offered, and has accepted, a contract;

- employees who fail to meet the performance and behavioural expectations of managers can have a detrimental impact on the performance of others;

- the process of correcting a hiring mistake can be difficult, prolonged, and costly to all those involved;

- employing new and better-qualified members of staff to replace those that are unwilling or unable to adapt to new requirements is often the only effective long-term strategy for improving the operational performance of functions and departments.

Pre-recruitment phase

Decide on scale of project and timescales

Decide whether demand for labour can be met by increasing flexibility and utilization of existing workforce

Liaise with other stakeholders to develop strategy

Prepare and agree on employment package and degree of discretion in wage or salary

Agree on contractual details, such as probationary period

Key recruitment activities

Carry out job analysis and produce up-to-date job descriptions

Choose between internal and external labour markets

Decide which communication medium to use

Decide on standards to be applied and 'ideal' person specification

Key selection activities

Prepare competency statements and frameworks

Decide on which selection approaches and instruments to use

Decide on shortlisting criteria

Build checks and safeguards into selection decisions

Document and store selection criteria and applicants' profiles against these

Train staff in interview, questioning, and feedback techniques

Post-selection activities

Check references and consider any other relevant evidence for contra-indicators

If appropriate, carry out medical, and employment eligibility tests

Prepare employment offer documents

Keep on file records of those not offered position but who may be suitable for alternative job

Provide feedback for unsuccessful candidates, which creates positive feeling towards the organization

Post-employment activities

Prepare appropriate socialization and induction experiences

Design opportunities for informal discussions and formal review of performance at appropriate time

Confirm or terminate employment at end of probationary period

Attempt to validate selection criteria, score against key criteria, and measure of job performance

Agree training and development programme

Cost whole exercise and produce useful metrics, in terms of time, money, and other resources used

Learn from the whole experience, share and agree on this learning, and use it in subsequent recruitment and selection exercises

Timeline

Figure 7.1 A strategic overview of the recruitment and selection process

The aphorism 'if you can't change people, change the people' helps to explain the extent to which the introduction of new people with different attitudes, competency profiles, and, above all, a stronger work ethic can bring about a transformation in performance capability throughout the organization. While not always the case, new CEOs brought in to 'recover' organizations that have been struggling, frequently go through a process of evaluating existing senior managers and quickly replacing those who in their opinion don't have the necessary attributes to work in a new corporate environment, with staff they know or who impress in an assessment and selection process. But even the most experienced leaders and managers can be influenced by first impressions, a refusal or inability to consider contra-evidence, and a selective approach to reviewing the available information.

Consider HRM Insight 7.1, in which an important and costly mistake was avoided only by the timely intervention of an HR professional.

HRM INSIGHT 7.1 The legal practice that nearly got it wrong

Celia Johnson had been employed by Richard Curtis, senior partner in the law firm Curtis, Bowers, and Smith, to bring some structure and order to the firm's HR provision. Up to her appointment, the HR function had effectively been limited to a part-time administrator and Curtis, who looked after all recruitment and reward matters. In an increasingly competitive recruitment environment, the firm had been struggling to attract and retain experienced lawyers, some of whom, in addition to their fee-earning roles, also had to manage different departments within the firm. Richard, aware of the need to strengthen his managerial team, was always on the lookout for new staff.

The firm had no recruitment strategy as such: recruitment was very ad hoc and relied on word of mouth, external networks, and on following up enquiries and the CVs submitted by lawyers seeking to develop their careers. The firm didn't advertise positions and had no formal selection procedures, relying instead on informal mechanisms to hire new recruits.

This was of concern to Celia, who felt that even one bad appointment might have serious implications for the harmonious working relationships that characterized the firm. She wanted to replace the existing approach to hiring new staff with one that offered more rigour, checks, and a shared responsibility for the assessment and selection of candidates.

One Monday morning, not long after she arrived in the office, Richard called her to say that he had received a CV from someone who looked really promising and who would be worth having. As well as having a good track record as a fee-earner in a similar-sized law firm, Richard thought he might be useful in acting as temporary head of section for one of the partners who was about to go on maternity leave. Richard told Celia that he would give this person a call and ask him to come in to talk about the possibility of a job. Unfortunately, Celia could not be present at this meeting and was concerned when, after the two had met, Richard began to enthuse about the person's background and experience, concluding: 'He looks perfect. I'm sure he'll fit in and do a good job for us.'

Unknown to Celia, it appeared that the first informal discussion had turned into a formal interview and that Richard was about to make an offer of employment. To pre-empt this, she suggested to Richard that this first meeting should be seen very much as the informal and preliminary stage of a more thorough selection process, and that the next stage should be a formal interview, preceded by a presentation on the applicant's strategy for enhancing the firm's fee-earning capability. Richard reluctantly accepted her advice and the necessary arrangements were made to invite the applicant back the next week. This gave Celia time to talk to the other partners and senior managers about the applicant's CV and whether they had an opinion on his suitability. She also arranged for one of the other partners to join her and Richard to hear the presentation and to interview the candidate.

The candidate's presentation turned out to be superficial and limited. Moreover, he failed to impress in the interview, coming over as one-dimensional and inflexible. This was despite the impressive list of achievements that he had claimed in his CV. In the discussion that followed the candidate's departure, Celia told the two partners that one of the firm's senior managers had spoken to her about the candidate and had said that 'he shouldn't be touched with a barge pole'. It was alleged that, in one of his previous jobs, his behaviour had resulted in other staff leaving. Moreover, his claimed experience was, to say the least, clearly exaggerated.

A very different picture had now emerged from that which had originally been acquired by Richard Curtis and all three agreed that a letter would be sent informing the candidate that, in the light of all of the available evidence, it was not considered appropriate to offer him a position.

Questions

1. What are the particular difficulties associated with recruiting knowledge workers?

2. What might the firm do to develop a more effective and reliable recruitment strategy?

3. What costs might the firm have incurred if the candidate had been offered a position?

 Insights and Outcomes: visit the **online resources** at **www.oup.com/uk/banfield3e/** for answers to the HRM Insight questions.

In summary, the solution to many so-called 'people problems' is often associated with improving the effectiveness of the recruitment process, discriminating between potential stars and potential problem employees, and providing a workforce that delivers against current and future requirements (Ryan and Tippins, 2004). It is against this background that the role and contribution of the HR professional will be judged and evaluated. And if this is the challenge to be faced, there must be a debate about the way in which these objectives can be met, and about the specific practices and techniques that meet the criteria of 'best practice' or 'best fit', about which more will be said later in the chapter.

 RESEARCH INSIGHT 7.1

To take your learning further, you might want to read:

Klotz, A. C. et al. (2013) 'The role of trustworthiness in recruitment and selection: A review and guide for future research', *Journal of Organisational Behaviour*, 34(1).

This article examines the importance of trust and trustworthiness in the context of recruitment and selection. The importance of trust and fairness in HR was considered more generally in Chapter 5. In this article, perceptions of trust are linked to decision-making and outcomes in the process.

Different Perspectives, Different Challenges

One of the problems of a prescriptive approach to recruiting and selecting people—essentially telling people 'how to do it'—is that it fails to recognize the very different contexts and requirements that give a wider meaning and rationale to the process itself. Moreover, the 'traditional' approach tends to be operationally focused. As Millmore (2003) argues, this involves establishing job requirements through the process of job analysis, producing a person specification that identifies necessary and desirable personal characteristics, and then engaging in a selection process that is essentially about fitting applications to this specification. The process of assessing and selecting becomes one of applying agreed procedures and criteria in a technical and reductionist way. Recent developments, however, suggest that private sector organizations are taking a more strategic approach to hiring, considering applicants in terms of their organizational as well as job 'fit'. This point is considered in detail later in the chapter, but this more strategic and longer-term perspective is also consistent with recruiting and selecting talented people rather than individuals who fit a particular person specification linked to a job vacancy. The belief that values as well as skills and knowledge are important criteria in the assessment and selection of people represents a further development and a potentially complicating factor in deciding who to employ. It also raises the possibility of selection dilemmas arising as decision makers and selection panels are faced with someone who is strong on values but scores less impressively on job competency criteria and a different candidate who is experienced and meets all the job requirements but fails to show sufficient evidence of being committed to the required personal and organizational values. At that point, professional judgement has to be applied to resolve the dilemma (Rousseau and Barends, 2011).

> **STUDENT ACTIVITY 7.1**
>
> This exercise is designed to encourage you to think more widely than is often allowed where procedures and process requirements can be rigidly applied. The idea is to build a 'mind map' on a sheet of flip chart paper, and, as a group, think creatively about the kinds of behaviours, attributes, and personal characteristics 'the ideal' applicant would possess. It's not necessary to think of a specific job to do this because the activity is not designed with this in mind. Rather it is about getting you to think generically about what the organization is looking for when it employs someone. To make the exercise more interesting, split into two groups and separately construct mind maps. Compare the two versions and discuss differences and the thinking that led to these.

It could be argued that the thinking behind most recruitment and selection decisions is based on the belief that there is a strong correlation between the people that are finally selected and subsequent levels of job performance and productivity. In other words, selecting better people will have a greater positive economic impact than choosing less capable ones. This is the view taken by Mark Cook in the latest edition of his influential book on selection (Cook, 2016), although he admits that not all commentators are convinced that this is the case, citing other factors impacting on performance and productivity such as training, management style, and working conditions. The position taken here is consistent with that of Cook: without questioning the influence of such factors, we believe that in most cases it is difficult if not impossible to fully compensate for limited ability, poor attitude, and a reluctance to make a commitment to the organization that goes 'beyond contract' by training people, providing support, and through opportunities to develop. But what we would also argue is that many selection decisions fail to reflect this economic imperative but rather are influenced by a different agenda—the requirement to be seen to be fair and to treat all applicants equally by which we mean excluding information that might favour one applicant but not others. The question is whether the desire for procedural correctness rather than the importance of selecting people with the highest potential value dominates the process. In a 63-page document which sets out its recruitment and selection guidelines, the University of East Anglia (2016) states that a primary function of the guidelines is to:

> **help ensure equality of opportunity for all applicants and employees by promoting and maintaining professional standards, within a framework of consistency, fairness and good practice.**

And while they offer nine pages of policy and regulatory frameworks and state that selection has to be on merit, there is little that engages with what might be described as the economic or human capital issues that Cook and others see as being of greater or at least as of equal importance to procedural regulation. The objectives and expected outcomes of the guidelines are presented as:

- promote staff awareness of their role and responsibilities in recruitment and selection;
- assist managers in attracting, selecting, and retaining the most suitable candidates for the job;
- encourage a systematic and objective approach;
- help individuals identify their training and development needs with regard to recruitment and selection;
- ensure an active commitment to equal opportunities;
- ensure compliance with employment legislation with regard to recruitment and selection.

Of course, this is not about presenting a binary choice but rather highlighting the competing imperatives that affect the way recruitment and selection is practised in different sectors and organizations and about the consequences of overstating one over the other, but consistent with one of the central themes of the book, HR needs to be aware of the consequences of its actions and actual rather than intended outcomes and not simply concerned with regulating what it does and how things are done.

There is a further point to make and that is that selection is not only about the quality of applicants and their abilities but also about the selectors and other decision makers who are involved in the process. The competency and judgement of those involved can't be taken for granted and while the case for selection panels has been well made, it's not how many, but who that matters. So, one major challenge is to reconcile the potentially competing requirements of on the one hand selecting people who are going to add economic value to the organization and on the other to design and implement a fair and compliant process that reflects organizational values. A second is to consider the quality, experience, and capabilities of those who participate in the process of recruiting and selecting people. We almost always think about selection in terms of the qualities of applicants and candidates but not about the profile of the selectors and how they make decisions, and in the context of evidence-based management whether these decisions are validated.

There are also situations where recruitment reflects a more strategic and political imperative. As an example, consider the report produced by the Women and Work Commission (2006), which raised the issue of female under-representation in the science and engineering sectors, and the importance of developing strategic recruitment initiatives to overcome expected shortages in skilled engineers. The report linked this under-representation to poor-quality career advice in schools, to continued male domination of the engineering profession, and to persistent pay differences between men and women. In a more recent report, Silim and Crosse (2014) found that females interested in careers in the STEM subjects still found difficulties in being recruited onto appropriate university courses and faced discrimination from employers who used male only interview panels and male-dominated assessment centre exercises. Clearly, in situations where one demographic group is being excluded or is perceived to be excluded from particular career paths, a quite different recruitment perspective needs to be applied to address this societal problem.

Evidence of the shift towards a wider recruitment agenda is provided by the CIPD which, in its most recent recruitment factsheet, stated its own position when it said that:

> **The importance of diversity and inclusion should be taken into account at each stage of the recruitment process. The Government is currently spearheading a campaign to get employers to work towards 'name blind' recruitment to reduce bias in the recruitment process. The CIPD is supporting this by promoting it as a standard practice. Processes and systems should also be regularly reviewed to ensure hidden bias is removed and that talent is not blocked from entering the organization. Everyone taking part in activities such as shortlisting and interviewing should be aware of relevant legislation and the importance of avoiding discrimination.**
> **(CIPD, 2016)**

Moving away from specific demographic groups, particular organizations such as the UK National Health Service (NHS) are faced with multiple recruitment scenarios that require different approaches and emphases, which further undermines the simplistic notion that there is 'one best way' to carry out this activity. For example, the NHS, for the most senior and specialized medical posts is faced with an international if not global labour market within which to search for suitable applicants. In a time of high and rising employment levels, limited supply and significant competition, regulated budgets and high levels of demand, hospitals constantly have to replace people who leave, recruit new cohorts of nurses and medics, and use agency staff to fill short-term vacancies and to cover for absent employees. (Average annual sickness rates in the NHS in 2015 were 4 per cent (UK Government, 2015).)

The need for sustained high levels of recruitment also raises the relationship between retention problems linked to working conditions, pay, stress, and other factors, and one of the important questions that needs to be asked after 'how to successfully recruit' is why are we recruiting and are we recruiting too much! The need to link recruitment levels to other aspects of HR provides an additional lens through which recruitment and selection activities and procedures can be viewed.

The need to evaluate recruitment and selection from a cost as well as an effectiveness perspective is a further challenge. According to ACAS, by far the greatest expense involved in recruiting staff comes from the loss of productivity caused by the time it takes, twenty-eight weeks on average (this figure will vary depending on the type of work involved), for a new recruit to get up to speed, rather than the direct costs associated with advertising, administration, and management time. The analysis was based on figures drawn from five different sectors: retail, legal, accountancy, advertising, and IT and technology. Annually these costs for all sectors combined are estimated to be £4.13 billion, although this figure can only be taken as indicative rather than precise (ACAS, 2014).

According to the NHS Employers (2016), reducing agency spend is a strategic objective and involves hospital trusts in understanding the link between reducing the need for temporary recruitment and an over-reliance on recruitment agencies, and organizational culture and leadership, workforce planning strategies, and flexibility in the deployment of substantive staff. The guidance offered to employers to reduce their recruitment requirements and reduce the costs of recruitment includes:

- the collection of data and management information to allow them to build the foundation for a tailored flexible workforce strategy. This is about *knowing*;

- investing in new and more sophisticated software to help manage temporary staffing and rostering. This is about being more *efficient*;

- examining ways to use permanent staff more flexibly and trialling differing working patterns. This is about *flexibility and change*;

- creating a staff bank (a group of ex-employees or workers who are not on the payroll but are willing to work flexibly) and extending this to all parts of the organization. This is about *innovation*;

- reducing recruitment cycle times. This is about *system improvement*;

- ensuring that policy and practices are in place and implemented to improve the health and well-being of staff. This is about *reducing sickness absence*;

- exploring the possibility of developing a more sophisticated internal labour market that extends between NHS units. This is about *strategic change*;

- re-examining internal controls and governance to improve agency authorization and sign-off procedures. This is about *management control*.

The point being made is that those working in HR on recruitment and selection cannot limit their involvement to the process itself but need to be aware of whatever strategic objectives are being pursued, the direct and indirect financial costs of recruitment (explored later in the chapter), and the way in which recruitment needs and levels are influenced by wider organizational forces.

 For further insight into alternative challenges and the problem of skills shortage particularly in the public sector, see the Online Resources Extension Material 7.1.

Different Recruitment Situations

It should be clear by now that the recruitment and selection challenges facing management not only vary in their scale and complexity between organizations, but change over time and differ in terms of the influence of environmental pressures. Without necessarily being complete, the following list represents the situations most likely to be encountered by HR professionals.

- Replacement recruitment

  This might involve recruiting to replace any kind of employee, from the CEO of a plc to a manual worker in a factory.

- Recruiting for a new position/job

  The scale of this challenge may also be limited to one person, but because someone is needed to fill a new or revised position, the processes and implications are not identical to those of recruiting a replacement.

- Recruiting for a new build

    In this situation, the whole organizational unit is new—a new hotel or factory for example—and this creates differences in scale, complexity, and timescales.

- Recruitment needs that reflect long-term distortions in the supply and demand for labour

    These needs are often sector-specific or geographical in nature. Responses may involve developing new, and often overseas, labour markets and may feature an ethical, demographic, and political dimension.

- Recruitment that is used as an instrument of social engineering

    The challenge in this situation is less linked to labour shortages, than to desired changes in the composition and demographics of the labour force.

 For an integrated case study demonstrating what is involved in recruitment for a 'new-build' situation, visit the Online Resources Extension Material 7.2.

An Economic and Financial Perspective on Recruitment and Selection

The ability to differentiate between applicants, in terms of their suitability and 'fit' with a person specification and the organization's culture, is at the core of what recruiting and selecting involves. But this still leaves the question: what difference do different hiring decisions make to the organization and can these differences be given a financial value?

Cook (2016), in considering what the value of good employees actually means, offers an insight into the economic and financial dimension of employment decisions. His statement that 'The best is twice as good as the worst' and, by implication, the idea that the best adds at least double the economic value to the organization of a poor recruit has two important implications:

- Decisions about employing new staff can have either long-term financial costs or benefits for the organization. This means that the difference between the value of the contribution of the person employed, compared with that of one who was rejected, can be either positive or negative, depending on whether the 'right' employment decision was made. Of course, it is impossible to know precisely what the value of the contribution of someone rejected might have been but the argument is that employing the 'wrong' person and rejecting the 'right' one is likely to represent a significant loss of human capital for the organization. It was explained earlier that many organizations experience the negative outcomes of employing the wrong person (but at the time of selection seemed to be the right one), and have to bear the costs and losses of rectifying decisions that, when taken, seemed rational and defensible. In economic terms, this is what is known as an 'opportunity cost' and, in extreme cases, such costs can be very high, particularly at senior levels.

- It becomes even more important to understand both the 'real' costs of recruitment and selection, as opposed to those associated with direct expenditure, and the longer-term financial consequences that follow from the selection decisions.

 Signpost to Chapter 1: Managing People at Work: Challenges and Opportunities, for insights into the different economic value of employees.

According to Cook, failing to discriminate between the 'productive potential' of different potential employees can be detrimental, should the 'productive capacity' of employees differ greatly. By this he means where applicants do vary considerably in their suitability and human capital value. He poses two questions to illustrate this:

- How much do workers vary in their productive capacity and value to the organization?
- How much are these differences actually worth?

To complicate matters, both those questions can be asked at different time points. First, at the beginning of employment, then at some subsequent point to reflect changes in productive capacity and value. It is, as Cook recognizes, empirically difficult to calculate such values and costs precisely but at least there should be some attempt made to consider the appropriateness of hiring decisions in the context of those differences and values as employment progresses. So, in addition to asking questions about the fit between the selected applicant the job and the organization's values, HR also needs to be addressing the much more difficult but arguably more important question of whether those selected were the ones that possessed the highest productive value (can this be done?) and over time generated greater value outputs. The lower levels of productivity that the UK suffers from in comparison with other European economies can be explained in different ways but it is highly plausible that improvements in the quality of selection decisions could be one way of addressing this problem.

According to Edward P. Lazear (1998), however, the best and most productive employees are also likely to be the most expensive in terms of their recruitment and employment costs. This presents an interesting dilemma: is it better to employ the best people, irrespective of the costs involved, because their long-term value to the organization will be far greater than the costs of recruiting and paying them? Or, is it better to employ the cheapest people and minimize recruitment, selection, and employment costs, irrespective of the quality of those employed? Decisions on whether a cost-reduction or productivity-maximization strategy is to be adopted can only be made within a specific context and only after the implications of adopting one or the other have been fully explored. The reality for most organizations is that a position between the two extreme points on this continuum will be adopted, based on pragmatic considerations, with much depending on contextual factors such as the state of the labour market, the urgency of the recruitment requirement, and the organization's approach to recruitment.

Fitz-enz (2002) holds the view that:

> The hiring decision is often made too lightly; few organizations have stopped to figure out how costly the decision to hire a new employee is . . . every time the recruitment system cycles, the company incurs a cost and runs the risk of making a poor hiring decision. Even if the new hire is good, there is a productivity loss as the person moves up the learning curve. Any way you look at it, hiring is expensive, and one cannot ignore the importance of the selection process.

The implications arising from Cook, Lazear, and Fitz-enz are obvious. An economic approach to recruitment and selection must reflect the fact that decisions to appoint or reject an applicant will:

- affect the financial value of the contribution directly related to the newly employed worker over the duration of his or her employment;
- depending on the seniority of the position affect the productive contribution of co-workers and subordinates; and
- involve considerable direct and indirect expenditure and costs.

Over the period that an employee remains with an organization, the costs associated with recruitment and selection become proportionately less as the net value of the employee's contribution increases, assuming that a suitable person was employed. The reality is that few organizations have developed the kind of HR metrics that Lazear and Fitz-enz in particular, have developed in the USA, which allow the value of contributions and costs to be reliably calculated. In his new book, Fitz-enz (2010) develops what can be called a productivity approach to hiring. His basic approach is based on the belief that through the use of existing information and data and by creating new data flows, important new insights can be created about how recruitment can be made more effective and productive. Quoting from the experiences of one company in the USA, Fitz-enz argues that as more and more data points are added to what is already known, new statistical relationships and predictive correlations will be found that will improve decision-making in the hiring process. The results of changes made by the company in question (2010: 170–2) and based on the analysis of data produced the following results:

205

- recruitment methods became more effectively targeted;
- applicant flow increased by 25 per cent;
- hiring costs were reduced by one-third;
- key employee retention increased by over 12 per cent; and
- turnover was reduced by 48 per cent in year one alone.

Calculating Recruitment Costs

Fitz-enz (2002) offers the following formula for the calculation of what he calls 'cost per hire' (CPH):

$$CPH = \frac{AC + AF + RB + TC + RE + RC + NC + 10\%}{H}$$

Where:

AC = advertising costs;
AF = agency fees;
RB = referral bonus;
TC = travel costs;
RE = relocation costs;
RC = recruiter costs;
NC = the costs of processing unsolicited CVs;
H = the number of hires.

An alternative costing model, more appropriate to the UK, might be expressed as follows:

$$CPH = \frac{DA + GO + RE + C \text{ of } S + RC + EAF + TC + CLP + 10\%}{\text{Numbers involved}}$$

Where:

DA = direct administration costs—time plus rate of pay;
GO = a proportion of general overheads;
RE = recruitment expenses;
C of S = costs of selection—time of staff involved, selection materials;
RC = relocation costs;
EAF = external agency fees;
TC = training costs;
CLP = costs of lost production.

This is a potentially useful way of understanding and calculating hiring costs. But the other side of the equation involves estimating the net value of each hiring decision, recognizing that this can be negative as well as positive, although if it is negative for a significant period the organization would be expected to terminate the person's employment or take other remedial action.

 For guidance on how to avoid excessive and costly recruitment administration, see the Online Resources Extension Material 7.3.

 Signpost to Chapter 10: Workforce Planning and Measurement, for insights into measuring human capital values.

As an example, one of the author's postgraduate students, completing a similar calculation but not necessarily using the same formula, came up with a figure of £6,000 as the cost of replacing a single administrative worker in a local authority. It doesn't take much imagination to realize that organizations which are growing organically, creating new productive units, or which have high turnover rates are likely to experience very substantial, and possibly recurring, hiring costs. Whereas recruiting in the context of the first two situations (replacement and new positions) can be considered necessary and an opportunity to invest in new and talented staff, recruitment that is linked to excessive rates of labour turnover or the over-reliance on expensive recruitment agencies, is an unnecessary and unjustifiable cost.

The CIPD survey (2009) on recruitment, retention, and turnover provides more authoritative data on the economic costs of hiring. The survey found that the average cost of recruitment (i.e. of hiring someone) is estimated to be £4,000, rising to £6,125 when the full impact of turnover, training, and induction are taken into account. It also found that 47 per cent of organizations do not even measure the direct costs of recruitment. Whatever the methodology used, being able to put reasonably robust and consistently applied financial values on this important area of HR is becoming less an option, and more a requirement, if the 'true' economic costs of finding new and replacement labour are to be recognized fully.

> **RESEARCH INSIGHT 7.2**
>
> To take your learning further you might want to read this article:
>
> **Barrick, M. R. and Zimmerman, R. D. (2009) 'Hiring for retention and performance', *Human Resource Management*, 48(2), 183–206.**
>
> This study looks at variables with a view to predicting both the likelihood that recruited employees would perform well and be unlikely to resign from their jobs within the first one to two years of joining. A number of factors were identified that would predict performance and retention. Recruits who spent longer in previous roles, knew others in the organization, were conscientious and emotionally stable, were motivated to get the job, and who were confident in themselves and their decision-making were more likely to remain in their jobs and perform well in their roles.

Labour Markets

Labour markets can be virtual or physical, and they are important because they represent the source of an organization's supply of labour. External labour markets were originally geographical areas in which economically active jobseekers travelled to and from the place of work. These people were either in employment or unemployed and seeking work. Markets can be local, regional, national, or international in size, depending on the degree of scarcity and specialization of the skills and experience required. Historically, the physical limits of external labour markets were determined by travel-to-work times but, because work can now, for many, be from home and because many professionals are prepared to commute long distances, such physical limitations are less important than they used to be. Depending on the type of work and the degree of flexibility that an organization allows, potential employees can be found almost anywhere. Having said this, for many manufacturing businesses, service industries, and administrative work the local or regional labour market still represents the only realistic source of new and replacement labour.

But external labour markets are also contexts in which rates of pay are established and regulated which in turn affects the demand for labour. Generally, there will be an inverse relationship between the demand for labour and the wage rate: if the latter rises the former will fall. As we noted in Chapter 5, ideas of what represents a fair wage (rate) coexist with the so-called market rate, but while employers have some degree of flexibility in the rates of pay they offer to different occupational groups, at some point increases in regulated rates—National Minimum and Living Wage—will result in reduced demand for labour. Over the long term, this will become associated with increased productivity from the substitution of labour by technology. Certain professional groups, by restricting entry into their professions, can restrict supply and push up the cost of labour. As in the medical profession, where places at medical schools and post-qualification training opportunities are restricted. Increases in labour supply, through for example migration and demographic changes, is another factor that can affect the level of pay. From a recruitment perspective, employers have to decide on where to pitch pay levels to remain competitive. That means not paying below the market rate which would have the effect of increasing turnover as employees move to work for higher rates elsewhere, and make recruitment more difficult, but also not paying significantly above that which is needed to retain staff and recruit new workers. Some employers pay top rates to hire the best and most productive people, but many rates of pay in the public sector are centrally regulated and inflexible. One exception to this is in teaching. Historically, salary levels were determined by nationally agreed scales, a situation that resulted in a disconnect between the value of a new recruit or an existing member of staff and the value they represented. Recent changes to the rules governing pay now mean that the majority of secondary schools in the state sector enjoy much more flexibility in terms of starting salaries and differential payments. The reason for these changes is clear: paying more for better teachers means that pupils are likely to learn and develop more quickly. In a recent Department for Education publication (2013), it was claimed that:

> **Evidence shows that improving the quality of teaching is essential to raising standards in schools. According to the Sutton Trust, the difference between a very good teacher and a bad teacher may be equivalent to a whole year's education for a disadvantaged pupil.**

Internal labour markets represent a more contained and specific source of labour which is already employed by the organization in question. Depending on the strategy adopted, certain vacancies can be filled from within while all vacancies potentially can be filled by recourse to external sources. In Chapter 4 we identified the importance of filling more senior positions through career development and succession planning, that is through developing and promoting people from within. However, according to Grimshaw et al. (2001), as long ago as the turn of the century there was growing evidence of an erosion of principles associated with the traditional internal labour market within the UK employment system. They claimed that:

> **Examples of organizations that offer a combination of permanent employment contracts, a steady career progression from low skilled to high skilled posts, transparent and integrated pay structures and internal training are difficult to find. Instead, there appears to be a growing use of temporary employment agencies, external recruitment of specialist staff, a gradual dismantling of occupational skills and a fragmentation of the career and pay promotion path through de-layering, outsourcing, pay structure fragmentation and privatization of public services.**

The movement from permanent to flexible employment contracts is particularly prevalent among lower-paid occupations and is the subject of considerable debate and controversy. Zero-hours contracts are probably the 'best' example of employers moving towards relying almost entirely on the external labour market to meet changes in labour requirements. These contracts do not guarantee a minimum number of paid hours of work and paradoxically involve a situation where someone is employed but may not work for several days or even longer. According to the Office for National Statistics, 801,000 individuals identified themselves as working on such contracts for October to December 2015, representing 2.5 per cent of people in employment, although because of definitional issues it is difficult to be sure about the numbers involved.

Despite the controversy over the fairness of such contracts, and there is evidence that many young people find them acceptable, the question here is about the ease or difficulty in recruiting people to work on these terms. From an economic perspective, recruitment can only be possible if the terms are acceptable to sufficient people, but lack of alternative job prospects, demographic changes, or increases in labour supplies through migration may be factors that help to explain the existence and growth of such contracts. They may be acceptable to some but have to be accepted by others.

For large organizations, using the internal labour markets will always offer employers options and certainly promoting from within has obvious advantages, which are:

● staff are already known and their capabilities understood;

● promoting or moving staff within promotes retention and loyalty;

● benefits from investing in training and development can be realized; and

● knowledge and expertise can be retained and shared.

However, over-reliance on the internal market is not without its potential problems, one of which is that the lack of new employees can impact negatively on organizational vitality. This is known as stagnation.

> **KEY CONCEPT Stagnation**
>
> This term relates to the detrimental effect on creativity, change, and originality that is associated with relying largely or entirely on the existing workforce to fill vacancies. The lack of 'new blood' from outside, which can bring new ideas, challenge, and vitality into an organization, can contribute to the long-term decline of an organization that is too inward-looking in its search for new talent.

The contemporary concern expressed by leaders of the financial services and pharmaceutical industries over the ability to recruit the top talent from around the world post-Brexit demonstrates the importance of recruiting 'new blood' in certain industrial sectors to maintain competitiveness and innovation. This echoes the point made by Burrows (2004) who, in relation to the pharmaceutical sector, said:

> many organizations will not survive without the injection of new talent from outside, bringing world class skills and track records of addressing some of the challenges facing the industry.
>
> (p. 390)

The Role of Fairness in Recruitment

It is important that the recruitment and selection processes adopted by an organization are fair. This means that processes need to be as objective as possible and that only information relevant to the situation should be required. Decisions at all stages should be based solely on the merits of applicants and their suitability for the position in question. In one sense, these prescriptions are perfectly understandable, and would be supported by most people, but there is a real need to recognize that they may be more aspirational than realistic requirements. As we pointed out in Chapter 5, fairness can mean different things to different people and even those who believe they act in non-discriminatory ways may be unaware of their subconscious biases and prejudices. Applicants' perceptions of how they are treated may well be influenced by their own expectations and prior experiences. It should also be remembered that in attempting to create an 'equal playing field' for all candidates, selectors may lose sight of the strategic objective of the process which is to identify applicants who are qualified and experienced, will deliver a high level of job performance, get on with and support colleagues, deliver other contributions, and develop their potential. Anecdotal evidence abounds of decision makers picking applicants who turn out to be poor performers, but were selected as a result of fair and non-discriminatory procedures.

Employers clearly have a legal responsibility to ensure that selection processes do not allow either direct or indirect discrimination to occur on the grounds of race, religion or belief, sex, sexual orientation, disability, or age. The law allows for some exceptions to the above, known as 'genuine occupational qualifications', such as recruiting a male attendant for male-changing facilities at a swimming pool. Discrimination on the grounds of disability can, in some circumstances, be shown to be justifiable, but organizations are obliged to consider making reasonable adjustments in the work that needs to be done before excluding any such applicant for a job. A wheelchair user, for example, may have difficulties operating checkout facilities. It may be justifiable not to employ this person, but only if it can be shown that consideration was given to ways of altering the environment to allow the work to be done by a wheelchair user. A larger organization would be under a greater obligation to make this type of adjustment than would a small local shop, due to the relative affordability of such changes.

In practice ensuring a fair and lawful process is open to a wide degree of interpretation. This responsibility is perhaps set out in policy and more rigorously controlled in the public sector than elsewhere. For example a selection interview in the public sector is more likely to involve candidates being asked a series of identical questions to avoid the risk that any difference in treatment might be construed as discriminatory, whereas the private sector, particularly in small and medium-sized enterprises, are more likely to simply interview those candidates who appear strongest on paper without scoring each applicant during screening and are more likely to follow a more flexible discussion and probing style at interview. Experience, skills, resources, and time will affect the way the process is carried out. Neither process is necessarily discriminatory, and it might be argued that the private sector approach allows more flexibility to probe concerns. However, there is a greater risk that a potential claim of discrimination will be more difficult to defend with the more flexible approach. It could be argued that in the private sector competitive pressures mean that doing the right thing (for the company) is given equal importance with doing things right, whereas in the public sector procedural regularity (doing things right) takes priority.

Identifying Recruitment Requirements

In most organizations, the costs associated with employing the required number of people represent a significant proportion of the organizational budget. Having too many people in a particular section will quickly impact upon either the profitability of the organization or its ability to deliver required performance levels within the specified budget. When a vacancy arises, it is therefore important to consider whether the need for the tasks carried out has changed, whether a different skill set may be required, whether tasks might be redistributed among others in the organization, and whether forthcoming changes may impact upon current requirements. But it is possible to go beyond these considerations and view a vacancy in an existing job as an opportunity to redesign the organization of work. What this means, is that taking other connected jobs into account, the work done by six people (one of whom has left) could, with the involvement of the remaining five employees, be done by five through job enlargement, job enrichment, or the redesign of working environments, which is one approach to increasing productivity (Waber et al., 2014). This response also offers advantages for employees in the form of opportunities for personal development and increased rewards, and for the organization of reduced employment costs. Of course, it may be easier to simply replace, but what is easier may not in the longer term be better for the organization or its employees.

STUDENT ACTIVITY 7.2

In two groups, independently discuss and produce answers to the following questions. Come back together and present both sets of answers. Discuss any differences between the two and explore the reasons behind them.

1. In what way should the role of the line manager and HR specialist differ in terms of their decision-making responsibilities? What are the pros and cons of placing full responsibility for the recruitment of a direct report to the line manager?

2. Consider the role of the second level manager in a recruitment decision. What role should the line manager's manager play compared to the HR specialist and direct line manager in making a decision about whether to replace a role and what should his or her role be in the recruitment and selection process?

3. Who should be responsible for inducting new recruits? What are the key requirements for an effective induction programme? To help you with this task listen to the podcast at: https://soundcloud.com/cipd/podcast-89-rethinking-staff-inductions; this highlights the limitations of many induction programmes and indicates a new way of thinking about and designing the induction experience.

Once a decision has been taken to recruit, whatever the circumstances, most organizations implement a series of connected procedures that in their entirety constitute the process of recruiting and selecting employees. These procedures were outlined earlier in the chapter but it is important to consider them in more detail. Resulting from an analysis of the job which generates information about what the job involves, two documents are usually completed. The *job description*, sometimes referred to as the 'job specification', gives details of the purpose of the job, and of the tasks and responsibilities or areas of accountability that are assigned to the jobholder. The *person specification* details the skills, knowledge, and attitudes that should ideally be possessed by the jobholder to ensure he or she can meet objectives. It represents a profile of the 'ideal' person in relation to a range of personal attributes and characteristics relevant to the job in question, but as we noted earlier in the chapter, such an approach is time bound. It fails to look beyond the immediate job vacancy in terms of future requirements, and restricts the profile to those attributes that are only judged to be relevant to doing the job without taking into account what we might call 'organizational citizenship' requirements.

KEY CONCEPT Organizational citizenship

This relates to behaviour that extends beyond that which is necessary to carry out job duties and responsibility to the required standard. It is behaviour that represents a person's voluntary commitment to an organization or company that is not part of his or her contractual tasks (see Zhang, 2011).

The Person–Job Fit

The idea that the assessment and selection process allows managers to identify someone from among those remaining 'in the pool' who is the 'best qualified for the job' informs the thinking of many HR professionals. 'Best' is, however, a relative term, and while the objective might be to eliminate weaker candidates and be left with the 'best', being the 'best' may not, in fact, mean that this person has the necessary personal and technical competences to perform the job to the required standards. An alternative approach to selection, often described as 'criterion-referenced selection', is based on the principle that the 'best' of applicants may not possess the required competences for the job. If this second approach is taken, it is much more likely that a decision to appoint will not be made because none of the applicants meets the required standards. Such an approach is often associated with the readvertisement of positions, after none of the original applicants have been considered suitable. Not appointing and readvertising is an outcome that is far better than one in which the best applicant is appointed but who fails to meet performance expectations.

Both approaches fundamentally involve 'fitting' the person to the job and, in each, either the 'best fit' or the 'right fit' is chosen at the end of the process. This notion of fit can be seen as both attractive and yet, at the same time, worrying. It is attractive because it implies that, with sufficient preparation and care, it is possible to match the person to the job with the minimum of disruption and friction to the social fabric of the organization. It is worrying, however, because it implies that, as with physical objects such as machines, human beings can be treated as the equivalent of machine parts and somehow 'fitted' into the organization (i.e. the 'machine'). The belief that organizations can be understood as machines and managed as such is associated with the widespread use of the organization-as-machine metaphor, within which order, predictability, and control mechanisms are believed to result in efficient and non-problematic employee performance (Morgan, 1997). But the complex, and often unpredictable, nature of human behaviour and the high level of subjectivity that still surrounds the recruitment and selection process, despite its procedural regulation, means that seeing candidates as the equivalent of pieces in a jigsaw puzzle is both simplistic and unhelpful.

Part of the problem is not simply associated with the dangers of seeing organizations as machines, but with the limiting notion of 'fitting' someone exclusively to the job. Fitting people into the organization, in terms of its culture and values, as well as into a job makes this task even more challenging. The identification of personal characteristics associated with being an effective part of a dynamic and challenging working environment is, arguably, of equal importance to the assessment of applicants against a more specific set of job competences. The emphasis on certain personal traits and strengths, described by Welch and Welch (2005), suggests that, in some organizations, more importance is given to the ability of applicants to fit into the organizational culture and value system than is given to their fitting the requirements of a specific job. In this respect, generic rather than job-specific requirements come into play. Jack Welch is a highly rated organizational leader who believes strongly in hiring people who possess what he has found are characteristics positively related to their subsequent performance. Examples of these are:

- **Integrity**—this is about honesty, admitting to but learning from mistakes, taking responsibility, and playing to win but within the rules of the organization.

- **Intelligence**—this does not equate to educational attainment but rather certain key cognitive skills such as problem solving, logical reasoning, intellectual curiosity, and emotional sensitivity.

- **Maturity**—this is not about age but is linked to knowledge, judgement, and wisdom but particularly the ability to handle pressure and display confidence in the way he/she operates.

Welch also emphasizes the importance of what he calls the 4-E framework which reflects the value and importance of generic as well as job-specific requirements. This is about:

- positive *energy* and a strong work ethic;

- the ability to *energize others*;

- having the '*edge*' to take important decisions and confront challenging situations;

- *execution*—the ability to get the job done.

The assessment of applicants against the person specification takes place at different stages of the process:

1. At the point where CVs or application forms are submitted or as a result of more informal online conversations.

2. After the results of assessment centre activities and work sample tests have been collated.

3. At the shortlisting stage where information about candidates from different sources is considered.

4. At the selection interview which is usually the final stage in the assessment process.

Many organizations use an assessment matrix to allow the person specification requirements to be given a numerical and often weighted value. In other words, applicants at the final interview stage are scored against each of the criteria included in the specification. The result is an aggregate score for each candidate being interviewed, based on the collective decisions of the interviewing panel. One of the reasons why assessment matrices have become more widely used is that they represent evidence of the 'objectivity' of the assessment procedure which can be used to justify and defend the appointment decision. There is a danger, however, in assuming that the candidate who received the highest score is the one who should be appointed. This may be the case but not necessarily so. Much depends on what has been included and omitted from the specification and assessment matrix and the weighting of criteria. The design of the assessment matrix and particularly the weighting of the different criteria are critical variables that affect what the selection panel are looking for and score.

For an example of a selection matrix, see the Online Resources Extension Material 7.4.

STUDENT ACTIVITY 7.3

1. In a group, agree on a job that all are familiar with. Perhaps you could use a generic university lecturer position.

2. Produce a list of essential and desirable personal characteristics for the job. You will need to discuss these and reach collective agreement.

3. Design an assessment matrix with up to six requirements down the left-hand side with the weighting. Across the top use a scoring range and decide on the different scoring levels. Use a weighting scale of 1–5. You cannot give an actual score for each criterion within the limits of the activity but you must understand how criteria are scored and how the final aggregate score is made up.

4. Discuss the different scoring ranges selectors might use to score how well individual candidates performed against the criteria.

5. Collectively discuss your matrix and the issues that might arise with your tutor and get feedback on its strengths and weaknesses.

Attracting the Right Applicants

A recruitment and selection strategy that focuses on hiring well-qualified high performers, or at least those with the potential to be this type of person, is likely to be more demanding and challenging than one in which lower standards are applied, or selecting the 'best' from a set of applicants. Even when unemployment levels in the external labour markets are relatively high, better workers are less likely to be unemployed or will only temporarily be so. The challenge of attracting them becomes, therefore, much harder than when recruiting less qualified people. This is because high-potential and top-performing candidates who can deliver the best results are often:

- well recognized, valued, and nurtured by their current employers;

- unlikely to be looking for another job, because they are likely to enjoy well-paid and satisfying jobs;

- attractive to many employers when they do look and will often get more than one offer when they start looking;

- given a counteroffer to stay with their current employer;

- hard to convince that it is worthwhile to move to a new job in an unknown organization.

The process of attracting the right candidates is that HR activity which involves marketing the organization to potential candidates. There are many channels that can be used to make potential candidates aware of current and future vacancies, and these vary in degrees of formality and expense. Figure 7.2 shows the types of option available and the main features associated with each method. It should be noted that, while informal methods of recruitment, such as word of mouth, personal referrals, and the use of 'now recruiting' banners, can be very cost-effective, they may limit the pool of applicants. The Equality and Human Rights Commission warns specifically against the dangers of indirect discrimination inherent to word-of-mouth recruitment should the workforce consist predominantly of one gender or racial group.

213

Recruitment Advertising

Research into the effectiveness of different recruitment strategies offers interesting insights into what appears to work and what doesn't (CIPD, 2009). However, perhaps the biggest change in recruitment in recent years has been the move to online recruitment and the use of social media. As early as 2008, the Internet Advertising Bureau claimed that online recruitment advertising accounted for 32.9 per cent of total online advertising spend of £1.7 billion in the UK, in fact without the growth of online recruitment advertising the overall advertising market would have seen a 4.6 per cent decline. The shift to online recruitment advertising has happened so rapidly that it is difficult to quantify, as research thus far does not reflect the extent of this change. Research in this area still has to catch up, in fact the CIPD (2009) survey did not even ask participants about online advertising and social media, and only asked about the use of their own corporate websites for attracting applicants (Robert Walters, 2014).

The mostly widely used method for attracting applicants is recruitment advertising and as we have noted the biggest change in recent years has been the move to online recruitment. The use of newspapers

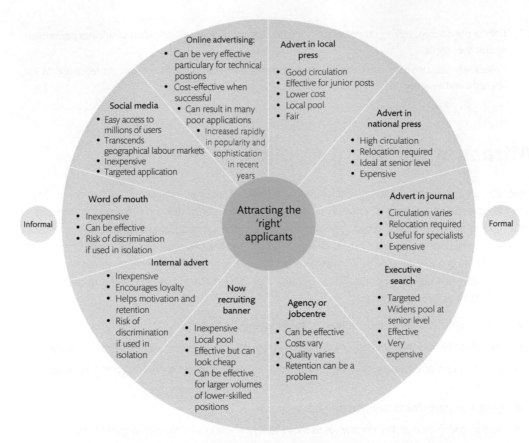

Figure 7.2 The recruitment 'wheel'—where and how to market vacancies

and trade journals for advertising has declined in popularity, although still popular within the professions. It has becoming increasingly rare for most organizations not to use some form of internet-based solution. Many websites including generic advertisers such as Monster (www.monster.com) and Totaljobs (www.totaljobs.co.uk) as well as regional websites and specialist websites for particular professions are now widely used to advertise vacancies. Virtually all the newspapers and journals that have relied upon the revenue generated by recruitment advertising have developed their own websites and this sector is still changing rapidly. Many websites have become much more sophisticated in recent years offering services to candidates such as job alerts, and careers advice and services to employers allowing better branding, CV search facilities, screening tools, and online application options to remain competitive. Online advertising tends to be cheaper than traditional methods and the switch away from printed media to online advertising was perhaps accelerated through the last economic downturn due to the costs pressures faced by organizations.

The Role of Social Media and Social Networking Sites

Social media is a broad category, encompassing practices such as podcasting, blogging, text messaging, internet videos, and HR email marketing, which are some of the more widespread applications used in recruitment.

Social networking sites have grown rapidly in popularity and there is an array of sites competing for members from more formal sites encouraging business networking such as LinkedIn to more informal sites such as Twitter and Facebook. LinkedIn (www.linkedin.com) now has over 60 million members, half of which are outside the USA. By its sixth anniversary, Facebook boasted over 400 million global users, twice the number at its fifth anniversary (Facebook, 5 February 2010) and Twitter (www.twitter.com) had 75 million users by January 2010, although arguably many of these are inactive or not economically active. There is no disputing the fact that social networking sites have direct access to many people and that these sites therefore present an opportunity to employers to attract potential applicants. However, the CIPD identified that only 7 per cent of employers use social networking sites such as LinkedIn to attract applicants. Employers are perhaps cautious about using these sites due to their informal approach and reputation for the ease with which inappropriate comments and material can be circulated. Many employers bar or discourage their use while at work because of the potential risks linked to claims of harassment in the workplace. Inappropriate comments shared through such sites can have negative consequences at work should these come to the attention of employers (Madia, 2011).

A report commissioned by Microsoft (www.euractiv.com, 1 February 2010) showed that 59 per cent of recruiters made use of data collected from the internet to evaluate candidates and that 41 per cent of UK recruiters, 16 per cent of German recruiters, and 14 per cent of French recruiters had rejected candidates on the basis of their online reputation. In the USA, 70 per cent of HR professionals have refused jobseekers based upon information found online. Whether this is morally or even legally defensible in light of discrimination legislation in countries that such practices occur is arguable, nonetheless employees should take care about how their personal information can be accessed as it would appear that employers are increasingly gathering such covert information where it is available and are using this to support recruitment decisions.

According to Broughton et al. (2011), and based on a survey conducted by a recruitment agency, more than half of all UK jobseekers use social media sites in their search for employment, including 18 per cent who use Facebook and 31 per cent who use LinkedIn. They claim that young people are increasingly using social media tools to build an online career presence and search for jobs. Another survey of over 30,000 graduates, students, and early career professionals worldwide found that in Europe, almost 100 per cent of survey participants would like to interact with employers online. The preference was for LinkedIn (48 per cent), with Facebook scoring 25 per cent.

The use of social media as a recruitment tool throws up opportunities and challenges for employers. Social media potentially offers speed, efficiency, and the ability to target and attract specific groups of people. It can provide a useful additional source of information on potential job candidates, especially since some data (at the personal as well as the professional level) may not be generated for recruitment, and therefore may provide candid supplementary information on the applicant. For candidates, it potentially offers multiple sources of information about the employer and the possibility of contact with existing employees to gain a more realistic job preview. Certainly, costs and the speeding up of the recruitment process are important advantages for employers who are using social media to support the process. Creating an online recruitment capability can involve considerable capital expenditure. Once set up, though, there is no significant cost associated with posting on a corporate vacancy board compared to placing job adverts in newspapers, professional journals, and jobcentres.

But in a case study on how Deloitte (2011) uses social media to recruit, a quite different advantage was noted. Deloitte created a real human connection between the company and prospective employees with personal bios, photos, and easy ways to contact and connect with them through the company's career website. In their view, this humanization of the recruitment process connects to people's feelings and desires to be treated as people and not simply as applicants. The study found that the use of social media became an enjoyable experience for those using it. Direct hires through social media represent only 2 per cent of the company's total hires but the indirect benefits of social media were considered much greater. The impression created by the Deloitte case study is that the use of social media facilitates rather than replaces traditional recruitment methods. At the same time, it is an important mechanism for communicating the company's brand message and supporting its attempt to become a preferred employer.

STUDENT ACTIVITY 7.4

Consider a selection of recruitment adverts from a variety of websites such as www.monster.co.uk, www.totaljobs.com, or www.fish4.co.uk for a job of your choice such as an administrator, sales representative, or other role.

1. Identify the qualities that make some adverts stand out more than others.

2. Produce a checklist of items that must be covered in a recruitment advert and items that would be interesting and attractive to potential applicants.

3. Add a set of guidelines to your checklist of areas to be checked to ensure that nothing which may discourage applications or that is potentially unlawful is included.

4. Rank the adverts according to the favourable impression they create and justify your decision.

PRACTITIONER INSIGHT **Francesca Fowler, former HR director at Nottingham Trent University and currently HR director at the University of Leeds. For this insight, Francesca drew upon her experiences at Nottingham.**

At Nottingham Trent University, recruitment is important to us for two reasons. It is not only an opportunity to bring new talent into the organization but we also challenge each vacancy that arises to be sure that we are recruiting for the right role. By following a thorough process, we ensure we are legally compliant and give careful consideration on whether to replace like for like or redesign the role. We then make sure that we use a thorough selection process to bring the best people into the organization. The risks of getting it wrong are high and it would be difficult and costly to address problems should we make the wrong decision.

We tend to advertise most of our vacancies online as well as using either local or national media to ensure we have good accessibility for equal opportunities purposes. We sometimes use a recruitment agency, usually only for more senior posts that are more difficult to fill, as this is a very expensive option.

Line managers are trained to be able to chair our structured interview panels to ensure they ask the right questions and probe sufficiently to be able to identify the best candidates. We also use psychometric tests to support selection decisions for more critical posts.

We carry out surveys among our recent recruits to help us to evaluate our recruitment process as it is important to us that candidates feel they were given an open and honest understanding of the role and the organization and their feedback helps us to make improvements in our future recruitment.

Our own website is an important recruitment tool for us. All our vacancies are advertised on our website along with supporting documentation such as job descriptions and person specifications. We like to take applications through the website as it helps us to effectively track and monitor our recruitment process as well as easily gathering all the data we need about candidates.

The important point to note about these different approaches and media platforms for communicating with and attracting prospective employees is that, depending on the numbers of people being recruited, the level and type of worker, and the importance of time and costs, different organizations will develop and use a mix of techniques and methods that works for them. All have potential advantages and disadvantages, and it is unrealistic and misleading to think that there is any 'right' way in which to recruit. What can be said is that, through experience and the ability to relate outcomes to the methods used, HR professionals should be able to reduce the costs involved and the cycle time, and improve the quality of recruits. In terms of what people are trying to achieve, and there will be differences here, objectives we might associate with recruitment and selection can be expressed in the aphorism—'never recruit the assholes and don't lose the stars!'

Recruiting new staff continues to pose problems and challenges, as HRM Insights 7.2 and 7.3 illustrate.

HRM INSIGHT 7.2 Recruitment practices at Thompson

CW Thompson is a privately owned business with over 2,000 employees. The vast majority of its recruitment is via referrals from existing staff and customers. Many new recruits are, in fact, the friends and relatives of existing staff, and the manager believes that this is one of the reasons why there is a strong sense of loyalty and team working. Thompson is based in an area with a high ethnic minority population, but the manager has only employed three people in the last four years from an ethnic minority—and two of these have left.

A local resident submits a complaint to the Equality and Human Rights Commission, which investigates and decides to prosecute the company. The business' defence is that it cannot afford to advertise all vacancies in the newspaper and that changing recruitment practices would displease the existing staff.

Questions

1. What low-cost options might the manager have used to advertise more fairly?

2. How might the manager ensure that members of staff are not displeased by changes to recruitment practices?

3. Given that the business employs over 2,000 employees, to what extent do you feel that the cost of advertising should be taken into consideration?

4. What might explain the decision of the two people to leave?

HRM INSIGHT 7.3 The case of LLT Solutions

LLT Solutions had a vacancy for a computer network administrator manager at one of its most prominent call centres, managing calls for global retail customers. The call centre was also a 'European hub', responsible for transferring queries to other European call centres. As this was a key role, the position was advertised nationally in the most widely recognized journal for network personnel and a thorough selection procedure was followed to select the preferred candidate.

The successful candidate accepted the offer and submitted one month's notice to his employer. That employer made the candidate a generous counteroffer, increasing his salary by 20 per cent, to beat the offer made. The employer also promised to make a number of changes to the role to address previously unresolved concerns about issues such as effective communication and involvement in corporate decision-making and projects. The candidate consequently withdrew his acceptance of the newly offered post three days before he was due to join.

Because no other suitable internal candidate was available, the position was readvertised the following month with a suitable closing date. The originally successful candidate applied again for the post, sending in an accompanying letter that explained that the promises made by his present employer had not been fulfilled and that he was still interested in joining the new business.

Questions

1. What are the pros and cons of making a 'counteroffer' if an employee resigns after an offer of employment is made by another organization?

2. In this example, what are the pros and cons to the recruiting organization of considering the same applicant a second time around?

3. What options does the recruiting company have in handling this application?

4. What would you do and why?

STUDENT ACTIVITY 7.5

This is a group activity and is designed to test your decision-making ability in different recruitment situations.

1. Split into two groups and work independently.

2. Use the following recruitment requirements:

- a vacancy for the head of finance in a multinational company
- a vacancy for a trainee heating engineer
- a vacancy for a general manager in a provincial hotel
- a vacancy for an HR manager in a law firm

3. Produce a job specification for the jobs you are working with.

4. Develop a recruitment strategy for each vacancy (or however many is practical), which means the employing company needs to identify suitable applicants/candidates. Identify the recruitment cycle time and estimated cost for each.

5. Come together as a whole group and share your decisions. Discuss any differences between the two subgroups and learn from each other. Use your tutor to give feedback.

Employer Branding

For many years organizations have invested in marketing products and services to their customers, consumers, service users, and clients to help maintain loyalty to their brand and corporate image, or identity or to promote the services that they provide. Employer branding from an HR perspective involves using a similar approach to HR issues and is used to describe how an organization promotes what it has to offer with regard to the attraction and retention of employees. This is an area of growing importance and many larger and global businesses have invested heavily in developing what they hope will be a distinctive brand image that will attract talented people to seek employment with them. The CIPD (2007) defines employer branding as:

a set of attributes and qualities—often intangible—that makes an organisation distinctive, promises a particular kind of employment experience, and appeals to those people who will thrive and perform to their best in its culture

According to Backhaus and Tikoo (2004), creating an employer branding is a three-step process:

1. A firm develops the 'value proposition' that is to be embodied in the brand. Using information about the organization's culture, management style, qualities of current employees, current employment image, and impressions of product or service quality, managers develop the value proposition which encapsulates the central message conveyed by the brand.

2. Following the development of the value proposition, the firm markets the value proposition to its targeted potential employees, recruiting agencies, placement, and other organizations involved in the recruitment business. This external marketing of the employer brand is designed primarily to attract the target population and create an external image and identity that results in the status of 'employer of preferred choice' being achieved.

3. Internal marketing of the employer brand through various communications channels. This is important because it carries the brand 'promise' made to recruits into the firm and incorporates it as part of the organizational culture. The objective here is to ensure that the value proposition which is at the core of the brand promise is actually delivered and experienced by employees.

Closely associated with the concept of employer branding is that of employer of preferred choice (Wilden et al., 2010). Organizations that achieve this status are looking to gain the following advantages:

- Ease in attracting quality talent.
- Good public relations when mentioned in articles and books citing the best companies, for example the *Sunday Times* survey of the Best Companies to Work For.

- High retention rates for current employees.

- Employees who experience the corporate brand are likely to support and represent the company in the external environment.

- It can reduce the costs of recruitment.

- Employee motivation can be easy to maintain because of the shared pride in the company.

RESEARCH INSIGHT 7.3

Sparrow, P. and Otaye, L. (2015) *Employer Branding: From Attraction to a Core HR Strategy* **(Centre for Performance led HR White Paper 15/01, Lancaster University Management School).**

To take your learning further you may want to read this paper by Sparrow and Otaye on employee branding. It considers branding as a form of contracting, a way of communicating key messages and information, and in terms of the impact on applicant behaviour.

Assessing and Selecting

Assessing the suitability of applicants at each stage of selection, starting from reviewing application forms or CVs, to evaluating psychometric test results and rating performance in interviews, is central to the process not only of hiring, but of hiring the right kind of people. As a result of 'knowing' how well applicants match the requirements of a person specification or competency framework, the next stage in the assessment process can be planned. This involves the use of techniques and tools that are designed to discriminate between shortlisted applicants, using legal, relevant, and predictive criteria. The requirement to assess and distinguish is both challenging and difficult, and the people involved need to apply not only a range of skills to the task but also experience in the exercise of managerial and professional judgement. Selection is therefore based on generating data about candidates which constitutes the evidential basis upon which individuals are seen as being more or less suitable. That evidence is then evaluated until the final decisions are taken about who to employ. It is conceivable that in the future AI systems will take over decision-making from humans but whether that will result in 'better' selection decisions being made remains unknown. What we can say, however, with some certainty is that the use of assessment methods which have the highest level of predictive validity will provide decision makers with the most useful evidence upon which to base their decisions. Whether they choose to use that evidence is another matter, and it would be naive to think that the process of selecting someone for a job, promotion, or redundancy doesn't have a political dimension.

Evidence from research carried out in the USA suggests a move away from restricting the assessment of specific applicant characteristics, such as educational attainments or cognitive ability, to a more holistic approach, as part of which assessors are interested in the 'whole person' and the full range of competencies that each person offers (O'Leary et al., 2002). Recognizing that effective job performance may be linked to other, perhaps less well-understood, skills and competencies is associated with the ideas of writers such as Daniel Goleman (1995, 1998), whose work on emotional intelligence has provided new insights into the relationship between what people are, how they behave, and job performance. In other words, how well people perform may involve the influence of factors and attributes that are not recognized or known by decision makers.

According to Cook (2016), assessment methods ideally need to meet the following criteria:

- **Reliability**—this is about consistency, for example if the same method was used on the same cohort of applicants would it produce the same results? Low levels of reliability raise doubts about the utility of the method in question. If two managers give different performance ratings to the same employee, then the method of managerial rating is flawed, using those managers. There is a point here that the reliability or otherwise of the method where the judgement of assessors is involved may reflect the skills and experience of the assessors rather than any inherent problem with the method.

- **Validity**—this means the method is able to identify and distinguish between weak and strong candidates. The concept of predictive validity, considered later, is critical to knowing which methods of assessing candidates are worth using.

- **Acceptability**—this is about procedural fairness to candidates, a point we considered in detail in Chapter 5.

- **Legality**—this means complying with relevant anti-discrimination legislation. However, in countries where different legislation requirements apply, the need to comply with legislation and judicial judgements may be more or less onerous.

- **Cost-effective**—this involves considering the resources used in the process and whether these are both necessary and used efficiently. Almost certainly where the wrong selection decision is taken the costs involved will not be compensated for by subsequent benefits but may be added to by the longer-term costs associated with the wrong decision. It goes without saying that the more senior the vacant position, the more time and resources will be used to support the final decision.

- **Easy to use**—probably the least important of the six criteria but this is about not using overcomplicated techniques and where the results can be understood by the decision takers.

Construct validity refers to the ability of a measurement tool (e.g. a survey, test) to actually measure the psychological concept or construct being studied—measuring intelligence for example by asking people questions would probably have a low level of construct validity—but the degree to which any assessment method can predict future job performance is critical. A high level of predictive validity implies that the method is actually measuring something of importance. Taking a generic and variable factor such as IQ, predictive validity is high when those who score high on the test perform well in the job and those who achieve low scores perform worst.

The Importance of Predictive Validity

According to O'Leary et al. (2002), the most important property of the assessment instruments used to measure or assess applicants against set criteria is their ability to predict future job performance, or job-related learning. In other words, does someone who scores well on the assessment instrument perform better on the job than someone whose score is poor? If the instruments and techniques are sufficiently reliable—meaning that they produce consistent results—the degree of predictive validity indicates which instruments and techniques are useful. Differences in test scores or ratings can then be used to identify which candidate is likely to be a better-performing employee. This is the evidence upon which distinguishing between candidates is based. The challenge for managers is, therefore, one of identifying the degree of predictive validity for the assessment instruments in use, or of those that might be used.

A complicating factor, however, is the approach taken to measuring job performance and how this is conceptualized. There are several ways this could be done: using performance ratings, salary progression, and promotion as indicators are well-known examples. But because low-scoring candidates are rarely hired, the ability to conduct systematic comparisons of job performance levels with both high- and low-scoring candidates is limited, although it is possible where cohorts rather than individuals are recruited. Think about cohorts of nurses and medics entering training or cohort entries into the armed forces.

One of the difficulties for those involved in using assessment instruments is, as Ryan and Tippins (2004) argue, that many of the research findings on recruiting staff have not been widely embraced by HR professionals. There are several reasons for this, including the failure of researchers to present their findings in an accessible and understandable way. The main reason, however, is perhaps that those using assessment instruments may have inaccurate beliefs about the predictive powers of the instruments they use. For example, in their US study, Rynes et al. (2004) found that 72 per cent of the HR managers they surveyed thought that the degree of applicant conscientiousness was a better predictor of job performance than intelligence, whereas the reverse is true. They argue that evidence shows that structured selection processes are better than less structured ones and suggest that, often, those involved in making selection decisions rely too much on what they call 'gut instinct' and 'chemistry'. This is a complex and difficult issue, and however much evidence is presented that emphasizes the use of one or a combination of assessment instruments, it remains the case, as we argued above, that the actual selection decision will involve some element of judgement and the application of personal experience of previous selection decisions.

As a result of reviewing a number of studies, Rynes et al. established the statistical relationships between commonly used assessment instruments and predictive validity as shown in Tables 7.1 and 7.2. In the earlier study by O'Leary et al. (2002), those instruments were found to have significantly lower levels of validity! So, while there is a pattern of results that establish levels of predictive ability for the main assessment methods in use, there is not complete agreement within the research community about how predictive these methods are.

These findings suggest that those instruments with a high predictive validity relative to others should be used, but this is an assumption that ignores the influence of contextual factors. For example, the skills and experience of interviewees will affect the actual level of predictive validity, with the use of inexperienced interviewers and deviations from 'best practice' resulting in considerably lower validity levels. What we need to emphasize here is not simply the potential of particular methods/instruments, but the way in which they are used, the qualities and experience of those involved, and the way in which different contributions to an assessment of the whole person are generated, evaluated, and combined with the judgement of the decision makers to produce a final selection decision.

Table 7.1 Statistical relationships between assessment instruments and predictive validity

Assessment instrument	Predictive validity
Work sample tests	0.54
Cognitive ability tests	0.51
Structured interviews	0.51
Job knowledge tests	0.48
Unstructured interviews	0.31
Biographical data	0.35
Assessment centre results	0.37
Reference checks	0.26

Source: Adapted from Rynes, S. L., Colbert, A., and Brown, K. G. (2002). Reproduced with permission.

Table 7.2 Instruments with lower levels of validity

Assessment instrument	Predictive validity
Job experience	0.18
Training and experience	0.11
Years of education	0.10
Graphology	0.02
Age	−0.01

Source: Adapted from O'Leary, B. S., Lindholm, M. L., Whitford, R. A., and Freeman, S. E. (2002). Reproduced with permission.

In the latest edition of his book on selection, Cook (2016) quotes US sources as indicating that any correlation below 0.3 has failed to establish any meaningful predictive validity and by implication cannot be relied upon in helping to make selection decisions. Where stronger correlations—0.5/0.6—are found between particular assessment methods/techniques and job performance, Cook states that these results explain between one-third and one-quarter of subsequent job performance and that it is unlikely that any assessable personal characteristic will produce higher correlations because job performance is also influenced by such factors as management behaviour, organizational climate, co-workers, and the working environment. The important conclusion that needs to be understood, is that while there are several very useful and predictive ways to assess how candidates might initially perform at work, job performance over time and in different jobs is much more difficult to establish by pre-employment assessment methods that produce evidence on only a limited range of personal attributes and characteristics, however reliable and valid these methods might be (Bozionelos, 2005). For a brief review of the validity of different selection methods, see Buzea (2007).

RESEARCH INSIGHT 7.4

To take your learning further you might want to read:

Macan, T. (2009) 'The employment interview: A review of current studies and directions for future research', *Human Resource Management Review*, 19, 203-18.

The article asks why 'structured' interviews have a higher predictive validity than unstructured ones, examines the constructs or characteristics that interviews 'measure', and investigates the applicant and interview factors that may affect the interview process.

An Applicant Perspective

One of the distinctive features of this book is the emphasis given to making sense of HR from an employee perspective. In bringing this chapter to a close, it is necessary therefore to ask: what does recruitment and selection mean to the person searching for a job and in particular what do applicants and candidates expect and experience from the hiring process? Inevitably, almost all of the research on this subject and, indeed, the approach taken by many writers of HR textbooks, essentially reflects a managerial perspective. This managerial tendency is understandable and to a degree justifiable, but without considering the applicants and how their behaviour and attitudes are influenced by the experiences they are required to go through, it is a one-sided and limited perspective. To compensate for this bias, more recent research has been carried out on the applicant perspective and experience (Dipboye et al., 2012).

Chambers (2002) makes the important distinction between factors that influence behavioural reactions among applicants and the consequences that follow from these reactions. This distinction is important because it shows that the consequences of positive or negative experiences, particularly at the selection stage, continue after the selection decision has been taken. As an example, consider the situation in which an internal applicant has received negative feedback from the chair of an interview panel, who is also his or her line manager. The effect, while not inevitable, is likely to be a degree of demotivation and possibly a questioning of self-worth. The long-term consequences may involve rethinking the 'psychological contract', reduced levels of job performance, and a worsening of interpersonal relationships.

Research quoted by Chambers points to the way in which applicant reactions to selection procedures are related to whether the procedures are perceived by the applicants as fair and just. The suggestion is that, if applicants perceive their experiences as unfair, unprofessional, or uncaring, they will take the decision not to continue with an application and to seek employment elsewhere. This reaction applies equally to internal and external job applications.

Chambers distinguishes between what he calls 'distributive justice', which is concerned with the perceived fairness of the outcome itself—for example, receiving or not receiving a job offer—and 'procedural justice', which is concerned with the perceived fairness of the procedures used to reach the outcome. (We considered these forms of fairness/justice in Chapter 5.) This is to do with feeling that the procedures used in assessment and selection have been valid, fair, and managed in a professional manner. He also offers a further form of justice, which he describes as 'interactional justice'. This relates to the interpersonal treatment of applicants as procedures are enacted and the manner in which information is conveyed and managed.

The important point to emerge from this brief consideration of an applicant perspective on recruitment and selection is that managers and HR professionals need to recognize that applicants are human beings who will become emotionally engaged in, and affected by, the way they are treated and what they are required to do. Decision-making is not something that only managers do; applicants are constantly evaluating their experiences and can decide at any point whether to continue with the process, up to, and including, declining the offer of a job. In tight labour markets and with an increasing proportion of knowledge workers in the labour force, traditional patterns of dependency, where managers were 'in control', are being eroded, to the point at which talented employees with high-performance potential are more selective about who they work for and the kind of work they do. The consequences for an organization that fails to understand this and bases its approach to recruitment and selection on twentieth- rather than twenty-first-century thinking and practices will almost certainly be costly and recurring.

Summary

- Recruitment and selection are important to maintain the strength of the human capital of an organization. This area therefore represents one of the main strategic challenges faced by line managers and HR professionals.

- Recruitment and selection involve known direct and indirect costs but the costs of making the wrong decisions about who to appoint—not appointing the 'right' person or appointing the 'wrong'—are unknown then and may never be fully appreciated, but can be significant and long lasting.

- Organizations are faced with different and changing recruitment requirements. As such there is no one 'right' way to recruit people; rather, managers have to develop recruitment strategies that fit the circumstances and combine efficiency with effectiveness.

- Procedural justice is an important element of the whole process where the need to discriminate between people is balanced by legislative compliance, fairness, and a respect for applicants as human beings.

- Despite developments in assessment instruments and high levels of procedural regulation, the final decision to hire or not remains, in many ways, a subjective one. Matching people to jobs and an organization still involves managers exercising professional judgement.

- Keeping the wrong people out of organizations is as important as selecting good people.

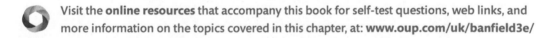 Visit the **online resources** that accompany this book for self-test questions, web links, and more information on the topics covered in this chapter, at: **www.oup.com/uk/banfield3e/**

? REVIEW QUESTIONS

1. Who should be involved in recruiting and selecting staff, and why? What roles will they play and why?

2. What are the arguments for fitting the job/organization to the person rather than fitting the person to the job/organization?

3. What do the concepts 'reliability' and 'validity' mean, and why are these important?

4. Making the right selection decision does not guarantee that the new recruit will stay—but what does?

5. From your own personal experiences of recruitment and selection, what role does the internet play? How do you feel organizations can get the maximum benefits from using internet-based technologies in recruitment?

Interest in values-based recruitment within the NHS generally has been growing for some years, but has been given a boost by a number of high-profile cases involving unacceptable behaviour in the way hospital staff have carried out their duties and responsibilities. The problem is less to do with competency but rather with behaviours in relation to patients and other hospital staff.

Alison Gibson, head of HR at Midshire, has been aware for some time about the work being done in the NHS to try to instil a stronger sense of its values into the way the service is being run. She recognizes that this is an area of concern that will be a mainstream issue for some time to come as part of the current reform agenda. From her perspective, too many complaints are being made by patients against medical staff about rudeness, lack of interest, poor communications, and lack of time to talk to them about their conditions and treatments. She knows staff are under increasing workload pressures but is equally aware that this doesn't excuse some of the things patients are concerned about. She has had discussions with the CEO about this and knows that he is committed to exploring ways to reduce the complaints. In addition, interprofessional tensions within the Trust seem to be increasing and arguments between colleagues have been reported to her. She is well aware that these reported incidents are the tip of the iceberg, but she doesn't know how big a problem it is. People seem to be doing their jobs, but without a clear understanding of the way the Trust wants to develop, particularly its commitment to working collaboratively and in multifunctional teams. It also wants to become much more transparent in the way it operates, particularly with regard to the way medical and other mistakes and errors are viewed. The CEO has made it clear to all staff that year-on-year improvements in efficiency and productivity will have to be met if the Trust is to stay within budget. This means that behaviours contributing to openness and continuous learning and knowledge sharing need to be encouraged.

Alison has been discussing these challenges with her HR team as part of the process of creating a new five-year HR strategy. A key element of this will be the changes she wants to be made in the way hospital staff are recruited and selected. As far as she is concerned, for far too long the same old approach has been taken—job descriptions form the basis of the process which in turn lead to person specifications. But she knows many job descriptions are out of date or inaccurate, person specifications are too generic, failing to discriminate between applicants. There is no explicit reference to individual and Trust values in the selection process. Moreover, the main method of assessing candidates is still by the panel interview which consists only of people from the host department or section.

Alison is determined to address these limitations and deficiencies in the selection process and has charged the head of recruitment and selection, Gavin Wilson, with the responsibility of producing a new selection strategy. She has given him the following remit:

1. Ensure that whatever is proposed does not compromise the ability to maintain high standards of job competence across the Trust.

2. Embed values in all aspects of the recruitment and selection process.

3. Develop a statement of employee values relevant to all levels and functions that will serve as an aid to selection and subsequently appraisal of performance and which reflect what the Trust expects its employees to be and do.

4. Suggest changes to the existing approach to selection that will focus on the assessment of behaviour and highlight those applicants that are likely to express the values contained in the employee value statement. Note that job competency will be established through other information sources such as CVs and application forms, job competency interviews, aptitude tests (where appropriate), and work tests.

5. Establish five key indicators or measures of performance that will allow the Trust to know whether or the extent to which this new emphasis on value-based selection is affecting how people behave in the Trust.

Taking the role of Gavin and his team, work on the five questions with the objective of making a presentation to Alison Gibson and the Trust's CEO. (You can use the exercise as a seminar presentation with your tutor taking Alison's role.)

» FURTHER READING

Barrick, M. R. and Zimmerman, R. D. (2009) 'Hiring for retention and performance', *Human Resource Management*, 48(2), 183–206.

CIPD (2015) *A Head for Hiring: The Behavioural Science of Recruitment and Selection* [Research Report].

Incomes Data Services (2008) *Employer branding, HR studies*.

Parry, E. and Tyson, S. (2008) 'An analysis of the use and success of online recruitment methods in the UK', *Human Resource Management Journal*, 18(3), 257–74.

Patterson, F. et al. (2015) *Recruiting for Values in Healthcare: A Preliminary Review of the Evidence*, Advances in Health Science Education.

||\ REFERENCES

ACAS (2014) http://www.acas.org.uk/index. aspx?articleid=4857

Backhaus, K. and Tikoo, S. (2004) 'Conceptualizing and researching employer branding', *Career Development International*, 9(5).

Barrick, M. R. and Zimmerman, R. D. (2009) 'Hiring for retention and performance', *Human Resource Management*, 48(2), 183–206.

Bozionelos, N. (2005) 'When the inferior candidate is offered the job: The selection interview as a political and power game', *Human Relations*, 58(12), 1605–31.

Broughton, A. et al. (2011) *The Use of Social Media in the Recruitment Process*, Institute for Employment Studies.

Burrows, C. (2004) 'Enriching the talent pool: Injecting new blood from outside the industry', *International Journal of Medical Marketing*, 4(4), 390–2.

Buzea, C. (2007) http://carmen.buzea.ro/ Buzea_c_2007_The_predictive_validity_of_ selection_methods_in_staffing_activities.pdf

Chambers, B. A. (2002) 'Applicant reactions and their consequences: Review, advice, and recommendations for future research', *International Journal of Management Review*, 4, December, 317–33.

CIPD (2007) *Employer Branding: A No-Nonsense Approach*, www.cipd.co.uk

CIPD (2009) *Recruitment, Retention and Turnover Survey*, www.cipd.co.uk

CIPD (2016) 'Recruitment factsheet: An overview'.

Collins, J. (2001) *From Good to Great*, Random House.

Cook, M. (2016) *Personnel Selection*, Wiley Blackwell.

DeLeon, M. (2015) 'What really happens when you hire the wrong candidate', *Entrepreneur*, 9 April, at: https://www.entrepreneur.com/article/244730

Deloitte (2011) 'How Deloitte uses social media to recruit', at: http://linkhumans.com/blog/how-to-use-social-media-to-recruit-deloitte-case-study

Department for Education (2013) 'New pay policies reward best teachers', at: https://www.gov.uk/government/news/new-pay-policies-reward-best-teachers

Dipboye, R. L. et al. (2012) 'The selection interview from the interviewer and applicant perspectives: Can't have one without the other', in R. L. Dipboye et al. (eds.), *Oxford Handbook of Assessment and Selection*, Oxford University Press.

Fitz-enz, J. (2002) *How to Measure Human Resource Management*, McGraw-Hill.

Fitz-enz, J. (2010) *The New HR Analytics*, AMACOM.

Goleman, D. (1995) *Emotional Intelligence*, Bantam.

Goleman, D. (1998) *Working with Emotional Intelligence*, Bantam.

Gratton, L. (2000) 'A real step change', *People Management*, 16 March, 26–30.

Grimshaw, K. G. et al. (2001) 'Organisations and the transformation of the internal labour market', *Work, Employment and Society*, 15(1), 25–54, at: https://www.researchgate.net/profile/Damian_Grimshaw2/publication/224892318_Organisations_and_the_Transformation_of_the_Internal_Labour_Market/links/5746114408ae9ace84243721.pdf

Internet Advertising Bureau (2008) Fact Sheet, at: https://iabuk.net/sites/default/files/research-docs/Online%20adspend%20factsheet%20-%20H1%202008.pdf

Klotz, A. C. et al. (2013) The role of trustworthiness in recruitment and selection: A review and guide for future research', *Journal of Organisational Behaviour*, 34(S1).

Lazear, E. P. (1998) *Personnel Economics for Managers*, Wiley.

Macan, T. (2009) 'The employment interview: A review of current studies and directions for future research', *Human Resource Management Review*, 19, 203–18, at: http://mavweb.mnsu.edu/howard/The%20employment%20interview.pdf

Madia, S. A. (2011) 'Best practices for using social media as a recruitment strategy', *Strategic HR Review*, 10(6), 19–24.

Michaels, E., Handfield-Jones, H., and Axelrod, B. (2001) *The War for Talent*, Harvard Business School Press.

Millmore, M. (2003) 'Just how extensive is the practice of strategic recruitment and selection?', *Irish Journal of Management*, 24(1).

Morgan, G. (1997) *Images of Organization*, 2nd edn, Sage.

NHS Employers (2016) *Reducing Agency Spend*, at: http://www.nhsemployers.org/your-workforce/plan/agency-workers/reducing-agency-spend

O'Leary, B. S. et al. (2002) 'Selecting the best and brightest: Leveraging human capital', *Human Resource Management*, 41(3), 325–40.

Rousseau, D. M. and Barends, E. G. R. (2011) 'Becoming an evidence-based HR practitioner', *Human Resource Management Journal*, 21(3), 221–35.

Ryan, A. M. and Tippins, N. T. (2004) 'Attracting and selecting: What psychological research tells us', *Human Resource Management*, 43(4), 305–18.

Rynes, S. L., Colbert, A., and Brown, K. G. (2002) 'HR professionals' beliefs about effective human resource practices: Correspondence between research and practice', *Human Resource Management*, 41(2), 149–74.

Silim, A. and Crosse, C. (2014) *Report on Women in Engineering: Fixing the Talent Pipeline*, Institute for Public Policy Research, at: http://www.ippr.org/files/publications/pdf/women-in-engineering_Sept2014.pdf?noredirect=1

Sparrow, P. and Otaye, L. (2015) *Employer Branding: From Attraction to a Core HR Strategy*, Centre for Performance-led HR, Lancaster University.

Ueno, A. (2010) 'What are the fundamental features supporting service quality?', *Journal of Services Marketing*, 24(1), 74–86.

UK Government (2015) 'NHS sickness absence rates—September 2015 provisional statistics', at: https://www.gov.uk/government/statistics/nhs-sickness-absence-rates-september-2015-provisional-statistics

University of East Anglia (2016) 'Recruitment and selection guidelines', at: https://www.uea.ac.uk/documents/2506781/2686727/Recruitment+and+Selection+Guidelines.pdf/93374dc4-6ff1-4847-bfe9-e76a961cb61d

Waber, B. et al. (2014) 'Workspaces that move people', *Harvard Business Review* (October).

Walters, R. (2014) 'Using social media in the recruitment process: An insight whitepaper', at: https://www.robertwalters.co.uk/content/dam/robert-walters/country/united-kingdom/files/whitepapers/rw-social-media-whitepaper.pdf

Welch, J. and Welch, S. (2005) *Winning*, HarperCollins.

Wilden, R. et al. (2010) 'Employer branding: Strategic implications for staff recruitment', *Journal of Marketing Management* (March).

Women and Work Commission (2006) *Shaping a Fairer Future*, Department of Trade and Industry, at: http://news.bbc.co.uk/1/shared/bsp/hi/pdfs/27_02_06_wwc_paygap.pdf

Managing Employee Relations

8

Key Terms

Trade union An organization that is independent of an employer and funded by member contributions, the function of which is to represent worker interests in relations between workers and employers.

Collective bargaining The process of negotiation between trade union representatives and employers, or employer representatives, to establish by agreement the terms and conditions of employment of a group of employees.

Collective agreement A written statement defining the arrangements agreed between a union and employer, and the terms that will apply. Such agreements are only legally enforceable if this is expressly stated or if the collective agreement is referred to in individual written terms and conditions of employment.

Psychological contract The obligations that an employer and an employee, or group of employees, perceive to exist between each other as part of the employment relationship, comprising both expectations of each other and promises made to each other.

Employee engagement A workplace approach resulting in the psychological and social conditions that encourage all members of an organization to give their best each day, become committed to their organization's goals and values, and motivated to contribute to organizational success. An engaged employee is one who is fully absorbed by and enthusiastic about their work and so takes positive action to further the organization's interests.

Learning Objectives

As a result of reading this chapter and using the online resources, you should be able to:

- understand the importance of maintaining good relations with employees, through involvement, engagement, and through effective communication and consultation;

- recognize the importance of the psychological contract at work and how to manage this to support organizational objectives;

- evaluate the contemporary role of trade unions and know how to manage effective union relationships through partnership;

- recognize the difference between consultation and collective bargaining, and how to avoid disruption due to collective disputes; and

- apply key theoretical and conceptual contributions to the analysis of individual and collective behaviour.

Introduction

The relationship between an employer and its employees lies at the heart of what makes an organization effective. The employees of an organization have the power to allow an organization to meet and exceed its objectives, or to fail. Highly motivated employees work more productively and, if they feel engaged with their employer, will make a greater contribution towards its overall direction and success. Demotivated employees, on the other hand, can also have an impact on the organization, but in different and more negative ways. This can include individual and less visible expressions of dissatisfaction, such as high absenteeism, poor timekeeping, and low productivity, as well as collective action, such as strikes and working to rule, all of which undermine the organization's ability to ensure its output, financial health, and long-term competitiveness.

While the long-term decline in British manufacturing can, in part, be explained by the emergence of low-cost economies in the Far East, it is also worth remembering that those industries which experienced a rapid and close-to-terminal decline in the 1970s and 1980s—the most well-known of which were motor manufacturing, shipbuilding, and steel production—were industries that were renowned for 'bad' industrial relations, low morale, and high levels of industrial conflict. (Of these, only motor manufacturing has regained something approaching its old prominence.) As a general statement, organizations that are able to establish and maintain good relations with employees and their representatives are those that will not only avoid the weakening effects of an under-producing and uncooperative workforce, but gain the advantages that result from a workforce that is motivated and committed: in other words, an engaged workforce. The expectation is that this workforce will understand that its long-term interests are better served by working in partnership with management, rather than by challenging them in the pursuit of its own short-term interests. Understanding why certain groups of workers continue to adopt a more adversarial approach to their employers is one of the key objectives of this chapter.

It is important to recognize that getting an organization's employment relations 'right' does not have the same significance as having an effective recruitment or training strategy. It is actually of *more* importance, because the state of an organization's individual and collective employment relations has a pervasive influence on how the other aspects of managing people are carried out. It is inconceivable that strategies to drive performance forward, initiatives to increase the level of employee utilization, and attempts to access the world of discretionary effort will be successful if the general state of employment relations is poor and unsatisfactory, and if there is little trust between managers and employees. Effective employee relations (ER) provide a framework conducive to a positive psychological environment within which performance discussions and other employment matters can take place. As a result, employees should be confident about expressing their views in the expectation that these will be taken into account when final decisions are made. But to be able to manage performance or gain employee support for change, an employer must first have a constructive relationship with its employees.

The Origins and Scope of Industrial (or Employment) Relations

What is now called 'employment relations' or 'employee relations' was originally known as 'industrial relations' and this has its origins in the 1960s as a separate academic field of study and as an area of managerial responsibility located within the emerging field of personnel management. As was explained in Chapter 2, the importance of industrial relations in the second half of the last century shaped and influenced the development of initially personnel management and then human resource management (HRM). But this does not mean that interest in the employee–employer relationship is a relatively recent phenomenon. The contractual relationship that is at the heart of employment has been of interest to economists, sociologists, and lawyers since at least the middle of the nineteenth century and, arguably, since even earlier.

This contract provides a set of rights, responsibilities, and obligations that structure the behaviour of both parties, and represents the basis of what constitutes the normative system of regulation and control within the workplace. For many writers on political economy, the perceived and actual inequalities between the individual worker and his or her employer, based on the ownership of the means of production (*capital*), is closely associated with worker resistance to aspects of the Industrial Revolution, particularly in those industries where machinery began to replace labour-intensive production methods, and the rise of craft guilds in the eighteenth century and the trade union movement in the latter part of the nineteenth century. Even today, these differences are seen as being at the heart of what many believe to be the source of conflict between employers and workers (Sorenson, 2006).

After the end of the Second World War, and in the immediate aftermath of reconstruction and read-justment to post-war conditions, trade unions and employers re-established relationships and proceed-ed to build new frameworks for the collective regulation of work and employment although many of those that came into being owed much to pre-war antecedents. The system of Whitely Councils, for example, established after the end of the First World War to provide a comprehensive collective bar-gaining framework for a range of industries, survived well into the second half of the twentieth century, although almost all of those that remained were in the public sector. Pay settlements in the public sector are now often reached through pay review bodies (NHS Pay Review Body, 2016). These are 'independent' bodies that make recommendations to government after hearing evidence from relevant parties. This fact reflects the way in which trade union presence and activity has become concentrated in public sector institutions, with relatively low levels of unionization in the private sector with the exception of transport and communications.

What became a feature of post-Second World War industrial relations was the increase in industrial con-flict, particularly strikes, experienced by companies in heavy engineering, manufacturing, and, increasingly, in parts of the public sector. The so-called 'Winter of Discontent' of 1978–9 was the culmination of trade union activity in pursuit of pay claims that were higher than government pay policy allowed and began in private industry, before spreading to local authorities and other public sector workers.

The incidence and frequency of strike action were not on the same scale as that which was experienced in the 1920s, but, nevertheless, the disruption caused to production, competitiveness, and public service were considered serious problems that needed urgent attention. The so-called 'British disease', repre-sented by a strike-prone and inefficient workforce, became an uncomfortable, but not entirely unjustified, description of what was wrong with industrial relations at that time (Crafts, 2011; Ingram and Metcalfe, 1991).

The twenty-first century represents a very different era of employment relations, almost unrecognizable from the 1970s and early 1980s except in relation to the public sector and parts of the transport sector. The Office of National Statistics (2016) reported that the number of working days lost due to labour disputes (170,000 days) was the second lowest annual total since records began in 1891. At the time of writing, disputes in the railway sector have become significant, and have serious underlying causes. However, the general pattern of disputes in the twenty-first century has not fundamentally altered.

This does not mean that ER and staff engagement is any less important. In 2009, *Engaging for Success*, a report to government on enhancing performance through employee engagement, argued that levels of engagement matter because employee engagement can correlate with performance, and there is evidence that *improving* engagement correlates with *improving* performance. While industrial conflict still exists and its causes are still relevant today, the relationship between employ-ers and employees, many of whom are not trade unionists, has evolved and become much more cooperative and focused on preserving jobs, employment, and opportunities. It could be argued with some justification that engagement and positive relationships are now the norm and that outbreaks of collective industrial conflict are the exception not the rule, although the precise nature of ER varies between industries and over time.

STUDENT ACTIVITY 8.1

Read CIPD (2015) 'Getting under the Skin of Conflict: Tracing the Experiences of Employees'.

- What does it say about the causes of workplace conflict?
- How is conflict conceptualized and what does it express?
- What are the main mechanisms for managing conflict and what determines whether these are successful or not?
- Can conflict be eliminated from the workplace? If not, why not?

To add an extra dimension to the activity, split into two groups. One subgroup represents employer interests and presents arguments based on the premise that strikes and other forms of workplace conflict are unnecessary and harmful to the long-term interests of workers. The second subgroup, representing trade union interests, makes its case that strikes are not only justified but the only way to protect worker interests and terms and conditions of employment. The whole group should then consider the two arguments and reach an appropriate conclusion.

The influence of academics

The 1960s saw the emergence of a group of academics who had a particular interest in trade unions and industrial relations. Among the most influential were John Dunlop (1958), Richard Hyman (1975), Alan Flanders (1970), and Alan Fox (1966). These, and others who shared their concerns about the state of industrial relations, were interested in trying to identify the underlying dynamics and structural forces that were leading workers towards trade unionism and predisposing them towards industrial action. They were particularly concerned with developing theoretical contributions that offered insights into the:

- political and institutional role of trade unions, and the impact that trade union activity had on employment and wages;
- relationship between trade union leaders and members;
- causes of strikes and conflict resolution; and
- role and influence of management and employers in shaping the way in which industrial relations developed.

Dunlop (1958) developed a theory of industrial relations that projected them as a subsystem of society, on a par with the economic and political subsystems, which overlapped and influenced each other. Although the suggestion that industrial relations was equivalent in importance and impact to the two other societal subsystems is much more contentious now than it was in the 1960s, the central components of his theory are still relevant (Kaufman, 2002). They provide important conceptual and explanatory tools that can be used by those who are trying to interpret the way in which the 'system' functions, and can be summarized as:

- what he describes as *actors* in the system. These are the representatives of management, employees and their representatives, and specialist government agencies who have an industrial relations function;
- the *context or environment* within which the actors operate and which determines the material conditions of work and employment;
- the *ideology or belief systems* that each 'actor' possesses and is influenced by, and which help to determine the way in which particular groups relate to other 'actors' within the system; and
- the *system outputs*, which are expressed in terms of rules, that give the system a degree of stability and maintain order, although these should be seen as provisional and conditional rather than as permanent.

The importance of rules and rule-making processes is central to understanding the primary 'function' of the industrial relations system. One way of understanding why rules are important is to consider the limitations inherent in the formal contract of employment. By this, we mean that, while the employer agrees to the rate of pay, fringe benefits, holidays, and other conditions of employment, the commitment of the employee is quite different. He or she agrees to accept a role that is subordinate to that of management, in the sense of accepting managerial authority, and to carry out the duties associated with the job for which he or she has been employed. But there is an important area of indeterminacy in the formal contract of employment, in terms of levels of job performance that will be delivered and sustained, and in the acceptance of specific management orders. As Hyman and Brough (1975) argued, an employee makes a commitment to obey:

> **Yet such a promise is neither unambiguous nor unconditional; and its interpretation is thus a source of potential conflict.**

They quote Gouldner (1954), who asks:

> **Which commands has the worker promised to obey? Are these commands limited to the production of goods and services only? Under the terms of the contract, may an employer legitimately issue a command unnecessary for production? Who decides this anyhow, worker or employer?**

This recognition that there is a degree of indeterminacy in all employment contracts means that one, or both, of the workplace actors, or an external third party, must establish additional rules to ensure that there is the necessary level of normative order, and therefore stability, within workplaces and nationally. If this does not happen, the tendency will be for the lack of normative regulation to lead to higher levels of uncertainty, instability, and conflict than would otherwise have been the case. But not only is the contract of employment limited in what it regulates—it is also asymmetrical in nature. This means that it favours the employer rather than the employee, because it prescribes what the employer has to provide but leaves indeterminate what the employee is required to give in terms of performance-related behaviour. It might be said, therefore, that the objective of any employment relations system is order and stability and the minimization of conflict.

A more recent way of establishing a normative order is through building employee commitment to the enterprise. This may be through an approach to partnership working with trade unions and/or through ensuring employee engagement. The Trades Union Congress (TUC, 2002) describe partnership working as a:

> **grown-up relationship between bosses and workers**

arguing that

> **when bosses and employees work together in partnership, businesses increase productivity and profitability, they have less staff turnover and less sickness absence.**

Historically, the predominant trade union and employer approach to the resolution of industrial conflict was based on negotiating compromise settlements and taking industrial action to put pressure on the other party to settle. The idea of partnership working is based on the premise that there are alternative ways of resolving differences between employers and employees based on working to prevent conflict being generated in the first place rather than trying to resolve it after it has been generated. The problem with this position is that it is based on certain assumptions about the nature and causes of industrial conflict; that these are not deeply rooted and structural but rather are more superficial and manageable, assumptions that are not shared by all parties.

Both partnership working and staff engagement are a means of increasing 'employee voice' where employees/trade unions are seen not as a problem but central to the solution. The *Engaging for Success* report in 2009 authored by David Macleod and Nita Clarke highlights four enablers to building employee engagement:

- a strong *strategic narrative* about the organization;
- *engaging managers* who focus on people;
- *employee voice* ensuring employees are invited to contribute their experience, expertise, and ideas; and
- *integrity* where the values on the wall are those reflected in day-to-day behaviours.

David Guest notes:

> much of the literature on engagement is either silent or muddled about employee voice but that engagement would be strengthened as a concept and an instrument of organizational policy if it took fuller account of voice.
>
> (in Johnstone and Ackers, 2015)

So, the search for order and stability not only goes on through the formal national institutions of the employment relations system but through the development of workplace relationships that facilitate cooperation, involvement, communication, and conflict prevention.

STUDENT ACTIVITY 8.2

Read Partnership Agreement: An Agreement between the Department of Health, NHS Employers, and NHS Trade Unions (Department of Health, 2012). This agreement outlines the principles agreed for working in partnership. After reading it, consider the following questions:

1. How does this resonate with your understanding of partnership working?
2. How is 'employee voice' expressed in the agreement?
3. What are the key elements of any partnership agreement?
4. What kind of problems might be experienced in making such agreements work?

232

Rules in employment relations

Rules in employment relations fall into two main categories, as set out below.

Procedural rules

Procedural rules are those that establish how the actors in the system will respond and behave in given situations. For example, if managers and union representatives fail to reach agreement about annual pay increases, they may have already agreed on ways in which to resolve the impasse and avoid industrial conflict. This may involve third-party intervention, a cooling-off period, or some other mechanism for facilitating agreement. These rules fulfil the important role of maintaining system stability and avoid either party taking arbitrary action.

There is, however, a second category of procedural rules that has a quite different function. In this case, rules are agreed that determine how other kinds of rules and decisions in many aspects of ER will be determined. Again, a simple example will illustrate how these rules work. Consider the important issue of what employees will be paid for the work that they do. Payment can be based on hours worked, production achieved, or performance attained—but who makes this decision? Is this something that management alone is to determine, or should it be decided by the employees themselves or through the intervention of a third party? These are important questions, the answers to which will have an important impact on the economic health of the organization and on the quality of the relationships between managers and employees. Another kind of procedural rules regulate action in the context, for example, of disciple, where disciplinary procedures (sets of rules) are invoked when someone is accused of breaking organizational rules. Such procedural rules are assumed to make the management of discipline fairer, more consistent, and less arbitrary.

These rule-making processes, that is rules about how both procedural and substantive rules are made, are at the heart of any employment relations system and can be expressed in terms of:

- *Unilateral regulation*, under which managers, unions, or employees create rules that regulate a particular part of the employment relationship. For example, on the question of overtime and the rates that are paid, managers might feel that this is something that they alone need to regulate and decide upon.

- On the other hand, trade unionism is based on the belief in, and commitment to, what is called *joint regulation*, more usually known as 'collective bargaining', under which both parties meet and, through the process of negotiation, reach a joint decision on rules, such as those that regulate the allocation and payment of overtime working, pay, and certain employment procedures. Unions have consistently striven to extend the application of joint regulation to as many aspects of the organization as possible, in an attempt to increase the protection that they can provide to their members and to enhance their own influence.

Procedural rules that originate outside of the employing organization or national institutions of the employment relations system can be created through *legal and judicial processes*. The UK Parliament, the European Union, and associated judicial bodies make and interpret laws that regulate work and employment. In fact, it might be argued that the relative importance of each of these rule-making processes has changed significantly over the past fifty years, with the influence of the EU and UK judicial processes increasing, while that of trade union unilateral regulation and joint regulation has been decreasing in both extent and influence. This view is consistent with the evidence of the relative decline in trade unionism and the increasing difficulty that unions experience in maintaining the idea and practice of joint determination through collective bargaining, particularly those that represent workers in the private sector. Think about the Working Time Regulations (WTR) and the National Minimum Wage (NMW) as examples of how complex sets of rules over working time and payment are made by external parties rather than by unilateral or joint regulation.

Substantive rules

These are the rules that are generated by rule-making processes, such as joint determination and unilateral decision-making. Once again considering pay as an example, these represent the actual rules that say what a person's basic pay will be and what any additional payments for extra work done might be. As explained above, the 'working week'—an area of particular importance for both employees and employers—is now, for many workers, regulated by the WTR following an EU directive and the substantive rules that have been established take precedence over any that were agreed by collective bargaining or imposed by employers. Substantive rules regulate how much people get paid, their hours of work, holiday entitlement, and so on. Many of these are contained in the formal contract of employment but, as explained earlier, this only regulates certain aspects of an employee's behaviour and performance at work. In a constantly changing environment, new conditions and situations arise that need to be regulated and, through the processes for creating new rules or amending old ones, the body of substantive rules is constantly being amended. Substantive rules, whether incorporated in the contract of employment or agreed as part of the process of maintaining order and stability at the informal level, are the outcome of procedural regulation, which in the workplace will be a mixture of managerial unilateral regulation, formal joint regulation, or informal regulation, which can be joint or unilateral worker regulation.

> **HRM INSIGHT 8.1 The rail disputes (2016–17)**
>
> In 2016 two disputes affecting the London Underground and Southern Railways arose. Once again, there were questions about the state of employment relations and the power of trade unions, and both disputes illustrate the role of rules within the ER system. The first dispute involving the RMT union and London Transport is about the decision of London Transport to eliminate some 800 ticket office staff and to close a number of underground ticket offices. Mick Cash, leader of the RMT union, is reported to have said:
>
> It has now also been shown that at management level there is agreement with the union that the cuts have been a disastrous mistake and that the staff need to be put back on the stations
> (RMT, 2017)
>
> The union representing the Underground office staff, TSSA, said:
>
> TSSA members on London Underground are set to take strike at the weekend after another round of talks with London Underground (LU) and Advice & Conciliation Advisory Service (ACAS) have again failed to make any progress to resolve our dispute about severe ongoing and increasing dangerous understaffing

233

of the Tube following the 800 job cuts made by London's Tory Mayor, Boris Johnson, shortly before he left office in May last year.

Management have admitted that too many jobs have been cut too quickly and have agreed to hire more staff to man stations, but the unions want a bigger recruitment drive and are continuing to call strikes and apply an overtime ban.

(TSSA, 2017)

The question is why are the two unions taking industrial action? Is it because of the job cuts, which represent a change in substantive rules on employment levels, or is it because of safety concerns linked to the office closures? Changes in rules governing numbers employed and changes in working conditions are common causes of industrial action.

In the case of Southern Railways and the RMT and ASLEF unions, the reason for the ongoing dispute is different. No job losses are involved and neither guards nor drivers will lose money or job security; this dispute is about rules governing 'who does what'. The company has proposed that drivers take over responsibility for closing train doors, using new technology that has been approved by the safety regulator. But the unions are opposing moving this responsibility from guards to drivers on safety grounds.

The point of this HRM Insight is that in ER making new rules creates its own set of challenges but so does changing existing rules where the proposed changes affect trade union representation and interests. We might say that industries where trade unions enjoy recognition and negotiating rights are those where change driven by management and linked to technological or financial considerations is likely to be resisted by the unions because of the real or perceived threat that the change poses to the union itself and/or its members. The desire and ability to resist change, however, rests largely on the power of the unions and their particular ideology. Both are key variables in any ER system, and its distribution between employers/managers and trade unions/workers can help to explain the behaviour of the main actors in the system.

Questions

1. What rules had changed and why did the unions oppose them?
2. Are both disputes about rail safety or preserving existing terms and conditions of work?
3. Why are the unions able to resist the changes management wanted to introduce?
4. What options does management have in both disputes to introduce the changes they believe are necessary and justified?

One of the key findings of the 2011 study by van Wanrooy et al. (2013) focused on the changes in the pattern of workplace regulation since the 2004 equivalent study. They found that the most prevalent arrangement through which employees are represented is the trade union. After two decades of substantial decline, union membership and representation (the two are not necessarily the same) was relatively stable among all but the smallest private sector workplaces over the period between 1998 and 2004. Non-union representation remained relatively uncommon; this presumably means staff associations were still rare. Since the 2004 study, the prevalence of workplace union representation has continued to fall in small private sector workplaces, which is probably accounted for by the growth in SMEs, but has proved relatively robust in other parts of the economy.

One of the particularly interesting findings relates to the way managers view trade unions. The survey found that:

● The percentage of workplace managers who were not in favour of union membership was 18 per cent, not significantly different from 17 per cent in 2004.

● In 2011, 24 per cent agreed that unions help to find ways to improve workplace performance (no significant change from 21 per cent in 2004), but despite the relatively low proportion of managers who see unions playing a positive and cooperative role in working to improve organizational performance, the traditional view of unions as always opposing change, despite recent evidence to the contrary, is clearly an inappropriate generalization for a significant number of organizations.

- The percentage who agreed that they would rather consult directly with employees than with unions rose from 77 per cent to 80 per cent. This is particularly significant because it adds further weight to the argument that ER, at least in the private sector, continues to develop along individualist rather than collectivist lines.

In the section of the report covering collective bargaining or joint regulation of terms and conditions of employment (pp. 22–3), the survey found that union influence had continued to decline since 2004, and that in the private sector, although formal rights to negotiate over pay changed little, the scope of collective bargaining in the unionized sector declined dramatically. It is clear from the survey findings that union influence over pay has been in decline for at least three decades, a trend that can in part be accounted for by the loss of trade union bargaining power. The survey found that:

- By 2011 only 7 per cent of private sector workplaces bargained with unions over pay for any of their employees and just under one-sixth of private sector employees (16 per cent) had their pay set by collective bargaining. These figures have remained fairly stable since 2004.

- Public sector pay bargaining remained robust even though the coverage of collective bargaining significantly fell.

- 36 per cent of public sector managers and 67 per cent of private sector managers said that they did not negotiate on any of the seven key areas of employment, from pay, hours, training, grievance, and discipline, etc.; these figures were largely unchanged from 2004.

Noting that these figures refer only to those workplaces that had union representation, it is clear that the majority of UK employees are in establishments that do not recognize them or where representation is limited in scope.

What can be inferred from the study is that collective bargaining as a procedural method of creating substantive rules is declining in coverage and probably scope, being replaced in the private sector by unilateral management regulation.

235

KEY CONCEPT Managerial prerogative

The concept of managerial prerogative is central to understanding the sources of tension within employment relations and the ongoing struggle between managers and trade unions, in particular over the 'rights' of each party. 'Prerogative' means the right to make decisions and to establish rules that are essential in allowing the production system to operate efficiently and effectively. Historically, managers have tended to guard their prerogative and have tried to prevent trade unions from eroding it. If trade union power has increased as a result of economic or political change, and has strengthened their representative and negotiating role, managerial rights have been eroded and pushed back; if trade union power has been weakened by the movement of capital and restrictive legislation, managers have been able to reassert their rights 'to manage' and to restrict trade union involvement in the decision-making process. In extreme cases, this has involved the removal of recognition and the restriction or elimination of bargaining rights. This is an aspect of employment relations that is never completely resolved, but is rather in a state of dynamic tension (Ronnmar, 2006).

Rules and legitimacy

There is one further category of rules that needs to be explained, and this concerns the form that the rules take and their legitimacy. The idea that people at work operate within two organizational environments has long been recognized (Watson, 2012), and this distinction represents one of the main themes of this book, where behaviour and relationships at work are regulated by the 'formal organization' but also influenced through informal processes and dynamics. Gouldner (1954) shows how the informal regulation of work and working practices can often modify and in certain circumstances undermine formal regulation.

At one level, the environment represented by the formal organization consists of the formally approved, usually by management, procedural and substantive rules. These rules are legitimized, through being known and approved by management, and regulate how people are supposed to behave at work.

The concept of the 'informal organization', however, suggests that this informal world, represented by the day-to-day interaction between managers and employees, can develop its own social and work-related norms (rules). These are often unknown to senior managers and may be in conflict with the formal rules that have emerged from 'more legitimate' processes. Such rules may lack the legitimacy of formally derived rules, but can nevertheless exert a powerful influence on the behaviour of the managers and employees affected by them. The reason why it is important to understand the importance of informal rules is that, while much of our behaviour is regulated and controlled in ways known to management, other aspects are not, for example:

- levels of discretionary effort;
- output and performance levels, up to a point;
- the level of cooperation offered to management;
- the degree of employee flexibility.

In situations in which there is a lack of trust between employees and managers, and in which employees exercise some degree of control over the production/work process, it is likely that employees, either as individuals or groups, will limit their performance, creating a body of informal and, as far as management is concerned, often unknown rules that regulate what employees are prepared and not prepared to do. The challenge that contemporary managers face is not simply to discover and change these rules, but to understand the reasons why they exist. The reality for many employees, however, is that while some are able to continue to engage in the informal regulation of work the majority cannot and do not in any meaningful way.

 Signpost to Chapter 5: Ethics and Leadership in HRM, for information on the criteria used to determine fairness and legitimacy.

 STUDENT ACTIVITY 8.3

Alvin Gouldner's (1954) classic study of an unofficial strike and its causes remains one of the outstanding contributions to our understanding of the interaction between the formal and informal systems of work. The task is to read the first chapter of the book in order to answer the following questions:

1. What is meant by the term 'indulgency patterns'?

2. Why did the original managers appear to allow the workers to break the formal rules?

3. Why was legitimacy an important issue in the conflict that led to the strike?

4. What role did management play in events leading up to the strike?

The whole book is available at https://libcom.org/files/gouldner-alvin--wildcat-strike-a-study-in-worker-management-relationships.pdf

---

RESEARCH INSIGHT 8.1

To extend your learning, you may wish to read:

Breslin, D. and Wood, G. (2016) 'Rule breaking in social care: Hierarchy, contentiousness and informal rules', *Work, Employment and Society*, 30(5).

The article illustrates, in the context of a particular organizational setting, how informal rules emerge and come into conflict with formal regulation. Read the article and think carefully about the reasons why informal rules were created, their purpose, and how management reacted to them.

Figure 8.1 represents a way of understanding the essential elements of an industrial relations system and how, as these change over time, the system produces new institutions, different patterns of rule-making, and new ways of preventing/resolving conflict. The important point to note is that the system must be understood as dynamic, rather than static, and is influenced by forces that are often outside the control of the main participants and interest groups. A particularly good example of this inability to control the system can be seen in the way in which the effects of internationalization and globalization have changed the forces of competition in manufacturing and service industries. This has resulted in growth in the knowledge economy and the numbers of knowledge workers, a decline in manufacturing jobs, and a corresponding fall in private sector union density. Because the public sector environment has so far remained relatively immune from the employment effects of the globalization of trade and competition, trade union membership and influence in this sector have been preserved. As the private sector increases its involvement in the provision of public sector services, however, and as old labour supply monopolies come under increasing pressure, it is inevitable that the form of regulation, union membership patterns, and the influence of trade unions will change in the public sector too.

Figure 8.1 is also useful in that it represents a model that can be applied both to national 'systems' and to those that exist within each organization. It can be used to explain why:

- the frequency and pattern of industrial conflict changes and differs between sectors and industries;
- new methods of reaching agreement on work and employment have been created;
- trade unions have a history of mergers and reorganization, and of developing new services for their members;
- more emphasis is now placed on individual, rather than collective, employment relations, as employers and managers use different and more effective strategies to gain acceptance and commitment from their employees;
- governments periodically intervene in the system in an attempt to 'correct' any imbalances of power and to limit the ability of the main parties to damage the social or economic fabric of society.

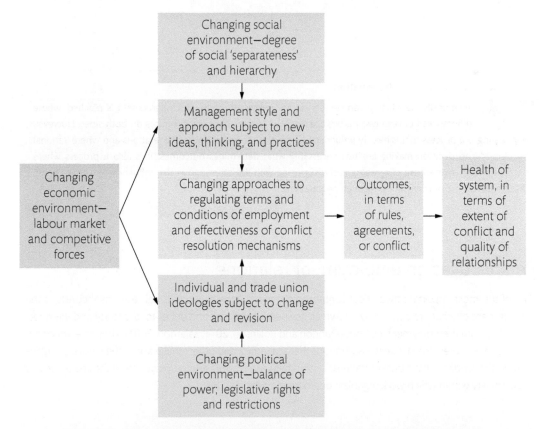

Figure 8.1 A diagrammatical representation of an employment relations system

HRM INSIGHT 8.2 The junior doctors' dispute (2015–16)

The 2015–16 junior doctors' strike in the NHS is an example of an industrial dispute that involves all the main actors, and illustrates the complexity of different interests and decision-making that can be found in major industrial disputes. The junior (and trainee) doctors in the NHS have a centrally negotiated contract of employment. The contract, negotiated in 2000, was in large part negotiated to take account of the Working Time Directive and the related UK law, i.e. the WTR (1998). It had largely done its job and significantly reduced the contractual hours trainee doctors worked. All parties, the government, the employers, and the trade unions (the British Medical Association (BMA)), accepted the contract was no longer fit for purpose. Years of renegotiating commenced without agreement, and in 2015 the government decided to introduce/impose the new contract. The BMA balloted members for industrial action and received overwhelming support. Days of action followed along with further attempts to reach agreement. A number of chief executives of NHS organizations signed a letter of support saying they believed the new contract was fair, only to withdraw their support in the way this was interpreted by the secretary of state for health to Parliament. It seemed to many that the industrial dispute was in fact a political dispute dressed up as a trade dispute. Further negotiations took place alongside further days of action. Agreement on a new contract was reached with the BMA in May 2016, subject to a ballot from junior doctors. They voted against accepting the new contract. The junior doctors' leader resigned. Government and trade unions had negotiated an agreement that was not supported by all NHS trust employers who have increasingly distanced themselves from the dispute, not supported by rank-and-file junior doctors, and embarrassed the BMA who supported the revised contract. Then, because of the ballot, the BMA had to sanction and approve further strike action. The question is: what is the strike really about and why is it proving so difficult to reach agreement?

Questions

1. How did the BMA seek to legitimize industrial action?

2. Was there any sense of a political dimension being present in the dispute? If so, what form did it take?

3. Was the dispute about patient safety or payment for working 'unsocial hours'?

KEY CONCEPT Negotiation

Technically, negotiating can be seen as the process through which agreement is reached, where differences between two parties are resolved as a result of compromises on both sides. However, negotiating is a process that is heavily influenced by political pressures and considerations and where 'rational behaviour' and decision-making are not necessarily what determines outcomes. It is also a process where perceptions of costs—those of agreeing and disagreeing with the other party—also influence outcomes. Some disagreements are never resolved through negotiations.

Perspectives on employment relations

One of the most important theoretical contributions made by the early industrial relations theorists, is the development of what are commonly known as perspectives on, or approaches to, the study and interpretation of industrial/employment relations (Dundon and Rollinson, 2011; Salamon, 2001). These are important because they express the different assumptions that academics and others make about the nature of organizations, the fundamental nature of the relationship between workers and employers, and the characteristics of the society within which work organizations exist and function.

The three perspectives that are most frequently referred to are:

- the unitary perspective, which sees organizations and societies working together towards a common objective, with a general acceptance of managerial authority and shared values and interests;
- *pluralism*—a perspective which recognizes the legitimate existence of different groups which pursue different objectives within a general framework of cooperation and ideological agreement, but where differences in priorities and interests can result in outbreaks of conflict, but conflict based on material differences or interests rather than on opposing ideologies; and
- the *radical*, or Marxist, perspective which suggests that class wealth and power creates a hierarchy in which workers will always be subordinate to owners and their agents and dependent upon these for employment. This perspective sees workers as being exploited by the property-owning classes and made subject to unacceptable working conditions. Trade unions represent the political and economic interests of workers and conflict is seen as endemic in a system where irreconcilable differences are structural not superficial. Workers within this system necessarily have to accommodate themselves to it but at the same time seek to change it.

The point about these three perspectives is that they represent different lenses through which employment relations can be seen and interpreted, but the idea that each can have a set of advantages and disadvantages is unhelpful and misleading. Rather we need to try to establish which perspective accords to 'reality' or whether all three are essentially ideological in nature. The difficulty for students is in distinguishing whether these perspectives are presented as descriptions of what *is*, or in a normative sense as prescriptions of what should *be*. The veracity of these perspectives can never be proven in any definitive sense, although the behaviour of employers, trade unions, and workers indicates particular ideological preferences and positions, but these can change as circumstances change. Two examples are worth noting here. First, the rejection by Rupert Murdoch of union recognition and continued collective bargaining with newspaper unions in 1986 represented the end of the dominant pluralistic industrial relations system in that industry to be replaced by one that was based on managerial control and an employer determined framework of terms and conditions of employment. The reasons behind the Wapping dispute are complex and still controversial and how the dispute was and still is presented depends on which version is read, but essentially the ability of unions to challenge management and promote their own and their members' interests was severely restricted.

The second example relates to motor manufacturing. In the 1970s and 1980s the industry was associated with frequent industrial action much of it informal in nature and a high level of union militancy. As international competition increased the UK car industry began to decline; factories closed and fewer cars were produced. There was a genuine existential threat hanging over the industry. The old system of joint regulation, union influence, managerial failures, and poor productivity came to be seen as incompatible with a modern and competitive industry. As more of the UK's car manufacturing became foreign owned and managed new ways of working were introduced, new models designed, and employment relations became transformed. Unions began to see that the future lay with working *with* management not opposing them and that change had to be embraced rather than opposed; a new era emerged characterized by a different form of pluralism, where managers and employee representatives, recognizing shared and common interests, worked together to transform the industry (Lambert, 2011).

Many of the criticisms levelled against each perspective are based on a questioning of the assumptions that underpin them, and while it is important to assess the veracity of these assumptions, because many are based on a particular and different economic and political ideology, it means that belief and interpretation rather than 'fact' becomes the reference point for establishing the validity of the perspectives. Put simply, these perspectives reflect what people believe as well as what 'exists'.

See Online Resources Extension Material 8.1 for further insights into employment relations perspectives.

RESEARCH INSIGHT 8.2

To take your learning further, you may wish to read:

Gall, G. (2012) 'Richard Hyman: An assessment of his Industrial Relations: A Marxist introduction', *Capital & Class*, 36(1), 135–49.

As you read this reappraisal of Hyman's theoretical contribution to our understanding of industrial relations, consider whether Hyman's analysis is valid and whether the Marxist perspective has anything of value to say to managers and those who work in employment relations today.

What Is a Trade Union?

A 'trade union' is a body that both collectively and individually represents the interests of its members, predominantly in the context of employment, but increasingly in relation to the provision of a wider range of personal services. The union is therefore concerned with the relations between workers and their employer. Many, but far fewer than in the second half of the twentieth century, organizations formally recognize one, or more, trade unions for representation or negotiation purposes. Equally many, predominantly in the private sector, do not. The form of recognition adopted might be restricted to recognition of a particular union to represent individual employees, or groups of employees, in procedures such as dismissal and grievance procedures, but will often extend to the recognition of unions for collective negotiation over issues such as terms and conditions, including pay. It should be noted that formal recognition comes about when an employer is willing to negotiate, rather than simply to recognize or consult with, a trade union.

Trade unions are a worldwide phenomenon and are associated with industrialization, the fracturing of old social relations and dependencies, and the experience on the part of labour of greater economic uncertainty and insecurity. Their form, practices, and ideologies differ between countries. For example, Japanese unions are based largely on individual companies, rather than on national associations, and are known for their commitment to a close working relationship with management. Their fundamental purpose is the same as that of British trade unions, that is, to offer their members protection and defence from the arbitrary action of management and from the uncertainties of the economic system within which they are employed. What is different is the way in which each nation's trade unions try to deliver these outcomes and how successful they are.

Trade unions, in the absence of legal prohibition, thrive in situations in which:

- employees have limited, or no, protection from state or other judicial authorities;
- management show little concern for the interests or well-being of their employees;
- individual workers are relatively powerless to challenge management and are unable to restrict their power; and
- workers' experience of employment leaves them with a strong sense of grievance towards management, based on a feeling that they are being exploited and treated unfairly.

Of course, the corollary of this is that workers may experience none of the above and, as a consequence, may feel disinclined to join a trade union or to participate in any trade union activity.

Member commitment to the union can therefore be strong or weak, depending on the perceived need for unions and the degree to which members share the ideology of the union leadership. Those who subscribe to a radical and Marxist-informed ideology are likely to have a much more adversarial relationship with employers and managers than will the representatives of a union that adopts a neo-pluralist perspective. It might be argued, therefore, that the contemporary existence of trade unions, and the relationship they have with employers and managers, is as much a function of the attitude and behaviour of employers and managers as it is of any independent motivation that affects the predisposition of workers to join, or to remain outside of, trade union representation.

The most well-known definition of a trade union was provided by the Webbs, who said it was:

> **a continuous association of wage earners for the purpose of maintaining or improving the conditions of their working lives.**
> **(Webb and Webb, 1920)**

A more contemporary definition can be found in the Trade Union and Labour Relations (Consolidation) Act 1992 (the 1992 Act), which defined a trade union as:

> **an organisation ... consisting wholly or mainly of workers of one or more descriptions whose principal purpose includes the regulation of relations between workers of that description and employers or employers' associations.**

Both definitions are similar and emphasize the union's regulatory and rule-making function, although the purpose of this activity, beyond reference to maintaining or improving the conditions of the working lives of members, is not made particularly clear.

Dunlop (in Kaufman, 2002), on the other hand, offers a much more helpful definition of what trade unions 'are for' and what this involves them in doing. He argues that, while people join unions for many different reasons, unions are fundamentally concerned with the following.

- **Industrial jurisprudence** This means that unions are involved in grievance and arbitration procedures, rules governing promotion, transfers, discipline, and dismissals, etc. Being able to participate in the regulation of such critically important policies and decisions provides a degree of protection and security from arbitrary action on the part of managers, but also helps to establish a more legitimate normative order. Dunlop calls this the 'human rights aspect of the workplace'.

- **The economic regulation of employment** This is concerned with what and how people are paid, the benefits they enjoy, their hours of work, and the terms of the wage–work bargain. This aspect of trade union activity is much more a reflection of the resource status of employees, the economic value they generate through using their physical and intellectual capital, and what they can expect in return from managers as rewards for their wealth-creating contributions.

Union recognition

There is no obligation for employers to negotiate with a union. If no voluntary recognition agreement is in place, however, a union can apply for recognition to the Central Arbitration Committee (CAC) if it can show that it has at least 10 per cent membership among the group it wishes to represent, and if it can secure a vote in favour of recognition from at least 40 per cent of the workers in that group. While recognition is usually expressed in some form of written agreement, it may be implied by the common practices undertaken by the organization. The CAC received thirty-eight applications for trade unions' recognition in the year ending March 2015 (Central Arbitration Committee, 2016).

It should be noted that public and political opinions about unions, and the extent of their rights and immunities, has swung in different directions throughout recent history, depending on the government in power at the time. As a generalization, however, it might be argued that, since the curbing of trade union power during the years of the Thatcher government in the 1980s, subsequent legislative changes have concentrated on protecting the rights of individual workers and union members rather than on restoring the collective rights and power of trade unions.

HRM INSIGHT 8.3 ABC Pharmaceuticals

ABC Pharmaceuticals is a global business with a manufacturing plant in the Republic of Ireland that is responsible for the production of the active ingredients used in a wide range of pharmaceutical products. The site employs over 400 skilled employees and has not had any union representation since the facility was built in the late 1970s. While the company does have union representation at some of its other manufacturing sites in Europe, its vision of the Irish site was that it would stay non-unionized. The decision by senior management not to recognize any union for either negotiation or representational purposes was based on the company's philosophy that its employees' best interests would be served through the creation of a single-status working environment. This would provide an excellent reward-and-recognition package and facilitate communication with employees at all levels.

From an operational perspective, it was also important to create a high level of flexibility in working practices, so that the plant could adapt and respond quickly to the continuing changes in product development, manufacturing processes, and market demand, all of which are features of the pharmaceutical industry.

To allow for employee representation, the company created the specific role of 'employee representative'. This role provides both individuals and groups of employees who have grievances or other difficulties with a route, involving defined procedure, by which they can raise issues and express their concerns to management. Management will then consult with the representative in solving the problem and in delivering a solution in the way that best meets the employees' and the business' needs.

There is a strong emphasis on communications at the site and it is a multilevel activity, involving crew/team meetings, individual discussions, general employee meetings, a newsletter (both internal and external), and the use of email/intranet.

Because of the nature of continuous change, any changes that are mooted are discussed within teams that are both directly and indirectly affected, and within specialized forums, such as safety committees. For the majority of employees, this system works very well and representatives play an important part in dealing with a wide range of concerns and issues, very few of which, to date, have required outside intervention of any sort.

There is a small minority of employees, however, who feel that they would like the right to join a trade union and have its presence formally recognized. The effectiveness of the employee representative role and management's engagement with employees has not, however, resulted in any sense of dissatisfaction among the majority of employees about the way in which grievances and concerns have been dealt with.

Questions

1. Is there a case to be made that the interests of employees would be better served by union recognition and gaining negotiating rights?

2. Would recognizing trade unions result in an increase in differences and disagreements between managers and employees? If so, why, and what would they be likely to involve?

3. To what extent are the success of the plant and the stability of employment and wages a function of its non-unionized status?

4. If you were a national trade union official trying to achieve union recognition in the plant, what arguments would you present to management and employees to try to persuade them to accept this objective?

STUDENT ACTIVITY 8.4

This activity could be the basis of a seminar presentation as it involves research and analysis.

1. Nationally, what are the current patterns of trade unionism and how have density levels changed from those of twenty-five years ago?

2. What explanations can be offered for changes in unionization and density levels?

3. What is the union situation in the private sector compared to the public sector?

4. Why do unions have such a limited presence and influence in the private sector?

5. Thinking about the recent junior doctors' dispute again, why is the BMA so successful in representing and protecting the employment interests of its members?

Rights, obligations, and immunities of trade unions, members, and representatives

Within the law, employees have individual rights, such as the right against discrimination on the grounds of being a union member. The trade union also has certain rights, obligations, and immunities from certain kinds of legal action, such as not being sued by employers in certain circumstances where the union is representing its employees. These rights, obligations, and immunities are summarized in Table 8.1.

The contemporary role of trade unions

Like many organizations, trade unions have had to adjust to a rapid change in the arena of ER over the last thirty years. As earlier noted, unions were originally formed to provide a collective voice to assert and defend employee rights; today's trade unions have been forced to look more critically at the role they play in the workplace and in wider society as they are confronted by greater government regulation of employment and an increasingly individualist workforce. In many instances, trade unions have struggled to come to terms with their changing environment and loss of influence, particularly with governments. The traditional and more confrontational approach, associated with the radical perspective, is unattractive to many current and potential members, in today's buoyant and flexible labour market which offers alternative job opportunities and the chance to become self-employed; many have become less dependent on the unions and/or have been alienated by their ideologies.

If a collective agreement on pay and conditions is in place, union members and non-union members alike benefit from the pay deals negotiated. With the rise in 'no win, no fee' offers of legal assistance from solicitors, the legal service offered by unions is less of a concern and many employees may choose not to pay a union subscription even if collective agreements are in place. Unions have, therefore, had to find alternative ways to attract members and have also been faced with the need to control costs, lose jobs, and reduce the burden of administrative expenses in much the same way as have many other organizations. Union mergers are one way that unions can maintain their independence and to be seen to be more relevant to the world they must adapt to survive. In many ways, they have had to become more sensitive and aware of what their members or prospective members actually want, and become more 'business-like' in how they operate, without losing sight of their basic *raison d'etre*.

Unions do, however, continue to play an important and influential role in many organizations and it is important that, if such a relationship exists, employers are careful to manage it in a constructive manner. Managed well, the relationship can promote useful dialogue, and can contribute towards effective decision-making and a positive working climate. If the relationship is managed poorly, then the results can be, at best,

Table 8.1 Individual rights and trade union immunities

Employee rights	Trade union rights	Trade union immunities
• Not to be discriminated against on the grounds of belonging or not belonging to a trade union. • Not to be dismissed during the first 12 weeks of industrial action. • Not to be selectively dismissed for participating in industrial action.	• The right to be consulted about redundancies and transfers. • Rights to certain types of information to facilitate meaningful consultation and collective bargaining. • Representatives' rights to paid time off for duties and training. • Right to appoint safety representatives.	• Immunity from being sued for compensation for economic loss suffered as a result of industrial action, provided that certain balloting and communication rules have been followed. • Immunity is not extended to secondary action. • Immunity is lost unless unofficial action is repudiated within 24 hours.

disruptive; at worst, if there is feeling of mistrust, there can be constant friction and outbreaks of conflict and the consequences to both interest groups can be damaging.

The Department for Business, Innovation and Skills reported in 2015 that approximately 6.4 million employees in the UK were trade union members in 2014. Trade union membership reached a peak in 1979, and declined sharply through the 1980s and early 1990s before stabilizing. However, despite this broad stability, the proportion of UK employees who are in a trade union declined because union membership levels did not keep pace with the increase in the total number of employees—the working population increased faster than the growth in union membership. The report also notes that female employees are more likely to be trade union members. The proportion of female employees who were in a trade union was around 28 per cent in 2014 compared to 22 per cent for male employees.

The question of union militancy is an interesting one to raise in the context of changes in employment, demographics, migration, and the feminization of important professions, and the trend towards moderation in trade union attitudes to relations with employers (Dobbins and Dundon, 2012). Historically, militancy which we define as the propensity to take industrial action was linked to the traditional heavy industries of coal, steel, engineering as well as motor manufacturing and transport. Of these, as we noted earlier, only transport has retained significant levels of unionization and representational rights as well as retaining an ideology more adversarial in nature than found in other sectors, but the key to understanding the presence of militancy is linked not only to the union's ideological position but also to its access to power. In the context of unionization in the UK power has been based on two quite unrelated sources:

1. On the protection that the law offers unions in terms of immunity from civil claims for damages from employers and the legal rights to engage in certain kinds of industrial practices such as taking unofficial strike action and secondary action in support of another union. These protections have evolved and changed over time. The current political environment is one where union protection and rights/immunities are more likely to contract than increase.

2. The ability to control the supply of labour and maintain a high level of employer dependency on the workforce. Historically, where union action can inflict high levels of costs on employers, while at the same time experiencing low levels of costs for the unions/members achieved through gaining a monopoly over the supply of labour, then unions have been able to gain concessions from employers.

So, for example, the print unions in the 1970s and 1980s were among the most powerful of that era precisely because the costs to employers of strike action was high and because the unions were able to enforce a closed shop agreement where only union members could work on particular jobs. Today, the unions with the most power and an inclination to use it to protect or advance the interests of their members are associated with transport—railways in particular—and as we have seen hospital doctors. Although public sector unions are associated with strike action, despite being able to influence the supply of labour (for example teachers and doctors need to be qualified and registered), the key question is whether they can inflict sufficient damage/costs on their employers to force concessions from them. Understanding why some strikes are successful while others are not requires us not only to consider the power and inclinations of unions to take industrial action but also the ability and determination of employers to accept the costs of that action.

This relationships between the respective costs associated with industrial action can be represented by the following two hypotheses.

1. When the costs of disagreeing with unions are higher than the costs of agreeing then employers acting rationally should decide to accede to union demands.

2. When the costs of agreeing with union demands are higher than the costs of continuing to disagree, employers acting rationally should continue to disagree and reject union demands.

The same hypotheses could be applied to the union position during a strike or other expressions of industrial conflict. The problem with this 'logical' approach to decision-making is that it is very difficult to quantify the different kinds of costs incurred by both parties, which change over the course of the conflict period. Second, the decision makers may not be able to act rationally as personal feelings and emotions are increasingly likely to influence different positions and negotiating stances the longer the dispute is unresolved.

But basing employment relationships on a win–lose outcome, where one party's gains are at the expense of the other's losses, and where industrial disputes are often resolved by reference to the costs being incurred compared to the gains that might be made, has obvious limitations—winners can still be losers! Working in a more cooperative way where outcomes of the relationship are more win–win than win–lose, although this does not mean the wins are equal on both sides, has clearly become a more attractive option to many private sector unions, but also one that also offers benefits to those in the public sector. This approach is what is meant by partnership working, one that is being actively pursued in the NHS (Royles, 2015).

Collective bargaining

An employer can recognize unions at a number of levels. We will see in Chapter 9 that all employees can be accompanied by a union representative of their choice in formal disciplinary meetings; this right may be expressed in the form of a recognition agreement with a particular union.

 Signpost to Chapter 9: Managing Misconduct, for further information on disciplinary and grievance meetings.

Employers can also recognize a union as the party with which they will consult on issues affecting the organization, and about specific areas of concern such as redundancies, transfer of legal ownership, and changes to pension provisions.

Some employers also recognize one or more unions for the purposes of representing the interests of members in collective bargaining arrangements. The distinction between consultation and bargaining is important and, from a managerial viewpoint, should not be confused. Trade unions will always tend to prefer to bargain, rather than be consulted, because 'bargaining' implies that any important decision has yet to be made, and is subject to trade union influence and, where appropriate, pressure and sanctions. Consultation, on the other hand, implies that management retains the final right to make the decision, but wishes to keep representatives informed of its intentions and is prepared to listen to what they have to say. Traditionally, representative consultation has been in the form of joint consultative committees (JCCs) or works councils as they are sometimes known, and can involve non-unionized employees (staff committees) or union members where the union may or may not be recognized by the employer for the purpose of collective bargaining. The committees are made up of managers and employee representatives who come together on a regular basis to discuss issues of mutual concern. The requirement that employers engage in individual consultation with employees is a legal requirement when the issue involves redundancies. According to ACAS (2014) consultation can be understood as:

> the process by which management and employees or their representatives jointly examine and discuss issues of mutual concern. It involves seeking acceptable solutions to problems through a genuine exchange of views and information. Consultation does not remove the right of managers to manage—they must still make the final decision—but it does impose an obligation that the views of employees will be sought and considered before decisions are taken. Indeed, in certain circumstances consultation with independent recognized trade unions is a legal requirement.

It is worth noting that a preference for consultation reflects a unitarist approach to ER while collective bargaining a more pluralistic one.

To engage with an employer in collective bargaining, a union must ask the employer in writing if they will agree to recognize them voluntarily. The written request must:

- give the name of the union;
- identify which employees will be represented by the union when it's recognized, sometimes known as the bargaining unit; and
- state that the union is making the request under Schedule A1 of the 1992 Act.

The employer has ten days to respond to the request and can choose to:

- agree to recognize the union voluntarily and begin collective bargaining;
- reject the request—the union may then apply for statutory recognition; or
- refuse the initial request but agree to negotiate.

When a union is recognized for bargaining purposes, it has certain rights (see Table 8.1). The information that should be disclosed is covered by the 1992 Act. This includes information about the company's business, the categories of workers covered by the recognition agreement, and broader categories of information, such as information which, were it not disclosed, would impede the union's ability to negotiate, and which it is good industrial relations practice to disclose. There are also exclusions if it might, for example, be damaging to the company to disclose the information. A union can make complaints for failure to disclose information to the CAC (see www.cac.gov.uk).

Negotiating committees may consist of a number of union representatives, including company shop stewards and full-time regional officials employed by the union. For negotiation purposes, two or more unions may also form a joint negotiating committee. Negotiation may take place at different levels, from local negotiations covering a group of workers at one or more sites, to national-level negotiations, if there is a national agreement in place. Employers may be members of employers' associations and, should the need arise, may draw upon the advice and expertise of experienced management negotiators. There may also be scope to establish a second tier of negotiation, usually involving either more senior levels within the unions or management, or involving external bodies, in an attempt to resolve negotiations should the original negotiating committee fail to reach agreement.

Collective bargaining has four dimensions over which each party has an interest in influencing.

- **Scope:** This relates to the range of issues that are subject to joint regulation.
- **Form:** This explains whether the bargaining is formal or informal.
- **Level:** This relates to whether the bargaining is at company or national level.
- **Unit:** This relates to the bargaining unit, which identifies the group of employees covered by the resulting collective agreement. The unit can change, depending on what is being negotiated.

HRM INSIGHT 8.4 Goldsmith's Pies

Goldsmith's Pies employs around 800 people, manufacturing pies and ready meals for the retail sector. The 650 hourly paid employees fall into two distinct groups for collective bargaining purposes. The food manufacturing team are represented by the Food, Bakers and Allied Workers Union (FBAWU). The maintenance team of twenty-five mechanical and electrical employees who are responsible for maintaining and repairing the food processing equipment, are represented by Unite, which incorporated engineering workers through various mergers and amalgamations.

Earlier in the year, the FBAWU negotiated a pay increase of 2 per cent for the manufacturing employees and this was accepted by ballot. The maintenance team negotiations are more problematic. This group feels that it is underpaid. The workers are particularly unhappy with the management team's suggestion that they should become multiskilled (electricians learning mechanical skills and vice versa) to bring about productivity savings that will fund pay increases. They have also taken exception to new working practices, which include all employees being required to wear wellingtons in production areas and a move away from hairnets and cloth caps to disposable 'mop cap'-style headwear to reduce the risk of hair contamination in the products.

The local representatives of Unite have refused to recommend the offer of 2 per cent and, as a result, members have rejected this in a show of hands. The management team does not wish to offend the majority of its employees in manufacturing by offering bigger increases to one group compared to another.

Questions

1. What options might Goldsmith's Pies have to resolve this dispute?
2. What might be the potential consequences of industrial action?
3. What recommendations would you make to try to move discussions forward?
4. What recommendations would you make to avoid this type of dispute arising in future?

Industrial action

Industrial action can have a damaging effect on an employer and its customers. It is the ultimate expression of pressure that a group of workers can inflict upon managers in an attempt to coerce management to agree to workers' demands. Equally, industrial action can have a negative effect on employees through loss of earnings and the possibility that prolonged action will result in job losses or at least job uncertainty. The nature of strike action has changed over the last few decades from indefinite and prolonged strikes to a series of 'days of action' or sporadic short periods of strike action of fixed duration, a trend that reflects the changing balance of power between unions and employers and the weakening of collective identity. The willingness to engage in serious and damaging industrial action for many trade unionists has been replaced by more 'token' strikes, with employees trying to minimize the costs to themselves while creating conditions which might result in employers seeking to reach agreement on favourable terms to the strikers.

In organizing industrial action, a union is encouraging its members to break their contractual obligation to attend work and hence, in turn, cause the organization to break its contractual obligation to customers, clients, and suppliers. On the face of it, such actions are unlawful and, were it not for the immunities granted to unions in such circumstances, they would be sued for compensation for the economic loss that results from these actions. Interestingly, individual employees have no such protection and could be sued for damages caused by their breach of contract although this doesn't happen very often. It is often difficult to establish individual liability and employers are generally reluctant to damage long-term relations (UK Government, 2016).

Procedures required to secure immunity

In order to secure immunity from being sued for damages (known as 'tort'), there are a number of conditions that the union must meet, which include:

● the action must be taken 'in contemplation or furtherance of a trade dispute';
● the union must conduct a secret postal ballot under strict conditions, involving every member who may be involved in the action;
● following the specific requirements about notifying the employer of the ballot, providing the employer with copies of the ballot paper, and with the numbers and categories of employee to be balloted;
● the ballot paper should state whether the union is calling for either strike action or action short of a strike;
● specific conditions must be met with regard to calling action and notifying the employer of action to be taken;
● the 2016 Trade Union Act made further provisions over the balloting process. Previously, a strike ballot only needed a simple majority of those voting for a strike to enjoy continued legal protection.

CHAPTER EIGHT MANAGING EMPLOYEE RELATIONS

247

The new Act, however, introduced a new minimum voter turnout (i.e. that at least 50 per cent of those entitled to vote do so) and an additional minimum support threshold applying in some important public services (i.e. that at least 40 per cent of those entitled to vote must vote 'yes');

- the new Act also changed the rules over the period over which the ballot decision remained 'live'. Previously, industrial action must have taken place within four to eight weeks of the ballot and action could have continued indefinitely, provided the dispute remained live. This provision has been repealed by the new Act and currently the ballot mandate expires after six months, or up to nine months if both sides agree.

For a brief guide to the Act, see Moss (2016).

Types of industrial action

- **Strike action** A 'strike' is a temporary withdrawal of labour. This might involve a complete stoppage of work over a number of days or a series of shorter strikes of perhaps a day, or even a number of hours, at a time. Some strikes have lasted months and even years! Strikes are often accompanied by a number of employees picketing, that is, standing at the entrance to 'encourage' other employees, customers, and suppliers not to enter the premises or to cross the picket line. Over the years, legislation has significantly reduced the use of picketing and banned it as a form of secondary action.

- **Action short of a strike** Most types of action short of a strike still consist of a breach of contract. Examples include a 'go slow', under which employees refuse to carry out specific tasks that are not specified in the employment contract. However, there is little evidence that the 'go slow' is officially and collectively practised today. Types of action that do not necessarily consist of a breach of contract include a 'work to rule', under which employees do the bare minimum to meet their contractual obligations; and an 'overtime ban', under which employees withdraw from voluntary overtime.

- **Unofficial industrial action** If action is taken by members, or is called by a union representative, and does not follow the strict conditions for balloting for industrial action referred to above, then the union must repudiate or disown it within twenty-four hours to maintain its immunity. This involves the principal executive committee, president, or general secretary of the union writing to withdraw support from the union representatives who called the action and all those involved in the action. Writing to all of these participants deems the action to be unofficial, and warns them that there is no protection from unfair dismissal, providing that *all* of those participating in the action are dismissed.

The above forms of non-strike industrial action are typical of what we can call 'the old industrial relations', which reflected an era of large-scale industrial conflict, collectivist action, and an ideological commitment to the values of trade unionism (Phillips, 2009). Of course, the 'old' model still exists in certain industries and sectors although as we have argued on a much-reduced scale. But the idea of a newer model, one based on reduced trade union power and influence, a decline in adversarialism, a fragmented and heterogeneous labour force, and the growing importance of the individual as opposed to the collective in terms of decision-making and the pursuit of interests, is one that has been occupying the theorists for some years. Change has undoubtedly taken place and continues to create new patterns of relationships at work and in employment generally and while it is difficult to predict the future shape of employment relations, the trends identified from the turn of the century are likely to continue to affect many aspects of the ER system. By that we mean that collective action will be replaced by individual action in enterprises where unions are absent or have limited power. Individual negotiations, something discussed in the final section of the chapter, may replace collective bargaining; more semi-informal regulation of work and performance will involve both managers and employees in a more explicit and open way and people who are dissatisfied with pay or conditions will leave and seek alternative employment rather than stay, or if they do stay express their discontent in more subtle ways. In reality, elements of the old forms of industrial action will stay in parts of the economy where unions have a presence, but coexist with new forms of individual action (Tanguy, 2011).

RESEARCH INSIGHT 8.3

To take your learning further, read the following:

Taylor, R. (2001) *The Future of Employment Relations*, Economic and Social Research Council.

This study explores the ways that economic and industrial change will affect the role of trade unions and influence the development of new patterns of employment relations.

Strategies for Improving Poor Industrial Relations

Most organizations are genuinely interested in improving relationships with trade unionists and their workplace representatives with the aim of building stronger and more effective organizations and providing better working conditions and rewards for their employees, but what specific actions can they take? The following actions make sense if both parties are committed to working together to resolve differences and increase levels of personal and institutional trust.

- Be clear on the rules and the distinction between normal working duties and union duties.
- Train, coach, and support the union representatives and line managers.
- Communicate directly with employees, as well as with union representatives, to prevent messages being distorted.
- Listen to employee concerns and rectify these wherever possible before the union representatives get involved.
- Apply the same consistent rules to union representatives as to all employees.
- Invite union representatives and managers to participate in joint training.
- Enlist help and support, and encourage senior dialogue with full-time union staff.
- Offer additional observer and participant places at consultation and negotiation meetings to other managers and representatives of non-union members to remove the mystery of such meetings.
- Take responsibility for the negotiations: managerial representatives should be given the authority to act, not be only a messenger.
- Brief managers and staff promptly, and publish minutes and notes following all collective meetings.
- Be consistent and clear.
- Ensure that all first-line managers are well trained to make appropriate decisions to avoid the need for an overruling decision to be made.
- Establish clear scope and objectives, along with joint commitment to outcomes of meetings, before commencing consultation or negotiation.
- Ensure that all relevant business decisions, corporate objectives, and organizational values are expressed and communicated in all communications, discussions, and negotiations.

249

PRACTITIONER INSIGHT Dan Goulding, former employee of an international motor manufacturer in the UK; currently occupies a senior HR role in the hospitality and leisure sector

The role that ER plays within an organization has evolved during the past decade. As an HR professional working within ER you are there to deliver the requirements of the company while ensuring employees are treated with fairness. This often means that a consistent approach needs to be applied to what people are paid and how they are treated.

Negotiations for this group have previously involved local branch union leaders meeting with senior managers. The series of meetings has lasted several months and, if this has gone beyond the normal settlement due date, increases have been backdated. The hospital trust has resisted this claim in previous years by stating that, in years of low inflation, it is hard to find a way to accommodate this change without the organization incurring significant additional employment costs.

This year, the union supporting the ancillary workers has made it clear that this unfair term must finally be addressed and that, while it does not wish to pursue industrial action, it may have no alternative given the strength of feeling about this disparity among its members.

Questions

1. What mistakes have potentially been made in previous years' negotiations?
2. What options might be available to the hospital trust to help to resolve this disagreement?
3. What strategies might be employed over the course of the negotiations to resolve this issue?
4. What recommendations might you make to improve future negotiations?

The psychological contract

We began this chapter by explaining the importance of trust between employees and managers, and how the quality of relations between them impacted on other aspects of HRM. Reference was also made to the importance of the informal dimension of employment—an idea that captures the day-to-day interaction

Table 8.2 Characteristics of good and poor industrial relations

Good industrial relations	Poor industrial relations
Regular opportunities for dialogue between parties	Each party is critical of the other
Accessibility to appropriate levels between both parties	Adversarial relationship between parties
Helpful, impartial, and realistic union support for employee in disputes and disciplinary matters	Unquestioning support of union for all employees in all disputes
Understanding of each party's role	Lack of union understanding of organizational objectives
Practical and realistic approaches	
Short, effective, and realistic bargaining	Little appreciation among union representatives of potential consequences of poor organizational performance
Open-minded parties	
Readiness of each party to back down and change direction	Lack of trust between parties
	Unions encourage negativity towards organization to build their own power base
Well-defined and clear mechanisms for allowing and managing distinct time off for union duties	Drawn-out, unrealistic bargaining
	Union representatives see union job as main role and union duties interfere with main job purpose
Organization takes responsibility for joint training and coaching of managers and representatives involved in the relationship	Over-reliance of organization on union to train representatives and lack of involvement of managers in training
Rapid resolution of issues at lowest possible level prior to union and senior management involvement	Over-reliance of organization on union and senior managers or HR to resolve disputes

between people who have to work together to produce goods and services and survive the pressures and stresses of work. Both of these aspects of what can be described as the 'human', as opposed to the 'institutional', aspect of employment relations are expressed in the concept of the 'psychological contract' (Hiltrop, 1996).

The psychological contract refers to the obligations that an employer and an employee, or group of employees, perceive to exist between each other as part of the employment relationship, and consists of both expectations of each other and promises made to each other. Rousseau (1995) captured the relationship between the psychological contract, trust, and performance when she wrote:

> When two people working interdependently, such as a worker and a supervisor, agree on the terms of the contract, performance should be satisfactory from both parties' perspectives. As individuals work through their understandings of each other's commitments over time, a degree of mutual predictability becomes possible: 'I know what you want from me and I know what I want from you.' Commitments understood on both sides may be based on communication, customs and past practices. Regardless of how it is achieved, mutual predictability is a powerful factor in coordinating effort and planning.

Arguably, the psychological contract is more important as a determinant of behaviour than is the formal contract because of the way it connects to employees' everyday experiences of work and of being managed. Indeed, as the frequency and intensity of strikes and other forms of formal, collective industrial action have diminished, perceived managerial violations of the psychological contract may explain the continued persistence of dissatisfaction and conflict at work, which as we noted above, is expressed at the individual and informal as well as the collective, formal level.

The references made in Chapter 1 to the rise in the frequency of stress-related illness and absenteeism, high turnover rates, and the withholding of discretionary effort may suggest that conflict has not necessarily been removed from the system but has become expressed in different forms. Moreover, it seems now to be expressed in ways that do not fit easily with the formal and collective mechanisms of conflict resolution that are associated with the 'old' industrial relations.

Guest (2004) recognizes that the transition from the 'old' industrial relations with its emphasis on collectivism, strong trade unions, and collective regulation to the 'new' employment relations characterized by individualism, different demographics, changing values, and greater cooperation, requires new and more appropriate perspectives to help make sense of these changes and developments. He argues that:

> In these changing circumstances, we need a rather different conceptual framework around which to focus our analysis and research. Arguably, a key challenge for the future is how to explore the employment relationship in settings where collective arrangements either do not exist, have decayed, or address only a minority of the workforce or a small part of what is considered important in the ongoing employer–employee relationship.

He believes that adopting a psychological perspective, one based on the concept of the psychological contract offers an alternative or at least a complementary analytic framework for making sense of the changing world of work and employment. He defines the psychological contract as:

> The perception of both parties to the employment relationship ... of the reciprocal promises and obligations implied in that relationship.

This definition implies a continuing process of negotiating and renegotiating resulting in agreement over a range of issues which may change in importance as circumstances change. Central to this notion that employees and individual managers negotiate to maintain order and stability, however provisional this might be, is the concept of reciprocity. Gouldner (1954), whose work we referred to earlier, believed that the stability of informal agreements, understandings, and 'contracts' between workers and managers depended on both parties keeping their side of the bargain. From an employee perspective, the inability or failure of managers to maintain the privileges, concessions, and opportunities valued by people may result in conflict, withdrawal of cooperation, weakening levels of engagement, and increased levels of sickness absence and turnover. Rousseau (2005) adds:

The extent to which an employee feels 'engaged' with their employer and therefore feels duty bound, morally obliged, or genuinely motivated to do all that is within their capability to contribute towards an organization's success is heavily influenced by the psychological contract.

Put simply, the psychological contract affects what an employee is willing to do, based upon the belief that over the long term the individual and group will be treated fairly by their manager(s) and be rewarded for their performance and contribution, but not necessarily on a day-to-day basis. Trust is a key ingredient of the maintenance of the psychological contract and this is not surprisingly tested in circumstances of organizational change (think again of the wildcat strike and its causes). Feelings of trust and mistrust are constantly affected by the way the change process is managed as well as by the substance of the change itself. Smollan (2013) found that perceptions of organizational justice during change were important contributors to the creation and erosion of trust in management. We can now see the clear link between the psychological contract, trust, and perceptions of justice and fairness.

Good managers, perhaps instinctively, develop productive psychological contracts from the early stages of a relationship being formed because of their understanding of what is important to employees and their ability to build a sense of mutual reciprocity. Ensuring that high expectations are clearly understood and accepted by all employees, and are rewarded with promises about involvement, development, and recognition, is the key to utilizing the psychological contract effectively to the organization's advantage. This is perhaps easier to achieve in smaller, more flexible, organizations because managers and employees are more closely engaged in 'production', but the principle applies generally. Organizations that experience low morale, frequent complaints from employees, and a general lethargy may well be those within which the psychological contract may be perceived to have been broken by either party, with neither even aware that it has happened!

Table 8.3 shows characteristics of employer and employees under positive and 'broken' psychological contracts.

Table 8.3 Employer/employee characteristics under positive and 'broken' psychological contracts

Party to contract	Positive psychological contract	Broken psychological contract
Employer	Is supportive	Offers only subjective evaluation
	Encourages two-way communication	Pays lip service to employees' views
		Engages only in pseudo-consultation
	Is consistent and fair	Is inconsistent in the way he/she treats people
		Reneges on commitments
	Sets clear standards	Is lacking in trust
	Keeps to commitments	Decision-making is controlled at senior level
	Offers objective evaluation of performance	Actions are motivated by need for personal approval and acceptance rather than team success
	Engages in meaningful dialogue	
	Offers a high level of empowerment and engagement	Feels threatened
Employee	Has strong sense of obligation	Questions job security
	Is trustworthy and honest	Lacks loyalty

(Continued)

Party to contract	Positive psychological contract	Broken psychological contract
	Makes maximum use of working time	Has low expectations
	Is reliable	Considers that appearances are more important than delivery of performance
	Is loyal	
	Is open-minded	
	Feels secure	
	Is confident	
	Has high expectations	

To conclude, employment relations is not just about trade unions and the institutions that support the collective bargaining process. Despite the continuing existence of both there is today much more awareness on the part of managers and employees of the importance of the informal dimension of working relations. If the 'old' style of industrial relations was about negotiations over pay and conditions, conflict and mistrust, the 'new' employment relations is more focused on understanding ways to improve relationships and developing strategies that drive improvements in performance and productivity which also enhance the quality of people's working lives. Of course, it would be naive to suggest that there has been a complete transformation in attitudes on both sides but it would be equally wrong to suggest that there have not been major changes in the way relationships at work are structured and managed.

Summary

- What originally was known as 'industrial relations' reflected an era in which 'old industries', the collective institutions of employers and workers, and the management of industrial conflict were the dominant features. This 'area' of HRM has, for some but not all, changed in important ways. First, the tendency to talk about 'employment' rather than 'industrial relations' represents a broadening of the subject to include all employment contexts, irrespective of whether these involve the collective representation of workers or not.

- The change in emphasis represented by the renaming of the field meant that unionization and collective relations are no longer assumed to be the norm or the starting point, particularly for HR professionals and line managers. Nor is conflict seen as inevitable and, as new management practices were introduced by Japanese and other overseas companies, a different mindset and approach to relations between managers and employees began to emerge, based much more on a mixed unitary–pluralist perspective and cooperative attitudes.

- The notion of ER takes this evolutionary trend even further, because of the emphasis this term gives to the primacy of individual over collective relations. This is consistent with the idea that the employment contract and the psychological contract are both important in understanding the dynamic behaviour of relations and relationships at work.

- In organizations where trade unions are recognized the terms and conditions of employment and the employment relationship are largely governed by agreements between the trade union and the employer. However, the extent of union recognition and union membership is declining. Many employment rights that were originally established through collective negotiation have been incorporated into legislation and the extent of the societal role of trade unions is perhaps therefore seen as less important than it has been viewed in the past.

- European legislation has been a key factor in establishing obligations upon employers to consult with their workforce, whether or not there is a recognized union in place.
- In more recent years the emphasis on the employer in honouring the psychological contract that exists between an employer and its employees has grown in importance and is now recognized as a key element in maintaining positive ER.

 Visit the **online resources** that accompany this book for self-test questions, web links, and more information on the topics covered in this chapter, at: **www.oup.com/uk/banfield3e/**

 ## REVIEW QUESTIONS

1. To what extent are the causes of industrial conflict post 2000 similar or different to those of conflict in the 1970s and 1980s?

2. What are likely to be the most important consequences for the management of people of an increasing emphasis on the individualization of employment relations?

3. In the absence of trade unions and collective bargaining, what can employers do to ensure that their workers have the ability to communicate with and influence management?

4. What are the essential differences between a 'formal' and an 'informal' approach to employment relations?

5. How are organizations that are non-unionized best advised to approach ER and consultation?

CASE STUDY   The claim for union representation

William Beckett Plastics is a small plastics manufacturing business based in Sheffield. It employs fifty people, the majority of whom are shop-floor operatives. The managing director, William Beckett, bought the company twenty years ago and has built it into a £3 million business that sells plastic components in over thirty countries. It has never been unionized, and relations between management and employees have always been fairly informal and amicable.

The MD's main contribution to the business was in the development of its business and marketing strategy, and he was heavily involved in expanding its national and international markets. While he maintained strategic control of the business, operational responsibility was in the hands of the production director and production manager, who were in day-to-day control of production and the two shifts of operatives that constituted thirty-four out of a total of fifty-five employees.

Unexpectedly, William Beckett received a letter from the Unite union seeking recognition and representational rights on behalf of the company's production operatives. He was initially surprised at the request—he had no idea that there had been discussions among his employees about union representation. Overcoming this, he remained unconvinced that there was sufficient overall support within the employee group for a change from the existing informal and direct model of ER, based upon management taking decisions on pay, benefits, and other employment matters in the best interests of the company. He decided, therefore, to write to each employee, reminding them of the benefits they had enjoyed in working for a company that, in his opinion, had treated them fairly and with consideration. At the same time, he wrote to Unite expressing the view that he did not believe their claim enjoyed sufficient support to be accepted.

255

In response, the union sought advice from ACAS and made an application to the CAC for union recognition. After passing the initial CAC test of acceptability, the union was given twenty days to agree on the representational and collective bargaining unit it wished to base its claim on. Believing that, at best, the union had the support of a handful of shop-floor operatives, the MD decided, with the assistance of the Electoral Reform Society, to ballot all fifty-five employees—a figure that included thirty-four operatives. He felt that any decision he might take needed to be based on a clear understanding of what all of his staff wanted, not only a small minority of them.

Almost all of the administrative staff voted for the status quo. Of the thirty-four shop-floor operatives, twenty-four returned valid ballot papers, of which ten represented a vote for union representation, two for a system of non-union employee representatives, and twelve for the status quo. As a result of the ballot, the union was disinclined to pursue the matter further, feeling that it had insufficient support from a bargaining unit based on all employees.

On reflection, the MD realized that there must have been something wrong for a significant number of shop-floor workers to feel that they needed independent union representation. After discussing the matter with his senior management colleagues, they all agreed that management had become complacent about the shop floor and had effectively become psychologically disengaged from the workers, even though it was in day-to-day contact with them. To avoid a similar situation occurring in the future, management had to make changes to the way in which employment relations were handled.

Questions

1. What procedures and criteria does the CAC apply in deciding on whether a union claim for recognition and representation rights succeeds?

2. What had management failed to do that resulted in the claim for representation being made and why had this happened?

3. What options were available to the MD in changing the way in which relations with his employees were managed?

4. As the MD, what would you have done and why?

 Insights and Outcomes: visit the **online resources** at **www.oup.com/uk/banfield3e/** for an account of the developments that followed the final ballot.

 FURTHER READING

Colling, T. and Terry, M. (eds.) (2010) *Industrial Relations: Theory and Practice*, Wiley.

Faragher, J. (2016) 'Unions: Is anyone listening?', at: http://www.cipd.co.uk/pm/peoplemanagement/b/weblog/archive/2016/08/24/unions-is-anyone-istenng.aspx?utm_medium=email&utm_source=cipd&utm_campaign=cipdupdate&utm_term=963101&utm_content=310816-6901-15136-20160831063044-Read%20People%20Management%20%27s%20report

Wright, C. F. (2011) 'What role for trade unions in future workplace relations?', ACAS discussion paper. www.engageforsuccess.org

ACAS (2014) Employee communications and consultation, at: http://www.acas.org.uk/media/pdf/i/g/Employee-communications-and-consultation.pdf

Breslin, D. and Wood, G. (2015) 'Rule breaking in social care: Hierarchy, contentiousness and informal rules', *Work, Employment and Society*, August, at: http://wes.sagepub.com/content/early/2016/04/22/0950017015595956.full.pdf+html

Central Arbitration Committee (2016) Annual Reports.

CIPD (2015) *Getting under the Skin of Conflict: Tracing the Experiences of Employees* [survey report], at: https://www.cipd.co.uk/Images/getting-under-skin-workplace-conflict_2015-tracing-experiences-employees_tcm18-10800.pdf

Crafts, N. (2011) 'Competition cured the "British disease"', at: http://voxeu.org/article/competition-cured-british-disease

Department for Business Innovation and Skills (2015) *Trade Union Membership 2014*, Statistical Bulletin.

Department of Health (2012) *Partnership Agreement: An Agreement between the Department of Health NHS Employers and NHS Trade Unions*, February, at: https://www.gov.uk/government/publications/partnership-agreement

Dobbins, T. and Dundon, T. (2012) 'Partnership and militancy as a contradictory dialectic in the labour process', paper for 30th International Labour Process Conference, University of Stockholm, 27–9 March.

Dundon, T. and Rollinson, D. (2011) *Understanding Employment Relations*, McGraw-Hill.

Dunlop, J. (1958) *Industrial Relations Systems*, Holt & Co.

Engaging for Success (2009) 'Enhancing performance through employee engagement', at: http://engageforsuccess.org/wp-content/uploads/2015/08/file52215.pdf

Flanders, A. (1970) *Management and Unions*, Faber & Faber.

Fox, A. (1966) *Industrial Sociology and Industrial Relations*, Royal Commission Research Paper No. 3, HMSO.

Gall, G. (2012) 'Richard Hyman: An assessment of his industrial relations: A Marxist Introduction', *Capital & Class*, 36(1), 135–49.

Gouldner, A. (1954) *Wildcat Strike*, Antioch Press.

Guest, D. E. (2004) 'The psychology of the employment relationship: An analysis based on the psychological contract', *Applied Psychology: An International Review*, 53(4), 541–55.

Hiltrop, J. M. (1996) 'Managing the changing psychological contract', *Employee Relations*, 18(1), 36–49.

Hyman, R. (1975) *Industrial Relations: A Marxist Introduction*, Macmillan.

Hyman, R. and Brough, I. (1975) *Social Values and Industrial Relations*, Blackwell.

Ingram, P. and Metcalfe, D. (1991) 'Strike incidence and duration in British manufacturing industry in the 1980s', CEP discussion paper.

Johnstone, S. and Ackers, P. (2015) *Finding a Voice at Work*, Oxford University Press, pp. 44–66.

Kaufman, B. E. (2002) 'Reflections on six decades in industrial relations: An interview with John Dunlop', *Industrial and Labor Relations Review*, 55(2), 324–48.

Lambert, R. (2011) *The Labour Market and Employment Relations Beyond the Recession*. Warwick Papers in Industrial Relations Number 93, at: https://www2.warwick.ac.uk/fac/soc/wbs/research/irru/wpir/wpir_93.pdf

Macleod, D. and Clarke, N. (2009) *Engaging for Success: Enhancing Performance Through Employee Engagement*, government report, at: http://dera.ioe.ac.uk/1810/1/file52215.pdf

Moss, R. (2016) 'Trade Union Act becomes law', *Personnel Today*, 5 May, at: http://www.personneltoday.com/hr/trade-union-act-2016-becomes-law

NHS Pay Review Body (2016) *29th Report*, at: https://www.gov.uk/government/uploads/system/uploads/attachment_data/file/506030/54488_Cm_9210_NHS_PRB_2016_Web_Accessible_NEW.PDF

Phillips, J. (2009) 'Workplace conflict and the origins of the 1984–1985 miners' strike in Scotland', *Twentieth Century British History*, 20(2), 152–73.

RMT (2017) press release, 27 January, at: https://www.rmt.org.uk/news/rmt-confirms-further-strike-dates-in-tube-dispute

Ronnmar, M. (2006) 'The managerial prerogative and the employee's obligation to work: Comparative perspectives on functional flexibility', *Industrial Law Journal*, 35(1): 56–74.

Rousseau, D. M. (1995) *Psychological Contracts in Organisations*, Sage.

Rousseau, D. M. (2005) *Ideals: Idiosyncratic Deals Employees Bargain for Themselves*, M.E. Sharp.

Royles D. (2015) 'Maintaining employer—Union partner relationships is critical', *HR Magazine*, 28 August, at: http://www.hrmagazine.co.uk/article-details/dean-royles-maintaining-employer-union-partner-relationships-is-critical

Salamon, M. (2001) *Industrial Relations: Theory and Practice*, 4th edn, Prentice Hall.

Smollan, R. K. (2013) 'Trust in change managers: the role of affect', *Journal of Organizational Change Management*, 26(4), 725–47.

Sorenson, M. K. (2006) 'Capital and labour: Can the conflict be solved?, *Interdisciplinary Journal of International Studies*, 4(1).

Tanguy, J. (2011) 'Collective and individual conflicts in the workplace: Evidence from France', at: http://congres.afse.fr/docs/2011/284354article_jtanguy_afse2011.pdf

Taylor, R. (2001) *The Future of Employment Relations*, Economic and Social Research Council, at: http://

www.dphu.org/uploads/attachements/books/books_5037_0.pdf

TSSA (2017) press release, 4 January, at: https://www.tssa.org.uk/en/Your-union/Your-company/company-pages/london-underground/index.cfm/acas-tube-talks-fail-to-make-progress

TUC (2002) *Partnership Works*, at: https://www.tuc.org.uk/about-tuc/congress/congress-2002/general-council-report-2002-chapter-4

UK Government (2016) 'Taking part in industrial action and strikes', at: https://www.gov.uk/industrial-action-strikes/your-employment-rights-during-industrial-action

Van Wanrooy, B. et al. (2013) *The 2011 Workplace Employment Relations Study*, at: https://www.gov.uk/government/uploads/system/uploads/attachment_data/file/336651/bis-14-1008-WERS-first-findings-report-fourth-edition-july-2014.pdf

Watson, T. J. (2012) *Sociology, Work and Organisation*, Routledge.

Webb, S. and Webb, B. (1920) *The History of Trade Unionism 1866–1920*, Longman.

Managing Misconduct

9

Key Terms

Misconduct Behaviour that transgresses contractual arrangements, work rules, established norms of performance, or other standards that can be seen as reasonable and necessary for the effective employment and management of people at work; behaviour that is deemed to be unacceptable by reference to formally established norms.

Discipline The formal measures taken, sanctions applied, and outcomes achieved by management in response to perceived acts of misconduct.

Grievance The formalization of a claim that one or more persons, either co-workers or management, have acted wrongly towards another person(s) and, as a consequence, inflicted physical or psychological harm on that person, or others. This may involve an act of misconduct.

Mediation An alternative form of dispute resolution. A voluntary process where an independent facilitator assists two or more parties to explore options for resolving a dispute, disagreement, or problem situation by attempting to reach a mutually acceptable agreement. The overriding aim of workplace mediation is to restore and maintain the employment relationship whenever possible.

Learning Objectives

As a result of reading this chapter and using the online resources, you should be able to:

- deliver an organization's approach to unacceptable behaviour and misconduct to reflect its wider managerial philosophy and values;

- understand what is meant by, and the role of, discipline and grievance at work;

- apply the law covering employee rights and procedural regulation thoughtfully and with regard to its consequences;

- understand the importance of acting ethically in discipline and grievance management;

- recognize the consequences of failing to manage effectively disciplinary and grievance issues in the workplace; and

- develop effective processes for handling grievances at work.

Introduction

The management of discipline and grievance features highly on the HR agenda of most UK organizations and can consume a considerable amount of time on the part of HR professionals and line managers, as well as involving considerable financial and reputational costs. A recent CIPD report (2011) indicated that the mean number of formal disciplinary cases in respondent organizations over the previous twelve months was 16.5 cases but that 2.5 per cent of organizations had more than one hundred cases. The mean number of formal grievance cases was 22.3. While it is difficult to give precise figures on the national picture of disciplinary and grievance cases, the medium-term growth in the number of employment tribunal cases dealing with claims of unfair dismissal suggests that either employers are initiating more disciplinary cases, or that employees are questioning the legitimacy of such action, or both. The number of tribunal claims in 2015 was 67 per cent lower than in 2013 which was the year that the new fee structure was introduced (Ministry of Justice, 2015). The effect of the new fee structure has been to reduce cases being brought to tribunals, not to reduce the frequency of disciplinary and grievance cases arising in the workplace. Therefore, care has to be exercised in interpreting official statistics on the incidence of grievance and disciplinary cases arising annually in the UK.

Further evidence for the growing importance of this aspect of HR can be found in the limited, but high-profile, number of cases of constructive dismissal, in which alleged failure by employers to respond adequately to employee grievances over issues such as harassment, bullying, and sexual discrimination have resulted in damaging and costly claims for compensation. More recently a number of high-profile whistle-blowing cases have been covered in the media. These stem from the reality or perception that legitimate concerns expressed over alleged wrongdoings at work have been ignored or not been taken seriously, with, perversely, the whistle-blower being disciplined and accused of breaking confidentiality rules resulting in constructive dismissal claims. Such cases highlight the danger of ignoring or failing to investigate behaviour at work that undermines the contractual, statutory, and human rights of employees.

The fact that employees are becoming increasingly aware of their 'rights' is neither contentious nor surprising. The preparedness of many managerial and professional staff to raise grievances over the way in which they have been treated suggests that organizations, and particularly their HR functions, will need to pay particular attention to this growing tendency and to the reasons for it. In a recent case, a female employee who left the army following disciplinary action after she failed to attend an evening parade due to child care problems took her claim to an employment tribunal. Despite an attempt to claim over £1 million in damages, she was awarded just £17,010 for 'hurt feelings', as she was told she was not 'pulling her weight'. However, the legal costs for the taxpayer incurred by the MoD are estimated to have been in the region of £100,000. This demonstrates the need for organizations to manage discipline and grievance cases effectively and that the potential costs of getting it wrong are very significant, for employee morale, brand reputation, and for the balance sheet.

Yet it would be unwise to assume that grievances are restricted to professional-level employees and it would be even more simplistic to assume that acts of misconduct resulting in formal disciplinary action are to be found only within the ranks of shop-floor workers and their equivalent. Of particular significance to our understanding of the challenges that management face in responding to both types of misconduct is the recognition that such problems occur at all levels within the organization and involve professional, white-collar, and manual employees.

Although small in number, some cases of serious misconduct involving financial irregularities and the breaching of important protocols involve top management. In the USA, two hedge fund managers for Bear Stearns, who managed a pair of sub-prime laden hedge funds until their $1.4 billion collapse in June 2007, were accused of misleading investors about the health of the funds (*Daily Telegraph*, 11 November 2009). This was a very high-profile case, given that this type of activity is widely regarded to have been what led to the credit crunch and subsequent recession in 2008–9. While acquitted of criminal charges following a four-week trial (the standard of proof is of course much higher in criminal as opposed to civil cases), these types of cases highlight the new kind of behaviour that can give rise to disciplinary action and the challenges facing HR in dealing with them. In another high-profile case, Dr Raj Mattu, a surgeon, won £1.22 million in damages after raising concerns about overcrowding of wards in Walsgrave Hospital in Coventry in 2001. He claimed he was 'vilified and bullied' as a result of raising his concerns (*Daily Mail*, 5 February 2016). This case not only highlights the consequences of HR 'getting it wrong', but gives some indication of the management time and legal costs of a case that took fifteen years to reach a conclusion.

Despite the belief that the management of misconduct may become more significant in the years ahead, it would be misleading to suggest that the typical organization experiences more than a handful of cases each year. Factors such as size, sector, and employee characteristics have an influence on the actual number of cases that require resolution. Moreover, the preference by most progressive HR professionals for trying to manage grievances and discipline, as far as possible, at the informal level further complicates any meaningful attempt to establish the number of incidents of misconduct that actually occur. But even if such cases are limited in number, responding to them can consume significant amounts of management time and resources, and the more difficult and complex cases often generate intense emotional pressures for those directly involved. This may result in psychological damage to individuals who believe that they have been treated unfairly and without proper regard to the circumstances and explanations that led to the action or behaviour resulting in disciplinary proceedings.

Organizations that consistently fail to act within defined legal and procedural frameworks, and which show scant regard for any wider ethical considerations, can also acquire damaging reputations as a result of the way in which they treat their staff. This, in turn, can affect their ability to recruit and retain top-quality people. The implications and consequences of 'getting things wrong' or, for reasons only known to those managers directly involved, of acting precipitously and without regard to the consequences, can go beyond reputational damage. Collective responses, in the form of strikes and other expressions of industrial conflict, can be triggered by a sense of injustice and disproportionality over managerial behaviour.

261

KEY CONCEPT Whistle-blowing

A whistle-blower is a person who exposes any kind of information or activity that is deemed illegal, unethical, or not correct within an organization. To be covered by whistle-blowing law, a worker who makes a disclosure must reasonably believe two things. The first is that they are acting in the public's interest. The second is that they must reasonably believe that the disclosure tends to show past, present, or future wrongdoing in defined categories such as criminal offences, miscarriages of justice, and health and safety.

STUDENT ACTIVITY 9.1

Read the relevant parts of the following two publications on whistle-blowing and consider their implications for the way organizations should treat those who have grievances and act as whistle-blowers.

1. *Whistleblowing: Guidance for Employees and Code of Practice* (Department for Business, Innovation and Skills, March 2015), available at: https://www.gov.uk/government/publications/whistleblowwhistleblowing-guidance-and-code-of-practice-for-employers

2. Sir Robert Francis, *Freedom to Speak up Review* (2015), available at: https://www.gov.uk/government/publications/sir-robert-francis-freedom-to-speak-up-review

---

Signpost to Chapter 5: Ethics and Leadership in HRM for a more detailed exploration of the ethics of whistle-blowing.

Protection for whistle-blowers is contained in the Employment Rights Act 1996 as amended by the Public Interest Disclosure Act 1998 (PIDA). Where a worker makes a protected disclosure, they have the right not to be subject to detrimental action by their employer for making that disclosure. Francis (2015) highlights that the legislation is limited in its effectiveness, as it only provides a series of remedies after discipline has been carried out, including loss of employment. He believes that too often, this is too late. The reason for the emphasis given to whistle-blowing and the use of disciplinary action in response is that this relatively recent phenomenon represents a new aspect of employee behaviour for which disciplinary procedures are being applied. Different organizations have different positions and policies on how to respond to serious disclosures by employees involving alleged breaches of confidentiality, but all are faced with the challenge of acting ethically and legally in the action they choose to take. It is becoming increasingly difficult for employers to use the threat or use of discipline to suppress the legal rights of employees to disclose wrongdoing but where a case of misconduct on the part of an employee is made, such cases are almost certainly going to be more complicated and challenging than those covering more straightforward breaches of works rules.

Failure to respond effectively

The important point that arises from the above situation is that the consequences of failing to act appropriately in the management of discipline and grievance do matter. Few senior managers will be so cavalier as to disregard these consequences in the lead they offer to those given specific responsibility for this key part of the HR agenda. One of the difficulties faced by HR professionals, however, is that they can never be sure that they are in full control of the situation that they are required to manage. Often they become involved after an incident has already taken place, with initial action having already been taken by line managers. The type of question that a manager may ask, along the lines of 'I've sacked someone: is that ok?', or 'I've just given someone a written warning', illustrates that HR professionals are often faced with having to recover a situation that may already, by the time they are involved, have become more serious than it needed to be. As will be made clear later, the key challenge facing HR, beyond the procedural management of discipline and grievance, is the ability to influence the actions of other participants, particularly line managers, whose own agendas and interests may take precedence over any wider organizational interests (Jones and Saundry, 2012).

While the arbitrary and inconsistent treatment of staff will never be entirely eliminated, there is an increasing awareness among line managers and HR professionals that their organizations need to develop more effective approaches and mechanisms for the management of discipline and grievance. This is not simply because of changing ethical, contractual, and legal considerations, but stems from the simple recognition that getting it wrong can result in serious and damaging consequences for all parties. The position promoted by organizations such as ACAS and the CIPD is that the discipline and grievance 'mindset' should recognize the importance of developing preventative strategies as well as effective procedural regulation, based on a better understanding of why such cases arise in the first place and of their underlying causes.

Choices in the Handling of Discipline

Organizations that might claim to have efficient and well-used disciplinary and grievance procedures may have less reason to feel self-satisfied than organizations that only infrequently need such procedures to be invoked. In the latter type of organization, it is clear that employee behaviour is such that disciplinary and grievance procedures need rarely to be used. But it is also self-evident that even where such cases are rare it would be foolish not to have robust and reliable mechanisms for dealing with them. The effective management of grievance and discipline involves therefore:

- understanding the causes of misconduct, how this is manifested, and its severity; and
- developing interventions and strategies that are aimed at limiting the damage caused by such cases as well as resolving the conflict between the parties involved.

The position taken here is that the role of HR is not simply about managing the resolution of discipline and grievance cases, but also includes investigating and addressing the reasons that contribute to their existence, however difficult and challenging this may be.

As far as acts of employee misconduct are concerned, the following may be relevant factors:

- deficiencies and failings on the part of the individual;
- external pressures and circumstances that have a temporary effect on individual performance and behaviour;
- management style and practices;
- the working environment;
- personal relationships;
- changes in people's employment status and security;
- misunderstandings and genuine mistakes;
- changes in standards, expectations, and social norms, resulting in behaviour that was previously considered acceptable becoming unacceptable; and
- failure to understand and adapt to external legislative changes.

From an HR perspective, it is important to establish which of the above explanations is relevant to each individual case of misconduct and whether, over time, any discernible patterns emerge that might justify a more strategic intervention to address particularly important causal factors. If a general criticism can be made of HR in the way that misconduct is managed, it is that often each case is treated individually, narrowly, and in isolation. Making sense of the situation by trying to locate incidents of unacceptable behaviour in a wider context can be seen as an important contribution to the effective resolution of patterns of behaviour.

'Making sense' goes beyond a simple investigation of the circumstances surrounding an incident, and involves the application of a more holistic and integrated approach, including diagnosis, interpretation, and motivation/intention. Such an approach should both inform the way in which each case is handled and contribute to an outcome that is, as far as possible, fair to all parties and appropriate in the circumstances.

But the importance of choice in the management of misconduct goes beyond the question of exploratory processes and procedural regulation, and extends into the more complex world of management philosophy, values, and beliefs. Consider, for example, the purpose and function of discipline in contemporary organizations. Interestingly, the use of, and need for, discipline seems at odds with developments in contemporary management thinking, with its emphasis on commitment, employee-centred HR practices, and the search for higher levels of performance and discretionary effort. This emphasis on the importance of employees as the key, if not the only, source of competitive advantage has led many writers to question some of the more traditional approaches to managing people, which include the use of sanctions and punishment to 'manage misconduct'.

Pfeffer and Veiga (1999, quoted in Frost et al., 2002), for example, argue that numerous studies have demonstrated that very significant economic benefits can be gained through the implementation of high-performance or high-commitment management practices, but that there is little evidence to suggest that disciplining staff contributes to these outcomes. On the contrary, there is extensive anecdotal evidence to suggest that disciplining—particularly, but not exclusively, if this is done in a way that is perceived to be arbitrary and unfair—creates exactly the opposite effect to that which is desired.

Moreover, the growth in the knowledge economy, in which highly skilled knowledge workers are increasingly replacing manual employees as an organization's key resource, might mean that traditional approaches to discipline, as well as hierarchical control, are unlikely to be appropriate and effective managerial practices when applied to such employees. In an economic environment of sustained low unemployment, growing flexible working arrangements, and an increasing body of legislative rights and duties that protect the individual from arbitrary and unfair disciplinary action, the ability of employers to maintain traditional approaches to disciplining staff has become increasingly compromised as well as its effective-ness questioned.

While the need for an appropriate response to instances of misconduct is a necessity for many organ-izations, what is increasingly important is that such responses are seen as proportionate, transparent, and fair, not only by those who are directly affected by them, but by their peers. A failure to deliver against these criteria not only undermines the integrity of HR, but affects the reputation of the organization, and is likely to have a detrimental effect on the attitudes and behaviour of other employees over time. In a somewhat perverse sense, the management of misconduct must involve a degree of consent and legitimization from those who are directly and indirectly affected by it. In the same way that applicants applying for jobs need to feel that they have been treated fairly and with 'procedural justice', so too do those subjected to disciplinary action (Konovsky, 2000). Taking a holistic view of the causes of misconduct at work, it seems clear that, as with misconduct and unacceptable behaviour in wider society, improved management practices alone are unlikely to eradicate the need for disciplinary action as the human con-dition contains the potential in some people to behave in unacceptable ways. Going back to the ideas of Robert Sutton we considered in Chapter 1, keeping the wrong kind of people out of the organization in the first place is often the starting point of any strategy that is concerned with the reduction of and need for disciplinary action.

There is, however, an important alternative perspective on grievance and discipline to be considered and this involves looking at the reasons for and implications associated with *not* taking appropriate and timely action to address certain types of misconduct particularly that associated with the bullying of subordinates by their managers. Bullying by co-workers is of course as important in terms of its potential effects but where managers are involved such behaviour is considered by many to be more prevalent and insidious. This can occur as a cultural expression, where patterns of behaviour involving the unethical exploitation of managerial power are seen to reflect a 'macho style' of management allowed if not endorsed by organiza-tional leaders. It can also involve individual managers who feel able to engage in bullying behaviour in an environment where no one feels confident about raising formal complaints about such behaviour, as they feel that protecting the institution takes precedence over addressing the problem. As with whistle-blowers, raising grievances with senior managers and HR about the behaviour of individual managers is not without risks and few are prepared to take those risks, preferring instead to leave or simply learn to live with the situation. The view that we express is supported by data from different surveys into bullying and harass-ment (CIPD, 2015). Research from the charity Family Lives found that in a poll of more than 1,500 work-ers, 91 per cent felt their organization did not deal with bullying at work adequately. It also found that 66 per cent of respondents witnessed bullying at work, with more than two-fifths (43 per cent) claiming they were bullied by their line manager, 38 per cent bullied by a colleague, and 20 per cent bullied by a senior manager or chief executive. Although by no means representative, individual comments presented in the charity's report and quoted in *People Management* (2015) editorial highlight the sense of uncertainty and insecurity those experiencing bullying behaviour feel. One respondent said:

HR are there to protect management and the organization. You are made to feel a trouble maker.

And another said:

Management are very weak and choose to ignore problems, bullying or otherwise, rather than to deal with them.

It may be the case, therefore, that one approach to the management of certain types of misconduct by managers is to ignore the problem and do nothing, hoping the situation will settle down or resolve itself. As we note later in the chapter, bullying in particular is difficult to establish in any objective way, where 'firm' management is considered acceptable by some but perceived as bullying by others, which might explain a cautionary approach taken by HR. But an approach characterized by denial, the protection of senior managers, the refusal to 'see' what is obvious to many and an overriding concern with the reputa-tion of the organization while understandable is at best likely to only contain the problem and at worst exacerbate it.

Alternatives to Disciplining People

This need to consider alternative ways of managing misconduct emerges from the meanings associated with the act of discipline. Many dictionary definitions equate 'discipline' with 'punishment', seeing it as a way of exercising control, and enforcing compliance and order, along with obedience. Discipline is almost always seen as being coercive—forcing people to change their behaviour. It is also seen in terms of a system of rules, the purpose of which is to improve and correct behaviour. Discipline is traditionally associated with 'what management does to employees' and usually involves the application, or implied use, of sanctions, ultimately ending in an individual being dismissed in cases of gross or persistent misconduct. But in less serious cases, the act of misconduct may require a less serious response: one that involves verbal or written warnings, demotion, or job change. Whichever action is considered appropriate, the underlying assumption associated with the use of sanctions is that they will have the effect of dissuading the individual involved from continuing to act in unacceptable ways and will set an example to others. The analogy to the criminal justice system, under which laws, procedures, and punishments are applied to reduce or eliminate unacceptable behaviour in the wider society, is difficult to avoid. So, too, is the ongoing debate between those who favour harsher and more coercive punishments, and those who believe that an interest in understanding why people engage in criminal activities is the only way to develop more effective ways of dealing with such behaviour, based on prevention and education rather than punishment.

In fact, the word 'discipline' has its roots in the word 'disciple' and implies teaching or training. From this perspective, managers and employees might view disciplinary procedures as a mechanism for solving serious behavioural problems rather than as some sort of stick with which managers can beat or punish their employees. Of course, the reality for the majority of organizations is that a dual strategy, combining elements of both approaches, is likely to be seen as the most effective approach. This approach should neither be too 'hard' nor too 'soft', although the relative weight given to each is likely to vary in ways that reflect organizational values, management philosophy, and experience. Many progressive organizations are trying to shift the balance to prevention and resolving issues early and informally wherever possible.

The idea that the choice of 'HR' instruments or approaches to people management problems must be heavily influenced by their relative effectiveness in delivering the required outcomes is an argument made throughout this book. In the case of disciplining employees and in the eyes of many, the model adopted by many organizations seems to be based on a wholly different relationship. According to Bingham (2014), even companies that have adopted what they call 'progressive discipline' in reality retain the essence of traditional approaches to discipline which is based on punishment, coercive training, limited communications, and inappropriate assumptions about human nature. She argues that 'progressive' discipline still involves the four-step process (verbal warning, written warning, final written warning or suspension, and termination), with HR professionals trained to end each step by delivering the not-so-hopeful refrain: 'Failure to correct the problem may result in further disciplinary action, up to and including possible termination'.

She argues that:

> The problem is that punishment is not instructive. It cannot teach a new behavior or solve a problem. You may be able to stop a person from doing something or even coerce him to act in a more desirable way, but the desired behavior will never be permanently learned unless the person recognizes the impact of the problem and takes ownership to solve it.

She believes the attraction of this model is that it avoids or limits the possibility of legal claims against the company and that compliance with the law and company policy is the objective, not the solution of problems or unacceptable behaviour. Instead, she argues for what she calls a 'respectful' approach to discipline, based on the following beliefs:

1. That because 95 per cent of employees are responsible adults (it's the bad apples or assholes that are the problem), if a problem does develop and is brought to their attention, they will want to solve it.

2. By using adult communication, showing confidence and trust, and involving the employee in finding a solution, you will get the desired results.

Table 9.1 Contrasting approaches to discipline

	Traditional discipline system	Counselling/mediation model
Goal	Discipline and procedural compliance	Problem solving and changing behaviour
Problem ownership	HR and line manager	Employee
HR mindset	Following procedure and building a case linked to punishment	Understanding what the cause of the problem is and addressing it
Outcome	Fear, anger, and resentment	Learning and a commitment to change behaviour or decision to leave

An approach based on counselling and shared management of the problem is presented in Table 9.1.

Another interesting development in the thinking about employee misconduct and discipline relates to the level of formality characterizing the process. The idea that early intervention and maintaining an informal approach for as long as is possible and appropriate is one that the joint ACAS/CIPD report on workplace trends has identified (ACAS/CIPD, 2015). Dix, writing in section 3 of the report says:

> The whole idea of informality—having a quiet word before any disciplinary or grievance proce-dures kick in—requires line managers to be able to use their own personal discretion in the way they handle individual problems. Unfortunately . . . centralised HR functions are tending to favour consistency and equity over improvisation.

As the report points out, the success of an approach which values informality and early intervention by the line manager depends on whether line managers themselves have the confidence to engage in this way and have the confidence of those in HR who may be reluctant to cede control to the line. The report unfortunately found that:

> The evidence on confidence is not good. The ER article describes a 'palpable fear' amongst junior managers of 'internal criticism' should they get things wrong. And, the report states, increasing pressures to reduce absence levels, particularly in the public sector, 'have made it more difficult to adopt nuanced and informal resolutions that take into account the circumstances of each case'.
> (Saundry et al., 2016)

It's interesting that the need to show procedural compliance and a consistent approach to misconduct, while in one sense understandable, has had the effect of severely limiting the opportunities of introducing if not a different then a complementary approach to the way disciplinary cases are dealt with.

The conventional view that management needs to act firmly and fairly in dealing with acts of misconduct is one that few would argue against. HR also have to have regard for the effectiveness and proportionality in the way they respond to situations of an alleged breach of rules and standards. In other words, while disci-plining staff is necessary and inevitable in cases in which individuals 'step out of line', the reality is, however, often more complicated and challenging than this deceptively simple proposition suggests. Consider HRM Insight 9.1, which demonstrates the importance of proportionality in handling discipline.

HRM INSIGHT 9.1 The case of the Queen's Medical Centre

In a well-documented case some years ago, the Queen's Medical Centre in Nottingham, UK suspended a consultant and senior lecturer in neurosurgery, who had eighteen years' experience. The suspension resulted from an allegation that the individual had taken a second helping of soup in the restaurant without paying for it. In his defence, he stated that he had simply added more croutons to his soup. Three patients awaiting surgery on the day of suspension had their operations postponed. One week after his suspension, the brain surgeon was reinstated. The incident was featured in the national media throughout the week of his suspension, despite the surgeon's lack of willingness to comment.

A more recent case of an employee being dismissed for what seems to be a similar 'misdemeanour'—for allegedly stealing a fried egg sandwich—was reported in the *Evening Standard* (2017).

Questions

1. Why was it considered necessary to invoke the hospital's disciplinary procedure?

2. What alternative forms of action might the HR function have taken in this example?

3. What was the overall impact of this incident likely to be in terms of the conduct and standards at the Medical Centre?

4. What recommendations might the HR function make following this incident?

5. To what degree do the likely consequences following from disciplinary action need to be considered, if at all, in deciding on the appropriate action?

Now consider the issues in Student Activity 9.2 and think about the most appropriate and effective ways of dealing with the situation and resolving the issues raised.

STUDENT ACTIVITY 9.2

A manager approaches you in confidence. She feels out of her depth with working relationships in one of her teams, and needs some urgent help and advice. She has a team of six staff, all relatively senior. The team leader is new to the post, having recently been promoted. She tells her manager she needs some support in managing one of her team who constantly undermines her in meetings and doesn't follow up the tasks he has been assigned by her. She believes it is because he has little or no respect for women managers. The male staff member, a Muslim, has also contacted the manager, saying he is thinking of raising a formal grievance about his team leader. He says she makes it hard for him to attend morning prayers and makes him feel uncomfortable, making condescending remarks in the office about fasting.

The manager feels the situation is tense and believes it will spill over into disciplinary and grievance issues if something doesn't change soon.

Split into two groups and consider the questions below, then come together and explore any differences in the way you have answered the questions. What might explain any differences observed?

1. As an HR professional, what are the issues raised by the case study?

2. Again, in an HR role, what advice would you offer to resolve the situation?

3. Is the situation one of grievance and/or discipline or is it about something else?

Consequences of Poor Decisions in Handling Disciplinary Matters

In the case highlighted by HRM Insight 9.1 the decision was eventually taken not to initiate any disciplinary action against the consultant, but the damage done to his professional standing (he was, to all intents and purposes, accused of stealing), the stress and inconvenience caused to his patients, and the damage done to the hospital's reputation were all real. There is also a question of perceived fairness to employees of different status. The hospital, in this case, had established a precedent prior to this incident in dealing with similar situations, but with much more junior, and therefore less high-profile, employees. Without knowing the details and background to the case, it is difficult to comment on the motives and intentions of those who took the decision to suspend the consultant, but it can be seen as an example of a response that is almost pre-programmed. The stimulus, in this case, was the accusation of wrongdoing and this immediately triggered the formal response to 'invoke procedure'. This arguably excessive, and potentially dangerous, reliance on a predetermined course of action may be attractive in terms of its consistency and formal rationality, but it does raise serious questions about the exercise of managerial judgement and the role of HR in the decision-making process. Above all, it raises questions about the kind of organizational environment that elevates simple mistakes or relatively minor breaches of organizational rules to the status of major incidents.

The importance of an organization's environment to the frequency and management of both disciplinary and grievance cases cannot be overstated (Rollinson et al., 1996). Consider these two very different statements, which relate to the making of mistakes: 'If you make a mistake in this place, you get fired'; 'People should be able to work in a blame-free environment, where mistakes are both tolerated and encouraged.' Of course, these two statements, based on different student experiences of work placements, reflect two extreme points on a continuum of managerial tolerance and discretionary behaviour. The mid-point would be an organizational environment that has a balanced, and arguably more sensible, approach to mistakes. Choices exist as to how individual organizations decide on the general principles they use to determine the way in which they approach cases of misconduct. A number of organizations now have adopted a 'no blame', 'fair blame', or a 'just culture' approach, the aim being to encourage transparency and to help employees feel safe in admitting to or knowing about mistakes. The rationale behind this approach to discipline is that it encourages openness which facilitates organizational learning without which improvements in systems, procedures, and changes in behaviour are unlikely to happen (Boysen, 2013).

The concept of mistakes is, however, more problematic than it may often seem. Mistakes differ in relation to their severity and consequences; many are the result of employees trying to do things differently and better, and errors or mistakes that result from this type of situation are often necessary parts of the learning experience. Clearly, disciplining a person who is acting in the best interests of the organization, however misguided, is probably not the most appropriate managerial response. But where behaviour is wilful, goes against clear operating procedures and standards, and has serious negative consequences, describing this also as 'a mistake' fails to do justice to the differences in the two situations.

Unconventional Approaches to Discipline at Work

In the Online Resources Extension Material 1.1 we referred to the distinctive features of the Men's Wearhouse, a US clothing company started by George Zimmer, which stands out from many other clothing retailers because of its distinctive philosophy of management, values, and employment practices. It also represents a company that takes a rather unconventional approach to misconduct and discipline: the distinctive philosophy of its founder shapes the way in which individual acts of misconduct are interpreted and managed. O'Reilly and Pfeffer (2000) are concerned with how great companies achieve extraordinary results with ordinary people. They use the Men's Wearhouse to illustrate the point that its success is not because of tight hierarchical and financial controls or performance management systems, but rather because of its values and philosophy.

This commitment to creating an environment through which successful business and customer satisfaction emerges from satisfied and 'turned-on' employees means that the company puts its people first. But O'Reilly and Pfeffer found that the company drew on a pool of labour that was not always the 'best', recruited staff who had personal problems and difficulties, and those who may have had limited educational and achievement experiences. The implication is that some of the company's employees would 'break the rules', which, in most other organizations, would result in disciplinary action being taken. In the Men's

Wearhouse, however, an action such as stealing would not necessarily result in dismissal. The company's executive vice president for human development explains this rather surprising position:

> what George has seen . . . are people who have never been treated particularly well, and that when you treat them well and give them a second and sometimes a third chance, even when they've ripped off a pair of socks, even when they've taken a deposit and put it into their pocket and not returned it for several days . . . you try to re-educate the person . . . We've looked at how to help ourselves and other people get better than most of the world thought we could ever be.
> (O'Reilly and Pfeffer, 2000)

The obvious question that emerges from this brief account of the attitude towards employee behaviour and discipline at the Men's Wearhouse is 'why?' Why does its management accept behaviour that would lead other companies immediately towards disciplinary action? O'Reilly and Pfeffer believe that the answer lies in the way such an approach generates a strong and sustained sense of reciprocation. They argue that:

> By exceeding people's expectations concerning the chances they will be given, the dignity and respect with which they will be treated, and the opportunities they will have, the company builds an incredible sense of loyalty and commitment.

In other words, there is a 'payoff'. By not taking action that would be considered by others to be both legitimate and appropriate, the company's management is able to generate a powerful and sustainable response in terms of positive attitudes and performance-enhancing behaviours that would be difficult to achieve by other means. Paradoxically, choosing not to discipline someone in circumstances under which management would be entitled to do so can result in outcomes that are highly valued and, indeed, necessary for the long-term success of the organization. Of course, this is not about 'unending forgiveness' but rather one that sees most examples of misconduct as being redeemable, where the person involved can be given the opportunity to learn and change and in the process become a better person and a better employee. It is difficult to know in the UK whether such an approach characterizes all but a very few organizations, but efforts to keep allegations of misconduct informal for as long as possible suggest that some elements of the Men's Wearhouse approach may be more prevalent than thought.

One of the key learning points that arises from the way the company deals with mistakes and misconduct is that its approach reflects a wider set of values and beliefs about its employees and how they should be managed. The Men's Wearhouse, despite its recent merger and the replacement of Zimmer as CEO, still rose to number 50 in the *Fortune* 100 best companies to work for in America in 2013, based to a large extent on the ability to bring to life the following employee-centred corporate culture. This is what Doug Ewart, President and CEO said:

> Trust and respect are the cornerstones of our philosophy; our collective honesty, sincerity, integrity, responsiveness, authenticity, mutual goodwill, and caring for each other will allow us individually and as a company to achieve maximum success. They are also the cornerstones of our values; nurturing creativity, growing together, admitting to mistakes, promoting a happy and healthy lifestyle, enhancing a sense of community, and striving toward becoming self-actualized people. This Code of Business Conduct will help you ensure that these core values, our mission, and our integrity are internalized and perpetuated as we grow individually and as a company.

See the Men's Wearhouse company philosophy and code of conduct.

Admitting mistakes—encouraging openness

Part of the Men's Wearhouse mission statement refers to 'admitting our mistakes' and it is this that provides a link to our second example of unconventional approaches to misconduct and discipline. It is taken from chapter 5 of Jerry Harvey's seminal work *The Abeline Paradox* (1988). In this chapter, Harvey tells the story of 'Captain Asoh and the Concept of Grace'; this account of motives, intent, honesty, genuine mistakes, and the power of forgiveness is summarized as follows.

Captain Asoh was the pilot of a Japanese airliner that landed in line with the runway at San Francisco airport but, unfortunately, 2.5 miles short, out in the Bay. No one was injured and very little damage was done, but a serious mistake had been made and those culpable needed to be identified and if appropriate punished. At a resulting inquiry, at which all of those who were involved in the incident attended, Asoh took the stand first and was asked by the chief investigator how he had managed to land his plane in the sea, rather than at the airport. To this, he replied: 'As you Americans say, Asoh, he f*** up!'

His admission of personal responsibility, refusal to attach blame to others, and honesty were both surprising and unexpected, to the point that the investigation had little more to do than tidy up the technical details. Perhaps people are not encouraged or supposed to display such characteristics in contemporary organizations, but the question that remained to be answered was: 'What do we do with Captain Asoh?'

Harvey's reference to this story is rooted in his earlier observation that, while it is now generally recognized that organizations need people who are prepared to take risks and, in the process, possibly make mistakes (on the grounds that, if you don't make mistakes, you are unlikely to have tried anything of significance), the managers of these organizations and those who support the managers (HR) aren't actually very good at forgiving those who make genuine mistakes or when things don't work out as intended! As a consequence of the fear of being found out and being criticized and punished, people at all levels become very adept at concealing the truth from others, and often from themselves, to the point at which it is difficult to distinguish truth from lies. Asoh was different, because he told the truth as he saw it, he didn't try to blame someone else, and he didn't lie. We know why this behaviour is not as common as it arguably should be—but why is it important at all? Harvey's argument is that the truth is important because it provides the basis for human connection. It relieves our alienation from one another and prevents us from being psychologically separated from those upon whom we lean for basic emotional support, which, he believes, is a fundamental human need and is characteristic of a healthy psychological state.

One of the interesting things about Asoh's admission that he made a mistake and his being prepared to accept personal responsibility for this is, according to Harvey, an increasingly rare phenomenon. The heart of the Captain Asoh story is not only about the acceptance of personal responsibility and honesty, but also about the reactions of those who were sitting in judgement over his wrongdoing. According to Harvey, what Asoh provided was an opportunity for these people to apply something that seems to be singularly absent from many organizations today: forgiveness. This can be thought of as 'the willingness to give up resentment, and in its highest form, the extension of grace', which is defined as 'forgiveness raised to the highest level in the form of unmerited favour' (Harvey, 1988).

So why should Asoh have been forgiven? There are two key reasons. First, because he was honest enough to admit his mistake—he was an excellent employee with an unblemished record and he never intended to cause harm or danger to anyone, so what purpose would have been served by punishing him? His competence to continue flying may need to have been tested but what purpose would have been served by firing him? Would it have prevented similar mistakes being made? Second, the act of forgiveness is also an act of giving, and giving is a particularly human need and characteristic. The act of forgiving is, therefore, an act of altruism from which both parties gain.

The story of Captain Asoh (and it is unclear even to Harvey whether it is apocryphal or not) often produces quite diverse reaction among those who are familiar with it. For some, the references to forgiveness, the extension of grace, and altruistic behaviour have little relevance to HR as it tries to shed its humanist/welfare traditions along the road towards 'a seat at the top table' and strives to increase its contribution to the 'bottom line'. Harvey, on the other hand, would consider this to be a mistake for two reasons. Altruism is an experience that is fundamentally human and good, as well as deeply satisfying to the giver, but it is also an essential requirement for survival. As Harvey puts it, 'cultures that lack the capacity for altruistic forgiveness and grace die' or at least become dysfunctional and increasingly limited and ineffective. But there is a more pragmatic reason: as we said above, forgiving and giving creates a reciprocal reaction from those in receipt. The sense of gratitude generated when someone in authority does not exercise the right to discipline and punish, or when management decides to give someone a second chance, can be a very powerful experience for those directly involved. It can also be the basis of an enhanced sense of obligation—the desire to show that the decision was the right one—and it can result in new, and stronger, personal relationships. These are the very outcomes that are associated with a high-commitment, high-performance environment. But such a policy is not without risk! What if Captain Asoh had been given a second chance and allowed to continue to fly and had another accident which killed people? In contemporary organizations, few situations will mirror that of a pilot flying an airliner so the consequences of that kind of mistake are highly unlikely to be experienced, which means that the risks associated with a more tolerant and learning-orientated response towards genuine mistakes and people trying new things that don't quite work out the first time, may be far less than the benefits that might result.

For information on the Civil Aviation Authority's approach to pilot error in the UK, see Parker (2012).

STUDENT ACTIVITY 9.3

Read the *Harvard Business Review* article by Campbell et al. (1985) 'Discipline without punishment—At last'.

The basic premise of the article is that punishing people rarely achieves changes in behaviour and the constant use of discipline as an instrument of change or retribution may not be as effective as people believe. After reading the article, consider whether such an approach to discipline as it advocates could work or whether it is idealistic and will eventually fail. The exercise could be undertaken in the form of a debate between two parties, one advocating the traditional approach and the other that articulated by Campbell et al., with the tutor summarizing the respective arguments and providing feedback.

A More Conventional Approach to Misconduct

Despite raising legitimate questions about the purpose, form, and effectiveness of more traditional disciplinary practices, it would be unrealistic to argue against the necessity of some form of institutional framework and procedural regulation to help to manage cases of misconduct or poor performance, even for the most forward-looking and employee-centred organization. The reasons for this are linked to:

● the existence of more prescriptive legislative provision in the field of employee rights, employer responsibilities, and procedural requirements. This means that all organizations need to develop a reliable and defensible capability for dealing with cases of discipline and grievance;

● the constant pressure to increase performance at the individual and organizational level has led many organizations to view 'poor or unacceptable performance', linked to absence, failure to meet performance targets, and general 'bloody-mindedness', as potential cases of misconduct, with the implication that more, rather than fewer, cases will need to be dealt with;

● societal changes in what is considered acceptable behaviour, with respect to language, attitudes, and how people at work generally behave towards others, and the imposition of new standards and norms governing social interaction;

● the ACAS Code of Practice on Discipline and Grievance (2015b) which sets out principles for handling disciplinary and grievance situations in the workplace. It came into effect on 11 March 2015, replacing the code issued in 2009. Employment tribunals will take the code into account when considering relevant cases.

As a consequence of these influences, people's behaviour and conduct at work has become increasingly subject to more prescriptive normative frameworks and procedures that are designed to deal with breaches in these norms. For the majority of employees, and in most circumstances, such standards will be known and complied with. In other cases, in which conduct falls short of established standards, or in which action

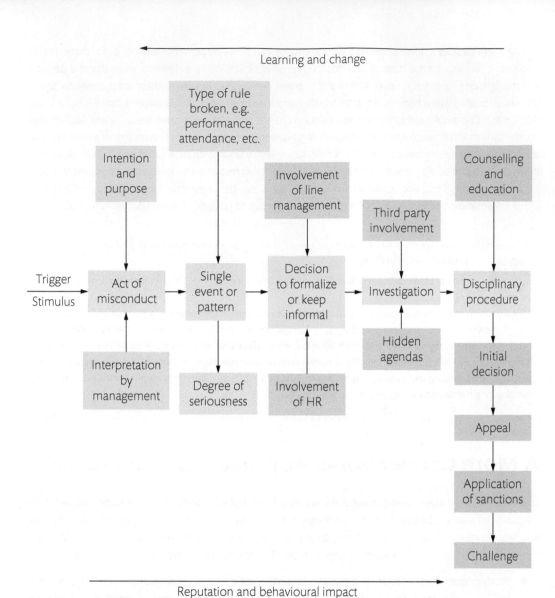

Figure 9.1 A model of the disciplinary process

such as educational and training provision has been used in preference to formal disciplinary proceedings and has failed to produce the desired effect, the need for effective ways of dealing with misconduct becomes necessary, and it to this that we now turn (Younson, 2002). Figure 9.1 represents a typical model of the disciplinary process.

RESEARCH INSIGHT 9.1

To take your learning further, you might want to read:

Saundry, R. and Wibberley, G. (2012) 'Managing individual conflict in the private sector: A case study' (iROWE, Lancashire Business School).

This paper offers detailed insights into workplace conflicts and disagreements and the approach taken by the company in question to develop a coherent and effective grievance and disciplinary system. After reading it, consider what some of its key findings and applications are and whether they would be helpful to all organizations.

The Relationship between Minor and Major Breaches in Standards

Figure 9.2 shows the relationship between minor and major breaches of standards at work and the relationship between the seriousness of the incident and formality of the response. For every major breach in standards, resulting in either dismissal or action short of dismissal, there will be more minor breaches of behavioural standards and rules, which are formally addressed. There will in turn be more minor incidents involving standards addressed informally and even more incidents of non-conformity that go either unnoticed or unaddressed. The longer these are allowed to continue, the more management, by its own act of omission (i.e. by doing nothing), legitimizes them. Early intervention, almost inevitably by the appropriate line manager, is important to provide guidance and interpretation of the status of the action or behaviour, and helps to resolve any uncertainties over its acceptability and seriousness. In a number of cases, minor breaches of conduct can escalate to more serious concerns if, during the course of investigation, the employee tries to 'cover up' the mistake or fails to show any recognition of the legitimacy of managerial concerns. From a policy perspective, while minor breaches and infringements may not need to be dealt with formally, not responding at all sends the wrong message and can be counterproductive.

We have presented the argument that the key to managing misconduct successfully is to address standards of compliance/non-compliance at the informal and minor level to prevent any escalation in the frequency or seriousness of the problem and that ignoring or, even worse, condoning and tacitly supporting wrongdoing and rule breaking will only result in the situation becoming more serious. If an organization is over-reliant on the use of formal procedures to address conduct, this suggests that the standards and objectives of the organization are not being made clear and that the existing culture encourages non-compliance across the board. Again, we can see the importance of the organizational environment to the patterns of misconduct and to management responses to these.

As indicated earlier, the need to invoke formal disciplinary procedures can be indicative of other issues within an organization and might reflect, for example, poor recruitment and selection practices, lack of training and development, unfair pay and reward structures, or poor communications and employee relations. It may also reflect key characteristics of the labour force, such as position in the hierarchy, the type of work carried out, and the degree to which people work in what might be described as a 'factory or canteen

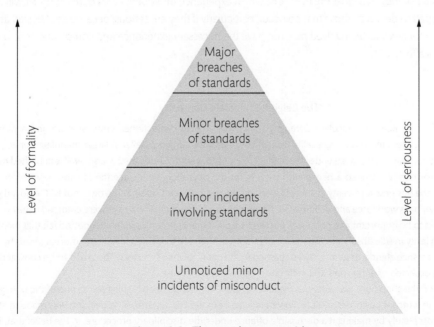

Figure 9.2 The conduct pyramid

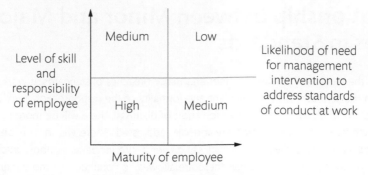

Figure 9.3 The correlation of disciplinary cases with employee skill/responsibility and maturity

culture' or where there is a kind of unseen (except to a few) subculture existing which condones illegal or questionable management practices. These terms are meant to cover any working environment in which employees have a more instrumental attitude to work, often involving less skilled or manually based work, in which employees and management perceive themselves to be in an adversarial relationship, or where there is a strong sense of loyalty and identification with fellow employees, such as in the police force. The greater the extent to which employees identify with the position of management and the wider interests of the organization, the less the likelihood of employees deliberately engaging in misconduct. As far as developing effective strategies for dealing with misconduct are concerned, this hypothesis offers a way forward that is not limited to using procedures to manage the misconduct but includes its prevention.

Figure 9.3 demonstrates how the extent to which management relies upon its formal disciplinary procedures will depend upon the make-up of an organization. Organizations employing younger employees to carry out roles requiring lower skills are likely to experience more disciplinary issues than those employing more mature and longer serving employees in jobs that require higher levels of skill and responsibility. This means that the frequency and seriousness of disciplinary cases is likely to be strongly correlated to the demographic characteristics of the workforce, knowledge of which can help management to pre-empt patterns of misconduct and to take appropriate preventative action. But as the cases of Rolls-Royce (Williams, 2017) and Enron, which we considered in Chapter 1, indicate, more serious, although fewer, cases of misconduct are likely to be associated with senior management personnel.

There is a risk, however, that organizations which experience infrequent cases of misconduct will be less well equipped to deal with those that do occur, particularly if they are serious, because the HR staff and line managers who need to be involved may not have the necessary experience and competencies to manage these cases effectively.

HRM INSIGHT 9.2 The Belgian Chocolate Company

The Belgian Chocolate Company (BCC) was a small confectioner, employing around a hundred people to produce speciality Belgian chocolates for a major retailer. A larger manufacturer acquired it, and the company was placed under the management of Townends Chocolates, a large, well-established manufacturer. Townends recruited a new plant manager for the operation, to replace the previous owner who had managed the business for twenty years before selling the company and retiring. The owner of BCC enjoyed good relations with his workforce and a culture had developed in which not all works rules were enforced if they weren't considered to be important and necessary. But the new plant manager took a different line and felt that there was too much laxity in rule observance on the factory floor. He intended to introduce new and more rigorous hygiene and performance standards as already established in the main Townends factory. There had to be consistence in what was expected of employees and in the enforcement of works rules.

Eating on the shop floor was a serious hygiene concern, which had been highlighted as one of the unhygienic practices in a recent customer audit. Following advice from the HR department a decision was made to stamp this out completely by making it a dismissible offence under the disciplinary procedure, in the belief that, if the consequences were so severe, then the behaviour would stop immediately. The Townends management team briefed the whole workforce by attaching a notice to their wage slips—and was shocked when the first offender was caught eating in the factory only days later. In the subsequent disciplinary hearing, the reason given was that sampling product on the shop floor had been standard practice for years to ensure the quality of the product. The staff representative in attendance stated that this was no more serious than office staff failing to wash their hands on each re-entry into the factory from the office area, which was a regular occurrence.

The plant manager issued a final written warning due to the mitigating reasons given and sent a further brief, via wage slips, that eating on the shop floor for any reason and failure to wash hands on entering factory areas would constitute dismissible offences. Several days later, the plant manager witnessed the staff representative entering the factory from the office without washing her hands. She was taken into the office for an investigation and was suspended pending a disciplinary hearing. When she informed a colleague later that evening of what had taken place, a petition was signed by the majority of employees, and submitted to the plant manager, that threatened that they would 'down tools' unless their staff representative was reinstated.

Questions

1. Why was this case not quite as straightforward as it might seem to be?

2. Is the enforcement of works rules only about the use of discipline?

3. What fundamental assumptions did the HR department and the new management team make?

4. In the context of change management, what should HR and the works manager have done to achieve a more successful transition to the desired state of employee behaviour?

 Insights and Outcomes: visit the **online resources** at **www.oup.com/uk/banfield3e/** to find out details about what actually happened and how this situation was handled.

Disciplinary Procedures and the Role of the Law

The need to have disciplinary procedures is determined by ACAS codes of practice, which were first introduced in the 1970s and have been updated at regular intervals.

Most larger organizations have established disciplinary procedures that are in line with the ACAS guidelines, which recommend, among other things, that a disciplinary procedure is made up of several stages or warnings. Under the recommendations, if an employee is involved in a minor breach of work rules, in the first instance, the employer is advised to address what is essentially a minor problem through informal conversations. If this fails to improve standards, the formal warnings can be used progressively. The minimum standards in the 2015 ACAS code of practice which were put in place when the Statutory Discipline and Grievance Procedures (set out by the Employment Act 2002) were repealed, must be complied with by all organizations, and tribunals are legally obliged to take this into account when considering cases. For example, employers must offer employees the right to be accompanied to a disciplinary hearing by a work colleague or duly accredited union representative. In these circumstances, employees can insist that disciplinary proceedings are delayed by up to five days to allow arrangements for their chosen representative to be present at the hearing.

The additional recommendations from ACAS no longer include the recommendation for a formal verbal warning stage that was in place prior to 2002. Instead, they place a stronger emphasis on the use of informal action wherever possible to resolve issues and encourage employers to consider the use of mediation to resolve disputes in the workplace. This more recent emphasis on not escalating matters for relatively minor breaches or failings is shown by the following advice given to employers by ACAS:

> Cases of minor misconduct or unsatisfactory performance are usually best dealt with informally. A quiet word is often all that is required to improve an employee's conduct or performance. In some cases additional training, coaching and advice may be what is needed. An informal approach may be particularly helpful in small firms, where problems can be resolved quickly and confidentially.

There will be situations where matters are more serious or where an informal approach has been tried but is not working.
(ACAS, 2015b: 10)

 See Online Resources Extension Material 9.1 for information on stages in the disciplinary process.

Gross misconduct

'Gross misconduct' is the term used to describe breaches of standards and rules that are serious and unacceptable in any circumstances. Gross misconduct is behaviour on the part of the employee, that is so serious that it destroys the relationship of trust between the employer and the employee. If a case of gross misconduct is identified, the likelihood is that, if the investigation provides evidence that supports the charge, the individual will face dismissal even though it may be his or her first offence. Examples of offences given by ACAS that can be regarded as gross misconduct are:

- theft or fraud;
- physical violence or bullying;
- deliberate and serious damage to property;
- serious misuse of organization's property or name;
- deliberately accessing internet sites containing pornographic, offensive, or obscene material;
- serious insubordination;
- unlawful discrimination or harassment;
- bringing the organization into serious disrepute;
- serious incapability at work brought on by alcohol or illegal drugs;
- causing loss, damage, or injury through serious negligence;
- a serious breach of health and safety rules;
- a serious breach of confidence.

What constitutes acts of gross misconduct can be determined by individual organizations in the light of their particular circumstances and requirements. Examples should be incorporated into employee handbooks or made known to employees in other appropriate ways. As in all cases of discipline, procedural regularity and the reasonableness of management's action will be the criteria used by an employment tribunal in the event of a subsequent claim for unfair dismissal brought by the individual concerned.

 For discussion about record keeping and the question of witness confidentiality see the Online Resources Extension Materials 9.2 and 9.3.

 STUDENT ACTIVITY 9.4

Read the briefing paper by Pinsent Masons (employment lawyers) entitled 'Dismissing for misconduct: The difference between "gross" and "serious" misconduct' (2012), available at: http://www.pinsentmasons.com/Documents/e-bulletin/Employment/2012-07-27.html
Discuss within the group the differences between the two and try to think of examples of behaviour that can be categorized as gross or serious misconduct.

The role of HR and line managers

The exact role of HR and line managers in carrying out disciplinary procedures varies between organizations (Rollinson et al., 1996). HR can be present in an active role, either as the party responsible for leading the investigation or the party taking the disciplinary action. In other organizations, one, or both, of these roles may be performed by a line manager and a more senior manager, with HR taking more of an advisory role, either within the meeting or independent from the meeting. There is no correct way of doing things. In SMEs, which are unlikely to have a dedicated HR function, the use of external HR consultants and/or employment lawyers working with the owner or MD is a more likely model. It is, however, advisable to have at least two representatives present, to divide the roles of leading the investigation and making the disciplinary decision, so that there is a degree of impartiality in the decision-making process. Many organizations specify in their disciplinary procedures who will be in attendance, at what level, and in what capacity. For example, a larger organization may wish to involve a more senior level of manager in more serious offences, for which the consequences of making an incorrect decision are wider reaching. But, ideally, the investigations should be distinct from the hearing and should involve different parties.

In what they describe as an important but under-researched aspect of workplace discipline, Saundry and Jones (2010) found that in all the organizations they looked at as part of the research project, responsibility for investigations, disciplinary hearings, and disciplinary decisions rested with line and operational management. The role of HR professionals was to provide advice on the application of procedure and the legal and organizational implications of disciplinary decisions. They also found that most operational managers saw HR practitioners as providing a degree of objectivity and fair play in disciplinary proceedings which suggests that they are aware of the importance of ensuring procedural fairness in the process.

Interestingly, their research suggested that those working in HR did not necessarily align with the managers they were advising. There was a general view that if left to their own devices, line and operational managers would be prone to procedural irregularities and inconsistent decisions that would leave the organization vulnerable to legal action. HR professionals saw their job more in terms of protecting the interests of the 'organization', ensuring its reputation was not threatened by harmful publicity over 'botched' dismissals or prolonged and unsuccessful tribunal cases. Working with line managers didn't appear to mean being subordinate to them in cases where procedure was not applied in the way intended. On the other hand, it may be that HR does work closely with line managers to ensure that employees who have become unsuitable, problematic, or wish to leave and move on are managed out of the organization in a sensible and agreed way, supported in most cases by a financial settlement.

> **KEY CONCEPT Settlement agreements (known as compromise agreements before 29 July 2013)**
>
> A settlement agreement is a legally binding agreement signed by both parties which formally brings to an end the contract of employment on specific terms that must be agreed by both parties. It is recognized by statute and is the only way you can validly waive your employment law rights. It usually provides for a severance payment, in return for which you agree not to pursue any claim or grievance you may have in an employment tribunal.

According to Landau (2011), employers have for many years used compromise agreements as a mechanism for preventing possible future complaints to an industrial tribunal and to resolve disciplinary cases, although they are also used to facilitate more senior employees leaving the organization on equitable terms. The major reasons for using the compromise agreement (other than to settle an existing claim) are to remove an employee on the grounds of poor performance or misconduct, to avoid legal challenge in redundancy situations, and to make it easier to remove senior staff without embarrassment. There is an argument that employers can 'buy off' a person's employment rights and this is of course what is fundamentally involved. On the other hand, the individual may be prepared to accept a substantial and tax-free payment, without damage to his/her reputation, rather than go through the stressful and uncertain process of an industrial tribunal claim (Martin Searle Solicitors).

One other aspect of the way discipline was seen differently by HR and the line manager is, according to Saundry and Jones (2010), over flexibility. We mentioned earlier that keeping disciplinary cases within the informal domain for as long as possible—a position endorsed by ACAS—ran the risk of inconsistencies arising in the way different cases are handled. Their research highlighted this issue, but with line managers being associated with a more flexible approach to the application of disciplinary procedures in cases where the 'offence' was, for them, not particularly serious, and HR appearing to favour a more consistent approach.

> **For HR professionals, however, such approaches, (flexibility) opened up a 'pandora's box' of nepotism and inequity with far reaching organizational and legal implications.**

What the report also makes clear, is that the actual approach taken to discipline not only reflects cultural variables but the status, experience, and the kind of relationship HR has with line managers who are the main decision makers.

> **Our research certainly suggested that a combination of inexperienced HR managers and a new generation of operational managers who lack the knowledge and confidence to deal with issues informally, was tending to strengthen the dominance of formal procedure. This was exacerbated where the HR function was remote (both physically and organizationally) from the workplace. Here, HR professionals had little knowledge of the work process and the workforce and had no emotional stake in the outcome of disciplinary decisions. In such cases, the key determinant inevitably became the rigid application of consistency.**

We might suggest, therefore, that the question of maturity and experience of both HR and managers, and particularly the relationship they have will be significant factors in the way disciplinary cases are handled and resolved, and arguably in respect of the fairness and acceptability, in the outcomes of these cases.

The above quotation points to an interesting paradox within HR, one we identified earlier. HR, despite its association with people and the people management function, can in fact become detached from the human dimension of work, lack any real understanding of employees as people, and act more as a centralized instrument of procedural regulation and conformity. The Practitioner Insight focuses on disciplinary processes and line manager involvement with HR and offers some support for the argument developed above.

PRACTITIONER INSIGHT Katy Edmonds, HR Manager, IFA Ltd, founded in 2001

At Independent Forgings and Alloys Ltd, we have around 120 employees and it is very rare that we need to use formal disciplinary procedures. I have worked in larger organizations where line managers are not as confident and were therefore over-reliant on using disciplinary procedures to enforce rules and standards and needed much more support and intervention from HR to do so. More of my work in this area now involves coaching and supporting line managers to identify problems early on and to nip them in the bud. I find that managers' behaviour is more important in maintaining standards than having an effective disciplinary procedure. If you've got good managers, you rarely need to use formal disciplinary procedures as they will set clear standards and identify potential problems early on and deal with them informally before problems escalate.

When it comes to grievances again having approachable managers helps avoid disputes escalating. If someone has a concern that could potentially be a problem this is best dealt with quickly at the lowest possible level. Where there is a problem and it is not possible to meet the employee's expectations it can be helpful for the employee to speak to their manager's manager and this may need a more formal process. When grievances arise, this tends to be where employees are not happy about a proposed change and it is often possible to be flexible to try and accommodate employees. It is helpful to have an open mind and to make sure the employee feels they have been listened to. It also helps if managers have the maturity to be ready to change their mind in the face of good evidence rather than being belligerent.

RESEARCH INSIGHT 9.2

To take your learning further, you might want to read:

Royles, D. and Kapur, N. (2016) 'A new way forward for disciplinaries', *Health Service Journal*, **28 June.**

This article, by an NHS HR director and a whistle-blower, provides contrasting views on reforming disciplinary procedures in the NHS and points to the challenges and opportunities of reforming disciplinary practices in a large and complex bureaucratic organization.

Appeals

Under the ACAS code of practice, employees must be given the right of appeal when dismissed, or where action is taken short of dismissal. In fact, failure to offer the right of appeal may result in a tribunal finding a dismissal to be automatically unfair, that is, making such a decision regardless of the merits of the case. The ACAS code of practice states that the right of appeal should be offered with all formal warnings. Procedures will often have a time limit and will state that the appeal must be in writing. Usually organizations, for clarity, will have a clear appeal process rather than rely on their grievance procedure as the mechanism for submitting appeals. Appeals should be dealt with speedily and, wherever possible, should be heard at a meeting by a person with greater authority than whoever took the original decision. If this is not possible, the appeal should nonetheless be as impartial a meeting as possible. The purpose is to hear grounds for appeal, paying particular attention to new evidence. If the original decision is felt to be unfair or unreasonable, it should be overturned—although it would be idealistic to suggest that the decision on appeal is not, occasionally, influenced by other considerations.

279

Managing Specific Types of Behaviour

There are certain specific types of 'new' behaviours that have become increasingly prominent in the contemporary workplace for which disciplinary action is often considered not only appropriate but necessary. We mentioned harassment and bullying earlier as examples of a growing contemporary phenomenon experienced by people at work. Where a formal complaint of harassment or bullying is made or comes to the attention of the organization, disciplinary action up to and including dismissal may be necessary. The point to make here is that both forms of unacceptable behaviour are rarely isolated events but more continuing patterns of behaviour which in one sense are more serious precisely because they are likely to be experienced over time.

In these circumstances while it is the perception of the victim that constitutes harassment—and here it is important to state that both are experienced subjectively—an investigation will need to be conducted to establish what has taken place and whether, if at all, formal action is needed to address these kinds of inappropriate behaviour. The problem is, with bullying in particular, the same language and behaviour used by a manager for example would for certain people be seen as within acceptable limits but by others as going well beyond what could be considered reasonable. Much therefore depends on people's tolerance levels and what an organization sets as its standards.

It is advisable to have separate harassment policies in place alongside disciplinary procedures to deal with harassment and bullying, and some organizations go further by developing 'dignity at work' policies and procedures to manage both the expectation of the organization and in dealing with behaviour that breaches these guidelines.

According to the CIPD (2016), the Equality Act 2010 defines harassment as:

unwanted conduct related to a relevant protected characteristic, which has the purpose or effect of violating an individual's dignity or creating an intimidating, hostile, degrading, humiliating or offensive environment for that individual

Bullying is not specifically defined in law but ACAS (2015c) defines bullying as:

> Behaviour which . . . may be characterised as offensive, intimidating, malicious or insulting behaviour, an abuse or misuse of power through means intended to undermine, humiliate, denigrate or injure the recipient.

These two definitions are clearly very similar and it is arguable that the two terms represent different kinds of behaviour.

The problem with both kinds of behaviour lies in their inherent subjectivity although in extreme cases there is unlikely to be much doubt about the validity of accusations. In many other cases, in the absence of clear and comprehensive guidelines and standards, proving that someone has been harassed or bullied is potentially challenging.

Another area where it is advisable to have separate policies in place is misconduct relating to the use of alcohol or illegal drugs. Organizations will wish to have rules in place making it clear that it is unacceptable for employees to report to work under the influence of alcohol or illegal drugs. However, employees have a right to privacy under the Human Rights Act (1998) which extends to being tested for the presence of either alcohol or drugs. A clear policy can help make it clear when testing might be requested and what action might be taken should any employee refuse to comply with such a request. There may also be occasions where it is appropriate and reasonable to suspend disciplinary processes to allow an employee time to take professional advice and undergo rehabilitation to encourage those with difficulties to be open about seeking help and sorting out their problems. Many organizations will treat employees who have drug or alcohol dependency as matters of capability, dealing with the problem under the employer's sickness and capability procedures; it becomes a medical rather than a disciplinary issue. Employees in particular industries and occupations such as an airline pilot who attend work under the influence of drugs or alcohol are much more likely to be subject to immediate disciplinary procedures for obvious reasons.

Absence Management

Absence is considered in more detail in Chapter 10 but in the context of measurement not as a potential disciplinary issue. According to the Confederation for British Industry (CBI) (2013) absence from work cost the UK economy £14 billion in 2012. The average employee took 5.3 days' sickness absence during the year; absenteeism was higher in the public sector at seven days per year. The control and management of employee absence is therefore an important role for both the line manager and HR practitioner as organizations cannot afford to fail to take steps to ensure that it is kept to the minimum level possible. Employees' absence can be controlled using either disciplinary or capability procedures linked to distinct absence management procedures. But it is worth noting that most sickness absence from work is not work-related. According to the Black and Frost Report (2011) only around one-fifth of working days lost to sickness absence are work-related (around 22 million days due to work-related ill health and a further 4.4 million to workplace injury). By implication, the causes of this form of absence are linked to extraneous factors which may not be easily addressed through disciplinary procedures, although the consequences for organizations of persistent absence can be particularly damaging for small businesses.

 Signpost to Chapter 10: Workforce Planning and Measurement, for further insights into absence issues.

Organizations are also increasingly investing in health and well-being initiatives to improve employee health and avoid and reduce sickness absence. The basic premise is that while it may be unavoidable for employees to take time off due to illness from time to time, organizations can monitor and review absence. Where levels are high, action can be taken, as the employee is not capable of fulfilling their contractual obligation to attend work on a regular basis. Under UK legislation as long as the employer follows a fair procedure and takes all reasonable steps to support an employee to attend regularly then ultimately an employee may be fairly dismissed for sustained poor attendance.

As an example of how organizations approach absence, Rolls-Royce developed a new sickness absence management policy that has benefited employees and the company by reducing absence and the associated costs. Before the initiative, staff sickness absence levels varied from around 3 per cent to 9 per cent. Rolls-Royce calculated that if it could reduce absence levels by 10 per cent it would make significant savings. Key to its policy were the following initiatives:

- Implementing a company-wide absence management policy, explaining the responsibilities of managers, human resources, and occupational health advisers.

- Early rehabilitation. Anyone absent for more than four weeks benefits from an action plan, including physiotherapy services (for both work- and non-work-related injuries).

- Introducing an IT programme that monitors employee absence, records the reasons for the absence, and calculates costs (Health and Safety Executive, 2015).

The obvious point to make about this case is that discipline doesn't feature as a key element in the company's policy, but that doesn't mean it isn't appropriate for individual cases where employees are felt to be being untruthful about their condition. According to Turner (2013):

> An employee's absence from work due to illness or injury is usually not their fault. However, there can be situations where the circumstances which caused the illness were within the employee's control, in which case the employer may be entitled to treat any further absence as a conduct issue.

In the UK, to qualify for statutory sick pay, employees are required to complete a self-certification form for absences up to one week and obtain a medical certificate for absences greater than one week. Following widespread criticism about the system in the UK over the ease with which employees can obtain the required medical certification for absences exceeding one week, a new 'fit notes' system was introduced in April 2010, allowing medical practitioners more scope to advise employers about the types of work an employee with health problems may still be fit to carry out. The Department of Work and Pensions (2013) undertook a survey of employers as an evaluation of the fit note. Of respondents, 71 per cent agreed the fit note was helpful and around half agreed it had made a difference to their employer's willingness to make changes to help them return to work.

Grievance Procedures

Grievances can be thought of as complaints made by one employee against another or against a manager and, as such, they will not normally be raised by management against an employee. While having the potential to involve breaches of company rules, they do not relate to the most common causes of disciplinary action, which often involve unacceptable performance, poor attendance, or misconduct.

The ACAS code of practice defines grievances as:

> concerns, problems or complaints that employees raise with their employers.

This may be considered too restrictive a definition in terms of the realities of employment under which it is well known for a grievance to be raised by one employee against another, or by an employee against a manager, or by a manager against a manager. Such complaints are, in effect, claims that the behaviour of one party in relation to the other is unacceptable, in that it involves unfair and discriminatory treatment, failure to act within designated procedures, or the belief that the employer has failed to meet its common law duty of care. This means that the employer must take reasonable action to protect its employees from any harmful or damaging experiences that are not an inevitable part of the occupation or environment in question. For example, a soldier accepts that the risk of injury and even death is part of what being an infantry soldier involves, but being bullied during training, being denied proper equipment in the field, or failure to ensure psychiatric care to help him or her to come to terms with the after effects of battle would be considered unacceptable and grounds for raising a grievance, or its equivalent, with the appropriate authorities. Some of these concerns, if escalated, could be covered under PIDA 1998.

As with cases of discipline, it is easy to make the mistake of seeing grievances in isolation from the social and work contexts in which they arise. Many grievances reflect what might be described as 'damaged relationships' rather than individual and isolated acts. It is well known, for example, that many employees who leave an organization often do so because of difficulties with working relationships: they don't 'leave their job', they 'leave their manager', or they leave because of the stresses of working with certain colleagues. This means that many grievances are never formally raised with management but are instead resolved by the 'aggrieved' party leaving the organization. Exit interviews can indicate whether an individual is being 'pushed out' by the inability or reluctance of management to resolve a stressful, damaging, or in some other way unacceptable situation. If HR is unaware of such situations directly or fails to use the information made available in exit interview records, the original cause of the grievance will continue to affect other relationships, with the likelihood of similar consequences continuing to occur (Wilkinson, 2007).

The need to have grievance procedures in place is governed by the ACAS codes of practice, which were first introduced in the 1970s and have been updated by ACAS at regular intervals. The ACAS code of practice lays out a process whereby, if an employee submits a grievance, this must be heard by an appropriate level of management and a response given within a reasonable time frame. The employee then has the opportunity to appeal against any decision given. Further details of codes of practice and guidelines can be obtained from the ACAS website (www.acas.org). Failure to comply with codes of practice can result in increased awards being made if a future complaint is found to be successful in an employment tribunal. These codes of practice do not govern collective disputes raised by more than one employee.

In reality, most companies have established procedures for handling employee grievances and recognize the value of handling complaints quickly and sensitively at the earliest opportunity, and of their being handled by the closest level of management to the employee who has made the complaint.

According to ACAS (2015d), the management of grievances should be based on:

- employees recognizing the importance of informing the employer that a grievance exists and what it is about;
- the appropriate line manager having informal discussions with the person who raised the grievance, in the first instance;
- moving to a formal meeting where informal resolution looks unlikely;
- allowing employees to be accompanied at any formal meeting with a representative;
- having written grievance procedures in place and available to all staff;
- the right of appeal.

Frequent causes of grievances

Most grievances can be linked to the following:

- unacceptable language and images, initiation rituals, and other forms of informal shop/office-floor behaviour;
- harassment and bullying;
- victimization and unfair discriminatory treatment;
- unreasonable and 'unlawful' requests to take certain action that might, for example, involve breaking health and safety regulations;

- failure to honour promises or obligations, for example, over the payment of bonuses or other forms of reward;

- differential application of common terms and conditions of employment.

While the basis and legitimacy of certain cases of grievance can be more readily established by looking at the 'hard' evidence, the majority are more difficult to verify simply because they involve perceptions, expectations, and different views as to what is 'acceptable'.

Consider the two following scenarios.

- The captain of a Royal Navy warship is recalled from his ship because two members of his crew have lodged complaints about his 'authoritative style of management'. The remaining crew members may have shared this grievance but not formally recorded their concerns, or may have been perfectly happy with the captain's behaviour and have considered it to be within the bounds of what could be considered 'acceptable'.

- A male manager relieves a female subordinate of responsibility for one key account on grounds that the employee has failed to meet basic performance criteria, and is subsequently accused of bullying and harassment.

Neither situation represents a clear-cut case of harassment or bullying, but it is also obvious that the possibility exists for a grievance to be brought. In the second scenario, it might be argued that the female employee lodging a grievance might have done so to protect herself from possible disciplinary action and reflects the efforts of the individual to rationalize the damaging effect that the manager's decision has had on both her self-esteem and her standing within the company. Suffice to say that some grievances have their own 'history' and complicating factors, and cannot be taken at face value. On the other hand, many grievances are made by people who genuinely feel that they have been treated wrongly by some other member of the organization and who feel that the only way to resolve the situation, apart from leaving, is to lodge a formal grievance with the line manager or HR department.

While registering a grievance invariably implies some degree of formalization, the response from the HR department, at that early stage, may not itself be formal. Much depends on the organization's general approach to such situations as well as its grievance procedure, which, since the Employment Rights Act 1996, is a legal requirement for all organizations that employ at least twenty employees. Consider the situation of a female employee of an engineering company, who works in the dispatch department with several male colleagues. She complains to her supervisor about the language used by one of her male colleagues, which she finds offensive and unacceptable. On being informed of the 'grievance', which is not yet formally registered as such, the HR officer arranges an informal meeting with the two employees to establish the 'facts' of the case. During the meeting, it transpires that the offensive language complained about was also used by the female employee to her male colleague, and that the real problem is that their personal relationship has deteriorated over time. The response of the HR officer is, metaphorically, to help them 'bury the hatchet' with a strong suggestion that they sort themselves out. Keeping the response informal not only avoids the consequences of early formalization, through which positions become entrenched, but also encourages the two parties to take responsibility for managing the problem themselves and probably results in a more satisfactory, and less damaging, outcome.

Complaints about a manager

The experience of many specialist mediators suggests that interpersonal conflict cannot always be resolved by applying formal grievance procedures, and this has led to a greater emphasis on more informal and less threatening resolution mechanisms. But the use of an informal approach to grievance resolution depends on both parties agreeing to this, which may not always be possible. As we noted above, some grievances have 'history', and relate to a number of incidents and exchanges. Interestingly, the number of grievances registered may not simply reflect an increase in incidents of interpersonal conflict, but also that organizations have failed to develop mechanisms and competences for dealing with such incidents. It may be that employers experience difficulties in managing the underlying causes of grievances because managers lack the awareness and skills to deal with this form of conflict.

RESEARCH INSIGHT 9.3

To take your learning further you might want to read the following article, which provides an interesting view on the management of discipline in the UK.

Suff, R. (2010) 'Dispute resolution survey: Managing discipline', *IRS Employment Review,* **26 April.**

Summary

- The vast majority of employees will not need to be disciplined by their employer because their performance and behaviour will be well within the bounds of what is considered appropriate and acceptable. The need to discipline someone should be, therefore, an unusual, and possibly exceptional, act.

- There will always be circumstances, however, that require an organization to take formal disciplinary measures to deal with a situation that is unacceptable. The reasons why such action is considered necessary are mainly to do with poor performance, absenteeism, and a failure to comply with works rules, such as those relating to safe working practices, along with dishonesty and behaviour that infringes the rights of others.

- Formal disciplinary procedures are typically used to address such situations, but the adoption of a more informal and flexible approach, including the use of mediation as part of a more sophisticated and less prescriptive strategy is becoming more widespread and is actively encouraged under ACAS guidelines. This is certainly the case when dealing with employee grievances.

- The role of HR in this field is to ensure that legal requirements are met, that consistency of treatment is maintained, and that employee rights are protected. But it must be recognized that this role has to go beyond the implementation of procedure. The need to explore underlying causes and influences, and, wherever possible, to address these is also an HR requirement.

- Grievances can potentially present more challenges to management and require careful investigation of all aspects of each case. Often cultural, gender, and race issues are involved. Behaviours that were acceptable in the context of a certain group of employees become less so when the demographic of the workforce changes. If grievances are individual in nature, the resolution of the complaint may be achieved more acceptably through informal processes of discussion and mediation, rather than through creating an adversarial situation by invoking formal procedure. If, however, there is a discernible pattern of grievances, for example, from female employees who are concerned about sexist behaviour, then HR is faced with a different challenge—one of influencing attitudes and changing perceptions.

- Some organizations have introduced disciplinary policies that don't involve traditional punishments. The question that needs to be asked is are these more or less effective at addressing behavioural issues than more traditional approaches? What does the evidence suggest?

Visit the **online resources** that accompany this book for self-test questions, web links, and more information on the topics covered in this chapter, at: **www.oup.com/uk/banfield3e/**

REVIEW QUESTIONS

1. What are the respective responsibilities of HR and line managers in the management of discipline and grievances?

2. What contribution might an organization's CEO make to ensure that these issues are effectively managed?

3. How does the philosophy of management affect the way in which misconduct and unacceptable behaviour is managed?

4. What are the features of a working organization environment that might be associated with low levels of misconduct and interpersonal conflict?

5. What are the advantages and limitations of relying on formal procedures to manage misconduct?

6. Under what circumstances should an informal approach to discipline and grievance be taken?

CASE STUDY   Unauthorized breaks at Brown Packaging

David Brown Packaging is a small, but highly efficient, supplier of packaging materials to the engineering industry. David, who is both the owner and MD of the company, set it up eighteen years ago. Over the years, his business has expanded and now involves selling to national and regional customers, in addition to a growing number of overseas organizations. The company manufactures and supplies good-quality products, produced to high technical specification and delivered through a just-in-time production system. This means that the company has to be highly responsive and flexible to changing customer requirements.

The culture of the company has been shaped by David and his two senior managers, Alan Davis, director of production, and Chris Wilson, who is in charge of quality and R&D. Through their emphasis on quality standards, individual responsibility, and efficient organization, the company has forged a well-deserved reputation for reliability and innovation. On the employee side, considerable resources have been invested in operator training, with all shop-floor staff qualified to at least NVQ Level 2. The company's employment policies are progressive, pay is locally competitive, and there is little evidence that the workforce is either dissatisfied with their conditions of employment or with how management treats them. The company has been able to create an environment in which standards of performance and commitment are high, but not at the expense of employees feeling good about their jobs. It's essentially an 'OK' place to work.

On Friday, 26 May, David had been invited to play in a corporate golf day at one of the local courses and had invited one of his friends, Bob White, to join him. Bob, as well as being his golfing partner, was also an HR consultant who had helped David to develop his HR strategy some years ago and he was familiar with the set-up there. Bob arrived at the factory around 1 p.m., left his car in the car park, and travelled to the competition in David's car.

The factory was operating a two-shift system at that time and the afternoon shift ran from 2 p.m. to 10 p.m., with a 30-minute break at 6 p.m. There were, during this time, twelve people on the shop floor working on machines and dispatching products to customer orders. Each team of six operatives was led by a supervisor, who was responsible for meeting the production targets and for ensuring that the operatives knew what was expected of them. The works manager, Richard Allenby, who had overall responsibility for the shift, was not on duty that day and the two supervisors were left in charge.

At around 7 p.m., David and Bob arrived back at the factory to transfer Bob's golfing equipment into his car. On arrival, most of the shift was playing football in the car park outside of the normal break time and, despite recognizing David, continued to play. Clearly, this was both surprising and disturbing although, given the circumstances, it was difficult to know what might explain the situation. David Brown decided not to confront the situation there and then, but to raise the issue first thing on Monday morning. To say that he was angry and annoyed was something of an understatement. As he drove away, he also expressed his disappointment with what he had experienced. Because of his professional interest, Bob asked David to let him know how the situation was handled.

Questions

1. Consider the action that David Brown should take in response to the situation.

2. Is there any form of managerial response that might be considered more effective than initiating formal disciplinary proceedings?

3. What objectives would management be seeking to achieve in the way in which the situation was handled?

4. If some form of disciplinary response were to be considered appropriate, who should be disciplined and what form should this take?

5. What are the dangers inherent to management being perceived to be acting disproportionately and unfairly?

 ## FURTHER READING

CIPD (2016) 'Discipline and grievances at work', at: http://www.cipd.co.uk/hr-resources/factsheets/discipline-grievances-at-work.aspx#link_0

Department for Business, Innovation and Skills (2009) *Avoiding and Resolving Discipline and Grievance Issues at Work*, BIS.

Simpson, S. (2015) 'Disciplinary procedures: 10 common breaches of the ACAS code of practice', *Personnel Today*, 15 April, at: http://www.personneltoday.com/hr/disciplinary-procedures-10-common-breaches-of-the-acas-code-of-practice

 ## REFERENCES

ACAS (2015a) *Discipline and Grievances at Work*, ACAS Guide, at: http://www.acas.org.uk/media/pdf/b/l/Discipline-and-grievances-Acas-guide.pdf

ACAS (2015b) *Code of Practice on Disciplinary and Grievance Procedures*, March, at: http://www.acas.org.uk/media/pdf/f/m/Acas-Code-of-Practice-1-on-disciplinary-and-grievance-procedures.pdf

ACAS (2015c) 'Bullying and harassment at work: Guidance for employees' [advice leaflet], at: http://www.acas.org.uk/index.aspx?articleid=797

ACAS (2015d) *Raising a Grievance at Work*, at: http://www.acas.org.uk/?articleid=1670

ACAS/CIPD (2015) *Workplace Trends of 2015*, at: http://www.acas.org.uk/media/pdf/t/e/Workplace-trends-of-20151.pdf

Bingham, S. (2014) 'A respectful way to discipline employees', at: http://www.huffingtonpost.com/great-work-cultures/a-respectful-way-to-disci_b_5853024.html

Black, C. and Frost, D. (2011) *Health at Work—An Independent Review of Sickness Absence*, at: https://www.gov.uk/government/uploads/system/uploads/attachment_data/file/181060/health-at-work.pdf

Boysen, P. G. (2013) 'Just culture: A foundation for balanced accountability and patient safety', *Ochsner Journal*, 13(3), 400–6, at: http://www.ncbi.nlm.nih.gov/pmc/articles/PMC3776518

Campbell, D. N. et al. (1985) 'Discipline without punishment—At last', *Harvard Business Review* (July).

CBI (2013) *Annual Absence Survey, at:* www.cbi.org.uk

CIPD (2011) *Conflict Management* [survey report], March.

CIPD (2015) 'Employers fail to deal with bullying at work adequately, say majority of staff', *People Management*, 13 January.

CIPD (2016) *Harassment and Bullying at Work* [revised August].

Department for Business, Innovation and Skills (2015) *Whistleblowing—Guidance for Employees and Code of Practice*, at: https://www.gov.uk/government/uploads/system/uploads/attachment_data/file/415175/bis-15-200-whistleblowing-guidance-for-employers-and-code-of-practice.pdf

Department of Work and Pensions (2013) *Evaluation of the Statement of Fitness for Work (Fitnote)*, June.

Evening Standard (2017) 'King George Hospital workers weigh up strikes after porter is sacked "for taking £4 breakfast"', 10 February.

Francis, R., Sir (2015) *Freedom to Speak up Review*, at: https://www.gov.uk/government/publications/sir-robert-francis-freedom-to-speak-up-review

Frost, P. J., Nord, W. R., and Krefting, L. A. (2002) *HRM Reality*, 2nd edn, Prentice Hall.

Harvey, J. (1988) *The Abeline Paradox and Other Meditations on Management*, Jossey-Bass.

Health and Safety Executive (2015) http://www.hse.gov.uk/business/casestudy/rollsroyce.htm

Jones, C. and Saundry, R. (2012) 'The practice of discipline: Evaluating the roles and relationship between managers and HR professionals', *Human Resource Management Journal*, 22(3), 252–66.

Konovsky, M. A. (2000) 'Understanding procedural justice and its impact on business organizations', *Journal of Management*, 26(3), 489–511.

Landau, P. (2011) 'What is a compromise agreement?', *Guardian*, 23 March, at: https://www.theguardian.com/careers/careers-blog/compromise-agreement-workplace-disputes

Martin Searle Solicitors [n.d.] 'Factsheet: Settlement agreement advice for employees', at: http://www.ms-solicitors.co.uk/employee/settlement-agreements/factsheet-settlement-agreement-advice-for-employees

Men's Wearhouse [n.d.] http://images.menswearhouse.com/is/content/TMW/4.0/Content/WCM%20Pages/Corporate%20Responsibility/TMW_Corporate_Responsibility2.pdf

Ministry of Justice (2015) *Tribunal Statistics* [September], at: https://www.gov.uk/government/collections/tribunals-statistics

O'Reilly, C. A. and Pfeffer, J. (2000) *Hidden Value*, Harvard Business School Press.

Parker, S. (2012) 'Just culture in UK civil aviation' [presentation], at: https://ec.europa.eu/transport/sites/transport/files/modes/air/events/doc/2012-04-19-seminar/uk-caa.pdf

People Management (2015) 'Employers fail to deal with bullying at work adequately, say majority of staff', 13 January.

Pfeffer, J. and Veiga, J. F. (1999) 'Putting people first for organizational success', *Academy of Management*, 13(2), 37–48.

Pinsent Masons (2012) 'Dismissing for misconduct: The difference between "gross" and "serious" misconduct', at: http://www.pinsentmasons.com/Documents/e-bulletin/Employment/2012-07-27.html

Rollinson, D. et al. (1996) 'Supervisor and manager styles in handling discipline and grievance', *Personnel Review*, 25(4), 38–55.

Royles, D. and Kapur, N. (2016) 'A new way forward for disciplinaries', *Health Service Journal*, 28 June, at: http://www.ajustnhs.com/wp-content/uploads/2012/06/Dean-Royles-Narinder-Kapur-HSJ-June-2016-p.pdf

Saundry, R. and Jones, C. (2010) 'Managing workplace discipline: Who holds the key?', ACAS research paper, at: http://www.acas.org.uk/media/pdf/a/h/Managing-workplace-discipline-who-holds-the-key-accessible-version.pdf

Saundry, R. et al. (2016) 'Managing workplace conflict: Formal and informal approaches', *Human Resource Management International Digest*, 24(1), 16–18.

Saundry, R. and Wibberley, G. (2012) 'Managing individual conflict in the private sector: A case study', iROWE, Lancashire Business School, at: http://www.acas.org.uk/media/pdf/6/b/0512_Managing_individual_conflict_in_the_private_sector-accessible-version-Mar-12.pdf

Suff, R. (2010) 'Dispute resolution survey: Managing discipline', *IRS Employment Review*, 26 April, at: http://www.xperthr.co.uk/article/101779/irs-2010-dispute-resolution-survey–managing-discipline.aspx

Turner, J. (2013) 'When can sickness absence be treated as a conduct issue?', *Personnel Today*, 7 October.

Wilkinson, K. (2007) 'Are exit interviews of any value—Do leavers really tell the truth?', *People Management*, 29 September.

Williams, C. (2017) 'Rolls-Royce's former senior management implicated in bribes and corruption, High Court finds', *Daily Telegraph*, 17 January, at: http://www.telegraph.co.uk/business/2017/01/17/rolls-royces-former-senior-management-implicated-bribes-corruption

Younson, F. (2002) 'A lack of discipline', *People Management*, 8(12), 13 June, p. 17.

HRM Processes

Workforce Planning and Measurement

10

Introduction

WP is one of the core activities of the HR function and in its most basic form is concerned with producing answers to three questions:

1. How many people do we need now and in the future to enable the organization to produce or deliver the goods and services it is committed to delivering to its customers and users?

2. What skills and abilities do these people need to possess to do the jobs they are employed for and will be expected to do in the future?

3. How can we ensure that the relationship between the demand for labour (quantity and quality) is broadly in line with the supply of labour employed by the organization at any one point in time, and that the costs of employing these people is effectively controlled?

Organizational size and complexity are factors that influence the development of the WP function beyond its core activities and responsibilities with organizations such as the NHS, the BBC, and many of the largest private sector companies incorporating additional activities such as:

- succession planning;
- flexible working;
- retention planning;
- skills audits and long-range forecasting;
- talent management;
- job design and multi-skilling;
- outsourcing; and
- career planning;

but all of these are activities that support and facilitate the core requirements of matching supply with demand and maintaining control over employment costs.

According to the CIPD (2016b), WP is:

getting the right number of people with the right skills employed in the right place at the right time to deliver an organisation's short- and long-term objectives. It covers a diverse range of activities, such as succession planning, flexible working, job design, and many more

a definition that notably fails to mention the costs of employment at all. 'Strategic' is a prefix that is increasingly used before most of the core HR activities, such as reward or recruitment, and thinking about WP in a more strategic way may offer additional insights into what it involves. The Hay Consulting Group (2012), for example, argues for the integration of workforce supply and demand analysis into the strategic planning cycle to ensure organizations have the 'five rights'—the right number of people, with the right skills, in the right place, at the right level, and at the right cost. They see this as what strategic workforce planning (SWP) actually means. They claim that demographic and workforce changes mean that direct people costs make up an average of 40 per cent of organizational costs, and that almost half of the workforce are in complex, knowledge-intensive roles that are fundamental to organizational success and profitability, although not all workers and jobs would fit this description. They argue that:

A talented and aligned workforce is crucial for bringing strategy to life and ensuring an organisation delivers on its objectives.

And conclude:

The cost therefore of getting workforce planning wrong can be significant.

The recognition that WP is not just about numbers and reconciling supply and demand estimates but involves a much more strategic understanding of changes in the workforce and the way organizations 'exist' in relation to their environment, seems to be the driver for change in the way WP is understood and operates in contemporary organizations. More will be said about the evolution of the function later in the chapter, but it is interesting to look at the way the workforce has and continues to change and the pressures organizations have to cope with when making workforce decisions.

As far as the workforce is concerned, the Hay Group's paper 'Tomorrow's workforce' identifies four important trends that are not only affecting the size and composition of the workforce but the expectations of those who are or will be part of it:

1. **Ageing**—according to the US Census Bureau, Europe's loss of 'baby boomers' from the workforce and the low birth rate mean that the active workforce will decline by 29 per cent by 2050. Of course, migration can help to compensate for this reduction but as point 2 makes clear, the loss of indigenous highly skilled professional workers is far less likely to be made up through increased migration than lower-skilled workers. Political decisions currently being taken will determine whether this decline is as serious as the predictions suggest.

2. **Skills and qualifications gap**—despite investment in higher education, there are significant gaps in skills in scientific, technical, engineering, and maths disciplines, with an estimated 80 per cent of the talent gap in organizations resulting from a shortage of highly qualified candidates in these areas.

3. **Higher costs for scarce skills**—linked to the skills gap, critical skills attract a market premium for those organizations that fail to develop and retain key workers. This means that having an effective and sustainable retention and development strategy may be the only way of avoiding having to pay increasing rates of pay for scarce labour.

4. **Changing career patterns and expectations**—the traditional career with retirement in a person's early sixties has been replaced with expectations of a longer working life, multiple careers, and flexible employment patterns. Many people are living and working longer either through desire or circumstances.

One of the consequences of these developments, is that those involved in WP are having to recognize that it is people that they are dealing with not 'resources' and that a human/employee as well as an organizational perspective needs to be applied to the decision-making process. Furthermore, as a report published by the Conference Board argued in the early part of the new millennium (Young, 2006), they have to operate at a much more specific level than before. The report claimed that:

> **Companies need to differentiate between jobs that are mission-critical and those that are not. They may need to identify employees who are at risk for attrition or who would be most difficult to replace. The real power of strategic workforce planning comes from its ability to home in on critical segments, rather than managing its human capital as if it were a faceless multitude.**

Many of the largest organizations where planning is still an essential requirement—think of the time it takes to train nurses and doctors—still plan for the future but at the same time the value of complex workforce plans tends to be limited by increasingly uncertain environments, where the 'future' is less and less known and where environmental changes can render large-scale plans very quickly redundant. The 'workforce plan' can be too cumbersome to be useful. In addition, they are arguably less useful than a focus on a particular segment of the workforce or on a particular part of the organization which is critical to overall success. This focus is consistent with what Boudreau and Ramstad called 'pivot points'—identifying those strategically important areas of work and the people who carry them out and giving them particular attention.

 Signpost to Chapter 4: Talent Management: Strategies and Models, for insights into the relationship between workforce planning and talent management.

As with other aspects of the HR function, there is a process of evolution taking place in the thinking and practice of what was originally called 'manpower planning', although not all organizations have experienced the same progression. For small and medium-sized enterprises (SMEs), although staffing decisions are probably more critical than for those employing thousands, carrying out the most basic of the WP function is probably all that is necessary. More is said about the transition of WP methodologies later in the chapter.

STUDENT ACTIVITY 10.1

Listen to the CIPD Podcast 46—Workforce Planning at http://www.cipd.co.uk/hr-resources/podcasts/46-workforce-planning.aspx

Then answer the following questions:

1. What, from a practitioner perspective, are the WP priorities and main activities discussed in the podcast?
2. What does the podcast add to what we have already said about WP?
3. What differences in WP would you expect to find in a much larger organization?

An Economic Perspective on WP

The central theme of this book is that human resource management (HRM) is not just about people, or human resources. It is also concerned with how people are managed and used at work and about their economic value in relation to the costs of employing them. As we have stated, those involved in WP are not simply concerned with balancing supply with demand in a constantly changing environment, but about dealing with operational and strategic requirements and issues. The HR professional, working with line managers, has a key role to play in ensuring that an optimum balance is struck between the number and quality of people employed, the associated employment costs, the organization's requirements for productive capacity, and financial/budgetary constraints.

Although the economic and financial imperatives vary between the public and private sectors—and most commentators would argue that, historically, these are much more influential in the private sector, which is growing in size (ONS, 2015)—people, in theory, in the private sector, at least, are rarely employed for any reason other than that they are an economic resource necessary for the creation of goods and services. This means that WP is not simply about meeting the demand for labour, but also involves understanding and managing the costs associated with employing any given number of people. As has been seen recently with the NHS, while there might be issues around meeting the rising demand for medical staff, budgetary constraints are increasingly affecting the ability of hospital trusts to fill vacant positions. According to a recent King's Fund study:

> The unprecedented slowdown in the growth of NHS funding in England since 2010 has meant that the NHS has had to pursue the most ambitious programme of productivity improvement since its foundation in order to close the gap between need and available funding.
> (Appleby, 2014)

The report found that there was an annual need for an initial 3 per cent increase in productivity across the NHS, as a whole, followed by an increase of 4.7 per cent to meet the anticipated funding shortfall, which in the context of a historical annual growth in productivity from 1995 to 2010 of only 0.4 per cent, would imply major changes in organization and working practices. It is clear that the challenge for HR and the NHS' senior leadership is not just about filling posts but creating a much more efficient and productive environment—in fact creating different ways of working if the service is to be preserved in its current form. WP is then about getting the right number of people with the required skills and competences in post at the right time, but this has to be achieved within changing budgetary constraints and has to reflect the organization's ability to pay the costs of employment (Imison et al., 2016).

From an economic perspective, employees represent a cost as well as a source of added value. While the costs of employing someone are relatively easy to calculate, the value they bring is not. This is key to understanding that WP is not simply about the production of 'manpower plans' and futuristic scenario planning, but needs to be seen as an important dimension of almost all aspects of HR. In particular, it connects to the implementation and effectiveness of an organization's recruitment and reward strategies, its labour reduction strategies, the continual search for improvements in productivity, and the consequences that follow from this in relation to changes in the demand for labour. From a managerial and economic perspective, the continued search for efficiency savings and productivity improvements that may well involve reduced head counts and lower overall employment costs is a rational response to a tighter fiscal framework, but its impact on the interests of individual employees and trade unions is often perceived quite differently. These situations demonstrate once again that the interests of employers and employees, together with their trade unions, can come into conflict. (As an example, see https://fullfact.org/health/junior-doctors-pay-short-introduction-dispute, for an explanation of the recent conflict between the government and junior doctors over their new contract.)

Generally speaking, those affected by job insecurity, changes in contractual arrangements, and pay/benefit cuts will resist them in whatever ways they can. Employers on the other hand will seek to find ways of pushing through changes in the numbers of people they employ and/or wage cuts, although historically wages have proved resistant to downward pressures, with the exception being experiences during the 2007–8 recession. Using people more flexibly, increasing their skill and capability range, and working more efficiently have been the main strategies for increasing labour productivity, which if demand remains constant will normally result in fewer hours being worked or fewer people being employed. The increasing use of zero-hours contracts reflects the way some, mainly lower-paying employers, are taking the idea of flexibility in labour contracts even further than before (ACAS, 2016). Unless trade unions can mobilize sufficient political power to resist or delay these changes, the question that has to be answered is: how do employers deliver the required cutbacks in employment or reduction in employment costs that are needed in the present or required in the future? The following insight illustrates the kinds of challenges facing managers in the way they seek to balance employment numbers, costs, and changing levels of demand for labour.

HRM INSIGHT 10.1 Reducing employment costs

Multiplex Manufacturing is a family-run business based in a northern industrial city. It employs 120 people in total who are all employed on one site. The breakdown of the 120 staff is as set out below.

Thirty are skilled workers on full-time contracts which equate to 38 hours per week. All thirty have been with the company for five years or more and are key to the business. Seven of the thirty are female. Turnover levels are low as the company has a good reputation for paying above-market rates and is known as a 'good employer' in the area. Overtime has been running at approximately 10 per cent per week.

Sixty-five are operatives who assemble the products, package them, and prepare them for dispatch. Some are responsible for stock control and materials handling. Approximately half of this group is female and the length of service varies from several weeks to twenty years. Annual turnover is above that of the skilled group and averages 10 per cent. Overtime has been approximately 15 per cent.

Twenty are administrative and technical workers who work in the office and are engaged in production planning, secretarial work, sales and marketing, and finance. Unlike the 'factory floor' staff, those in this group are paid monthly salaries.

The final group consists of five managers. The MD is the daughter of the original owner, her brother is production director, and the other three head up sales and marketing, production planning and quality control, and product development and technical support.

Over time, more and more of the company's products have been sold abroad and now exports represent 80 per cent of output. It has an annual turnover of £5 million, with plans to grow this to £10 million, and is in the process of negotiating a bank loan to fund its expansion plans. Employment costs represent 50 per cent of turnover.

After having its best year ever, with profits reaching three-quarters of a million pounds in 2007, the world recession hit and within weeks orders fell by 30 per cent and it quickly became apparent to the MD that things would remain very difficult for some time. At that reduced level of output, the finance director calculated that the business would cease to exist as a viable concern within three months. At that point, it was impossible for management to know how long the recession would last, but there was a belief that, with the depreciation of the pound against most other currencies and economic growth in the Far East, if the company could survive, and make the necessary changes in its workforce and employment costs, it would be well placed to take advantage of these opportunities. But it needed a survival strategy!

Because the company has very little internal HR expertise, you have been hired to advise them on what actions need to be taken to cut employment costs by 20 per cent over a twelve-month period. While you have a relatively free hand, you must identify actions that have the potential to achieve the required costs savings, but it is equally important that the changes do not undermine employee motivation and commitment to the company. It is equally important to retain 'core' employees whose skills are critical to the company's future success yet at the same time trying to ensure that what is being proposed is as fair to everyone as possible.

Working in groups and with the intention of producing a presentation that summarizes your thinking and ideas, you are required to outline:

1. Your general strategy for achieving the required employment costs reduction.

2. In detail where the savings would come from—making realistic assumptions about wages and salaries.

3. What actions you would take to ensure the cuts were perceived as fair.

4. What you would do to ensure motivation and productivity levels remained high.

 Insights and Outcomes: visit the **online resources** at **www.oup.com/uk/banfield3e/** for answers to the HRM Insight questions.

The long-term trend in Western economies is for organizations to operate more efficiently with fewer employees—a fact that reflects increasing labour productivity partly through the strategies mentioned above but increasingly as a result of advances in technology which for many jobs can be used as a labour substitute. Note however that companies can experience different scenarios:

- an absolute fall in number of people employed—head count;

- an absolute fall in hours worked where head count remains the same or falls;

- an absolute reduction in employment costs where head count and hours worked can remain constant or fall, in which case wage rates/overtime rates fall or head count/overtime hours are cut;

- relative reductions in numbers employed/employment costs, where growth in the overall budget is higher than growth in employment numbers/labour costs;

- relative increases in numbers employed/employment costs where the growth in these is higher than the growth in the overall budget.

This does not mean, however, that fewer people are economically active or that there are fewer jobs available. Part of the difficulty is that new job creation, while increasing the number of people in work often involves part-time or casual work. So while certain organizations may be adding to their labour force the actual numbers employed may well be associated with a relative fall in hours worked. Remember in Chapter 1, we highlighted the increasing number of doctors who choose to work part-time during their career. Conversely, where the public sector is shedding jobs and/or reducing employment costs, many job losses will be full-time and permanent, which is where the greatest long-term costs savings can be made (Philpott, 2010). Since the recession of 2007–8, while there has been an increase in those working on more flexible contracts the numbers of those working full and part-time has increased to the point where the employment rate is the highest on record. The ONS (2015) has established that comparing the estimates for full-time and part-time employment by sex for April to June 2015 with those for a year earlier, the number of:

- men working full-time increased by 153,000 to reach 14.36 million;
- men working part-time increased by 21,000 to reach 2.14 million;
- women working full-time increased by 198,000 to reach 8.40 million;
- women working part-time fell by 18,000 to reach 6.13 million.

Where the *general* trend of employment is upwards, reflecting economic expansion, the job of workforce planners is to meet rising demand for labour from the available supply, which may be relatively inflexible and result in rising wages as employers compete for scarce supplies, or seek to find additional supplies through accessing different labour markets or increasing the productivity of the people they already employ. Again, we are not talking about choosing one strategy but an organization combining the three we have identified, to achieve the maximum economic gain/savings combined with consistently delivering the required quantity and quality of labour.

RESEARCH INSIGHT 10.1

To further your learning, you may wish to read the following:

Boxall, P. (2013) 'Mutuality in the management of human resources: assessing the quality of alignment in employment relationships', *Human Resource Management Journal,* **23(1).**

The article explores the extent to which the interests of the individual and the organization are or can become aligned in the search for commitment to increasing employee capabilities and flexibility.

Managing a planned reduction in the labour force or labour costs in recessionary periods presents a different set of challenges. Organizations can face unpredictable changes in competitive and financial conditions, falling product/service demand, unfavourable movements in exchange rates, increased costs of employing people, and tightening budgetary constraints. As a result, they can quickly find that they are employing too much labour at too high a cost and quickly need to reduce either employment numbers, or hours worked, or overall employment costs. WP strategies need to be developed that allow organizations to respond quickly to changing demand conditions. A comprehensive range of WP strategies that are appropriate to different demand and supply conditions is presented in Table 10.1, but for a detailed exploration of HR actions appropriate to a recessionary situation, see Teague and Roche (2014).

The following situation represents the kinds of environmental change that impact directly on employers' costs.

In response to proposed increases in the number of statutory holidays from twenty to twenty-eight days, Bob Cotton, the chief executive of the British Hospitality Association, commented that the change represented an additional 3.5 per cent on payroll costs. Whatever the social case for such changes, the impact on employment costs cannot be avoided:

> If you start pushing up the wage bill too high you start shedding labour to pay for those left in work.
> (Wallop, 2006)

His comment captures the pressures and dilemmas that employers have in deciding on their employment strategies. But one of the most significant consequences of the 2007–8 recession was the emergence of pay freezes and absolute pay reductions in organizations that had to respond in a much more radical way to budgetary and market changes. For the first time in many years, organizations were able not only to resist demands for pay increases but actually freeze or even reduce wages either in addition to or as an alternative to shedding labour. The threat to many private sector businesses was an existential one rather than one of

Table 10.1 Management strategies related to changes in the demand and supply for labour

A *short-term fall* in the demand for labour can involve:

- reducing or eliminating overtime working
- postponing the recruitment of workers to replace those who have left
- freezing establishment numbers
- ceasing the use of agency staff

A *short-term rise* in the demand for labour can involve:

- increasing advertising spend and improving its effectiveness
- increasing the use of temporary staff and short-term contract workers
- using 'golden hellos' to attract new recruits
- increasing overtime

A *long-term fall* in the demand for labour can involve:

- moving some employees from full-time to part-time contracts
- introducing short-time working
- introducing voluntary or compulsory redundancy

A *long-term shortage* of labour can involve:

- developing alternative labour markets (e.g. overseas recruitment)
- substituting technology for labour
- increasing the degree of functional flexibility through changes in training strategies
- introducing flexible working strategies
- improving the perceived value of the reward package

declining or falling growth and radical, often brutal, reductions in labour costs were necessary for their survival. The more recent collapse in oil and gas prices has had a similar effect on employment numbers and terms and conditions in many of the country's oil companies (see Chapter 4).

On the other hand, a numerical shortage of labour or qualitative imbalances can have a serious effect on the organization's ability to meet demand for its goods and services. This can result in reduced revenues, lost orders, and dissatisfied customers: having too few employees of the right quality can have equally serious financial consequences as having too many employees! Depending on the degree of volatility and change in the product market, organizations can be faced by quite rapid turnarounds in their financial situation, where labour force reductions are quickly followed by the need to expand employment in critical areas. To make it more complicated an organization can suffer from a surplus and a shortage of labour—different kinds of course—at the same time. The challenge for WP is to reconcile changes in the supply and demand for labour, and to produce, as far as possible, a labour force that can be flexed in terms of numbers and quality in response to changes in demand. To achieve this while avoiding the creation of damaging conflict with the employees and their representative institutions is, it might be argued, the 'holy grail' of WP. The fact that few organizations seem to have been able to achieve this goal is testimony to the difficulties and challenges facing the HR professional in this aspect of their work. (See Agency Central (2014) for a detailed explanation of changing supply and demand levels in UK construction.)

PRACTITIONER INSIGHT Steven Ned, director of HR and organizational development and deputy chief executive, Sheffield Children's Hospital, NHS Trust

In the NHS, WP is driven by the rapid pace of technological and organizational change, advances in treatment and techniques, and the rising expectations of patients and service users. Another key factor is the long-term planning timelines involved in training medical staff today for situations that can only be predicted ten or fifteen years ahead.

Problems with WP are often conflated with poor or overambitious service planning. Making better WP decisions means that management has to be 'more savvy' about the situation we are faced with. In particular, we need to be able to have much more confidence in the indicators we use to tell us what the situation is in relation to numbers, capabilities, and costs, and avoid the mistake of simply relying on the data themselves. We need to avoid the situation of being 'data rich and insight light'.

Contemporary WP is no longer a purely internal function about head count and resources—this is only one of its dimensions. It also needs to have an external focus, looking at the changing environment in which we have to operate, and ensuring that we can meet the ambitions of the health service and support it on its ongoing transformational journey. The NHS Five Year Forward View paints a picture of rapid change. The success of WP is inextricably linked to the ability to deliver the service changes. For example, the current national priority being given to mental health can only be reflected in improved mental health provision if the numbers and skills of those working in this area, together with appropriate facilities, are delivered.

WP today is not just about head-count numbers: it also involves contributing to the challenge of improving employee and service productivity. This can be achieved in two ways. First, by looking at wage costs and efficiency levels. Second, by looking towards increasing the level of employee engagement, which we know plays a major part in levels of discretionary effort—'going the extra mile', which in turns affects productivity.

But a major challenge over the next five years is to address the financial costs of employment, which look set to involve ongoing public sector pay restraint, as well as pay increases in other sectors, and reductions in agency spend. This will require productivity increases, which means the cost of inputs falls in relation to outputs. But the reality is that the long-term trend in productivity in the NHS has been static or slightly negative since 1997. This means that if this weakness in productivity growth is to be addressed, WP will need to support and be engaged with a continuing programme of change and improvement—more from the same rather than more of the same.

The tools of WP are becoming more sophisticated and reliable. They allow managers to demonstrate a more direct link between cause and effect and returns on investments. But we still have to avoid the errors of previous years, particularly the mistake of seeing planning as a simple linear process—it's not quite as simple as that! We also need to be better at building contingencies into our plans and recognizing the virtue of flexibility so that we can mitigate the effects of things that we cannot predict now. The new reality is of a WP system that needs constant refinement to get it as good as we can; perfection is a dangerous illusion. As an example, the information needed to guide both local and national WP activities and objectives is never complete and in key areas often has failed to keep pace with the growing complexity of NHS providers. Recent research by the King's Fund (Addicott et al., 2015) identified large data gaps on primary and community care, use of agency and bank staff, vacancy rates, and independent/voluntary sector providers. Without up-to-date and accurate information WP at the local level may be compromised: at the national level it almost certainly will be.

For an explanation of the different interests between employers and employees in relation to the challenges of balancing supply requirements with demand, see the Online Resources Extension Material 10.1. The company referred to in the Extension Material is still in business and employs over one hundred people manufacturing sophisticated process control equipment.

The Planning Process

Planning, generally, is integral to any organized activity. It often is not only an option, but a necessity. Most organizations, particularly larger ones, engage in some form of planning as part of the process of strategic and operational management. Given that people are a critical organizational resource and source of significant cost, it is logical that managers need to plan for meeting the organization's human resource requirements. This is particularly the case if labour markets are tight, as time taken to train people is a cost.

Planning, however, is a process that has been associated with spectacular failures and white elephants. In the 1960s, the Labour government under Harold Wilson produced a 'national plan', which claimed to be a blueprint for managing the whole economy—but its use and value, and indeed relevance, were soon questioned, as the economic environment on which it based its assumptions and forecasts changed. The eventual failure of Communism can be linked to the inefficiencies and defects of its centralized economic planning system, under which resources, production targets, and markets were determined centrally, with little regard for what people wanted and needed.

The assumptions that both of these centralized planning models were based upon quickly lost their validity as social, political, and economic forces changed the environments to which the economic plans related. A plan, as with a strategy, is only as good and as useful as the assumptions about the future internal and external environment on which it is based are accurate. Understanding the limitations and fragility of planning and plans is as important to the HR planner as is the potential value that the planning process and the resultant HR plans offer. Given the rapidly changing environments in which most organizations operate, human resource plans must be flexible. They must be adapted constantly to reflect changes in the environment if they are to retain their potential utility. Planning that is seen more as a discrete event and mechanistic activity than as an ongoing and adaptive process is unlikely to contribute much of value to organizational effectiveness. Indeed, it may be harmful to organizational interests.

WP, if based on poor data, limited forecasting models, and an inability to see the wider HR and business picture, can result in inaccurate and misleading estimates of supply and demand numbers, resulting in either a costly surplus or shortage of employees. As John Bramham (1994), one of the most influential writers on this subject, stated:

> In preparing 'plans' the need for flexibility is stressed. No plan in any fixed sense will be relevant for long. The success of planning in an organization will be judged by how well the organization can anticipate or adapt to the unforeseen.

This is a view supported by Bratton and Gold (1999) who state that:

> The domination of equations, which mechanistically provide for solutions for problems based on the behaviour of people, may actually become divorced from the real world and have a good chance of missing the real problems. Hence the poor reputation of manpower planning.

We are in an era in which almost all organizations are struggling to cope with an unprecedented level of change and it would be too simplistic to see planning as being able to 'see' or predict the future.

This view was echoed in an Institute for Employment Studies report that concluded:

> When it concerns human resources, there are the more specific criticisms that it is over quantitative and neglects the qualitative aspects of contribution. The issue has become not how many people should be employed, but ensuring that all members of staff are making an effective contribution.
> (Reilly, 1996)

The importance of this statement lies in the recognition that numbers, in themselves, are less important than what people contribute, the behaviours they exhibit, and the potential they possess. The HR planner and the whole approach to planning now need to reflect the importance of distinguishing between the numbers of people in employment and what they actually do and are capable of doing at work.

Many of the problems associated with what was known, in the 1980s and early 1990s, as 'manpower planning' were linked to the following:

- the planning process was more a series of activities than an ongoing process, meaning that information from the internal and external environments was often outdated and irrelevant;

- the idea that a plan, in the form of a single document, once written was complete, was attractive but misguided. The danger is that people come to believe that the contents of the plan and what it forecasts are fixed in time rather than contingent and provisional;

- it focused too heavily on the quantitative aspect of employment and neglected issues of variability in contribution and performance;

- the lack of flexibility and ability to frequently change planning scenarios and forecasts meant that many plans quickly became out of date;

- forecasting and predicting future economic conditions, and attempts to reconcile these with the organization's workforce requirements, were often carried out without being sufficiently integrated in the organization's strategic planning process.

More recent attempts to explain and justify the role of WP emphasize the need not to try to predict the future, but to use planning to challenge assumptions about the future and to engage in more sophisticated 'scenario planning' activities. WP is now much more about finding ways to achieve a better internal integration of HR activities, to be clearer about what the workforce requirements will be in the future, in terms of skill and competency requirements, and how these needs can be met. Quality, potential, and 'fit', rather than simply numbers, of employees required is seen as a particularly important dimension of the planning process and its outcomes.

Table 10.2 provides a summary of the essential features of the HR planning process, and the actions needed to ensure that each key feature can be effectively managed and add value to the organization.

As was made clear in Chapter 2, HRM is associated with a degree of terminological complexity and confusion that is rarely found in other management functions with the result that both students and practitioners are often confused about the meaning(s) of commonly used terms and expressions. In the context of this chapter, the central question is whether the term manpower planning carries essentially the same meaning as HRP or the more recent term, WP, as adopted in this chapter.

According to Bramham (1994), one of the earliest writers on the subject:

> There is a big difference between human resource planning and manpower planning . . . in terms of process and purpose.

He argues that WP is concerned with motivating people and involves processes in which costs, numbers, control, and systems interact. On the other hand, manpower planning is concerned with the numerical requirements of forecasting. Despite this, he accepts that there are important areas of overlap and interconnection.

It might be argued that Bramham's position on this issue has, to a degree, been superseded by a simple change in definition, driven by the need to avoid the use of discriminatory language, and by the incorporation of the more restrictive forecasting function into the wider and more encompassing WP activity. If there is a meaningful and useful distinction to be made, it is probably based on the differences between strategic and operational requirements and focus. If this is a defensible point of view, it justifies Bramham's position and allows WP to be defined as:

> involving the strategic alignment of an organization's human capital with its business direction, and employing the use of methodical processes in analysing the current workforce, determining future workforce needs, identifying the gap between the present and future, and implementing solutions so the organization can accomplish its mission, goals, and objectives.
> (HR Society, 2013)

Manpower planning can be thought of as:

> Part of the wider HRP function, but having a more operational focus and purpose that involves identifying the numbers of people required at appropriate skill levels across a given shift or production pattern in order to meet production or work requirements.
> (Bramham, 1994)

While WP is generally seen to be interchangeable with terms that describe the same kinds of activities and responsibilities, there is another term that needs to be considered because this might usefully describe different interests and priorities. Workforce analytics describes the growing interest in metrics and managing human capital costs which have strong foundations in quantitative analysis. Called workforce analytics by some, human capital metrics by others, this next generation of WP goes beyond head count to examine the relationships among key variables, such as:

- employee demographics;
- costs;
- job categories; and
- outcomes, such as turnover, performance, customer satisfaction, and revenue.

Table 10.2 Features of effective WP

Essential feature	Essential actions
Based on organization's objectives	The workforce plan should grow out of the organization's objectives and strategic aims. For example, expansion plans may require a greater focus on recruitment, while upgrading skills may be necessary if technological advancement is required.
Flexible	The workforce plan may need to change to ensure that organizational objectives are met in the event of unseen demands or change. These might be market changes, such as a recession resulting in job losses to save costs, or internal unexpected change, such as the resignation of unexpected numbers of key personnel, leading to refocused efforts in recruitment and retention.
Built-in contingencies	There may be aspects of the plan that allow for resource to be diverted elsewhere in the event of unplanned events. For example, temporary or interim staff may be required to cover unexpected absence.
Defined value-added outcomes	All activity should be carefully scrutinized to examine whether it truly adds value. For example, an increased number of staff committee meetings with the intention of improving communications may actually escalate the number of complaints and encourage more time away from productive work.
Regularly reviewed	Objectives set early in the year may no longer be relevant as the year progresses. For example, there may have been plans for a programme of management training, which might be cancelled in the event of a decision to make a layer of management redundant.
Overall strategic direction	All aspects of the plan should directly or indirectly contribute towards the overall strategic direction of the business. For example, improved induction procedures may enhance productivity, despite more time away from direct work in the initial weeks, because of enhanced long-term retention of staff.
Timelines identified	Plans should include a time frame over which activity will be completed. For example, succession planning may be an annual activity, reviewed at a set time each year.
Priorities identified	There may be some aspects of the workforce plan that are more important than others and activity may be prioritized, particularly if there are seasonal demands. A retail chain may be more focused on recruiting, rather than training, new staff during the lead-up to Christmas and may focus on training for development during the quieter times of the year.
Resource identified	Different levels of workforce support may be required for different aspects of the plan and the plan should take account of the availability of staff to support activity.
Acknowledges reactive requirements	Remember that allowing time for the day-to-day reactive issues is just as important and often more valued. A prompt reaction to an unexpected challenge can stop problems from quickly escalating further; effective plans acknowledge this valuable role.

Table 10.3 The major strands and evolution of WP

Traditional	Analyses supply–demand gap and creates plan to address future staffing needs.
Strategic WP	Engages business leaders in a high-level discussion of business strategy and its broad workforce implications, but also, at the operational level focuses on more precise numbers.
Forecasting and scenario modelling	Uses internal and external data to create forecasts incorporating multiple what-if scenarios, which enable executives to evaluate strategic options.
Workforce analytics	Mines current and historical employee data to identify key relationships among variables.
	Analyses relationships between workforce and business data (human capital metrics).
Human capital planning	Segments jobs based on their mission-criticality.
	Makes different levels of workforce investment in each segment.
	Focuses on broad trends over three–four-year period rather than precise head count and near-term plans.

According to Fitz-enz in his latest book on the new HR analytics (2010), the real focus now for organizations is on predicting the economic value of their investments in human capital, which involves among other things measuring what is important, integrating predictions based on detailed data into the wider HR field, developing better metrics, and developing employee value propositions. While most organizations are unlikely to be implementing all these new quantitative practices the 'direction of travel' is likely to be towards incorporating many of the activities and relationships being advocated by Fitz-enz and others who share his ideas and beliefs into a more sophisticated WP paradigm. Table 10.3 highlights the main strands of WP.

One of the important changes in the evolution of the WP function is the way that it has moved from being only concerned about forecasting changes in the demand and supply for labour into a more sophisticated and integral part of HR. This has been driven, in part, by the growing use of a contingent, flexible, and diverse workforce. While full-time working is still the predominant form of employment, the use of part-time staff, zero-hours contracts, seasonal workers, contract workers, and temporary staff has grown considerably. While there is ongoing debate about whether this more complicated employment model is a reflection of employer interests or expresses social and demographic changes that benefit employees there can be little doubt that many employers see a flexible labour force, both in terms of hours worked and costs, as critical to their economic success and survival. As the mix of employment arrangements becomes more diverse, WP becomes an important tool for managing these relationships and for evaluating the costs and benefits of different staffing models and scenarios.

RESEARCH INSIGHT 10.2

To take your learning further, you may want to read the following:

Rubery et al. (2016) 'Flexibility bites back: The multiple and hidden costs of flexible employment policies', *Human Resource Management Journal,* **26(3), 235–51.**

The article challenges the UK's labour market flexibility, with the authors arguing that far from being the cause of a UK 'jobs miracle', flexibility in employment brings costs in job quality and productivity that are detrimental to individuals, society, and the economy.

While an ability to predict changes in the external environment is still valued as a contribution to effective decision-making in the employment of people, the limitations and uncertainties of 'knowing' what the external environment will look like at any point in time are better understood today than they perhaps used to be. What have also changed and become increasingly important influences on what WP represents can be expressed in terms of:

● the importance of the organization's internal environment, particularly the impact on its labour requirements of such activities as succession planning, competency development, retention levels, productivity, and efficiency initiatives;

● a movement away from the notion that organizations can always be proactive when it comes to planning human resources, based on the unsustainable belief that future environmental conditions can be accurately predicted; reactivity is considered a perfectly reasonable response to rapid environmental change;

● a greater recognition that WP is increasingly associated with both strategic and operational dimensions;

● the importance of flexibility in HR plans;

● the critical need for management thinking and organizations to be able to adapt quickly to environmental changes;

● the need for HR practitioners to develop appropriate planning tools and provide managers with a range of options in terms of known and 'predicted' environmental conditions.

> **KEY CONCEPT** **Whole-time equivalents (WTEs)**
>
> This is a quantitative measurement of the number of staff available to or in the establishment that allows for staff on different employment contracts to be reflected in the 'head count'. A simple system of weighting operates, under which a full-time employee working a nominal 35 hours—or whatever is the company or industry standard working week—is allocated a weighting of 1. A part-time worker who works half the standard hours is weighted 0.5; one who works two days each week is weighted at 0.4. As organizations, particularly the NHS, move to more employee-friendly and flexible contracts, the actual numbers of nurses and doctors, for example, can increase while the WTE figure falls. Expanding the output of medical schools can, paradoxically, be associated with a fall in general practitioner WTEs because more GPs work on a part-time basis.

From a senior management perspective, the perceived effectiveness and value of HR's contribution to the planning and management of human resources is less to do with whether those involved are reactive or proactive, or whether they have a 'manpower plan' or not, and more to do with whether they are effective in meeting the organization's labour requirements, within existing budgetary constraints; in other words outcomes are more important than processes. They must also provide 'solutions' that fit the strategic and operational requirements of the organization. The general criticisms levelled against HR departments outlined in Chapter 2, in terms of the relevance of priorities and activities, can be revisited in the context of WP. The HR department is likely to be criticized because of its inability to distinguish between the HR plan and an HR plan for the organization, and because it is slow to respond to changing resource requirements. Such criticism is likely to be compounded by a perception that its contribution to WP is marginal and ineffective, at least as far as delivering against the organization's capacity and capability requirements are concerned. The HR department may be 'behind the curve' when it comes to meeting expectations of its contributions to WP. This may well mean that it is as legitimate and appropriate for HR to concentrate energy on actions that help to overcome unexpected problems in meeting quantity and quality targets as it is for HR to engage in preplanned and proactive activities, such as forecasting future demand and supply conditions. WP has a short-term relevance and value as well as a long-term dimension and, as was pointed out recently to one of the authors, the long term is getting shorter! Stacey's (2011) concept of organizational agility is one that has interesting applications to HR's role in WP.

Table 10.4 Constructing the workforce plan—key questions and sources of information

Key question	Useful sources of information
What are the purpose, strategy, and objectives of the WP function?	• Organizational objectives • Department objectives • Job descriptions
What are the strengths and weaknesses of the current labour force?	• SWOT analysis • Customer service survey
How do we classify positions and grades?	• Manpower plan • Grading structure • Job evaluation scheme • Job descriptions
What are the external labour market changes?	• Market data • Jobcentre Plus statistics
What are the age, skill, gender, and ethnicity profiles?	• Personal records • Training files
What forthcoming legislation may affect us?	• Consultation papers • Recently reported case law • New regulations
What is our current demographic and ethnic spread compared to the community?	• Equal opportunities monitoring data demographics analysis • Data from Equality and Human Rights Commission
How do we retain specialist skills?	• Turnover data • Skills audit • Appraisal data
Do we have the right organizational structure for future demands?	• Organizational structures • Organization's strategic aims and objectives
What skills will we need in future?	• New product development strategy • Organization's strategic aims and objectives

Despite the recognition that making effective contributions in the field of WP sometimes involves the HR practitioner reacting to unforeseen events, constructing some sort of HR plan, the key features of which reflect a detailed understanding of the organization's internal and external environments, is still considered an important tool for the management of employment numbers, employment costs, and the quality of an organization's human resources. Its construction and format are likely to differ depending on the requirements of different organizations, but, as a guide to the key issues against which the plan needs to deliver, Table 10.4 provides a useful summary.

Measurement and Metrics

Historically, measurement in HR was very much associated with WP and involved the production of estimates or 'precise' measures covering:

- Changes in the existing supply of labour as a result of:
  - people leaving the organization, often described as 'labour wastage', or 'labour turnover' if losses are replaced by the recruitment of new employees;

- people being absent from work because of illness or other reasons;
- the loss of productive time resulting from wasteful working practices and lower-than-acceptable performance levels.

- Changes in the demand for labour, which can only meaningfully result from an assessment of changes in:
  - production levels and work requirements;
  - establishment numbers;
  - changes in employment budgets;
  - the expansion or contraction of productive capacity;
  - changes in labour productivity and working methods;
  - the application of new technology.

Developing reliable demand forecasting models has always been more difficult to achieve than measuring changes in the supply of labour, for the simple reason that variations in the demand for an organization's products or services can never be predicted with a sufficient degree of certainty. Quantitative methods of identifying future demand requirements include:

- Trend analysis, where demand levels for specific types of worker are based on known factors and historical data and these can then be predicted as the known factor values change. For example, in a hotel, if a cleaner can clean ten rooms in one shift and the hotel has 100 rooms, ten cleaners are required with 100 per cent occupancy rates. But as occupancy rates change over the year, expected reductions in occupancy rates, say to 80 per cent, would require only eight cleaners. However, small movements in demand either way and for a limited duration may not necessarily involve any changes in the number of employees but rather in the number of hours worked and paid for.

- Ratio analysis determines future HR demand based on ratios between assumed causal factors and the number of employees needed. It differs from trend analysis in that it does not require significant historical data. Establishing ratios of supervisors to staff, sales staff to annual sales volumes, and drivers to the number of weekly/yearly items to be delivered allow predictions about the demand for workers/managers based on changes in the independent variable. However, this method can be crude and often overstates labour requirements. For example, increasing the size of a delivery lorry would mean fewer drivers even if the number of parcels increased. Improvements in efficiency, working arrangements, and the use of technology all make fixed ratios of questionable value. However, in cases such as fruit picking where the work remains much the same, increases in acreage of strawberries to be picked would help to predict changes in the demand for pickers given what is known about the average weight of strawberries one competent worker can pick per hour/day.

- Regression analysis is a method of estimating demand based on statistical analysis of relationships, either single or multiple. The closer the correlation to one the stronger the relationship. Obviously, it is important to select appropriate independent variables that correlate highly and over time with the dependent variable—the demand for labour.

There are qualitative approaches to demand forecasting which include:

- managerial judgement (sometimes referred to as the Delphi technique). This really involves taking a holistic and flexible view of the company's strategic plans, its external environment, and any other salient factors and reaching a judgement about its future labour requirements based on expert opinion; and

- scenario planning which involves creating different future states the company might find itself in and creating estimates for its labour requirements based on these; in other words, the organization develops several 'plans' which reflect different scenarios. An organization could create three different estimates accordingly, one for a constant economic situation (e.g. zero growth), a second for some anticipated economic growth (e.g. 5 per cent growth), and a third for the possibility of economic decline (e.g. 5 per cent reduction). But most scenario planning exercises are much more sophisticated than this example suggests.

Difficulties of accurate demand forecasting are particularly acute in the private sector, but even in the public sector, in which services rather than products dominate and markets are generally less volatile, changes in funding and budgetary pressures can also affect the ability to make long-term predictions about demand requirements.

Changes in demand can often be linked to known changes in labour supply, for example, a known level of wastage, and can be used to establish demand requirements in terms of replacing people who leave. Knowledge of wastage levels is also an important factor in making decisions about demand requirements over the longer term. On the one hand, if an organization is expanding, simply replacing labour that is lost will not deliver the numbers and quality of employees required, leading to the need for additional recruitment. On the other hand, an organization that needs to make reductions in its labour force as a result, for example, of a decision to outsource may be able to avoid or limit the need for compulsory redundancies by not replacing the numbers of people who are predicted to leave over a given period. Recruitment then becomes a strategy relevant to both situations—reducing it when demand falls and increasing it when demand increases.

Before we move on to consider some of the most commonly used measurement techniques, it is important to make the point that the results of these calculations do not, in themselves, represent anything other than a contribution to subsequent decisions about how organizations manage situations of labour surplus or shortage. Depending on expectations of future requirements, managers may choose to accept a short-term surplus in the knowledge that demand will increase in the medium term and that the cost of a short-term reduction strategy, followed by the costs of hiring new staff, would be more than the costs associated with running a short- to medium-term surplus. Much depends on the organization's ability to live with short-term surpluses, and on its philosophy towards its employees and their welfare.

Equally, shortages of labour do not necessarily result in new recruitment. There are other ways to meet demand requirements, through, for example, the use of overtime working, reorganizing working methods, and introducing new contractual arrangements for existing staff. There is no single 'correct' strategy for managing surpluses or shortages for all organizations; rather, it is a matter of choosing the one that best fits, or a combination of several that fit the particular circumstances of each individual organization in ways that minimize costs, maximize productivity, and, as far as possible, also reflect the interests of employees. As shown in HRM Insight 10.2, the situations faced by managers in responding to changes in their workforce, even though the numbers involved might be relatively few, can be complicated and challenging.

HRM INSIGHT 10.2 **The case of Sunside Leisure**

Sunside Leisure is a privately owned business, which operates a number of leisure facilities: including hotels, leisure centres, sports facilities, gyms, and swimming pools. The organization employs around 500 staff in total. The HR team consists of an HR director, an HR manager, and two administrators. In three months' time, the HR manager is due to start maternity leave and will therefore be out of the business for between six and twelve months. She has indicated that she will probably take only six months off and, after this time, intends to return on a full-time basis. Additionally, one of the HR administrators is due to go on maternity leave in six weeks' time. She has indicated that she will probably be on leave for twelve months and may wish to return part-time, for two or three days each week.

The team is committed to the following activities in addition to the normal day-to-day recruitment, adminis-tration, induction, performance management, and communications activity:

- delivery of equal opportunities training to fifty managers and team leaders (consisting of five one-day work-shops, which were originally going to be delivered by the HR manager in four months' time);

- wage negotiations covering fifty staff who transferred under TUPE from facilities that were originally man-aged by the local council, which are likely to be sensitive due to a disparity in rates between the different facilities;

- restructuring of the catering teams, including outsourcing to third-party caterers of ten employees and po-tentially reducing the requirement for a team leader;

- a recruitment campaign to increase head count at two leisure centres for the increased summer demand and to provide 'out-of-school' summer sports clubs for 5–12-year-olds in the area.

Questions

1. What options might the HR director consider for covering the periods of maternity leave in the department?
2. What additional resources might be required and where might they be found?
3. How might the HR plans be affected by the current situation and how can these effects be minimized?

Absence

Absence through sickness or because of other reasons represents a significant cost to most organizations. In 2007 it was estimated to have cost UK businesses over £13.4 billion (CBI, 2007). In 2013, according to PwC, sick days are costing UK employers about £29 billion a year, with British workers taking up to four times as many days off than rival economies. It found UK workers have an average of 9.1 sick days each year, nearly double the amount workers in the US take (4.9 days) and four times more than Asia-Pacific (2.2 days). The Western Europe average is 7.3 days. The study of 2,500 UK businesses also showed sick leave accounts for nearly 90 per cent of a company's absence bill, which includes compassionate leave and industrial action. It found while UK employees are taking fewer unscheduled absence days than two years ago (9.8 days in 2013 compared to 10.1 days in 2011), the number of sick days has risen (9.1 days in 2013, compared to 8.7 days in 2011), as well as the associated cost of staff sickness. It is estimated that sick days now account for £28.8 billion of the UK's overall £31.1 billion absence bill (Newcombe, 2013).

A more recent survey of UK absenteeism claimed that while absence costs vary considerably within and between sectors, the median annual absence cost per employee is £522, which is less than in previous years, corresponding with the decrease in absence levels (CIPD, 2016a). More interestingly, the survey also showed that a WP approach to absence does not just involve monitoring and measuring it but in addition involves developing strategies for its reduction. Two-fifths of organizations reported that they had a target in place to reduce absence, rising to 48 per cent of those that believe it is possible to reduce absence. Targets are more common in organizations with higher levels of absence. In addition, targets are more likely to be found in larger organizations and in the public sector, which probably reflects the way HR is structured in those organiza-tions. Somewhat worryingly, only 25 per cent of organizations, regardless of sector, achieved their 2014 target absence level, and a further 38 per cent almost achieved it, but just under two-fifths failed to achieve their target, with larger organizations most likely to fail. There is no explanation as to why the targets were not met but we might speculate that this is a reflection of an HR department that is 'active' but not particularly effective.

As far as average days lost are concerned, the CIPD survey found that the average level of employee absence had increased slightly compared with 2014, from 6.6 to 6.9 days per employee, although it remains lower than in 2013 (7.6 days). There is, however, considerable variation in absence levels across and within sectors. Average absence has increased most in the public sector (where it is now 50 per cent higher than in the private sector), while it has decreased slightly in manufacturing and production. The level of absence also tends to be higher in larger organizations, regardless of sector. Given that the majority of recorded cases of absence are sickness-related, the significantly higher sickness levels among public sector workers raises a number of interesting questions. It is unlikely that those who work in the public sector are generally more unhealthy than private sector employees; a much more likely explanation lies in the generosity of public sector sick pay schemes and the cultural acceptability of certain levels of sickness absence, although ACAS state that most sickness absence is genuine (Bevan, 2016).

The difference in these figures compared to those produced by the PwC report is difficult to explain without looking at the details of the respective methodologies, but these differences in reported absence levels do focus attention on the challenges associated with measuring accurately and consistently workforce data. At the organizational compared to national or sector levels, this is much easier to achieve. Statistical trends show long-term changes in the levels of absence and as we have noted these are affected by a number of key variables such as type of work, economic sector, and the generosity of sick pay schemes. The latest ACAS booklet that covers attendance management (2014) highlights patterns of absence that are broadly unchanging although they do vary from organization to organization because they are influenced not just by levels of illness, but also by management style, culture, traditions of behaviour, and working conditions; sickness absence levels can indicate not just physical and psychological issues but cultural problems too.

Research quoted in the ACAS booklet has shown that these patterns often display a number of common features:

- young people tend to have more frequent, but shorter periods of sickness than older people;
- manual workers generally have higher levels of absence than office workers;
- office workers have higher levels of stress-related illness than manual workers;
- unauthorized absence is more common among new starters; longer-serving workers get to know the organization's standards and stay within the framework;
- sickness-related absence due to work-related accidents is also greater for new or inexperienced workers.

But the report did not confront the kind of cultural issues that we have identified as explaining some of the differences in sickness absence levels between the public and private sectors and between large and small organizations.

> **KEY CONCEPT Presenteeism**
>
> The problem of workers being on the job but, because of illness or other medical conditions, not fully functioning, can cut individual productivity by one-third or more. In fact, presenteeism appears to be a much costlier problem than its productivity-reducing counterpart, absenteeism. And, unlike absenteeism, presenteeism is not always apparent: you know when someone does not show up for work, but you often cannot tell when—or how much—illness or a medical condition is hindering someone's performance (see Hemp (2004)).

While it is inevitable that the majority of employees will be unable to attend work from time to time due to ill health, it is a fact that some employees will take more time off than others. Employers tend to expect that employees will only take time off when they are genuinely unable to work, but there will always be occasions on which employees take time off, claiming ill health, when they might have come to work, known euphemistically as 'taking a sickie'.

Absence rates vary between different organizations and between different types of job. It might be argued that it is easy to manage with minor illness if the working environment is warm and comfortable, compared to more physically demanding environments, and that more motivated employees with a greater degree of responsibility will be less inclined to take time off when they are ill. The propensity to take time off may also be linked to the extent to which the psychological environment is positive and supportive or threatening.

Whatever the reason for absence, there is no doubt that it impacts on the organization's ability to meet its objectives and puts pressure on those who have to cover the extra workload. According to ACAS (2014), the effects of high absence levels are wide-ranging and affect everyone in the organization: managers and employees, together with their representatives, who collectively need to work to keep absence under control and to minimize its costs.

The costs of unacceptably high levels of absence are normally expressed financially, and are based on calculating the value of lost production and sick payments. These financial measures also include:

- the costs of additional staffing levels and overtime working to cover anticipated absences;
- the cost of replacement labour;
- costs associated with delayed production and disruptions to planning schedules;
- costs associated with loss of quality or service levels;
- costs resulting from low morale and dissatisfaction.

Monitoring absence rates forms a key element of absence management and most organizations track absenteeism on a weekly, or monthly, basis to monitor the effectiveness of absence management strategies. This often involves calculating absence using a formula and comparing the resultant figure with an internal or external benchmark standard.

The *absence rate* is usually calculated as follows:

$$\frac{\text{Number of days absence within team}}{\text{Number of working days available}} \times 100$$

For example, a team of five people who each work five days a week, less bank holidays, can work a total of (365–104–8) 253 days each, making a team total of 1,265 potential working days. If 50 days were to be lost through absence, the team's absence rate would be:

$$\frac{50 \times 100}{1,265} = 3.95$$

A calculation for the whole organization is similarly based on the time lost as a result of absence. The formula usually used for calculating the *lost time rate* is:

$$\frac{\text{Total absence in days / hours over a given period}}{\text{Total time in days / hours available over the period}} \times 100$$

In the case of a hotel, for example, we can work out total hours available per month by multiplying each employee's monthly contracted time (remembering that this figure will reflect different employment contracts) and adding the individual totals together. This assumes, of course, that the hotel actually monitors and records absences, aggregates the time lost through absence, expressed preferably in hours, and calculates the lost time rate. By using the same calculation on a departmental basis, it is possible to develop a more detailed pattern of absences that will be useful in deciding on what corrective action to take.

One of the limitations of the lost time rate calculation is that it cannot distinguish the pattern of absence in terms of whether few employees are taking long periods of absence or whether many employees have infrequent bouts of absence. Consequently, the calculation of what is known as the *frequency rate* is often preferred to, or used in conjunction with, the lost time rate. The formula for this is:

$$\frac{\text{Number of spells of absence over a given period}}{\text{Number of workers employed over the period}} \times 100$$

A similar calculation can also be used to establish the individual frequency rate, expressed in terms of:

$$\frac{\text{Number of employees with one or more spells of absence over a given period}}{\text{Number of workers employed over the period}} \times 100$$

The Bradford absence index is useful because it gives weighting to the frequency of absences, reflecting the belief that many frequent spells of absence are more disruptive and costly than fewer, longer absences, which can be more easily managed because it is easier to make contingency plans. The index is calculated by using the formula:

$$\text{Index} = S \times S \times H$$

Where:
S = the number of recorded absences;
H = the total number of hours absent.
The formula can be applied to each individual and to the organization as a whole.

As an example, consider two hotel employees, one a porter and the other a chef. If the porter were to be absent on five separate days during a month, totalling forty hours, his or her absence index would be:

$$\text{Index} = 5 \times 5 \times 40 = 1,000$$

The index for the chef, who was absent only once during the month for one week, would be:

$$\text{Index} = 1 \times 1 \times 40 = 40$$

The problem with this method of calculating absence, as with the others, is that it cannot show the actual costs of any given level or individual pattern of absence. It might be argued that, although the index for the chef is much lower, his or her absence in the month might be more of a problem than that of the porter simply because of the chef's more valuable contribution and the revenue lost in the restaurant because of his or her absence. Not all employees have the same value in terms of their contribution to the organization and the costs of absence will vary in relation to the value of work that is lost.

Turnover

'Turnover' differs from 'wastage' only in the sense that the use of the former term relates to those who leave an organization and are replaced, while the latter relates only to the number of those who leave. For practical purposes, both relate to the loss of people and the terms can be used interchangeably.

According to a CIPD survey (2015), the median rate of labour turnover increased in 2014, reversing the decline observed in previous years. More than three-quarters of the organizations surveyed experienced challenges retaining staff, with many taking steps to address retention by improving pay and benefits. The recent rise in turnover rates reflects a healthier and growing economy and supports the theory that turnover rates are inversely related to the rate of unemployment, so that when unemployment falls turnover rates rise. As the CIPD survey points out, by far the most important reason for people leaving their jobs is a voluntary decision to leave, with the presumption that most will leave to look for another job.

While the need to replace those who leave and/or recruit to new posts will always be a key part of what workforce planners do, retaining skilled people is increasingly important in times of economic growth. Of course, different economic sectors and specific organizations will experience their own particular priorities and challenges. But understanding why people stay within jobs and organizations and taking action to increase retention levels is assuming strategic significance. We have mentioned the use of financial rewards in the context of improving retention but other approaches such as increasing learning and development opportunities and improving line managers' people skills are also used. CIPD research (2015) emphasizes the value of non-financial and intangible rewards (such as recognition and praise) in ensuring employees feel valued and appreciated, a point raised in Chapter 13 on managing rewards.

While there are situations in which high wastage rates may actually help an organization to resolve a situation of labour surplus, persistently high rates outside of the organization's or industry benchmark range are usually a cause for concern: when skilled and experienced employees decide to leave, it usually represents a significant loss and a cost to the organization. Finding suitable candidates to replace leavers takes time and resources in terms of recruitment and training (Chapter 7 deals with recruitment costs).

It is inevitable, however, that, from time to time, employees will choose to leave and either pursue careers elsewhere, retire, take a career break, or return to education. These are examples of what is known as 'voluntary quits'. In addition to employees who choose to leave, there are a small number who are dismissed or who are performance managed out of the organization. High turnover rates create particular pressures for the HR department, which is primarily responsible for replacing those who leave, but also for line managers who face disruption to production and service standards. This is the necessary result of having to induct and train new employees, who are usually less experienced and productive compared to those they replace: it takes time before new recruits perform at their optimum levels. The result is a reduced ability to meet objectives, reduced levels of productivity, and higher unit costs. It is therefore important for managers to measure labour turnover, monitor its impact, and take appropriate action to minimize its effects. As far as the latter is concerned, this should at least involve operating efficient and effective replacement procedures, but the effective management of turnover also involves understanding and dealing with its underlying causes.

The highest rate of labour turnover tends to be among those who have recently joined an organization. The reason why longer-serving employees are more likely to stay is mainly because they become used to the work and the business and have an established relationship with those around them. It can be thought of as a kind of investment that people make in an organization where the returns are enjoyed largely although not entirely from remaining. Opportunities for development, promotion, and increased status also tend to increase over time, balanced of course, by those that might be available somewhere else. Factors that affect labour turnover can be categorized as:

- pull factors: which organizations have little or no control over, such as moving to a new location, arrival of children, and retirement, but particularly higher wages/salaries; and
- push factors: which organizations have control over, such as dissatisfaction with work, managerial behaviour, lack of promotional/developmental opportunities, and relatively low pay.

STUDENT ACTIVITY 10.2

Read the 2015 ACAS guide on induction, available at: http://www.acas.org.uk/media/pdf/3/0/Starting-staff-induction.pdf. After reading the guide, list the main mistakes that employers can make in the way they deal with new starters. What are the key characteristics of an effective induction programme?

KEY CONCEPT The survival curve

The survival curve measures the number of new starters (normally those who start together or over a short period) who are still there after, say, twelve months. The survival rate can be calculated by dividing the number who started with those left at monthly intervals.

Measuring turnover

Turnover is typically measured over a twelve-month period to smooth out seasonal differences, but can be tracked weekly or monthly to provide a more detailed and contemporary understanding of what is happening.

When I first moved into HR I found it was essential to listen to my customers, understand what their requirements were, and to try to accommodate these requirements within the wider HR framework. I have continued to develop and build relationships with my customers during my career. It is vital as an HR professional to devote time and effort to building trust and relationships with those who depend on you and need your advice and support.

To enhance the customer relationship, it is vital as an HR professional that you ensure your customers are trained in ER if you want them to deliver the HR agenda. B, improving their competence and confidence in this area they will be better equipped to work with you. This relates particularly to line managers who need to be informed and made aware of what the organization's key ER policies are, so they are able to buy into them.

ER can take two forms within an organization: it can be seen as the internal police within the organization that ensures compliance with policies and procedures or it can work in partnership with the internal customers of the organization to deliver its HR agenda. Working in partnership ensures that relationships are built which will allow the HR professional to influence other stakeholders and through this increase the chances of successfully delivering the HR agenda.

The ER framework within which an organization operates will be shaped by the legislation and the policies and procedures which are applied. It is essential as an HR professional that you are aware of these and also of any future legislation which will impact upon this area.

During my time in manufacturing I had good relations with the unions. I found that it is possible to work in partnership together for the benefit of the company and union members. When this relationship has been strained, particularly around pay reviews, it has sometimes resulted in industrial action by union members which was detrimental not only to the company but to those involved in the industrial action. This is because even if the company accedes to union wage demands to avoid prolonging the action, the need to restrict increases in the overall wage bill is often associated with a reduced head count and loss of employment.

When dealing with individual cases involving disciplinary action, it is essential to undertake proper preparation and collect and retain supporting documentation. My experiences have shown that when this is not followed management are exposed to claims of unfair or unreasonable conduct, and any subsequent employment tribunal cases become more difficult to defend.

ER in the future will continue to be governed by legislation and by a company's own policies and procedures. Those working in this field of HR have an important opportunity and responsibility to work in partnership with other organizational stakeholders in such a way as to deliver the organization's HR strategy, which ultimately contributes to the bottom line.

The points made about improving ER in the Practitioner Insight offered suggestions to managers about how to deal with union representatives and build understanding and trust between the two parties. Dan Goulding's reflections point towards specific actions the ER professional can take in dealing with his internal 'customers' to maximize his effectiveness and deliver the outcomes expected of him and his ER colleagues. But how does an organization know whether its ER are good or poor, and in need of improvement? What good and poor mean is of course subjective and debatable, but there has to be some correlation between what managers and trade union representatives do or don't do well and how these actions affect institutional and personal relationships. Table 8.2 offers an indication of what both parties could do to strengthen relationships.

HRM INSIGHT 8.5 Resolving conflict at work

The following insight provides an opportunity for a practical activity to resolve a particular employment relations problem. Read the case and answer the following questions.

Southlands Hospital Trust employs a wide variety of different employees. The ancillary hospital staff have a 39-hour working week, compared to a 37-hour working week for nursing and professional staff. Over the last three years, the union, as part of the collective negotiating process, requested a reduction in the working week of ancillary staff from 39 hours to 37 hours, to match those in professional positions, with no loss in overall weekly pay.

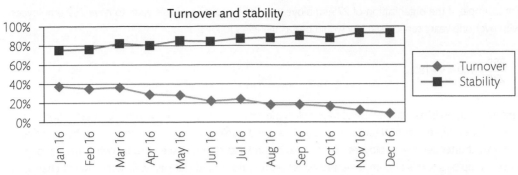

Figure 10.1 Annual labour turnover and stability tracked monthly as a percentage (2016)

Turnover is calculated as follows:

$$\frac{\text{Number of leavers over a given period}}{\text{Number employed at the period end}} \times 100$$

For example, if twenty-five people left over the last twelve months and the current number of employees is 275, turnover would be calculated as:

$$\frac{25}{275} \times 100 = 9.09\%$$

Variations on this method involve taking the average number employed during the period. For example, in an organization employing 235 people at the start of the period and 275 at the end, with 25 leavers, the calculation would be:

$$\frac{25 \times 100}{(235 + 275)/2} = 9.8\%$$

Figure 10.1 shows how annual turnover can be tracked on a monthly basis to show trends. In the graph, annual labour turnover within this organization is showing a downward trend throughout the twelve-month period. Note that turnover and stability rates always move in the opposite directions.

Stability

'Stability' is a useful measure to accompany turnover and can give a better reflection of the retention of employees than can turnover. If turnover is high, it is difficult to establish which employees are those that are leaving without carrying out more in-depth analysis. It may be that new employees are poorly inducted and often leave within the first few weeks, and that longer-serving staff tend to stay. Or it might be the case that a large portion of longer-serving employees are nearing retirement and that the increase in turnover is due to a demographic 'surge'.

Stability is a measure of the percentage of employees with more than a stipulated amount of service. For example, it may be useful to know what percentage of staff has over one year's service and can therefore be assumed to have become experienced and qualified. Stability can be calculated as follows:

$$\frac{\text{Number of staff with over one year service over a given period}}{\text{Number of staff employed at the period end}} \times 100$$

For example, if the organization of 275 employees in the turnover example were to have 259 employees with over one year's service, stability would be calculated as follows:

$$\frac{259}{275} \times 100 = 94.18\%$$

This information is particularly useful to establish the kind of problem from which the organization is suffering. For example, if annual turnover is 45 per cent and stability is 90 per cent, then it can be seen that it is mostly shorter-serving employees who are leaving and that retention seems to be better among longer-serving employees. It is also important to assess both turnover and stability against the overall change in numbers employed. For example, stability figures will fall during expansion, due to the number of new positions created, and turnover may be very high, along with very high stability, if an organization reduces in size resulting in little recruitment and large numbers of redundancies. Figure 10.1 also shows an organization with increasing stability among its workforce throughout 2016.

Vitality

Some organizations, particularly larger ones with a variety of more senior positions, may have policies that encourage and promote the development of staff, and which try to balance external recruitment to more senior positions with internal promotions. 'Vitality' is a method of measuring the balance of internal promotion versus external recruitment or loss of employees. Although much less commonly measured than turnover, it can be a useful measure of career development and employee satisfaction.

Recruitment vitality is measured as follows:

$$\frac{\text{Number of roles filled by internal promotion} - \text{number of roles filled externally}}{\text{Number of positions filled}} \times 100$$

High negative scores indicate a preference for external recruitment, suggesting that if there is little opportunity for internal promotion, then it is likely that internal potential is not being tapped. High positive scores indicate that most posts are being filled internally and that external markets are not being fully exploited to bring in new ideas, skills, and methods of working.

A similar calculation can be made for *turnover vitality*:

$$\frac{\begin{array}{c}\text{Number of roles vacated due to internal promotion} - \\ \text{number of roles vacated due to departure}\end{array}}{\text{Number of roles being vacant}} \times 100\%$$

High negative scores indicate that employees are leaving to advance their careers, while high positive scores indicate that employees rarely leave to pursue careers externally and benefit from internal promotion as a preference.

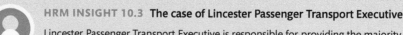

HRM INSIGHT 10.3 The case of Lincester Passenger Transport Executive

Lincester Passenger Transport Executive is responsible for providing the majority of local passenger transport for the town of Lincester. There are 150 drivers employed across a variety of shifts, providing a bus service seven days a week to the general public. The organization also employs ten maintenance and twenty administration and managerial staff. Turnover has risen among drivers over the last five years, from 10 to 25 per cent. Driving staff are expensive to recruit and train. In addition, 25 per cent of the drivers will be eligible for retirement in the next five years.

Questions

1. List as many reasons as you can think of that might contribute to the high levels of labour turnover among driving staff. How might you establish the 'real' reasons for the turnover of drivers?

2. What range of HR activities might the Lincester Passenger Transport Executive consider over the next twelve months to help to improve retention?

3. What HR metrics should the organization track and how might information be gathered to monitor any improvement in employee retention that might be achieved?

4. What strategies might managers consider to deal with the retirement problem?

Measurement in HR—the Wider Debate

One of the central objectives of this book is not only to provide insights into what skills and knowledge HR practitioners and line managers need to manage employees effectively, and how these activities might be carried out. It also explains why these activities are important and the consequences that might follow from doing them, not doing them well, or not doing them at all. This approach is particularly important as far as measurement and the use of metrics in HR are concerned, and the issues surrounding the development of wider and more sophisticated approaches to measurement now need to be considered.

To put this issue into a wider context, it is necessary to recognize that the increasing use of metrics to monitor organizational performance is not restricted to HR. The public sector, in particular, has been subject to the development and application of many different performance measures and targets, and there is an extensive literature on the experiences and effects of performance measurement strategies (Propper and Wilson, 2003).

In the USA the work of writers such as Jac Fitz-enz (2010) and Huselid et al. (2005) and in the UK Mayo (2001) and Bucknall and Wei (2006), in measuring the economic value of employee performance and producing measures that allow the financial costs of employee behaviour to be calculated, has been instrumental in bringing the debate about measurement in HR to centre stage. Paul Mooney (2001) in particular, provides a powerful argument in support of the use of measurement in HR. He starts off his chapter on HR metrics by quoting W. Edwards Deming:

You don't have to do this—survival isn't compulsory.

This is Mooney's way of stressing the importance he attaches to the extensive use of measurement in HR. He is particularly critical of the HR community because of its reluctance to understand why measurement is important and the value it can provide. He claims that while almost every other facet of business has committed to measuring its contribution and effectiveness, HR has been reluctant to go down this route, and argues that this is directly linked to the lack of status and respect from which many in HR suffer. But is this the cause or effect of HR failing to engage with the measurement debate?

He goes on:

The absence of quantification forces HR departments to remain on the periphery of strategic decision-making, rather than occupying the central role which the importance of the function requires (Mooney, 2001)

With this comment, Mooney reinforces the importance of the distinction that Ulrich (1996) makes between HR activities and HR outcomes, under which what HR 'does' is less important to its organizational standing and reputation among other stakeholders than what it achieves, or its outcomes. Measurement of these 'deliverables' and the added value they represent is now seen as a critical part of what managing the HR function involves and it affects WP.

Part of the problem with measurement in HR is the belief that the economic value or effectiveness of people and HR activities cannot be calculated, and Fitz-enz (2000) accepts that there are difficulties associated with measuring the economic effectiveness of people, particularly in service and professional work, although less so in manufacturing. But he, like Mooney, is a strong believer in the importance of incorporating rigorous measurement systems into the HR function, arguing that:

> **The bottom line is that although it is not easy to evaluate staff work in quantitative terms, it can be and is being done**
> (Fitz-enz, 2000)

This strategic approach to measurement has significantly different implications for HR practitioners than the measurements associated with WP and its association with absence and turnover rates. Mooney argues that it is the management and effective reduction of absence and turnover that has the potential for reducing the financial costs of employment, not the measurement of the rates alone. The application of a strategic rather than an operational perspective on the use of metrics in HR provides an important insight into the way thinking about metrics has changed over time. In an endorsement of Huselid et al. (2005), M. J. Carey, a senior US HR professional, said:

> **Their focus is not HR metrics, but metrics in the context of business strategy. Rather than asking, 'how do we measure HR' they ask, 'what do we need to measure about the workforce to deliver strategy'.**

In their book, Huselid et al. make a number of key points which reflect their whole approach to developing workforce metrics:

- Workforce performance and management is not simply a 'people' issue that is the responsibility of HR professionals; rather, it must be a shared responsibility with line managers.
- Strategic success requires both line managers and HR professionals to adopt a different perspective on what constitutes workforce successes. This means that a focus on standardization, cost reduction, and maintaining the status quo needs to be replaced with a different mindset; one in which differentiation, segmentation, and achieving outcomes that are strategically valuable dominate.
- Workforce measurement systems need to go beyond the operational and serving a monitoring and comparative function (benchmarking), to become strategic. That is, they have to focus on aspects of the workforce and its performance that will confer competitive advantage. (In this context think about what we said in Chapter 3 about what being strategic actually means.)

This strategic approach to measurement and its link to outcomes means that rather than HR developing useful but not necessarily connected and integrated measures, they need to develop a set of measures that link:

- The effectiveness of what HR does and what it is capable of doing in terms of its:
  - HR management systems;
  - HR practices; and
  - the competencies of its staff;

to:

- leadership and workforce behaviours;
- workforce competencies; and
- workforce mindset and culture.

These can then be directly related to:

- financial success;
- customer satisfaction; and
- operational performance.

Research by Anderson (2007), commissioned by the CIPD, into organizational evaluation practices has led to important developments in how the returns from training can be conceptualized and calculated. Her work highlights different approaches to calculating returns on training with the concept of 'return on expectations' replacing or coexisting with more conventional ideas about return on investment. Anderson argues that different organizations have different evaluation requirements and that a 'one size fits all' approach is misleading and unhelpful. Importantly, she considers the strategic significance of engaging in meaningful evaluation activities and how this can help to generate stronger integration between training and other HR activities. Again, with reference to the training function, the report by Mavin et al. (2010) suggests an approach to the evaluation of training that involves sixteen factors in what is called the learning transfer system inventory. Both examples illustrate how measurement in HR and a stronger focus on measuring what is useful and important is evolving and becoming more sophisticated. Yet the question remains: what is HR doing with the data?

Returning to the contribution of Andrew Mayo, he is another influential writer who believes in the importance of quantification in HR. He is committed to the principle that everything can be quantified, and in ways that facilitate improved management and organizational change. He claims that:

> Whether we are talking about the capability or potential of people, the culture in which they work ... measures for these can be found and tracked.

(Mayo, 2001)

Mayo's main contribution is in his work on measuring the asset value of employees, rather than on measuring absence or turnover levels. His more sophisticated approach involves measuring:

- people's human capital, which varies between employees, can rise as a result of personal and competency growth, and collectively represents the totality of human capital available to the organization;

- aspects of the working environment, such as leadership, the level of practical support available to employees, the extent of team and cooperative working, the extent of learning and development, and the effective use of rewards and recognition;

- the financial and non-financial value to the organization generated by each/all employees.

He argues that, while employees do represent a cost in terms of their wages/salaries and other benefits, they are also an asset, in the sense that they create and add value. He is also clear that some employees represent a net cost, in the sense that the value of their contribution is less than the costs of employing them. Some employees become 'liabilities', and it is important that managers are able, through appropriate measurement activities, to identify these employees, as well as those who represent a high positive asset value.

The ability to calculate each person's *human asset worth* (HAW), and give it a numerical value that can be tracked over time and which can be compared with that of other employees, is based on the following formula:

$$HAW = \frac{EC \times IAM}{1000}$$

Where:

HAW = human asset worth;

EC = employment costs;

IAM = individual asset multiplier.

Essentially, Mayo's model is based on knowing what it costs to employ a person, and this is not only their wage or salary, but a more complete understanding of the costs associated with employment and the value of those factors, such as capability, potential, contribution, and what he terms 'alignment to organizational values', that collectively express the person's gross asset worth or value (Mayo, 2001: 82–3).

There are, of course, questions that can be asked about the methodology and assumptions that underlie Mayo's model, but his concern with finding ways of measuring, and thereby distinguishing, individual asset values is understandable when so little is known about this area.

A more recent contribution to the search for effective and reliable ways of calculating key human resource costs, benefits, and outcomes comes from one of the UK's leading HR organizations—Mercer Human Resource Consulting (Bucknall and Wei, 2006). In their introduction, the authors set out the rationale for using measures in HR. The reasons are to:

- determine how well HR is operating and contributing;
- determine how efficient and effective the HR function is overall;
- help establish key features of the organizational climate and how well it is performing;
- improve the productivity of all staff; and
- maximize the return on human capital.

They also set out certain important principles which reflect Mercer's extensive experience in the field of workforce management. The following are important because they reflect a clear focus and approach to planning and resource management; they provide a set of guidelines that indicate how best to create maximum value for an organization's human resources. They suggest that managers:

- Recognize that WP and management should be seen as a form of asset management based on business needs and performance drivers. This emphasis implicitly rejects the notion that jobs can be created and people employed, or continue to be employed, for reasons that cannot be justified by key business considerations.

- Segment employees and focus on groups that have the greatest potential impact for adding value or reducing costs.

- Consider and focus on three critical dimensions of the workforce:
  - capabilities;
  - behaviours; and
  - attitudes.

- Determine which workforce characteristics contribute most to the creation of value and at what cost.

- Establish priorities and drive through changes in how things are done.

STUDENT ACTIVITY 10.4

Obtain a copy of *Magic Numbers for Human Resource Management* (Bucknall, H., and Wei, Z. (Wiley, 2006)) and look at chapter 8 which shows you how to calculate HR staff as a percentage of total staff.

1. Use the ratio provided to calculate the HR ratios in organizations from which it is possible to collect the required data.

2. Compare the different ratios and explore the reasons for the differences.

3. Establish whether organizations that have a high HR staff to total staff ratio are more or less productive than those with low ratios—and how this can be measured.

4. Think of strategies that reduce the HR ratio and consequently the costs of running the HR function, while increasing current levels of HR contribution and effectiveness.

Measurement in HR—Some Important Reservations

Despite the enthusiasm for measurement, the debate about its relevance, value, and consequences is by no means one-sided. The purpose of this final section is to address some of the concerns associated with the increasing use of measurement and its extension to different areas of the HR function.

The first point to make relates to the collection of data that allows measurements to be made of the chosen parameter or variable. Without appropriate monitoring and recording systems, and without the accumulation of reliable data, managers can often find that they are presented with 'snapshots' rather than meaningful trends. Actions based on partial, flawed, or misleading data will undermine the ability of measurement to improve HR's contribution to organizational performance: they might result in the wrong decisions being taken. The arguments we developed about evidence-based management earlier in the book are relevant here: how reliable as well as useful is the data being generated?

Weaknesses and limitations in HR measurements is one fairly obvious problem that organizations have to confront. According to Cascio and Boudreau (2011), even where HR develops more comprehensive measurement systems, organizations typically 'hit a wall'. They claim that:

> Despite even more comprehensive databases and ever more sophisticated HR data analysis and reporting, HR measures only rarely drive strategic change . . . and that there is a large gap between the expectations of the measurement systems and their true effects.

Comparing HR with other management functions such as accounting and finance, Cascio and Boudreau argue that HR develops measures to justify itself and the investments made in the function and/or to try to prove a cause–effect relationship between HR programmes and activities and organizational outcomes. When in fact the other two functions are less concerned about how their services are delivered, and more on the quality of the outcomes. They go on:

> Most HR measures today focus on how the HR function is using and deploying its resources and whether those resources are used efficiently. If the HR organization is ultimately to be accountable for improving talent decisions . . . HR professionals must take a broader and more complete perspective on how measurements can drive strategic change.

Mooney (2001) confronts the same challenge when he suggests that managers need to consider the following criteria in deciding on their strategy on measurement.

● **The relevance of the chosen measure to the overall business performance**

If the data relates to an aspect of employment or HR that is of no, or limited, value (defined by the appropriate stakeholders), little is gained from expending energy and resources in measuring it. Becker et al. (2001), in their work on measurement in HR, make a similar point when they question how well existing HR measures capture the 'strategic HR drivers'. They go on to claim that there is often a disconnect between what is measured and what is important.

● **The amount of control that the HR function has over a particular measure**

The phenomenon or behaviour that is of interest to managers—for example, employee satisfaction with organizational leadership—is a result of a wide range of experiences outside the control of HR.

The question arises: is this something that the HR department should measure if it can't do much to influence these experiences?

- **The ease and reliability of data collection**

  This raises questions about whether decisions on what to measure are unduly influenced by the ease with which data can be collected and analysed, rather than driven by the value and importance of the phenomena to which the data relates.

- **Data quality**

  This relates to the reliability and integrity of the data, and the way in which it is analysed and interpreted. The key question is: what does the data actually show and can it be relied upon?

Pfeffer and Sutton (2000) are two writers who, while accepting the potential value that appropriate and reliable measures can bring, are concerned to highlight the pitfalls and problems that managers face when the measurement process 'goes wrong'. They begin their chapter, 'When measurement obstructs good judgement', by claiming that:

> **Measures and the measurement process, especially badly designed or unnecessarily complex measures, are amongst the biggest barriers to turning knowledge into action.**
> (Pfeffer and Sutton, 2000)

They are particularly concerned about the many examples of measurement processes that fuel destructive behaviour, rather than helping managers deal with it. They also claim that, even when such destructive measurement practices are identified, little is done to correct things.

Perhaps the most well-known, but nevertheless important, observation that they make is that measures focus particular attention on what is measured, often at the expense of other equally—or perhaps more—important behaviours. They point out that measures affect what people do, as well as what they notice and ignore, arguing that, as a consequence:

> **everyone knows that what gets measured gets done, and that what is not measured gets ignored.**

In addressing the potential and actual problems that managers experience with measurement, Pfeffer and Sutton offer the following suggestions:

- Effective measurement systems that drive behaviour need to be simple enough to focus attention on key elements and fair enough that employees believe in and support them.

- Measurements need to guide and direct behaviour, but not be so powerful and coercive that they become substitutes for judgement and wisdom. Managers need to interpret and ascribe meanings to what the measures are producing. The meaning may not be immediately apparent and managers may be unwilling to accept the 'correct' interpretation if this seems to reflect badly upon their actions.

- Managers should avoid the overuse of 'end-of-process' measures, which can provide insights into how well or badly something has gone—but, because these are 'end' measures, it is often too late to correct a problem. Consider the use of evaluation questionnaires that ask students what they feel about a module after they have completed it. 'In-process' measures instead allow for the correction of mistakes and for more effective control in time to make a difference.

In their later book, Pfeffer and Sutton (2006) address the wider issue of the evidential basis upon which managers take strategic decisions that impact on their employees. As part of a powerful critique on management practices that lack a strong evidential support base, they consider the widespread practice of benchmarking and whether this 'best practice' HR activity will deliver the outcomes expected of it. The point they make is that there is far too much 'casual benchmarking' taking place, with practices being copied without those who are doing the comparison and benchmarking against another company fully understanding the underlying logic that drives these practices. In other words, they really don't understand why someone else's strategies, policies, and HR practices are in fact better and end up trying to imitate what others do. They argue that much of what successful organizations do and achieve is less to do with superficial behaviours, rituals, and practices and much more to do with the organization's basic values and beliefs—in other words its philosophy, a point made in Chapter 1. This suggests that too many measures that HR initiates may be more superficial and limited rather than deeply rooted and of strategic significance.

They also make the important point that comparisons with other organizations, particularly where external benchmarking is involved, fail to reflect the different strategies, competitive environments, and business models that define the uniqueness of the comparator organization. The implication is that external benchmarking runs the risk of establishing a disconnect between the underlying rationale and drivers of success from the more obvious measures of their success.

The following student activity provides a very powerful example of what can go wrong when performance measures and targets are imposed on one organization simply because they worked somewhere else.

STUDENT ACTIVITY 10.5

Read the case:

Kerr, S. (2003) 'The best laid incentive plans', *Harvard Business Review*, **81(1), 27–37.**

1. Explain what the case has to say about the relationship between data and actual behaviour.

2. In groups, discuss the examples of employees responding in unexpected and undesirable ways to the measures to which they were subject. In particular, try to explain their motivations and objectives.

3. Explore the underlying assumptions made by Hiram Phillips and his consultants about the use of the measures and the behaviour of employees.

4. Evaluate the choice of the performance measures imposed on the company and its employees. Consider alternative and more effective ones.

5. Given the original objectives, present your own ideas on the use of measures to improve performance.

Summary

- HR professionals are increasingly required to take a more strategic role within their organizations, but the ability to operate strategically and the invitation to do so are heavily dependent on their ability to show clearly and consistently how their contribution can add value and contribute to organizational performance.

- Understanding how employees create value and measuring the value-creation processes is the challenge that the HR professional faces.

- Organizations, because they are unique, need to develop different approaches to the measurement of the things that are important to them and which help them create value, either through the reduction of costs (e.g. those of sickness absence) or through increasing the asset value of their employees.

- One of the most important things that HR needs to know about are the consequences of its actions and policies, and whether these are positive, neutral, or negative.

- WP is an obvious aspect of HR that requires reliable and useful measurement tools and approaches, but there are many others that seem to be increasingly subject to measurement and evaluation.

- In considering what to measure and how, two things stand out. First, measures are not ends in themselves, but means to ends. In other words, they contribute to the achievement of objectives and outcomes that matter to organizational stakeholders; if they do not, they fail the functionality test. Second, deciding on what to measure involves managerial judgement and choices that reflect questions of importance: that which is easy to measure may not be as important and useful to HR and the organization as things that are not.

- What many managers often fail to realize is that the introduction of HR measures does not simply represent a technical innovation or initiative. For those affected by measures and targets, their significance and impact is likely to be perceived and experienced in a rather different way: measures and targets can become instruments of coercion and punishment, and, because employees react to this perception, they can distort behaviour.

- Moving HR measurements from an internal to a strategic focus is not just a question of developing new measures and metrics: it is strongly linked to the ability of HR itself to develop a more strategic role.

Visit the **online resources** that accompany this book for self-test questions, web links, and more information on the topics covered in this chapter, at: **www.oup.com/uk/banfield3e/**

? REVIEW QUESTIONS

1. How is WP different from what used to be known as manpower planning?

2. What are the quantitative and qualitative aspects of WP?

3. What are the implications for WP of flexible employment patterns?

4. Why can the use of targets and measurements of performance distort behaviour and lead to the manipulation of figures, and how can this consequence be avoided?

5. What are the key contributions to effective WP that HR professionals and line managers must make?

6. What does strategic WP mean and involve?

Q CASE STUDY   Absence management—the case of Mid-shire Council

Mid-shire Council employs over 3,000 employees and is the largest employer in its local area, which has a population of 400,000 people. A brief overview of its workforce characteristics is as follows:

- 51 per cent work on a part-time basis;
- 32 per cent are male;
- over 50 per cent are aged 40 plus;
- 90 per cent are classified as white British;
- less than 1 per cent consider themselves to have a disability;
- over 30 per cent have worked at Mid-shire for over ten years.

Compared to the overall national average of eight days' absence per employee per year, Mid-shire continues to have a high level of absence. Over the past few years, managing absence has become a strategic priority for the Council, and it has invested considerable amounts of time and resources to try to reduce absence levels.

The average number of days absent per employee for the last few years is as follows:

- 2011–12   11 days
- 2012–13   12 days
- 2013–14   16 days
- 2014–15   14 days
- 2015–16   13 days

There was a reduction in absence between 2013–14 and 2014–15, which can be attributed to some of the absence management interventions that were put into place. However, the magnitude of the problem hasn't really changed. This is despite providing absence data to managers, the introduction of new absence management policy and procedures, and the provision of training for managers.

The absence management policy is a comprehensive document, which details the responsibilities of all parties when managing absence. It also details the procedures that have been followed. This includes the requirement that managers carry out a return-to-work interview after every absence. Mid-shire has also identified a set of 'trigger points', which means that, after a specified number of days or occasions of absence, a counselling interview will take place between the manager and the employee. The organization has made some progress in reducing its absence levels. It has also set some ambitious future targets for the average number of days' absence per employee over each of the coming four years, as follows.

- 2016–17   12 days
- 2017–18   11 days
- 2018–19   10 days
- 2019–20   9 days

There is confidence that the absence levels can be reduced further because of the commitment of the organization to achieving this. Senior managers have this as one of their strategic priorities, and this has been communicated to managers and employees throughout the organization.

Questions

1. Is it possible to distinguish symptoms from underlying causes in explaining absence at Mid-shire?
2. Taking the average salary of Mid-shire staff as £28,000, with an add-on to cover other employment costs of 35 per cent, calculate the costs to the Council of the last two years of absence.
3. Does the demographic profile of the organization have an impact on absence?
4. Are there any absence management interventions that the organization has not covered which could be made to try to improve the situation and help to achieve the planned reductions in absence?
5. What would be your strategy for addressing the absence problem at Mid-shire, recognizing that the workforce is heavily unionized?

FURTHER READING

Crush, P. (2011) 'Strategic workforce planning is just the business for the savvy HR director', *HR Magazine*, 11 August.

Incomes Data Services (2011) *Workforce Planning. HR Studies.*

Kearns, P. (2000) *Measuring and Managing Employee Performance*, FT/Prentice Hall.

Mayo, A. (2015) 'Strategic workforce planning: A vital business activity', *Strategic HR Review*, 14(5).

Wilkinson, A. and Johnstone, S. (eds.) (2016) *Encyclopedia of Human Resource Management*, Edward Elgar.

REFERENCES

ACAS (2014) *Managing Attendance and Employee Turnover*, at: www.acas.org.uk

ACAS (2016) *Zero Hours Contracts*, at: http://www.acas.org.uk/index.aspx?articleid=4468

Addicott, R. et al. (2015) 'Workforce planning in the NHS', paper for the King's Fund, at: https://www.kingsfund.org.uk/sites/files/kf/field/field_publication_file/Workforce-planning-NHS-Kings-Fund-Apr-15.pdf

Agency Central (2014) http://www.agencycentral. co.uk/articles/2015-11/skill-shortages-in-construction-industry.htm

Anderson, V. (2007) *The Value of Learning from Return on Investment to Return on Expectation*, CIPD.

Appleby, C. et al. (2014) *The NHS Productivity Challenge Experience from the Front Line*, King's Fund, at: http://ignacioriesgo.es/wp-content/uploads/2014/09/NHS-productivity-Kings-Fund1.pdf

Becker, B. E., Huselid, M. A., and Ulrich, D. (2001) *The HR Scorecard*, Harvard Business School Press.

Bevan, S. (2016) 'Do public sector workers really take more sick leave?', Lancaster University Management School, at: http://www.lancaster.ac.uk/lums/news/comment/do-public-sector-workers-really-take-more-sick-leave

Boxall, P. (2013) 'Mutuality in the management of human resources: Assessing the quality of alignment in employment relationships', *Human Resource Management Journal*, 23(1).

Bramham, J. (1994) *Human Resource Planning*, IPD.

Bratton, J. and Gold, J. (1999) *Human Resource Management*, 2nd edn, Macmillan Business.

Bucknall, H. and Wei, Z. (2006) *Magic Numbers for Human Resource Management*, Wiley.

Cascio, W. and Boudreau, J. (2011) *Investing in People*, Pearson Educational.

CBI (2007) 'Workplace absence rises amid concerns over long-term sickness: CBI/AXA survey', press release, at: www.cbi.org.uk

CIPD (2015) *Show Me the Money! The Behavioural Science of Reward* [research report].

CIPD (2016a) *Absence Management. Annual Survey Report*, at: https://www.cipd.co.uk/Images/absence-management_2016_tcm18-16360.pdf

CIPD (2016b) Workforce Planning Factsheet, at: https://www.cipd.co.uk/knowledge/strategy/organisational-development/workforce-planning-factsheet

Fitz-enz, J. (2000) *The ROI of Human Capital*, AMACOM.

Fitz-enz, J. (2010) *HR Analytics*, AMACOM

Hemp, P. (2004) 'Presenteeism: At work—But out of it', *Harvard Business Review*, October.

HR Society (2013) *The Complete Guide to Workforce Planning*, at: http://hrsociety.co.uk/resources/knowledge_resources/Workforce-planning-chapter-one_draft_02.pdf

Huselid, M. A. et al. (2005) *The Workforce Scorecard*, Harvard Business Review Press.

Imison, C. et al. (2016) *Reshaping the Workforce to Deliver the Care Patients Need*, Nuffield Trust.

Jacobson, D. (2013) '16 HR metrics smart HR departments track', at: http://www.globoforce.com/gfblog/2013/16-hr-metrics-to-track

Mavin, S. et al. (2010) *The Evaluation of Learning and Development in the Workplace: A Review of the Literature*, at: https://www.northumbria.ac.uk/static/5007/hrpdf/hefce/hefce_litreview.pdf

Mayo, A. (2001) *The Human Value of the Enterprise*, Nicholas Brealey.

Mooney, P. (2001) *Turbo-Charging the HR Function*, CIPD.

Newcombe, T. (2013) 'Sick leave costs UK employers £29 billion a year, says PwC', *HR*, 15 July, at: http://www.hrmagazine.co.uk/article-details/sick-leave-costs-uk-employers-29-billion-a-year-says-pwc

ONS (2015) *Statistical Bulletin Public Sector Employment*, at: http://www.ons.gov.uk/employmentandlabourmarket/peopleinwork/employmentandemployeetypes/bulletins/uklabourmarket/2015-08-12

Pfeffer, J. and Sutton, R. I. (2000) *The Knowing–Doing Gap*, Harvard Business School Press.

Pfeffer, J. and Sutton, R. I. (2006) *Hard Facts*, Harvard Business School Press.

Philpott, J. (2010) *The 2010 Jobs Recovery*, CIPD.

Propper, C. and Wilson, D. (2003) 'The use and usefulness of performance measures in the public sector', *Oxford Review of Economic Policy*, 19(2), 250–67.

Reilly, P. (1996) *Human Resource Planning: An Introduction*, IES Report No 312, at: http://www.employment-studies.co.uk

Rubery, J. et al. (2016) 'Flexibility bites back: The multiple and hidden costs of flexible employment policies', *Human Resource Management Journal*, 26(3), 235–51.

Stacey, R. (2011) *Strategic Management and Organisational Dynamics: The Challenge of Complexity to Ways of Thinking about Organisations*, Pearson Education.

Teague, P. and Roche, W. K. (2014) 'Recessionary bundles: HR practices in the Irish economic crisis. *Human Resource Management Journal*, 24(2), 176–92.

Wallop, H. (2006) 'Bank holidays time off law "will penalise firms"', *Daily Telegraph*, 28 August.

Young, M. B. (2006) *Strategic Workforce Planning: Forecasting Human Capital Needs to Execute Business Strategy*, Conference Board, at: http://www.hrma.ca/wp-content/uploads/2012/10/Strategic-Workforce-Planning-Conf-Brd-May-2009.pdf

Learning, Training, and Development

11

Key Terms

Learning A fundamental and natural human process involving growth and change. Learning is about behavioural modification. It cannot be seen, but is inferred from differences in what we know, believe, and can do. Learning is the way in which we can improve and be different from that which we were. Learning needs to be understood as both a process and an outcome.

Training Can best be understood as planned, structured, and often formalized learning experiences that seek to develop specific skills and knowledge needed for effective job performance. Historically, employees have learned many of the competencies they need to perform effectively by being trained.

Development A term often used to describe changes in the whole person and what they can do. It reflects the belief that all people have the potential to be more and do more, and that this potential needs to be developed as well as utilized. People can develop to a limited degree through training, but development implies the employment of a much wider range of learning experiences and methods, such as coaching and mentoring, not all of which are necessarily connected to the working environment.

Competence The combination of skills, knowledge, and experience that results in a person's ability to carry out specific tasks and procedures to a required standard. Can be equated to 'know-how' (Gladstone, 2000). A specific competency can also be understood as an underlying characteristic of a person, that is, a trait, a belief, an ability, or an attitude, that distinguishes one person from another and explains differences in job performance (Rothwell, 2004).

Human resource development This term came into usage in the late 1980s and early 1990s, and is used by many writers, but fewer practitioners, in preference to training. Its relationship to training is similar to that between human resource management (HRM) and personnel management, in that it represents a more holistic and strategic approach to learning than does training (Walton, 1999).

Coaching A process in which a 'coach' supports an individual to develop his or her skills through a series of structured conversations by exploring the nature of challenges faced at work and helping the individual to identify the best approaches to those challenges to achieve the desired outcomes.

Mentoring The development of a relationship between a more senior person in an organization and more junior person, often as part of a development programme, involving the experienced person using his or her greater knowledge and expertise to accelerate the junior colleague's development.

Learning Objectives

As a result of reading this chapter and using the online resources, you should be able to:

- understand how people learn and recognize that training represents only one way in which people can learn at work;

- understand and explain why training and development (T&D) are important to an organization and to its employees;

- identify different approaches to delivering learning;

- recognize the relationship between learning, development, and performance; and

- understand the importance of evaluating training and other approaches to work-based learning.

Introduction

Humans are designed to learn: people who don't learn rarely survive or prosper. While we are born with different levels of inherited capabilities and potential, we are all programmed to learn and, through learning, grow as individuals. But some people seem to learn more than others, learn more quickly, and attain higher levels of performance. The ability to learn is strongly associated with intelligence, with nature and nurture explaining differences in this variable. Learning is a common characteristic, but also one that distinguishes one person from another in that some people seem to be 'better learners'. From the day we are born, we embark on a lifelong journey of learning. We are the most versatile of all animals and are able to adapt to the widest variety of environments, because of our capacity to learn the skills, knowledge, and best approach to be successful in the environment in which we find ourselves. The make-up of the human brain is much the same whether we choose to live and work in a fast-paced city environment or to adopt a subsistence lifestyle in a remote area with very low population density. However, the capabilities we must acquire to survive and succeed in these different environments are themselves vastly different and we require very different learning experiences to enable us to develop the necessary skills to survive and do well in each.

Most people will thrive when exposed to positive learning experiences and will continue to enjoy learning throughout their lives, but it is important to recognize that people can also be damaged by negative experiences of learning, particularly as children. This can have a lasting effect on their motivation to learn later in life, as adults. Nevertheless, learning new skills and acquiring knowledge, and therefore becoming better equipped to survive and succeed, are important to everyone because these connect to a person's sense of achievement and self-esteem.

STUDENT ACTIVITY 11.1

Some years ago, one of the authors discovered an unusual and interesting website that invited people to write in with 'their most dangerous idea'. He checked it out and found that the head of learning at a US university claimed that schools were bad for children and should be closed. His argument was based on the belief that learning in schools involves children being spoon-fed information and repeatedly tested to see if they can regurgitate it. This creates stressed-out children and adults who avoid all learning because it reminds them of their school experiences. He concluded his entry by saying that 'we need to produce adults who love learning and can think for themselves'.

Create a discussion group to share learning experiences. Use the questions below as starting points. Are there any patterns in the collective experiences of students? What conclusions can you reach? You can also use the results of the activity to make a presentation to your tutor and receive feedback on your work.

1. In the context of your own experience of learning, what were the things that you enjoyed about learning and what didn't you like?

2. Think about the learning achievements that have been particularly important to you. Why were they important and how did you change as a result of these experiences?

3. How can we make learning enjoyable and meaningful for adults, particularly those who have experienced learning failures earlier in life?

We can learn in many different ways, not all of which produce the kinds of outcomes to which either the individual or the training professional is committed. Learning at work, and for work, involves particular difficulties and challenges. Training, as a way of learning, is, from a managerial perspective, usually seen in instrumental terms. This means that learning is linked to the acquisition of new or increased competencies and capabilities which are used in the production of goods or services. These competencies and capabilities are only needed because they help to create value and wealth for the company. Quite simply, people and their capabilities are used by those who employ and manage them to generate goods and services that have a social or financial value but at the same time represent an investment from the individual in his/her future.

That both parties theoretically enjoy economic benefits from education and training is recognized by Woessmann (2014) who said:

> If a more educated person contributes a larger marginal product to the production process of a firm, in a market economy the firm will pay the person higher earnings accordingly. To the extent that the increases in future income streams are valued higher than the initial costs, the investment in education will be viewed as worthwhile from an economic perspective.

 Signpost to Chapter 1: Managing People at Work: Challenges and Opportunities, for information of the different value people represent as economic resources.

People are employed not only for what they already know and can do, but also for what they may subsequently learn to do. The ability to and a motivation to learn are then central to what is learned, and in the context of recruitment and selection represent one of the most important criteria for deciding who to employ and who not to. It is precisely because of the dynamic nature of the working environment, where employees are constantly expected to update their knowledge, learn new skills, and acquire new capabilities that the ability to learn is so important. There is a presumption, therefore, that all employees will not only work, but will also continue to learn. Peter Cheese, CEO of the CIPD, captured this dynamic which links changes in work and organizations to the importance and value of learning when he said in his introduction to a recent report on learning in the workplace:

> In this changing world of work, learning as a capability has to evolve and it has to be accessible, agile and flexible. Many interventions are now best delivered in the flow of work activity, not in a classroom. Digital technologies enable learning to be available anytime and anywhere with many also choosing to learn in their own time and often from their own sources of learning and knowledge.
> (Overton and Dixon, 2016)

To be effective and to continue to make a positive contribution to the employing organization, employees need to be active learners. But it is also important to recognize that, if an employee believes that the only beneficiary from his or her improved competence is the employer, learning through training will inevitably be seen as something he or she is required, rather than wants, to do. In extreme cases certain forms of training are perceived to be coercive, which raises important questions about learning and motivation. The positive motivation to learn cannot be taken for granted and must be nurtured, so that employees see learning as important for themselves as well as for the organization. Motivation is about the drives and needs within each person that direct and influence their behaviours. People are constantly interpreting their environment by reference to their own and others' interests, and act accordingly. Unless employees *want* to learn, they will be neutral towards it or try to avoid being involved. Coercing people to learn rarely works and is often counterproductive. If they are forced to participate in training, the most that will happen is that they will 'be there'. The reality is that the desired learning will not take place because those attending the activity lack the motivation to learn from it and may be determined not to.

It is not uncommon to find examples of individuals who have transgressed works rules or codes of behaviour, often in the context of anti-discrimination policies, to be 'sent for training' in an attempt to rectify unacceptable behaviour. For those involved, the training is likely to feel more like a punishment than any meaningful learning opportunity. Rather than change attitudes or behaviour such experiences are much more likely to have negative consequences. Such 'learning experiences' are of little or no value, consume valuable resources, and rarely achieve their intended objectives. The obvious question is why are they considered useful at all? Punishing people through forced attendance on certain types of training courses is an aspect of HR that is difficult to understand or indeed justify.

Few training events are likely to be experienced by those participating as coercive, but how many are considered effective? Knowing why good intentions surrounding training interventions don't achieve their intended outcomes is the purpose of HRM Insight 11.1.

HRM INSIGHT 11.1 Team briefing training at Delta Ltd

Delta Ltd employs over 200 people providing an outsourced call centre response for a large financial company. Each team has a team leader who is responsible for the day-to-day performance and management of the teams, ensuring that customers receive a prompt and friendly response to telephone queries. As part of Delta's strategic intention to improve communications across the business, the management team decided to revise their team brief. This was based on feedback from a recent opinion survey which suggested that employee interest in the briefings was low, that the briefings were rushed and largely consisted of a manager reading from a script. The senior management team therefore redesigned the briefing format to include sections about local performance and local news that were to be completed by the line manager along with an interactive section which would consider a particular problem area chosen by the team leader and their team to discuss and resolve issues.

Prior to the introduction of the new briefing, the senior managers met with the HR and training adviser to design and deliver an interactive training workshop to support the line managers to develop skills and confidence in delivering team briefing. The senior managers assisted with the training and agreed to attend a sample of briefings before and after training to support the desired improvements. The line managers all attended training and the feedback was very positive with everyone agreeing that the training was informative, enjoyable, and helpful. Two months after the training another opinion survey was conducted and the results from this survey showed no improvement in the responses from staff about their team briefings. The senior managers gathered further information from team members which suggested that briefings continued to be rushed and read from a script, with low interest for those involved.

Questions

1. What might be the reasons for the failure to change behaviour?

2. What alternatives might have been considered to embed a positive and sustained behavioural change in this situation?

'Learning' was 'Training'

One of the aims of this chapter is to clarify the often-experienced confusion between training and learning. It is a mistake to think of these as separate and independent activities. Training is a way of generating learning, based on the use of certain techniques and methods. As long ago as the 1960s, Magee and Thayer (1961) explained this relationship when they said:

> **The central process in training is learning.**

Training has, however, been subject to sustained criticism precisely because it is felt that it does not represent a powerful and reliable means of generating the learning managers and employees require. More specific criticisms are considered later in this section. The problem that people such as Martyn Sloman (2001) have with training is twofold. First, it is often badly designed and delivered, or based on a faulty diagnosis of training needs. Second, it is considered an inappropriate way of meeting certain learning requirements for which other, more individualized, learning methods, such as coaching and mentoring, are more likely to produce the required results. While the purpose of training is to generate learning, whether it does so and whether it meets the expectations of different stakeholders is problematic and uncertain.

Tom Boydell (2003) summarized the position of many who feel that HR professionals have placed too much emphasis and reliance on training when he asserted:

> I think most learning does not arise as a result of training. If you ask yourself, or a group of people, to identify 4 or 5 or whatever really important things you or they have learned in the past year/2 years of life so far, I would be surprised if many came as the result of training—i.e. of someone else telling or showing you, deciding for you, what the right answer is, the best way to do things, the correct way to be.

Over time, learning became increasingly structured, planned, and formalized. Training was seen as the means by which people could learn what they needed to know and do. Training itself became a profession. As Davis and Davis (1998) concluded:

> Training, with great impetus from the exigencies of two world wars became a function within organizations, and its processes became formalized. Like other work, training itself became work and was assigned to the people who performed it. This became the basis assumption about the place of training in organizations for almost half a century and is still the basic concept that governs how learning takes place in most organizations.

In response to this outdated concept, a more relevant vision of what training and the role of the trainer means and represents has emerged. In one sense, this 'new vision' presents a much stronger functional role for training, which involves, according to a joint CIPD/Towards Maturity report (2015), ensuring:

> that there is a clear line of sight between L&D activity and organisational performance

and that the role of tomorrow's learning and development specialist will be as facilitator and creator of network connections, social mentor, and curator of knowledge and learning resources in addition to occupying a strategic position within the HR and performance environments (Jeffery, 2016).

The critical question then becomes:

> Can training be reformulated and reframed, so that it can overcome many of its limitations and deliver valued contributions to the development of employees and facilitate improved organizational performance?

Perhaps, as an example of the way forward, those responsible for the management of training could and should incorporate the principles and practices associated with the theory of accelerated learning, which we consider towards the end of the chapter and which represents a more humanistic and effective learning paradigm. It seems to us that the shift within the training profession from an emphasis on training to one of learning is, in one sense, absolutely appropriate and justified. Learning is the key to change, improved performance, and personal growth. The central question is:

> How can we achieve this in the most effective and efficient ways possible?

It also must be recognized that, in the same way that 'learning got left out of training' we might also conclude that 'people have been left out of learning'. Perhaps there is even a link between these two statements. Certainly, we would argue that understanding the human dimension of learning is critical to any efforts to make training more effective: if training is seen only in terms of models, procedures, budgets, activities, and roles, it will continue to disappoint and fail to deliver. The human dimension has to be at the heart of the training experience. As learning becomes less an option and more a necessity, the failure to create learning is increasingly unacceptable and costly to employees and organizations. The problem is not one of not knowing how to meet this challenge, but of learning how to use what we know about what works and what doesn't, and understanding why.

⊕ For examples of different types of training, see Online Resources Extension Material 11.1.

Why train employees?

Consider for a moment how T&D fits into the HR and organizational agendas. In Chapter 1, the development of the human resource was explained as a key objective of organizations linked to the way that human knowledge and skills is linked by many to organizational performance and competitive advantage. Developing the resource is one of the fundamental objectives of people management, because it is through employees' growth and development that they increase their asset value and acquire new, or higher, capabilities that organizations need and managers can utilize.

But training can also be seen to be in the interests of employees who, through planned and structured learning, can acquire new competencies and capabilities, which they own. It adds to the value of their human capital. This not only increases their value to the employer, but increases their attractiveness to other employers: it enhances their employability and value in the labour market. In practical terms, this can result in increases in pay (skill- and qualification-based pay are part of many organizations' reward strategies) or lead to offers of more rewarding jobs elsewhere.

As well as supporting both employee and managerial interests, training is important because of the way in which it has the potential for facilitating:

- organizational change;
- functional flexibility;
- attitudinal change;
- statutory compliance.

Using a mechanical metaphor, effective training, as part of a strategy for learning and personal development, is arguably the most powerful 'lever' managers can use to achieve these important objectives. It is rare for major new organizational initiatives not to be linked to training of some sort or another, but there is a danger that training can be overloaded with expectation and used inappropriately or unrealistically. Training can be ineffective as well as effective—much depends on whether training is the 'right' lever to pull and, of course, on who is pulling it! To add a further layer of complication, but necessarily so, the same training experience can be both effective and ineffective for different participants! The choice of training method and the techniques that are used to stimulate interest and generate learning will also influence the effectiveness of training. As with other aspects of HR, the need to take a holistic and critical perspective on training is the only way to answer questions about its effectiveness and failure to deliver what it promises to do. This means that trying to understand and explain different training outcomes involves taking a much more holistic and systems approach than is often the case, where blame for failure is often attributed to inadequacies in instruction or lack of interest on the part of trainees. We also need to distinguish and recognize symptoms of failure from underlying causes.

RESEARCH INSIGHT 11.1

To take your learning further, you might want to read:

Sloman, M. and Webster, L. (2005) 'Training to learning', *Training and Development*, **59(9), 58–63.**

This article offers an interesting insight into the problems of training. Partly, they argue, these are due to changes in the nature of work and the kind of employees on which organizations increasingly depend for their long-term success, that is, those they describe as 'knowledge workers'. They claim that traditional classroom-based training courses are likely to be of limited value to the learning and development of this category of employee and that a 'shift is taking place from training to learning'.

Table 11.1 The six 'Es' of training—why organizations train employees

Engage	Effective training provides the opportunity for employees to connect with the organization, and with its policies and methods of working. It helps to ensure that employees 'buy into' or engage with the organization's culture. It helps to make employees feel valued and develop working relationships with their colleagues.
Educate	Training can help to educate or increase the knowledge and awareness of individuals and teams.
Enhance	Training can help to enhance or improve the skills and competence of individuals and teams within an organization.
Empower	By properly training employees, an organization can increase the accountability of teams and individuals, and can ensure that faster, better quality decisions can be made, while avoiding the need to pass decision-making unnecessarily up the organizational chain.
Energize	Participation in training can help to energize, motivate, and inspire employees. It provides an opportunity to take a step back and allows people to consider how they can best contribute towards the effectiveness of the organization.
Enlighten	Training can also be an effective means of helping individuals to see things in a different way. It can help employees reach an often sudden conclusion that there is a better, more effective, way of doing something and can help to unlock previously untapped potential.

Training can also be an expensive activity and the resources needed to equip a specialized T&D function do not come cheaply. Off-the-job training will incur the cost of either purchasing the professional training support or of providing a skilled person in the organization to design and deliver the training. Often both will be involved. In addition, there is the cost of releasing employees and covering their work for the period during which they are undergoing training. Additionally, there will be costs involved with expenses that are incurred by trainers and trainees, including facilities and materials. So why do organizations bother with the expense? Why not simply recruit someone who is fully trained already?

More often than not, it is not possible to recruit the ideal person with the exact skills needed for the job. Even when good candidates are available, they will still need to learn the unique systems, processes, and procedures operating within the organization. In addition, change is a feature of most organizations, and, as a consequence, so is the need to learn the new skills necessary for adapting to changing products, technologies, and markets. Technology, in particular, is constantly being improved and updated; new working arrangements are frequently introduced as a result of reorganization and attempts to re-engineer operating processes and procedures, and all of these require the employee to learn new things.

Training, for many, is therefore an essential part of surviving change and maintaining the currency of what they know and what they can do. Table 11.1 presents the main justifications and potential advantages of training.

STUDENT ACTIVITY 11.3

This can be done individually or as a seminar activity. Think about your experiences of attending training courses. Choose one that was a positive experience and another which failed to live up to your expectations. You can substitute a training course with a university learning experience. Write or talk about both experiences in terms of the following:

- The degree of control exercised by the trainer/lecturer and the participants.
- The degree of participation and engagement of participants in the learning process.
- The level of motivation shown by participants.

- The nature of your feelings during the experiences (e.g. enjoyment, enthusiasm, satisfaction, boredom, frustration).
- The extent to which your 'real' learning needs were met.
- The extent to which the learning experiences affected your job performance/progress.
- Comparing the two sets of responses, reach appropriate conclusions about what is linked to successful and unsuccessful training/learning.

The idea that training helps to prepare people for the changes they are likely to experience throughout their working lives, as well as helping to build job competences has always been at the core of what training represents as a managerial intervention. But the context in which training now operates is very different from that in the last two decades of the twentieth century. Today, according to a CIPD report (2015):

> in order to thrive in a volatile, uncertain, complex and ambiguous (VUCA) context, organisations need to be adaptive, agile and ambidextrous.

This means that the training function needs to be much more responsive, innovative, and integrated within the business, rather than being seen as a somewhat detached and marginal activity. The report found that only 56 per cent of L&D professionals agree that their activities were aligned to the organization's strategic goals and this must indicate that doubts or uncertainties exist about the purpose and value of the training function and its strategic value. This concern over the contribution training makes is given added weight by the findings that just 53 per cent of L&D professionals agree that the 'course' is only one of many options for building skills and performance. This suggests that 47 per cent of those surveyed believe that the training course retains its central role in delivering the required learning outcomes. The report did find however that the difference in approach and practice between those that were 'course reliant' and those that had embraced a more extensive range of learning interventions was becoming more marked. What the report describes as 'top deck' organizations reduced the focus on classroom training and learning administration and are over 50 per cent more likely to be focusing roles on coaching and mentoring, technology, infrastructure, and online delivery.

So, the evidence from this survey at least, indicates that while many of the more innovative and forward-looking organizations had developed a range of learning interventions which were suitable for different requirements, with training being one, a significant number of organizations and their L&D professionals were still relying far too much on training as the solution for most learning and performance enhancing requirements. Learning was almost certainly training thirty or so years ago but despite the fact that the emphasis now in forward-looking organizations is on a range of different and more effective learning interventions, there is still significant reliance on trainer-based formal training programmes with the completion of 'course' the measure of success and effectiveness. On the other hand, it would be wrong to reject the relevance of training: not everyone is a knowledge worker, not all improvements in performance can be achieved through coaching and mentoring, and the acquisition of basic skills is for many smaller businesses still best achieved through formal training. In their investigation into training Hutchinson and Purcell (2007) said:

> These traditional approaches to training, however, as a top-down, formal provision of courses, with the line manager role essentially that of a gatekeeper, are increasingly at odds with the reality and practical meaning of modern learning and development. It's important to recognize the emphasis placed on formal training, and its value, and not to throw the baby out with the bath water. But all organizations recognized that although formal training provision was necessary, it is by no means sufficient.

HRM INSIGHT 11.2 Taylor's Laundry Services

Taylor's is a medium-sized, privately owned business, employing around 200 people. It supplies industrial clothing to a variety of private and public sector customers, and provides a regular laundry service for those customers who require it. Most employees work in the laundry, ensuring that garments are properly washed, dried, and sorted for return to customers within a short time frame. Most jobs have relatively low skill requirements and new recruits are regarded as being able to pick up the work very quickly on the job. They are therefore put straight on the job on their first day in the business, having been shown where the fire exits are and how to operate the washing and drying machinery.

Time off the job for training is seen as costly, so people pick up the job by asking more experienced staff what to do. Staff turnover is high, with even relatively new employees passing on skills to new recruits.

Questions

1. What kind of training would this organization benefit from?

2. What cost is the company incurring as a result of the lack of effective training provision?

3. How is the lack of a training function impacting on other HR issues?

4. How would you design a realistic training intervention(s) that would address the above problems?

See the Online Resources Extension Material 11.2 for an explanation of the relationship between training and working.

Criticisms of training

While the theoretical case for training is undeniable, the reality is often disappointing. There is a sense that training—or, perhaps more accurately, those with training responsibilities—have too often failed to deliver what has been promised and expected, to the point at which the credibility of the training function has been compromised. Criticisms of the effectiveness of training are not new (Megginson et al., 1993), but, worryingly, persist. Davis and Davis (1998) suggest that one explanation for training's credibility problem is because 'learning got left out'.

They, at least, would agree that, if not left out, learning must either have been neglected or that the central role of learning in training has not been fully understood or articulated. They offer two reasons for this worrying neglect.

- Training, frequently seen as a response to a performance problem, has become routinized and, under pressure to provide a response, trainers have failed to reflect on the reasons for its successes and failures.
  - Particular factors that have a bearing on whether training 'works' are:
    - trainee motivation;
    - the importance of practice, transfer, and application;
    - the critical role of the line manager in supporting trainees.
- Trainers themselves often lack sufficient understanding of learning theories and, while they may be knowledgeable about the technique, subject matter, or procedure, many are not professional trainers. This is an important point because it suggests that, whatever the inherent limitations of training are, the key to its success or failure can be the personal and professional qualities of those who train, and the extent to which they can effectively manage the whole training process.

But the evidence that we have on the use of training does suggest organizations are relying less on this kind of collective intervention and more on those that focus on the individual, although much seems to depend on the purpose of the intervention. For example, the CIPD (2008) learning and development survey noted that within the companies surveyed, the use of training courses remained static, whereas the use of both coaching and in-house development programmes is on the increase. Even before the CIPD reported, the *IRS Management Review* emphasized the trend away from training to learning. Describing training as a reactive activity designed to resolve short-term operational deficiencies rather than being connected to the long-term needs of the individual or the business, the review made the point that:

> **organisations have recognised that the traditional ad hoc approach to training is incompatible with the need to adapt quickly to changing business circumstances.**
> (*IRS Management Review*, 1998)

This distinction between training and learning was explored in an earlier article by Sloman (2004), who reflected on the limitations of course-based training and its emphasis on content, instruction, and the passive involvement of trainees, associated with prescribed but not always achieved behavioural change. He concluded that learning was the way forward, generated by:

- motivated participants;
- self-direction; and
- work-based processes and locations.

In addition to uncertainties over whether learning is, or can be, generated through training, there is the added problem of line managers failing to understand their training-related responsibilities. According to Cosgrove and Speed, cited by Rothwell (1996), senior managers often fail to specify what they expect from the training function and training professionals, in an attempt to please everyone and gain support for their work, raise unrealistic expectations of what training can deliver. They fail to understand the importance of integrating it with corporate strategy.

Rothwell (1996) shares with Ulrich (1998) the view that, historically, training has been focused too much on activities, such as organizing and delivering courses, rather than on hard results and valued outcomes. Moreover, Rothwell believes that many customers of training mistakenly believe that high-profile training activity automatically means results and that offering more training inevitably improves performance. Both assumptions are questionable. In his critique of traditional approaches to training, he argues that the main problems that need to be overcome in any attempt to 'reframe' training are as follows.

- **Its lack of focus**

  There are too many terms in the field—education, development, etc.—and different job titles within the training community create confusion about what people actually do and what training actually means.

- **Its lack of management support**

  Senior executives and line management often express concerns over training's importance, costs, credibility, and effectiveness, and fail to understand their own responsibilities.

- **It is not conducted and managed systematically**

  Poorly carried out training needs analysis fails to identify the nature of the performance problem; training methods and materials are not carefully matched with training requirements and little is done to ensure that transfer of learning takes place.

- **It is not linked to other organizational initiatives**

  Training is often undertaken in isolation from other HR practices and management initiatives, and, however effective it might have been, quickly loses its impact because of this 'lack of connectivity'. Training becomes something that is bolted on, rather than integrated and embedded.

- **It can be used unrealistically to try to achieve attitudinal change, which is rarely, if at all, achievable through conventional training interventions**

In such areas as diversity, equal opportunities, and racial awareness, deeply rooted prejudices, beliefs, and behaviours are unlikely to be touched and changed through instruction or course-based training. Training can, if properly designed and managed, help employees to acquire knowledge and skills; it is much more difficult to believe that it can change the way in which they think and see the world.

HRM Insight 11.3 illustrates some of these issues.

HRM INSIGHT 11.3 Paul Kearns's story of an unhelpful director

Many years ago, when I had only been in my new job as head of training for a couple of weeks, our technical director came into my office and asked me if I could organize some presentation skills training for his team of engineers. I have to admit that I did not particularly like the way he just expected me to deal with his requests immediately, without any prior discussion. So, my first reaction was, 'Can we sit down and talk about exactly what you want?' This was not the reaction he had been used to from my predecessor. He seemed impatient and more or less intimated, 'What is there to talk about?' As far as he was concerned, it was a simple matter of sending his engineers on a course.

What Kearns was reacting to was the superficial level of engagement shown by the director, reflecting what was probably a belief that training itself was an unproblematic and a superficial process and needed little thought given to intended outcomes, processes, participants, and choices.

Source: Kearns, P. (2005) *Evaluating the ROI from Learning* (London: CIPD).

Questions

1. What did Kearns want to talk to the director about and why?

2. If Kearns had simply done what he had been asked and organized presentation skills training for the engineers, what might the outcomes have been?

3. What strategy might Kearns adopt to try to change the attitude of the director towards training and the role of training experts?

Figure 11.1 shows some of the defective thinking and practice that characterized some, but not all, traditional training experiences. But if the employee's experience of training reflects even parts of the approach to training presented in the diagram, the probability of any positive and lasting outcomes being created is likely to be low or non-existent. In fact, it might even be negative, because employees may be deterred from any further participation in training by the negative experiences of a flawed process. The specific weaknesses and problems associated with this model are not difficult to identify and include:

- the lack of direct involvement and ownership of trainees;

- the assumption that other people—line managers and trainers—know what employees need to learn and that reliable processes exist to identify learning requirements;

- the practice of subjecting employees, who may have quite different interests, skills, knowledge, and motivation, to the same training programmes;

- the belief that taking employees 'off the job' and out of their working environment facilitates learning;

- the belief that the transfer and application of any new learning that might occur is not problematic;

- the failure to recognize that employees learn as much, if not more, from informal processes and interactions than they do from planned and formalized interventions;

- the idea that training can be wholly managed and controlled by others and still be effective.

 See the Online Resources Extension Material 11.3 for information on the training cycle.

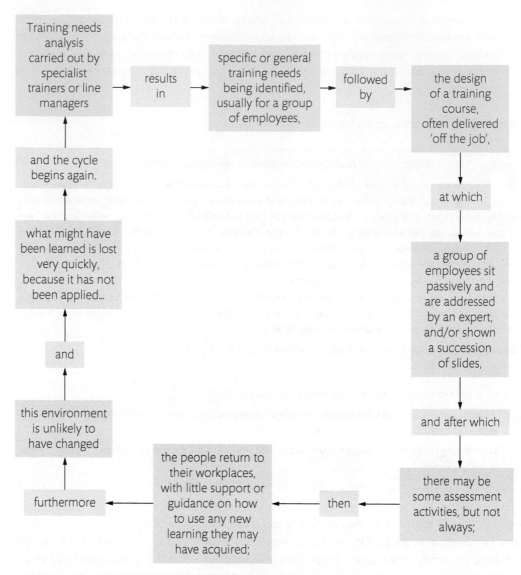

Figure 11.1 A flawed model of the training cycle

STUDENT ACTIVITY 11.4 Fixing the problem

Look carefully at Figure 11.1 and answer the following questions.

1. Taking each stage in turn, identify what changes and improvements should be made.

2. How might the trainees contribute to each stage of the model?

3. What might line managers contribute?

As a result of answering the above questions, design your own improved model of the training process. You can carry this out as a group activity, and present your results for discussion and evaluation to your tutor.

On a more optimistic note

A combination of budgetary pressures and the need for training to re-establish its credibility as a 'value-adding' activity has resulted in an improved understanding of what training can and cannot achieve, and a more effective use of training interventions. According to Peter Cresswell (in Hope, 2006), general manager for consultancy services at Siemens:

> Over the years training has improved considerably. We are now looking at how effective the training has actually been. It is important that organizations know what they want out of training and are able to measure it, to prove that they have achieved their objectives.

Evidence from recent research into the way many organizations have redefined and aligned their T&D functions shows that traditional models and thinking about training have been replaced with more effective and valued approaches. This is based in part on a closer integration between training and business strategy. Of particular interest is the way in which the 'business partner' model of HR is driving training in a more strategic and focused direction (Hirsh and Tamkin, 2005).

What emerges from many of these examples of new thinking and practices in training is the importance of the following (Hope, 2006):

- employees who want to participate actively in their own learning;
- close working relationships between trainers and line managers that result in agreement on training plans, skill and competency needs, and line support for learners;
- accurate diagnosis of T&D needs;
- opportunities for the reinforcement of learning through practice;
- designing bespoke training solutions rather than offering 'courses for all';
- a connection between the delivery of training, its evaluation, and the planning and design of future training interventions (i.e. a cycle of learning and application); and
- a strong relationship between the required learning outcomes and the learning methods employed.

The skills, sensitivity, and commitment of the trainer will always be a key factor that explains different training outcomes, so the answer to the 'who trains' question will be as important as how training is delivered. Line managers are not generally associated with the direct delivery of training; it is something that is more frequently associated with professional trainers but, consistent with our argument that much of HR is delivered through 'the line', it's reasonable to ask why not, given the obvious advantages that the line manager has in terms of knowing the employees, the skills and knowledge required, their application, and the social context in which they need to be applied. In the CIPD report by Hutchinson and Purcell (2007), line managers were in fact associated with an extensive range of training and learning-related activities, either directly or indirectly. These were:

- induction activities—for example, arranging for a 'buddy' to guide and advise the new starter, and encouraging shadowing or working alongside a member of staff in meeting clients/project work;
- giving access to challenging work or being a member of a project team;
- job rotation and the development of multiskilling so the individual is better able to contribute to the work of the section, team, or department;
- coaching and guidance—where the line manager works with a member of staff in dealing with a difficult business or service issue or the use of technology;
- the provision of informal training activities—often over the lunch period, where the team meets to consider a particular development/issue;
- arranging for the secondment of an individual to work in another section or location for a limited period to broaden experience and build networks;
- identification of external training programmes not provided for by the organization but which are directly related to the skill needs of the team; and
- providing formal training, as in delivering the training courses.

Different Perceptions of Training

In addition to the debate about whether, and under what circumstances, training delivers the required learning outcomes, significant differences have been expressed over the economic status of training (Kearns, 2005).

Training as a cost

As argued earlier, there are direct and indirect costs involved in training employees that have to be paid for, either from a central training budget or from budgets devolved to line managers. Training can also be perceived as an overhead, that is, a charge on all income-generating departments irrespective of whether they actually benefit from any centralized training provision. Seen as a cost, training is likely to be limited in scope and intensity: costs, generally, are something to be reduced. It might be thought that organizations that employ low-skilled workers are more likely to see the costs of training in a negative way, believing that adequate supplies of labour in the external labour market can meet all of their skill requirements. Surprisingly, however, the perception that training is a cost to be minimized is not restricted to such companies. Pfeffer (1998) provides evidence of national differences in the amount of training provided among motor manufacturing plants. He presents data that shows Japanese plants providing 364 hours of training in the first six months for new employees, while the respective figures for European and Australian plants are 178 hours and 40 hours respectively. One can speculate that, in the latter two examples, training is seen more as a cost to be controlled rather than as an investment, although there may well be other explanations for the difference.

In their study of human resource practices in UK companies, Truss et al. (1997) provide similar evidence of minimal levels of training being provided. In one large retailing and distribution company it was found that less than half of the employees received any training in the year prior to the research. In only two of the other seven organizations studied did more than half of the respondents indicate that they had received the training they needed to do their job.

Calculating Costs

According to Mayo (2001), the majority of adult learning comes from experience and experimentation which arguably involves little in the way of direct costs. The inference is that the most effective ways of learning do not require high levels of financial investment in order to increase the asset value of employees through enhancing their capabilities and competences. This low cost/high value approach to learning contrasts markedly with the fact that countries and organizations spend large amounts of money on training their employees. In 2000, US industry spent $62 billion annually on employee development, a figure which in 2010 was estimated to be nearer $100 billion (Fitx-enz, 2010), and probably higher today even if we only take inflation into account. While it is difficult to allocate this expenditure into the four main categories of learning—education, training, experience, and learning—from others, training costs are likely to represent the bulk of this amount.

Those who view training as a cost are influenced by three important considerations:

● the costs of training are borne in the present and can be easily calculated, assuming the necessary data is available, while the benefits from training accrue in the future;

● investments in training may not produce the expected or required learning and/or improvements in job performance even though traineees may be satisfied with their training; and

● trainees who benefit from training may leave the organisation and take their knowledge and skills elsewhere.

According to Fitz-enz (2000), the future benefits are far less uncertain than some would believe. His claim that if you spend time and money helping people learn and grow you make a deposit in their loyalty bank . . . and that the attitude that training simply helps people find other jobs is stupid, short-sighted and self-centered

suggests *that* the costs of training will almost certainly be compensated for by the tangible and intangible benefits and positive outcomes that will, in 95 per cent of people, almost certainly be realized. The reality may well be that the figure of 95 per cent is at the high end of the range measuring those employees who 'pay back' the costs of their development. Much of course depends on other factors such as the organizational culture and nature of the psychological contract between employees and management.

Notwithstanding the views of Fitz-enz and others like him who are committed to the principle and practice of developing employees, training and education, and to a lesser extent learning from experience and from others, do involve costs which need to be identified and measured. The following are the main cost categories that should be considered when planning and designing learning interventions:

1. **Design and development costs**: these are largely generated by:
   - time spent by trainers on identifying learning needs, consulting with managers, and designing the programme;
   - costs of external designers and developers;
   - other direct design and development costs (e.g. purchase of copyrights, travel, expenses);
   - costs of producing bespoke materials and purchasing off-the-shelf resources.

2. **Promotional costs**: most organizations devote efforts to promoting and marketing their training programmes which may involve in-house and external expertise.

3. **Administration costs**: an allowance must be made for the time taken by the training department in administrating the training programme. This will typically be a factor of the number of students:
   - hours of administration required per student;
   - direct administration costs per student (e.g. joining materials, registration fees);
   - maintaining training records.

4. **Staffing costs and management time**: this relates to the delivery of the training, whether it involves trainers/educators, instructors, coaches, mentors, or being self-administered (e.g. workbooks, computer-based training, online training). These costs are usually related to participants based on:
   - the number of students who will be going through the programme;
   - hours of group training (whether classroom-based, delivered in real time, online);
   - hours of one-to-one training (typically face to face, but also by telephone, videoconferencing, in real-time, online);
   - hours of self-study training;
   - additional staff hours (preparation time, the time needed to review or mark submitted work or the time needed to correspond by email or bulletin boards with online students);
   - staff expenses (e.g. travel, accommodation, subsistence).

   But an often ignored cost is that associated with lost work/production time, as participants often have to stop working to learn. The so-called opportunity costs are the costs associated with the participant not creating value while learning. Although these may be difficult to calculate, they are nevertheless real and may be significant.

5. **Materials**: traditional course-based education and training may not involve significant expenditure on materials but the delivery of online courses invariably involves considerable and ongoing expenditure to produce quality materials and resources (Schechter, 2009).

6. **Facilities:** depending on whether training is based on existing in-house resources or involves more expensive external facilities. The cost of premises, accommodation, and subsistence needs to be factored in to the cost calculations.

7. **Direct student tuition/course costs:** many management development courses involving externally awarded qualifications can be very expensive.

8. **Evaluation costs:** the cost of evaluating learning depends very much on the methodology used. Some approaches are rudimentary and involve little more than self-administered questionnaires but evaluation approaches that involve a considerable number of metrics, different stakeholders, and different time periods will involve considerable staff time.

Training as an investment

Seen from this perspective, training represents a key instrument in developing capacity and capability to support organizational objectives. During periods of economic difficulty, such as that seen towards the end of the last decade, it is particularly important that organizations are able to see the economic benefit of investing in training. The training budget can be seen as an easy target to reduce costs and unless spend can be justified then it is likely to be one of the first things to be forfeited. As Kearns (2005) states:

We should think of it as an important lever through which we can gain competitive advantage.

This means, however, that the contribution which training makes needs to be systematically evaluated and that some attempt must be made to calculate the returns on investment in training. Pfeffer (1998) again provides interesting examples of organizations that spend heavily on training and relate this spend to changes in key performance indicators. He cites the Men's Wearhouse, whose sustained growth in revenues and net earnings is linked to its investment in people. According to Pfeffer (1998):

The key to its success has been how it treats its people and particularly the emphasis it has placed on training, an approach that separates it from many of its competitors.

Interestingly, while claiming that training is an investment, Pfeffer accepts that return on investment (ROI) calculations are difficult, if not impossible, and that successful firms who invest heavily in training:

do so almost as a matter of faith and because of their belief in the connection between people and profits.

We might adopt Herzberg's comment here: 'it works whether you can prove it or not!' (Youngsang and Ployhart, 2014).

This belief in the beneficial effects of training and other developmental activities has helped to justify the huge sums of money spent on these activities annually: we mentioned earlier the situation in the USA and this is mirrored in the UK where in 2013 nearly £43 billion was spent nationally by employers, with 66 per cent claiming that they had trained their staff over the previous twelve months. Significantly, however, the survey that produced these figures was not talking about the quality or effectiveness of training, only the spend and coverage of training. It is worth noting that of this £43 billion nearly half went on the wages of providers (UK Government, 2014). The conclusion has to be that there is or can be a big difference between expenditure on and investment in training.

Another problem is that of trying to establish the returns on the expenditure made in training. From an investment perspective, the financial benefits of training cannot be measured in terms of student reactions, nor the amount of learning that has been achieved; not even the extent to which behaviour may have changed. The real benefits come from improved performance—traditionally the hardest training outcome to forecast or measure. The challenges of putting a financial value on different training outcomes are genuine and significant. How for example can we put a financial value on any increased loyalty that results from employees having benefited from training their employer has provided for them? Nevertheless, those writers and managers who see training first and foremost as an investment argue that it is vital to avoid easy measures of outcomes, or at least don't rely entirely on these, but to look for hard, financial measures that allow the ROI on training to be calculated. The following benefit categories can be used for this purpose, but it is important to note that they are not necessarily mutually exclusive—in some respects they provide alternative ways of looking at the same underlying benefit, which reduces the risk of counting the same benefit twice.

Labour savings

These occur where, as a result of the training, less effort is needed to achieve current levels of output. People who are more skilful as a result of training will be able to reduce the time needed to carry out any operation which is under their control. This can have the effect of reducing unit labour costs. But labour savings will only be realized if the labour applied to a job can really be reduced, whether this comes as a result of redundancies, transfers of staff to new positions, or reallocations of work. If the time savings simply result in more slack, then there is no saving.

Productivity increases

These occur where, as a result of training, additional output can be achieved with the same level of effort or within the same time standards. This implies that the organization requires or desires more output in this particular area. If it does not, then it might be better to express the benefit as a cost saving.

Other cost savings

Cost savings can be achieved in a variety of ways, not just through savings in labour, and this category allows organizations to take account of these. Examples include fewer machine breakdowns resulting in lower maintenance costs and lower staff turnover which reduces recruitment and training costs.

Greater flexibility

Training that increases functional flexibility, which means that people can do different jobs or become more specialized, can reduce the need for temporary hires to cover for holidays and absence which in turn reduces overall employment costs.

Income generation

In some job positions, it may be possible for new income to be generated as a direct result of training. Sometimes this can be satisfactorily recorded as a productivity increase, but there will be times when a more direct and specific analysis is required. Examples include a higher success rate in bidding for new work/contracts, higher sales, and greater innovation. The latter might not be easy to put a financial value to, but training in quality improvement techniques can result in new ideas and suggestions for improvements in production and manufacturing processes that can sometimes have a major financial impact (see Shepherd, 1999).

Signpost to Chapter 3: A Strategic Perspective on HRM, for insights into how training and learning can be related to competitive advantage.

HRM INSIGHT 11.4 The German engineering company

Some years ago, one of the authors was part of a group of staff and students on a visit to Germany. The purpose of the visit was broadly educational, and involved visiting different organizations to learn about management and how businesses in Germany were run. One of the companies visited was a medium-sized engineering company that manufactured a range of products used in the construction industry.

342

The Measurement and Evaluation of Training

The need to evaluate and measure the effectiveness in training is intrinsically linked to the justification for carrying out training, which can be justified in both economic and humanistic terms but is generally understood in terms of the increased contribution that employees and teams make to the organization. The evaluation of training has been debated continuously for the last fifty years, yet it remains difficult to directly quantify training outcomes and the link between attending training and subsequent changes in behaviour and the effect these have upon the organization. Fitz-enz (2010) argues that while trainers have historically maintained that the value of their programmes cannot or cannot easily be measured, this is not necessarily the case, offering examples of how returns on training can be either estimated or calculated. One of the earliest and best-known studies on the evaluation of training was that of Kirkpatrick (1998), who first proposed four levels of training evaluation. Kirkpatrick explained that the levels are increasingly more complex, and perhaps more costly to evaluate, but that for evaluation to be meaningful it should be across all four levels:

1 Reactions—what the trainees thought and felt about the training.

2 Learning—the increased knowledge and skills.

3 Behaviour—and the change in behaviour and improved performance on the job.

4 Results—the impact upon the organization of the training.

Where Kirkpatrick's model describes what should be evaluated the case for *why* should be linked to the following reasons:

1 **Proving**—to prove something has happened as a result of T&D activity.

2 **Controlling**—to demonstrate that the standards of delivery have been monitored.

3 **Improving**—to demonstrate that the review of current programmes and activities will ensure that they become better in future.

4 **Learning**—to demonstrate that evaluation is an integral part of the whole learning and development process itself.

It can be helpful to consider both models when designing training evaluation so that consideration can be given to what to evaluate and why. There are, however, difficulties in measuring the above in an objective manner that is valid in relation to the required outcome. Traditional post-course questionnaires may measure the satisfaction of trainees following attending training. However, this does not mean that learning has taken place or that this learning will be transferred to the workplace and within what time frame. Similarly, an evaluative test at the end of training may be helpful to assess knowledge, but this does not mean that it will be applied for the benefit of the relevant organization. It is therefore difficult to accurately measure ROI in training. Nonetheless this area remains a key focus for HR and training specialists as well as line managers in order that they may justify this continued expense. Arguably, the difficulty of evaluating the outcomes and value of informal learning activities are even more challenging than formal programmes, but Mattox (2012) offers insights into how this can be achieved. Valerie Anderson (2006) has been the leading UK writer on training evaluation and her research and insights have changed the nature of the debate, particularly on the different forms that returns on training investments can take. While many of the different models and approaches to training evaluation are of interest and of potential value, what is rarely acknowledged is that the process is or may well be an inherently political one. By that we mean that the need to show evidence of success may influence the way data is collected, what data is chosen as relevant, and how data is interpreted. Different stakeholders may view the same training experience differently (here we are thinking about management development programmes as well as nationally funded skills development schemes) where the reputation of the training function may be affected by the outcome of specific programmes. Where funding is dependent on agreed outcomes being achieved, then the risk of being less than objective is obviously present. But participant views on the training experiences they have experienced may also reflect personal and organizational issues that can affect the reliability of the feedback they provide. While the attractiveness of evidence-based management is difficult to deny, real care needs to be taken in the determination of whether the evidence generated through training evaluation is, or to what extent it is, objective and reliable: by no means any easy task!

RESEARCH INSIGHT 11.2

Read the following to take your learning further:

Anderson, V. (2008) 'View from the top: Executive perceptions of the value of learning', *Strategic HR Review,* **7(4).**

The article provides insights into what executives expect learning to deliver at an organizational level, the challenges of aligning learning to strategic priorities, and the ways in which HR professionals are measuring and reporting on the value of learning. A trend away from ROI approaches to 'return on expectation' assessments of the value of learning is identified.

The Practitioner Insight from Beverly Hodson highlights the importance of training and its evaluation at Northern Foods.

PRACTITIONER INSIGHT Beverly Hodson, former group learning and development manager, Northern Foods plc

Learning and development is widely recognized at Northern Foods as being an important part of our success. We are made up of a number of business units and these have different cultures. Some units are more proactive and more forward-thinking than others and here T&D is further up the agenda and is more targeted. Those units demonstrating best practice have mapped out their strategic plan and have clear and measurable outcomes and an associated return on the investment for T&D that link to this plan.

Measuring the ROI for training is an area with which many businesses struggle. However, for us it is critical to show this return to justify the training budget and to ensure that it is not an easy target for cuts when considering our annual budgets. Training is only part of this picture and individual development supported by good line managers is recognized as being one the most effective ways of learning with the strongest long-term benefit.

Our most effective learning is targeted development, where individuals are given the opportunity to learn new skills by engaging in real experience outside their normal responsibilities, like a project, with good line manager support. We have found it is better to focus on building an employee's strengths and mitigating their weaknesses rather than focusing on weaknesses. Effective line manager support is so important in ensuring that employees reach their maximum potential, that this is a key area of focus for us in terms of learning and development. We have a broad range of managers with different levels of skills and it is important for us to improve consistency in this area. This goes beyond learning and training and has involved us identifying what 'good management' looks like in our organization, identifying current capabilities, and helping managers move towards best practice. This entails developing management tools such as our 'capability model', which maps out the skills, knowledge, and talent required, as well as developing managers to be able to manage as effectively as possible.

Developments in Workplace Learning

The debate referred to earlier about training and learning involved two key issues.

First, questions were raised about the limitations of training, particularly with regards to over-reliance on training courses and the role of the trainer as 'expert', and whether such criticisms undermined the credibility of training as a planned and structured source of learning. We concluded that training continues to have a role to play, but only if the responsible parties respond to criticisms from participants and line managers, and begin to develop practices that are grounded in appropriate theories and principles of learning, and which also reflect actual business requirements.

Second, the trend away from 'training' towards 'learning' suggests that non-course-based approaches and practices need to be developed to reflect developments in the nature of the work and workers. This means that structured learning, defined as learning that is planned and is associated with specific outcomes, should be more individualized and learner-centred rather than 'imposed from above', and should wherever possible be embedded in the working environment.

This recognition that the workplace, rather than the training room, should be the primary context in which learning is located is a theme shared by many of the writers to whom we have already referred. 'Workplace learning', or 'work-based learning', is associated with the following contemporary beliefs:

- that the workplace, in terms of its physical and social environments, is a site for learning and offers a range of learning opportunities;
- that many of these opportunities are informal and opportunistic rather than formal and planned;
- that the workplace needs to be understood as a learning, as well as a working, environment;
- that working and learning are inextricably linked.

What emerges from this brief reference to the learning environment is the importance of context. Whether learning emerges from the ongoing social interaction at the place of work or as a result of more planned and structured training interventions, the influence on these experiences of a wider set of factors cannot be ignored. If HR professionals are genuinely interested in increasing the effectiveness of workplace learning, it will be necessary to address barriers to learning that may exist in the workplace itself, in addition to developing more effective learning interventions (Billet and Choy, 2013).

Coaching

Coaching is becoming a more commonly used tool to support employee development at work. The CIPD (2008) learning and development survey reported that 70 per cent of organizations surveyed use coaching as a method of developing their workforce. However, it can be defined in different ways and can be confused with mentoring and counselling.

Coaching in a work context shares many of the characteristics of coaching in sport. It generally refers to a process where a coach supports an individual to develop his or her skills through a structured conversation which explores the nature of the challenges faced at work and helps the individual to identify the best approaches to those challenges to achieve the desired outcomes. This may, for example, involve discussing situations at work to analyse the root cause and identify desired outcomes, followed by a process to choose the best options for achieving the outcome and evaluating the impact of actions taken. There is also an important motivational dimension to coaching that develops as the relationship between coach and coachee strengthens. Coaching should not be confused with either mentoring or counselling, although the boundaries between them can become blurred. Mentoring has some similarities but tends to involve a much more senior person using their greater knowledge and expertise to support the development of a more junior person within an organization. Coaching, in comparison, is perhaps more associated with developing a specific skill set that has been previously identified either formally or informally as an area for development. While it may be a line manager who is coaching a team member it may also be a functional expert, more experienced colleague, or third party appointed for the specific purpose of developing that skill set further. Counselling more typically refers to a process of support for an individual with personal problems often relating to either mental or physical health.

Coaching can be a very effective mechanism for developing employee skills, particularly in complex environments. Many organizations are investing in either coaching training for managers or are employing the expertise of externally sourced coaches to support the development of their employees.

According to the CIPD (2015), coaching targets high performance and improvement at work and usually focuses on specific skills and goals, although it may also have an impact on an individual's personal attributes such as social interaction or confidence. Anecdotal evidence suggests that coaching, through the relationship that develops between the two parties, can have a particularly strong effect on the coachee's emotional engagement to their work as well as in the more obvious impact on skills and technique. The process can last for a relatively short defined period of time, or form the basis of an ongoing relationship and style of managing (Knights and Poppleton, 2008).

STUDENT ACTIVITY 11.5

Read the conference paper by Valerie Anderson 'The line manager as coach: An assessment of coaching characteristics reported by line managers', available at: http://www.ufhrd.co.uk/wordpress/wp-content/uploads/2009/07/3-12-refereed-paper.pdf. After reading the article:

- Summarize the positive and negative experiences of line managers as coaches.
- Identify the factors that affect the line manager from taking on this role.
- Based on your own experiences, think about whether you have been coached by your manager and reflect on the effects and outcomes.
- Consider whether you have the capabilities to coach others; if not, what would you need to do to acquire these?

Although there is a lack of agreement among coaching professionals about precise definitions, there are some generally agreed characteristics of what coaching in organizations means and involves:

- It is essentially a non-directive form of development, though this isn't a hard-and-fast rule.
- It focuses on improving performance and developing individuals' skills.
- Personal issues may be discussed but the emphasis is on performance at work.
- Coaching activities have both organizational and individual goals.
- It provides people with feedback on both their strengths and their weaknesses.
- It is a skilled activity, which should be delivered by people who are trained to do so. This can be line managers and others trained in basic coaching skills. On the other hand, informal coaching from peers and co-workers may well be an effective, if limited, form of coaching that is often unrecognized.

Research by the CIPD (2008) found that a tension frequently exists between the personal and organizational dimension of coaching and the extent to which structure is both necessary and enabling. At the centre of this dilemma is the fact that, as many empirical studies, coaching experts, and most practitioners would stress, the quality of the coaching relationship is the single most important determinant of success in coaching. Therefore, the most significant challenge for organizations is that of determining the appropriate level of structure and support to enable coaching relationships to be as effective as possible in the organization in which it takes place. The key question is then about the kind and level of support and resources—in the form of systems, structures, and processes—that should be provided to facilitate this critical relationship, and how to link coaching as a development activity to the needs of the individual and the organization. To use the sporting comparison, coaching of individuals, in team sports, is done in ways that recognize the other members of the team and the importance of enhancing the performance and achievement of the team.

Mentoring

Mentoring is often associated with coaching and the two terms may be used by some interchangeably. To a degree, this close association is justified because both processes use the same or similar models and skills such as questioning, listening, clarifying, and reframing. Traditionally, however, mentoring in the workplace has tended to describe a relationship in which a more experienced colleague uses his or her greater knowledge and understanding of the work or workplace to support the development of a more junior or inexperienced member of staff and is associated with more long-term development than short-term performance. A mentor can be understood as someone who is:

a more experienced individual willing to share knowledge with someone less experienced in a relationship of mutual trust

but we need to add something about helping the mentee see and think about things differently and to find creative solutions to problems to capture the potential power than mentoring offers.

Mentoring, as with coaching, certainly involves the establishment of a relationship between two people but tends to have a different purpose often linked to succession planning and career development. As such, mentoring is more likely to be used as part of a talent management strategy and limited to high-potential individuals. Mentoring relationships work best when they move beyond the directive approach of a senior colleague 'telling it how it is', to one where both learn from each other. An effective mentoring relationship is a learning opportunity for both parties, and, if effective, an experience valued by both parties. A more recent association has seen mentoring used to encourage inclusive employment practices and equal opportunities, for example where a senior female or ethnic minority leader mentors a more junior colleague from a similar background. Reverse mentoring (where a more junior colleague mentors a senior leader) can also be effective in encouraging sharing and learning across generations and/or between role levels.

The Growth of e-Learning

E-learning has enjoyed a rapid growth over the last ten years and although not restricted to the workplace in terms of delivery and learning location can still be considered an example of learning for work. It can be understood as learning that is delivered, enabled, or mediated using electronic technology for the explicit purpose of training in organizations. But Martyn Sloman's influential book on e-learning (2001) places this new approach to learning in a wider context. He argued that this development is not simply about the use of technology, claiming that:

> Today's training professionals are operating at the beginning of a revolution. Importantly, it is about much more than the arrival of a new platform for the delivery of training. The context in which the trainer operates, internal and external relationships and the role of training itself can be expected to undergo profound changes.

But as with most new developments in HR, the emergence of e-learning has not been without controversy. Central to this has been the role of technology and whether the development of advanced learning systems and electronic platforms have the potential to transform learning and training as Sloman suggests. The role of technology seems to be at the core of disagreements over precisely what e-learning represents, with people like Elliott Masie (www.masie.com), for example, not only arguing that e-learning is not about computers and computing, but that the 'e' should be an abbreviation for 'experience', not 'electronic'. The point he is making is that there is real danger in concentrating on systems, portals, and technology-driven 'learning solutions', and in seeing them as ends rather than means. As Sloman (2001) says:

> There is a danger of becoming seduced by the functionality of the technology rather than concentrating on its use.

Since Sloman's earlier work, e-learning has developed at a pace, as new technologies have emerged and been adapted to support learning, not simply linked to individual development interests and requirements but in response to the organizational need for agility and responsiveness. Overton (2011) found that a growing number of firms believe that technology can help them become more agile (72 per cent). They believe that learning technologies will help them respond faster to changing business conditions, and help them release new products faster and respond to organizational change (77 per cent). Traditional notions about how and where people learn are being overturned as old dependencies on trainers and trainer-led courses are being replaced by new flexible opportunities and the individualization of learning. As the CIPD reported, the trend identified by Overton and Dixon (2016):

> is likely to deepen with the further spread of apps (mini programmes designed for smartphones), and the increasing need for people to learn everything from languages to budget forecasting as their job roles are stretched. The more people learn on connected devices, the more their workplace will need to connect with that aspect of their learning lives. It is evident that the boundaries between workplace learning and leisure time will become blurred.

See the Online Resources Extension Material 11.4 which presents the case for e-learning.

Forms of e-learning

- **Web-based training**

  In corporate training, technology is used primarily to deliver content to the end user without significant interaction with (or support from) training professionals, peers, or managers.

- **Interactive online learning**

  Particularly used in further and higher education, but also in organizations with their own intranet, the emphasis here is on the delivery of courses and support material online. Platforms such as Blackboard also provide opportunities for exchanges of information, interaction with tutors, collaborative activities, and, depending on the nature of the course, assessment and online feedback. There has also been a very significant growth in the private sector, with specialist companies offering a range of generic and bespoke e-learning solutions (Alcock, 2005). Webinars are increasingly being used as an alternative to face-to-face learning environments and online communities of practitioners represent a powerful learning resource.

- **Informal e-learning**

  Beyond these 'course-based' approaches to e-learning are the growing opportunities for technology to support informal learning in the workplace. In many knowledge-intensive organizations, technology is linked with knowledge management strategies and developing intranet capabilities to facilitate knowledge exchange linked to 'communities of practice'.

- **Standalone e-learning materials**

  These take the form of CD ROM-based learning. In this case, there is no support provision or interaction outside of the CD ROM-based material.

348

Understanding and Managing the Learning Process

So far, this chapter has focused on the role of training in organizations and developments in learning methods. What has only been indirectly alluded to—the actual way in which learning takes place—is now addressed. The emphasis is on how people learn and the relationship between this (process) and what they learn (outcomes). Without an understanding of the process of learning, learning as a key HR intervention cannot effectively be managed and the potential inherent in all employees to be and do more will only partially be realized.

Learning, as a process, has several important characteristics:

- you cannot see it happening—it is essentially a cognitive process;

- you can only see that learning has taken place through changes in the way people think, behave, and work;

- people may well have learned something new or already possess a valued competency, but may choose not to use and display it;

- 'real' learning relates to knowledge, skills, and attitudes that are embedded within the individual. Some learning can be described as temporary and superficial, which can be easily lost;

- no one can learn for you. HR professionals and line managers can help others to learn, provide 'learning-rich' learning environments, and support learning with a wide range of resources, but learning is only something that individuals can do (i.e. learning happens within);

- we may choose not to engage in certain kinds of learning because of being apprehensive about what we might learn about ourselves or about others, or because we cannot see its relevance. This means that employees need to feel positive about the outcomes of the learning process before they make a commitment to learn. In other words, the motivation to learn is a precondition of successful learning.

From personal experience and research findings, the amount of what is learned, i.e. the effectiveness of learning experiences, is not only affected by individual motivation but by how people are required to learn and the environment in which learning takes place. Consider the following statements about the relative effectiveness of different learning experiences, and their implications for the design of learning experiences. From your own experiences, compare lectures with group problem-solving activities as a way of linking learning effectiveness with learning experiences.

People remember (learn):

10 per cent of what they read;

20 per cent of what they hear;

30 per cent of what they see;

50 per cent of what they see and hear;

70 per cent of what they talk over with others;

80 per cent of what they use in real life;

95 per cent of what they teach someone.

The Kolb learning cycle

Perhaps the best-known representation of how learning is created was presented by David Kolb (1984). His 'learning cycle' offers important insights into the different ways in which people can learn, and into the choices and preferences that exist in our own learning.

The theory is based on the fact that our learning experiences are not discrete experiences, but form part of the constantly evolving view that we develop of the world around us. It is a model that reflects the importance of learning from the consequences of our own, and others', actions. This enables us to understand, interact with, and manipulate our environment to our advantage. For example, children initially learn to eat with their fingers and to associate eating with pleasure, not only because of the taste, but also because it removes the discomfort of being hungry. They then learn to use a spoon, so that they can eat food that cannot be eaten easily with their hands and, eventually, they learn to use cutlery to enable them to eat without making a mess. Each of these learning experiences builds on the last and becomes part of an increasingly complex pattern of behaviour, including social skills and rules used at mealtimes. This learning process is cyclical and each part of the learning builds upon the last.

Kolb defined how people learn from their experiences by going through the following four steps.

● Concrete experience (activist learning style)

This is the stage in learning during which the learner carries out an action that has observable consequences. Kolb used the example of a child touching a hot stove. In a work context, it might be easier

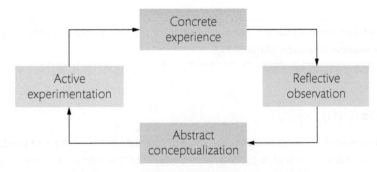

Figure 11.2 Kolb's experiential learning cycle
Source: Kolb, David A., *Experiential Learning: Experience as a Source of Learning*, © 1984, p. 42, Fig. 3.1. Adapted with the permission of Pearson Education Inc., New York.

to imagine selecting a computer icon that you have not previously used and the function of which you do not understand.

● Reflective observation (reflecting learning style)

This is the stage in learning during which the learner reflects upon their action and the outcome of that action. In Kolb's action, the child realizes that the stove burned his hand and it hurts. In our work context example, you might reflect upon the fact that the icon in a word processing package created a large indented dot on the page.

● Abstract conceptualization (theorizing learning style)

This is the stage in learning during which the learner develops a theory that can be applied to similar scenarios. In Kolb's example, the child theorizes and draws the conclusion that touching a hot surface will hurt. In our example about learning to use a computer, the learner may draw the conclusion that the icon can be used to create a bullet point in a piece of text.

● Active experimentation (pragmatist learning style)

This is the stage in learning during which the learner tests the theory out to see if the correct conclusion has been drawn. In Kolb's example, the child may put his hand near the stove to see if it feels hot. In our word processing example, the learner may type text and select the icon again to see if, in fact, this icon does enable the learner to create bullet points within a document.

In turn, this cycle can lead to further experience. For example, Kolb's child might begin to learn about other items that are hot; our computer learner may go on to explore other icons, such as numbered bullet points. Hence the learning process is ongoing and cyclical.

Kolb's model, while generally seen as capturing important learning concepts, has been criticized on two grounds:

1. Because it represents an essentially individualistic approach to learning and fails to reflect social learning experiences. According to Wheeler (2012):

> **Kolb's model frames individual exploration of the world, and can be seen in a number of activities such as problem based learning, inquiry based learning and experiential learning. Although none of these preclude a social element of learning such as collaboration or group discussion, individual constructivism tends to rely on the ability of the learner to be an autonomous and independent self-learner.**

2. Despite the continued popularity of Kolb's model and the derivative learning styles popularized by Honey and Mumford (2006), Wheeler believes that its continued relevance is threatened by new learning opportunities linked to technology. He states:

> **One view is that the experiential learning model is increasingly irrelevant in an age where social media, and social learning are increasingly prevalent.**

 For more information about the Honey and Mumford (2006) model of learning styles, see the Online Resources Extension Material 11.5.

Steps in learning

Learning is not always an easy process. Despite the sense of achievement that can be attained, sometimes it can be a difficult and uncomfortable process, particularly when the learner is developing unfamiliar skills or learning about more difficult concepts. We have seen how Kolb described learning as a cycle of experience, through to experimentation, but this model does not address the emotional experience that

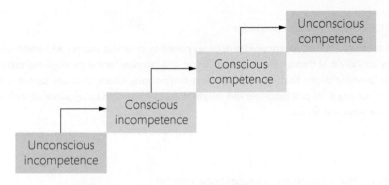

Figure 11.3 The conscious competence model

Source: Although widely used in training circles, the original source of this model is unknown.

we can go through when struggling to learn something new. Learning is usually not a surprise experience that 'pops up' at random and helps us to realize that the world operates in a particular way. More often than not, we go through a deliberate process of acquiring knowledge and skills. Once mastered, it is difficult to understand what we found about learning that skill to be such a challenging experience. A useful way of understanding how learning progresses from one stage to another is presented in Figure 11.3. This model is useful in that it highlights the different stages through which the learner progresses until full competence is attained.

Within the 'conscious competence' model, the learner starts from a position of being unaware of the nature of the learning need. For example, before you start to learn to drive, it looks a bit tricky, but you know that it is something to do with pedals and a steering wheel. This is referred to as being in a state of 'unconscious incompetence' (Stage 1), that is, the learner is unaware of his or her lack of competence. The first step in learning is to become aware of that shortfall and to move to a state of 'conscious incompetence' (Stage 2). Our learner driver, at this point, is struggling to master the basic manoeuvres in his or her car and may well frequently stall or crunch gears, and will need to be told exactly what to do by the instructor. As skills are acquired, the learner climbs another step, into 'conscious competence' (Stage 3). At this point, our learner may pass his or her test, but is still conscious of each of the actions that contribute towards driving, such as changing gear or the observation and signalling routine 'mirror, signal, manoeuvre'. Eventually, once the skills become very familiar, the learner is no longer conscious of each of the individual actions that make up the new skill. This is described as 'unconscious competence' (Stage 4) and, for our driver, will represent the point at which driving becomes automatic, that is, the driver is no longer conscious of observations and actions that have become predictable. This state of unconscious competence is similar to that described by the term 'tacit knowledge'. At this point, knowledge and know-how have become embedded within the individual to the point at which the ability to carry out a series of operations, such as driving, fitting a boiler, or operating a piece of machinery, have become 'second nature'.

Trainers can mistakenly assume trainees to be at Stage 2 and focus effort towards achieving Stage 3, when often trainees are only at Stage 1. The trainer assumes that the trainee is aware of, and understands the importance of meeting a skill, or competency deficiency and of the benefits from learning. This is not the case if trainees are still at the stage of unconscious incompetence: they will not be able to address achieving conscious competence until they've become consciously and fully aware of their own *in*competence. This is a fundamental reason for the failure of many training activities, and emphasizes the importance of trainers not making unfounded assumptions about trainee awareness and motivation. If the awareness of skill and deficiency is low or non-existent—that is, if the learner is at the unconscious incompetence stage—the trainee or learner will simply not see the need for learning. It is essential to establish *awareness* of a weakness or training need prior to attempting the training needed to move trainees from Stage 2 to Stage 3.

A term used to describe knowledge of things gained from various sources and which is internalized by an individual through the process of 'doing' and practice. Tacit knowledge represents for many people the achievement of the final stage—unconscious competence, where tasks are carried out based on experience and learning from past successes and failures without the person being aware of the link between knowledge, know-how, and action.

Applications of the conscious competence model

It is important, in the context of the working environment, to understand that each of the above stages has to be mastered before moving on to the next stage. A learner will not be able to learn unless he or she becomes aware of what it is that he or she is not doing effectively. It can be very disconcerting, particularly for an employee who has carried out their duties in a particular way for a long time, to discover that this is no longer regarded as being the most effective method of doing things. It is therefore important to be sensitive and empathic as a trainer, and to structure training so that skills can be learned in easily achievable steps that will allow the learner quickly to develop conscious competence. This will ensure that the learner has the satisfaction of having mastered one skill before attempting to move on to the next item. A music student, for example, will first learn to master relatively easy short tunes before moving on to more complex pieces of music. In the working/learning environment, it is important to consider what can be successfully achieved by which methods to maintain employee satisfaction, motivation, and achievement.

If a learner becomes overwhelmed by the magnitude of what is not known and by the scale of what needs to be learned, there is a probability that he or she will become defensive and uncooperative. This might result in loss of motivation, denial about his or her shortcomings, and negative attitudes towards the training. It is important, therefore, that a 'safe' psychological learning environment is created, in which shortcomings can be openly addressed without unnecessary concern on the part of the learner. In more challenging training on personal management styles or attitudes, the organization may prefer to consider using an external independent trainer. Organizations may put trainees on courses with people they don't work with, to encourage openness and participation.

Mountainside Training Centre was asked to run a week-long outward bound-style training course for managers of Henry Associates Finance and Investments (HAFI). HAFI wanted to get the most from investing in this expensive training, so training consisted of long days, starting at 8.30 a.m. and continuing into the evenings. The training included an overnight exercise during which participants were required to continue throughout the night by splitting into two shifts. Participants were also expected to network in the evenings by socializing together, leaving little time for rest and personal reflection.

The training centre recommended that the groups follow the Kolb learning cycle by doing an activity, receiving feedback, and producing guidelines and action plans as a team for the next exercise. The training therefore consisted mainly of outdoor activities, followed by discussions about what had gone wrong in order to learn from mistakes made and to improve team performance in the next exercise. The exercises were of increasing duration and complexity, and trainees were encouraged to develop weaknesses by having a go at roles they wouldn't normally play. Feedback included detailed comments about personal style from the trainers and from other group members. People who were not natural leaders were expected to lead the group; people naturally good at problem solving were expected to let others try out their ideas and be more considerate to team members, and so on.

To make the most of this expensive training, underpinning theory on subjects including management, team working, motivation, and communication was given to trainees as documents and books. These were to be read outside of the structured activity (managers were expected to study this in their own time).

Andragogy

Malcolm Knowles developed the concept of adult learning to distinguish this kind of learning from that experienced by children (Smith, 2010). He coined the term 'andragogy' as the adult equivalent of pedagogy. According to Knowles, andragogy, as a description of adult learning begins at the point in a person's development when the individual acquires a concept of self and of the need to exercise self-direction. As a child, we are taught and are dependent on others for what and how we learn; as adults, we need to take control over our learning. The problem is, however, that much 'adult learning' is still based on the principles and practices of pedagogy and this creates a tension between what the adult person feels and needs and the learning experiences he/she is put through. This tension is expressed through low levels of motivation, resistance to be told what to learn, and challenges to those in control of the learning curriculum and learning methods.

His theory of adult learning is based on the following assumptions:

- **The need to know**—adult learners need to know why they need to learn something before undertaking to learn it.

- **Learner self-concept**—adults need to be responsible for their own decisions and to be treated as capable of self-direction.

- **Role of learners' experience**—adult learners have a variety of experiences of life which represent the richest resource for learning. These experiences are however imbued with bias and presupposition which needs to be addressed.

- **Readiness to learn**—adults are ready to learn those things they need to know in order to cope effectively with life situations.

- **Orientation to learning**—adults are motivated to learn to the extent that they perceive that it will help them perform tasks they confront in their life situations.

Moving forward—the power of accelerated learning

A consistent theme in this chapter is that looking at, and correcting, deficiencies in how people learn and how they are trained can improve the value and effectiveness of training. We would argue that, through understanding how these two processes can be improved, both employees and managers will benefit. What 'accelerated learning' offers is a set of principles, values, and practices that represent an alternative to conventional approaches to learning, particularly the use of course-based training, which have the potential of generating enjoyable and productive learning experiences. Proponents of accelerated learning reject learning based on mechanization, standardization, external control, 'one size fits all', behaviouristic conditioning, and an emphasis on instruction and passive listening, suggesting instead a very different, but more effective, approach (Meier, 2000).

Meier compares what he calls 'traditional learning' with 'accelerated learning', using the dimensions shown in Table 11.2.

Table 11.2 A comparison of traditional learning and accelerated learning characteristics

Traditional learning	Accelerated learning
Rigid	Flexible
Sombre and serious	Enjoyable
Single-pathed	Multi-pathed
Competitive	Collaborative
Behaviouristic	Humanistic
Verbal	Multisensory
Controlling	Nurturing
Cognitive	Cognitive, emotional, and physical
Means-centred	Results-based

Meier argues that any approach to, or philosophy of, learning is underpinned by a set of assumptions about what people need to optimize their learning. As far as accelerated learning is concerned, these assumptions are as follows.

A positive learning environment

People learn best when their social, physical, and emotional environments are positive, supportive, and stimulating.

Total learner involvement

Active involvement and responsibility are key to effective and sustained learning. Meier points out that learning is not a spectator sport, but participatory.

Collaboration among learners

People generally learn best in an environment characterized by working together with others. Learning can, and often does, happen through what a person does on his or her own, but effective and deeper learning is often associated with groups and teams engaging in a shared learning experience.

Variety that appeals to all learning preferences and styles

Learning becomes 'accelerated' and more effective when the full range of people's senses and energies are engaged and used in learning.

Contextual learning

Again, the importance of context is emphasized. Learning 'out of context' and in isolation from the working environment is harder to absorb, and can easily be lost. Meier believes that:

> **the best learning comes from doing the work itself in a continual process of 'real world' immersion, feedback, reflection, evaluation and re-immersion.**

Based on the characteristics and assumptions of accelerated learning, Meier offers what he describes as a 'universalistic' model of learning (2000: 53). This features four phases or components all of which must be present in one form or another, or, according to Meier, no real learning occurs. The four phases or components are:

preparation—the arousal of interest;

presentation—the initial encounter and involvement with new areas of knowledge or skill;

practice—the integration and embedding of the new knowledge or skill; and

performance—applying the knowledge or skill to the job.

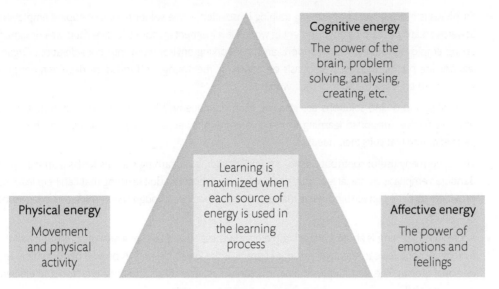

Figure 11.4 The energy triangle

Finally, and to continue the thinking behind the ideas associated with accelerated learning, we want to offer an interesting and challenging hypothesis: that enjoyment and learning outcomes are positively correlated to the amount and variety of energy consumed in the learning experience. Consider, as an example, being involved in business simulation or skills development exercises, as opposed to sitting in a lecture theatre listening to a PowerPoint presentation. Which learning experience consumes most energy and which is likely to be the most productive type of learning? The concept of the 'energy triangle' presented in Figure 11.4 describes the three types of energy that need to be utilized in learning.

 STUDENT ACTIVITY 11.7

1. Think of two learning situations, one of which was enjoyable and productive, and one that wasn't. Rate both on a scale of 1–10, with 10 the most enjoyable and productive.

2. On a scale of 1–10, rate each of the two experiences in relation to the three types of energy generated/used, with 1=low and 10=very high. Add the three values together.

3. Compare the ratings from task 1 to the aggregate energy score in task 2 and establish whether the hypothesis has validity.

Summary

- Human beings learn throughout their lives; to be effective and continue to make a positive contribution to an employing organization, employees need to be active learners. Equally to get the best from their employees, organizations should provide an environment that ensures that the learning and development of their employees is ongoing, reflects both organizational and individual needs, and exists in the formal/informal domains.

- Training is one method of bringing about learning among employees. While it forms an important part of learning and development, it is not always the case that learning from training is effectively transferred to a change in behaviour to enhance the performance of individuals and teams. Effective evaluation of T&D is essential to show a positive ROI for an organization and to therefore demonstrate that the activity is valuable and worthwhile.

- Emphasis is moving away from seeing training in isolation as the solution for developing employees towards creating a learning environment at work. Development is more effective if it is well designed, taking employee requirements, support, and the working environment into consideration. Organizations are placing increased emphasis on coaching, mentoring, and in-house development programmes to enhance the skills of their workforce.

- E-learning and online solutions are growing in importance and becoming more sophisticated to ensure effective, supported learning with a greater flexibility allowing learners to work at their own pace at a time that suits their needs.

- There are many useful contributions to our understanding of learning such as Kolb's learning cycle, Bandura's emphasis on social learning, and Knowles's concept of adult learning that can help learning providers to better understand what makes learning effective, although their limitations need to be recognized.

- Accelerated learning is about enhancing the effectiveness and uptake of learning by ensuring all the factors are conducive to effective learning. Learning is the key to change, improved performance, and personal growth. The central question is: how can we achieve this in the most effective and efficient ways possible?

Visit the **online resources** that accompany this book for self-test questions, web links, and more information on the topics covered in this chapter, at: **www.oup.com/uk/banfield3e/**

REVIEW QUESTIONS

1. What does 'from training to learning' mean and why has this shift in emphasis come about?

2. In what ways does e-learning facilitate the individualization of learning?

3. What does an employee-centred approach to learning involve and what are its implications for trainers?

4. What are the respective roles of the HR professional and the line manager in generating learning at work?

5. Why is the motivational state of learners important to the outcome of learning interventions?

6. How can HR demonstrate the economic and business case for learning and development activities?

CASE STUDY   A strategic perspective on development

Smith Associates is a middle-ranking but nationally established accountancy and financial services company with a turnover in 2016 of £78 million. It employees approximately 800 staff, split between professionally qualified accountants, financial experts and management consultants, administrative and support staff, and IT specialists. All thirty-one partners that manage the company have come up through the ranks after being recruited directly from UK universities. It has an HR department, the director of which reports to the senior partner, although she does not sit on the management board and has little input into the development of the company's HR strategy.

The culture of Smith Associates is not dissimilar to other professional organizations and could be described as somewhat conservative. Change is slow to happen and where if something is seen to work the consensus will probably be, 'why change!' Recruitment into the professional accountancy ranks is still based exclusively on the Russell Group universities, heavily influenced by interviews with the partners and degree class. As a consequence, the demographic of the professional staff is heavily biased towards white males who share similar backgrounds. Over the years, however, as the national university demographic profile has changed so too has the annual intake into the company's graduate development programme, but only gradually. The top tier of management reflects the company's historical recruitment policy and will only change over time.

Two things have put pressure on the partners to reassess their approach to recruitment and management development. One is the recognition that their company is not attracting the best applicants and that far too many who enter as graduate recruits leave within five years of joining. Together with the restricted approach to recruitment, this means that it is experiencing difficulties in meeting the expectations of its clients and providing the kind of professional staff to support the company's expanding range of services. The second is that, as a result of recent staff surveys, it is increasingly evident that there are issues over the lack of career development opportunities, which partly explains the rise in turnover rates and the lack of enough suitably qualified with the right mix of professional, managerial, and leadership qualities.

The company has a long-established professional qualification route, the suitability of which is not in doubt. But its record of management and leadership development is at best patchy, and to both HR director and the managing partner, ineffective, based as it is on the assumption that younger staff will acquire the necessary competencies through working with more experienced managers.

After discussing these developments and issues, it was agreed that two new initiatives needed to be taken and headed by the HR director who would present proposals to the managing partner within two months.

Questions

Assuming the role of HR director, you are required to:

1. Develop a new recruitment and selection strategy that will address the existing problems and generate a more diverse annual intake (approximately twenty) into the company's graduate development scheme. The strategy is not about diversity per se but about generating intakes that reflect social change and provide people with the potential to become senior managers and effective leaders of teams. You need to explain what your strategy is and how it will be implemented.

2. Develop a career development strategy for existing staff. This requires you to show how the 'stars' will be identified, what development opportunities they will be provided with and what role the partners will be expected to play.

CHAPTER ELEVEN LEARNING, TRAINING, AND DEVELOPMENT

>> FURTHER READING

Bandura, A. (1971) *Social Learning Theory*, at: http://www.esludwig.com/uploads/2/6/1/0/26105457/bandura_sociallearningtheory.pdf

Beard, C. and Wilson, J. P. (2013) *Experiential Learning*, Kogan Page.

Beevers, K. and Rea, A. (2016) *Learning and Development Practice in the Workplace*, 3rd edn, CIPD.

CIPD (2014) *L&D: New Challenges, New Approaches*, at: https://www.cipd.co.uk/binaries/l-and-d_2014-new-challenges-new-approaches.pdf

CIPD (2016) Factsheet: Learning methods, at: http://www.cipd.co.uk/hr-resources/factsheets/learning-methods.aspx

Gibbs, D. and Gosper, M. (2006) 'The upside-down world of e-learning', *Journal of Learning Design*, 1(2), at: https://www.jld.edu.au/article/view/16/12

Van Dam, N. (2012) 'Designing learning for a 21st century workforce', *T+D*, 66(4), 48–53.

REFERENCES

Alcock, M. (2005) 'Time for e-learning to be handed back to the trainers?', at: http://www.trainingreference.co.uk

Anderson, V. (2006) *The Value of Learning: A New Model of Value and Evaluation*, at: http://www.cipd.co.uk/NR/rdonlyres/94842E50-F775-4154-975F-8D4BE72846C7/0/valoflearnnwmodvalca.pdf

Anderson, V. (2008) 'View from the top: executive perceptions of the value of learning', *Strategic HR Review*, 7(4), 11–16.

Boydell, T. (2003) 'Difference between training and learning', at: http://www.trainingzone.co.uk

CIPD (2008) 'Reflections on the 2008 learning and development survey: Latest trends in learning training and development survey report', at: http://www.cipd.co.uk

CIPD (2012) 'From e-learning to "gameful" employment', *Research Insight* (April), at: https://www.cipd.co.uk/Images/from-e-learning-to-gameful-employment_2012_tcm18-9175.pdf

CIPD (2015) Coaching and mentoring factsheet, December, at: http://www.cipd.co.uk/hr-resources/factsheets/coaching-mentoring.aspx

CIPD & Towards Maturity (2015) *L&D: Evolving Roles, Enhancing Skills*, at: http://www.towardsmaturity.org/ldskills2015

Davis, J. R. and Davis, A. B. (1998) *Effective Training Strategies*, Berrett-Koehler.

Fitz-enz, J. (2000) *The ROI of Human Capital*, AMACOM.

Fitz-enz, J. (2010) *The New HR Analytics*, AMACOM.

Garrett, J. (2014) 'Is Mentoring the new black?', *Training Journal*, 1 February, at: https://www.trainingjournal.com/articles/feature/mentoring-new-black

Gladstone, B. (2000) *From Know-How to Knowledge*, Spiro Press.

Hirsh, W. and Tamkin, P. (2005) *Planning Training for Your Business*, IES Report 422.

Honey, P. and Mumford, A. (2006) *The Learning Styles Questionnaire*, Peter Honey Publications.

Hope, K. (2006) 'Class act', *People Management*, 15 September, p. 16.

Hutchinson, S. and Purcell, J. (2007) *Learning and the Line: The Role of Line Managers in Training, Earning and Development*, CIPD.

IRS (1998) 'Using human resources to achieve strategic objectives: Learning strategies review', *IRS Management Review*, 8.

Jeffery, R. (2016) 'Five lessons for the future of L&D', *People Management*, 26 January, at: http://www.cipd.co.uk/pm/peoplemanagement/b/weblog/archive/2016/01/26/five-lessons-for-the-future-of-l-amp-d.aspx

Kearns, P. (2005) *Evaluating the ROI from Learning*, CIPD.

Kirkpatrick, D. L. (1998) *Evaluating Training Programs*, 2nd edn, Berrett-Koehler.

Knights, A. and Poppleton, A. (2008) *Developing Coaching Capability in Organisations*, CIPD.

Kolb, D. A. (1984) *Experiential Learning: Experience as a Source of Learning*, Pearson Education.

McGhee, W. and Thayer, P. (1961) *Training in Business and Industry*, Wiley.

Mattox, J. R. (2012) 'Measuring the effectiveness of informal learning methodologies', *T+D*, 66(2), 48–53.

Mayo, A. (2001) *The Human Value of the Enterprise*, Nicholas Brealey.

Megginson, D., Banfield, P., and Joy-Matthews, J. (1993) *Human Resource Development*, Kogan Page.

Meier, D. (2000) *The Accelerated Learning Handbook*, McGraw-Hill.

Overton, L. (2011) 'Towards maturity: 2011 benchmark study with learning and development specialists from 600 organisations', Towards Maturity, at: http://www.towardsmaturity.org/2011benchmark

Overton, L. and Dixon, G. (2016) *Preparing for the Future of Learning*, CIPD.

Pfeffer, J. (1998) *Hidden Equation*, HBS Press.

Quality Magazine (2009) http://www.qualitymag.com/articles/86204-don-t-punish-employees-with-training, 27 January.

Rothwell, W. J. (1996) *Beyond Training and Development: State-of-the-Art Strategies for Enhancing Human Performance*, AMACOM/American Management Association.

Schechter, H. B. (2009) 'The cost of e-learning', *e-learn Magazine*, July, at: http://elearnmag.acm.org/featured.cfm?aid=1595447

Shepherd, C. (1999) *Assessing the ROI of Training*, at: http://www.fastrak-consulting.co.uk/tactix/Features/tngroi/tngroi.htm

Sloman, M. (2001) *The e-Learning Revolution*, CIPD.

Sloman, M. (2004) 'Learner drivers', *People Management*, 2 September, p. 36.

Sloman, M. and Webster, L. (2005) 'Training to learning', *Training and Development*, 59(9), 58–63.

Smith, M. K. (2010) 'Andragogy: What is it and does it help thinking about adult learning?', at: http://infed.org/mobi/andragogy-what-is-it-and-does-it-help-thinking-about-adult-learning

Truss, C. et al. (1997) 'Soft and hard models of human resource management: A reappraisal', *Journal of Management Studies*, 34(1), 53–73.

UK Government (2014) *The Future of Apprenticeships in England*, at: https://www.gov.uk/government/uploads/system/uploads/attachment_data/file/302235/bis-14-597-future-of-apprenticeships-in-england-funding-reform-technical-consultatation.pdf

Ulrich, D. (1998) 'A new mandate for human resources', *Harvard Business Review*, 76(1), 125–34.

Walton, J. (1999) *Strategic Human Resource Development*, Pearson Education.

Wheeler, S. (2012) 'Recycling Kolb', at: http://www.steve-wheeler.co.uk/2012/06/recycling-kolb.html

Woessmann, L. (2014) *The Economic Case for Education*, European Commission.

Youngsang, K. and Ployhart, Robert E. (2014) 'The effects of staffing and training on firm productivity and profit growth before, during, and after the great recession', *Journal of Applied Psychology*, 99(3).

Managing Performance

12

Introduction

One of the difficulties in trying to make sense of what PM 'is' and what it might mean for managers and employees, as Armstrong and Baron (1998) state, is that:

> **performance management is a fairly imprecise term, and performance management processes manifest themselves in many different forms. There is no one right way of managing performance.**

What can be said with some certainty, however, is that PM is not synonymous with the appraisal process, which is one technique (or instrument) used by many organizations to 'manage' performance. Unfortunately, in many organizations appraisal techniques often constitute the only formal method of managing performance. A much more sophisticated and useful conceptualization is provided by Lockett (1992), who emphasized the need to see PM in an ecological way, within which the different elements of a living system interact and influence each other, rather than as a series of unrelated functions and activities.

In Chapter 1 we identified employee utilization as one of the fundamental objectives of management. In contemporary organizations, PM is the aspect of management closely associated with delivering this objective. Simply having a PM system in place does not, however, guarantee higher levels of performance than would otherwise have existed without the 'benefit' of the system's formal features. As with many other aspects of HR, formal and material rationality are not necessarily synonymous. By this we mean that the effectiveness of PM systems is problematic and *net gains* in performance can be far lower than anticipated. The reality of unintended consequences is frequently experienced by managers who fail to think through all the likely effects of their plans and policies!

The search for higher levels of individual and team performance is important to all organizations, and ways must be found to ensure that performance levels are sustained and enhanced. Despite improvements in equipment, materials, and processes, organizational performance is still linked to the quality of people that an organization employs and what they do at work. You can have the best equipment and systems in your sector, and the most up-to-date processes, but if you don't have the right number and quality of people doing what is needed, the organization will not function properly. 'Managing performance' fundamentally means that employees know what is expected of them and act in ways that contribute to the best interests of the organization (and the individual). But what this means and how it is delivered for each individual organization will inevitably differ because each faces a unique set of circumstances and challenges. There are no universal solutions to PM problems and each organization must, through a process of diagnosis, action, evaluation, and learning, develop its own strategy and practices.

According to Mabey et al. (1998), PM refers to a set of techniques and procedures that serve to:

- provide information on the contribution of human resources to the strategic objectives of the organization;
- form a framework of techniques to secure the maximum output for any given level of inputs;
- provide a means of inspecting how well individual performance-enhancing processes actually deliver performance in relation to targets and objectives.

They define PM as:

> **A framework in which performance by individuals can be directed, monitored, motivated and refined.**
> (Mabey et al., 1998)

While useful, this attempt to define PM suffers from one fundamental fault—it sees performance only in terms of individual capabilities and effort. Of course, individual talents are important to performance but there are increasingly situations where the performance of a unit or part of an organization reflects the efforts and contributions of many people working towards a common goal. Individualizing performance detracts from seeing the wider and more integrated picture. Consider for example a school. The head teacher will obviously have an important and sometimes critical role to play but to deny the contributions of the other staff is to engage in the over-personalization of performance.

In its recent survey of PM, the CIPD (2015) supports this more holistic approach to conceptualizing PM which brings together many of the elements of good people management practice, including learning and development, measurement of performance, and organizational development. They argue that for this very reason the activity is complex, is seen by different people in different ways, and is often misunderstood.

In their later book on the subject, Armstrong and Baron (2004) define PM as:

a process which contributes to the effective management of individuals and teams in order to achieve high levels of organisational performance.

The problem with this approach is that it reflects a rather simplistic and questionable assumption that managing performance is unproblematic and that simply being engaged in this activity results in certain desired outcomes being achieved. There are countless examples of PM strategies simply failing to work or not working as well as expected and the reasons for this range from poor design and implementation weaknesses to employee resistance and poor communications. Referring once again to the criticism levelled at HR, activities and outcomes are not necessarily related—there are many mediating factors that have to be factored in and effectively managed before means and ends are more closely related. Their argument that PM is:

a strategy which relates to every activity of the organisation set in the context of its human resource policies, culture, style and communications systems

is also one that requires questioning. First, defining PM as a strategy is not particularly helpful when it is expressed in such a holistic way; seeing every aspect of an organization at every level from a PM perspective, while theoretically of interest is more aspirational than practical. As with rewards, there are likely to be distinctive strategies *within* PM and certain of these are considered later in the chapter. These strategies are based on a set of assumptions about human behaviour, the key drivers of performance, and the ability to manage performance that need to be evaluated and their evidential base assessed.

But drawing together the different contributions about what PM is or should be (remember the distinction between positive and normative statements) the following points seem to reflect a broad consensus about PM.

- It should possess both *strategic and operational* dimensions, where small and regular improvements in processes, technology, and behaviours reflect wider performance improvement strategies and contribute to the achievement of short- and long-term goals and objectives.

- It should reflect a degree of *integration* based on the different PM strategies working together rather than being isolated and disconnected.

- The emphasis needs to be on performance improvement through *effective* PM in all aspects of performance.

- Recognizing that performance improvements come as much from *system changes* as they do from system improvements.

- Working relationships and what people feel about their work and their organization—in other words the *affective domain*—is critical to how people perform at work and the standards they achieve.

Effective PM relies as much on the informal as the formal domain. In the latter, the role of planning, establishing formal objectives, creating strategies, and deciding on performance measures are important. In the former, organizational culture, individual motivation, expectations, levels of commitment, trust, and perceptions of shared interests are important considerations and factors that affect performance.

The PM Cycle—Key Activities

Figure 12.1 presents the key activities and areas of responsibility associated with an integrated and holistic PM system. The fundamental importance given to evaluating the effectiveness of the individual and the cumulative effects of these activities is consistent with Ulrich's emphasis on the outcomes of HR interventions rather than on activities per se (Ulrich, 1998).

PM should not be seen as a once-a-year task, but as an ongoing process or cycle. Figure 12.1 shows that the first step in this cycle is for the organization to define its long-term strategy and strategic intentions. The objectives of the organization define the goals and targets over a given time period and will need to be regularly assessed to establish their alignment with the strategy. For example, these might express the levels of service to be provided, or the level of sales or profitability, or future planned activities.

To be able to measure progress/success at regular intervals, key measures, or metrics, need to be established. Unless an organization defines what is important and how this will be measured, it will be difficult to assign the necessary resource to ensure that the objectives are, as far as possible, achieved. Once this is

363

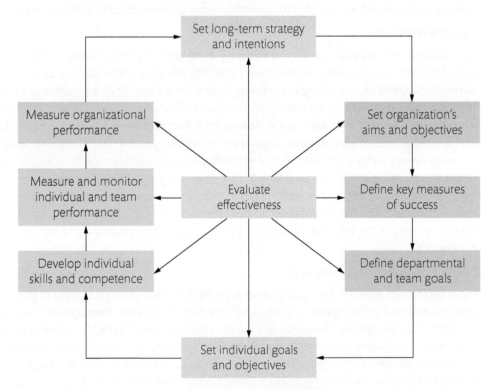

Figure 12.1 Model of PM

agreed, it is easier to decide which team will be responsible for each element that contributes towards the overall objectives. The organizational objectives can then be translated into departmental and team goals, and then into individual goals and objectives. The individual objectives are often agreed and finalized during an appraisal interview, a process which will be explored in greater detail later in the chapter.

The next step in the process is to develop the skills and abilities of the individuals and teams, to ensure that they are able to maximize and focus their efforts towards achieving their objectives. The performance of individuals and teams is then measured, and the results can be pooled to establish a regular measure of the organization's performance. Increasingly, key performance outcomes are a function of teams rather than of individuals, although the relative importance of one or the other depends on the nature of the work being undertaken and the social organization of work.

The importance of conceptualizing PM as a process rather than an event or several discrete events cannot be overstated. The idea of a continuous cycle of integrated activities as illustrated by Figure 12.1 is useful, but what it does not do is make reference to the obstacles and problems facing managers in their efforts to improve performance through implementing the cycle. As with many aspects of HR, knowing what should be done is one thing but being able to successfully implement it is quite another!

In addition to implementing the above performance cycle or a similar version there are a number of associated principles or practices that could contribute to an organization's PM thinking and strategies. They are:

- **Everyone should know what to, and what not to do**

  It is as important to establish what *not* to do as what *is* to be done: doing 'more' is not particularly helpful or sensible if this involves doing more of the wrong thing! Simply asking the individual to undertake more activities, without first establishing if there are any that are no longer required or which should be replaced with a more efficient activity, can be both detrimental to the organization and demotivating to employees, who may struggle with a seemingly ever-increasing workload. Performance improvements can be achieved by eliminating errors, reducing or eliminating wasted and unproductive time, and taking out of processes elements that have no value and simply consume resources. In many sports, individual and team performance can be improved by reducing or eliminating mistakes and errors.

- **Everyone contributes**

  It is important for employees, as well as managers, to contribute to the effective management of performance. Line managers do not know everything, nor should they be seen as the only stakeholder capable of contributing to improving performance. The position adopted here is that employees are fundamentally responsible for their own performance, in the same way that they are responsible for their own learning and development. Excluding them from any initiatives to improve performance makes no sense, and will almost certainly result in initiatives failing to deliver or being only partially successful. Even if such initiatives involve only annual objective setting, employee involvement in the process is likely to contribute to higher individual motivation, greater legitimation of the process, and increased commitment. Contemporary thinking about improving employee performance has moved away from simply communicating what needs to be done, towards recognizing the importance of achieving the employee's active support, and engagement in the process.

- **Everyone develops the necessary skills**

  For an organization to maximize its performance, every employee should be encouraged to grow by acquiring new skills and competences that will enhance their effectiveness. Development need not be restricted to HR-organized training courses, but can include a range of formal and informal learning experiences, including secondments, coaching, and project work. The link between performance and its management and learning has already been considered in detail, and developing capabilities that not only improve job performance but facilitate functional flexibility and wider contributions is an obvious performance-enhancing strategy.

● **Managers must have the necessary skills**

Ask a group of managers if they are effective in managing the performance of their teams and most, if not all, will probably say that they are. But if you were to ask those that they manage the same question, a different picture might emerge. The existence of this 'perception gap' suggests that there are important issues around what is known by managers, and what is unknown or hidden from them. For example, employees might feel that they are working hard and trying to do their best, but, for differing reasons, some of which will be to do with the quality of interpersonal relationships, this endeavour is not recognized. What is critical to the effective management of performance is the contribution of line managers to the engagement of their staff in the delivery of performance. To be effective in this role, managers need a range of technical and process skills, without which their ability to influence employee performance will inevitably be compromised. It might be argued, therefore, that employee performance is as much a function of the quality of managers as it is of the skills and competences of employees. Holbeche and Matthews (2012) emphasize the important role line managers play in creating a working environment that is both challenging and encouraging. This distinguishes their role in ensuring employees' work is aligned with organizational objectives and that they are at the same time engaged with their work, which is about wanting to do it and do it well.

● **Managers measure and monitor**

We have already emphasized that effective PM cannot be 'done' once a year. The process is ongoing and, to be effective, managers need to measure performance on an ongoing basis to ensure that it remains on track and that employees are supported and guided in their efforts as well as continuously developing their skills. What is critical, however, is the decision about what is to be measured as an indicator of changes in performance. Measuring the wrong thing is probably worse than not measuring anything! We explored this point in the context of performance-related pay schemes in an earlier chapter and it was clear from the evidence reviewed that serious problems occur when the wrong indicators are used in PM systems. Distinguishing PM as a process, rather than an event, helps to identify the nature of the management engagement process and avoids situations developing in which it is 'the time' to do something, such as 'the time' to carry out annual staff appraisals. It also means that moving towards a situation where real-time monitoring of performance changes becomes possible. While we locate the measurement and monitoring of performance as a management responsibility this does not necessarily mean that only formally designated managers are involved. Where management responsibilities have been devolved to individuals and teams then it is likely that a joint approach to this requirement will be taken.

RESEARCH INSIGHT 12.1

Read the following two articles to take your learning further:

Goh, S. C. (2012) 'Making performance measurement systems more effective in public sector organizations', *Measuring Business Excellence*, **16(1).**

The author argues that problems with improving performance in public sector organizations is due to a lack of focus in the implementation of performance improvement programmes.

Rogers, E. W. and Wright, P. M. (1998) 'Measuring organizational performance in strategic human resource management: Looking beyond the lamppost' (CAHRS Working Paper, Ithaca, NY: Cornell University), pp. 98–24.

This article claims that one of the key challenges for strategic HRM is to devise meaningful ways of measuring organizational performance. It goes on to suggest what these might be.

After reading both articles, consider the challenges of measuring performance and what can be done to improve it.

PRACTITIONER INSIGHT David Lloyd, PM consultant: an HR consultant's view of PM in practice

One of the most challenging questions managers need to address is precisely what is meant by PM? All too often people in the same organization hold different views about what it means and what it involves the organization doing. Very often it is seen in a very limited way—being equated to the pursuit of targets and individual objectives. While there is nothing wrong with the pursuit of targets, on its own it can damage long-term performance, e.g. by producing unintended consequences. Emphasizing quantitative targets can negatively impact on the quality of goods and service and indeed lead to unethical behaviour with damaging consequences.

The PM system in any organization must be capable of understanding and describing the value its goods and services create for its customers and the processes that create this value. All targets whether at an organizational, team, or individual level must be aligned to and support customer value and the processes that create this value in terms of goods and service. Without this understanding and alignment goods and service can be created that meet targets but which are not fit for purpose and do not create meaningful customer value.

PM, in my experience, involves prioritizing three key elements. First, the organization needs to have a sense of where it is going—knowing what its long-term vision for itself is and continually reinforcing this to all levels and all employees. The second element is the organizational philosophy and core values that will guide the organization along its journey, particularly at times of uncertainty and change. Third, a coherent set of policies and practice that define the framework within which individual and team contributions can be assessed and validated. So, the three elements of any PM system are a vision and certainty of purpose, a coherent business and management philosophy, and a set of policies and practice to define effectiveness and efficiency.

An organization is a work system and therefore PM must be a system to support the overall purpose and goals of the organization as a work system. Remember 80 per cent of the purpose of a work system is dependent on the design and management of the work system and only 20 per cent is dependent on the performance of individuals. The PM system must also be aligned to other support systems and initiatives (e.g. communications, quality, investment, technology).

It is essential and critical that HR does not design PM policies and practices that create 'silos' whether these be functional or process-based, but rather works to integrate and connect different aspects of the wider performance system. This means they need to take a holistic and systems approach to performance and avoid an unduly bureaucratic emphasis on procedural conformity. Above all, HR needs to understand the concept of added value and the importance of meeting internal and external customer requirements.

Making Sense of Performance

'Performance' is a term used frequently in HR, but it has no precise or agreed meaning: it can mean different things to different stakeholders and this can create problems in 'what' is managed. Just let your mind wander and think of what you associate the word 'performance' with. You may think of actors who 'perform' on the stage or cinema set, who entertain an audience. Those who have delivered an outstanding performance can then be nominated for awards, with those considered to have performed better than any of the other nominated persons receiving the highest award—perhaps an Oscar. You may also associate performance with sport and athletes, who constantly strive to reduce the time they take to run a set distance, increase the weights they can lift, or the height they can jump. Such initial associations confirm that 'performance' is not something that is restricted to the world of employment and work, and there may be much that we can learn from these other contexts in which improved performance is an important objective.

But performance is also of vital importance to the way in which organizations are managed and to what people do at work. How well businesses perform often determines their status, financial value, and survivability. The performance of each employee and how well they work together as teams is an enduring managerial concern.

Whatever the industry, the level at which people function or the jobs being performed, managers are faced with four fundamental questions:

- What are the key determinants of organizational performance?
- How well are my staff currently performing in their jobs?
- How can employee, including managers, performance be improved?
- What are the causes of underperformance, again directed to employees and managers?

Pfeffer and O'Reilly (2000) provide a useful starting point to the analysis of organizational performance. They begin by asking the question:

What's the most important factor for success in today's knowledge-based economy?

In other words, what will make some organizations more successful, and therefore more likely to survive and prosper, than others? Pfeffer and O'Reilly quote from the McKinsey report, *The War for Talent*, to present the 'conventional' answer to these questions—that superior organizational performance will come from the superior performance of talented people. The implication of this view is, therefore, that the performance 'problem' is solved by employing only the most talented people, who, it is assumed, will naturally perform to their capability to deliver the high levels of performance that organizations require. If only it were that simple! (Human Resource Management Association, 2012).

One important drawback to adopting this PM strategy is that there are a finite number of exceptionally talented people around and, if all organizations are trying to employ them, the following might happen:

- because demand will exceed supply, the cost of employing such talent will increase to the point at which their productivity will fall;
- because they can command high prices, these people are much more likely to change employers more frequently than other employees, which means that what they can give to an organization is transitory;
- undue emphasis on potentially high performers may well result in 'ordinary' performers becoming disillusioned, and less committed to their work and organization, which can result in reduced performance;
- there is no guarantee that even the most talented staff will always perform to their potential—capability has to be engaged and harnessed, and this cannot be taken for granted.

There is, of course, persuasive anecdotal evidence that those with exceptional talent are often crucial to organizations becoming, and remaining, successful and the importance of recruiting the best possible employees or of refusing to employ those that don't meet a minimum specification is undeniable. So, too, is the need to retain talented staff, so that their capability and potential has a chance of being realized over the longer term.

 Signpost to Chapter 4: Talent Management: Strategies and Models, for an explanation of different ways talent can be conceptualized and used.

But the real challenge facing organizations is in understanding the 'secret' of high performance. According to Pfeffer and O'Reilly (2000), this means creating cultures and systems in which talented staff can actually use their talents. They go beyond this, however, and emphasize that the key to long-term organizational success is to ensure that management practices are in place that ensure extraordinary results from almost everybody (Pfeffer and O'Reilly, 2000: 2). Their emphasis on the environment in which people work and perform, which can liberate the potential of all employees, is an important step forward in understanding the limitations of concentrating a PM strategy on individuals without having any regard for the quality and characteristics of the social and psychological environment in which they work.

Having made the point that organizational success comes from driving the performance of all employees, rather than simply recruiting highly talented people, the McKinsey report offers insights into what companies should do to become successful, suggesting that recruiting high performers is only part of a set of requirements that drive performance of both people and the organization.

Part of the problem associated with managing performance is that people often interpret it in different ways, which, as was noted earlier, causes confusion and uncertainty. Just consider having a conversation with a subordinate about his/her performance and presenting a case for improvements: the reply you would almost certainly receive is, 'What do you mean by performance?'

First, managing performance isn't only about job performance, although this is the primary and often exclusive focus of PA. Performance can relate to what the team or group achieves and the outcomes of the production or service unit. Given that, from an HR perspective, our primary interest is on employee performance, it is recognized that the higher the organizational focus, the more factors such as pricing, product development, investment decisions, and currency fluctuations influence the performance of the organization measured in financial and economic terms. But, as we saw in the coverage of strategic HRM in Chapter 3, there is an increasing recognition that the human resource and human capital are critical to the success of most organizations. It is the cumulative effect of all people performing well rather than any one individual's performance achievements that in almost all circumstances makes a difference to the organization.

We can also conceptualize performance not only in terms of outcomes but in the way these outcomes are achieved. This is not an unimportant point! Long-term performance improvements and successes are what most organizations aspire to and while short-term improvements are of course important indicators of success they may actually be misleading and indicative not of success that is founded on improved fundamentals but on highly questionable business practices and dysfunctional management behaviour. Many PA schemes, particularly those for managers, produce overall performance ratings on how the manager behaved in achieving (or otherwise) their objectives and contributed to their subordinates achieving theirs.

So, in managing performance, we have to decide on:

- Exactly what we mean by performance and whose performance we are focusing on.
- How performance improvements are achieved and targets met.
- The timescale over which performance changes are monitored.
- The causal factors that are strongly associated with performance changes.
- The key interrelationships where one person's performance is influenced by others and other system influences.

The uncertainty over what performance is and means is compounded by several related concepts, certain of which may help to explain changes in performance levels while others represent quite different phenomena. Consider the following and try to become familiar with their meanings and significance.

 See the Online Resources Extension Material 12.1 for further discussion of the concept of performance and productivity.

Productivity

This is a concept that links the inputs to a production process to its outputs, expressed in quantitative or financial terms. According to the OECD (2001) productivity is commonly defined as a ratio of a volume measure of output to a volume measure of input use. While quantitative input–output measures are useful in certain contexts, and because they exclude the impact of price changes, using financial measures of both is often preferred.

Applied to the individual, it can be thought of as being close to performance but conceptually is different. Improved performance may be a contributing factor in increased productivity but the reverse cannot be claimed. Productivity is a key indicator of how well an organization uses its resources both human and material and it can be measured much more precisely at the aggregate rather than the individual level. Historically, in the engineering and manufacturing sectors, but more recently in many service sector industries, productivity has been the preferred concept that managers use and measure. The end of chapter case study shows how improved worker performance can drive organizational productivity.

STUDENT ACTIVITY 12.2

Read the Harvard Business Review article 'No-nonsense guide to measuring productivity' by W. Bruce Chew (1998), available at: https://hbr.org/1988/01/no-nonsense-guide-to-measuring-productivity

Think of two different organizations, one public sector and one private sector, and devise one or more productivity measures that would be useful and realistic.

Efficiency

This can be understood as the comparison of what is actually produced compared with what can potentially be achieved with the same resources. Efficiency is much more of an engineering than a behavioural concept, where from a technological perspective the maximum capacity of a productive system can be calculated and efficiency levels precisely measured. In a behavioural context, efficiency is much more difficult to measure, although conceptually we can see that efficiency is a key factor in determining the level of productivity.

Effectiveness

This can be understood as the relationship between targets or objectives set and what is actually achieved. If the targets or objectives are not particularly stretching or are impossible to meet, however, whether an employee is considered effective or not is more a function of the target or objective-setting process than of anything that the employee might do. Judgements about being effective are usually made without reference to any costs that have been incurred and can be highly subjective where targets or objectives are hard to measure. As such, effectiveness is a more contentious and subjective concept than productivity and efficiency as well as being less useful unless targets are properly set.

Effort

This is a difficult concept to precisely define as it has meaning outside of the employment context. We might think that effort is linked to the intensity of work, that is, how hard an employee works: it might be about how much energy a person puts into work or another activity such as sport. But effort is not necessarily linked to desired outcomes where effort is misplaced or not directed towards things that are of value. People who have a strong work ethic are, however, likely to put a great deal more effort into their work compared to those who are less strongly motivated, and are also likely to be committed and high-performing employees. Increases in focused effort are almost certainly going to affect performance and productivity levels.

Discretionary effort

This term captures the belief that employees only give a part of what they are capable of and that moving to higher levels is, to a degree, at their discretion, rather than subject to management control. From a managerial perspective, reducing the amount of discretionary effort employees retain through the way productive systems are controlled by technology and work systems, with people subordinate to them, is an understandable objective, but one that is much more difficult to achieve with knowledge workers. Achieving sustained, high levels of discretionary effort will in many work situations remain problematic for managers in the absence of either very effective work controls or incentive schemes, which are considered in detail in Chapter 13.

Contribution

This is a broader concept than performance and less precise than efficiency and productivity. Contribution is seen as what employees can do in addition to doing their jobs. What needs to be understood about work is that most people are capable of contributing more than their job performance, although whether they feel motivated to do so is another question. Contributing ideas and suggestions that result in process improvements and cost savings is rarely seen as part of someone's job but this is often because the importance of these 'wider contributions' is never articulated or where restrictive job descriptions explicitly limit and discourage anything than transcends job boundaries (Konrad, 2006).

Fundamentally, performance is about achievement, but what explains what people achieve in life? Looking at the many different contributions to our understanding of what explains different levels of performance, we can identify those that can be considered key. These are:

1. **Innate** and/or learned abilities.

2. **Motivation,** which is the inner desire to do something which may also be an innate condition or one influenced by external factors such as rewards, or a sense of fairness.

3. **Practice.** Certainly, in a sporting context and in areas such as music, practice and the search for perfection go hand in hand. The idea that with experience of doing something over and over again we become better at whatever it might be is supported by many who have achieved the highest levels of performance. Danny Willetts, the 2016 winner of the Masters Golf Tournament ascribes his success not to his abilities but to hard work and practice!

4. **Opportunity.** Many people are often surprised by what they have achieved in life, thinking that they lacked ability more than anything when the real problem was never being given the chance to show what they are really capable of doing. HRM Insight 12.1 illustrates this point very well.

HRM INSIGHT 12.1 The story of Kidane Cousland

Kidane Cousland, 24, was given the Sword of Honour at Sandhurst Royal Military Academy in 2016, beating candidates from Oxford and Cambridge to finish top of his class. He initially worked his way up the ranks, later attending Sandhurst, and became one of only a handful of mixed-race officers to ever be given the prestigious award, graduating as the best of his 200-strong intake. Cousland is the son of a single mother, who never knew his father, and grew up on a tough north London housing estate. At the age of 11, he was unable to read, but he and his brothers have all gone on to become leading talents in their respective fields, with one of the trio a famed artist, and the other became the first black British dancer to be accepted into the Royal Ballet. He is reported to have said that if it had not been for joining the Army he would have been dead or in prison.

Questions

1. What might explain his success after his early years of underperformance and underachievement?

2. Why wasn't his performance potential realized earlier in his life?

3. How can a person's potential be identified?

Source: 'From Tottenham to Sandhurst', *Mail Online* (15 April 2016).

Taking all these dimensions of performance into account we suggest the following conceptualization:

Individual performance = a function of (A, M, O, P) where:

A = abilities, innate and acquired

M = motivation, internally and externally located

O = opportunity

P = practice

Two important conclusions follow from this:

1. Not all employees are capable of the same levels of performance. All organizations contain people who have different existing capabilities and differences in potential. Employees, in other words, are different in terms of their innate capabilities and in terms of what they want to and can achieve. Using a sporting analogy, however hard most footballers try, the majority will never perform at the level of David Beckham or Wayne Rooney, or others who are exceptionally talented and driven. While effort is important, it is not the same as inherent or acquired talent or capability. 'Trying hard', if this effort is focused and directed to desired outcomes, is clearly an important element in performance, but effort alone is rarely sufficient to explain high-performing employees. In observing changes in management thinking and philosophy, driven by the ideas of such writers as Charles Handy and Tom Peters, John Lockett (1992) argues that one key feature of this shift in thinking is the emphasis from effort towards performance. He claims that:

   > There is an urgent need for people at work to achieve results—results which meet the company's performance requirements. Scoring 'A' for effort is no longer relevant, unless that effort is harnessed towards those requirements.

2. Simply achieving set objectives is not necessarily an indication of high performance if the targets or objectives set are too low and do not realistically stretch an individual or reflect his or her capability. This means that, while one individual might achieve more than another, they might actually be seen as a lower performer because, while one achieved all that they were capable of, the other did not. Using objectives to manage performance, while an attractive proposition, can therefore be difficult and fraught with dangers, particularly if objectives change and if they are expressed in qualitative ways which often involves the need to apply subjective judgements in establishing whether they have been achieved or not.

We can summarize this section by claiming that maximum performance is achieved when employees use their capabilities to the fullest, drawing on all their physical, intellectual, and emotional energies, and when they are set targets and objectives that stretch the individual (or team) to the highest sustainable level of performance.

Low Performance: Understanding the Problem

Perhaps the most consistent theme throughout this book has been the importance placed on how the situation or problem is framed. In other words, making sure we can see the situation/problem from different perspectives before proposing a solution. As far as managing performance is concerned, there is a tendency, often unconsciously followed, to frame the performance problem as being about getting people to improve their performance. This in turn leads to suggestions about incentive schemes, training, disciplinary action, and improved PA systems. But another approach is to focus much more on the reasons why current performance is lower than expected and what could be considered as reasonable. Making sense of the reasons for low performance is often the foundation for making better decisions about how to improve it.

The use of a sporting analogy helps to identify explanations for low and unsatisfactory performance problems. An experienced golfer with a handicap of 15 regularly performs to this standard at his club. On a golfing holiday with some friends, he played three of the top links courses in Scotland and returned scores well in excess of his handicap—i.e. he performed badly. Consider the possible explanations for this.

- It might be that the three courses were more difficult than his own, and that his poor performance was simply a function of the newness and level of difficulty of the courses. He played as well as he normally did, but because the courses were harder than he was used to, his performance fell relative to the challenge he faced.

- They were courses he had not played before and he lacked information on course layouts, bunkers, and distances. Basically, performing poorly first time round was not to be unexpected.

- The playing conditions might have been a factor in his poor performance. The wind might have been blowing, it might have been raining—i.e. the physical environment might have played a part.

- He might have lacked the level and range of skills to perform well in a more challenging environment. The courses might simply have been too tough for his skills and experience.

- There might have been something about him on those days that affected his performance: he might not have been in the right frame of mind, or he might have been nervous or a little over-awed by the occasion. He might have been physically below par, without the energy to deliver a sustained performance over the course. He might have lacked motivation to go out and play well. Collectively, these factors relate to the person's state of mind, and his psychological and physical well-being.

- Finally, he might have been missing help from his club professional or coach, who would normally give him tips on what he was doing wrong, offering constructive advice on what to do differently to improve his performance—i.e. he lacked some of the necessary support to help his performance.

This sporting analogy is useful because it suggests that we can draw upon our own experiences of performance, many of which may lie outside the world of work, to help us to understand human behaviour and the factors that influence our performance at work. The obvious point to make is that poor performance is often situational and temporary while other situations are explained by the relationship between what people can do, are good at doing, and the job they are in.

STUDENT ACTIVITY 12.3

There is an often unquestioned assumption that the work people do is necessary and important and that the organization benefits from work being successfully carried out. However, the feeling that some of the work people do is not particularly important and may not in fact be necessary has long been recognized. Performing such work well may seem to be desirable but if the work itself contributes little and in fact may be hindering organizational performance does it really matter whether it is done well or badly? The question about the value of work undertaken should always be considered in addition to how well the work is being performed. Parkinson's law is the belief that work expands to fit the available time, the implication being that some of the work we do is unnecessary.

Read the original article by Parkinson published in the *Economist* on 19 November 1955: 'Parkinson's Law' (http://www.economist.com/node/14116121), then consider the proposition that reducing working hours or the time allocated for a particular task is a way towards increasing worker productivity. Think of what might need to happen to facilitate such changes.

In addition to the possible explanations offered above for performance problems, W. E. Deming, cited in Rothwell (1996: 12), provides a further insight into where the most frequently experienced performance problems are to be found. Deming holds the view that what workers do or do not do is not the main reason why organizations experience these problems. He argues:

> **The workers are handicapped by the system, and the system belongs to management.**

Rothwell, in supporting this emphasis on managerial responsibility, claims that:

> **As little as 20% of all human performance problems are attributable to individual employees; as much as 80% of all such problems is attributable to the work environments or systems in which employees work.**

Deciding on appropriate strategies to address performance problems must begin from a clear understanding about the nature of the problem and its causes. While some and arguably many performance issues can be explained in terms of human deficiencies—skills, motivation, attitudes to work, etc.—even where they are part of the problem they may not be the most important explanations. In their influential book on improving performance, Rummler and Brache adopt a systems approach to the analysis of performance which sees different elements of the system as interrelated and often interdependent. They quote John Muir who said:

> **When we try to pick anything by itself, we find it hitched to everything else in the universe.**
> **(1995: 15)**

They go on to argue that:

> **we have found that everything in an organization's internal and external ecosystems is connected. To improve organizational and individual performance, we need to understand these connections.**

They offer an analysis of organizations as interdependent systems based on three levels of analysis, each associated with a range of performance relevant variables.

- First, at the organizational level, the variables that affect performance are its strategies, goals, measures, structure, and the way resources are allocated and deployed.

- At the process level—where the work gets done—a range of different cross-functional work processes interact to produce work outputs. Here, variables such as efficiency levels, resources, communications, standards, and expectations come into play.

- The third level—the job/performer level—involves people doing jobs that are linked to work processes where variables such as hiring standards, rewards, and training affect performance levels.

Taking the three levels of performance and relating them to the three key requirements of deciding on goals, design, and management, Rummler and Brache offer a model of performance that is multifaceted and highly integrated, as outlined in Figure 12.2.

	Goals	Design	Management
Organizational Level	Organizational Goals	Organizational Design	Organization Management
Process Level	Process Goals	Process Design	Process Management
Job/Performer Level	Job Goals	Job Design	Job Management

Figure 12.2 Rummler and Brache (1995) model of performance

Source: Rummler, G. and Brache, B. (2012) *Improving Performance: How to Manage the White Space on the Organizational Chart*, 3rd edition, Jossey-Bass. Reproduced with kind permission of Wiley.

Figure 12.2 suggests that no one single 'performance lever' will achieve the kinds of performance improvements and standards organizations are looking for, and that a more holistic and integrated approach will be needed to achieve sustained improvements. Managers also need to be able to distinguish between different 'performance situations' which may from time to time arise and require attention. We conclude this section by identifying some of the more common situations that can, in the absence of effective managerial action, become serious and even endemic.

People absent from work

If people are not at work, they cannot perform and their absence will also result in falls in productivity levels. Sick pay and fixed employment costs mean that, even though people are absent from work, the costs of employing them largely remain the same, or may even increase as replacement labour has to be hired, while their added-value contributions become zero. The higher the level of absence and the longer the time for which people are away from work, the bigger the performance loss becomes. The challenge for management then becomes one of finding effective ways of reducing absenteeism and its direct and indirect costs.

 Signpost to Chapter 10: Workforce Planning and Measurement, for insights into the management of absence.

People at work who don't perform—presenteeism

Given the need to become as competitive and efficient as possible, pressures to increase performance are found in most organizations. Employees who are physically absent from work represent one kind of problem, but those who just turn up to 'do their jobs' and no more present a different challenge to management. If people don't want to perform at any level other than that with which they are comfortable, then there can be a serious under-utilization of labour that, sooner or later, affects the performance of the organization itself. Examples of employees who do as little as possible are more likely to be found in organizations that are protected from financial and competitive pressures. In serious cases, a culture of underperforming can develop, which can be more difficult to change than cases of individual underperformance. But presenteeism is also associated with people being at work who are suffering from some kind of medical condition which reduces their performance and productivity. The reasons for the two kinds of underperformance are different—one is attitudinal and the other medical, but the consequences are broadly similar.

Legitimizing low standards

Although not obviously a problem, the existence of high performers who coexist with those who are satisfied with, or are allowed to deliver, lower levels of performance does create certain challenges and difficulties. If there are no negative consequences for being a low performer, why should a low performer want to improve? Moreover, what message does this send to high performers if it doesn't matter? Not addressing the problem of low performance can paradoxically result in its legitimization, making subsequent attempts to address the problem more difficult than they would otherwise have been.

Raising performance expectations and standards

How can managers stimulate people to raise their 'average' level of performance to sustainably higher levels? This is not about raising performance on a temporary basis, although this can be important under crisis circumstances. It is about leveraging everyone's performance to a new and higher level that becomes the new performance base line. The Hay Group (Jirasinghe and Houldsworth, 2006) has found that many organizations adopt a performance-enhancing strategy that combines elements from two broad approaches. Some give an emphasis to improving performance through the development of employees (a 'soft' approach), while others prefer one based on measurement (a 'hard' approach). The conclusion reached is that the most successful companies adopt a balanced and rounded approach, combining elements of both, including measures on teamwork, long-term thinking, building human capital, developing and managing talent, increasing employee engagement, and commitment to their jobs/the organization.

Removing the barriers to higher performance

The final situation that has to be managed is fundamentally different to the other four. If management feels that there are performance problems, the often-implicit assumption is that employees need to be encouraged, induced, or paid for additional effort or performance, and an effective mix of antecedents and consequences are often designed to impact on employee behaviour. In many cases in which job performance and wider contribution linked to the exercise of discretionary effort give cause for concern, the problem is less to do with lack of ability or motivation and more to do with the existence of 'organizational blockages'. Quite simply, this means that there are influences that originate in the culture, working environment, or management behaviour that act to suppress employees' natural desire to 'give more'. The challenge is, therefore, to clear the blockages that are preventing people from improving their performance. Knowing where to look is often the first step in any performance-enhancing strategy!

HRM INSIGHT 12.2 Managing the performance of managers at GE

In his book about his experiences as the CEO of GE (General Electric), one of the most successful USA-based global businesses listed on the New York Stock Exchange, Jack Welch describes the mechanism used throughout GE to manage performance (Welch and Byrne, 2003). In this approach, an employee's performance is described in terms of their performance against the previous year's objectives with 'A' performers being in the top 20 per cent, 'B' performers being in the middle 70 per cent in terms of performance, and 'C' performers defined as the bottom 10 per cent. Under this model, the company insisted that every manager identify the lowest-performing 10 per cent. Failure to do so would result in the manager being categorized as a 'C' performer. In Welch's words, 'the underperformers generally had to go', presumably meaning that, in most cases, those identified as the lowest-performing 10 per cent would generally lose their job or be encouraged to leave. Welch also expresses the view that anyone in this category should not have received any pay rise.

Then read Olsen (2013) before answering the questions.

Questions

1. What advantages might be achieved by an organization in implementing this model?

2. What might the disadvantages be to the organization and what impact might this approach have on the employees of the organization?

3. Consider the above model from the point of view of a manager of a team of ten people. What dilemmas might a manager face if asked to rate his or her team against this model?

4. What are the legal and ethical implications of using this system to identify the poorest performing 10 per cent of the salaried workforce, given the intention to terminate the employment of employees in this group under the strategy described?

5. How might the top 20 per cent of performers be positively and negatively affected by this policy?

Motivation and Performance

The subject of motivation properly belongs to the discipline of psychology and the study of human behaviour, but it has long been used in HR to try to generate insights into the performance-focused behaviour of people at work and the factors and conditions that impact on their work. It is not the intention here to provide a systematic account of motivational theories, nor of the extensive range of research outputs that have been produced on this subject (Kanfer, 2008).

However, it is worth noting the growing interest in what is called positive psychology (Compton, 2005; Peterson, 2006), which emphasizes the positive aspects of human behaviour and the use of the power of positive emotions to focus attention on what people can do well and what they find rewarding and self-fulfilling. Positive psychology is associated with the humanist tradition in psychology, linked to such writers as Maslow, McGregor, and Herzberg.

KEY CONCEPT Motivation

Motivation is generally understood as a force that exists within people that initiates and directs behaviour. In this sense, it can also be seen as a force that drives behaviour in certain directions rather than others. The force and direction are linked to goals that people are assumed to desire and outcomes that they would prefer to avoid. While many of the things/goals that people's behaviour is directed towards are inherent (basic needs) others are learned or are environmentally shaped.

STUDENT ACTIVITY 12.4

Martin Seligman is one of the leading proponents of positive psychology, which emphasizes the importance of positive emotions in life and of the state of happiness for the human condition. Watch the presentation by Seligman and consider the concept of happiness and how this emotional state is related to behaviour at work, available at: https://www.youtube.com/watch?v=9FBxfd7DL3E. Evaluate the evidence and arguments he presents that link a state of happiness with performance.

One of the common themes of this group of writers is the importance of understanding motivation as an inner force, often associated with enduring needs or drives that shape and direct behaviour in the workplace, where either failure or success in achieving desired needs has consequences for what the employee does. The implicit assumption that connects motivation to performance is that the more managers know about the dynamics of motivation, the more they can acquire insights into what employees value from their work. In turn, this allows them to develop mechanisms and provide opportunities that allow employees to achieve their needs, while increasing their performance. There is an implicit belief held by many motivational theorists that work is or should be an experience through which people satisfy their inner needs for belonging, recognition, affection, power achievement, and self-actualization. Satisfying these needs is associated with high performance, although the precise relationship between the state of satisfaction or the search for it and performance is controversial and complex (Judge et al., 2009).

The search for a universalistic answer to the question of how to motivate people has produced numerous answers and a seemingly endless supply of motivational techniques and books, all purporting to provide an answer. And that is the point; there are many different answers to the question, all of which have the potential to address specific performance problems and situations, but none relate to all. What complicates this relationship even further, is that the question itself is both problematic and potentially misleading. Asking 'how do we motivate workers' implies that they are relatively passive players in a relationship that is largely controlled by others. This is sometimes described as *extrinsic motivation*, where factors and decisions 'outside' the individual represent the main context for understanding and influencing employee behaviour. But if we ask the question in a different way—how does the worker motivate himself/herself?—then the focus of interest and understanding moves to within people, with the challenge then being one of understanding the dynamics of self-motivation. An internal focus is often associated with the concept of *intrinsic motivation*, where forces and processes within the individual interact with the external environment and specific external influences such as reward systems, performance standards, and managerial expectations (Thomas, 2009).

One of the most stimulating and original contributions on employee motivation and performance is Amabile and Kramer (2007, 2011). While accepting the importance of talented people and the use of external influences, their research findings lead them to attach primary importance to people's perceptions, motivation for work, and emotional states which are not only in dynamic equilibrium within the individual but are also influenced by the environment the person is working in. They argue:

> If your organisation demands knowledge work from its people, then you undoubtedly appreciate the importance of sheer brainpower. You probably recruit high-intellect people and ensure they have access to good information. You probably also respect the power of incentives and use formal compensation systems to channel that intellectual energy down one path or another. But you might be overlooking another crucial driver of a knowledge worker's performance—that person's inner work life.

(Amabile and Kramer, 2007: 72)

For them, perception involves making sense of their environment and giving it meaning and significance; emotions represent their reactions to these external events and activities and determine 'how they feel', while the motivation for work determines how they will perform their duties, when, to what standard, and indeed whether to do it at all. Amabile and Kramer claim that:

> Every worker's performance is affected by the constant interplay of perceptions, emotions, and motivations triggered by workday events, including managerial action—yet inner work life remains mostly invisible to management, and that most managers are not in tune with the inner working lives of their people; nor do they appreciate how pervasive the effects of inner work life can be on performance.

(2007: 9)

It may be that in searching for ways to motivate people to improve their performance, managers have been overemphasizing, as well as overstating, their ability to shape the external environment and failing to recognize that behaviour is fundamentally determined by what goes on within people.

Their model of inner working lives is based on the dynamic interplay between three critical variables:

1. **Perceptions**/thoughts about the organization, managers, other people and self, their work and how they are regarded.

2. **Emotions** and feelings which represent reactions to events and experiences at work. These emotions are usually positive or negative and on balance influence their overall mood.

3. Their **motivation** to do things, which is influenced by their attitude towards work, their drives to do things, and the energy/commitment they are prepared to give to it.

The work of Amabile and Kramer points to a new understanding of employee motivation, based on the dynamic between perception, motivation, and feeling, which collectively explain part of people's behaviour, and the external environment consisting of co-workers, managers, systems, work procedures, and decisions that collectively influence but do not determine what people do and how they behave.

One of their key conclusions is that managers and the way they behave in relation to their subordinates represent the most important influence on employee behaviour and performance, because this influence affects the three elements of inner working life. They identified two ways that managers could exercise a positive influence on employees. First, by treating them as human beings and providing a supportive working environment where people's achievements were recognized and commended. Second, and more importantly, by managers actively facilitating the work of their subordinates which helps them in making progress and in achieving important outcomes—to themselves and the organization.

Quoting Peter Drucker, who said that:

> So much of what we call management consists of making it difficult for people to do work

they argue that when people are blocked from doing their jobs they form negative impressions of their co-workers, managers, and the organization—negative impressions which may not be articulated or known by managers—which result in feelings of frustration, unhappiness, and ultimately demotivation. This then affects performance in the short and long term. But when managers facilitate progress—and this facilitation can take different forms—then the effects on inner life dynamics are very different, creating positive emotions and feelings and increasing motivational drives, both of which have performance implications.

The findings of Amabile and Kramer support the belief that a person's behaviour at work is primarily a function of the interplay between two critical forces. On the one hand, what a person 'is like' and what defines them; second, the relationship between the people they work with, the work they do, and the way they are managed. But not all managers will feel confident enough or possess the necessary social skills and have the required levels of emotional intelligence to engage with their staff in the way suggested. Nevertheless, their emphasis on the critical role of managerial behaviour as a key variable in understanding employee performance is strongly supported by other researchers (Buckingham and Coffman, 1999). In their influential book on work and management, they discovered that building a strong workplace was the key to understanding employee and organizational performance and that this kind of workplace was heavily although not exclusively influenced by the behaviour of managers. The extensive research involving many thousands of employees found that twelve questions captured the essential requirements for attracting and developing a high-performing workforce. Giving positive answers to these questions, summarized below, was strongly correlated to a strong and productive workplace.

1. Do I know what is expected of me at work?
2. Do I have the right materials and equipment to do my job?
3. Do I have the opportunity to do good work every day?
4. Do I receive recognition for what I achieve?
5. Am I seen by my manager as a human being?
6. Is my development encouraged at work?
7. Do people listen to my views and ideas?
8. Can I relate through my job to the organization's mission?
9. Are my co-workers committed?
10. Do I have friends at work?
11. Do I talk to my manager about my progress?
12. Am I given specific opportunities to learn new things?

Buckingham and Coffman's analysis of their extensive data led them to make two defining statements:

1. That those employees who responded positively to the twelve questions also worked in organizations with higher levels of productivity, profit, staff retention, and customer satisfaction.
2. That the manager—not pay, benefits, perks, or a charismatic corporate leader—was the critical player in building and motivating a strong workforce.

The key role of the manager and his/her influence on the motivational state and performance of the employee is now increasingly recognized and accepted by researchers, consultants, and managers. On a personal level, several years ago, one of the authors was attending an international conference on HRM in Beirut. One of the speakers was a Frenchman, who had worked for more than twenty years as a senior HR executive for American Express and who, after leaving, had built up his own international PM consultancy. During a conversation about his work as a consultant, he made an interesting comment about his thinking on where most performance problems lie:

> Whenever I am asked by the CEO of a business to try to sort out their performance problems, I always say that I will only agree to work for them on the basis that I will not be recommending

any of the employees are made redundant as a way of solving the problem. Almost all problems of organizational underperformance are not due to what employees do or don't do—they are generally because of deficiencies in management.

The point of the story is that, while individual performance is an important factor in explaining organizational success, it rarely explains organizational failure. People can be working hard and achieving performance targets, but a business can still fail.

 Signpost to Chapter 1: Managing People at Work: Challenges and Opportunities, to refresh your memory about how managers can make a difference to employee performance.

The work of Nohria et al. (2008) offers further insights into the strategic value and implications that come from understanding what explains human motivation. They theorize that motivation is based on, and driven by, four basic things.

1. **The drive to acquire.** This may be largely seen as a materialistic need but extends beyond the obvious things such as money and better jobs to positive experiences that individuals value and gain satisfaction from.

2. **The drive to bond.** This emphasizes people's need to form relationships, be part of something more than their own existence, and where the need not to be excluded or marginalized leads most people to seek social acceptance and recognition.

3. **The drive to comprehend.** This need reflects the fundamental requirement for people to make sense of their situation, what they are being asked to do, and why. Knowing why is arguably more important than knowing what in terms of explaining behaviour! Humans are naturally curious and while differences between individuals do exist, most seek to become more aware of their environment and what others expect of them.

4. **The drive to defend.** The need to protect oneself and others from threats, uncertainty, unknown change, and, for example, the 'unfair' and unjustified decisions of managers.

Nohria et al. link these basic four drives to related motivational and performance strategies, as shown in Table 12.1.

The interesting feature of Nohria's work is that it links the main human needs/drives to distinctive although not mutually exclusive PM strategies, and the research of Amabile and Kramer and Buckingham provide strong empirical evidence for the importance of three of these strategies, with that linked to rewards appearing to be the least effective, a conclusion that is supported by some, although not all, of the research we quote in Chapter 13 on rewards.

Table 12.1 Nohria et al.'s (2008) basic drives and strategic focuses and responses

Basic drive	Strategic focus and response
Acquiring	Reward system
Bonding	Culture building
Comprehending	Job design and work organization
Defending	Develop trust and fairness

Source: Nohria, N., Groysberg, B., and Lee, L. E. (2008) 'Employee motivation: A powerful new model', *Harvard Business Review*, 86(7/8), 78–84.

These four strategies reflect an approach to PM that is based on an understanding of human motivation, seeing people as human beings first and workers second. But many other PM strategies are based on a different perspective—one that could be described as reflecting a more rational and process-driven rather than a relationship-based approach to influencing behaviour: the person becomes less important than the process! Those strategies that fall into this category are:

- objective setting and management by objectives;
- performance measurement and the creation of standards and formalized expectations;
- building flexibility; and
- PA.

Limitations of length mean that not all four strategies are looked at in detail, but given its popularity and prevalence within organizations coverage of the PA process is provided.

The PA process

PA is a process that is commonly used throughout many organizations to evaluate or appraise employee performance in the past and to consider how to improve it in the future. The timescale under consideration is often a year, but performance may be appraised over a shorter period, from as little as a few weeks for a newly hired employee completing a probationary period. A distinctive feature of many, less effective PA systems is that they are seen as a single 'event', rather than an ongoing process.

The process usually includes a preparation stage, completed by both the employee and the manager. This may involve filling in either a pre-appraisal form or a draft copy of the appraisal form, to be used in the PA meeting. To avoid favouritism and to ensure that a consistent approach is adopted across the organization, there may be some input in the preparation stage from the manager's manager. Often appraisals will cascade through an organization and the appraisals are completed in order of seniority to ensure that objectives are passed down through each level of employee.

The appraisal then typically takes place at a meeting between the employee and his or her manager, and discussions take place covering each of the elements of the employee's job that the manager and employee wish to consider. Table 12.2 gives some examples of the elements that are often included in an appraisal process.

A final record is then made of what was discussed and agreed at the meeting, including performance in the past, objectives for the future, and development plans to support the employee to achieve these targets. This document is then copied for each of the parties and forms the basis of ongoing assessment against the objectives set. The process is shown in Figure 12.3.

> **KEY CONCEPT** Appraisal
>
> Appraisal or the process of appraising someone involves one or more people depending on the model or approach taken. It involves the examination and assessment of a person's behaviour in relation to their performance over a period of time. It involves making judgements and based on these making decisions about future changes in behaviour with the objective of improving performance. It can involve the rating of a person's performance by a superior (in a managerial sense) with the rating being linked to subsequent decisions about rewards, development, or corrective action.

Like many if not all HR processes or procedures, PA suffers from defects; some reflect highly questionable assumptions about human nature, others about the rating process, and yet more express concerns about the evidence upon which the PA narrative is based (Coens and Jenkins, 2000). But perhaps the most

Table 12.2 Areas and issues that might be covered in an annual PA

Item	Details	Why might this be included?
Personal information	Name; department; service details; date commenced in role; date of appraisal meeting	To give context of the appraisal
Last year's objectives	Details of objectives set at last year's appraisal	To clarify what level of performance was required for the preceding year
Performance against last year's objectives	Details of the extent to which objectives were met	To assess the extent to which performance last year reached the expected standard
Performance rating	A grade or score relating to overall performance	To give a score relative to others in the organization—often linked to performance-related pay
Additional achievements	Other achievements during the previous year	To establish additional contribution during year that was not anticipated as part of objectives initially set
Summary of last year's development activity	Details of training and development activities last year and the benefits of these	To assess effectiveness of development activity over previous year
Employee's strengths	Manager's view about what an employee is good at	To praise and recognize the employee's best qualities
Employee's weaknesses	Manager's view about areas in which performance could be improved	To identify areas of skill, knowledge, or attitude that might be improved
Planned training	Training activity and courses scheduled for forthcoming year	To identify training courses to address training needs identified
Other planned development activity	Other development activity, such as projects, coaching, or secondment	To identify other planned activities to help to address weaknesses or to build skills and knowledge that will be required in future
Next year's objectives	Details of objectives for the forthcoming year, including measures and constraints	To agree standards expected of the employee over the coming year
Manager's summary	A summary of the manager's overall view of performance during the year	To record manager's overall view of employee
Senior manager's comments	A summary of the next level of management's view of the employee's performance	To provide an opportunity for the next level of management to ratify the process and provide feedback
Employee's comments	An opportunity for the employee to make his or her own comments	To provide an opportunity for employee to comment, including areas of agreement or disagreement
Signatures	Signatures and dates of acceptance of the record of meeting	Ensures interested parties acknowledge receipt of the formal record

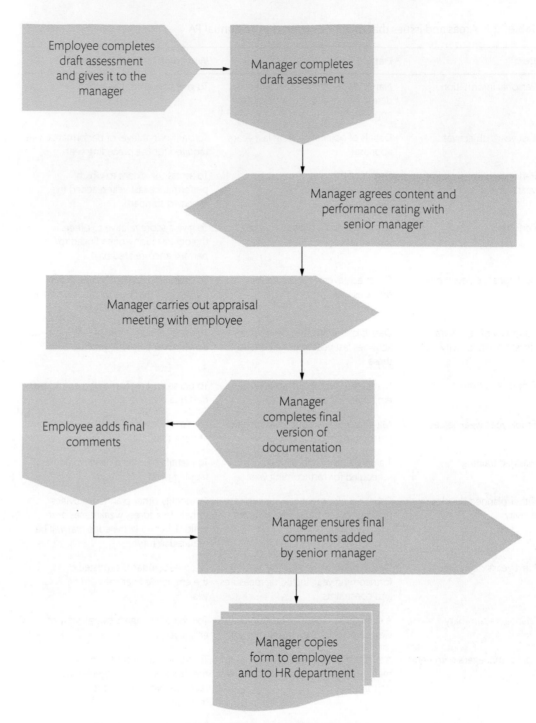

Figure 12.3 A typical PA process

worrying criticism of all, is that PA systems rarely impact positively on performance, a criticism which if evidentially based makes their continued use somewhat paradoxical. But of course, as Coens and Jenkins point out, many PA systems serve a range of different purposes other than performance improvement (Buckingham and Goodall, 2015).

Rating performance

Many appraisals require the manager to rate the performance of each employee in order to compare performance among colleagues as well as rate against established criteria. Rating systems can also be used to link performance to pay. They can be a useful indication to an employee of the extent to which the company recognizes their contribution; a lower score can be an effective way of alerting an employee that they need to improve.

Manager-allocated rating scales

Rating scales vary in complexity. A simple method of rating performance might be to ask the manager to choose a rating using a scale (see Table 12.3). In this example, the manager chooses the rating that is most appropriate for the employee, given the manager's knowledge of that employee's overall performance since the last appraisal. While this system is easy to implement and relatively simple, the rating is highly subjective and will be susceptible to a manager making a judgement based upon his or her overall perception of the employee, rather than on hard indicators of actual performance.

Objective-based rating scales

One way of trying to avoid the subjectivity of a rating scale is for the manager to assess an employee's performance against the objectives set and to allocate a rating based upon the extent to which these objectives are met (see Table 12.4). Providing that the objectives were set in such a way that the required target level of performance was clearly defined, then the rating allocated can reflect this.

Table 12.3 Example of a performance rating scale

Rating	Description
Outstanding	Employee demonstrates a level of performance that substantially exceeds that expected. Demonstrates an outstanding ability to meet all challenges within current role
Above standard	Employee has demonstrated a level of performance above that expected and has met challenges with a high degree of proficiency
Satisfactory	Employee's performance is at a standard that is satisfactory and acceptable
Needs some improvement	Some areas of performance need to be improved to reach a satisfactory level; more than a typical level of supervision required to meet objectives
Poor	Performance falls below the expected standard and unsatisfactory performance needs to be addressed, with considerable input required from supervision

Table 12.4 Example of an objective-based rating scale

Rating	Description
Exceeds	Employee measurably exceeds all objectives in every respect
Fulfils	Employee has met all agreed objectives to a standard that is fully satisfactory
Developing	Employee is relatively new to role and has met objectives to a satisfactory level, given level of experience and training
Below standard	Some areas of objectives not met, and employee requires more support and supervision than should be necessary to achieve objectives

The advantage of linking the rating to objectives is that the rating will more closely reflect the employee's actual performance. You will notice, in the example in Table 12.4, we have referred to the level of support and supervision provided to an employee, which may exceed that normally expected for any given level of performance. It is possible that an employee has only reached certain objectives as a result of levels of support and supervision that should not be necessary, and the organization may wish to take this into account in rating performance. Ratings such as these are often then linked to the pay award given to an employee.

Points-based rating scales

There are also a variety of systems for rating job performance that allocate points to different aspects of the job that employees perform. To be effective, points-based appraisal rating systems require comprehensive, reliable, and consistent information on performance against each job element or objective. Unless it is possible to meet these criteria, these systems are unlikely to possess the necessary credibility to be accepted and legitimized.

The value of rating performance

In general, the more objective a system is, the more value there is to rating performance because the rating given will actually relate to job performance. In reality, there are many jobs in which it is relatively easy to measure and rate performance, such as the sales levels achieved by a sales representative or the number of calls answered per hour by a telephone enquiry receptionist. Even in these examples, however, outside factors, such as the demand for these services, will influence performance levels.

The more complex a PA system is, the more effort and time needs to go into designing, maintaining, and implementing it. HR professionals, often seen as the guardians of the appraisal process, must have regard for the time spent by managers in carrying out appraisals and completing the associated paperwork or online forms. A degree of sensitivity, and awareness of the loopholes and 'shortcuts' that can develop, is also required, otherwise the appraisal process can become increasingly detached and ineffective as a positive contribution to improved performance. But criticisms of the rating process point to important and often unavoidable weaknesses, and deficiencies in the way ratings are given and the effect they have, particularly the undermining effects of managers sitting in judgement on their subordinates and the biases that inevitably intrude into the assessment not only of an employee's performance, but of the person (Rock et al., 2014).

RESEARCH INSIGHT 12.2

To take your learning further, read:

Dusteroff, C. et al. (2013) 'The effects of performance rating, leader–member exchange, perceived utility, and organizational justice on performance appraisal satisfaction', *Journal of Business Ethics*, 119(2), 1–9.

The article considers the role of fairness and justice in the way appraisals are carried out and the effect the ratings have on employee behaviour.

Setting Objectives

A key factor in the success of any organization is its ability to ensure that everyone clearly understands what they are required to do to contribute to its success. Everyone has a part to play in achieving the organization objectives, and setting objectives for individuals and teams is an important part of any PM process.

SMART is an acronym used to describe key characteristics of appraisal objectives:

S   specific (one end result is clearly described);

M   measurable outcome (the outcome can be measured);

A   agreed (manager and report agree the outcome);

R   realistic (i.e. what is the maximum that can realistically be achieved including target and stretch);

T   timely (i.e. by when will it be achieved).

It is also important to remember that objectives can become outdated as circumstances change, and management must respond quickly to new situations and demands.

Tracking progress and amending objectives to reflect new conditions and priorities is an essential part of 'managing objectives' if employees are to stay focused on what's important, rather than on what was originally agreed. Whatever objectives are agreed it is important to understand that these could, paradoxically, limit employee performance, in that they prevent or inhibit employees from responding to other needs or engaging in other value-added activities that are not incorporated in an employee's formal objectives.

Direct objectives

Most organizations will have a financial budget to which it must adhere. Some sections of the organization will be responsible for bringing money in through bidding for funding, achieving sales, or raising funds. Other teams will require resources that have a cost attached to them and the team may be responsible for securing the most effective resource possible within the predetermined cost. If an individual or team is responsible for a section of this budget, this might be expressed as a direct objective as follows:

Achieve sales of £500,000 in lingerie by the end of December 2011

Many objectives that can be quantified, either by using financial values, percentage changes, or physical quantities, and expressed in these ways, represent a stronger motivational influence on employee behaviour because progress towards the agreed objectives can be monitored and displayed. If this is not possible, an alternative approach to agreeing objectives is required, possibly expressing these in a qualitative way. The problem with this approach, however, is that it becomes more difficult to agree on measures that accurately express progress and achievement.

Indirect objectives

Key performance indicators (KPIs)

It may also be possible to have a measure in place the achievement of which, although not referred to directly in the organization's central objectives, contributes to these objectives being met. Such objectives become supportive or secondary, rather than primary. It is therefore important to adopt these measures and set targets, which are often referred to as key performance indicators (KPIs). An example might be:

Attract an average of 5,000 visitors per month to Mayfield Hall Museum throughout the next summer season

In this example, the KPI is visitor numbers and this directly correlates to revenue generated from ticket sales.

Project measures

If objectives cannot easily be expressed in terms of numbers that are directly or indirectly related to the organization's main aims and objectives, then targets might also be expressed in terms of delivery of a project that, if completed successfully, will contribute towards the organization achieving its strategic objectives. An example might be:

Re-tender the combined schools' catering contract for the Stokehampton district, incorporating government guidelines on healthy eating and maintaining current overall costs for the three years commencing on 1 April 2020.

The drawbacks of setting objectives

It should be noted that some jobs lend themselves more readily to objective setting than do others. For example, a sales representative with a clearly defined sales target is perhaps in a role better suited to objectives than an administrator, who may need to respond flexibly to manage a variable, and at times unpredictable, workload.

Setting objectives presumes that required actions or outputs can be predicted, but sometimes this simply is not the case. Many jobs consist of complex patterns of decision-making and long-term strategic planning, and the flexibility and creativity needed to deliver success in these roles can be stifled by rigid objectives. Many employees will have the self-motivation and capability to add value to an organization, identifying what needs to be done and how best to contribute to this in the absence of, or regardless of, what objectives are set. Furthermore, this creative capability can be further stifled if the attainment of prescribed objectives is related to future pay awards, which can have the effect of narrowly focusing people's efforts onto that which directly influences bonus/commission payments.

Giving Effective Feedback

Employees and managers generally benefit from honest, objective feedback about how things are going. A constant exchange of information, often generated through what might be described as 'performance conversations', helps everyone to stay on track and the organization to stay competitive. Problems come to the surface before they get out of hand, information that can improve performance gets to the right people before it's too late, and people build stronger working relationships because of feedback.

Effective feedback helps an employee to understand how others perceive their behaviour and performance. It may not always be welcome if it contains implied or explicit criticisms, but it is an essential part of any PM system. The purpose of giving feedback is not to change employees and try to mould them into what their manager would like them to be. It is about furnishing them with information about their behaviour and performance. Helping employees to understand how they are perceived at work, and not only by their line manager, gives them the opportunity to learn about themselves and to decide whether they need to change in some way or another.

Effective feedback, then, offers people information about themselves in a way that leaves them with a choice about how to act. The objective of giving feedback is to clarify and not judge. To be effective, the receiver needs to feel empowered and motivated to change and this can be achieved if the feedback is delivered in ways that do not damage the employee's self-esteem. Any negative feedback needs to be balanced by feedback that is positive and encouraging, so that the overall effect of the experience works to improve the employee's sense of worth and value, and motivates them to do better. That is the 'best practice' or prescriptive model for giving feedback. The reality for many, however, is quite different, and whether intentional or not, feedback given insensitively and without regard to its effects can cause long-term damage to a person's self-esteem and relationship with others. On the other hand, where criticism or negative comments are justified, then such outcomes may be inevitable if not desired (Steelman and Rutkowski, 2004).

360° feedback

One of the more recent developments in the use of appraisals to manage performance is 360-degree (360°) feedback. This involves seeking contributions about what a person achieves and how he or she operates not only from the line manager, but from others who are in contact with the person and are in a position to offer such feedback. Using this process, an employee, but more often a manager, can receive structured feedback from a variety of sources to assist him or her in improving performance. Typically, a questionnaire is sent to a selection of colleagues, subordinates, and, possibly, external contacts. The completed questionnaires are returned anonymously to an independent third party. The same questionnaire is also completed by the employee and by his or her manager, and the responses are compared between each group.

To be effective, feedback to the employee of the results should ideally be undertaken by a trained facilitator, who can help the employee to understand his or her own strengths and weaknesses, and can use the information to produce a development plan. While this tool can be extremely effective in helping an employee to understand exactly how he or she is perceived, the process must be properly managed. The employee is unlikely to benefit unless he or she remains open-minded and willing to participate in the process. Without a reasonable degree of trust, the process of seeking feedback at different levels might be detrimental to working relationships. Other staff may be reluctant to comment, and may need encouragement to be open and honest, and reassured that responses are anonymous. The feedback will also be more meaningful if any scores and responses are supported by examples and written comments to aid clarification. The design of the questionnaire is also crucial. While generic, 'off-the-shelf' questionnaires are available, organizations may benefit from designing their own process relevant to the skill sets they deem to be important to their own managers and teams (Coomber, 2006).

Development Plans

A development plan is an important tool to help an individual plan how he or she can best maximize his or her skills and knowledge. This can form part of an appraisal process, but a more detailed development plan can help to enhance the development of any individual. For example, an organization may wish to use development plans to fast-track employees who are identified as having high potential (Stringer and Cheloha, 2003). Typically, development plans will list all structured activity that is designed to address specific development needs. This might be to help build upon weaker areas, to develop existing skills and knowledge, or to develop new skills and expertise in readiness for future challenges. An effective development plan will encompass a broad range of developmental activity and should have only a small element of development reliant on attendance of training courses. Other activities may involve coaching or mentoring, participation in project work, secondment to another role or department, and opportunities to carry out new tasks or be exposed to new situations and challenges in the workplace.

Managing Problem Performance

Earlier, we made reference to a situation with which managers are often confronted—that of performance that is consistently below what is reasonable and acceptable. In a worst-case scenario, managers will ignore the problem or rationalize it away, interpreting it as less of a problem than it really is. But problems of underperformance are rarely solved by pretending that they don't exist, and the effective management of performance not only involves developing systems and procedures, but also engaging with those employees whose behaviour is unacceptable.

In serious cases involving managerial staff, this may involve managing people out of the organization through the use of what are referred to as 'compromise' or 'settlement agreements'. These are contracts that end the employment relationship by mutual agreement, and involve the employee giving up his or her employment protection rights in exchange for a financial payment, and often a favourable reference. In cases in which the problem is considered irretrievable, often involving a breakdown in the relationship between employee and management, rather than invoke disciplinary procedure leading to dismissal, management may wish to consider a solution to the problem that is less damaging for both parties (ACAS, 2013).

In less serious situations, management can consider the mechanisms that normally lie outside an existing disciplinary process.

- **An informal performance review**

  This involves a meeting between a manager and an employee to highlight areas of concern with the employee's current performance, to discuss and set targets for improvement, and, if appropriate, to arrange support and training to achieve these targets.

- **A formal performance review**

  This is a meeting between a manager, often with an HR practitioner or another manager present, and the employee, who should be informed of the right to be accompanied by a representative. At a formal meeting, concerns about performance can be discussed, targets set for improvement, and consequences of failure to improve can be highlighted, which may ultimately include demotion, transfer, or termination of employment. A timescale for improvement, training, and support can also be agreed.

Both types of review should be based on the principles that employees need to be given the opportunity to improve their performance before further action is taken, and that raising concerns informally first is preferable to invoking formal procedure or action. Both types of meeting are, however, likely to cover the same content, including:

- discussing areas of concern;
- setting targets and timescales for improvement; and
- agreeing appropriate training and support.

Summary

- PM is something that takes place in all organizations—it is a generalized activity existing at different levels and taking different forms. In its formal expression PM is manifested through a range of interventions, strategies, and processes that are subject to different levels of managerial influence. Informally, performance is subject to a set of rules, conventions, and standards that often reflect the attempts by employees to defend themselves against attempts by managers to increase performance expectations and requirements.

- The dominant discourse on PM is one where managers are working to increase performance, and productivity, by developing new and more effective interventions, but it is sometimes necessary to see PM through an employee prism, where protecting, defending, and engaging in negotiations with managers over performance levels characterizes the process. Once again, we see in HR the importance of recognizing and understanding the importance of the informal as well as the formal domain and the need to make sense of how one interacts with the other.

- As we have noted, improving performance is not as important to an organization as improving productivity although the latter may be influenced by the former and many productivity improvement initiatives involve ways of increasing employee effort and performance.

- It is important to recognize that many formal performance initiatives fail to deliver long-term sustainable improvements in performance either among employee groups and/or at the organizational level. Those that use rewards to induce performance increases suffer from what Herzberg described as short-term performance improvements but long-term productivity declines with this tendency explained by an increase in costs which may be greater than the value of any increase in performance.

- The work of the motivational theorists we referred to suggests that more effective strategies for growing performance lie in building workplaces with strong positive emotions, opportunities to grow and perform, and managers who encourage, support, and facilitate the work of their staff. This is a position supported by writers such as Amabile, Kramer, and Buckingham.

- Approaches based on PA, although widely adopted seem far less effective and the many critical comments and reviews of traditional PA schemes suggest that their widespread use is, for the most part, at odds with their actual effectiveness.

- A systems perspective on performance linked for example to the work of Rummler and Brache leads to the conclusion that subunit or organizational performance is not simply a consequence of what employers do but reflects work design, resource allocation, and the quality of managers.

- What can be said with confidence, is that there are no organizational 'levers' to pull that will have the effect of increasing performance to higher and sustainable levels. Most of the evidence we have reviewed suggests that in the long term only those strategies that involve culture change, relationships, opportunities, trust, and fairness are likely to succeed. 'Buying' performance improvements may have a short-term relevance, but it comes with financial costs. Forcing increases in performance, because of a lack of legitimacy and consent, will hardly ever work in situations where employees have choices about where to work and under what conditions.

389

 Visit the **online resources** that accompany this book for self-test questions, web links, and more information on the topics covered in this chapter, at: **www.oup.com/uk/banfield3e/**

? REVIEW QUESTIONS

1. What are the key features of the working environment that have an impact on an employee's level of performance?

2. How does 'performance' differ from 'productivity' and what is the relationship between the two?

3. What kind of appraiser biases might be found in the PA process and how might these be managed?

4. What are the features of high-performance work practices?

5. What does the concept 'discretionary effort' mean and why is this important in managing performance?

6. To what extent is 'poor' performance a reflection on management rather than employees?

7. What explains underperformance and what strategies are available to management in the way underperformance is managed?

CASE STUDY   The case of the light machine shop

In situations in which managers are under pressure to increase pay in a way that does not increase wage costs, which might decrease labour productivity, agreements with groups of employees to link increases to changes in employee behaviour can result in improvements in productivity. In other words, agreements can generate added value or reduced cost, with either the savings or increased output values becoming the source of increased payments. Employees, through greater utilization of their intellectual and physical labour, effectively pay for their own pay increases. The management of United Steels, within which the light machine shop (LMS) was located, was faced with a similar situation. The shop stewards representing the fifty workers employed in the LMS had submitted a pay claim, but after discussions with Peter Wilson, employment relations manager for United Steels, they agreed to consider a proposal for a productivity agreement.

The LMS was one small department in a complex of steel-producing and heavy engineering facilities, and was physically on the perimeter of the complex, well away from where most of the senior managers were located. It was essentially a fabrication shop, in which products such as steel frames, tables, and panels were made.

Peter discussed the options with his team and it was decided that a scheme should be designed that would generate increased revenue, which could be shared between the company and the employees covered by the scheme. He asked George Black, one of the employee relations officers, to come up with an idea that might deliver the required objectives. George looked at the current system of working and payment, and found the following:

- All employees were paid an hourly rate based on their skill level. This was known as the 'consolidated time rate' and was paid irrespective of the amount of work each completed. There was an unspoken understanding within the shop of the level of output that was needed before management began to show a concern about performance levels.

- Each job allocated by the shop foreman to a worker had a time allowance attached to it. This allowed time figure was the result of a time study, under which the foreman would apply time study practices to arrive at a time that was neither too easy nor too difficult to meet. All new jobs had to be timed by the foreman and an allowed time determined. Existing jobs were often subject to retiming as design changes altered the 'amount of work' that was involved.

- Workers were able to increase their weekly wages by completing jobs that had an aggregate allowed time in excess of forty hours (a 40-hour week was in place). If, for example, an individual completed jobs having an allowed time of forty-seven hours, he would receive forty-seven times his hourly rate.

- Individual performance could only effectively be increased by workers increasing their focused effort, i.e. by working harder and smarter, and by using their skills to full effect.

- Current management attitudes and practices meant that the decisions on performance levels were largely in the hands of the workers.

- The shop foreman was only in contact with his line manager infrequently and the HR representatives were rarely seen on the shop floor. He spent most of his time with the workers he was managing and was particularly influenced by the strong trade union presence, manifested by two experienced shop stewards who had worked in the shop for many years. He didn't want any trouble that might involve senior management and he was very much interested in a 'negotiated order'.

George was relatively inexperienced in designing 'productivity' schemes, but, after discussing the best approach to take with a colleague, he came up with the following proposal.

- The scheme would be based on the ability of workers to earn a non-consolidated bonus by increasing their weekly output of steel components.

- The principle underpinning the scheme would be the relationship between allowed times and actual times. The time the workers *actually* took to complete each job or part of a job would be recorded, along with the *allowed* time, on each job card issued by the shop foreman.
- All job cards for the previous six months would be collected and the aggregate allowed times calculated. The aggregate actual times would also be calculated and compared to the allowed times using the formula:

$$\frac{\text{Allowed times}}{\text{Actual times}}$$

The data collected produced the following base-line index:

$$\frac{57,850}{52,000} \times 100 = 111$$

- A 13-week moving average would be used to iron out weekly fluctuations in output, with the first bonus payment being paid in week 13.
- Bonus payments would be paid to each worker pro rata to his or her skill grade, with skilled workers receiving 100 per cent bonus, semi-skilled workers receiving 90 per cent, and those designated as unskilled, 80 per cent.
- Actual payments, at 100 per cent, would be £15 per week for every percentage point by which the productivity index exceeded its base line.

Questions

1. What were management's objectives in designing this scheme?
2. Was the scheme about performance or productivity?
3. If the index were to increase from its base line, what might the explanations for this be?
4. Are there any potential flaws in the scheme?
5. How do you think the behaviour of the workers in the LMS would have changed as a result of the scheme being implemented? Would their behaviour have reflected what the HR staff expected?

 Insights and Outcomes: visit the **online resources** at **www.oup.com/uk/banfield3e/** for an account of why the bonus scheme failed and the lessons that were learned.

 FURTHER READING

Brown, D. (2010) 'Performance management: Can the practice ever deliver the policy?', Institute for Employment Studies, at: http://www.employment-studies.co.uk/resource/performance-management-can-practice-ever-deliver-policy

Haines, V. Y. and St-Onges, S. (2012) 'Performance management effectiveness: Practices or context?', *International Journal of Human Resource Management*, 23(6), 1158–75.

Hoffman, E. and Bueno, B. (2013) 'Choosing the right performance metrics', *Workspan*, 56(9), 33–7.

Hutchinson, S. (2013) *Performance Management: Theory and Practice*, CIPD.

Rogers, E. W. and Wright, P. M. (1998) 'Measuring organizational performance in strategic human resource management: Looking beyond the lamp-post', at: http://digitalcommons.ilr.cornell.edu/cgi/viewcontent.cgi?article=1134&context=cahrswp

Stewart, H. (2012) *The Happy Manifesto*, Kogan Page.

REFERENCES

ACAS (2013) Settlement Agreements, at: http://www.acas.org.uk/index.aspx?articleid=4395

Amabile, T. M. and Kramer, S. J. (2007) 'Inner work life', *Harvard Business Review*, 85(5), 72–83.

Amabile, T. M. and Kramer, S. (2011) *The Progress Principle*, Harvard Business Review Press.

Armstrong, M. and Baron, A. (1998) *Performance Management: The New Realities*, CIPD.

Armstrong, M. and Baron, A. (2004) *Managing Performance: Performance Management in Action*, CIPD.

Brailsford, D. (2013) 'Five steps to peak performance', *Management Focus* (autumn), at: http://www.som.cranfield.ac.uk/som/dinamic-content/news/documents/manfocus35/management_focus_issue_35_15_steps.pdf

Buckingham, M. and Coffman, C. (1999) *First Break All the Rules*, Pocket Books.

Buckingham, M. and Goodall, A. (2015) 'Reinventing performance management: How one company is rethinking peer feedback and the annual review, and trying to design a system to fuel improvement', *Harvard Business Review*, 93(4), 40–50.

Chew, W. B. (1998) 'No-Nonsense Guide to Measuring Productivity', *Harvard Business Review* (January), at: https://hbr.org/1988/01/no-nonsense-guide-to-measuring-productivity

CIPD (2015) *Performance Management: An Overview* [revised September].

Coens, T. and Jenkins, M. (2000) *Abolishing Performance Appraisals*, Berrett-Koehler.

Compton, W. C. (2005) *An Introduction to Positive Psychology*, Thomson/Wadsworth.

Coomber, J. (2006) 'Feedback—360 degree', at: http://www.cipd.co.uk

Dusteroff, C. et al. (2013) 'The effects of performance rating, leader–member exchange, perceived utility, and organizational justice on performance appraisal satisfaction', *Journal of Business Ethics*, 119(2), 1–9.

Economist (1955) 'Parkinson's Law', 19 November, at: http://www.economist.com/node/14116121

Goh, S. C. (2012) 'Making performance measurement systems more effective in public sector organizations', *Measuring Business Excellence*, 16(1).

Holbeche, L. and Matthews, G. (2012) *Engaged*, Jossey-Bass.

Human Resource Management Association (2012) 'The best and the rest: Revisiting the norm of normality of individual performance, research briefing', at: http://www.hrma.ca/wp-content/uploads/2012/11/rb-the-best-and-the-rest.pdf

Jirasinghe, D. and Houldsworth, E. (2006) *Managing and Measuring Employee Performance*, Kogan Page.

Judge, T. A. et al. (2009) 'The job satisfaction–job performance relationship: A qualitative and quantitative review', *Psychological Bulletin*, 127(3), 376–407.

Kanfer, R. et al. (2008) *Motivation Past, Present and Future*, Routledge.

Kolb, D. A. (1984) *Experiential Learning: Experience as a Source of Learning*, Pearson Education.

Konrad, A. M. (2006) 'Engaging employees through high-involvement work practices', at: http://iveybusinessjournal.com/publication/engaging-employees-through-high-involvement-work-practices

Lockett, J. (1992) *Effective Performance Management: A Strategic Guide to Getting the Best from People*, Kogan Page.

Mabey, C., Salaman, G., and Story, J. (1998) *Human Resource Management: A Strategic Introduction*, Blackwell.

Nohria, N., Groysberg, B., and Lee, L. E. (2008) 'Employee motivation: A powerful new model', *Harvard Business Review*, 86(7–8), 78–84.

OECD (2001) *Measuring Productivity: Measurement of Aggregate and Industry Level Productivity Growth*, at: https://www.oecd.org/std/productivity-stats/2352458.pdf

Olsen, E. G. (2013) 'Microsoft, GE and the futility of ranking employees', *Fortune*, at: http://fortune.com/2013/11/18/microsoft-ge-and-the-futility-of-ranking-employees

Peterson, C. (2006) *A Primer in Positive Psychology*, Oxford University Press.

Pfeffer, J. and O'Reilly, C. A. (2000) *Hidden Value*, Harvard Business School Press.

Rock, D., Davis, J., and Jones, B. (2014) 'Kill your performance ratings', *Strategy+Business*, 76 (autumn), 75–83.

Rothwell, W. (1996) *Beyond Training and Developing*, AMACOM.

Rummler, G. A. and Brache, A. P. (1995) *Improving Performance: How to Manage the White Space on the Organization Chart*, Jossey-Bass.

Steelman, L. A. and Rutkowski, K. A. (2004) 'Moderators of employee reactions to negative feedback', *Journal of Managerial Psychology*, 19(1), 6–18.

Stringer, R. A. and Cheloha, R. S. (2003) 'The power of a development plan', *Human Resource Planning*, 26(4), 10–17.

Thomas, Kenneth W. (2009) *Intrinsic Motivation at Work: What Really Drives Employee Engagement*, Berrett-Koehler.

Ulrich, D. (1998) 'A new mandate for human resources', *Harvard Business Review*, 76(1), 124–34.

Welch, J. and Byrne, J. A. (2003) *Straight from the Gut*, Warner Books.

13 Managing Rewards

Introduction

According to the CIPD (Arkin, 2005), there has never been a better time to become a specialist in reward management. This view is based on evidence generated by the Institute's 2005 annual reward survey (CIPD, 2005), which found that demand for such expertise was growing, with more organizations taking on specialist reward practitioners. There seems little doubt that since Arkin made his remark little has changed that challenges this view. Interesting as this trend might be for those wishing to develop a career in the field, the real significance of the report lies in the way in which it casts light on the forces and pressures influencing reward practices, and the challenges facing managers in the way in which they respond to these pressures.

But why are rewards, and the way in which they are managed and experienced at work, such an important part of HRM? A useful starting point is recognizing that rewards are a basic element of the employment relationship, and have a critical influence on the satisfaction and commitment of employees. Organizations that fail to understand this fundamental relationship are likely to be less competitive and successful than those that do, and which deliver consistently effective reward policies and practices. Quite simply, employees who are frustrated and dissatisfied with the rewards they receive will express this through how they behave and perform in their jobs; in ways that are unlikely to be in the interests of the organization. Organizations that make mistakes in the way in which they manage rewards are almost certainly going to experience damaging consequences, in the forms of low productivity, higher turnover, and a general lack of employee engagement. The bigger the mistakes, the higher the costs the organization is likely to experience. As an example, decisions that led to the use of highly incentivized bonus schemes in the banking and finance sector prior to the recession of 2008–9 have been directly linked to the questionable and unethical promotion and sale of what in retrospect turned out to be almost worthless securities. Selling more to gain a higher bonus irrespective of the consequences became, in many organizations, an institutionalized practice with at the time unanticipated consequence (Siegert, 2014).

It is similarly important to recognize that the way in which rewards are managed will also, either directly or indirectly, impact on other aspects of HR. For example, a sense of unfairness and dissatisfaction with pay will probably affect the form and level of industrial conflict, and the preparedness of employees to participate with management in a more collaborative approach to employee relations. In other words, feeling that managers are rewarding people unfairly or not meeting their 'legitimate' expectations in relation to changes in the reward package is likely to influence and contaminate employees' general perception of management and the organization.

On the other hand, there is a view that getting rewards 'right' offers important positive outcomes. As Paul Bissell (in Arkin, 2005) observed:

> **Organizations are realizing what a powerful lever reward is and how it needs to complement their other business strategies, whereas historically people have tended to view it in glorious isolation.**

What this means is that reward management is not simply about the basic issues of paying people fairly in relation to market rates, the job they do, and how well they perform in the job, but extends to the impact of reward decisions on recruitment, retention, training, flexibility, and performance, in addition to their effect on morale and commitment and particularly on the psychological contract. It is self-evident that, without satisfactory rewards, the organization will not be able either to attract or retain the calibre of employee it requires, with the right skills and competencies to deliver the contributions that the organization needs in order to be successful and competitive. In fact, it would not be an exaggeration to suggest that rewards have a significance that pervades almost every aspect of employment and work. Because rewards, in their different forms, have such an important influence on relationships and behaviour in the formal and informal domains it is unsurprising that they occupy a central position within HRM.

As we have indicated, one of the most challenging aspects of managing rewards is to do with fairness. Because the concept of fairness is inherently subjective—by that we mean that individuals create their own meaning as to what is fair or unfair—opportunities for different views as to what is fair or not abound. In an attempt to establish the fairness of rewards in a more objective way, Vaughan-Whitehead (2010), in conjunction with the International Labour Office, developed the following criteria which can be used by management to test the fairness or otherwise of different aspects and forms of wages/salaries, although there still remains an element of subjectivity in some.

● **Payment of wages:** a wage which is regularly and formally paid in full to the workers.

● **Living wage:** a wage that ensures minimum acceptable living standards.

● **Minimum wage:** a wage which respects the minimum wage regulations.

● **Prevailing wage:** a wage which is comparable to wages in similar enterprises in the same sector.

● **Payment of working time:** a wage which does not generate excessive working hours and properly rewards normal working hours and overtime.

● **Pay systems:** a wage that leads to a balanced wage structure/composition between the basic wage and additional bonuses and benefits. A wage that reflects different levels of education, skills, and professional experience, as well as rewarding individual and collective performance. A wage that complies with regulations on social insurance payments and paid holidays and is not dominated by disciplinary wage sanctions.

● **Communication and social dialogue:** a wage on which workers receive sufficient information in advance (through an individual work contract), in the course of the production process (through regular communication channels) and at the time of the wage payment (with a detailed pay slip). A wage that is negotiated individually (between the employee and his or her own individual employer) and if appropriate collectively (notably through collective bargaining between the employer and the workers' representatives who are freely accepted in the company).

● **Wage discrimination/wage disparity:** an equal wage for equal work that does not lead to wage discrimination and does not generate unjustified and high wage differentials within the company.

● **Real wages:** a wage that progresses at least in proportion to increases in the cost of living.

● **Wage share:** a wage that progresses proportionally along with enterprise sales and profit growth and which does not lead to a fall in the wage share in enterprise performance growth.

● **Wage costs:** a wage whose progression does not lead to a dramatic reduction in wage costs within total production costs and as a percentage of employment.

● **Work intensity, technology, and increases in skill:** a wage that progresses along with changes in intensity at work, technological content, and the evolving skills and tasks.

Realistically, some rather than all these criteria will be incorporated into decision-making processes and they only relate to wages and not other reward types, but at least they offer ways of addressing the fairness challenge. But fairness is more usually established by subjective criteria. This often involves employees looking to other employees, and comparing what they do and what they get paid. Internal and external pay relationships, sometimes referred to as relativities and differentials, are used to legitimize pay claims and defend existing pay relationships. Relative pay can be as important to people as the real value of pay because it expresses implied or explicit status differences between and within occupations. Judgements about what is fair and what is not fair are also found in relation to the reward experiences of male and female employees doing the same or similar work. If differences in pay or benefits exist that cannot be justified by differences in the value of jobs, the feeling of unfairness that often follows can ultimately involve the aggrieved party challenging the employer through an equal pay claim.

But there is another form of fairness in addition to that associated with comparisons and objective criteria and that is expressed through the concept of procedural justice. Tyler and Bies (1990) suggest that it is procedural justice—associated with how decisions are taken over rewards—that is the key to understanding perceptions of 'felt fairness' rather than distributive justice—the substantive outcomes that express reward levels and relationships. This led Suff et al. (2007: 6) to claim that:

This has important implications for employers, who might do well to focus their investment in time spent getting reward processes right rather than on the size of reward at stake.

 Signpost to Chapter 5: Ethics and Leadership in HRM, for a more detailed exploration of what fairness means.

While the issue of pay and reward is fundamental to the behaviour and performance of employees, it is also arguably one of the most contentious and difficult areas of HR to manage. It is perhaps for this reason that the remuneration packages of reward specialists tend to be significantly greater than those enjoyed by the majority of HR generalists (CIPD, 2005). This level of recognition of the important role and contribution played by reward specialists is partly due to the scale and range of reward matters. From managing the payroll, pensions, and other contractual benefits, those involved also have to make critical decisions on wage and salary levels, pay increases, and sort out the never-ending disputes and disagreements over bonus payments. The costs of the pay and the total reward packages represent, for most organizations, a significant proportion of their total budget and these costs need to be managed effectively to ensure that they remain within acceptable limits. Reward specialists not only have to ensure that employees are fairly and adequately paid (both highly subjective), but must also avoid significant overpayment, in the context of what the organization can afford to pay to remain competitive and stay in business or within budget.

Managing rewards can also involve large-scale, sector-based pay modernization projects, which seek to replace ageing and ineffective pay policies with common pay structures, based on national job evaluation frameworks and harmonized conditions of employment. The NHS' Agenda for Change project is a good example of a major reward management initiative and, in this case, linked the development of a new national competency framework to a simplified structure of jobs and payment levels (Department of Health, 2004).

The challenging nature of reward management is also the result of the increasingly complicated nature of the 'reward package'. Rewards are far from being solely about pay. According to Thompson (2002):

> the era in which reward was just about cash and benefits is gone forever; increasingly the emphasis in leading organizations is on a total reward approach, including more intangible rewards like the work environment and quality of life considerations, the opportunity for advancement and recognition, and flexible working.

Moreover, as reward systems are integrated with other areas of HR, and have to respond to external pressures and legislative change, it becomes increasingly difficult to envisage a situation in which managers have, in some finite sense, 'solved the problem'. It is much more sensible to conceptualize reward management as an ongoing process—an attempt to reconcile the interests and expectations of different organizational stakeholders—that is undertaken in the knowledge that these different interests and expectations can never be fully met or reconciled. As Daniels (2000) alleges:

> Few organizations are satisfied with their reward and recognition systems. Furthermore, every change in these systems results in someone else becoming unhappy. Most often, management becomes cynical, because no matter what they try, nobody is satisfied.

 For information on payment frequency and annualized hours, see the Online Resources Extension Material 13.1.

Differences over what constitutes 'fair' and 'effective' reward systems and uncertainties about the behavioural impact of particular rewards and reward practices make the job of the HR practitioner working in this field particularly problematic and challenging. There are neither simple nor universal answers or prescriptions that are guaranteed to work. What emerges from the different academic contributions, research findings, and individual experiences, is that there is no consensus on how organizations should be rewarding their employees. Nor is there any certainty that the use of particular rewards will actually generate the behaviours and outcomes desired by managers. Furthermore, not all commentators hold the same view as to the effects on behaviour of particular types of reward.

A good example of the polarization of opinion over the use of rewards can be seen in the arguments relating to the use of rewards to encourage higher levels of individual performance, that is, those relating to performance-related pay (PRP), a question considered in detail later in the chapter. Many managers and employees genuinely believe that rewards used in this way do have a positive impact on employee motivation and, used appropriately, can increase individual performance levels. This reflects the belief that employees attempt to restrict performance levels to below what is sustainable unless they are offered incentives to perform at higher levels. On the other hand, writers such as Herzberg (2003) and Kohn (1993a) have consistently taken the view that such rewards not only fail to deliver intended outcomes, but actually distort behaviour and have a long-term detrimental effect on productivity. Kohn even equates these additional payments with bribes and argues that they should not be used, despite the fact that many managers and employees believe that people will do a better job if they have been promised some kind of reward or incentive. More will be said about this later.

 Signpost to Chapter 12: Managing Performance, for insights into the relationship between rewards and performance.

The difficulties faced by managers in determining the most appropriate and effective reward strategy for their organizations are not only highlighted in the academic literature, but also in the realities of organizational life. The dilemma managers face is that, while employees value rewards and generally would like more of them, rewards, as we mentioned earlier, can be very costly for the organization. If pay is the predominant form of reward, overpaying employees can be an expensive mistake. One of the realities of reward management is that mistakes are not easily rectified—giving rewards is much easier than trying to take them away. At the same time, it is natural to expect that employees will want to maximize their remuneration and reward levels, to reflect their own views about their value and the contribution that they believe they make to the organization. This tension between what employees feel they are worth and what managers consider it is economically prudent to pay is often at the heart of disagreements and conflict between the two parties, particularly where financial rewards are involved. This is a good example of the way dialectics—the struggle between opposing forces and interests—manifests itself within organizations and through industrial disputes. But it isn't simply about employees wanting to increase their pay without limitations or employers wanting to pay as little as possible. First, both parties have a vested interest in reaching compromise because excessive demands will inevitably result, if met, in job losses and business failures. Underpaying for employers affects recruitment, retention, and performance requirements. Within the two extremes, the two parties will almost certainly express opposing interests where the rewards involve significant financial costs or gains.

It is quite easy, therefore, to understand the ongoing existence of tensions and disagreements over pay, a state that is caused by a number of factors. For example, if an organization were to seek the opinions of its employees on this subject, it would be far more likely to find that they considered themselves underpaid rather than overpaid. Whether they would consider themselves to be under- rather than over-rewarded is a separate question, but given that pay is the most visible and, arguably, the most important reward provided by employment, the tendency for employees to believe that they are paid less than they feel they deserve helps to explain why pay is often the cause of industrial conflict and less obvious but still important displays of discontent. Differences over rewards are never fully resolved because the reasons for their existence are endemic within the organization; the realistic goal from an HR perspective is that rewards are effectively controlled and managed. Student Activity 13.1 is designed to provide insights into the complexities and apparent paradoxes associated with the use and perception of rewards.

Language and perception are critical to understanding the meanings associated with certain reward situations. Consider the following statements and explain what they mean, giving examples if possible:

- a reward can be seen as a punishment;

- a reward can become a bribe;

- the award of an annual bonus can result in disappointment and a loss of trust;

- the offer of a pay increase is rejected by union officials as 'insulting';

- a pay increase is also perceived as a pay decrease.

Different Reward Perspectives

One of the central themes of this book has been the importance of focusing on the meaning of phenomena, to better understand their significance for different stakeholders and the way people are managed at work. In the case of rewards, we can create a deeper understanding of what they represent by looking at them from different perspectives. The following represent the most useful ways of looking at rewards. They provide insight into the complex relationships of meanings that managers and employees are faced with in the way rewards are made sense of and used in the workplace.

Rewards represent instruments of social control

Rewards can, in one sense, represent instruments for controlling behaviour. By behaviour we do not simply mean performance-related behaviour but behaviour in its widest sense. The presence or absence of different kinds of rewards influence decisions to join, stay, and leave an organization. They influence people's perceptions of what is fair and unfair in relation to the way they are rewarded, and have an effect on people's emotional state. Rewarding people serves to confirm the 'rightness' of particular behaviours and reinforces that behaviour such that people associate a particular reward with a particular behaviour.

Consider their use, first, in a non-employment context. Anyone who has visited Disney SeaWorld theme parks will almost certainly have observed the use of rewards to reinforce desired behaviour in animals. When a seal, dolphin, or killer whale performs an act correctly, the trainers pat it, praise it, and feed it fish as a reward for doing the right thing. This is what is known as 'instrumental conditioning', which involves desired behaviours being immediately rewarded. The animal quickly begins to associate certain behaviours with particular consequences, i.e. the reward, and because the reward is desired, it quickly learns to associate one with the other.

Children similarly learn through the use of various kinds of reward. Being well behaved can become associated with sweets and chocolate, extra TV time, and special rights. Interestingly, however, while the use of rewards to train animals seems to work most of the time, the same can't be said for children, who don't seem to play to the same set of rules as animals! The reason is because even children 'think' about the exchange and begin to understand what is happening. When rewards are applied to animals they are invariably used to train them to develop or exhibit a range of desired behaviours without the animals engaging with the experience in a deeper cognitive way; used to control the behaviour of children and people at work—a form of social conditioning—rewards are frequently associated with manipulation as adults try to induce children to behave in ways they would prefer not to commit to and managers attempt to push people in certain directions some of which may not be particularly attractive. This raises questions and feelings about the legitimate use of rewards as instruments of social control (Kohn, 1993a).

The use of rewards to influence behaviour is associated, among others, with the work of B. F. Skinner. He developed the concept of operant conditioning, which means changing behaviour by the use of reinforcement that is given after the desired behavioural response. An operant refers to any behaviour that acts on the environment and leads to consequences. Skinner identified three types of responses or reinforcers that can follow behaviour:

- **Neutral**: responses from the environment that neither increase nor decrease the probability of a behaviour being repeated.
- **Positive**: responses from the environment, not just from management, increase the probability of a behaviour being repeated (rewards).
- **Negative**: responses from the environment decrease the likelihood of a behaviour being repeated (punishment). Punishment is thought to decrease the prospect of a particular behaviour being repeated (Cherry, 2016).

Perhaps the central assumption underpinning the use of PRP schemes, is that employees will 'work harder' out of a desire for reward. But will their behaviour be determined by the contingent reward or influenced by it, and what might mediate the impact of the reward? Behaviour is also influenced through negative reinforcement—the withholding of rewards. While there seems to be a consensus that positive reinforcement is much more likely to generate the required kinds of responses, at least this is the view of some commentators, might the threat of certain rewards being removed or withheld have a similar effect? It is impossible to offer a general answer to this question, although the Pareto effect seems to offer some help here. This suggests that managers seeking to exercise some degree of control over employee behaviour through rewards should use positive reinforcement 80 per cent of the time and negative reinforcement 20 per cent of the time.

But consider a situation where rewards are withheld or changed in ways that lack legitimacy: promises not kept, managerial changes that undermine or alter the psychological contract and reward relationships. Is withdrawing or withholding a reward a form of punishment and if so how do people react? It is important to remember that, just as rewards have the potential to give pleasure and satisfy a fundamental need if they are given, withholding or withdrawing them has the potential to hurt and undermine employee interests. From a behavioural perspective, managers need to try to predict the reactions that follow from using rewards in different ways. The motives of managers, the legitimacy of their action, and how their decisions are perceived will all influence the way people react to rewards being given, removed, or withheld.

Kohn (1993a) argues that rewards and punishment are not really opposites, but different sides of the same coin. He suggests that the giving and the withholding of a reward represent strategies that amount to manipulating behaviour. In this sense, a reward represents an extrinsic—i.e. externally located—source of motivation that, according to Kohn, does not alter a person's emotional or cognitive commitment which are far more important factors in explaining people's behaviour at work. This is not to say that rewards in the form of extrinsically generated influences cannot affect behaviour, rather, their impact is generally likely to be less than other motivational forces. In terms of positive rewards and their behavioural impact, it is important to establish:

- Which kinds of rewards are likely to have the most behavioural impact—extrinsic or intrinsic?
- How should rewards be used to reward or punish and in what circumstances?
- Which rewards have the potential to exert the greatest behavioural impact on employees?
- What kind of unintended behavioural consequences might follow from using rewards in certain ways?

It is also necessary to establish the validity of the assumptions underpinning the use of rewards to influence behaviour, particularly whether:

- People pursue certain objectives/outcomes that reflect what is important to them alone.
- People think about their responses and make rational decisions about what is in their best interests.

- Positive reinforcers are needed because people will not normally behave as required.
- People are driven by the same drives/needs and whether these remain constant in relation to changes in people's developmental life cycle.
- Manipulating behaviour is ethically acceptable.

Rewards Express Organizational Values

Seen from an organizational perspective, rewards express much about what the organization wishes to project to the outside world. Rewards in the form of pay and benefits, but increasing those that facilitate personal development, represent an important component of an organization's image which it seeks to present to external stakeholders and potential employees; being a high payer, offering an extensive range of benefits, and providing development opportunities not only projects a positive brand image but attracts potential new recruits.

Rewards and reward practices also reflect aspects of the organization's internal culture, expressing beliefs about the importance of fairness, equality, the status of the individual/collective, and access to opportunities. From this perspective, rewards also constitute:

- the size and composition of the compensation package;
- the medium through which formal and informal contracting takes place; and
- reasons why people want to work for and stay with/leave an organization.

Different people will be attracted to or deterred from an organization by, among other things, the reward package presented by it to the outside world and rewards in this sense will communicate something about what it would be like working for that organization. Rewards are an important factor in people's decision not simply to join but to stay.

Rewards Represent a Strategic Resource

Viewing rewards simply in terms of 'the compensation package' limits our ability to see them from a strategic perspective, by which we mean the way rewards can be used to support an organization's business strategy, facilitate flexible working, and confer competitive advantage. Of course, rewards that have a strategic impact can only contribute to rather than cause these outcomes. Nevertheless, this contribution can be significant. Designing pay and reward systems that are integrated, consistent with organizational values and priorities, and clearly linked to desired behavioural and performance outputs are more than transactional characteristics. The situation, however, is that, as Daniels commented above, few organizations seem to be able to translate aspiration into reality and reward management for many involves satisfying more limited operational and transactional objectives. Despite this, it seems that the idea of developing a strategic approach to rewards and using them in a more thoughtful, integrated, and focused way *is* increasingly of interest to senior managers and reward specialists. In Chapter 4 we saw how the strategic use of rewards was linked to a strategy of segmentation and differentiation of the labour force in the context of an organization's talent management strategy.

Rewards seen from a financial perspective

In labour-intensive organizations, pay and labour costs, which include National Insurance, pensions, and benefits, are frequently found to be the largest element of the organization's total costs and relatively small increases in the firm's wages/employment bill can have a disproportionate effect on its overall cost base. This relationship applies far less to capital-intensive industries such as oil and gas but particularly so in the hotel, entertainment, and leisure sectors. Taking the example of the National Minimum Wage (NMW), research has found evidence that its impact on wage costs has been partly offset by increases in productivity at the organizational level but there was no conclusive evidence that the NMW is directly affecting firm profitability. Organizations are constrained by competitive pressures from increasing prices as profitability may be affected (Riley and Bondibene, 2015). But in the absence of compensating productivity improvements—and the UK lags behind many of its international competitors in productivity growth—increased basic pay for all employees will increase employment costs which have to be absorbed by the organization or passed on in the form of higher charges/prices. For example, in a report written by KPMG (2015) on the economic impact of the National Living Wage the authors found that universal adoption of the new wage rates would add £11.1 billion or 1.3 per cent to the national wage bill. For employers, its impact would vary and depend on the numbers of low-paid employees involved, but in traditional low-paying industries the financial cost of this legislation could be very significant. Moreover, as the report points out, where existing wage relationships are disturbed by the new rates, pressure is likely to mount from those higher in the wage hierarchy for the restoration of established pay differentials. The important point to remember, however, is, as Pfeffer (1998a) has pointed out, wage rates do not mean the same thing as wage costs which reflect rates and labour productivity. This means that high wage rates can be associated with low wage costs. Germany offers a good example of this kind of relationship, but increasing rates without improvements in productivity will usually result in wage cost increases. From an economic and financial perspective wage and employment costs are rarely unimportant and where the industry involved is labour-intensive *and* high paying often the survival of the business depends on keeping these under tight control.

Rewards seen from a managerial perspective

The ability to exercise control over resources allows managers to exercise power. Control over the range and level of rewards available in an organization, in addition to their hierarchical roles, provides managers the means by which employees can be induced or persuaded to alter some of the things they do at work in ways that are valued and desired by managers. Rewards in this sense become 'levers of control'. But not all rewards operate in this way, only those rewards that are at the discretion of management or are contingent on other factors. To understand the significance of rewards from this perspective it is useful to consider the concept of the *negotiation of order*. This idea is based on the recognition that while the formal employment contract sets out basic terms and conditions of employment and carries with it expectations of what people will do at work in exchange for their employment rights, it does not prescribe precisely, and never can, everything they do or how exactly they perform their job. There is an element of discretion in relation to the amount of effort employees give and the levels of performance they attain (the concept of discretionary effort is explored in Chapter 12). Nor is it possible for managers to prevent discontent and conflict if people feel they are being unfairly treated. Rewards provide one way in which managers can maintain order through their role in 'buying compliance'. Gouldner's (1954) classic study of industrial conflict identified what he called 'patterns of indulgency', where individual managers rewarded their staff by waiving certain company rules, offering them concessions, and allowing questionable work practices to operate in exchange for the men's agreement to meet production targets. We referred to his pioneering study in Chapter 1. More recently, financial rewards have been used to induce people to improve attendance and reduce absence levels in addition to those directed at performance. But there are two problems with using rewards to buy compliance. First, they stop managers looking for more longer-term and effective solutions to the problems in question. Second, using rewards in this way creates a transactional mindset where everything that involves discretionary behaviour comes with a price!

> **KEY CONCEPT The negotiation of order**
>
> The negotiation of order has its origins in the writings of sociologists such as Gouldner, Park, and Strauss. These authors saw society and institutions as made up of different interest groups that needed to be constantly working to creating order and flexibility, a process that involves a succession of conflicts, assimilations, and accommodations. Social order achieved through shared agreements and understanding is

not fixed or binding for all time, and must be reconstituted continually, or worked out. The theory highlights emergence, change, and temporality, the embedded and contextual nature of order, and the omnipresence of specific power relations. Rewards of different kinds represent an important means of influencing the way order is continuously being renegotiated and agreed (Strauss, 1978).

Rewards seen from a political perspective

Perhaps the most obvious point to make here is that rewards and particularly pay are closely linked to political differences found within the employment context. By political we mean different interests expressed through institutional relationships within and external to the organization. We explored the causes and symptoms of industrial conflict in Chapter 8 so the link between disagreements over the allocation of resources and rewards from employers to employees is one that has already been established. Historically, disagreement and conflict over pay has been the most frequent reason given for collective industrial action. Many of the major strikes in the first half of the twentieth century were over pay increases or attempts by employers to cut pay. At the time of writing, although it is difficult to establish the significance of pay precisely, the national strike by junior doctors was at least in part about the payment of premium rates of pay for working 'unsociable hours'. Arguments in the informal domain over the terms of the effort bargain, while not necessarily expressed through overt conflict, are capable of contributing to increased levels of cognitive dissonance, and unfairness where people affected feel a disconnect and inner tension over the pay/rewards they receive. Rewards, in addition to any monetary value they have, also express power and status and relationships are often expressed through the different kinds and levels of rewards people enjoy. In extreme, but not unknown cases, the use of rewards is associated with corrupt practices and the illegitimate use of power. Even when used legally, certain reward practices—think of excessive executive pay and the payment of bank bonuses—have been questioned in terms of ethical acceptability.

There are numerous current examples where those in positions of power and influence use rewards to bribe people and to subvert proper processes. Corrupt payments have been exposed in football and in athletics. Questionable practices have been identified within the NHS where those responsible for recommending and purchasing drugs in certain NHS trusts have enjoyed lavish entertainment and accommodation at conferences organized by pharmaceutical companies (Heighton et al., 2015). Less obviously corrupt is the practice of promoting people (promotion can be seen as a reward) for reasons other than merit. The point is that while in almost all cases rewards used in employment and within organizations are used in the right way and for the right reasons it would be naive not to recognize the potential for power to corrupt or at least shape the way people who enjoy it behave.

That rewards can and should be seen from these different perspectives means that managing them is far less straightforward than might be imagined. This is because, from a managerial position, making 'the right' reward decisions and developing the 'right' reward strategies often involves trade-offs and compromises. For example, avoiding disputes over pay might mean an employer overpays and has then to deal with the rising cost of pay. Trying to meet employee requirements for fair pay can trigger responses from other individuals or groups whose pay, as a result, has declined relative to another individual or group. Using rewards to drive performance can create a culture of expectation, affect people's perceptions, and undermine managerial control. Daniel's point earlier that most managers struggle to manage pay and rewards effectively begins to make more sense than it perhaps did before!

Characteristics of rewards

We should not take it for granted that all organizational stakeholders share the same views about what constitutes a reward and the value that any reward represents. As Thompson (2002) argues:

we need to re-think what is and what is not a reward

403

To establish clarity about what constitutes a reward, we would argue that, whatever form it takes, a reward must have the following characteristics:

- It must have a value in itself or because of what it represents; a reward for example can have a material and/or a symbolic value. In other words, its value is linked to the fulfilment of a basic human need or one that is socially acquired.

- It must be relevant and important to the individual. A company car, for example, is not important to the employee who either cannot drive or has no need of a car, and free membership of a fitness club is unlikely to be attractive to someone who has no interest in physical activity.

- It must be associated with or serve a purpose. A reward is something that produces or is intended to produce an effect or outcome that is desired by one party or the other.

- A reward needs to have an attitudinal or behavioural effect on the person receiving the reward, although the actual effect may not be that which was intended.

- There must be conscious recognition on the part of the receiver that an act of 'rewarding' has taken place. Even though the giver of the reward has the intention of rewarding, unless the receiver acknowledges the 'reward transaction' it cannot be said to have taken place. Whatever the intention of the 'giver', it is the receiver who effectively gives meaning to an exchange or transaction, and managers must be at least aware of the possibility that their motivation and intentions may be misinterpreted or misconstrued by the receiver.

The Status of Rewards

Rewards vary in terms of their status, by which we mean their distinctiveness and the likely effect they have on people. The most important reward categories are set out below.

Rewards as rights

Rewards become rights largely through the process of agreeing the formal contract of employment which establishes the terms and conditions associated with the job and working for the organization. Many of the expressed terms of the contract refer to what the employer is contracted to provide to the employee, in the form of a set wage or salary, holidays, pension, sick pay entitlements, and so on. These represent what the Americans call forms of 'compensation for having to work', and the benefits that employers provide over and above the financial package are seen as additional to the core package. These rewards, or forms of compensation, need to be understood as a set of rights associated with being employed by a particular organization, which continue to be provided for as long as the contract remains in place. Over time, employers have been adding to these contractual rights particularly through the expansion of additional 'fringe benefits'; benefits associated not only with the job but with being employed. But these 'rights' are given as compensation or in exchange for what the employee agrees to provide to the employer—time, effort, acceptance of authority, and so on. As we noted in Chapter 8, the formal contract of employment is asymmetrical in nature. This means that while the rewards, as rights, associated with it are relatively fixed, the effort, performance, and other important contributions expected from employees are not. This situation helps to explain why certain rewards are contingent. But as far as rewards as rights are concerned, the impact or effect of receiving them is paradoxical in the sense that there is little evidence of an obvious behavioural or psychological response. Consider the weekly or monthly pay cheque. When employees open their pay slips, do they see what they have been paid as a reward or as something to which they have a right because they have earned it? Here, again, we see evidence to support the argument that rewards need to be seen in the context of reciprocation, that is, an exchange relationship, rather than as isolated and detached acts of benevolence. It is also worth considering the behavioural effect on the employee of being paid as opposed to not being paid. Being paid (i.e. rewarded through pay) may not elicit any obvious behavioural consequences. It might generate a sense of reassurance; it might reinforce the degree to which the individual identifies with the organization; it might create a sense of obligation to those in control. But these effects can be difficult to discern and may not be obviously expressed in what the employee does or in how he or she performs at work. What is more predictable, however, is the effect on the employee's behaviour of not being paid, not being paid on time, or not being paid the right amount, and of not being given the benefits to which he or she is entitled. Failing to deliver rewards that have the status of rights will almost certainly generate a much more obvious, and potentially damaging, response simply because these rewards are both expected and contractually determined.

Rewards that are conditional or contingent

Within the employment relationship, many rewards made available to employees are additional to those prescribed in the employment contract. As was noted above, the asymmetrical nature of the formal contract means that both formally and informally managers and their staff discuss, negotiate, and compromise over job performance, flexibility, responsibilities, and so on. This is the process of agreeing the terms of what Behrend (1975) called 'the effort bargain'. Behrend argued that employees have a tendency to regulate and limit their effort to a level or range which reflects their interpretation of what is meant by a fair day's work for a fair day's pay. A central assumption underpinning the effort bargain is the belief that workers operate at two different levels of effort–performance. One reflects their basic pay; the second, a higher one that can only be accessed through and by additional payments. From a managerial perspective, incentive payments are designed to essentially buy into this higher effort level but the point about these incentives is that the extra reward on offer is only paid when certain conditions and outcomes have been met. Incentives are not rewards in themselves; only the promise of specified rewards which are given if agreed targets, objectives, and outcomes are met (Armstrong, 2002). This might involve acquiring new competencies, for which extra pay would be given, achieving agreed levels of output or production, meeting sales targets, or meeting personal/business objectives. It would be too restrictive to suggest that this type of reward is only associated with performance criteria, but many of the reward schemes that are based on the 'conditionality principle' are associated with some measure of job performance and are frequently linked to what is generally understood as PRP. Not all contingent rewards take the form of pay/money but in relation to PRP—more of which is said later—this is the usual and expected kind of reward.

The point about this category of rewards is that they are not 'freestanding', in the sense that they are acquired simply as a result of being employed. They are related to some measure of how we actually behave or perform at work, and are experienced only if predetermined conditions and criteria are met. According to Armstrong:

> **Financial incentives aim to motivate people to achieve their objectives by focusing on predetermined specific targets and priorities ... Financial rewards provide financial recognition for achievement.**

Certain kinds of rewards can, therefore, take the form of promises of what will, or might, be experienced by employees at some future date. While many promises provide a clear understanding of what the employee has to do or achieve for the reward to be given, some are more ambiguous. Consider, for example, an employer who is struggling to make money in difficult trading conditions and who pays his staff below market rates for the jobs they are doing, on the grounds that he 'can't afford to pay more now', but 'promises' to increase pay when conditions and profitability improve. In this case, it is the employer who decides when levels of profitability justify increased pay and, despite the reasonable expectations of his employees, the pay increases may never materialize, with fairly predictable consequences for the quality of relationships between those employees and management. Contingent rewards are found in almost all organizations and while it might be thought likely that they would operate predominantly in the formal domain the reality is that they have an important role to play in the informal organization linked to the process of negotiating order.

KEY CONCEPT Expectation

This is one of the most powerful and important concepts in the field of reward management. It focuses attention on the behavioural impact of different 'reward experiences' and on whether the amount or form of any given reward creates a positive or negative response. The more people expect, whether this is considered reasonable or not, is not the point; what is, is that expectations, if not met, will result in disappointment and behaviours that reflect this emotional state. Conversely, the less an employee expects, the lower the likelihood of disappointment with what he or she receives.

Many years ago, when one of the authors worked in the steel industry he had a conversation with the works manager over the complicated bonus scheme that measured productivity for several of the departments in the steel works. When he asked the manager how it was possible for the scheme to measure accurately weekly changes in productivity the manager said that it really didn't matter because he adjusted the input data to ensure that the workers' expectations of a decent and regular bonus were as far as possible always met. This may raise ethical questions but his behaviour served important purposes which he considered justified manipulating the productivity data.

Rewards that are discretionary

These are rewards that are neither based on contractual rights nor on meeting specified conditions, but which result from managers and employees deciding to reward others in ways that only make sense in the context of their own circumstances, relationships, and working environment. For example, without it being part of any formal agreement or incentive scheme, an owner of a business might, in the light of a good year's results, decide to give his or her staff a week's fully paid holiday in the Mediterranean, or a night out at the pub with dinner thrown in. Alternatively, he or she might provide a one-off payment to reflect the contribution of the workforce to the organization's success, as was the case with the American Shoe Corporation in HRM Insight 13.1. There is no promise of repeating the reward and, even if the company achieves similar results in the future, the owner may decide to invest the sum potentially available as a bonus, in new capital equipment, or even pay it as dividends to the shareholders. Discretionary rewards are often not planned, and therefore employees have no expectation of receiving them. Discretionary rewards that become regular can, however, increase employees' expectation that they will receive them, with predictable consequences when they cease.

But what does discretionary actually mean? According to Pritchett (2013), the label applied to a bonus is not determinative and what may be thought of by an employer as completely discretionary may well not be. This is a legally grey area, and where significant sums are withheld based on the discretionary nature of the scheme litigation may result. If a bonus payment has become a contractual entitlement, it must be paid to avoid potential claims of breach of contract. On the other hand, where the bonus is genuinely discretionary an employer can exercise that discretion and choose to pay or not to pay without incurring legal liability. Of course, many discretionary awards are non-monetary and do not involve any form of contracting.

Because employees have no legitimate expectation of discretionary awards they are often surprised when they receive them; the greater the surprise, the greater impact such rewards have.

KEY CONCEPT Reciprocation

Reciprocation relates to the effect that certain kinds of rewards generate. This can take the form of an obligation or predisposition to give something back to the person or organization responsible for the original reward. Reciprocation also suggests that rewards are never simply one person giving to another, but represent a more complex, and often unspoken, exchange that has positive outcomes for both parties. The concept emphasizes the idea that the act of rewarding, particularly if rewards are discretionary, valued, and represent genuine motives, can, in turn, result in the recipient rewarding the giver, albeit in different, but no less important, ways. Altruism involves giving rewards without the expectation of anything being given in return. In work organizations, giving without expectation of receiving anything in return may exist but even where people act altruistically those who receive may still choose to reciprocate.

HRM INSIGHT 13.1 The American Shoe Corporation

The American Shoe Corporation (ASC) is a long-established and family-owned business, with manufacturing plants in West Virginia and Pennsylvania. It has some 250 employees, many of whom are from the same families and have worked for the company for many years. In recent years, the industry generally had been damaged by overseas competition from low-cost producers and several other US shoe producers had outsourced their manufacturing operations, laid off part of their workforce, or, in some cases, gone out of business.

On the day before the company was due to announce its results for the preceding financial year, employees received letters asking them to attend a meeting on the following Monday morning with the works manager of the two respective factories. The reaction to this letter was predictable. Many anticipated bad news and expected that some would be told their jobs had to go, and, by the time of the meeting, there was an air of pessimistic apprehension among the two groups of workers.

Both works managers began the meeting by sharing the same message with their staff. The head of the company, in the light of a reasonable set of results and to reflect his gratitude and appreciation for the commitment and loyalty showed by his staff, was awarding each worker $1,000 for each complete year of service, with a pro rata payment for those with less than one year's service. For some, this meant payments of over $20,000 and for those whose husband or wife worked there, this meant a combined amount of even more.

The reaction of many employees was a mixture of surprise, disbelief, and a deep sense of appreciation, with some reduced to tears. They knew that this would be unlikely to be repeated, but they also knew that the payments genuinely reflected the beliefs and philosophy of the company's owner, who did try to treat his employees as part of a wider family.

Questions

1. What might the motives of the company's owner have been in deciding to reward his staff in this way?

2. What effect do you think the decision had on the behaviour of his staff?

3. Would the same effects on employee behaviour have been achieved by giving the same overall amount paid as an increase in base pay over the next three years or as improvements in the benefit package, rather than in the form of a 'loyalty reward'?

4. Are there any negative consequences that might follow from this act?

5. Think of other examples of circumstances in which discretionary rewards might be used to positive effect.

Reward Strategy

All organizations are constantly making decisions about rewards: some are made within the informal domain and reflect the natural interactions between people at the same and at different hierarchical levels but many others reflect what could be described as having strategic significance. These rewards and reward decisions exist largely within the formal domain and collectively represent the organization's intentions regarding the types of rewards it wishes to emphasize, the terms and conditions regulating their availability, and the beliefs and values the organizations intend to reflect in the way it manages rewards. Reward decisions that are more operational in character would include developing and implementing the rules associated with variable pay systems, payments associated with the termination of employment, and rewards linked to appraisal schemes; we might equate operational reward decisions to design, implementation, and monitoring. Strategic reward decisions are those that reflect and support corporate strategy, express organizational values, and facilitate key HR activities. Examples would include the determination of pay levels and pay relationships, meeting workforce planning requirements by providing appropriate incentives to join or remain, and facilitating flexible working arrangements. Strategic in this sense means that the decisions either have or are intended to have a long-term impact, affect large numbers of employees, and are consistent with organizational objectives. Reward decisions can have an intended strategic impact without necessarily reflecting a coherent reward strategy, but there is an increasing expectation that organizations will develop a more focused and directional approach to their reward decisions and this is what is generally meant by the term reward strategy. By coherent we mean the decisions make sense in relation to each other: by directional we mean that reward decisions are meant to achieve a purpose and that collectively the intended outcomes of these various decisions point in the same direction and move the organization forward along its intended pathway.

 Signpost to Chapter 3: A Strategic Perspective on HRM, for an explanation of the concept of strategy.

A reward strategy can be seen to equate to the intended strategic outcome and objectives and the means by which these are expected to be achieved. A reward system can be thought of as the operationalization of the strategy, consisting of the policies, processes, practices, and procedures that are in place at any one time but which can change as the strategy changes and evolves. A reward system can also be seen as a system of rules represented by its policies, practices, etc. where certain rules regulate the amount and form of the reward (substantive reward rules) and other rules (procedural) establish matters of frequency, eligibility, conditionality, and reward status.

Consistent with our explanation of what reward strategy means and can be understood as, a leading reward consultancy has defined it as a set of ideas that:

> **determine the direction in which reward management innovations and developments should go to support the business strategy, how they should be integrated, the priority that should be given to initiatives and the pace at which they should be implemented.**
> (Rewards Consulting, 2015)

It is important to emphasize that reward strategies can exist at different levels and relate to different human resource requirements. For example, an overarching strategy can act as a framework within which specific reward strategies directed towards market competitiveness, talent management, gender, and performance can exist in a coherent way. And in the 'real world' many smaller and medium-sized enterprises may not have any formal and explicitly articulated strategies, relying more on a pragmatic and responsive approach to the way rewards are decided and managed: not having an explicit and articulated strategy may be a strategy in itself because it implies flexibility. Having a strategy does not mean it is working or will continue to work in the future; as we have pointed out, simply having a strategy says nothing about its effectiveness. What further complicates attempts to make sense of an organization's reward strategy is the problem of distinguishing what managers say the strategy is and what is actually experienced. Argyris (2000) called these two different positions the *espoused theory of action*—for example what managers say the reward strategy is—and *theories in use* which relates to the decisions actually taken and policies enacted. Argyris believed this commonly experienced paradox of human behaviour characterizes organizational life and in the context of reward strategy means that:

> **people consistently act inconsistently, unaware of the contradiction between their espoused theory and their theory in use, between the way they think they are acting and the way they really act.**
> (2002: 131)

An example of this contradiction can be found in the way some organizations promote the importance of fairness in pay while at the same time legitimizing unjustified pay differences between men and women.

One of the obvious points to emerge from this distinction is that having a reward strategy and articulating it is one thing; turning it into 'reality' in ways that eliminate or radically reduce the contradiction Argyris was talking about is quite another. If this objective is not achieved, the credibility and therefore the effectiveness of the strategy is almost certainly going to be affected.

Adopting Tyson's (1997) conceptualization of strategy and applying it to rewards, the expectation is that reward strategies should be:

- emergent and flexible;
- consistent between the formal and informal domains;
- future-oriented with an emphasis on change and adaptation; and
- subject to effective managerial influence and control.

Having attempted to clarify what reward strategy means, what does reward management mean? According to Armstrong et al. (2010), reward management is represented by or based on:

> **a philosophy in the form of a set of beliefs and guiding principles that are consistent with those values and help enact them. These include beliefs in the need to achieve fairness, equity, consistency and transparency in operating the ward system.**
> (2010: 35)

We would reject this definition, preferring instead to see an organization's philosophy as, together with its strategic objectives, the underpinning inputs into its reward strategy. We would argue that while many people do equate reward strategy with reward management this can create unnecessary terminological confusion. Reward management or managing rewards is more usefully seen as the overall process of shaping, changing, and controlling the reward strategy and system and in so doing affecting the actual behaviour of people in desirable and intended ways.

To try to create a clearer understanding of what these different elements of the 'reward world' might mean and how they are related, consider Figure 13.1.

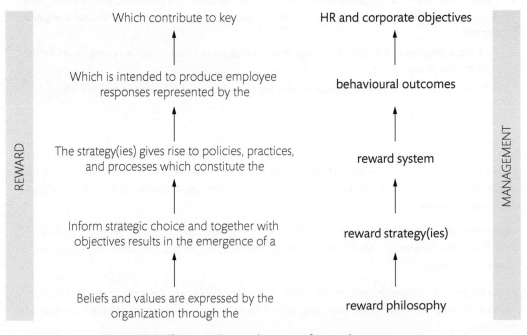

Figure 13.1 The constituent elements of reward management

From a practitioner perspective, developing a conceptual grasp of the 'world of rewards' is important because it helps to focus their thinking and decisions on things that matter and that can make a difference. Of equal importance is the need to develop reward strategies that work, so that they deliver the behaviours and other outcomes the organization needs to be successful.

Reward strategies need to be about something and have clearly defined expectations and objectives. Within HR they tend to be about:

- **Approaches to basic pay and conditions of employment**—here organizations need to decide how competitive they wish to be in the labour market but at the same time having regard to affordability.

- **Talent management**—here organizations need to decide on the package of rewards needed to attract, retain, and motivate those whose human capital value makes them particularly important employees.

- **Driving performance**—here organizations need to develop strategies that incentivize and encourage employees to increase their effort and performance to a consistently higher level without creating dysfunctional behaviours.

- **Non-financial rewards**—here the emphasis is on strategies that affect employees at the psychological and social level and are designed to connect to people's inner needs and drives.

- **Meeting individual and organizational needs for self and professional development**—here rewards take the form of opportunities for broadening and deepening experiences within and outside of work, allowing employees to learn, grow, and meet career aspirations.

- **'Fringe benefits'**—where strategies focus on the range, availability, and conditions associated with additional benefits to basic terms and conditions of employment by virtue of seniority, achievement, and hierarchical level.

STUDENT ACTIVITY 13.2

1. In two groups, list all rewards that members have experienced throughout their working experiences.

2. Consider the effects that the different rewards had on their behaviour and performance—which have been associated with generally positive behavioural and attitudinal changes or alternatively have had a negative impact?

3. Each group presents to the other its findings, then the class discuss the implications of the results for the management of rewards.

4. What general conclusions are you reaching? What are the implications for developing a reward strategy?

The concept of *total rewards* has been a central feature of the reward literature for some time now. It reflects the idea that an organization's reward strategy should be based on a much more holistic view of the relationship between different kinds of rewards and behavioural outcomes. According to the CIPD (2015) total rewards encompasses:

> all aspects of work that are valued by employees, including elements such as learning and development opportunities and/or an attractive working environment, in addition to the wider pay and benefits package.

Figure 13.2 provides an insight into the full range of rewards available to the organization although it is important to stress that these evolve over time, both in terms of relative importance to the individual, and their impact.

Monetary Rewards	Benefits
• Basic pay and allowances	• Pensions
• Bonuses	• Sick pay
• Commission payments	• Flexible working arrangements
• Overtime	• Subsidized means, loans, etc.
• Conditions payments	• Fitness and health benefits
• Premium payments	• Company cars
	• Travel allowances
Psychological and Social	**Learning and Development**
• Recognition	• Promotion
• Praise	• Training/learning
• Being valued	• New experiences
• Being part of a community	• Sabbaticals
• Achievement	• Increased employability

Figure 13.2 A model of total rewards

Figure 13.2 is, however, limited as it focuses only on employee interests; in a broader and more strategic sense the concept should reflect the interests of employees and the organization. For the employer, this can mean higher levels of commitment and engagement, work flexibility, retention, and motivation. For employees, it means meeting expectations of fair and equitable treatment, providing additional earning opportunities, and recognition of their 'human' needs. This more sophisticated interpretation of what a total rewards strategy represents also suggests that the different kinds of reward categories highlighted above are used in a more flexible and strategic way, often involving a much more discriminatory approach in the way rewards are used in the management of different employee groups.

For some commentators, however (Brown, 2014), the concept of total rewards has become:

increasingly meaningless and outdated in our post-recessionary economy of austerity and inequality. Its generic and unthinking application in uniform flexible benefits packages risks isolating the rewards profession into an administrative backwater.

Instead, Brown (2014) argues for a new approach which he calls 'smart rewards' which consists of four components:

1. a simpler and clearer focus on a few core values and principles;

2. a stronger basis in evidence and measurement;

3. more emphasis on employee engagement through rewards; and

4. improved and more open communications and line management involvement in the management of rewards.

Brown believes that by adapting and tailoring this approach it is much more likely to create the genuinely business-enhancing and employee-engaging reward practices and outcomes that HR professionals and senior managers are or should be seeking to achieve.

Whatever progress has been made in modelling reward approaches and strategies, there is a view that organizations still struggle to deliver the kind of effective strategies that achieve the objectives and outcomes senior management require (Cox et al., 2010). They argue that this is because many reward strategies are badly designed and implemented and fail to meet the expectations and preferences of employees. Interestingly, they also claim that while strategy is supposed to be about choice and competitive differentiation, where organizations simply benchmark their own reward strategies against others and copy external practices, the outcome is strategies that are not strategic! After reviewing the evidence on the effectiveness of different kinds of reward strategies, they conclude:

> Admittedly, there is some statistical evidence of positive associations between some forms of pay system and organisational productivity and performance. In particular, group-based pay systems such as profit-sharing and employee share ownership plans seem to fare well in evaluations. But managers continue to express widespread dissatisfaction with the effectiveness of pay systems and their outcomes, and in general, there is limited research evidence to support the relative success or failure of particular reward-strategy approaches and their constituent policies

As Cox et al. claim, developing a reward strategy is a challenge for many organizations, which as we have argued, is somewhat surprising, given their potential power. But it may be the magnitude and complexity of the challenge itself that explains, at least in part, this worrying disconnect. As far back as 2007, the CIPD reported that only 35 per cent of managers surveyed in their study had a written reward strategy, while 91 per cent believed that implementing one was either difficult or very difficult, with reported problems being linked to changing external environments, legal changes, and line manager resistance. In the more recent CIPD (2015) reward survey little seems to have changed. Although there is limited explicit reference to the use of reward strategies, there are indications that little in the way of strategic thinking and action was found. Although the data referred only to pay, the report found that only 19 per cent of respondents had data on the spread of pay within the organization, while the rest did not collect any data on earnings spread and relationships. The reasons for this are not really known, but the report asked the important question: how are employers able to work out the effectiveness of their reward spend if they are unable to provide basic pay data? It goes on by asking how is the reward function going to be able to demonstrate itself as a strategic function that adds value for the business, rather than being seen as an administrative department dealing with the day-to-day issues, most of which will end up being done by software—and robots in the near future? Certainly, while the survey may not be representative of all organizations, the lack of evidence of strategic thinking on rewards and the minimal development and application of distinctive reward strategies is cause for concern. What still remains to be considered is the evidence, apparently limited, that connects the use of reward strategies to outcomes. More is said about this later in the chapter.

In concluding this section on reward strategy, the point that perhaps needs making more than any other, is that there appears to be a significant gap between the rhetoric of developing a strategic approach to the management of rewards and the reality that exists within many organizations, which suggests limited strategic thinking and action. There is evidence from some of the leading high-tech businesses that the total rewards model is in evidence and that employees are benefiting from both a flexible and a holistic reward strategy which emphasizes material *and* social/psychological rewards (Glassdoor, 2015). But the findings from the CIPD (2015) rewards survey suggest that this is far from typical. The belief that reward levers can be easily manipulated to change behaviour is, for many, more aspirational than achievable; organizations simply don't work that way. The difficulty of the challenge associated with developing new and more effective reward strategies is probably greater than most managers think, particularly those associated with the development of high-performance working environments. Many of the rewards found to be effective in such contexts are non-materialistic and relate to the psychological well-being of employees and are the product of positive relationships and a distinctive organizational culture. Pfeffer (1998b) recognized this and the difficulty in delivering them:

> Creating a fun, challenging and empowered work environment in which individuals are able to use their abilities to do meaningful jobs for which they are shown appreciation is likely to be a more certain way to enhance motivation and performance—even though creating such an environment may be more difficult and take more time than merely turning the reward lever.

It could be argued that strategies associated with total and smart rewards, for the majority of organizations, are either underdeveloped or only partially effective. The largely untapped potential of the effective use of rewards awaits to be realized.

Money and Its Use as an Incentive: An Evidence-Based Approach

Perhaps one of the oldest controversies in reward management is the use of financial incentives and the extent to which they impact on performance. Years ago, in a TV recording (source unknown) Herzberg, in promoting his two-fact theory of motivation claimed:

it works whether you believe in it or not.

In many ways, the debate about the importance of money and the use of financial incentives reflects something similar—financial incentives, for many people, work whether you believe it or not. Some people believe they do or can work under particular conditions while others are adamant in their rejection of their claimed effectiveness. The difficulty with trying to cut through the sometimes questionable claims and counterclaims is that the evidence on this question is incredibly inconsistent. Furthermore, people's views and positions do reflect beliefs as well as 'hard facts' and are not easily changed in response to evidence which questions and undermines them. Part of the problem of 'knowing' whether incentives improve performance is linked to the difficulty of deciding what to choose and measure as an indicator of changed performance. Kessler and Purcell (1992) made the point:

> **There are major difficulties in finding measures of PRP effectiveness. The bottom line measure of effectiveness for any payment system is arguably an improvement in overall organisational performance, assumed to flow from improved individual performance. It is, however, clear that the complex range of factors interacting to determine organisational performance make it difficult to isolate the impact of a payment system alone.**

We would go further in highlighting the problematic nature of directly linking a payment method to organizational performance measures; even at the level of individual performance or group performance there are still difficulties in trying to establish cause–effect relationships. The best that can sometimes be achieved is a strong association based on observable and believable changes between the operation of the incentive effect and the resultant change in output/performance. Perhaps the most convincing case for using financial incentives is to be found in relatively simple piece rate systems applied to physical and quantifiable production environments where the association between the piece work system and output can be clearly established.

STUDENT ACTIVITY 13.3

This is best carried out as part of a group exercise. For each of the following occupations/jobs decide whether each would be suitable for a PRP scheme. To do this you need to establish criteria that help you decide whether and how performance can be measured. Then, for those you think could benefit from such a scheme identify what measures of performance could be used in the scheme and the problems that might be experienced if these measures were used.

- GPs
- secondary school teachers
- nurses

- HR professionals
- local government CEOs
- chief constables

Review and discuss your findings.

Notwithstanding the measurement and relationship challenges in trying to make sense of these inconsistent and opposing views about financial incentives, we also need to address the closely related question of the motivational power of money. Space prohibits a detailed review of those theories of motivation that might cast light on this question, and several contributions to the debate were briefly considered in Chapter 12, but certain ones are worth noting here, with perhaps the most frequently referred to coming from the experiences and writings of F. W. Taylor (1998). Taylor believed that workers who placed a high value on money and had limited aspirations would respond positively to the prospect of earning more through increasing their effort–performance. He based this belief on the view that if employers wanted their workers to show initiative and commit to managerial work expectations, then they must be given some special incentive which could take the form of promotion, higher wages through generous piece-work prices, better working conditions, and so on. It was the prospect of earning more that exerted the motivational effect whether the extra payments came from hitting standard or exceeding it. Certainly, in the engineering sector during most of the post-war period the idea that workers operated to two differ-ent standards of effort–performance was accepted by all parties. The non-incentivized level was linked to basic pay but the second and higher level was only made available through the use of incentive payments built into PRP schemes. The range of performance increases usually referred to was between one-quarter and one-third. In other words, workers retained sufficient discretionary effort to increase output within that range. It is difficult to know whether in today's service and knowledge-dominated economy the same beliefs still exist and whether the effort–performance gap is as great as it was. Given human motivation and the nature of working relationships, it is likely that levels of discretionary effort continue to be subject to some form of incentive. Taylor did not believe that workers are only interested in money, but he was realistic enough to recognize that depending on the individuals and the circumstances many are.

Surveys of employees which ask them to rate the importance of money and other aspects of their reward packages have consistently shown that pay (this is not quite the same as more pay) is rated less highly than might have been thought, taking Taylor's 'economic man' theory into account. This view that pay may have far less of an impact on employees' day-to-day behaviour than other forms of reward is supported by research undertaken by Sanders and Sidney, the HR consultancy. Quoting from their findings that employ-ees value work friendships as much as pay, Deeks (2000) reported that:

> Of the 313 employees surveyed, 80 per cent claimed that they enjoyed going to work mainly because of the people they worked with. Two-thirds indicated that the workplace community influenced whether they stayed with an organization. A further 62 per cent said that the workplace community had alleviated other areas of dissatisfaction, such as pay.

In a more recent survey (Mayson, 2013), respondents were asked to identify the three most important moti-vating factors from a list of ten. Providing employees with an enjoyable job was the most highly rated, followed by a competitive base salary and pension, third was how well employees get on with the people they work with. Base salary was listed as the second most important motivator (49 per cent of employees chose it as one of their top three factors). But other financial incentives were found to be much less so: performance-related bonuses ranked as eighth most important motivator (only 13 per cent selected it in their top three).

Yet the use of financial incentives is commonly practised by employers, with 43 per cent of respondents indicating that their employer uses some form of financial bonus. Personal performance-related bonuses were the most common reward scheme in operation (13 per cent), with bonuses related to business performance

(10 per cent), and PRP increments (6 per cent) the next most popular. The data produced by this survey is by no means consistent as far as the power and importance of money is concerned because three-quarters of respondents rated the impact of financial incentives from important to very important, suggesting that they did have a behavioural impact in some form or other on the majority of respondents. In research carried out in South Africa into intergenerational reward differences, Bussin and Van Rooy (2014) found significant differences in reward preferences across generational boundaries. This raises the question as to whether money and financial incentives are more important to certain generational groups as well as changing in importance as individuals/generations move through their development life cycles. The evidence on the importance of money as a motivator overall suggests that broad generalizations need to be replaced by a recognition that a number of influential situational and contextual factors affect its impact on employee behaviour.

RESEARCH INSIGHT 13.1

Read the following to take your learning further:

Bussin, M. and Van Rooy, D. J. (2014) 'Total rewards strategy for a multigenerational workforce in a financial institution', *SA Journal of Human Resource Management,* **12(1).**

The article shows that the value of rewards reflects generational differences, which has implications for developing effective reward strategies. The article suggests the importance of reward flexibility rather than a one-size-fits-all approach.

The evidence so far suggests that while financial incentives are relatively ineffective motivators for most staff (this does not mean money is not important), for the majority of people, but again depending on their circumstances, improving the workplace and developing better employee–management relationships are more likely to have a stronger behavioural impact on people and facilitate higher-performing teams. This distinction between the effectiveness of financial incentives and the importance of money may help to explain the confusing and inconsistent picture that is emerging over the motivational impact of financial incentives, which offers support to those in both camps.

But one of the most consistent critics of financial incentives and incentive-based payment systems, Alfie Kohn (1993a, 1993b), has no doubts about his position. The starting point for Kohn's critique is the acceptance that, as in the UK, many US managers, and those that advise them, believe in the redemptive power of rewards and in the validity of agency theory (which seems to be the basis of Taylor's position on incentives). This theory suggests that the main or only way to encourage people to act in the interests of owners/senior managers is to tie in extra pay with high levels of performance. But his research—based on numerous articles, studies, and experiments, not all of which are industry-based—indicates that rewards:

typically undermine the very processes they are intended to enhance.

These problems appear to go beyond the design and implementation of incentive-based pay systems. Kohn (1993b) argues that:

the failure of any given incentive programme is due less to a glitch in that program than to the inadequacy of the psychological assumptions that ground all such plans.

Kohn suggests that financial incentives, in their many different forms, not only achieve (at best) temporary compliance or short-term behavioural changes that may be manifested in improved performance, but do not alter the attitudes that underlie behaviour. This is a very similar view to Herzberg (2003) in his famous article on employee motivation, in which he distinguished 'movement' from 'motivation'. Herzberg saw incentives as having the capacity to 'move' people, with further movement only being achieved by more incentives. Motivation, on the other hand, is based on an inner force, under which behaviour comes primarily from a person wanting to do something rather than from external stimulation, which he describes as being equivalent to bribes.

415

What, then, are the reasons that rewards, in the form of incentives, fail? Kohn (1993a) suggests the following factors.

- **Pay is not a motivator**

  This is not meant to imply that money is unimportant or that paying less than is considered fair is acceptable, but rather that paying people more will not encourage them to do better or more work over the long term. There is, as we noted above, evidence that the promise of additional pay, if it has a sufficiently strong incentive effect, can move/motivate people but the question is for how long and at what cost.

- **Rewards punish**

  This is about feeling controlled and manipulated by managers, if the rewards that employees expect or hope to receive are withheld or withdrawn or linked to unreasonable conditions and requirements.

- **Rewards rupture relationships**

  The pursuit of personal rewards has the effect of reducing cooperation and fracturing relationships: individually based incentive schemes individualize work.

- **Rewards ignore reasons**

  The use of incentives is often an easier way of trying to address problems of behaviour and performance than exploring and understanding the underlying causes of the problems.

- **Rewards discourage risk taking**

  Because employee behaviour is increasingly focused on trying to achieve the incentive payment, behaviour that is not seen to be relevant to this is downgraded, even though it still might be important to the organization.

- **Rewards undermine interest**

  This is about the way in which the use of extrinsic controls and influences are thought to undermine employee commitment and interest in their work, because they reduce interest in anything else and create an unhealthy dependency.

Kohn's articles and criticisms of using rewards to generate commitment and improved performance produced a predictable response from many managers, consultants, and other academics, whose views were also published in the *Harvard Business Review* (Bennett Stewart et al., 1993). In the article, the contributors argued that:

- Rewards should not be confused with incentives and people should be rewarded for a job well done. Companies should not stop paying for performance, but should avoid using incentives. The problem with this argument is that it leaves open to interpretation what the reward will be for in relation to improved performance and the form of reward.

- While much of what Kohn says about the limits of behaviourist psychology and the instrumental use of incentives has a degree of validity, integrating the use of incentives and gain-sharing, as part of a wider strategy of work reorganization and participative working, can achieve very significant results.

- Incentive schemes have a limited time during which they can be effective and, within this time frame, they can be important elements of a wider reward package.

- Many rewards are not perceived as bribes, but as equitable outcomes that reflect the contributions that people have made.

- While the negative aspects of using piece rates and merit pay to reinforce task-oriented behaviour are understood, appropriate rewards for improved performance make sense intuitively and practically, and they are neither wrong nor intrinsically demotivating.

It is possible to reconcile the differences between Kohn's position and those who, while accepting some of his arguments, believe that he has gone too far in appearing to reject any positive outcomes from using rewards to influence employee behaviour. Both are, to a certain extent, 'right' and, while incentive-based rewards may have a part to play in influencing employee performance, over-reliance on such rewards is dangerous. Metaphorically, in rejecting the possible beneficial effects of incentives, we might be throwing out the baby with the bathwater! On the other hand, there are many recent examples in the UK and USA where financial incentives incorporated into bonus schemes have had almost the precise effect that Kohn predicted. In response to a *Financial Times* article on bankers' bonuses one anonymous commentator said:

> On the psychology of pay, there are battles between those who think pay for performance works, and the opposite. But I have observed that the more you make rewards specific to transactions, the more you erode concern for the organisation beyond the local team (what I used to term the 'boat's not sinking at my end' attitude). Hence the pay for failure issues.
> (Hill, 2016)

Another important contribution to this debate is made by Pfeffer and Sutton (2006: ch. 5) who address the role and impact of financial incentives directly in their book. Their starting point is to accept that many, if not all of management's decisions on pay policy and the use of incentives are based on several deeply held, widely shared, and intertwined beliefs and assumptions about what motivates people at work. But they are also clear that these basic assumptions are part of the problem—they are only assumptions! And because organizations fail to adequately test their validity and contextual applicability, they often result in pay policies and practices that fail to produce the kind of employee behaviour that managers want. A view that supports much of what Kohn argues.

The assumed motivational effect of financial incentives is based on the twin beliefs that the desire for more 'pay' does or can affect the behaviour of most employees, and that performance can be increased primarily or only through an increase in employee effort levels and that this results in improved performance. But the question as to the sustainability of the increased performance and of any unintended consequences associated with the way the incentive works remains. As Pfeffer and Sutton quite rightly point out, if performance problems result from factors other than restricted effort, then using financial incentives to raise effort and through this individual performance will inevitably fail. The diagnosis of performance problems then becomes a critical element in the decision whether to employ an incentive scheme.

But their review of the evidence on the use of financial incentives allows them to claim that:

> There is no question that financial incentives motivate people and, under the right conditions, can drive big increases in performance and productivity
> (2006: 121)

while recognizing that critical to this outcome are the conditions and contextual features of the environment in which such schemes are applied. It is clear from their research that while the basic assumption about the motivational impact of financial incentives may well have a degree of general validity, many of the failures associated with such schemes are caused by:

1. The failure to accurately diagnose the underlying causes of performance problems.

2. Weaknesses in the design and implementation of financial incentive schemes.

3. Organizational factors and conditions which are not consistent with or accommodative to what are relatively simplistic and one-dimensional interventions.

Research by Rynes et al. (2004) into the importance of pay to employees produced a number of very interesting conclusions and takes our understanding of this enduring question to a different level. They argue that surveys that directly ask employees how important pay is to them are likely to understate pay's true importance. In other words, people are more likely to under-report than to over-report the importance of pay as a motivational factor in most situations. Put another way, their research suggests that pay is much more important in people's actual choices and behaviours than it is in their self-reports of what motivates them. They go on to claim that:

In general, there appears to be a consistent (but incorrect) message to practitioners that pay is not a very effective motivator—a message that, if believed, could cause practitioners to seriously underestimate the motivational potential of a well-designed compensation system.

One of the reasons they offer to explain this inconsistency in what people say about money and how they behave in situations where money is used in a motivational way, is that most people share a common tendency to say things which are socially desirable. In other words, because being seen to be driven by the money motive—socially undesirable—is considered to clash with other social values they therefore have an unconscious tendency to underplay its importance to them. They quote several influential research studies where the impact of pay on behaviour was carefully studied and report that in these studies pay indeed showed a more significant effect on performance, primarily in the form of productivity increases.

As a result of their research, Rynes et al. present three important but not necessarily consistent views on money as a motivating force.

1. There is strong evidence that pay is a powerful motivator—perhaps the most powerful potential motivator—of performance. But the emphasis on potential is significant because they recognize that many payment systems which claim to tie additional pay to increased performance fail to do this effectively. In other words, the relationship is often unclear and weak because of failures in the way the schemes are designed and implemented.

2. The broad usefulness of money as well as its many symbolic meanings suggests that, far from being a mere lower-order motivator, pay can assist in obtaining virtually any level on Maslow's motivational hierarchy, including social esteem and self-actualization.

3. There is also evidence that pay is not the only motivator and that it may not always be the most important—much depends on contingent factors. So, with this recognition of the importance of contingency in relation to motivational impact of pay, Rynes et al. seem to reflect, if not the consensus on this question—there isn't one—a view that is at least consistent with other studies into pay, its importance and effectiveness as a motivator.

In trying to make sense of the inconsistent evidential base on the importance of financial incentives as a driver of performance, we need to question:

- The research methodologies used to test the relationship.
- The design of incentive schemes which may offer insufficient incentives to produce more and/or use the wrong measure of performance/output.
- Whether people are inconsistent in the way they report on the importance of money as a motivator.
- The impact of mediating factors that conceal the 'true' nature of the relationship.
- The causes of performance problems.

The views and beliefs of the experienced manager and HR consultant in the Practitioner Insight offer some interesting insights into the pay–performance relationship.

PRACTITIONER INSIGHT Judy Crook, HR consultant

I want to say a few things about the use of payments linked to performance or production, based on my experience of working in manufacturing and sales environments.

The most important difference between manufacturing and service-based organizations, including the public sector, is the ability to carry out meaningful, objective, and consistent measures of performance. Many PRP schemes outside of the manufacturing sector may look good on paper but they often fail because the reward/bonus is often based on questionable measures of performance. This not only undermines the integrity of the scheme but can be costly to the company. Manufacturing and sales environments allow for the physical measure of production/sales and the translation of this into financial values which support easily constructed measures of individual and team performance.

But even in environments where measurements are relatively easy to establish, things can still go wrong. Any bonus scheme needs to be designed carefully to ensure that the scheme is driving the behaviours the company wants from its workers. This is not always fully understood.

There are two key objectives that need to be met in designing bonus schemes. First, to ensure that the behaviours the bonus scheme is designed to encourage are linked to company, team, and individual targets. For example, if you design a bonus scheme for sales people that only rewards sales it will result in behaviour that maximizes sales numbers. But the problem with this is that important considerations, like the margin the salesperson generates, are not seen as important because they have not been recognized in the scheme. The result is likely to be more sales but at the expense of lower margins. A salesperson should be targeted on sales and margin to make sure they don't sell at the lowest price.

Second, ensure the bonus scheme targets are stretching but achievable, otherwise they can demotivate employees. This is not always easy to achieve, but HR professionals and line managers need to work together to try to get the right balance between targets that are too easy and those that are too hard. The introduction of such schemes also needs careful consideration. For example, making sure that all those employees involved know the purpose of the scheme and its operating rules well in advance of the scheme starting. Regular monitoring and updates should be undertaken throughout the year to increase the motivational effect of the schemes, to drive performance, to create healthy competition, and to share best practice. Bonus schemes don't manage themselves!

It is also important to look at the 'small print' of these schemes. For example, what are the rules governing eligibility? Do workers need to have been employed for a certain time to participate? Will bonuses be paid on a proportionate basis depending on how long they have worked? What happens if someone leaves but is still entitled to a bonus that is only realizable after the date of leaving? These are important questions that need answering before the scheme is introduced. Finally, from a management point of view it is vital that these schemes and bonus payments are not seen to be part of the terms and conditions of employment of participating workers and may be changed at any time by management in accordance with the rules of the scheme.

In my experience, well-designed and managed bonus schemes can benefit the business and the employees, but these outcomes don't happen by accident. They happen by applying the right kinds of design principles and operating rules, and by adopting performance measures that can be relied on.

STUDENT ACTIVITY 13.4

Read the Work Foundation Report by Kay (2014) into the use of PRP in the public sector and answer the questions below.

1. What are the main findings of the report?

2. Do these findings support or question any of the views or theories on money as a motivator summarized above?

3. From a strategic perspective what are the risks and benefits of implementing incentive-based PRP schemes?

4. List the conditions under which financial incentives are likely to succeed and fail, making clear the criteria used in reaching your decisions.

Payment Systems

Payment systems refers to the way pay is determined. Although indirectly the way people are paid has a bearing on the amount they receive, this is more about the 'how and why' rather than the 'what' question; it is about the procedural rules that regulate payment rather than the form or level of payment. Payment systems not only determine how base pay is calculated but they also establish how additional payments and other rewards are made available to employees. Payment systems indirectly affect the level of reward and establish the extent of discretion, or flexibility, managers have in rewarding/paying people. The actual determination of pay levels at least as far as basic rates/pay is concerned is also influenced by one or more 'political' processes:

- collective bargaining—employers negotiate with unions;
- pay bodies set wage rates for specific groups of workers;
- unilateral managerial decision-making—managers decide with reference to labour market conditions, benchmarks, and ability to pay considerations;
- legislation—nationally established rates of pay;
- individual negotiation.

Taking into account the way the payment system works and the political processes at play, managers need to ensure that:

- individual wages/salaries are not higher than they need to be in relation to the organization's recruitment and retention strategies and ability to pay;
- individual wages/salaries are high enough for the organization to remain competitive in the labour market;
- payment/reward systems provide opportunities for additional pay/rewards that have an additional motivating impact; and
- the importance of meeting the fairness criteria is recognized.

Movements in pay rates and wages/salaries depend on the organization's pay policy, but most are reviewed annually and reflect internal and external changes and the length of collective agreements. Employees expect to see adjustments in rates/salaries that reflect annual changes in the cost of living measured by the government's preferred measure (Consumer Price Index). This maintains the real value of wages and salaries. Increasing the real value of wages means higher than annual cost of living changes to rates/salaries and/or additional earnings based on bonuses, overtime, and allowances.

The use of job evaluation to determine a person's location on an internal pay structure—essentially a set of pay scales—is not considered here but details of how such schemes operate can be found on the Online Resources Extension Material and from ACAS (2016).

 For details of how job evaluation works, see the Online Resources Extension Material 13.2.

 Details of the most commonly used individual and group payment systems currently in use can be found in the Online Resources Extension Material 13.3.

Benefits

We have already explained that staff/employee benefits constitute an increasingly important part of the total rewards model, and while they don't constitute a payment scheme or system as such, and the benefits provided are in a non-cash form (pensions excluded), they can have a monetary value, and represent a distinctive part of the overall reward package. More and more companies are recognizing the importance of developing benefit strategies that are intended to influence staff behaviour and impact indirectly on performance

(Barton, 2011). But what leads employers to offer such benefits as additional rewards? There are several possible explanations:

1. certain kinds can be used to compensate for low pay;

2. some facilitate attendance and are necessary for certain jobs (e.g. company cars, subsidized travel);

3. other benefits may be subsidized or paid by the government and are simply administered by employers;

4. benefits are increasingly expected by certain categories of employees and are seen as critical to recruitment and retention strategies;

5. some benefits particularly those associated with the working environment reflect the philosophy of those who founded the business and are integral to the kind of organization they want to create.

With benefits that are 'rights', that is, they are specified by the employment contract, the question is whether they affect employee behaviour. We argued earlier that rewards that are based on rights rather than on the discretion of employers or on meeting certain conditions may have a limited behavioural impact on performance and contribution. Compared with the rest of Europe, it seems that the UK is less generous than other countries. Research quoted in *HR Magazine* found that in a ranking of fourteen European countries the UK came third from the bottom when taking into account factors such as unemployment benefits, maternity and paternity entitlements, annual leave, and sick pay (Frith, 2016). Only Switzerland and Ireland ranked lower, but the research did not consider the effect these benefits had on individuals and their relationship with work.

As far as discretionary benefits are concerned, most of the strategic developments are taking place with large private sector organizations, although research by Canada Life Group found that 26 per cent of UK employees don't receive workplace benefits from their employer. Businesses that did offer them said that their employee benefits schemes made important contributions to their HR strategies with retention, recruitment, and employee well-being cited most frequently (Sage UK).

Perhaps the most interesting development regarding the use of discretionary benefits is the way that some organizations are using them in a flexible and more strategic way. Research by Mercer, the internal benefits consultancy, found that the UK, despite lagging in legislative-based awards, was the leading European country when providing employees with a degree of choice over the benefits they wanted. Mercer UK head of flexible benefits, Kim Honess, said:

> **More and more we are seeing employers offering choice in employee benefit schemes because of rising benefit costs, a changing workforce, but also the need to mark themselves out as the employer of choice.**
>
> (Robert Half, n.d.)

There is evidence that the strategic use of flexible benefits is frequently linked to an organization's talent management strategy and used to support the recruitment and retention of senior managers and high-flying graduates. Barton (2011), in his study of Airbus, found that the company had developed a coherent stance on benefits that combined clear strategic objectives with flexibility in terms of what benefits were available and under what conditions, based on knowing the value of these benefits to different groups of managerial staff.

STUDENT ACTIVITY 13.5

Read the article by Barton and research more widely the use of benefit packages as part of an organization's reward strategy. Then:

● Build a profile of an employee as a newly recruited graduate trainee, middle manager, and finally a senior executive linking the kinds of benefits he/she might value most.

- Consider what 'a market for benefits' might mean. How would a system where benefits are bought and sold work and what would its advantages be?

- Outline a strategy for evaluating the effectiveness of a benefits strategy that was defined as an investment in human capital.

Summary

- Rewards and how they are managed constitute an important part of what HR professionals are responsible for. This importance is likely to grow, as the new class of knowledge workers applies different requirements and priorities to what they want their employers to provide for them.

- Managing rewards has never been particularly easy; it is almost certainly becoming more challenging as employers have to meet the reward expectations of an increasingly diverse labour force. Inevitably, this means that reward packages and 'solutions' will become more individualized, rather than be the product of collective negotiations, and will reflect changes in personal circumstances and priorities.

- The evidence suggests that rewards that meet an individual's intrinsic needs, that is, those that connect to his or her 'humanness', have a stronger and longer-lasting effect on his or her perception and behaviour than do those that are essentially materialistic in nature. Many of these rewards are generated in the working environment, and are given and received in an often informal and hidden (from HR) way. Examples of these might include praise from a manager, colleague, or customer; recognition for achievement; and opportunities to learn new skills.

- The psychological environment is once again identified as the context in which major influences on how an employee feels and behaves are located.

- As far as the formal reward arena is concerned, pay and benefits continue to remain contentious issues for management and this is, in an era of increasing competition and outsourcing of production and jobs, as much to do with costs as well as the effectiveness of different pay practices.

- The evidence on the efficacy of financial incentives and the importance of money to people varies and lacks consistency.

- One of the challenges facing HR and line management is to increase the overall value of the reward package without increasing its cost and this is being achieved by those who understand the value of non-financial rewards.

- Critically, organizations need to 'know' whether their reward practices and strategies are working in the intended way, and if they are not, take the necessary actions to address the problems encountered. It is not evident from the available evidence that this is in fact the case!

Visit the **online resources** that accompany this book for self-test questions, web links, and more information on the topics covered in this chapter, at: **www.oup.com/uk/banfield3e/**

? REVIEW QUESTIONS

1. What is the evidence on the motivational effect of financial incentives and why is it inconsistent?

2. What is PRP, and what are the pros and cons of implementing a PRP system?

3. How do intrinsic and extrinsic rewards differ, and why is this distinction important?

4. Why have organizations moved away from the piece rate pay systems that were so popular in the 1970s?

5. What reward strategies are contemporary organizations using and what are the objectives to which these strategies relate?

6. What do employees value and expect to receive from their job and the organization they work for?

 CASE STUDY The Star Hotel

The Star Group of hotels has twenty-six hotels throughout the UK, operating in the business, conference, and banqueting markets. While there is a London-based corporate HQ, hotel general managers have considerable discretion for deciding on wage and salary levels, and over any incentive or bonus schemes they may wish to introduce.

Strict financial controls are established through the budgeting process, and managers have to produce monthly revenue and expenditure forecasts for head office. The expectation is that agreed budgets will be met, because this allows HQ to be confident about revenue and cash flows. Strict control over staff and employment costs are expected to be in place and maintained, which should not exceed an agreed percentage of each hotel's monthly turnover figure.

Beating the performance standards represented by the monthly and annual budgets is seen by managers as the way in which to demonstrate to senior management that the hotel is being well managed and is financially successful. Equally important is the need to ensure that customers are satisfied with the services they receive when they use the hotel. This helps to ensure a strong customer base and long-term prosperity. A key role played by the conference and banqueting department, and by reception/reservations, is increasing the proportion of 'repeat business', as well as finding new business.

The Sheffield Star Hotel is located on the edge of the city, which is seeing a growth in the number of hotels operating within the city limits. The growth in competition without a corresponding increase in overall demand for hotel facilities might be a potential threat to the Sheffield Star and its general manager is keen to find ways of responding to this. He is also under pressure to increase bottom-line performance and is considering different cost-reduction strategies to achieve this. He is, however, convinced that increasing revenue and cash flow have to be the main way forward, because most obvious areas for cost savings have already been explored.

Table 13.1 summarizes the hotel's situation.

Table 13.1 The hotel's key financial, employment, and operational situation

Annual sales turnover	£6m
Gross profit	£1.2m
Employee WTEs	48
Annual payroll	£1.4m
Average monthly wage/salary bill	£278,000
Average room occupancy rate	69%
Average monthly sales ledger (i.e. outstanding debt)	£187,000
Average monthly restaurant sales	£89,000
Average monthly conference and banqueting sales	£215,000

Table 13.2 lists the hotel's departments and numbers of employees:

Table 13.2 The hotel's departments and related numbers of employees

Department	Numbers	FT	PT
Housekeeping	15	3	12
Reception, including telesales	7	7	0
Restaurant, including waiting staff	28	7	21
Sales and banqueting	5	5	0
Bar staff	11	3	8
Finance	3	3	0
Secretarial and admin	5	3	2
General manager	1	1	0
Operations manager	1	1	0
Maintenance	1	1	0
Total	77		

Note: A significant proportion of the bar and restaurant staff is casual workers. The remaining members of staff are either on part-time or full-time contracts.

The Task

The general manager believes that the way forward is to incentivize his staff to perform at higher levels of effectiveness. He holds the view that, if the right kind of incentive schemes can be designed, most of his employees will respond positively. He has invited your company of reward management consultants to work with him on this task.

These are the guidelines you have been given:

- as many employees as is practical to be included;
- individual, functional/departmental, and organizational schemes can be considered;
- a close relationship between changes in employee performance and contribution to the bottom line should be established;
- schemes should be based on the ability to measure changes in performance;
- the expectation is that benefits, in all cases, should exceed costs;
- different incentive schemes for different groups of employees can be considered.

The task is to prepare a presentation to the general manager, in which you outline your ideas for incentivizing the hotel's employees. The presentation should include details on the following:

- who should be and who should not be considered for incentivizing, with reasons;
- your ideas/plans for incentivizing any two groups of employees, showing clearly how you would measure the performance of each group (note that a group can be one person or all employees);
- the problems that the hotel might encounter, in general, from its attempts to incentivize staff and the specific problems that might be experienced in the two schemes considered as part of the above point.

 Insights and Outcomes: visit the online resources at www.oup.com/uk/banfield3e/ for examples of incentive schemes that were developed by the hotel's management.

» FURTHER READING

Armstrong, M., Brown, D., and Reilly, P. (2010) *Evidence-Based Reward Management: Creating Measurable Business Impact from Your Pay and Reward Practices*, Kogan Page.

Frey, B. S. and Gallus, J. (2014) 'The power of awards', *Economic Voice*, 11(1).

IDS (2011) *Total Reward. HR Studies.*

Pepper, A. et al. (2013) 'Are long-term incentive plans an effective and efficient way of motivating senior executives?', *Human Resource Management Journal*, 23(1), at: http://eprints.lse.ac.uk/41818/1/Are%20 long%20term%20incentive%20plans.pdf

Trevor, J. (2009) 'Can pay be strategic?', in S. Corby, S. Palmer, and E. Lindop (eds.), *Rethinking Reward*, Palgrave Macmillan.

REFERENCES

ACAS Booklet, Job Evaluation: Considerations and Risks, at: http://www.acas.org.uk/index. aspx?articleid=682

Argyris, C. (2000) *On Organisational Learning*, Blackwell.

Arkin, A. (2005) 'Eyes on the prize', *People Management*, 10 February, p. 28.

Armstrong, M. (2002) *Employee Rewards*, CIPD.

Armstrong, M. (2010) *Handbook of Reward Management Practice: Improving Performance Through Reward*, Kogan Page.

Barton, T. (2011) 'Reach for the sky', *Employee Benefits* (February), at: https://www.employeebenefits. co.uk/issues/february-2011/airbus-reaches-for-the-sky-with-staff-benefits

Behrend, H. (1975) 'The effort bargain', *Industrial and Labor Relations Review*, 10(4).

Bennett Stewart, G., Appelbaum, E., Beer, M., and Lebby, A. M. (1993) 'Rethinking rewards', *Harvard Business Review*, 71(6), 37–49.

Brown, D. (2014) 'The future of reward management: From total reward strategies to smart rewards', *Compensation Benefits Review*, 46(3), 147–51.

Bussin, M. and Van Rooy, D. J. (2014) Total rewards strategy for a multigenerational workforce in a financial institution', *SA Journal of Human Resource Management*, 12(1).

Cherry, K. (2016) 'What is operant conditioning and how does it work?', *Psychology, Very Well.*

CIPD (2007) *Annual Reward Management Survey.*

CIPD (2015) *Reward Management Survey.*

Cox, A. et al. (2010) *Reward Strategy: Time for a More Realistic Reconceptualization and Interpretation?*, at: http://www.interscience.wiley.com

Daniels, A.C. (2000) *Bringing out the Best in People*, McGraw-Hill.

Deeks, E. (2000) 'Mates lighten workload', *People Management*, 12 October, p. 9.

Department of Health (2004) 'Agenda for change: What will it mean for you? A guide for staff', at: http:// www.dh.gov.uk

Frith, B. (2016) 'UK has one of the most frugal benefits systems in Europe', *Employee Benefits*, 18 February.

Glassdoor (2015) 'Facebook #1 among top 25 UK companies for pay & benefits', at: https://www. glassdoor.co.uk/blog/facebook-1-top-25-uk-companies-pay-benefits

Gouldner, A. (1954) *Wildcat Strike*, Antioch Press.

Half, R. [n.d.] 'Can flexible benefits help retain talented workers?', at: https://www.roberthalf. co.uk/news-insights/advice-managers/staff-retention/can-flexible-benefits-help-retain-talented-workers

Heighton, L. et al. (2015) 'Lavish trips laid on by drugs firms to "sway" NHS staff', *The Telegraph*, 22 July.

Herzberg, F. (2003) 'One more time: How do you motivate people?', *Harvard Business Review*, 81(1), 87–96.

Hill, A. (2016) 'Bonuses are bad for bankers and even worse for banks', *Financial Times*, 25 January, at: https://www.ft.com/content/da1a2df6-c058-11e5-846f-79b0e3d20eaf

Kay, R. (2014) *A Review of the Evidence on the Impact, Effectiveness and Value for Money of Performance-related Pay in the Public Sector*, Work Foundation, at: https://www.gov.uk/government/uploads/system/ uploads/attachment_data/file/381600/PRP_final_ report_TWF_Nov_2014.pdf

Kessler, I. and Purcell, J. (1992) 'Performance-related pay: Objectives and application', *Human Resource Management Journal*, 2(3), 16–33.

Kohn, A. (1993a) *Punished by Rewards*, Houghton Mifflin.

Kohn, A. (1993b) 'Why incentive plans cannot work', *Harvard Business Review*, 71(5), 54–63.

KPMG (2015) *The Living Wage: An Economic Impact Assessment*.

Mayson, H. (2013) 'Beyond the bonus: Driving employee performance', Institute of Leadership and Management, at: https://www.i-l-m.com/Insight/inspire/2013/October/beyond-the-bonus-research

Pfeffer J. (1998a) 'Six dangerous myths about pay', *Harvard Business Review* (May–June).

Pfeffer, J. (1998b) *The Human Equation: Building Profits by Putting People First*, Harvard Business School Press.

Pfeffer, J. and Sutton, R. I. (2006) *Hard Facts, Dangerous Half-Truths, and Total Nonsense: Profiting from Evidence-based Management*, Harvard Business School Press.

Pritchett, N. (2013) 'Discretionary bonuses: when can employers not pay?', at: http://www.shoosmiths.co.uk/client-resources/legal-updates/discretionary-bonuses-when-can-employers-not-pay-5862.aspx

Rewards Consulting (2015) 'What is reward strategy?', at: http://rewardsconsulting.co.uk/resources/articles/what-is-reward-strategy

Riley, R. and Bondibene, C. R. (2015) *The Impact of the National Minimum Wage on UK Businesses*, National Institute of Economic and Social Research and Centre for Macroeconomics, Report to the Low Pay Commission.

Rynes, S. L. et al. (2004) 'The importance of pay in employee motivation: Discrepancies between what people say and what they do', *Human Resource Management*, 43(4), 381–94.

Sage UK http://www.sage.co.uk/business-advice/employing-people/employee-benefits-and-incentives-packages#

Siegert, C. (2014) 'Bonuses and managerial misbehaviour', *European Economic Review*, 68 (May), 93–105.

Strauss, A. L. (1978) *A Review Symposium: Anselm L. Strauss—Negotiations: Varieties, Contexts, Processes, and Social Order*, Jossey-Bass.

Suff, P. et al. (2007) *Paying for Performance: New Trends in Performance-Related Pay*, Institute for Employment Studies.

Taylor, F. W. (1998) *The Principles of Scientific Management*, Dover.

Thompson, P. (2002) *Total Reward*, CIPD.

Tyler, T. R. and Bies, R. J. (1990) 'Beyond formal procedures: The interpersonal context of procedural justice', in J. S. Carroll (ed.), *Applied Social Psychology and Organisational Settings*, Lawrence Erlbaum.

Tyson, S. (1997) *The Practice of Human Resource Strategy*, Pearson Education.

Vaughan-Whitehead, D. (2010) *Fair Wages: Strengthening Corporate Social Responsibility*, Edward Elgar.

Glossary

Ambiguity A lack of clarity or meaning in something: the difficulty in seeing and understanding, for example, the relationship between HR activities and individual/organizational outcomes.

Appraisal The examination and assessment of a person's behaviour in relation to their performance over a period of time. It involves making judgements and based on these making decisions about future changes in behaviour with the objective of improving performance. It can involve the rating of a person's performance by a superior (in a managerial sense) with the rating being linked to subsequent decisions about rewards, development, or corrective action.

Assessment The tools and techniques used by an organization to identify and measure, either qualitatively or quantitatively, the skills, knowledge, and potential of applicants.

Benefit Normally contractually agreed non-pay additions to the wage or salary, provided by an employer as part of the overall employment package.

Bonus An additional, but variable, payment associated with individual, group, or organizational performance.

Career planning The activities and policies that link a person's current and future capabilities to development decisions, future job opportunities, and promotion.

Career and succession management Formal and informal processes that ensure talented people are developed and available to fill strategically important roles.

Coaching A process in which a 'coach' supports an individual to develop his/her skills through a series of structured conversations by exploring the nature of challenges faced at work and helping the individual to identify the best approaches to those challenges to achieve the desired outcomes.

Collective agreement A written statement defining the arrangements agreed between a union and employer. Such agreements are only legally enforceable if this is expressly stated or if the collective agreement is referred to in individual written terms and conditions of employment.

Collective bargaining The process of negotiation between trade union representatives and employers, or employer representatives, to establish by agreement the terms and conditions of employment of a group of employees.

Competence The combination of skills, knowledge, and experience that results in a person's ability to carry out specific tasks and procedures to a required standard. A specific competency can also be understood as an underlying characteristic of a person (i.e. a trait, belief, ability, or attitude, that distinguishes one person from another and explains differences in job performance).

Contribution Something wider than performance: relates to what a person does 'beyond contract' that is of value to the organization.

Culture The shared beliefs, values, and understandings that define and distinguish one group from another. It is what Hofstede and Hofstede call 'the collective programming of the mind'.

Culture shock The psychological and emotional reaction associated with exposure to different cultural environments.

Development Changes in a person and in what they can do. It reflects the belief that all people have the potential to be more and do more, and that this potential needs to be developed as well as utilized. People can develop to a limited degree through training, but development implies the employment of a much wider range of learning experiences and methods, such as coaching and mentoring, not all of which are necessarily connected to the working environment.

Dialectic The tension that arises as a result of conflicting ideas, interacting forces, or competing interests. The term can also be used to explain the process of reconciling opposing or differing opinions and interests by means of argument and discussion. It is assumed that the constant need for adaptation and change can result in differences and conflict over different stakeholder interests and in the legitimacy of managerial decision-making rights.

Differentiation The practice of distinguishing people based on their innate and acquired talents and developing different and focused HR policies and practices that reflect the special value these people represent to the organization.

Discipline The formal measures taken, sanctions applied, and outcomes achieved by management in response to perceived acts of misconduct.

Employee engagement A workplace approach resulting in the psychological and social conditions that encourage all members of an organization to give their best each day, become committed to their organization's goals and values, and motivated to contribute to organizational success.

Ethical dilemmas These represent situations where ethical choices have to be made and where different criteria or standards come into consideration.

Ethics The branch of philosophy that deals with morality: what is good and bad, right and wrong. Ethics is about the choice and application of values and standards to establish the social acceptability of behaviour and action.

Evidence-based management This is about translating principles based on best evidence into organizational practices. By focusing on issues about which there is a clear evidential base the assumption is that the practice of managing will improve and lead to better outcomes.

Expatriate worker An employee deployed overseas, usually sourced from his/her country of origin.

Expectation The behavioural impact of different 'reward experiences' and on whether the amount or form of any given reward creates a positive or negative response. The more people expect, whether this is considered reasonable or not, is not the point; what is, is that expectations, if not met, will result in disappointment and behaviours that reflect this emotional state.

External recruitment The process of identifying and attracting potential employees to an organization to fill current or future vacancies.

Fairness An inherently subjective term that describes behaviour or outcomes in terms of criteria, standards, and expectations.

Global organization An organization that employs a workforce in different countries throughout the world, with a view to maximizing performance by sourcing or providing goods and/or services in a globally based market, and in which decisions are driven by markets rather than by geography.

Grievance The formalization of a claim that someone, either a co-worker or management, has acted wrongly towards another, and, as a consequence, inflicted physical or psychological harm on that person. This may involve an act, or acts, of misconduct.

Hiring or employing The overall process of taking on new staff from outside the organization.

Horizontal integration Relates to the link between different HR activities and practices, and emphasizes the importance of looking at what HR does holistically, rather than as separate and disconnected elements. The concept also expresses the need for consistency in the sense that the way in which the activities are carried out reflects understood and agreed strategic objectives. For example, adopting an individualist, rather than a collectivist, approach to the management of people implies the use of individual reward and development practices if consistency in practice is to be achieved.

Human capital metrics *see* Workforce analytics

Human resource development Used by many writers, but fewer practitioners, in preference to the term 'training'. Its relationship to training is similar to that between HRM and personnel management, in that it represents a more holistic and strategic approach to learning than does training.

Human resource function A term that can be used in a specific sense to mean the HR department, but in its wider sense it relates to all activities and responsibilities connected to managing people, which includes the role played by organizational leaders, line, and departmental managers.

Human resource management (HRM) A late twentieth-century approach to the management of employees, which sees people as a key organizational resource that needs to be developed and utilized to support the organization's operational and strategic objectives.

Human resources (HR) An alternative to 'people'; also the term used by organizations to describe the specialized department that deals with the administration and management of employees.

Incentive The prospect or promise of a reward that is conditional upon an agreed performance outcome being achieved.

Internal recruitment The process of identifying current employees who may be suitable for newly created vacancies or for replacing staff who leave.

Leadership The act of leading: an organizational position/role that confers power and authority on individuals and confers upon them specific responsibilities and requirements.

Learning A fundamental and natural human process involving growth and change. Learning is about behavioural modification. It is inferred from differences in what we know, believe, and can do. Learning is the way in which we can improve and be different from that which we were.

Managerial prerogative 'Prerogative' means the right to make decisions and to establish rules that are essential in allowing the production system to operate efficiently and effectively, and, historically, managers have tended to guard their prerogative and have tried to prevent trade unions from eroding it.

Mediation An alternative form of dispute resolution. A voluntary process where an independent facilitator assists two or more parties to explore options for resolving a dispute, disagreement, or problem situation by attempting to reach a mutually acceptable agreement.

Mental models Images, representations, or schemes of how we perceive and understand the world around us. Like all models, mental models are abstractions of reality. The models we use represent simplifications of the 'real' world and therefore can never represent all that exists in that world we are trying to understand. No matter how well constructed, all models are imperfect in some context or time.

Mentoring The development of a relationship between a more senior person in an organization and more junior person, often as part of a development programme, involving the experienced person using his/her greater knowledge and expertise to accelerate the junior colleague's development.

Metrics What and how something is measured. HR metrics focus on key aspects of the labour force, its behaviours, costs, and contributions. The use of measures is increasingly associated with important features of the HR function, as part of the process of evaluating its efficiency and effectiveness.

Misconduct Behaviour that transgresses contractual arrangements, work rules, established norms of performance, or other standards that can be seen as reasonable and necessary for the effective employment and management of people at work; behaviour that is deemed to be unacceptable by reference to formally established norms.

Motivation A force that exists within people that initiates and directs behaviour. In this sense, it can also be seen as a force that drives behaviour in certain directions rather than others. The force and direction are linked to goals that people are assumed to desire and outcomes that they would prefer to avoid.

Multinational companies (MNCs) Companies that have a national base, but which operate and trade in multiple countries.

National culture A complex system of norms, social values, behaviours, expectations, and legal frameworks that gives an identity to a particular country.

Negotiation Technically, negotiating is the process through which agreement is reached; where differences between two parties are resolved as a result of mutual compromise.

Negotiation of order Has its origins in the writings of sociologists such as Gouldner, Park, and Strauss who saw society and institutions as made up of different interest groups that needed to be constantly working to create order and flexibility, a process that involves a succession of conflicts, assimilations, and accommodations. Social order achieved through shared agreements and understanding is not fixed or binding for all time and must be reconstituted continually, or worked out. The theory highlights emergence, change, and temporality, the embedded and contextual nature of order, and the omnipresence of specific power relations. Rewards of different kinds represent an important means of influencing the way order is continually being renegotiated and agreed.

Organizational blockages Practices, behaviours, or structural/cultural characteristics that inhibit, punish, or prevent people from being productive.

Organizational citizenship Behaviour that extends beyond that which is necessary to carry out job duties and responsibility to the required standard. It is behaviour that represents a person's voluntary commitment to an organization or company that is not part of his/her contractual tasks.

Organizational memory The accumulated body of data, information, and knowledge created in the course of an organization's existence (also known as institutional/corporate memory).

Paradox A concept that describes a situation which contains conflicting and possibly contradictory ideas, behaviours, and/or elements.

Pay Regular and contractually agreed monetary rewards, usually linked to position or job and paid as a wage/salary.

Performance The relationship between a person's capabilities and what the person actually achieves, usually related to a person's job.

Performance appraisal A process for reviewing the past performance of an employee, and agreeing future objectives and development activities.

Performance management The set of practices through which work is defined and reviewed, capabilities are developed, and rewards are distributed.

Personnel management The name given to the specialized management function that developed after the Second World War which assumed responsibility for the employment, payment, and training of employees.

Philosophy An enduring framework of beliefs, values, and ways of doing things that can exist at the individual and organizational levels. A shared philosophy is a powerful way of creating a common purpose and set of expectations as to how people behave.

Planning A set of techniques, an approach, and a mindset, all of which relate to achieving specified objectives. It should be understood as a process, rather than a time-constrained event.

Positivism The term used to describe an approach to the study of society, or phenomena that relies specifically on scientific evidence, such as experiments and statistics, and the discovery of facts, to reveal the 'true' nature of how society operates or the phenomenon being studied.

Potential What people are capable of doing. Potential implies that what people are capable of doing is not being utilized, but could develop as a result of learning and experience.

Presenteeism The problem of workers being present on the job but, because of illness or other medical conditions, not fully functioning.

Productivity An economic concept that relates to and measures input–output relationships.

Psychological contract The obligations that an employer and an employee perceive to exist between them as part of the employment relationship, and which comprises mutual expectations and promises.

Reciprocity A response to a positive action with another positive action. People who are treated well by their manager or the organization may well reciprocate with higher levels of loyalty and commitment and deliver higher levels of discretionary effort. It tends to be generated when that which is done to someone and valued is unexpected and discretionary—and is probably symbolic rather than material in form.

Reification The process of giving things that are inanimate (e.g. social constructs) human characteristics such that they become an independent, living entity. For example, when we talk about organizations as having objectives, of thinking, of having a conscience we reify them. The same thing happens to HRM/HR—it is almost always, but wrongly, represented as having an independent existence, because we often have to simplify complex phenomena.

Rewards Can be both material and symbolic in form; both are outcomes of the employment and psychological contracts.

Selection The process, culminating in the decision to fill a vacancy from internal or external applicants, used by the organization to choose the most suitable candidate from a pool of applicants.

Settlement agreement A legally binding agreement signed by both parties which formally brings to an end the contract of employment on specific terms that must be agreed by both parties. It is recognized by statute and is the only way you can validly waive your employment law rights.

Social capital Relates to the value of personal networks, relationships, and cooperative behaviour between people.

Social constructionism A theory of knowledge that examines the development of jointly constructed understandings of the world, based on experience, that form the basis for shared assumptions about what is real in the world.

Stagnation The detrimental effect on creativity, change, and originality that is associated with relying largely or entirely on the existing workforce to fill job vacancies. The lack of 'new blood' from outside, which can bring new ideas, challenge, and vitality into an organization, can contribute to the long-term decline of an organization that is too inward-looking in its search for new talent.

Strategic A particular mindset and approach defined by a more integrated and holistic view of the world of business and management.

Strategic advantage Actions that follow on from specific strategies which make the organization better and different from its competitors or those against which it is benchmarked.

Strategy A coherent way of doing things that is intended to produce required outcomes and results.

Survival curve Measures the number of new recruits (normally those who start together or over a short period) who are still there after, say, twelve months. The survival rate can be calculated by dividing the number who started with those left at monthly intervals.

Tacit knowledge Relates to knowledge of things gained from various sources and internalized by an individual, through the process of 'doing' and practice. Represents for many people the achievement of the final stage—unconscious competence, where tasks are carried out based on experience and learning from past successes and failures without the person being aware of the link between knowledge, know-how, and action.

Talent Used generically, this describes people's knowledge, skills, and capabilities and means the same as human capital. Also used to describe special, higher, and scarce skills/capabilities. Talent is what people have and what they can do.

Talent management Formal attempts aimed at identifying, developing, and using people who have been designated as talented.

Trade union An organization that is independent of an employer and funded by member contributions, the function of which is to represent worker interests in relations between workers and employers.

Training Planned, structured, and often formalized learning experiences that seek to develop specific skills and knowledge needed for effective job performance. Historically, employees have learned many of the competencies they need to perform effectively by being trained.

Trust A characteristic of a relationship between two people or between people and an organization. It involves having faith, confidence, and belief in another.

Unintended consequences Outcomes that are not foreseen or intended by a purposeful action (also called unanticipated/unforeseen consequences). They can be positive but are more often negative.

Vertical integration Relates to the link between policies and practices associated with the management of people, and the wider business objectives. Vertical integration can be based on the cascading down of corporate priorities and objectives, which then inform HR policies, practices, etc. Alternatively, it can be based on representatives of HR informing senior management of the current and future state of human resource capacity and capabilities, which helps to ensure that corporate strategy is grounded in a realistic understanding of what is available to deliver the strategy.

Whistle-blower A person who exposes information or activity relative to an organization that is deemed illegal, unethical, or not correct.

Whole-time equivalents (WTEs) A quantitative measurement of the number of staff available to or in the establishment that allows for staff on different employment contracts to be reflected in the 'head count'.

Workforce analytics A more quantitative approach to workforce planning, relying on data analysis to identify longer-term trends to diagnose future problems/issues.

Workforce planning (WP) Originally known as 'manpower planning' and previously described as 'human resource planning', this is concerned with planning and controlling the quantity and quality of labour available to an organization.

Index

441